LINGUISTICS
FOR
TEACHERS

LINGUISTICS FOR TEACHERS

Linda Miller Cleary
Michael D. Linn

University of Minnesota, Duluth

McGraw-Hill, Inc.
New York   St. Louis   San Francisco   Auckland   Bogotá
Caracas   Lisbon   London   Madrid   Mexico City   Milan
Montreal   New Delhi   San Juan   Singapore
Sydney   Tokyo   Toronto

This book was developed by STEVEN PENSINGER, Inc.

This book was set in Times Roman by The Clarinda Company.
The editors were Steve Pensinger and Scott Amerman.
The cover was designed by Carol Couch.
R. R. Donnelley & Sons Company was printer and binder.

This book is printed on acid-free paper.

LINGUISTICS FOR TEACHERS

Acknowledgments appear on pages 625–629, and on this page by reference.

6 7 8 9 0   DOC   DOC   9 0 9 8

ISBN 0-07-037946-7

Library of Congress Cataloging–in–Publication Data

Cleary, Linda Miller
    Linguistics for teachers / Linda Miller Cleary, Michael D. Linn.
       p.   cm.
    Includes bibliographical references and index.
    ISBN 0-07-037946-7
    1. Applied linguistics.   2. English language—Study and teaching.
I. Linn, Michael D.   II. Title.
P129.C56   1993
428'.0024372—dc20   92-26665

ABOUT
THE AUTHORS

LINDA MILLER CLEARY is an Associate Professor of English Education in the English Department of the University of Minnesota, Duluth. She taught English at the secondary level in Maine and California for thirteen years before completing an Ed.D. with emphasis in English education and a minor emphasis in linguistics at the University of Massachusetts, Amherst, in 1985. Her research has focused on studies of concentration and motivation of secondary school writers and on issues of literacy. She has authored *From the Other Side of the Desk: Students Speak Out About Writing* and co-edited *Children's Voices: Children Talk About Literacy* (both Heinemann Educational Books).

MICHAEL D. LINN, a professor of linguistics at the University of Minnesota, Duluth, has taught at Lamar State University and Virginian Commonwealth University. He earned his Ph.D. at the University of Minnesota, Twin Cities. He is currently president of the American Dialect Society and vice president of the International Society of Dialectologists and Geolinguists. Previous books include the two anthologies edited with Harold B. Allen: *Readings in Applied Linguistics* and *Dialect and Language Variation*.

v

This Book Is Lovingly Dedicated
to Jed and Sarah Cleary
and to Francie Linn

CONTENTS

PREFACE

This book reflects a deep and abiding concern with the relationship between the field of linguistics and the preparation of teachers. Discussions between us revealed a shared concern with the lack of texts linking the study of English linguistics with their practical classroom applications. Out of those discussions we developed *Linguistics for Teachers*. Instead of doing a revision of *Readings in Applied English Linguistics,* edited by Michael D. Linn and the late Harold B. Allen, we proposed the possibility of doing an entirely new book, one that stressed linguistics for teachers. A teacher must have a background in linguistic theory in order to understand changes that occur in language instruction. A background in theory becomes even more important for those teachers who are in multicultural classrooms. Yet research and theory alone do not sufficiently prepare the prospective teacher to go into the classroom. Without practical readings in pedagogy, teachers go into their classrooms unprepared for the tension that exists between methods derived from recent research and the well-entrenched traditional methods that are all too often practiced in the classroom. We felt it necessary to develop a single collection that combines the writings of important modern linguistic theorists with those of insightful practitioners to prepare teachers of reading, writing, and thinking.

In addition, certification requirements have changed. In 1986 the National Council of Teachers of English (NCTE) revised their *Guidelines for the Preparation of Teachers of English Language Arts.* These guidelines were adopted by the National Council for Accreditation of Teachers of Education (NCATE), a national organization which certifies the program of teacher education institutions wishing to be recognized for excellence and wishing to provide their students with reciprocal licensure in other states. In assembling the essays for this collection, we made sure that all NCTE/NCATE guidelines were met except the one indicates thorough preparation in one grammatical theory. Before assembling these essays, we also surveyed the state departments of education and found that the NCTE/NCATE guidelines in the area of language certification are either more rigorous or are commensurate with those of the individual states.

Because many of the articles have copious references, we have not provided an overall bibliography. A few important and pertinent references have been cited in the introductions. Advanced and serious students will also want to consult the annual *MLA International Bibliography* published by the Modern Language Association.

Whatever contribution this book can make to the preparation of teachers or to the general understanding of language would, of course, have been impossible without the primary work of the authors and publishers who have generously granted permission to reprint their material. For their consent, we are most grateful. We also want to extend our appreciation to those who were involved in the development of the text. Some of the more theoretical readings selected were used in a class called "Language in the Middle and High School Classroom," a course originally developed by Judith Solsken and Earl Seidman at the University of Massachusetts and subsequently taught there by Linda Miller Cleary. The students in that course offered valuable response to many of the articles. In addition, we offer particular appreciation to undergraduate and graduate students at the University of Minnesota, Duluth, who have taken Linn's course, Applied Linguistics, where we field tested this material. Many of them offered helpful responses and suggestions. Furthermore, we are grateful to Catherine Long who read and offered suggestions on the introductions. A special note of appreciation and gratitude is due to Robin Blatnik who spent many hours preparing the manuscript, writing to publishers for permission to reprint material, keeping track of the permissions slips once they were returned, and any typing when required. We would also like to thank, along with McGraw-Hill, Elizabeth Anne Duke of Virginia Commonwealth University, and Ronald Shook of Utah State University, for their helpful reviews of the manuscript.

Linda Miller Cleary
Michael D. Linn

A NOTE TO
THE READERS

If you already have a general knowledge of linguistics, the introductions to these sections will provide a quick view of the articles as they fit into your prior learning. These introductions will suggest further reading for those who develop interests in any of the areas presented.

If you are a beginner in the study of linguistics, read the introductions thoroughly, as they will provide useful connections for you between what you already might know about language and what you will need to learn. These links between prior knowledge and what you are about to read will be important to you in improving your comprehension of the text.

HISTORY OF ENGLISH AND ACQUISITION OF LANGUAGE

Humans are often described as talking animals, and certainly speech is a distinguishing characteristic of the species. While English, as we know it today, is a member of the Germanic branch of the Indo-European language, it has been evolving as long as humans have been talking. Its recent history is chronicled in Lee Pederson's opening article. For those of you who are not familiar with the history of English, Lee Pederson's opening article offers an effective review of the origin and evolution of English from the first Low German invaders in A.D. 449 to our present American English. This article provides broad background knowledge of how the language of the Anglo-Saxon invaders was modified by the French of the Norman invaders of 1066 and how Modern English emerged as a world language. Pederson's article further chronicles the early development of American English and details the influences of Native American, European, and African languages. The influence of both regional and social dialects on present-day American speech is also described. If you are interested in learning more about the history of the English language, you might consult any current text on the history of the English language. You will find one book particularly accessible:

McCrum, Robert Willian Cran, and Robert MacNeil. *The Story of English* (New York: Viking, 1986).

There is an educational television series of the same name. For those of you who are interested primarily in American English, two excellent books to consult are:

Dillard, J. L. *All-American English: A History of the English Language in America* (New York: Vintage, 1975).

1

Marckwardt, Albert H. *American English,* revised by J. L. Dillard (New York: Oxford, 1980).

You may find the following books tough going, but they are valuable scholarly books that will be useful to those who have had prior training in the history of language:

Bolton, W. F. *A Living Language: The History and Structure of English* (New York: Random House, 1982).
Pyles, Thomas, and John Algeo. *The Origins and Development of the English Language,* 3rd ed. (New York: Harcourt, Brace, Jovanovich, 1982).
Williams, Joseph M. *Origins of the English Language: A Social and Linguistic History* (New York: Free Press, 1975).

An excellent videotape is *American Tongues,* available from the Center for New American Media, 524 Broadway, New York, New York 10012.

In the next article, Karl Dykema outlines the classical Greek and Roman origins of the study of grammar and traces the debate between the proponents of *descriptive grammar,* a grammar that describes the way a particular language or dialect works, and the proponents of *prescriptive grammar,* a grammar that describes what is considered the "proper" way to speak or write a language. He points out that in spite of the widespread use of the prescriptive grammar and grammar-as-remedy movements, neither has been effective as an educational tool. Further discussion of this topic is found in the book's section on syntax. Students who are interested in reading further in the history of linguistics will find the following useful:

Caroll, John R. *The Study of Language: A Survey of Linguistics and Related Disciplines in America* (Cambridge: Harvard University Press, 1953).
Robbins, R. H. *A Short History of Linguistics,* 2d ed. (London: Longman, 1979).

Every human, barring neurological damage or social isolation, learns language. For the first half of this century, most linguists and psychologists believed that children learned language by imitating the speech of their parents. It was hypothesized that children learned new grammatical and semantic extensions by means of analogy. As a result, educational practice in the language arts curriculum during this period of time often stressed drills and rote memory.

However, following Noam Chomsky's publication of *Syntactic Structures* (Mouton, 1957) and his *Aspects of a Theory of Syntactic Structures* (MIT Press, 1964), the serious study of child language acquisition began. Chomsky hypothesized that children develop language too rapidly to learn it simply through imitation and that there must be some kind of language acquisition device that is activated when the child starts to hear language. Chomsky further felt that since children often use language to fit novel situations for which they have no model, linguistic extensions could not be the result of analogy. Those of you who are interested in this debate will find Chomsky's review of B. F. Skinner's "Verbal Behavior" [*Language* 35 (1959):25–58] stimulating.

Breyne Arlene Moskowitz's article supports Chomsky's claim that children are genetically endowed with a language learning capacity. She delineates some of the early stages that children go through as they learn language and demonstrates that they cannot learn by rote memory or imitation. If this is true, the study of child language acquisition demonstrates that extensive correction and rote drills are not a help in language acquisition and may even slow it up. In the next article, Jerome Bruner further emphasizes how the child cannot learn merely by imitation of the caretaker's speech. He describes how language acquisition occurs through interactions with parents for real purposes. Language acquisition is not complete by adolescence. As other areas of linguistics and classroom applications are examined, the book will address aspects of adolescent language development.

Those of you who are interested in child language acquisition should read some of the following:

Brown, Roger. *A First Language: The Early Stages* (Harvard University Press, 1973). This book also contains a section on ape communication.
Bruner, Jerome S. *Learning to Use Language* (New York: Norton, 1983).
Dale, Philip S. *Language Development: Structure and Function,* 2d ed. (New York: Holt, Rinehart and Winston, 1976).

The *Journal of Child Language* also has interesting articles, although some are quite technical. An excellent videotape on child language is *Nova*'s presentation *A First Language.*

In order for teachers to understand current language issues, it is necessary to know how the English language originated and evolved into its present state and to know how a child acquires language. Without an understanding of the history of language, it is difficult to understand the present language and instruction. Without a sense of how humans acquire language, one cannot know what classroom procedures help students refine and further develop their language skills.

Language, Culture, and the American Heritage

Lee Pederson

American speech and writing record the transactions of nearly four hundred years of social history. Dialects embody patterns of sound, syntax, and meaning; literature documents those spoken forms in poetry and prose. Through the process of communication a native language becomes the social inheritance of all its speakers. In describing the linguistic resources of American English this Dictionary becomes a property book for the American people.

A century before Noah Webster organized his first American dictionary (1806), Jonathan Edwards defined the materials of inquiry in remarkably modern terms, in words that should appeal to every reader, whether layman, linguist, or lexicographer:

> By *conversation,* I mean intelligent beings expressing their minds one to another in words, or other signs intentionally directed to us for our notice, whose immediate and main design is to be signification of the mind of him who gives it.

Defining language as intelligent conversation, Edwards recognized the conceptual, symbolic, and functional aspects of human communication: the engagement of thought, the use of signs, and the transmission of ideas from one mind to another.

Today the English language makes conversation possible among three hundred million native speakers who share its system of symbolic behavior. This number includes speakers of American, Australian, British, Canadian, Irish, New Zealand, and Scottish English as members of the most influential speech community in the history of civilization. Their common cultural heritage makes possible the use of a single language by the members of these different groups, but each national variety with all its regional and social dialects reflects unique social experience.

Such experience makes a national vocabulary the most accessible and productive source of cultural information. Words are the complex linguistic structures that transmit the native lexicon through the systems of sound, grammar, and meaning. Words are also cultural emblems, symbols with social meaning that preserve the experience of human activity. Emerson said that words are signs of natural facts and wrote: "The etymologist finds the deadest word to have been once a brilliant picture. Language is fossil poetry." He demonstrated by his own example, moreover, that words are also signs of sociohistorical facts by giving the American meaning to *transcendentalism.* Roger Williams, America's first anthropologist, recorded an Algonquian dialect, provided us with the earliest occurrences in English of *birchen bark* and *squash,* and coined the phrase *Indian affairs.* George Washington furnished the earliest citations for *Democrat* and *Republican* and himself was the first to receive the designation *favorite son.* Noah Webster made the earliest use of the phrase *American English* with characteristic impatience but ultimate accuracy: "In fifty years from this time [1806], the American-English will be spoken by more people than all other dialects of the language." Such thought, conversation, and social interaction shaped the national character and gave substance to the lexicon. Contributions came from every sector of the American culture: education, religion, government, and even lexicography.

As the central component of American English culture the national language transmits the essential messages of all other cultural systems. All of these are inseparable from language: *family* (kinship and marriage), *training* (education and economics), *values* (morality, ethics, and religious rites), *government* (political and social control), *technology* (artifacts of survival), and *fine arts* (artifacts of the creative imagination and of spiritual expression). From the earliest days on its first frontiers American English carried forward the messages of the culture and the experience of the past. As it did its work the national language established an identity and expressed native ideas in an American voice. This dictionary records that American voice and gives substance to its underlying systems, *language* and *culture.*

Thoreau recognized a national dictionary as "a very concentrated and trustworthy natural history of the people":

> What they have a word for, they have a thing for. A traveller may tell us that he *thinks* they used a pavement, or built their cabins in a certain form, or soaked their seed corn in water . . .; but when one gives us the word for these things, the question is settled,—that is a clincher. Let us know what words they had and how they used them, and we can infer almost all the rest. The lexicographer not only *says* that a certain people have or do a certain thing, but, being evidently a disinterested party, it may be allowed that he brings sufficient evidence to prove it. He does not so much assert as exhibit. He has no transient or private purposes to serve.

HISTORICAL BACKGROUND OF ENGLISH

This natural history of the American people is the essential gift of the mother tongue. With all speakers of the English language Americans share the results of fifteen hundred years of linguistic development, and English had itself evolved for a full millennium before the first American words were spoken in Virginia. Furthermore, as a member of the Germanic language group of the Indo-European language family, English shares an ultimate heritage with most of the modern languages of Europe and Asia and with the official languages of every government in North and South America.

The essential features of the Germanic languages are these: (1) consonant modification, especially the First Germanic Consonant Shift, captured in

Grimm's Law, that distinguishes the system from all other Indo-European consonant patterns, as illustrated by the correspondences between initial sounds in the Latin/English cognates *pater/father, tu/thou,* and *hortus/garden;* (2) vowel mutation in the specialization of Germanic vowels, diphthongs, and umlauted forms to give them values different from all other Indo-European vowel systems; (3) word stress on the first syllable; (4) seven classes of strong (irregular) verbs, such as *sing, sang, sung;* (5) three classes of weak (regular) verbs, such as *love, loved, loved;* (6) strong and weak adjectives that disappeared in Medieval English but endure elsewhere, as in the Modern German and Norwegian definite and indefinite articles; (7) a core vocabulary of common words. These shared characteristics define the thirteen modern Germanic languages: Danish, Faroese, Icelandic, Norwegian, Swedish, German, Yiddish, Low German, Dutch, Afrikaans, Flemish, Frisian, and English.

The history of the English language begins with the coming of invaders from the continent in A.D. 449, as reported in the Anglo-Saxon Chronicle. In the eighth century the Venerable Bede (A.D. 673–735) identified the Low Germans as Angles, Saxons, and Jutes. In Britain the Germans encountered their Indo-European relatives, the Celts, a Belgic tribe that had arrived some time after the advent of the Iron Age (700 B.C.) but before Caesar's invasions of 54 B.C. Like the Amerindians, the Celts left their greatest linguistic legacy in place names, such as *Avon, Bryn Mawr* (Welsh "great hill"), *Dover, Thames,* and probably *London.* Unlike the Amerindians, the Celts provided no vocabulary of flora, fauna, or cultural activities for the newcomers. This latter fact reflects differing geographical and cultural circumstances: the Celts and Germans were never separated by a distance greater than the narrow English Channel and shared a common Indo-European ancestry. Conversely, the Amerindians and English came from different environments thousands of miles apart, from homelands distinguished by their native forms of vegetation, animal life, and social behavior.

As the Low German dialects merged in England they gave rise to the Northumbrian, Mercian, and Saxon varieties of the language that is called Old English today. Three tenth-century texts show the close similarities of those dialects in their respective translations of Medieval Latin (Matthew 6:9) "Pater noster, qui est in caelis, sanctificetur nomen tuum . . .":

Northumbrian

Fader urer ðu arð in heofnas, sie gehalgad noma ðin . . .
Father our thou art in heaven, be hallowed name thy . . .

Mercian

Fæder ure ðu ðe in heofunum earð, beo gehalgad ðin noma . . .
Father our thou which in heaven art, be hallowed thy name . . .

West Saxon

Fæder ure ðu ðe eart on heofonum, si ðin nama gehalgod . . .
Father our thou which art in heaven, be thy name hallowed . . .

Despite differences in pronunciation, word formation, and syntax, simple and effective conversation was surely possible among speakers of the different regional dialects of English. Conversation was also possible between the English and their Viking neighbors from the north. That cultural interaction extended throughout the Old English period (449–1066) is evidenced in the greatest literary monument of the Anglo-Saxons, their epic poem *Beowulf,* which has a thoroughly Scandinavian setting and cast.

Words shared by Anglo-Saxons and Vikings include *bring, can, come, father, folk, hear, house, life, mother, man, mine, ride, see, sit, smile, sorrow, summer, thine, wife, will, winter,* and *wise.* In addition to hundreds of such intimate correspondences, the Scandinavians gave English many other familiar words through cultural interaction: *anger, fellow, happy, husband, meek, root, rotten, skill, skin, sky,* and *ugly.* A second and much greater influence was brought to bear on the language and culture after the events of 1066, when the French-speaking descendants of the Vikings arrived from Normandy.

FRENCH INFLUENCES

The Norman-French presence marked the beginning of great changes in English social behavior, reflecting a gradual evolution of institutional and conversational forms. The chronicles and other writings show that Old English was in transition before the coming of the Normans, and later poetry and prose record unmodified Germanic forms deep into the Middle English period. In England, French became the official language of the dominant culture and spread its influence into every social system. Earlier, on the continent, the Normans had adopted Frankish laws, developed a system of knightly conduct, and perfected the skills of cavalry warfare. Through force and friendship they gave the English a chivalric code, a parliamentary system of government, and one of the most distinctive architectural styles in all of European civilization. During the period of Norman dominion the English dialects evolved without a native prestige form. The Scandinavian remnant of earlier times emerged in the speech of the northern counties, and the regional dialects were broadly reorganized. In the process Middlesex became the pre-eminent focal area, and from its center arose the London Standard, the most influential social variety the language has ever known.

The dialects of fourteenth-century England were the immediate ancestors of the London Standard, based on the speech of the Southeast Midland region. The recorded usage of that era illustrates great linguistic change, a process that began more than two hundred years earlier through the mingling of English and

French. Causal relations for the change are hard to establish because phonological, grammatical, lexical, and cultural modifications were under way before the Battle of Hastings. Romance language words, such as *cheese, copper,* and *dish,* entered Low German dialects through Latin before the invasion of England in A.D. 449; from the same source came *cleric, psalm,* and *temple* with the Christianization of England in the seventh century. Late Romance loans in Old English include *pride* (French), *capon* and *castle* (French or Latin), and *apostle, epistle, lily,* and *peony* (Latin). Old English texts of the tenth century—the Vercelli Book, Exeter Book, Junius Codex, and *Beowulf* Codex—show the early simplification of weakly stressed vowels and inflectional patterns. During the reign of Edward the Confessor (1043–1066) a Norman association was firmly established between the king and his cousin, William the Conqueror, underscored by the installation of Robert of Jumiàeges as Archbishop of Canterbury in 1051.

During the next three hundred years the French presence altered the development of English through direct contributions and reinforcement of linguistic trends already under way. Four fricative consonants emerged as distinctive elements of the sound system during this period, the initial sounds of *veal, zeal,* and *thee,* as well as the medial sound in *leisure.* None of these were distinctive in Old English, which had only the fricatives of modern *feel, seal, thing,* and *pressure,* respectively. The single outright contribution of Norman French to the sound system of English was the diphthong of *joy.* French usage did accelerate the leveling of weakly stressed vowels, the simplification of noun, pronoun, and adjective inflections, and the transfer of many strong (irregular) verbs to weak (regular) conjugations. For example, Old English forms of modern *doom* included *domes* (genitive singular), *domas* (nominative plural), and *domum* (dative plural); all became *doomes* in Middle English. Strong verbs such as *creopan, helpan,* and *slæpan* became the weak verbs *creep, help,* and *sleep,* although a residue of the old patterns endures in the past forms *crept* and *slept,* as well as *holp* (pronounced like *hope*) in several current American dialects.

More French loan-words entered English during the fourteenth century than during any comparable period before or since. As the French language fell into disuse in England many of its culturally useful words were borrowed. Here the relationship between speech and writing is an important consideration. The documented evidence of the written forms is conservative and lags behind current usage. After King John lost the province of Normandy in 1204, French influence on English society began to decline. Before the Hundred Years' War (1337–1453) began, English speech had already returned as the native tongue of the nobility, and before the century closed, had replaced French in the courts, Parliament, schools, and finally in the highly formal documents of titles, deeds, and wills.

Chaucer composed *The Canterbury Tales* in his native Southeast Midland dialect and so demonstrated the appropriateness of London speech as a literary medium, but this did not mark the triumph of a standard language within the culture at large. Just two years before he began his masterwork, Chaucer worried about the diversity of current speech in his envoy for *Troilus and Criseyde* (1385):

And for ther is so gret diversite
In Englissh and in writyng of oure tonge,
So prey I god that non myswrite the(e),
Ne the(e) mysmetre for defaute of tonge.
And red wherso thow be, or elles songe,
That thow be understonde, God I biseche!
But yet to purpos of my rather speche.

He prayed that none miswrite, mismeter (wrongly scan the measures), or misunderstand the purpose of his earlier *(rather)* speech, his spoken words that became this "litel bok."

THE EMERGENCE OF MODERN ENGLISH

Chaucer had good reason for concern. The Great Vowel Shift was beginning a modification in quality of all long vowels and diphthongs, and the inconsistent treatment of weakly stressed vowels placed many syllables in jeopardy. The shift raised [a] to [æ] (and later[e]), [e] to [i] , [ɔ] to [o] , and [o] to [u].[1] The vowels formerly pronounced [i] and [u] became, respectively, [əi] (later [ai]) and [əu] (later [au]). Thus Chaucer's final vowels in *diversite* and *the(e)* rhyme with modern *they;* his pronoun *I* rhymes with modern *me;* his verb *write* rhymes with modern *feet; beseche* and *speche* rhyme with modern *aitch;* his pronoun *oure* rhymes with modern *boot.* Although metrical evidence is difficult to interpret, Chaucer quite possibly pronounced the weakly stressed *e* in *myswrite* and *elles* but ignored it in *tonge, understonde, speche,* and other words in this same stanza that comprise those seven iambic pentameter lines of rhyme royal.

At the outset of the early Modern English period (1500–1700) fewer than five million people in the world spoke English, as compared to twelve million speakers of French, ten million of German, nine million of Italian, and eight million of Spanish. During the next two centuries those "intelligent beings expressing their minds" in English included More, Tyndale, Milton, Newton, Locke, and Dryden. At its center was Elizabethan English, the language of Shakespeare, Marlowe, Bacon, Donne, Raleigh, Spenser, and the queen herself. From this stage of linguistic development came the earliest varieties of American English.

---

[1]All pronunciations in this article are in the notation of the International Phonetic Alphabet. The Pronunciation Key lists these symbols and their equivalents in the pronunciation system employed for this Dictionary.

By 1700 the number of English speakers had nearly doubled, while German, Italian, and Spanish had scarcely maintained their numbers of two centuries earlier, and only French surpassed the growth rate of English among the western European nations.

As an emergent world language English advanced with the spread of the London Standard and general education, with the loosening of class distinctions, and through the influence of what would today be called the mass media. By the year 1500 printed books in all of Europe included thirty-five thousand titles, most of which were in Latin. During the next hundred and forty years twenty thousand English titles appeared in print, and scribal composition of manuscripts became virtually a lost art. England regained its cultural self-reliance with those new sources of influence and the spread of empire. In 1579 E. K., the anonymous editor of Spenser's *The Shepheardes Calender,* commended his author and reflected the spirit of the age:

> For in my opinion it is one special prayse of many which are dew to this Poete, that he has labored to restore, as is their rightfull heritage, such good and naturall English words as have been long time out of use and almost cleane disherited. Which is the onely cause that our Mother tonge, which truely of it self is both ful enough for prose and stately enough for verse, hath long time ben counted more bare and barrein of both.

The English recognized the legitimacy of their native tongue for all modes of communication, including those technical fields formerly dominated by Latin and Greek. In his *Elementary* (1582) Richard Mulcaster defended the use of English and explained the implications of his work:

> For the account of our tongue, both in pen and speech, no man will doubt therof who is able to judge what those things be which any tongue be of account; which things I take to be three: the autority of the people which speak it, the matter and argument wherein the speech dealeth, the manifold use for which the speech serveth. For all which three our tongue needeth not give place to any of her peers.

Mulcaster and others wrote rules for pronunciation and grammar and tried to enrich the national word store. Earlier the Italians, Spanish, French, and Germans had done these same things for their own varieties of speech, as the transformation of local vernaculars into national languages characterized the Renaissance in every European country that it touched.

During the reign of Elizabeth (1558–1603) a language pattern developed that was to become the base form of early American English. London usage reflected the linguistic patriotism of the English Renaissance and accepted forms from a variety of regional and social dialects in the development of a spoken standard. Roger Ascham, Elizabeth's Latin tutor, was a Yorkshireman; Raleigh preserved his distinctive Devonshire speech throughout his life; Essex was from Hertfordshire; Sidney, from Kent; Shakespeare, from Warwickshire; of Welsh ancestry, John Donne emerged from the London merchant class. The language habits of all those speakers contributed to the shaping of the urban pattern and to the development of vigorous conversational speech.

THE BEGINNINGS OF AMERICAN ENGLISH

The fluid structure of Early Modern English underlies the formation of American English. Although the Great Vowel Shift had assigned new values to the long vowels, many British, Scottish, and Irish social dialects were slow to accept all of these emergent features. Morphology and syntax showed inventiveness and flexibility in word formation and adaptations, as with the free use of affixes in word building *(re-, de-, -ish, -ize)*, functional shift of parts of speech (nouns used as verbs, verbs as nouns, and both as adjectival or adverbial modifiers), frequent parenthetical expression, and phrase structures of predication, complementation, and coordination that reflect the intonational contours of the spoken language.

Drawn from that rapidly flowing stream, American English shows a much greater uniformity than its origins might suggest. Einar Haugen has called this evolution of the national language in American "Babel in reverse." The concept of the American melting pot can be found in the writing of St. John de Crèvecoeur, a Norman-French immigrant and the eponym of St. Johnsbury, Vermont. In the *Letters of an American Farmer* (1782) he provided the logic for a unified American language and culture:

> What attachment can a poor European emigrant have for a country where he had nothing. The knowledge of the language, the love of a few kindred as poor as himself, were the only cords that tied him; his country is now that which gives him land, bread, protection, and consequence: *Ubi panis ibi patria* [where there is bread, there is one's fatherland] is the motto of all emigrants. What is an American, this new man? He is either a European, or the descendant of a European, hence that strange mixture of blood, which you will find in no other country. I could point out to you a family whose grandfather was an Englishman, whose wife was Dutch, whose son married a French woman, and whose present four sons have now four wives of different nations. *He* is an American, who, leaving behind him all of his ancient prejudices and manners, receives new ones from the new mode of life he has embraced, the new government he obeys, and the new rank he holds. He becomes an American by being received in the broad lap of our great *Alma Mater* [Dear Mother]. Here individuals of all nations are melted into a new race of men, whose labors and posterity will one day cause great changes in the world. Americans are the western pilgrims, who are carrying along with them that great mass of art, science, vigor, and industry which began long since in the east; they will finish the great circle. The Americans were once scattered all over Europe; here they are incorporated into one of the finest systems of population which has ever appeared, and which will hereafter become distinct by the power of the different climates they inhabit. The American ought therefore to love this country better than that wherein either he or his forefathers were born.

The first substantial collection of immigrant literature appeared in New England, where writers worked with Elizabethan patterns and recorded a variety of occasional spellings and distinctive forms. In *The History of Plimmoth Plantation* (1620–1647) William Bradford wrote *burthen, fadom, furder, gifen (given), gusle (guzzle), trible (triple), vacabund (vagabond),* and *woules (wolves).* Roger Williams rhymed *abode/God, blood/good,* and *America/away* in *A Key to the Language of America* (1643). Ann Bradstreet paired *conceit/great, stood/flood,* and *satisfy/reality* in *The Tenth Muse, Lately Sprung Up in America* (1650). Two generations later Edward Taylor alternated *spoil* and *spile,* as well as *soot* and *sut,* and rhymed *is/kiss, far/cur,* and *vile/soil.*

Early American grammar also showed a great variety of forms. In 1630, aboard the *Arabella* and westward-bound, John Winthrop preached "A Model of Christian Charity" with the line "We must love brotherly without dissimulation: we must love one another with a pure heart fervently." Bradford used *rid, runned* (and *ranne*), *drunk, writ,* and *shrunk* as past forms of *ride, run, drink, write,* and *shrink,* respectively. Williams declared, "My disease is I know not what" and offered the interrogative form "Sleep you?" Mary Rowlandson wrote, "It is not my tongue or pen can express the sorrow of my heart . . ." in her captive narrative of 1675.

During these same years cultural activity all along the Atlantic seaboard produced the first Americanisms. The following native words, among hundreds of others, originated, gained special meaning, or entered the English language through American speech in the seventeenth century: *creek* (stream), *fat pine, green corn,* and *papoose* from Massachusetts; *catfish, corn* (maize), *mock*[ing]*bird, polecat* (skunk), and *raccoon* from Virginia; *Chippewa, ground hog, Manhattan,* and *Podunk* from New York; *gang* [of birds], *hominy, snakeroot,* and *Virginian* from Maryland; *frontier people, oyster rake, samp,* and *wampum* from Rhode Island; *grocery* (store), *hot cakes* (corn cakes), *peavine* (a climbing plant similar to the pea), and *sunfish* from Pennsylvania; *settlement* and *swampland* from Connecticut; *Dutch grass* (any one of various grasses) and *hickory nut* from South Carolina; *frontier* from New Jersey. Beyond the frontiers *pilot* (a guide over a land route) appeared in what is now Colorado, and *Miami* from what is now Illinois.

NATIVE AMERICAN INFLUENCES

These words suggest the importance of Amerindian loans, especially for artifacts and places. From the Algonquian dialects alone English and French in the New World borrowed more than a hundred terms that remain current in American speech. In addition to *Chippewa, hominy, Manhattan, papoose, Podunk, samp, squash,* and *wampum,* the eastern tribes provided *caribou, mackinaw, pone, Tammany, terrapin,* and *toboggan.* These often suggest multiple language contacts; as *caribou* and *toboggan* entered through Canadian French in the north, *barbecue, canoe,* and *cushaw* came out of the West Indies through Spanish. Spanish later transmitted *anaqua* (the Texas "knockaway" tree), *coyote,* and *peyote* from the Nahuatl Indian language of Mexico. From Quechua, probably through the cooperative efforts of French and Spanish, New Orleans' *lagniappe* appeared somewhat later. The American place names comprise the greatest Amerindian contribution. From *Appalachia* and the *Alleghenies,* across all five Great Lakes *(Erie, Ontario, Huron, Michigan,* and *Superior),* from *Chicago* to *Sitka,* Indian words cover the continent. Emblematic of American language and culture are the blends, such as *Bayou La Batre,* Alabama (Choctaw *bayuk* = "creek" + French *de la Batre* = "of the [artillery] battery"), and *Minneapolis,* Minnesota (Dakota *minne* = "water" + Greek/English (a)*polis* = "city"), or the loan translations *Spearfish,* South Dakota, *Warroad,* Minnesota, and *Yellow Dirt Creek,* Georgia, besides the Indian loans of the state names *Alabama* (tribe), *Dakota* (tribe), and *Minnesota* (Dakota *minne* = "water" + *sota* = "white").

LOANS FROM THE EUROPEAN LANGUAGES

Early loans from European languages correspond with Dutch, French, and German settlements in the coastal colonies and along the first interior frontiers. During their New Amsterdam experience the Dutch added to American English the words *boss, Bowery, coleslaw, cookie, sleigh, stoop,* and *waffle.* Later they gave more place names, such as *Catskill, Kinderhook,* and *Schuyler.* Although Thoreau spoke of *Yankee ingenuity* in 1843, the durable nickname probably had its origin in the Dutch diminutive for *John (Johnny), Jan (Janke).* Saint Nicholas, clipped to *Sint Klaas* in a Dutch dialect, became *Santa Claus* before the Revolutionary War.

French loans contrast sharply with the Dutch and later German contributions. Although they also gave English such ordinary household words as *chowder, gopher, pumpkin, sashay, shanty,* and *shivaree,* the enterprising French illustrate their experience in a distinctive set of loans. Explorers, missionaries, and frontier warriors made American words of *bateau, coulee, crevasse, levee, portage, prairie,* and *voyageur.* As the English, Dutch, and Swedes struggled to control the seaboard the French ranged across the interior and left their mark with the names of places at *Bienville, Cape Girardeau, Prairie du Chien,* and *Sault Sainte Marie.*

Early German loans on the frontier are difficult to ascertain. Like the Scandinavians and Anglo-Saxons in England, the Germans and the English spoke languages with a common word stock that still endures in the basic vocabularies of both cultures. For the same reason it is impossible to determine whether *nosh* (snack) and *schlemiel* are of Yiddish or German origin and whether *spook* and *dumb* (stupid) are of Dutch or German origin, because in each case the words occur in both languages. Only when the Germans established discrete territories, as the Dutch had in New York, did the loans begin to appear in significant numbers from Pennsylvania, Cincinnati, Chicago, Milwaukee, St. Louis, and east-central Texas. From early Pennsylvania, American English probably received *smearcase, ponhaws (pannhass* = "pan" + *hare* = "scrapple"), *rainworm,* and possibly George Washington's most familiar title, *The Father of His Country,* which first appeared as *Des Landes Vater* on a *Nord Amerikanische Kalender* for 1779.

THE AMERICAN FRONTIER

The frontier contributions of the Swedes and folk speakers of British, Irish, and Scottish dialects are virtually impossible to identify because they were soon united in a common culture. As Crèvecoeur described the people at the outbreak of the Revolution:

> They are a mixture of English, Scotch, Irish, French, Dutch, Germans, and Swedes. From this promiscuous breed, that race now called Americans have risen. The eastern provinces [i.e., the coastal colonies] must needs be expected, as being unmixed descendants of Englishmen.

Early frontier speech probably included the pronouns *hit* (for *it*), *hisn, ourn, theirn,* and *yourn,* the inflected verb forms *clumb, drug, holp,* and *riz,* the auxiliary construction *mought could* (or *might could*), and a large number of folk pronunciations and lexical items. Scottish forms, also appearing in the poetry of Burns, include *duds* (clothes), *gumption, hunkers, mountain billy* (hillbilly), *tow* (cloth), and the distinctive pronunciations reflected in *chimla (chimney), het (heated),* and *southron (southern),* as well as the simplification of consonant clusters, as in *kin' (kind)* and *sin' (since),* and the total assimilation of *l* after back vowels, as in *ca' (call), fu' (full),* and *howe (hollow).* From Irish sources probably came *mammy, moonshine,* and *mountain dew.* General English folk forms also included *clean, flat,* and *plumb* (meaning "completely"), *passel* (from *parcel*), and *sass* (from *sauce*). Many of these forms appear in Middle English, and all survive in current American Midland and Southern dialects.

THE EVOLUTION OF DIALECTS IN AMERICAN ENGLISH

During the eighteenth century the principal dialect regions of American English developed. These are the historic cultural areas. Every major regional dialect area, past and present, corresponds almost perfectly with a cultural area delimited by other social systems. The presbyters of Appalachia mark the pattern of Scottish settlement, the Dutch and German barns show a Germanic presence in the eastern and east-central states, the methods of cooking cornmeal in *pones, dodgers,* and *hush puppies* reflect the settlement patterns of various groups, and the superstitions connected with chicken clavicles *(wishbone, pulley bone,* or *lucky bone)* identify social groups, as do the southern greetings *hey* (for *hi*) and *Christmas Gift!* The styles of folk, blues, jazz, and rock music also correspond with cultural areas, contrasting the perfected forms of the Carter Family in Appalachia and Huddie Ledbetter in the Upper Delta, the rural blues of Richard Amerson and the urban blues of Bill Broonzy, the Kansas City jazz of Count Basie and the Chicago jazz of Bud Freeman, or the middle Georgia rock of the Allman Brothers and the southern California rock of the Eagles. All of these are as regionally distinctive as the voices of the musicians are. Wherever clear-cut boundaries of culture can be reconstructed on the basis of historical information from archaeology, music, graphic arts, or the social sciences, dialect differences can be predicted, based on the most persuasive kind of circumstantial evidence: the recorded experience of the forebears of a speech community.

Modern American seaboard dialects preserve the early system from Maine to the Florida Keys and along the Gulf shores to Brownsville, Texas. The coastal communities shared the evolution of urban British pronunciation, grammar, and vocabulary, but very different speech forms developed throughout the interior along the old frontier. Neither of these regions is a uniform cultural area, but remarkable concordances of speech endure. Early centers at Boston, New York, and Philadelphia were quite different from their southern counterparts at Richmond, Charleston, and New Orleans. Along the Atlantic and Gulf coasts, however, the dialects shared important features: the loss of a constricted *r* after vowels (making *popper* homophonous with *Papa*); a contrast of stressed vowels in *Mary, merry,* and *marry;* a most distinctive diphthong in *dues, news,* and *shoes* that approaches that in *few, music,* and *pupil;* the loss of *h* in *whip, white, wheelbarrow,* and similar words; and even a "broad *a*" in *hammer, pasture,* and *Saturday.* Besides the familiar British past form *et* (of *eat*), the coastal dialects also shared lexical features, such as *hog's head cheese, haslets* (or *harslets*), and *piazza* (porch).

The coastal pattern divides near the Potomac. To the north the language and culture drifted away from British influence more quickly than they did in the South, where the early planters of Jefferson's agrarian democracy required close association with British commerce, education, and industry. Southern coastal dialects preserved several other British features: the "clear *l*" of *lean* in *Billy* and *Nelly* as opposed to the "dark *l*" of *load,* a flapped *r* in *three* and *thresh,* as heard in some current British pronunciations of *very* (written humorously as *veddy*), and even an occasional back vowel in *pot* and *crop.* Along the Gulf Coast these forms had mixed currency, largely because of the powerful influence of New Orleans, a cultural center that dominated the entire interior of the South until the Civil War. Basic Northern and Southern contrasts persist from the Potomac to the mouth of the Rio Grande: the Southern drawls (patterns of diphthongs, lengthening, and intonation), the vowel of *ride* [a] (which northerners confuse with *rod* [ɑ]), the vowel of *bird* [ɜɪ] (which northerners associate with Brooklynese), a positional variant [əu] in *house* and *mouse* but not in *rouse* and *cows,* the plural pronoun *you-all (y'all),* the past form *drug* (of *drag*), and a large set of vocabulary forms, such as *mosquito hawk* (dragonfly), *crocus sack* (burlap bag), *snap beans* (string beans), and *tote* (carry).

The New Orleans focal area interrupts this pattern, extending its influence from Mobile Bay to beyond the Sabine River. A General Coastal and New Orleans contrast is marked by *serenade, bateau, clabber cheese,* and *mush* along the Southern coast, except in the area of New Orleans dominion, where *shivaree (charivari), pirogue, cream cheese,* and *cush-cush* prevail. Although *cush* and *cush-cush* have currency throughout the South, nowhere else is there a double form to match the New Orleans usage. Other distinctive terms are *flambeau* (makeshift torch), *(h)armonica* (instead of Southern *harp*), *lagniappe* (something extra, instead of South Carolina *brawtus,* Texas-Spanish *pilon,* and Florida-Minorcan *countra*), *wishbone* (instead of South Midland and Southern *pulley bone*), and *creole tomatoes* (instead of Northern *cherry tomatoes* and Southern *tommytoes*).

Unlike coastal speech, the Midland dialects of that transition area between the North and South grew up in the interior. From Pennsylvania to Georgia the eastern boundary of the Midland dialect area coincides with the geography of the old frontier. Settlers took the land in the great migrations out of Pennsylvania, Maryland, and Virginia during the half century that preceded the Revolutionary War (1725–1775). Thomas' discovery of the Cumberland Gap in 1750 provided a southern gateway to the Middle West, that passage into Kentucky for the ancestors of both Jefferson Davis and Abraham Lincoln. Before the War of 1812 the frontier extended out of Pittsburgh and down the Ohio River in the north and out of the Yadkin Valley of North Carolina in the south, across Tennessee and Kentucky along the Wilderness Trail of Pennsylvania's Daniel Boone.

Like other American dialects, the Midland varieties rose from a British-English base, but on the frontier the social composition was different. Six of the seven ethnic groups mentioned by Crèvecoeur spoke no British English before they arrived in North America. Later those residents of the interior Midland dialect areas were landbound without ports of entry to receive the influence of English culture and to share in the development of the prestigious London forms. More important, the frontier people occupied themselves mainly with survival in a hostile region. Those factors influenced the disparate groups in a uniform way: Midland dialects resisted the phonological changes under way in England and in the coastal colonies to the north and south; English, Irish, and Scottish folk speech reinforced the regional grammar and vocabulary, giving these American dialects identities of their own.

The Midland pattern contrasts most sharply with the interior varieties of Northern and Southern speech. With a domain that in modern times extends from western New England and upstate New York, along the southern shores of the Great Lakes and then northwestward into the upper Middle West, the Inland Northern dialect spread from its eastern source after the War of 1812. With the construction of the Erie Canal, the watercourse from Albany to Buffalo gave upstate New York and New England access to the Great Lakes, as had the construction of the earlier and slower roadways and the later, more efficient railroads. As Northern speech extended out of upper New Jersey and northern Pennsylvania a major dialect boundary was established with the southern limit of *darning needle* (dragonfly), *pail,* and *whiffletree,* contrasting with North Midland *snake feeder, bucket,* and *singletree.* From upstate New York and across Ohio, Indiana, Illinois, and Iowa westward, the division of Northern and North Midland remains apparent in the pronunciation of *fog* and *hog,* which are pronounced with the vowel of *father* in the North and the vowel of *dog* in the North Midland, in the pronunciation of the diphthong of *cow, house,* and *towel,* which is [æu] in the North Midland, beginning with a higher vowel that is closer to that of *lather,* and the existence of an excrescent *r* in *"warsh"* and *"Warshington"* in some Midland speech. More clearly distinctive are the Northern terms *stone wall, pail, swill, teeter-totter, faucet, pit* [of a cherry or peach], and *fire-fly* contrasting with the Midland terms *stone fence, bucket, slops, seesaw, spicket* (spigot), *seed,* and *lightning bug.* In the West the Northern/Midland distinction is most clearly heard in the pronunciation of *car, yard,* and similar words: the Northern pronunciation is marked by a vowel closer to the vowel of *father;* the Midland pronunciation, by one closer to the vowel of *saw.*

Prior to the Civil War other interior forms spread from south of the Great Lakes to the fringes of the plantation cultures from Virginia to Texas and gave rise to the principal Midland varieties, North and South. Between those contrasting cultures the Midland area is perhaps best divided by a phonological Mason-Dixon Line established by the pronunciation of the medial consonant of *greasy,* with an [s] to the north and a [z] to the south. On the Atlantic Coast the boundary replicates the historic Mason-Dixon Line, the common border of Pennsylvania and Maryland. Philadelphia, with the pronunciation [s], must be considered a Northern territory. Westward, however, this difference in pronunciation marks the division within the Midland territory, from Ohio to Missouri. Heading south, a traveler encounters the line at approximately the same place where grits replace hash browns on the breakfast menu, where greens appear at dinner, and where nice, white rice served with Indiana- or Kentucky-fried chicken are all pronounced with a vowel that northerners confuse with the vowel common to *cat, hat,* and *sat.* With this feature comes the first suggestion of the drawl, indigenous bluegrass music, and stock-car, instead of Indy-type or midget-automobile, racing. Along that same line the northern extent of Southern cultural penetration appears in these contrasts: North Midland *bunk, wishbone, husks, headcheese, fritters, bag,* and *turtle* versus South Midland *pallet, pulley bone, shucks, souse* (or *pressed meat*), *flitters, sack,* and *terrapin.*

South Midland speech is a Southern dialect, formerly called Hill Southern in contrast with the Upcountry and Lower Southern patterns (Plantation Southern) to the south and east. The principal South Midland/Southern boundary follows the Blue Ridge Mountains across Virginia, the Carolinas, and Georgia. In South Carolina and Georgia the boundary coincides with the hundred-eighty-day growing season for cotton, the waterways, the soil types, and the cultural organizations inseparable from the plantation systems devoted to the cultivation of indigo, rice, and cane as well as cotton.

Those geographical features and cultural factors underlie the Midland enclaves, as far south as the Florida panhandle, and their Southern counterparts as far north as the St. Francis Basin of Arkansas and the boot heel of Missouri, the cotton country around New Madrid. South Midland is marked by the presence of a constricted *r* after a vowel in *bird, car,* and *horse* and identical vowels in *right* and *ride,* whereas Southern preserves a diphthong in *right* and similar words. Lexical contrasts include South Midland *green beans, red worm, fireboard, French harp* (for *harmonica*), and *tow sack* (for *burlap bag*), versus Southern *snap beans, earthworm, mantelpiece, harp,* and *crocus sack.* In the east South Midland contrasts with Virginia Piedmont Southern with *snake feeder, peanuts,* and *terrapin* versus *snake doctor, goobers,* and *cooter.* In the Mississippi Valley the South Midland dialect occupies the territory by-passed by the plantation cultures as unsuitable for the production of cotton, cane, and rice.

Where the planters extended their operations north and west, as in upper Louisiana, west Tennessee, Arkansas, and east Texas, Lower Southern features outline the area. The Coastal and Gulf Plains were settled from the east, but the deltas of the Mississippi, Atchafalaya, Yazoo, Red, and St. Francis rivers received their populations from the south. As a result interior Southern areas do not show the predictable gradations of uniformity from east to west that are found in the North and North Midland regions.

These Southern dialects are distinguished by coastal forms and by the distinctive contributions of the New Orleans focal area. Coastal Southern pronunciation includes the loss of constricted *r* after vowels, the contrast between the stressed vowels of *Mary, merry,* and *marry,* a "clear *l*" in *Billy* and *Nelly,* and vocabulary items such as *mosquito hawk, crocus sack, hoghead cheese* (or *hog's head cheese*), and *red bug* (instead of *chigger*). Besides *locker* (for *closet*) and *flambeau* (for *makeshift lamp*), the domain of New Orleans is marked by the pervasiveness of *lagniappe, pirogue* (a dugout canoe), *cream cheese* (cottage cheese), *wishbone* (instead of South Midland and Southern *pulley bone*), and *(h)armonica* (instead of South Midland *French harp* or Southern *harp*). Such forms appear as far north as Lake Providence and Monroe, Louisiana, Yazoo City, Mississippi, and along the Gulf Coast beyond the Sabine River into Texas and eastward to Mobile Bay.

The speech of the West is complicated by the blending of Northern, Midland, and Southern forms, as well as by a heavy Spanish influence from Texas to California. The Northern Midland boundary extends over Iowa and cuts across South Dakota in a northwesterly direction. In Montana and Idaho the presence of North and South Midland features reflects the history of the frontier and the enterprises of cattle, agriculture, and mining. Throughout the Rocky Mountains and the urban West Coast the dialects of the early settlers determined the pattern. Seattle and San Francisco speech grew from an Inland Northern base quite similar to old-fashioned Chicago speech. Denver and Los Angeles also developed from that same base, although the Hispanic influence in both places and the successive waves of newcomers from the East, especially in Los Angeles, have obscured the regional pattern that endures with greater stability in Seattle and San Francisco. The Midland influence is strongest west of the Rockies, from Idaho to Arizona, and especially in the conservative speech of Boise, Salt Lake City, and Phoenix. On a train near Yuma, Arizona, during the Great Depression, Woody Guthrie heard the complexity of American speech in the New West as he was going to California:

> There was a big mixture of people here. I could hear the fast accents from the big Eastern joints. You heard the slow, easy-going voices of Southern swamp dwellers, and the people from the Southern hills and mountains. Then another would talk up, and it would be the dry, nosy twang of the folks from the flat wheat plains; or the dialect of the people that come from other countries, whose parents talked another tongue. Then you would hear the slow, outdoor voices of the men from Arizona, riding a short hop to get a job, see a girl, or to throw a little celebration. There was the deep, thick voices of two or three Negroes. It sounded mighty good to me.

THE INFLUENCE OF BILINGUALISM

In just that way, moving across the country, the national idiom grew through languages and dialects in contact. Spanish, French, and German bilingualism marks the regional patterns of Florida, Louisiana, and Pennsylvania, as well as of south Texas. Gullah, an English-based pidgin, developed in the Sea Islands and low country of South Carolina and Georgia. From that source many varieties of American black folk speech are derived, reflecting various stages of creolization as the dialects merge with the dominant patterns. Social dialects grew through urban and rural experiences throughout the country, many of these related to the Americanization of European bilinguals in the urban North and the integration of blacks in all sectors of society. These dialects are further conditioned and refined by formal and situational styles, including slang, ethnic variation, and patterns of usage reflecting socioeconomic class.

Before urban American Spanish gained prominence in San Antonio, Los Angeles, and Miami, that language had already made large contributions to English in the West. Besides the place names, extending from the *Rio Grande* to *Montana,* the Spanish vocabulary marks the cattle country with Western words: *arroyo, bronc(o), chaparral, canyon, cinch, corral, frijoles, hoosegow, lasso, lariat, mesa, mustang, patio, pinto, pronto, ranch, remuda, rodeo, sombrero,* and *tortilla.*

In bilingual communities Spanish speakers of English tend to avoid regional dialect forms in favor of terms from the general vocabulary, despite the distinctive accent and syntax carried over from the parent language. The same tendency appears among the French in Louisiana, who freely use their native loans, such as *banquette* (sidewalk), *boudin* (blood sausage), *faisdodo* (country dance), and *jambalaya,* as well as loan translations and adaptations, such as *coffee black, cream cheese* (cottage cheese), and *(h)armonica.* These same speakers resist the Southern regionalisms *pulley bone* and *snap beans.* German, Italian, Scandinavian, Slavic, Spanish, and Yiddish speakers reflect the same trend in the urban North, perhaps through learning from books rather than by simple oral acquisition, and perhaps through efforts to translate from their native tongues. In becoming Americans all of these people enriched the national language and culture. If examples are limited to food alone, Germans provided *bock beer* and *pretzels,* Italians brought *antipasto* and *pizza,* Scandinavians added *lingonberries* and *smorgasbord;* Slavs contributed *kolacky* and *kielbasa,* Yiddish-speaking Germans and Slavs gave *bagels* and *gefilte fish;* and Mexican Spanish provided the base for an endless variety of *enchiladas, burritos,* and *tacos* as its cooking entered the fast-food industry.

CONTRIBUTIONS FROM THE AFRICAN LANGUAGES

The full impact of African languages through Gullah and Plantation Creole remains to be properly assessed, but evidence suggests the influence is significant. Among African loans these have gained currency in the national language: *chigger, goober, gumbo, jazz, juke (-box, -joint,* and *-step), okra, voodoo,* and *yam.* Some are regionally restricted to the South: *cooter* (turtle), *cush* and *cushcush* (mush), and *pinder* (peanut). Others seem limited to the South Carolina and Georgia low country: *buckra* (white man), *det* (heavy), as in *det rain* and *det shower,* and *pinto* (coffin). In addition to the loan-words from Gullah (or "Geechee," the interior Georgia pattern), the creolization of that auxiliary language may have left its mark on American English phonology and grammar as well. As a contact vernacular or language of business (and the probable source of the word *pidgin*), Gullah provided a medium of communication for African slaves and their American supervisors. Thus the pidgin was a language native to neither group. In the development of Plantation Creole (from Portuguese *crioulo* = "white man") the language acquired the highly complex phonological and grammatical rules and complete vocabulary, features necessary in a self-reliant, independent language. General Southern features today include many correspondences with Plantation Creole, the creolized English black folk speech of the plantation cultures of cane, cotton, indigo, and rice. Southern vowel nasality often replaces nasal consonants in *am, been,* and *bacon,* but this feature occurs in Parisian and Louisiana French, as well as in Plantation Creole and West African languages. The simplification of consonant clusters, as in *des* (for *desk* and *desks*) or *tase* (for *taste* and *tastes*), is commonplace in all of those languages, as well as in the Scottish dialect of Robert Burns, who, like American southerners, black and white, often assimilated *l* after back vowels, as in *fa'* (fall) and *saut* (salt). Similarly, the pervasive deletion of articles, copulas, prepositions, and other function words, so characteristic of Gullah and its creolized extensions, is a feature regularly associated with the speech of French, German, and Spanish bilinguals. Nevertheless, this fact remains: large numbers of black and white speakers share those features across the lower South, especially in those areas dominated by the plantation cultures.

THE INFLUENCE OF SOCIAL DIALECTS

As creolization reflects the blending of languages and cultures, so slang, argot, and social dialects mark the activities of subcultures within the basic social structure. Although nothing as widespread as Cockney and Australian rhyming slang has developed in America, inventive usage here has steadily modified native speech. Most slang originates in the specialized conversations of particular groups, in which usage reinforces group identity and develops into private codes that may later gain wide acceptance. These include such now-familiar terms as *clout* and *gerrymander* from politics, *blues* and *jazz* from music, *headline* and *editorial* from journalism, and *by a nose, inside track, front-runner, shoo-in,* and *sure thing* from the vocabulary of horse racing. The distinctive words of other groups—pickpockets, CB operators, and computer specialists— suggest the ways in which the subcultures function and illustrate the ways in which language develops.

Social dialects also underlie the regional patterns of speech, reflecting absolute factors, such as age and ethnic origin, and relative factors, such as education and social position. As a healthy language is always changing, the age and experience of its speakers are recorded by incipient, dominant, and recessive forms, as demonstrated in the vocabulary of automobiles: the emergent *gas guzzler* and *pimpmobile,* the durable *sedan* and *limousine,* and the relic *tin lizzie* and *roadster.* Ethnic terms are the cultural birthrights of individual speakers and great linguistic resources for society at large. Yiddish *schlock, chutzpah, macher,* and *schmaltz* have moved from the Jewish communities to the national language, as have the specialized Sicilian terms *capo, Cosa Nostra,* and *Mafia* in urban American subcultures. Education reinforces language trends with the spread of generalized patterns of pronunciation, grammar, and vocabulary, but these are challenged by migrant accents in Chicago today just as they were in London four hundred years ago. As Latinos made *macho* an American word, blacks have put many Southern regionalisms, such as *funky, up-tight,* and *right on,* into common usage. The language reflects cultural patterns, refined and strengthened through association and social status.

Social dialects also mark the evolution of a language. In America the middle classes have generated great changes. These include the absorption of immigrant cultures at the lower level and influence upon the dominant culture at the higher level. As the linguistic and cultural forms are traditionally conservative in both aristocratic and folk groups, however different their social styles, middle-class society and speech alter those conventional patterns from below and from above. Just as members of the secular and regular clergy, educators, lawyers, politicians, and physicians helped shape the London Standard from the early Middle Ages through the English Renaissance because they were conversant with both the ruling class and the common people, so new patterns of American usage grow today through the influence of upper-middle-class dialects. Even stronger influences appear from the speech of the lower middle class, especially in urban centers, where clerks, cab drivers, and telephone operators come in contact with the entire community in their daily work.

Of these, ethnic dialects preserve the most complicated social varieties of language and reflect the essential spirit of American culture. As frontier societies developed distinctive regional patterns, Spanish, French, Dutch, Scandinavian, and German settlers used their native languages before adopting the dominant English dialect. English, Irish, and Scottish folk speech constituted probably the most influential ethnic varieties on the frontier, but these were modified by the language habits of their neighbors. In the process of Americanization, Europeans, Africans, and Asians gave the language some of its most familiar words: *chop suey, hamburger, hillbilly, juke box, pizza, prairie, rodeo, Santa Claus, smorgasbord,* and *tycoon.*

The national vocabulary reflects the intimacy of conversation and the evolution of democratic social forms. John Adams proposed that Congress establish an American Academy "for refining, correcting, improving, and ascertaining the English language." Later, when asked to preside over such activities, Thomas Jefferson responded:

> There are so many differences between us and England, of soil, climate, culture, productions, laws, religion, and government, that we must be left far behind the march of circumstances, were we to hold ourselves rigorously to their standard. If, like the French Academicians, it were proposed to *fix* our language, it would be fortunate that the step were not taken in the days of our Saxon ancestors, whose vocabulary would illy express the science of this day. Judicious neology can alone give strength and copiousness to language, and enable it to be the vehicle of new ideas.

Instead of rules from a National Academy of English, Americans accepted the common-law customs of intelligent conversation with all of its modifications through time and circumstance. Current usage, for example, may reject *illy express* and *judicious neology,* but history shows the correctness of Jefferson's message. He recognized the certainty of change, the function of language as a cultural tool, and the importance of thoughtful selection. Through common-law customs of speech and writing the national language develops words and records social facts. This Dictionary orders those materials of discourse and transmits the substance of the American heritage.

Where Our Grammar Came From

Karl W. Dykema

The title of this paper is too brief to be quite accurate. Perhaps with the following subtitle it does not promise too much: A partial account of the origin and development of the attitudes which commonly pass for grammatical in Western culture and particularly in English-speaking societies.

The etymology of *grammar* shows rather sharp changes in meaning: It starts with Greek *gramma, letter* (of the alphabet), itself a development from *graphein, draw* or *write*. The plural *grammata* develops in meaning through *letters* to *alphabet* to the *rudiments of writing,* to *the rudiments of learning*. The adjective form *grammatike* with *techne* meant the art of knowing one's letters. From this form comes the Latin *grammaticus*. The medieval vernacular forms with *r* are something of a mystery, appearing first in Old Provençal as *gramaira* and developing in English with a variety of spellings, often with only one *m* and ending in *er*. One of the more amusing forms is that with the first *r* dissimilated to *l, glamour*.

In present usage at least four senses can be distinguished which have an application to language: (1) The complete structural pattern of a language learned unconsciously by the child as he acquires his native tongue; (2) an attempt to describe objectively and systematically this fundamental structure, usually called descriptive grammar; (3) a partial description of the language based on puristic or pedagogical objectives, usually called prescriptive grammar; (4) a conviction held by a good many people that somewhere there is an authoritative book called a grammar, the conscientious memorization of which will eliminate all difficulties from their use of language. This I call grammar as remedy. It is mainly with the last two of these notions of grammar that I shall concern myself, prescriptive grammar and grammar as remedy, and how the earlier conceptions of grammar were metamorphosed into them.

As the etymology of the word suggests, Western grammar begins with the ancient Greeks. As early as Plato we find in the *Sophist* the statement that a word describing action is a verb (rhema), one which performs the action is a noun (onoma). Aristotle adds conjunctions (syndesmoi), recognizes that sentences have predicates, and is aware of three genders and of inflection (*Rhetoric,* etc.). The Stoics attempted to separate linguistic study from philosophy and made important contributions to the discipline. In their writings we find terms which are approximately equivalent to *noun, verb, conjunction, article, number, gender, case, voice, mood,* and *tense.*[1] But the direct source of most of our wide-

---

[1] R. H. Robins, *Ancient and Medieval Grammatical Theory in Europe* (London, 1951), pp. 20–35.

ly used grammatical terms is Dionysius Thrax's little *Techne Grammatike,* which Gilbert Murray recollects his great-uncle still using at the Merchants Taylors' School in the nineteenth century to learn Greek from.[2]

A few quotations from this little work will illustrate how close many of our school grammars still are to their source of more than 2000 years ago:

> A sentence is a combination of words, either in prose or verse, making complete sense. . . . Of discourse there are eight parts: noun, verb, participle, article, pronoun, preposition, adverb, and conjunction. . . . A noun is a part of discourse having cases, indicating a body (as 'stone') or a thing (as 'education'), and is used in a common and a peculiar way (i.e., is common or proper). . . . A verb is a word without case, admitting tenses, persons, and numbers, and indicating action and passion (i.e., being-acted-upon). . . . A pronoun is a word indicative of definite persons and is used in place of a noun. . . . The adverb is an uninflected part of discourse, used of a verb or subjoined to a verb. . . The conjunction is a word conjoining or connecting thought in some order and filling a gap in the expression.[3]

The few examples I have given emphasize analysis by meaning, because that is the aspect of classical grammar which our traditional grammar has dwelt upon. But the definitions of noun and verb, it should be observed, begin with formal distinctions—case and tense—and throughout the work there is clearly an awareness of the importance of structure in the functioning of the language. The contribution of the Greeks to linguistics was a great one, as Gilbert Murray and others have pointed out. But for twenty centuries their work was carried on by slavish and unimaginative imitators incapable of developing the work of their predecessors. Especially in the less highly inflected languages like English and French it did not occur to them that the inflectional devices of Latin and Greek must have some counterpart in the structure of the modern language.

Though today there are a few scholars in universities who assert that they pursue grammar for its own sake as an academic discipline, most people conceive of grammar only as a utilitarian thing, as a means of learning to use a language correctly. This notion was certainly completely absent from the thinking of Plato, Aristotle, and the Stoics, and probably from that of Dionysius Thrax. Grammar began as a philosophical inquiry into the nature of language. Now, for most people, it is merely a dogmatic means of achieving correctness. It is this transformation that I am mainly concerned with.

How the transformation took place is not easy to document. Perhaps the most plausible explanation lies in the familiar desire of younger teachers to regurgitate undigested fragments of what they have swallowed in the course of their higher education. All too often a high school teacher just out of college will use his college lecture notes as the foundation of his high school teaching, or a

---

[2]Gilbert Murray, *Greek Studies* (Oxford, 1964), p. 181.

[3]"The Grammar of Dionysius Thrax," translated . . . by Thos. Davidson, *Journal of Speculative Philosophy,* VIII (1874), 326–339.

teacher of undergraduates tries to give them exactly what he got in his graduate seminar.

Then there is the fundamental difference between the prevailing purposes of elementary and advanced instruction. Primary education is severely utilitarian; and though it can hardly be denied that, especially in our society, graduate instruction is often infected by utilitarianism, the speculative approach does persist, and inquiry for its own sake plays a major role. The curriculum at all levels of education is and has been determined partly by tradition, partly by immediate utilitarian objectives, partly by a desire to perpetuate the best elements of the cultural heritage. The application of these criteria is of ascending difficulty. Easiest is to accept without question the practice of one's predecessors; not much harder is to accept a limited practical goal and provide instruction intended to achieve it. Most difficult is to select critically what is most valuable in the cultural heritage, and the Romans weren't up to it.

Because of Greek prestige in the ancient world, less developed cultures borrowed extensively from that of Greece. The influence of Greek art, philosophy, and literature on Rome is familiar, but Greek grammar was quite as influential and became the model not only for grammars of Latin but of Syriac, Armenian, Hebrew, and possibly Arabic as well.

It could not be a good model. The structure of every language is peculiar to itself—though there are, of course, similarities between members of the same linguistic family—and the best description of it derives from a careful examination of the language itself, not from an attempt to fit it into the pattern of another. To be sure, both Greek and Latin are rich in inflections and the Latin of Varro was not much further away from the parent Indo-European than was the Greek of Dionysius Thrax; so the deformation imposed by the model was less distorting than when the same procedure was followed many centuries later and attempts were made to strait-jacket the modern vernaculars of Europe within the model of Latin grammar. For example, Greek had a definite article, Latin had none, though in Varro's *De Lingua Latina,* the term *articuli* is applied to the demonstratives *is* and *hic* (VIII, 45, 51). Latin has more cases but a different tense system and no dual. English has only two inflected active tenses against six for Latin, but many more periphrastic verbal constructions than had Latin.

The attention given to grammar by the ancients seems to have been considerable. Susemihl in his *History of Greek Literature in the Alexandrian Period* discusses over fifty grammarians. One of them, Aristophanes of Byzantium (ca. 257-ca. 180 B.C.), was librarian to Ptolemy Epiphanius, who imprisoned him to prevent the king of Pergamum from hiring him away.

Among the Romans, grammarians were also in demand. The slave Lutatius Daphnis, a grammarian, was bought for 700,000 sesterces, perhaps $35,000, which puts him about in the class of a lesser baseball player. Caesar put this Lutatius Daphnis in charge of the public libraries, though it was not until much later, according to Suetonius, that a regular salary of 100,000 sesterces was paid from the privy purse for Latin and Greek teachers of rhetoric (Suetonius, *Lives of the Caesars,* VIII, xviii). Caesar himself took part in one of the persisting grammatical quarrels of the time, that of the analogists and the anomalists, by producing a work called *De Analogia,* known to us only in fragments. Though he favored the analogists, who demanded complete inflectional consistency, it is significant that he wanted no radical departures from usage.[4] Suetonius also states that Claudius "invented three new letters and added them to the [Latin] alphabet, maintaining that they were greatly needed; he published a book on their theory when he was still in private life, and when he became emperor had no difficulty in bringing about their general use" (Suetonius, *Lives of the Caesars,* V, xli). Theodore Roosevelt was less successful when he tried to impose a few spelling reforms on the Government Printing Office; Congress refused to permit the changes.

Though Caesar favored the analogists, he was unwilling to depart from established usage. His position was that of many of his cultivated contemporaries, as it has been of many cultivated people ever since. The appeal of analogy is the appeal of logic, a creation of the Greeks and a tool that has been used with interesting and surprising effects in most areas of Western thought ever since. The foundation of Aristotelian logic is the syllogism. As the analogists applied the syllogism to language it worked like this: The form of the personal pronoun determines the form of the verb of which the pronoun is the subject. The form *you* is plural; therefore the form of the verb *be* which follows it must be plural; hence *you were,* not *you was.* So we have in cultivated English today only *you were.* But the cultivated dare not apply this syllogism to the intensive or reflexive, where the eighteenth-century practice of agreement with the notional number of the pronoun still persists. The eighteenth century had both *you was there yourself* and *you were there yourselves;* while we have *you were there yourselves* when the notional number of *you* is plural, but *you were there yourself* when it is singular.

Language has its own logic, which it is the function of the descriptive grammarian to discover if he can. Whatever it may be, it is not Aristotelian logic. But for two millennia our attitudes toward language have been colored by the assumption that the system of a language can be analyzed and prescribed by an intellectual tool that is inapplicable.

Conformity to a standard, or correctness if you like, is, of course, socially of the greatest importance. There is a long record of the penalties imposed on those who deviate from the standard, the earliest I know of being the account given in *Judges* (12, 4–6) of the forty and two thousand Ephraimites who were slain by the Gileadites because they pronounced *shibboleth sibboleth.* Later examples are less gory. Aristophanes in the *Lysistrata* (lines 81–206) ridicules the dialect of the Spartan women, though they are the allies of the Athenian women in their

---

[4]Jean Collart, *Varron, Grammairien Latin* (Paris, 1954), pp. 10, 19, 146; Robins, p. 58.

campaign of sexual frustration. Stephen Runciman in his *Byzantine Civilization* says "the Patriarch Nicetas in the Eleventh Century was laughed at for his Slavonic accent, and the statesman Margarites treated with disrespect in the Thirteenth because he spoke with a rough rustic voice."[5] And Chaucer's nun spoke the provincial French of the Benedictine nunnery of Stratford-Bow, the French of Paris—standard French—being to her unknown.

Conformity to the standard is what matters. But how is the standard to be determined? Quintilian, whom Professor T. W. Baldwin calls "The Supreme Authority" in his *Shakespeare's Small Latine and Lesse Greeke,* provides a most illuminating basis for discussion. In the *Institutes* Quintilian tells us that:

> Language is based on reason, antiquity, authority and usage. Reason finds its chief support in analogy and sometimes in etymology. As for antiquity, it is commended to us by the possession of a certain majesty, I might almost say sanctity. Authority as a rule we derive from orators and historians. For poets, owing to the necessities of metre, are allowed a certain licence. . . . The judgment of a supreme orator is placed on the same level as reason, and even error brings no disgrace, if it results from treading in the footsteps of such distinguished guides. Usage however is the surest pilot in speaking, and we should treat language as currency minted with the public stamp. But in all cases we have need of a critical judgment, . . . (I.vi. 1-3)

This is fuller than Horace's neater statement: "Use is the judge, and law, and rule of speech" *(De Arte Poetica, 72: Quem [usus] penes arbitrium est et ius et norma loquendi)* and shows more clearly why we have troubles. Usage "is the surest pilot" but "we have need of a critical judgment."

Quintilian has more to say on the matter:

> Usage remains to be discussed. For it would be almost laughable to prefer the language of the past to that of the present day, and what is ancient speech but ancient usage of speaking? But even here the critical faculty is necessary, and we must make up our minds what we mean by usage. If it be defined merely as the practice of the majority, we shall have a very dangerous rule affecting not merely style but life as well, a far more serious matter. For where is so much good to be found that what is right should please the majority? The practices of depilation, of dressing the hair in tiers, or of drinking to excess at the baths, although they may have thrust their way into society, cannot claim the support of usage, since there is something to blame in all of them (although we have usage on our side when we bathe or have our hair cut or take our meals together). So too in speech we must not accept as a rule of language words and phrases that have become a vicious habit with a number of persons. To say nothing of the language of the uneducated, so we are all of us well aware that whole theatres and the entire crowd of spectators will often commit *barbarisms* in the cries which they utter as one man. I will therefore define usage in speech as the agreed practice of educated men, just as where our way of life is concerned I should define it as the agreed practice of all good men. (I.vi. 43–45)

[5]Stephen Runciman, *Byzantine Civilization* (Meridian Books, New York, 1956), pp. 173, 176.

But Quintilian makes it quite apparent from the many examples he cites that educated men are not entirely agreed on their practice, and that they lean heavily on the authority of Greek usage:

> More recent scholars have instituted the practice of giving Greek nouns their Greek declension, although this is not always possible. Personally I prefer to follow the Latin method, so far as grace of diction will permit. For I should not like to say *Calypsonem* on the analogy of *Iunonem,* although Gaius Caesar in deference to antiquity does adopt this way of declining it. Current practice has however prevailed over his authority. In other words which can be declined in either way without impropriety, those who prefer it can employ the Greek form: they will not be speaking Latin, but will not on the other hand deserve censure. (I.v. 63–64)

A thorough knowledge of Greek, learned from slave-tutors, had long been common among educated Romans, but it was Varro who transferred the entire body of Greek grammatical scholarship to Latin in his *De Lingua Latina,* written between 57 and 45 B.C. Though of the original 25 books of that work only V through X survive relatively intact, we have a fairly good account of what was in the rest because Varro is the source which all later Latin grammarians follow, and they have apparently borrowed from him most faithfully.

Greek grammar, is, then, a development of Greek philosophy, an attempt to treat systematically an important aspect of human behavior. It is a late development which in Alexandrian culture is given a practical application through its use in the editing, elucidation, and interpretation of texts, especially that of Homer; and in the correction of solecisms. Since there was little of the speculative in the Romans, Varro's encyclopedic treatment of Latin language and literature was the ultimate source of a host of school texts.

What has been presented so far is a partial account of the development of philology, though this ancient term has been an ambiguous one for almost as long as it has existed—naturally enough, since it derives from the Greek roots usually translated as *love* and *word.* Some people love words as the means of argument, others because they are the foundation of literature, others still for their forms and relations in discourse. All these senses have been designated by the word since it first appeared in Greek, and in nineteenth-century France and Germany it normally included literary history, textual and literary criticism, and linguistics. (We might well revive the word; it would provide a single term by which we could describe ourselves along with chemists, historians, and the rest; we are philologists.)

The ancients called the various aspects of this study by a variety of names: *philologos, grammatikos, grammatistes, kritikos* in Greek; *philologus, grammaticus, litterator, criticus* in Latin. They were evidently no more certain of exactly what the terms signified than we are today with similar terms. Suetonius writes:

The term *grammaticus* became prevalent through Greek influence, but at first such men were called *litterati*. Cornelius Nepos, too, in a little book in which he explains the difference between *litteratus* and *eruditus* says that the former is commonly applied to those who can speak or write on any subject accurately, cleverly and with authority; but that it should strictly be used of interpreters of the poets, whom the Greeks call *grammatici*. That these were also called *litteratores* is shown by Messala Corvinus in one of his letters, in which he says, "I am not concerned with Furius Bibaculus, nor with Ticidas either, or with the *litterator* Cato." For he unquestionably refers to Valerius Cato, who was famous both as a poet and as a grammarian. Some however make a distinction between *litteratus* and *litterator,* as the Greeks do between *grammaticus* and *grammatista,* using the former of a master of his subject, the latter of one moderately proficient. Orbilius too supports this view by examples, saying: "In the days of our forefathers, when anyone's slaves were offered for sale, it was not usual except in special cases to advertise any one of them as *litteratus* but rather as *litterator,* implying that he had a smattering of letters, but was not a finished scholar."

The grammarians of early days taught rhetoric as well, and we have treatises from many men on both subjects. It was this custom, I think, which led those of later times also, although the two professions had now become distinct, nevertheless either to retain or to introduce certain kinds of exercises suited to the training of orators, such as problems, paraphrases, addresses, character sketches and similar things; doubtless that they might not turn over their pupils to the rhetoricians wholly ignorant and unprepared. But I observe that such instruction is now given up, because of the lack of application and the youth of some of the pupils; for I do not believe that it is because the subjects are underrated. I remember that at any rate when I was a young man, one of these teachers, Princeps by name, used to declaim and engage in discussion on alternate days; and that sometimes he would give instruction in the morning, and in the afternoon remove his desk and declaim. I used to hear, too, that within the memory of our forefathers some passed directly from the grammar school to the Forum and took their place among the most eminent advocates. (*On Grammarians,* iv)

Another writer who provides evidence on the Roman attitudes toward language is Aulus Gellius in his *Attic Nights.* Gellius represents the aristocrat's conviction that what he himself does must be right coupled with the conservative attitude that older practice is to be preferred:

Valerius Probus was once asked, as I learned from one of his friends, whether one ought to say *has urbis* or *has urbes* and *hanc turrem* or *hanc turrim.* "If," he replied, "you are either composing verse or writing prose and have to use those words, pay no attention to the musty, fusty rules of the grammarians, but consult your own ear as to what is to be said in any given place. What it favours will surely be the best." Then the one who had asked the question said: "What do you mean by 'consult my ear'?" and he told me that Probus answered: "Just as Vergil did his, when in different passages he had used *urbis* and *urbes,* following the taste and judgment of his ear. For in the first *Georgic,* which," said he, "I have read in a copy corrected by the poet's own hand, he wrote *urbis* with an *i. . . .*

But turn and change it so as to read *urbes,* and somehow you will make it duller and heavier. On the other hand, in the third *Aeneid* he wrote *urbes* with an *e:* . . .

Change this too so as to read *urbis* and the word will be too slender and colourless, so great indeed is the different effect of combination in the harmony of neighbouring sounds. . . .

These words have, I think, a more agreeable lightness than if you should use the form in *e* in both places." But the one who had asked the question, a boorish fellow surely and with untrained ear, said: "I don't just understand why you say that one form is better and more correct in one place and the other in the other." Then Probus, now somewhat impatient, retorted: "Don't trouble then to inquire whether you ought to say *urbis* or *urbes.* For since you are the kind of man that I see you are and err without detriment to yourself, you will lose nothing whichever you say." (XIII. xxi. 3–8)

And his attitude towards grammarians is expressed quite as explicitly in this passage:

Within my memory Aelius Melissus held the highest rank among the grammarians of his day at Rome; but in literary criticism he showed greater boastfulness and sophistry than real merit. Besides many other works which he wrote, he made a book which at the time when it was issued seemed to be one of remarkable learning. The title of the book was designed to be especially attractive to readers, for it was called *On Correctness in Speech.* Who, then would suppose that he could speak correctly or with propriety unless he had learned those rules of Melissus?

From that book I take these words: "*Matrona,* 'a matron,' is a woman who has given birth once; she who has done so more than once is called *mater familias,* 'mother of a family'; just so a sow which has had one litter is called *porcetra;* one which has had more, *scrofa.*" But to decide whether Melissus thought out this distinction between *matrona* and *mater familias* and that it was his own conjecture, or whether he read what someone else had written, surely requires soothsayers. For with regard to *porcetra* he has, it is true, the authority of Pomponius in the Atellan farce which bears that very title; but that "matron" was applied only to a woman who had given birth once, and "mother of the family" only to one who had done so more than once, can be proved by the authority of no ancient writer. . . . (XVIII. vi. 1–7)

By the Middle Ages the aristocrats were unlikely to have had much education, and the classical heritage was perpetuated by the grammarians, whose dogmatic victory was complete. Donatus (fl. 400) and Priscian (fl. 500) are the dominating figures. The name of the first, shortened to Donat or Donet, became synonymous with 'grammar' or 'lesson' in Old French and Middle English, and the grammar of the second survives in over a thousand manuscripts.[6] He also has the distinction of being consigned to Hell by Dante (*Inferno,* 15:110).

As an example of Priscian, here is the beginning of an analysis of the

[6]John Edwin Sandys, *A History of Classical Scholarship* (Cambridge, 1920), vol. 1, p. 230, note; p. 274.

Aeneid—this is not from his big grammar, which was in eighteen books, but from a smaller one, *Partitiones Duodecim Versuum Aeneidos Principalium:*

> Scan the verse, *Arma vi / rumque ca / no Tro / iae qui / primus ab / oris.* How many caesuras does it have? Two. What are they? Semiquinaria (penthemimeral) and semiseptenaria (hephthemimeral). How? The semiquinaria is *arma virumque cano* and the semiseptenaria is *arma virumque cano Troiae.* How many figures are there? Ten. For what reason? Because it consists of three dactyls and two spondees. How many parts of speech has this verse? Nine. How many nouns? Six: *arma, virum, Troiae, qui, primus, oris.* How many verbs? One: *cano.* How many prepositions? One: *ab.* How many conjunctions? One, *que.* Discuss each word; *arma,* what part of speech is it? Noun. Of what sort? Appelative (or common). What is its species? General. Its gender? Neuter. Why neuter? Because all nouns which end in *a* in the plural are unquestionably of neuter gender. Why is the singular not used? Because this noun signifies many and various things. . . .[7]

And this is not the end of the catechism on the opening line of Virgil. Evidently this sort of drill was to accompany the study of the poem from beginning to end, if the end was ever reached.

Increasingly in the Middle Ages the written heritage of Greece and Rome was accepted unquestioningly because literate men did not have a cultural background which would permit them to ask pertinent questions. We learn, for example, that one of the best sources for the text of Diogenes Laertius is a manuscript of about 1200 written by a scribe "who obviously knew no Greek."[8] To be sure, there were sometimes conflicts between the Christian heritage and the classical, usually resolved in favor of the Christian. In a medieval manuscript is a comment: "Concerning the words *scala* (step), and *scopa* (broom), we do not follow Donatus and the others who claim they are plural because we know that the Holy Ghost has ruled that they are singular." And it was comforting when the traditions of classical grammar could be given divine corroboration. For example: "The verb has three persons. This I hold to be divinely inspired, for our belief in the Trinity is thereby manifested in words." Or this: "Some maintain that there are more, some that there are fewer parts of speech. But the world-encircling church has only eight offices [Presumably Ostiariat, Lektorat, Exorzistat, Akolythat, Subdiakonat, Diakonat, Presbyterat, Episkopat]. I am convinced that this is through divine inspiration. Since it is through Latin that those who are chosen come most quickly to a knowledge of the Trinity and under its guidance find their way along the royal road into their heavenly home,

---

[7]Heinrich Keil, *Grammatici Latini* (Leipzig, 1859), vol. 3, p. 459.

[8]Diogenes Laertius, *Lives of Eminent Philosophers,* with an English translation by R. D. Hicks (Loeb Classical Library) (Cambridge & London, 1925), vol. 1, p. xxxv. (The quotations from Suetonius, Varro, Quintilian, and Aulus Gellius are from the translations in the Loeb Classical Library editions.)

it was necessary that the Latin language should be created with eight parts of speech."[9]

On the other hand, St. Boniface's (675–754) "sense of grammatical accuracy was so deeply shocked when he heard an ignorant priest administering the rite of baptism *in nomine Patria et Filia et Spiritus sancti* [that is, with complete disregard of the required case endings] that he almost doubted the validity of the rite."[10]

Up to about the twelfth century Donatus and Priscian, whose grammars were based ultimately on classical Latin, were followed unquestioningly except where there seemed to be a conflict with sacred texts. The Vulgate and various theological writings were in a later Latin which might disagree with classical grammar, as in the more frequent use of the personal pronouns.[11]

But in the twelfth century the reintroduction of Greek philosophy had a tremendous impact on medieval thought, as is best illustrated by the Aristotelianism of Aquinas. And St. Thomas, as might be expected, deals with philological matters in the *Summa Theologica,* and again as might be expected through the syllogism:

> It seems that in Holy Writ a word cannot have several senses, historical or literal, allegorical, tropological or moral, and anagogical. For many different senses in one text produce confusion and deception and destroy all force of argument. Hence no argument, but only fallacies, can be deduced from a multiplicity of propositions. But Holy Writ ought to be able to state the truth without any fallacy. Therefore in it there cannot be several senses to a word. (First Part, Question One, Article 10, Objection 1)

A more explicitly grammatical example is this one from the thirteenth century:

> For a complete sentence, two things are necessary, namely a subject and a predicate. The subject is that which is being discussed; it is what determines the person of the verb. The predicate is that which is expressed by the subject. Nouns were invented to provide subjects. . . . Verbs were invented to provide predicates.

This concept of grammar being something created is found in another thirteenth-century writer:

> Was he who invented grammar a grammarian? No, because the creation of grammar cannot be based on teaching since that would presuppose its existence. Grammar was invented. For the invention of grammar must precede grammar. So it was not the grammarian but the philosopher who created grammar, for the philosopher studies the nature of things and recognizes their essential qualities.[12]

---

[9]J. J. Baebler, *Beiträage zu einer Geschichte der lateinischen Grammatik im Mittelalter* (Halle a. S., 1885), p. 22/Hans Arens, *Sprachwissenschaft, der Gang ihrer Entwicklung von der Antike bis zur Gegenwart* (Munich, 1955), pp. 30, 31.
[10]Sandys, p. 469.
[11]Baebler, p. 22.
[12]Arens, pp. 32, 34.

The authority of the grammarian was occasionally challenged. In a seventeenth-century German satirical treatment of schoolmasters is this account of a fifteenth-century episode:

> The Emperor Sigismund came to the Council of Constance and said: "Videte patres, ut eradicetis schismam Hussitarium." There sat an old Bohemian pedant in the Council who was convinced that with this box on the ear to Priscian the Emperor had sinned against the Catholic Church as gravely as had John Hus and Hieronymus of Prague. So he said [in Latin]: Most Serene Highness, *schisma* is neuter gender." The emperor said [in German]: "How do you know that?" The old Bohemian pedant answered [now in German]: "Alexander Gallus says so." The emperor said: "Who is Alexander Gallus?" The Bohemian pedant answered: "He is a monk." "Yes," said Sigismund, "I am the Roman emperor, and my word is worth at least that of a monk." (Joh. Balthaser Schupp, *Der Teutsche Schulmeister,* 1663)[13]

It now remains to consider the transfer of these attitudes to the modern vernacular languages. But first a brief review of the three preceding stages. The first is the unique situation in Greece, which differed from that of any of the succeeding cultures in two significant ways: It was essentially a monolingual society, and at least during the period of its greatest intellectual and artistic achievement it knew nothing of formal grammar. Rome differed in both essentials. The cultivated Roman was educated in Greek, and formal grammar was a part of his Latin education, though this does not mean that he learned Greek through formal grammar. In the Middle Ages the two-language requirement for the educated, which was charac teristic of Rome, was continued, but with an important difference. Whereas for the Roman, Latin was a respectable language with a respectable literature, for the educated man of the Middle Ages his native vernacular was not respectable and at least at first had no important literature. Also he learned the language of scholarship and literature in a way quite different from that used by the Roman. He learned it with the aid of formal grammar.

Of these three stages, the third, the medieval, is much the longest; in formal education and scholarship it lasts well into the eighteenth century and therefore has a duration of well over a thousand years. Of course during the last two or three hundred of those years a great change had come over Europe, due partly to an intimate reacquaintance with the heritage of Greece and Rome. But in the field of philology this meant largely a return to the attitudes of the ancients. It also meant the transference of the whole philological approach—ancient and medieval—to the modern vernacular languages.

The history of vernacular grammars and of English grammars in particular comes next in this development, but there is no space for it here.

---

[13]Baebler, p. 118.

One consequence of this transfer must be illustrated: The ambivalence it has given us toward language. Here are some examples. Trollope in his *Autobiography* writes:

> The ordinary talk of ordinary people is carried on in short sharp expressive sentences, which very frequently are never completed,—the language of which even among educated people is often incorrect. The novel-writer in constructing his dialogue must so steer between absolute accuracy of language—which would give to his conversation an air of pedantry, and the slovenly inaccuracy of ordinary talkers, which if closely followed would offend by an appearance of grimace—as to produce upon the ear of his readers a sense of reality. If he be quite real he will seem to attempt to be funny. If he be quite correct he will seem to be unreal.[14]

The nineteenth-century German philologist Wilhelm Scherer, discussing the great dramatist Heinrich Kleist, remarks that "he did distinguished work in all forms. There dwells in his language an individual magic, though he has an uncertain control of German grammar."[15] And in a recent review in the *TLS* is this sentence: "He [Leonard Clark] died after completing the first draft of his book, *Yucatan Adventure,* which would have gained some grammar, while losing some of the punch of its author's virile enthusiasm, if it had been more carefully revised."[16]

In a detective story, Rex Stout has Archie Goodwin make this comment after one of the principal characters has said, "Yes. . . . We shall see.": "But what really settled it was her saying, "We shall see." He [Nero Wolfe] will always stretch a point, within reason, for people who use words as he thinks they should be used."[17] But in another story Wolfe is made to say, "If it's her again. . . ."[18]

And Mark Twain, who took Cooper severely to task for his "ungrammatical" English, did what was perhaps his best work, in *Huckleberry Finn,* by using a narrative device which relieved him of all responsibility for conforming to standard usage.

One of the most eloquent and emphatic in condemnation of the Latin grammatical tradition was Macaulay but, as you might guess, he is much too long to quote here.[19]

I conclude by returning to the four senses of the term grammar outlined at the beginning. Contemporary philologists who specialize in linguistics have, it seems to me, attempted to strip away the accretions of two thousand years and

---

[14] Anthony Trollope, *An Autobiography* (World's Classics, Oxford, 1953), p. 206.

[15] Wilhelm Scherer, *Geschichte der deutschen Literatur* (Knaur, Berlin, n.d.), p. 752.

[16] *Times Literary Supplement,* March 20, 1959, p. 156.

[17] Rex Stout, "Murder Is No Joke," *And Four to Go, A Nero Wolfe Foursome* (Viking, New York, 1958), p. 155.

[18] Rex Stout, "Too Many Women," *All Aces, A Nero Wolfe Omnibus* (Viking, New York, 1958), p. 237.

[19] T. B. Macaulay, "The London University," Edinburgh Review, February, 1826, in *Critical, Historical and Miscellaneous Essays and Poems* (Porter and Coats, Philadelphia, n.d.), vol. 3, pp. 631–634.

are turning to a rigorously descriptive approach, the seeds of which are to be found in the Greeks. Other philologists have other interests, such as literary history, literary criticism, and, of course, the problem of getting freshmen to write better. As an inescapable burden of their academic heritage, they have to bear the weight of the ancient and medieval grammatical tradition, which survives in the other two senses, prescriptive grammar and grammar as remedy. What I have tried to do is to give some account of how that tradition developed, how it was transmitted, and why much of it is essentially irrelevant to the problems the philologist faces today.[20]

The Acquisition of Language

Breyne Arlene Moskowitz

An adult who finds herself in a group of people speaking an unfamiliar foreign language may feel quite uncomfortable. The strange language sounds like gibberish: mysterious strings of sound, rising and falling in unpredictable patterns. Each person speaking the language knows when to speak, how to construct strings and how to interpret other people's strings, but the individual who does not know anything about the language cannot pick out separate words or sounds, let alone discern meanings. She may feel overwhelmed, ignorant and even childlike. It is possible that she is returning to a vague memory from her very early childhood, because the experience of an adult listening to a foreign language comes close to duplicating the experience of an infant listening to the "foreign" language spoken by everyone around her. Like the adult, the child is confronted with the task of learning a language about which she knows nothing.

The task of acquiring language is one for which the adult has lost most of her aptitude but one the child will perform with remarkable skill. Within a short span of time and with almost no direct instruction the child will analyze the language completely. In fact, although many subtle refinements are added between the ages of five and 10, most children have completed the greater part of the basic language-acquisition process by the age of five. By that time a child will have dissected the language into its minimal separable units of sound and meaning; she will have discovered the rules for recombining sounds into words, the meanings of individual words and the rules for recombining words into meaningful sentences, and she will have internalized the intricate patterns of taking turns in dialogue. All in all she will have established herself linguistically as a

---

[20]A somewhat shorter version of this paper was read to the Northeastern Ohio College English Group, Akron, 5 November 1960.

full-fledged member of a social community, informed about the most subtle details of her native language as it is spoken in a wide variety of situations.

The speed with which children accomplish the complex process of language acquisition is particularly impressive. Ten linguists working full time for 10 years to analyze the structure of the English language could not program a computer with the ability for language acquired by an average child in the first 10 or even five years of life. In spite of the scale of the task and even in spite of adverse conditions—emotional instability, physical disability and so on—children learn to speak. How do they go about it? By what process does a child learn language?

WHAT IS LANGUAGE?

In order to understand how language is learned it is necessary to understand what language is. The issue is confused by two factors. First, language is learned in early childhood, and adults have few memories of the intense effort that went into the learning process, just as they do not remember the process of learning to walk. Second, adults do have conscious memories of being taught the few grammatical rules that are prescribed as "correct" usage, or the norms of "standard" language. It is difficult for adults to dissociate their memories of school lessons from those of true language learning, but the rules learned in school are only the conventions of an educated society. They are arbitrary finishing touches of embroidery on a thick fabric of language that each child weaves for herself before arriving in the English teacher's classroom. The fabric is grammar: the set of rules that describe how to structure language.

The grammar of language includes rules of phonology, which describe how to put sounds together to form words; rules of syntax, which describe how to put words together to form sentences; rules of semantics, which describe how to interpret the meaning of words and sentences, and rules of pragmatics, which describe how to participate in a conversation, how to sequence sentences and how to anticipate the information needed by an interlocutor. The internal grammar each adult has constructed is identical with that of every other adult in all but a few superficial details. Therefore each adult can create or understand an infinite number of sentences she has never heard before. She knows what is acceptable as a word or a sentence and what is not acceptable, and her judgments on these issues concur with those of other adults. For example, speakers of English generally agree that the sentence "Ideas green sleep colorless furiously" is ungrammatical and that the sentence "Colorless green ideas sleep furiously" is grammatical but makes no sense semantically. There is similar agreement on the grammatical relations represented by word order. For example, it is clear that the sentences "John hit Mary" and "Mary hit John" have different meanings although they consist of the same words, and that the sentence "Flying planes can be dangerous" has two possible meanings. At the level of individual words all adult speakers can agree that "brick" is an English word, that "blick" is not an English word but could be one (that is, there is an accidental gap in the adult lexicon, or internal vocabulary) and that "bnick" is not an English word and could not be one.

How children go about learning the grammar that makes communication possible has always fascinated adults, particularly parents, psychologists and investigators of language. Until recently diary keeping was the primary method of study in this area. For example, in 1877 Charles Darwin published an account of his son's development that includes notes on language learning. Unfortunately most of the diarists used inconsistent or incomplete notations to record what they heard (or what they thought they heard), and most of the diaries were only partial listings of emerging types of sentences with inadequate information on developing word meanings. Although the very best of them, such as W. F. Leopold's classic *Speech Development of a Bilingual Child* continue to be a rich resource for contemporary investigators, advances in audio and video recording equipment have made modern diaries generally much more valuable. In the 1960's, however, new discoveries inspired linguists and psychologists to approach the study of language acquisition in a new, systematic way, oriented less toward long-term diary keeping and more toward a search for the patterns in a child's speech at any given time.

An event that revolutionized linguistics was the publication in 1957 of Noam Chomsky's *Syntactic Structures.* Chomsky's investigation of the structure of grammars revealed that language systems were far deeper and more complex than had been suspected. And of course if linguistics was more complicated, then language learning had to be more complicated. In the 21 years since the publication of *Syntactic Structures* the disciplines of linguistics and child language have come of age. The study of the acquisition of language has benefited not only from the increasingly sophisticated understanding of linguistics but also from the improved understanding of cognitive development as it is related to language. The improvements in recording technology have made experimentation in this area more reliable and more detailed, so that investigators framing new and deeper questions are able to accurately capture both rare occurrences and developing structures.

The picture that is emerging from the more sophisticated investigations reveals the child as an active language learner, continually analyzing what she hears and proceeding in a methodical, predictable way to put together the jigsaw puzzle of language. Different children learn language in similar ways. It is not known how many processes are involved in language learning, but the few that have been observed appear repeatedly, from child to child and from language to language. All the examples I shall discuss here concern children who are learning English, but identical processes have been observed in children learning French, Russian, Finnish, Chinese, Zulu and many other languages.

Children learn the systems of grammar—phonology, syntax, semantics, lexicon and pragmatics—by breaking each system down into its smallest combinable parts and then developing rules for combining the parts. In the first tw years of life a child spends much time working on one part of the task, disassembling the language to find the separate sounds that can be put together to form words and the separate words that can be put together to form sentences. After the age of two the basic process continues to be refined, and many more sounds and words are produced. The other part of language acquisition—developing rules for combining the basic elements of language—is carried out in a very methodical way: the most general rules are hypothesized first, and as time passes they are successively narrowed down by the addition of more precise rules applying to a more restricted set of sentences. The procedure is the same in any area of language learning, whether the child is acquiring syntax or phonology or semantics. For example, at the earliest stage of acquiring negatives a child does not have at her command the same range of negative structures that an adult does. She has constructed only a single very general rule: Attach "no" to the beginning of any sentence constructed by the other rules of grammar. At this stage all negative sentences will be formed according to that rule.

Throughout the acquisition process a child continually revises and refines the rules of her internal grammar, learning increasingly detailed subrules until she achieves a set of rules that enables her to create the full array of complex, adult sentences. The process of refinement continues at least until the age of 10 and probably considerably longer for most children. By the time a child is six or seven, however, the changes in her grammar may be so subtle and sophisticated that they go unnoticed. In general children approach language learning economically, devoting their energy to broad issues before dealing with specific ones. They cope with clear-cut questions first and sort out the details later, and they may adopt any one of a variety of methods for circumventing details of a language system they have not yet dealt with.

PREREQUISITES FOR LANGUAGE

Although some children verbalize much more than others and some increase the length of their utterances much faster than others, all children overgeneralize a single rule before learning to apply it more narrowly and before constructing other less widely applicable rules, and all children speak in one-word sentences before they speak in two-word sentences. The similarities in language learning for different children and different languages are so great that many linguists have believed at one time or another that the human brain is preprogrammed for language learning. Some linguists continue to believe language is innate and only the surface details of the particular language spoken in a child's environment need to be learned. The speed with which children learn language gives this view much appeal. As more parallels between language and other areas of cognition are revealed, however, there is greater reason to believe any language specialization that exists in the child is only one aspect of more general cognitive abilities of the brain.

Whatever the built-in properties the brain brings to the task of language learning may be, it is now known that a child who hears no language learns no language, and that a child learns only the language spoken in her environment. Most infants coo and babble during the first six months of life, but congenitally deaf children have been observed to cease babbling after six months, whereas normal infants continue to babble. A child does not learn language, however, simply by hearing it spoken. A boy with normal hearing but with deaf parents who communicated by the American Sign Language was exposed to television every day so that he would learn English. Because the child was asthmatic and was confined to his home he interacted only with people at home, where his family and all their visitors communicated in sign language. By the age of three he was fluent in sign language but neither understood nor spoke English. It appears that in order to learn a language a child must also be able to interact with real people in that language. A television set does not suffice as the sole medium for language learning because, even though it can ask questions, it cannot respond to a child's answers. A child, then, can develop language only if there is language in her environment and if she can employ that language to communicate with other people in her immediate environment.

CARETAKER SPEECH

In constructing a grammar children have only a limited amount of information available to them, namely the language they hear spoken around them. (Until about the age of three a child models her language on that of her parents; afterward the language of her peer group tends to become more important.) There is no question, however, that the language environments children inhabit are restructured, usually unintentionally, by the adults who take care of them. Recent studies show that there are several ways caretakers systematically modify the child's environment, making the task of language acquisition simpler.

Caretaker speech is a distinct speech register that differs from others in its simplified vocabulary, the systematic phonological simplification of some words, higher pitch, exaggerated intonation, short, simple sentences and a higher proportion of questions (among mothers) or imperatives (among fathers). Speech with the first two characteristics is formally designated Baby Talk. Baby Talk is a subsystem of caretaker speech that has been studied over a wide range of languages and cultures. Its characteristics appear to be universal: in languages as diverse as English, Arabic, Comanche and Gilyak (a Paleo-Siberian language) there are simplified vocabulary items for terms relating to food, toys, animals and body functions. Some words are phonologically simplified, frequently by the duplication of syllables, as in "wawa" for "water" and "choo-choo" for "train," or by the reduction of consonant clusters, as in "tummy" for "stomach" and "scambled eggs" for "scrambled eggs." (Many types of phonological simplification seem to mimic the phonological structure of an infant's own early vocabulary.)

Perhaps the most pervasive characteristic of caretaker speech is its syntactic simplification. While a child is still babbling, adults may address long, complex sentences to her, but as soon as she begins to utter meaningful, identifiable words they almost invariably speak to her in very simple sentences. Over the next few years of the child's language development the speech addressed to her by her caretakers may well be describable by a grammar only six months in advance of her own.

The functions of the various language modifications in caretaker speech are not equally apparent. It is possible that higher pitch and exaggerated intonation serve to alert a child to pay attention to what she is hearing. As for Baby Talk, there is no reason to believe the use of phonologically simplified words in any way affects a child's learning of pronunciation. Baby Talk may have only a psychological function, marking speech as being affectionate. On the other hand, syntactic simplification has a clear function. Consider the speech adults address to other adults; it is full of false starts and long, rambling, highly complex sentences. It is not surprising that elaborate theories of innate language ability arose during the years when linguists examined the speech adults addressed to adults and assumed that the speech addressed to children was similar. Indeed it is hard to imagine how a child could derive the rules of language from such input. The wide study of caretaker speech conducted over the past eight years has shown that children do not face this problem. Rather it appears they construct their initial grammars on the basis of the short, simple, grammatical sentences that are addressed to them in the first year or two they speak.

CORRECTING LANGUAGE

Caretakers simplify children's language-analysis task in other ways. For example, adults talk with other adults about complex ideas, but they talk with children about the here and now, minimizing discussion of feelings, displaced events and so on. Adults accept children's syntactic and phonological "errors," which are a normal part of the acquisition process. It is important to understand that when children make such errors, they are not producing flawed or incomplete replicas of adult sentences; they are producing sentences that are correct and grammatical with respect to their own current internalized grammar. Indeed, children's errors are essential data for students of child language because it is the consistent departures from the adult model that indicate the nature of a child's current hypotheses about the grammar of language. There are a number of memorized, unanalyzed sentences in any child's output of language. If a child says, "Nobody likes me," there is no way of knowing whether she has memorized the sentence intact or has figured out the rules for constructing the sentence. On the other hand, a sentence such as "Nobody don't like me" is clearly not a memorized form but one that reflects an intermediate stage of developing grammar.

Since each child's utterances at a particular stage are from her own point of view grammatically correct, it is not surprising that children are fairly impervious to correction of their language by adults, indeed to any attempts to teach them language. Consider the boy who lamented to his mother, "Nobody don't like me." His mother seized the opportunity to correct him, replying, "Nobody likes me." The child repeated his original version and the mother her modified one a total of eight times until in desperation the mother said, "Now listen carefully! Nobody likes me." Finally her son got the idea and dutifully replied, "Oh! Nobody don't likes me." As the example demonstrates, children do not always understand exactly what it is the adult is correcting. The information the adult is trying to impart may be at odds with the information in the child's head, namely the rules the child is postulating for producing language. The surface corrections of a sentence do not give the child a clue about how to revise the rule that produced the sentence.

It seems to be virtually impossible to speed up the language-learning process. Experiments conducted by Russian investigators show that it is extremely difficult to teach children a detail of language more than a few days before they would learn it themselves. Adults sometimes do, of course, attempt to teach children rules of language, expecting them to learn by imitation, but Courtney B. Cazden of Harvard University found that children benefit less from frequent adult correction of their errors than from true conversational interaction. Indeed, correcting errors can interrupt that interaction, which is, after all, the function of language. (One way children may try to secure such interaction is by asking "Why?" Children go through a stage of asking a question repeatedly. It serves to keep the conversation going, which may be the child's real aim. For example, a two-and-a-half-year-old named Stanford asked "Why?" and was given the nonsense answer: "Because the moon is made of green cheese." Although the response was not at all germane to the conversation, Stanford was happy with it and again asked "Why?" Many silly answers later the adult had tired of the conversation but Stanford had not. He was clearly not seeking information. What he needed was to practice the form of social conversation before dealing with its function. Asking "Why?" served that purpose well.)

In point of fact adults rarely correct children's ungrammatical sentences. For example, one mother, on hearing "Tommy fall my truck down," turned to Tommy with "Did you fall Stevie's truck down?" Since imitation seems to have little role in the language-acquisition process, however, it is probably just as well that most adults are either too charmed by children's errors or too busy to correct them.

Practice does appear to have an important function in the child's language-learning process. Many children have been observed purposefully practicing language when they are alone, for example in a crib or a playpen. Ruth H. Weir of Stanford University hid a tape recorder in her son's bedroom and recorded his talk after he was put to bed. She found that he played with words and phrases, stringing together sequences of similar sounds and of variations on a phrase or on the use of a word: "What color . . . what color blanket . . . what color mop . . . what color glass . . . what color TV . . . red ant . . . fire . . . like lipstick . . . blanket . . . now the blue blanket . . . what color TV . . . what color horse . . . then what color table . . . then what color fire . . . here yellow spoon." Children who do not have much opportunity to be alone may use dialogue in a similar fashion. When Weir tried to record the bedtime monologues of her second child, whose room adjoined that of the first, she obtained through-the-wall conversations instead.

THE ONE-WORD STAGE

The first stage of child language is one in which the maximum sentence length is one word; it is followed by a stage in which the maximum sentence length is two words. Early in the one-word stage there are only a few words in a child's vocabulary, but as months go by her lexicon expands with increasing rapidity. The early words are primarily concrete nouns and verbs; more abstract words such as adjectives are acquired later. By the time the child is uttering two-word sentences with some regularity, her lexicon may include hundreds of words.

When a child can say only one word at a time and knows only five words in all, choosing which one to say may not be a complex task. But how does she decide which word to say when she knows 100 words or more? Patricia M. Greenfield of the University of California at Los Angeles and Joshua H. Smith of Stanford have suggested that an important criterion is informativeness, that is, the child selects a word reflecting what is new in a particular situation. Greenfield and Smith also found that a newly acquired word is first used for naming and only later for asking for something.

Superficially the one-word stage seems easy to understand: a child says one word at a time, and so each word is a complete sentence with its own sentence intonation. Ten years ago a child in the one-word stage was thought to be learning word meanings but not syntax. Recently, however, students of child language have seen less of a distinction between the one-word stage as a period of word learning and the subsequent period, beginning with the two-word stage, as one of syntax acquisition. It now seems clear that the infant is engaged in an enormous amount of syntactic analysis in the one-word stage, and indeed that her syntactic abilities are reflected in her utterances and in her accurate perception of multiword sentences addressed to her.

Ronald Scollon of the University of Hawaii and Lois Bloom of Columbia University have pointed out independently that important patterns in word choice in the one-word stage can be found by examining larger segments of children's speech. Scollon observed that a 19-month-old named Brenda was able to use a vertical construction (a series of one-word sentences) to express what an adult might say with a horizontal construction (a multiword sentence). Brenda's pronunciation, which is represented phonetically below, was imperfect and

Scollon did not understand her words at the time. Later, when he transcribed the tape of their conversation, he heard the sound of a passing car immediately preceding the conversation and was able to identify Brenda's words as follows:

Brenda: "Car [pronounced 'ka']. Car. Car. Car."
Scollon: "What?"
Brenda: "Go. Go."
Scollon: [Undecipherable.]
Brenda: "Bus [pronounced 'baish']. Bus. Bus. Bus. Bus. Bus. Bus. Bus. Bus."
Scollon: "What? Oh, bicycle? Is that what you said?"
Brenda: "Not ['na']."
Scollon: "No?"
Brenda: "Not."
Scollon: "No. I got it wrong."

Brenda was not yet able to combine two words syntactically to express "Hearing that car reminds me that we went on the bus yesterday. No, not on a bicycle." She could express that concept, however, by combining words sequentially. Thus the one-word stage is not just a time for learning the meaning of words. In that period a child is developing hypotheses about putting words together in sentences, and she is already putting sentences together in meaningful groups. The next step will be to put two words together to form a single sentence.

THE TWO-WORD STAGE

The two-word stage is a time for experimenting with many binary semantic-syntactic relations such as possessor-possessed ("Mommy sock"), actor-action ("Cat sleeping") and action-object ("Drink soup"). When two-word sentences first began to appear in Brenda's speech, they were primarily of the following forms: subject noun and verb (as in "Monster go"), verb and object (as in "Read it") and verb or noun and location (as in "Bring home" and "Tree down"). She also continued to use vertical constructions in the two-word stage, providing herself with a means of expressing ideas that were still too advanced for her syntax. Therefore once again a description of Brenda's isolated sentences does not show her full abilities at this point in her linguistic development. Consider a later conversation Scollon had with Brenda:

Brenda: "Tape corder. Use it. Use it."
Scollon: "Use it for what?"
Brenda: "Talk. Corder talk. Brenda talk."

Brenda's use of vertical constructions to express concepts she is still unable to encode syntactically is just one example of a strategy employed by children in all areas of cognitive development. As Jean Piaget of the University of Geneva and Dan I. Slobin of the University of California at Berkeley put it, new forms are used for old functions and new functions are expressed by old forms. Long before Brenda acquired the complex syntactic form "Use the tape recorder to record me talking" she was able to use her old forms—two-word sentences and vertical construction—to express the new function. Later, when that function was old, she would develop new forms to express it. The controlled dovetailing of form and function can be observed in all areas of language acquisition. For example, before children acquire the past tense they may employ adverbs of time such as "yesterday" with present-tense verbs to express past time, saying "I do it yesterday" before "I dood it."

Bloom has provided a rare view of an intermediate stage between the one-word and the two-word stages in which the two-word construction—a new form—served only an old function. For several weeks Bloom's daughter Alison uttered two-word sentences all of which included the word "wida." Bloom tried hard to find the meaning of "wida" before realizing that it had no meaning. It was, she concluded, simply a placeholder. This case is the clearest ever reported of a new form preceding new functions. The two-word stage is an important time for practicing functions that will later have expanded forms and practicing forms that will later expand their functions.

TELEGRAPHIC SPEECH

There is no three-word stage in child language. For a few years after the end of the two-word stage children do produce rather short sentences, but the almost inviolable length constraints that characterized the first two stages have disappeared. The absence of a three-word stage has not been satisfactorily explained as yet; the answer may have to do with the fact that many basic semantic relations are binary and few are ternary. In any case a great deal is known about the sequential development in the language of the period following the two-word stage. Roger Brown of Harvard has named that language telegraphic speech. (It should be noted that there is no specific age at which a child enters any of these stages of language acquisition and further that there is no particular correlation between intelligence and speed of acquisition.)

Early telegraphic speech is characterized by short, simple sentences made up primarily of content words: words that are rich in semantic content, usually nouns and verbs. The speech is called telegraphic because the sentences lack function "words": tense endings on verbs and plural endings on nouns, prepositions, conjunctions, articles and so on. As the telegraphic-speech stage progresses, function words are gradually added to sentences. This process has possibly been studied more thoroughly than any other in language acquisition, and a fairly predictable order in the addition of function words has been observed. The same principles that govern the order of acquisition of function words in English have been shown to operate in many other languages, including some, such as Finnish and Russian, that express the same grammatical relations with particularly rich systems of noun and verb suffixes.

In English many grammatical relations are represented by a fixed word order. For example, in the sentence "The dog followed Jamie to school" it is clear it is the dog that did the following. Normal word order in English requires that the subject come before the verb, and so people who speak English recognize "the dog" as the subject of the sentence. In other languages a noun may be marked as a subject not by its position with respect to the other words in the sentence but by a noun suffix, so that in adult sentences word order may be quite flexible. Until children begin to acquire suffixes and other function words, however, they employ fixed word order to express grammatical relations no matter how flexible adult word order may be. In English the strong propensity to follow word order rigidly shows up in children's interpretations of passive sentences such as "Jamie was followed by the dog." At an early age children may interpret some passive sentences correctly, but by age three they begin to ignore the function words such as "was" and "by" in passive sentences and adopt the fixed word-order interpretation. In other words, since "Jamie" appears before the verb, Jamie is assumed to be the actor, or the noun doing the following.

FUNCTION WORDS

In spite of its grammatical dependence on word order, the English language makes use of enough function words to illustrate the basic principles that determine the order in which such words are acquired. The progressive tense ending "-ing," as in "He going," is acquired first, long before the present-tense third-person singular ending "-s," as in "He goes." The "-s" itself is acquired long before the past tense endings, as in "He goed." Once again the child proves to be a sensible linguist, learning first the tense that exhibits the least variation in form. The "-ing" ending is pronounced only one way, regardless of the pronunciation of the verb to which it is attached. The verb endings "-s" and "-ed," however, vary in their pronunciation: compare "cut(s)," "cuddles (z)," "crushes (əz)," "walked (t)," "played (d)" and "halted (əd)." (The vowel "ə," called "schwa," is pronounced like the unstressed word "a.") Furthermore, present progressive ("-ing") forms are used with greater frequency than any other tense in the speech children hear. Finally, no verb has an irregular "-ing" form, but some verbs do have irregular third-person present-tense singular forms and many have irregular past-tense forms. (The same pattern of learning earliest those forms that exhibit the least variation shows up much more dramatically in languages such as Finnish and Russian, where the paradigms of inflection are much richer.)

The past tense is acquired after the progressive and present tenses, because the relative time it represents is conceptually more difficult. The future tense ("will" and a verb) is formed regularly in English and is as predictable as the progressive tense, but it is a much more abstract concept than the past tense. Therefore it is acquired much later. In the same way the prepositions "in" and "on" appear earlier than any others, at about the same time as "-ing," but prepositions such as "behind" and "in front of," whose correct usage depends on the speaker's frame of reference, are acquired much later.

It is particularly interesting to note that there are three English morphemes that are pronounced identically but are acquired at different times. They are the plural "-s," the possessive "-s" and the third-person singular tense ending "-s," and they are acquired in the order of listing. Roman Jakobson of Harvard has suggested that the explanation of this phenomenon has to do with the complexity of the different relations the morphemes signal: the singular-plural distinction is at the word level, the possessive relates two nouns at the phrase level and the tense ending relates a noun and a verb at the clause level.

The forms of the verb "to be"—"is," "are" and so on—are among the last of the function words to be acquired, particularly in their present-tense forms. Past- and future-tense forms of "to be" carry tense information, of course, but present-tense forms are essentially meaningless, and omitting them is a very sensible strategy for a child who must maximize the information content of a sentence and place priorities on linguistic structures still to be tackled.

PLURALS

When there are competing pronunciations available, as in the case of the plural and past tenses, the process of sorting them out also follows a predictable pattern. Consider the acquisition of the English plural, in which six distinct stages can be observed. In English, as in many other (but not all) languages, nouns have both singular and plural forms. Children usually use the singular forms first, both in situations where the singular form would be appropriate and in situations where the plural form would be appropriate. In instances where the plural form is irregular in the adult model, however, a child may not recognize it as such and may use it in place of the singular or as a free variant of the singular. Thus in the first stage of acquisition, before either the concept of a plural or the linguistic devices for expressing a plural are acquired, a child may say "two cat" or point to "one feet."

When plurals begin to appear regularly, the child forms them according to the most general rule of English plural formation. At this point it is the child's overgeneralization of the rule, resulting in words such as "mans," "foots" or "feets," that shows she has hypothesized the rule: Add the sound /s/ or /z/ to the end of a word to make it plural. (The slashes indicate pronounced sounds, which are not to be confused with the letters used in spelling.)

For many children the overgeneralized forms of the irregular nouns are actually the earliest /s/ and /z/ plurals to appear, preceding "boys," "cats" and other regular forms by hours or days. The period of overgeneralization is considered to be the third stage in the acquisition of plurals because for many children there is an intermediate second stage in which irregular plurals such as "men" actually do appear. Concerned parents may regard the change from the second-stage "men" to the third-stage "mans" as a regression, but in reality it demonstrates progress from an individual memorized item to the application of a general rule.

In the third stage the small number of words that already end in a sound resembling /s/ or /z/, such as "house," "rose" and "bush," are used without any plural ending. Adults normally make such words plural by adding the suffix /əz/. Children usually relegate this detail to the remainder pile, to be dealt with at a later time. When they return to the problem, there is often a short fourth stage of perhaps a day, in which the child delightedly demonstrates her solution by tacking /əz/ endings indiscriminately onto nouns no matter what sound they end in and no matter how many other plural markings they may already have. A child may wake up one morning and throw herself into this stage with all the zeal of a kitten playing with its first ball of string.

Within a few days the novelty wears off and the child enters a less flamboyant fifth stage, in which only irregular plurals still deviate from the model forms. The rapid progression through the fourth stage does not mean that she suddenly focused her attention on the problem of /əz/ plurals. It is more likely that she had the problem at the back of her mind throughout the third stage. She was probably silently formulating hypotheses about the occurrence of /əz/ and testing them against the plurals she was hearing. Finding the right rule required discovering the phonological specification of the class of nouns that take /əz/ plurals.

Arriving at the sixth and final stage in the acquisition of plurals does not require the formulation of any new rules. All that is needed is the simple memorizing of irregular forms. Being rational, the child relegates such minor details to the lowest-priority remainder pile and turns her attention to more interesting linguistic questions. Hence a five-year-old may still not have entered the last stage. In fact, a child in the penultimate stage may not be at all receptive to being taught irregular plurals. For example, a child named Erica pointed to a picture of some "mouses," and her mother corrected her by saying "mice." Erica and her mother each repeated their own version two more times, and then Erica resolved the standoff by turning to a picture of "ducks." She avoided the picture of the mice for several days. Two years later, of course, Erica was perfectly able to say "mice."

NEGATIVE SENTENCES

One of the pioneering language-acquisition studies of the 1960s was undertaken at Harvard by a research group headed by Brown. The group studied the development in the language of three children over a period of several years. Two members of the group, Ursula Bellugi and Edward S. Klima, looked specifically at the changes in the children's negative sentences over the course of the project.

They found that negative structures, like other subsystems of the syntactic component of grammar, are acquired in an orderly, rule-governed way.

When the project began, the forms of negative sentences the children employed were quite simple. It appeared that they had incorporated the following rule into their grammar: To make a sentence negative attach "no" or "not" to the beginning of it. On rare occasions, possibly when a child had forgotten to anticipate the negative, "no" could be attached to the end of a sentence, but negative words could not appear inside a sentence.

In the next stage the children continued to follow this rule, but they had also hypothesized and incorporated into their grammars more complex rules that allowed them to generate sentences in which the negatives "no," "not," "can't" and "don't" appeared after the subject and before the verb. These rules constituted quite an advance over attaching a negative word externally to a sentence. Furthermore, some of the primitive imperative sentences constructed at this stage began with "don't" rather than "no." On the other hand, "can't" never appeared at the beginning of a sentence, and neither "can" nor "do" appeared as an auxiliary, as they do in adult speech: "I can do it." These facts suggest that at this point "can't" and "don't" were unanalyzed negative forms rather than contractions of "cannot" and "do not," but that although "can't" and "don't" each seemed to be interchangeable with "no," they were no longer interchangeable with each other.

In the third stage of acquiring negatives many more details of the negative system had appeared in the children's speech. The main feature of the system that still remained to be worked out was the use of pronouns in negative sentences. At this stage the children said "I didn't see something" and "I don't want somebody to wake me up." The pronouns "somebody" and "something" were later replaced with "nobody" and "nothing" and ultimately with the properly concorded forms "anybody" and "anything."

Many features of telegraphic speech were still evident in the third stage. The form "is" of the verb "to be" was frequently omitted, as in "This no good." In adult speech the auxiliary "do" often functions as a dummy verb to carry tense and other markings; for example, in "I didn't see it," "do" carries the tense and the negative. In the children's speech at this stage "do" appeared occasionally, but the children had not yet figured out its entire function. Therefore in some sentences the auxiliary "do" was omitted and the negative "not" appeared alone, as in "I not hurt him." In other sentences, such as "I didn't did it," the negative auxiliary form of "do" appears to be correct but is actually an unanalyzed, memorized item; at this stage the tense is regularly marked on the main verb, which in this example happens also to be "do."

Many children acquire negatives in the same way that the children in the Harvard study did, but subsequent investigations have shown that there is more than one way to learn a language. Carol B. Lord of U.C.L.A. identified a quite different strategy employed by a two-year-old named Jennifer. From 24 to 28 months Jennifer used "no" only as a single-word utterance. In order to produce a negative sentence she simply spoke an ordinary sentence with a higher pitch. For example, "I want put it on" spoken with a high pitch meant "I don't want to put it on." Lord noticed that many of the negative sentences adults addressed to Jennifer were spoken with an elevated pitch. Children tend to pay more attention to the beginning and ending of sentences, and in adult speech negative words usually appear in the middle of sentences. With good reason, then, Jennifer seemed to have hypothesized that one makes a sentence negative by uttering it with a higher pitch. Other children have been found to follow the same strategy. There are clearly variations in the hypotheses children make in the process of constructing grammar.

SEMANTICS

Up to this point I have mainly discussed the acquisition of syntactic rules, in part because in the years following the publication of Chomsky's *Syntactic Structures* child-language research in this area flourished. Syntactic rules, which govern the ordering of words in a sentence, are not all a child needs to know about language, however, and after the first flush of excitement over Chomsky's work investigators began to ask questions about other areas of language acquisition. Consider the development of the rules of semantics, which govern the way words are interpreted. Eve V. Clark of Stanford reexamined old diary studies and noticed that the development in the meaning of words during the first several months of the one-word stage seemed to follow a basic pattern.

The first time children in the studies used a word, Clark noted, it seemed to be as a proper noun, as the name of a specific object. Almost immediately, however, the children generalized the word based on some feature of the original object and used it to refer to many other objects. For example, a child named Hildegard first used "tick-tock" as the name for her father's watch, but she quickly broadened the meaning of the word, first to include all clocks, then all watches, then a gas meter, then a firehose wound on a spool and then a bathroom scale with a round dial. Her generalizations appear to be based on her observation of common features of shape: roundness, dials and so on. In general the children in the diary studies overextended meanings based on similarities of movement, texture, size and most frequently, shape.

As the children progressed, the meanings of words were narrowed down until eventually they more or less coincided with the meanings accepted by adult speakers of the language. The narrowing-down process has not been studied intensively, but it seems likely that the process has no fixed end point. Rather it appears that the meanings of words continue to expand and contract through adulthood, long after other types of language acquisition have ceased.

One of the problems encountered in trying to understand the acquisition of semantics is that it is often difficult to determine the precise meaning a child has constructed for a word. Some interesting observations have been made, however, concerning the development of the meanings of the pairs of words that function as opposites in adult language. Margaret Donaldson and George Balfour of the University of Edinburgh asked children from three to five years old which one of two cardboard trees had "more" apples on it. They asked other children of the same age which tree had "less" apples. (Each child was interviewed individually.) Almost all the children in both groups responded by pointing to the tree with more apples on it. Moreover, the children who had been asked to point to the tree with "less" apples showed no hesitation in choosing the tree with more apples. They did not act as though they did not know the meaning of "less"; rather they acted as if they did know the meaning and "less" meant "more."

Subsequent studies have revealed similar systematic error making in the acquisition of other pairs of opposites such as "same" and "different," "big" and "little," "wide" and "narrow" and "tall" and "short." In every case the pattern of learning is the same: one word of the pair is learned first and its meaning is overextended to apply to the other word in the pair. The first word learned is always the unmarked word of the pair, that is, the word adults use when they do not want to indicate either one of the opposites. (For example, in the case of "wide" and "narrow," "wide" is the unmarked word: asking "How wide is the road?" does not suggest that the road is wide, but asking "How narrow is the road?" does suggest that the road is narrow.)

Clark observed a more intricate pattern of error production in the acquisition of the words "before" and "after." Consider the four different types of sentence represented by (1) "He jumped the gate before he patted the dog," (2) "Before he patted the dog he jumped the gate," (3) "He patted the dog after he jumped the gate" and (4) "After he jumped the gate he patted the dog." Clark found that the way the children she observed interpreted sentences such as these could be divided into four stages.

In the first stage the children disregarded the words "before" and "after" in all four of these sentence types and assumed that the event of the first clause took place before the event of the second clause. With this order-of-mention strategy the first and fourth sentence types were interpreted correctly but the second and third sentence types were not. In the second stage sentences using "before" were interpreted correctly but an order-of-mention strategy was still adopted for sentences that used "after." Hence sentences of the fourth type were interpreted correctly but sentences of third type were not. In the next stage both the third and the fourth sentence types were interpreted incorrectly, suggesting that the children had adopted the strategy that "after" actually meant "before." Finally, in the fourth stage both "before" and "after" were interpreted appropriately.

It appears, then, that in learning the meaning of a pair of words such as "more" and "less" or "before" and "after" children acquire first the part of the meaning that is common to both words and only later the part of the meaning that distinguishes the two. Linguists have not yet developed satisfactory ways of separating the components of meaning that make up a single word, but it seems clear that when such components can be identified, it will be established that, for example, "more" and "less" have a large number of components in common and differ only in a single component specifying the people of the dimension. Beyond the studies of opposites there has been little investigation of the period of semantic acquisition that follows the early period of rampant overgeneralization. How children past the early stage learn the meanings of other kinds of words is still not well understood.

PHONOLOGY

Just as children overgeneralize word meanings and sentence structures, so do they overgeneralize sounds, using sounds they have learned in place of sounds they have not yet acquired. Just as a child may use the word "not" correctly in one sentence but instead of another negative word in a second sentence, so may she correctly contrast /p/ and /b/ at the beginnings of words but employ /p/ at the ends of words, regardless of whether the adult models end with /p/ or /b/. Children also acquire the details of the phonological system in very regular ways. The ways in which they acquire individual sounds, however, are highly idiosyncratic, and so for many years the patterns eluded diarists, who tended to look only at the order in which sounds were acquired. Jakobson made a major advance in this area by suggesting that it was not individual sounds children acquire in an orderly way but the distinctive features of sound, that is, the minimal differences, or contrasts, between sounds. In other words, when a child begins to contrast /p/ and /b/, she also begins to contrast all the other pairs of sounds that, like /p/ and /b/, differ only in the absence or presence of vocal-cord vibration. In English these pairs include /t/ and /d/, and /k/ and the hard /g/. It is the acquisition of this contrast and not of the six individual sounds that is predictable. Jakobson's extensive examination of the diary data for a wide variety of languages supported his theory. Almost all current work in phonological theory rests on the theory of distinctive features that grew out of his work.

My own recent work suggests that phonological units even more basic than the distinctive features play an important part in the early acquisition process. At an early stage, when there are relatively few words in a child's repertory, unanalyzed syllables appear to be the basic unit of the sound system. By designating these syllables as unanalyzed I mean that the child is not able to separate them into their component consonants and vowels. Only later in the acquisition process does such division into smaller units become possible. The gradual discovery of successively smaller units that can form the basis of the phonological system is an important part of the process.

At an even earlier stage, before a child has uttered any words, she is accomplishing a great deal of linguistic learning, working with a unit of phonological organization even more primitive than the syllable. That unit can be defined in terms of pitch contours. By the late babbling period children already control the intonation, or pitch modulation, contours of the language they are learning. At that stage the child sounds as if she is uttering reasonably long sentences, and adult listeners may have the impression they are not quite catching the child's words. There are no words to catch, only random strings of babbled sounds with recognizable, correctly produced question or statement intonation contours. The sounds may accidentally be similar to some of those found in adult English. These sentence-length utterances are called sentence units, and in the phonological system of the child at this stage they are comparable to the consonant-and-vowel segments, syllables and distinctive features that appear in the phonological systems of later stages. The syllables and segments that appear when the period of word learning begins are in no way related to the vast repertory of babbling sounds. Only the intonation contours are carried over from the babbling stage into the later period.

No matter what language environment a child grows up in, the intonation contours characteristic of adult speech in that environment are the linguistic information learned earliest. Some recent studies suggest that it is possible to identify the language environment of a child from her babbling intonation during the second year of life. Other studies suggest that children can be distinguished at an even earlier age on the basis of whether or not their language environment is a tone language, that is, a language in which words spoken with different pitches are identifiable as different words, even though they may have the same sequence of consonants and vowels. To put it another way, "ma" spoken with a high pitch and "ma" spoken with a low pitch can be as different to someone speaking a tone language as "ma" and "pa" are to someone speaking English. (Many African and Asian languages are tone languages.) Tones are learned very early, and entire tone systems are mastered long before other areas of phonology. The extremely early acquisition of pitch patterns may help to explain the difficulty adults have in learning the intonation of a second language.

PHONETICS

There is one significant way in which the acquisition of phonology differs from the acquisition of other language systems. As a child is acquiring the phonological system she must also learn the phonetic realization of the system: the actual details of physiological and acoustic phonetics, which call for the coordination of a complex set of muscle movements. Some children complete the process of learning how to pronounce things earlier than others, but differences of this kind are usually not related to the learning of the phonological system. Brown had what has become a classic conversation with a child who referred to a "fis." Brown repeated "fis," and the child indignantly corrected him, saying "fis." After several such exchanges Brown tried "fish," and the child, finally satisfied, replied, "Yes, fis." It is clear that although the child was still not able to pronounce the distinction between the sounds "s" and "sh," he knew such a systematic phonological distinction existed. Such phonetic muddying of the phonological waters complicates the study of this area of acquisition. Since the child's knowledge of the phonological system may not show up in her speech, it is not easy to determine what a child knows about the system without engaging in complex experimentation and creative hypothesizing.

Children whose phonological system produces only simple words such as "mama" and "papa" actually have a greater phonetic repertory than their utterances suggest. Evidence of that repertory is found in the late babbling stage, when children are working with sentence units and are making a large array of sounds. They do not lose their phonetic ability overnight, but they must constrain it systematically. Going on to the next-higher stage of language learning, the phonological system, is more important to the child than the details of facile pronunciation. Much later, after the phonological system has been acquired, the details of pronunciation receive more attention.

In the period following the babbling period the persisting phonetic facility gets less and less exercise. The vast majority of a child's utterances fail to reflect her real ability to pronounce things accurately; they do, however, reflect her growing ability to pronounce things systematically. (For a child who grows up learning only one language the movements of the muscles of the vocal tract ultimately become so overpracticed that it is difficult to learn new pronunciations during adulthood. On the other hand, people who learn at least two languages in early childhood appear to retain a greater flexibility of the vocal musculature and are more likely to learn to speak an additional language in their adult years without the "accent" of their native language.)

In learning to pronounce, then, a child must acquire a sound system that includes the divergent systems of phonology and phonetics. The acquisition of phonology differs from that of phonetics in requiring the creation of a representation of language in the mind of the child. This representation is necessary because of the abstract nature of the units of phonological structure. From only the acoustic signal of adult language the child must derive successively more abstract phonological units: first intonations, then syllables, then distinctive features and finally consonant-and-vowel segments. There are, for example, few clear segment boundaries in the acoustic signal the child receives, and so the consonant-and-vowel units could hardly be derived if the child had no internal representation of language.

At the same time that a child is building a phonological representation of language she is learning to manipulate all the phonetic variations of language, learning to produce each one precisely and automatically. The dual process of phonetics and phonology acquisition is one of the most difficult in all of language learning. Indeed, although a great deal of syntactic and semantic acquisition has yet to take place, it is usually at the completion of the process of learning to pronounce that adults consider a child to be a full-fledged language speaker and stop using any form of caretaker speech.

ABNORMAL LANGUAGE DEVELOPMENT

There seems to be little question that the human brain is best suited to language learning before puberty. Foreign languages are certainly learned most easily at that time. Furthermore, it has been observed that people who learn more than one language in childhood have an easier time learning additional languages in later years. It seems to be extremely important for a child to exercise the language-learning faculty. Children who are not exposed to any learnable language during the crucial years, for example children who are deaf before they can speak, generally grow up with the handicap of having little or no language. The handicap is unnecessary: deaf children of deaf parents who communicate by means of the American Sign Language do not grow up without language. They live in an environment where they can make full use of their language-learning abilities, and they are reasonably fluent in sign language by age three, right on the developmental schedule. Deaf children who grow up communicating by means of sign language have a much easier time learning English as a second language than deaf children in oral-speech programs learning English as a first language.

The study of child language acquisition has made important contributions to the study of abnormal speech development. Some investigators of child language have looked at children whose language development is abnormal in the hope of finding the conditions that are necessary and sufficient for normal development; others have looked at the development of language in normal children in the hope of helping children whose language development is abnormal. It now appears that many of the severe language abnormalities found in children can in some way be traced to interruptions of the normal acquisition process. The improved understanding of the normal process is being exploited to create treatment programs for children with such problems. In the past therapeutic methods for children with language problems have emphasized the memorizing of language routines, but methods now being developed would allow a child to work with her own language-learning abilities. For example, the American Sign Language has been taught successfully to several autistic children. Many of these nonverbal and antisocial children have learned in this way to communicate with therapists, in some cases becoming more socially responsive. (Why sign language should be so successful with some autistic children is unclear; it may have to do with the fact that a sign lasts longer than an auditory signal.)

There are still many questions to be answered in the various areas I have discussed, but in general a great deal of progress has been made in understanding child language over the past 20 years. The study of the acquisition of language has come of age. It is now a genuinely interdisciplinary field where psychologists, neurosurgeons and linguists work together to penetrate the mechanisms of perception and cognition as well as the mechanisms of language.

Learning the Mother Tongue

Jerome S. Bruner

Learning a native language is an accomplishment within the grasp of any toddler, yet discovering how children do it has eluded generations of philosophers. St. Augustine believed it was simple. Recollecting his own childhood, he said, "When they named any thing, and as they spoke turned towards it, I saw and remembered that they called what they would point out by the name they uttered. . . . And thus by constantly hearing words, as they occurred in various sentences, I collected gradually for what they stood; and having broken in my mouth to these signs, I thereby gave utterance to my will." But a look at children as they actually acquire language shows that St. Augustine was wrong and that other attempts to explain the feat err as badly in the opposite direction. What is more, as we try to understand how children learn their own language, we get an inkling of why it is so difficult for adults to learn a second language.

Thirty years ago, psychologies of learning held sway; language acquisition was explained using principles and methods that had little to do with language. Most started with nonsense syllables or random materials that were as far as researchers could get from the structure of language that permits the generation of rich and limitless statements, speculations, and poetry. Like G. K. Chesterton's drunk, they looked for the lost coin where the light was. And in the light of early learning theories, children appeared to acquire language by associating words with agents and objects and actions, by imitating their elders, and by a mysterious force called reinforcement. It was the old and tired Augustinian story dressed up in the language of behaviorism.

Learning theory led to a readiness, even a recklessness, to be rid of an inadequate account, one that could explain the growth of vocabulary but not how a four-year-old abstracts basic language rules and effortlessly combines old words to make an infinite string of new sentences. The stage was set for linguist Noam Chomsky's theory of LAD, the Language Acquisition Device, and for the Chomskyan revolution.

According to this view, language was not learned; it was recognized by virtue of an innate recognition routine through which children, when exposed to their local language, could abstract or extract its universal grammatical principles. Whatever the input of that local language, however degenerate, the output of LAD was the grammar of the language, a competence to generate all possible grammatical sentences and none (or very few) that were not. It was an extreme view, so extreme that it did not even consider meaning. In a stroke it freed a generation of psycholinguists from the dogma of association, imitation, and reinforcement and turned their attention to the problem of rule learning. By declaring learning theory dead, it opened the way for a new account. George Miller of

The Rockefeller University put it well: We had two theories of language learning—one of them, empiricist associationism, is impossible; the other, nativism, is miraculous. The void between the impossible and the miraculous remained to be filled.

Both explanations begin too late—when children say their first words. Long before children acquire language, they know something about their world. Before they can make verbal distinctions in speech, they have sorted the conceptual universe into useful categories and classes and can make distinctions about actions and agents and objects. As Roger Brown of Harvard University has written, "The concept . . . is there beforehand, waiting for the word to come along that names it." But the mystery of how children penetrate the communication system and learn to represent in language what they already know about the real world has not been solved. Although there is a well-packaged semantic content waiting, what children learn about language is not the same as what they know about the world. Yet the void begins to fill as soon as we recognize that children are not flying blind, that semantically speaking they have some target toward which language-learning efforts are directed: saying something or understanding something about events in a world that is already known.

If a child is in fact communicating, he has some end in mind—requesting something or indicating something or establishing some sort of personal relationship. The function of a communication has to be considered. As philosopher John Austin argued, an utterance cannot be analyzed out of its context of use, and its use must include the intention of the speaker and its interpretation in the light of conventional standards by the person addressed. A speaker may make a request in several ways: by using the conventional question form, by making a declarative statement, or by issuing a command.

Roger Brown observed young Adam from age two until he was four and found that his middle-class mother made requests using a question form: "Why don't you play with your ball now?" Once Adam came to appreciate what I shall call genuine *why* questions (i.e., "Why are you playing with your ball?"), he typically answered these—and these only—with the well-known "Because." There is no instance, either before or after he began to comprehend the genuine causal question, of his ever confusing a sham and a real *why* question.

Not only does conceptual knowledge precede true language, but so too does function. Children know, albeit in limited form, what they are trying to accomplish by communicating before they begin to use language to implement their efforts. Their initial gestures and vocalizations become increasingly stylized and conventional.

It has become plain in the last several years that Chomsky's original bold claim that any sample of language encountered by an infant was enough for the LAD to dig down to the grammatical rules simply is false. Language is not encountered willy-nilly by the child; it is instead encountered in a highly orderly interaction with the mother, who takes a crucial role in arranging the linguistic encounters of the child. What has emerged is a theory of mother-infant interaction in language acquisition—called the fine-tuning theory—that sees language mastery as involving the mother as much as it does the child. According to this theory, if the LAD exists, it hovers somewhere in the air between mother and child.

So today we have a new perspective that begins to grant a place to knowledge of the world, to knowledge of the function of communication, and to the hearer's interpretation of the speaker's intent. The new picture of language learning recognizes that the process depends on highly constrained and one-sided transactions between the child and the adult teacher. Language acquisition requires joint problem solving by mother and infant, and her response to her child's language is close tuned in a way that can be specified.

The child's entry into language is an entry into dialogue, and the dialogue is at first necessarily nonverbal and requires both members of the pair to interpret the communication and its intent. Their relationship is in the form of roles, and each "speech" is determined by a move of either partner. Initial control of the dialogue depends on the mother's interpretation, which is guided by a continually updated understanding of her child's competence.

Consider an infant learning to label objects. Anat Ninio and I observed Richard in his home every two weeks from his eighth month until he was two years old, video-taping his actions so that we could study them later. In this instance he and his mother are "reading" the pictures in a book. Before this kind of learning begins, certain things already have been established. Richard has learned about pointing as a pure indicating act, marking unusual or unexpected objects rather than things wanted immediately. He has also learned to understand that sounds refer in some singular way to objects or events. Richard and his mother, moreover, have long since established well-regulated turn-taking routines, which probably were developing as early as his third or fourth month. And finally, Richard has learned that books are to be looked at, not eaten or torn; that objects depicted are to be responded to in a particular way and with sounds in a pattern of dialogue.

For the mother's part, she (like all mothers we have observed) drastically limits her speech and maintains a steady regularity. In her dialogues with Richard she uses four types of speech in a strikingly fixed order. First, to get his attention, she says "Look." Second, with a distinctly rising inflection, she asks "What's that?" Third, she gives the picture a label, "It's an X." And finally, in response to his actions, she says "That's right."

In each case, a single verbal token accounts for from nearly half to more than 90 percent of the instances. The way Richard's mother uses the four speech constituents is closely linked to what her son says or does. When she varies her response, it is with good reason. If Richard responds, his mother replies, and if he initiates a cycle by pointing and vocalizing, then she responds even more often.

Her fine tuning is fine indeed. For example, if after her query Richard labels the picture, she will virtually always skip the label and jump to the response, "Yes." Like the other mothers we have studied, she is following ordinary polite rules for adult dialogue.

As Roger Brown has described the baby talk of adults, it appears to be an imitative version of how babies talk. Brown says, "Babies already talk like babies, so what is the earthly use of parents doing the same? Surely it is a parent's job to teach the adult language." He resolves the dilemma by noting, "What I think adults are chiefly trying to do, when they use [baby talk] with children, is to communicate, to understand and to be understood, to keep two minds focused on the same topic." Although I agree with Brown, I would like to point out that the content and intonation of the talk is baby talk, but the dialogue pattern is adult.

To ensure that two minds are indeed focused on a common topic, the mother develops a technique for showing her baby what feature a label refers to by making 90 percent of her labels refer to whole objects. Since half of the remainder of her speech is made up of proper names that also stand for the whole, she seems to create few difficulties, supposing that the child also responds to whole objects and not to their features.

The mother's (often quite unconscious) approach is exquisitely tuned. When the child responds to her "Look!" by looking, she follows immediately with a query. When the child responds to the query with a gesture or a smile, she supplies a label. But as soon as the child shows the ability to vocalize in a way that might indicate a label, she raises the ante. She withholds the label and repeats the query until the child vocalizes, then she gives the label.

Later, when the child has learned to respond with shorter vocalizations that correspond to words, she no longer accepts an indifferent vocalization. When the child begins producing a recognizable, constant label for an object, she holds out for it. Finally, the child produces appropriate words at the appropriate place in the dialogue. Even then the mother remains tuned to the developing pattern, helping her child recognize labels and make them increasingly accurate. For example, she develops two ways of asking "What's that?" One, with a falling intonation, inquires about those words for which she believes her child already knows the label; the other, with a rising intonation, marks words that are new.

Even in the simple labeling game, mother and child are well into making the distinction between the given and the new. It is of more than passing interest that the old or established labels are the ones around which the mother will shortly be elaborating comments and questions for new information:

> *Mother:* (with falling intonation): What's that?
> *Child:* Fishy.
> *Mother:* Yes, and see him swimming?

After the mother assumes her child has acquired a particular label, she generally drops the attention-getting "Look!" when they turn to the routine. In these petty particulars of language, the mother gives useful cues about the structure of their native tongue. She provides cues based not simply on her knowledge of the language but also on her continually changing knowledge of the child's ability to grasp particular distinctions, forms, or rules. The child is sensitized to certain constraints in the structure of their dialogue and does not seem to be directly imitating her. I say this because there is not much difference in the likelihood of a child's repeating a label after hearing it, whether the mother has imitated the child's label, simply said "Yes," or only laughed approvingly. In each case the child repeats the label about half the time, about the same rate as with *no* reply from the mother. Moreover, the child is eight times more likely to produce a label in response to "What's that?" than to the mother's uttering the label.

I do not mean to claim that children cannot or do not use imitation in acquiring language. Language must be partly based on imitation, but though the child may be imitating another, language learning involves solving problems by communicating in a dialogue. The child seems to be trying to get through to the mother just as hard as she is trying to reach her child.

Dialogue occurs in a context. When children first learn to communicate, it is always in highly concrete situations, as when mother or child calls attention to an object, asking for the aid or participation of the other. Formally conceived, the format of communication involves an intention, a set of procedures, and a goal. It presupposes shared knowledge of the world and a shared script by which mother and child can carry out reciprocal activity in that world. Formats obviously have utility for the child. They provide a simple, predictable bit of the world in which and about which to communicate. But they also have an important function for the mother in the mutual task of speech acquisition.

When a mother uses baby talk, her intonation broadens, her speech slows, and her grammar becomes less complex. In addition, baby talk virtually always starts with the here and now, with the format in which the two are operating. It permits the mother to tune her talk to the child's capabilities. She need not infer the child's general competence for language, but instead judges the child's performance on a specific task at a specific time.

A second major function of speech is requesting something of another person. Carolyn Roy and I have been studying its development during the first two years of life. Requesting requires an indication that you want *something* and *what* it is you want. In the earliest procedures used by children it is difficult to separate the two. First the child vocalizes with a characteristic intonation pattern while reaching eagerly for the desired nearby object—which is most often held by the mother. As in virtually all early exchanges, it is the mother's task to interpret, and she works at it in a surprisingly subtle way. During our analyses of Richard when he was from 10 to 24 months old and Jonathan when he was 11 to 18 months old, we noticed that their mothers frequently seemed to be teasing them or withholding obviously desired objects. Closer inspection indicated that it was not teasing at all. They were trying to establish whether the infants real-

MOTHER'S QUESTIONS WHEN CHILDREN REQUEST NEARBY OBJECTS

	Age in months		
Type of question	10-12	13-14	More than 15
About intention ("Do you want it?")	93%	90%	42%
About referent ("Do you want the x?")	7%	10%	58%
Number of questions	**27**	**29**	**12**

FORMS OF EARLY REQUESTS

	Age in months				
Request for:	10-12	13-14	15-16	17-18	20-24
Near and visible object	100%	74%	43%	22%	11%
Distant or invisible object	0	16%	24%	8%	24%
Shared activity	0	10%	14%	23%	36%
Supportive action	0	0	19%	47%	29%
Minutes of recording	**150**	**120**	**120**	**120**	**150**
Number of request/10 minutes	**1.5**	**1.6**	**1.8**	**4.3**	**2.3**

ADULT RESPONSES TO CHILDREN'S REQUESTS

	Age in months				
Type of response	10-12	13-14	15-16	17-18	20-24
Pronominal question					
Open question (who, what, which)	78%	55%	36%	8%	1%
Closed question (yes, no)	3%	10%	18%	30%	22%
Comment/Question (yes/no)	6%	27%	36%	25%	36%
Comment/Question on agency	8%	2%	0	20%	28%
"Language lesson"	6%	6%	9%	14%	4%
Request for reason	0	0	0	3%	5%
Other	0	0	1%	0	4%
Number of utterances	**36**	**51**	**22**	**116**	**100**

ly wanted what they were reaching for, urging them to make their intentions clearer.

When the two children requested nearby objects, the mothers were more likely to ask "Do you really want it?" than "Do you want the X?" The mother's first step is pragmatic, to establish the sincerity of the child's request.

Children make three types of requests, reflecting increasing sophistication in matters that have nothing to do with language. The first kind that emerges is directed at obtaining nearby, visible objects; this later expands to include distant or absent objects where the contextual understanding of words like "you, me," "this, that," and "here, there" is crucial. The second kind of request is directed at obtaining support for an action that is already in progress, and the third kind is used to persuade the mother to share some activity or experience.

When children first begin to request objects, they typically direct their attention and their reach, opening and closing their fists, accompanied by a characteristic intonation pattern. As this request expands, between 10 and 15 months, an observer immediately notes two changes. In reaching for distant objects, a child no longer looks solely at the desired object, but shifts his glance back and forth between the object and his mother. His call pattern also changes. It becomes more prolonged, or its rise and fall is repeated, and it is more insistent. Almost all of Richard's and Jonathan's requests for absent objects were for food, drink, or a book to be read, each having its habitual place. Each request involved the child's gesturing toward the place.

When consistent word forms appeared, they were initially idiosyncratic labels for objects, gradually becoming standard nouns that indicated the desired objects. The children also began initiating and ending their requests with smiles. The development of this pattern is paced by the child's knowledge, which is shared with the mother, of where things are located and of her willingness to fetch them if properly asked. Once the child begins requesting distant and absent objects, the mother has an opportunity to require that the desired object be specified. Sincerity ceases to be at issue, though two other conditions are imposed: control of agency (who is actually to obtain the requested object, with emphasis on the child's increasing independence) and control of "share" (whether the child has had enough).

Requests for joint activity contrast with object requests. I think they can be called precursors to invitation. They amount to the child asking the adult to share in an activity or an experience—to look out of the window into the garden together, to play Ride-a-cockhorse, to read together. They are the most playlike form of request, and in consequence they generate a considerable amount of language of considerable complexity. It is in this format that the issues of agency and share (or turn) emerge and produce important linguistic changes.

Joint activity requires what I call joint role enactment, and it takes three forms: one in which the adult is agent and the child recipient or experiencer (as in early book reading); another in which there is turn taking with the possibility of exchanging roles (as in peekaboo); and a third in which roles run parallel (as in looking around the garden together). Most of what falls into these categories is quite ritualized and predictable. There tend to be rounds and turns, and no specific outcome is required. The activity itself is rewarding. In this setting the child first deals with share and turn by adopting such forms of linguistic marking as *more* and *again.* These appear during joint role enactment and migrate rapidly into formats involving requests for distant objects.

It is also in joint role enactment that the baby's first consistent words appear and, beginning at 18 months, word combinations begin to explode. *More X* (with a noun) appears, and also combinations like *down slide, brrm brrm boo knee, Mummy ride,* and *Mummy read.* Indeed it is in these settings that full-blown ingratiatives appear in appropriate positions, such as prefacing a request with *nice Mummy.*

Characteristically, less than 5 percent of the mother's responses to a child's requests before he is 17 months old have to do with agency (or who is going to do, get, or control something). After 17 months, that figure rises to over 25 percent. At that juncture the mothers we studied began to demand that their children adhere more strictly to turn taking and role respecting. The demand can be made most easily when they are doing something together, for that is where the conditions for sharing are most clearly defined and least likely, since playful, to overstrain the child's capacity to wait for a turn. But the sharp increase in agency as a topic in their dialogue reflects as well the emergence of a difference in their wishes.

The mother may want the child to execute the act requested of her, and the child may have views contrary to his mother's about agency. In some instances this leads to little battles of will. In addition, the child's requests for support more often lead to negotiation between the pair than is the case when the clarity of the roles in their joint activity makes acceptance and refusal easier. A recurrent trend in development during the child's first year is the shifting of agency in all manner of exchanges from mother to infant. Even at nine to 12 months, Richard gradually began taking the lead in give-and-take games.

The same pattern holds in book reading, where Richard's transition was again quite rapid. Role shifting is very much part of the child's sense of script, and I believe it is typical of the kind of "real world" experience that makes it so astonishingly easy for children to master soon afterwards the deictic shifts, those contextual changes in the meaning of words that are essential to understanding the language. At about this time the child learns that I am *I* when I speak, but *you* when referred to by another, and so too with *you;* and eventually the child comes to understand the associated spatial words, *here* and *there, this* and *that, come* and *go.*

The prelinguistic communicative framework established in their dialogue by mother and child provides the setting for the child's acquisition of this language function. His problem solving in acquiring the deictic function is a *social* task: to find the procedure that will produce results, just as his prelinguistic communicative effort produced results, and the results needed can be interpreted in relation to role interactions.

For a number of years an emphasis on egocentrism in the young child has tended to blunt our awareness of the sensitivity of children to roles, of their

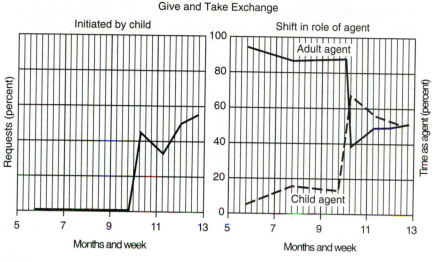

FIGURE 1

capacity to manage role shift and role transformation. Although there is little doubt that it is more difficult for a young child to take the view of others than it will be for him later, this aspect of development has been greatly exaggerated. In familiar and sufficiently simple situations the child is quite capable of taking another's view. In 1975 Michael Scaife and I discovered that babies in their first year shifted their glance to follow an adult's line of regard, and in 1976 Andrew Meltzoff found in our laboratory that babies only a few weeks old appeared to have a built-in mechanism for mimicking an adult's expression, since they obviously could not see their own faces. More recently, Marilyn Shatz has shown that quite young children are indeed able to "take another's position" when giving instructions, provided the task is simple enough.

According to Katherine Nelson and Janice Gruendel at Yale University, what seems to be egocentrism is often a matter of the child not being able to coordinate his own scripts with those of the questioner, although he is scrupulously following turn taking (which is definitely not egocentric). They found that when "egocentric" four-year-olds do manage to find a joint script, they produce dialogues like the following. Two children are sitting next to each other talking into toy telephones:

Gay: Hi.
Dan: Hi.
Gay: How are you?
Dan: Fine.
Gay: Who am I speaking to?
Dan: Daniel. This is your Daddy. I need to speak to you.

Gay: All right.

Dan: When I come home tonight we're gonna have . . . peanut butter and jelly sandwich . . . uh . . . at dinner time.

Gay: Uhmmm. Where're we going at dinner time?

Dan: Nowhere, but we're just gonna have dinner at 11 o'clock.

Gay: Well, I made a plan of going out tonight.

Dan: Well, that's what we're gonna do.

Gay: We're going out.

Dan: The plan, it's gonna be, that's gonna be, we're going to McDonald's.

Gay: Yeah, we're going to McDonald's. And ah, ah, ah, what they have for dinner tonight is hamburger.

Dan: Hamburger is coming. O.K., well, goodbye.

Gay: Bye.

The child takes into account his or her partner's point of view, phrases his turns properly, and says things that are relevant to the script they are working on jointly. That is surely not egocentrism. But even managing the deictic function of language provides evidence that children realize there are viewpoints other than their own.

The last type of request, the request for supportive action, has a very special property. It is tightly bound to the nature of the action in which the child is involved. To ask others for help in support of their own actions, children need at least two forms of knowledge. One of them represents the course of action and involves a goal and a set of means for getting to it. The second requirement is some grasp of what has been called the arguments of action: who does it, with what instrument, at what place, to whom, on what object, etc. Once children have mastered these they have a rudimentary understanding of the concepts that will later be encountered in case grammar.

The degree to which a child comes to understand the structure of tasks is the degree to which his requests for support in carrying them out become more differentiated. These requests do not appear with any marked frequency until he is 17 or 18 months old and consist of bringing the "work" or the "action" or the entire task to an adult: A music box needs rewinding, or two objects have to be put together. In time a child is able to do better than that. He may bring a tool to an adult or direct the adult's hand or pat the goal (the chair on which he wants up). He is selecting and highlighting relevant features of the action, though not in a fashion that depends on what the adult is doing. Finally, at about the age of two, with the development of adequate words to refer to particular aspects of the action, the child enters a new phase: He requests action by guiding it successively. The pacemaker of the verbal output is progress in the task itself.

Let me give an instance of this successive guidance system. Richard, as transpires, wishes to persuade his mother to get a toy telephone from the cupboard; she is seated (and very pregnant). Successively, he voices the following requests:

Mummy, Mummy; Mummy come . . . Up, up. . . . Cupboard. . . . Up cupboard, up cupboard; up cupboard. . . . Get up, get up. . . . Cupboard, cupboard. . . . Cupboard-up; Cupboard-up, cupboard-up. . . . Telephone. . . . Mummy. . . . Mummy get out telephone.

His mother objects and asks him what it is he wants after each of the first two requests. She is trying to get him to set forth his request in some "readable" order before she starts to respond—to give a reason in terms of the goal of the action. Richard, meanwhile, achieves something approaching a request in sentence form by organizing his successive utterances in a fashion that seems to be guided by his conception of the needed steps in the action. The initial grammar of the long string of task-related requests is, then, a kind of temporal grammar based on an understanding not only of the actions required, but also of the order in which these actions must be executed. This bit of child language is an interpersonal script based on a young child's knowledge of what is needed to reach the goal in the real world; it is the matrix in which language develops.

In looking closely at two of the four major communicative functions (indicating and requesting), we discovered a great deal of negotiating by the mother about pragmatic aspects of communication: not about truth-falsity and not about well-formedness, but about whether requests were sincere, whose turn it was, whether it should be done independently or not, whether reasons were clear or justified.

There is, of course, more to communication than indicating and requesting. Another major function of speech is affiliation, the forming of a basis for social exchange. This involves matters as diverse as learning to acknowledge presence, to take turns, and to enter what has been called the "cooperative principle" underlying all speech acts.

The final function is the use of communication for generating possible worlds, and it has little to do with asking for help or indicating things in the real world or, indeed, with maintaining social connection. The early utterances of the children we have studied show one clear-cut characteristic: Most of the talking by mother and by child is *not* about hard-nosed reality. It is about games, about imaginary things, about seemingly useless make-believe. What is involved in the generation of possible worlds is quite useful for both conceptual and communicative development—role playing, referring to nonpresent events, combining elements to exploit their variability, etc.

Had we gone on to look at the other two functions, affiliative activity during which mother and child learn the rules for interacting and the sort of play in which possible worlds are created, the case for mother-infant interaction would have been as strong. There is an enormous amount of teaching involved in transmitting the language, though very little of it has to do with language lessons proper. It has to do with making intentions clear, as speaker and as actor, and with overcoming difficulties in getting done in the real world what we want done by the mediation of communicating. And this is why learning a second language is so difficult. The moment we teach language as an explicit set of rules for generating well-formed strings out of context, the enterprise seems to go badly wrong. The rule in natural language learning is that language is learned in order to interact with someone about something the two of you share.

Where does that leave the problem of language acquisition? Well, to my way of thinking it brings it back into the sphere of problem solving—the problem being how to make our intentions known to others, how to communicate what we have in consciousness, what we want done in our behalf, how we wish to relate to others, and what in this or other worlds is possible.

Children still have to learn to use their native lexicons and to do so grammatically. They learn this in use, in order to get things done with words, and not as if they were ferreting out the disembodied rules of grammar. I think we have learned to look at language acquisition not as a solo flight by the child in search of rules, but as a transaction involving an active language learner and an equally active language teacher. That new insight will go a long way toward filling the gap between the impossible and the miraculous.

FOR FURTHER INFORMATION:

Clark, Herbert, and Eve Clark. 1977. *Psychology and Language: An Introduction to Psycholinguistics.* Harcourt Brace Jovanovich.

De Villiers, Jill G., and Peter A. de Villiers. 1978. *Language Acquisition.* Harvard University Press.

Miller, George A. 1977. *Spontaneous Apprentices: Children and Language.* The Seabury Press.

Snow, Catherine E., and Charles A. Ferguson, eds. 1977. *Talking to Children.* Cambridge University Press.

LANGUAGE AND CULTURE

In all cultures there is a relationship between thought and language. As children begin learning the language of their parents, they also start to become socialized into their parents' culture. Part of the enculturation of children involves learning the dialect of their parents and peers. In order to be effective teachers of the language arts, it is important to understand the relationship between language and culture and to see how the two interact. To be effective in multicultural classrooms, it is imperative to understand the nature and relationship between various regional, social, and ethnic dialects.

LANGUAGE AND THE CONSTRUCTION OF REALITY

Probably no area of linguistic study has provoked as much interest among the general public as has the question of how much does a language or dialect influence how one thinks. In educational circles some people think that language determines thought while others feel language only influences thought. In the first article, Lev Vygotsky proposes that as children begin learning language, they develop an inner speech or egocentric, self-directed speech that correlates with thinking processes. This inner speech is used by adults as well when they solve problems such as those in mathematics. In the second article, Benjamin Whorf examines the concept of time and matter as they appear in different cultures and uses the perceived differences to argue that the language we learn affects both the way we think and the way we perceive the world around us. The final article by Edward Finegan and Niko Besnier summarizes current thinking

67

on the relationship between thought and language. Students who would like to explore this relationship further are encouraged to read further in Whorf and Vygotsky. An excellent collection of articles by Whorf is *Language, Thought, and Reality: Selected Writings of Benjamin Lee Whorf,* edited by John B. Carroll (Cambridge: MIT Press, 1956). Two excellent translations of Vygotsky are *Thought and Language,* translated and revised by Alex Kosulin (Cambridge: MIT Press, 1986), and *Mind in Society: The Development of Higher Psychological Processes,* edited by Michael Cole, et al. (Cambridge: Harvard University Press, 1978).

DIALECTS, LANGUAGE, AND SCHOOLING

In the United States, work in regional dialects began in the 1930s as the *Linguistic Atlas of the United States and Canada* was developed, but because of financial difficulties only two regional atlases have been published to date. The first article in this section, "Varieties of American English" by Walt Wolfram, summarizes this work done by the American regional geographers, continues with a brief summary of social dialects, discusses the relationship between ethnicity and dialects, and finishes with a discussion on the relationship between varieties of English.

In recent years, no topic has been more controversial in the field of dialects than the relationship between nonstandard dialects and the teaching of standard English. In the sixties, this debate centered primarily around bidialectalism. In the seventies, some teachers argued that speakers of Black English Vernacular, that variety of Black English spoken primarily by black inner-city youths, should be taught standard English with the same methods used in teaching English as a foreign language. Since then, linguists have found this analogy to be unsound. Black English Vernacular, or any other ethnic dialect, is only a dialect of English and should be treated as such. The next three articles by Geneva Smitherman, William Labov, and Roger Abrahams discuss the nature of Black English Vernacular and the educational implications.

In the first of these, Smitherman discusses the ramifications of the federal case *Martin Luther King Junior Elementary School Children v. Ann Arbor School District Board* in which the court intervened on the behalf of the children who speak nonstandard dialects to require the school district to take appropriate specialized action to teach these children to read in the standard English used in the commercial world, the arts, sciences, and the professions. While concentrating on grammatical features, Labov discusses the nature of Black English Vernacular and argues that it is a dialect of English, and as with any other dialect, it is often more difficult to change features from this dialect to that of other dialects. In addition, Labov presents five strategies for teaching reading to speakers of Black English Vernacular. In the last of these three articles, Abrahams outlines and exemplifies many of the features of black English

Vernacular that might cause problems in communication between the teacher and black students.

In the next article, John Baugh applies the research that sociolinguists have done on Black English Vernacular to Chicano English to outline some of the potential problems that will affect an adequate definition and to emphasize that Chicano English is a dynamic and changing linguistic system. He emphasizes that it is important to treat Chicano children or Hispanics with respect and not to treat them as if they had all been stamped out of the same mold. In the next article, William Leap outlines the development of Native American Englishes and calls for a strategy that begins instruction with the students' existing language skills and then builds toward language fluencies as they are appropriate for the individual's community needs. The last two articles in this section examine gender and language. In the first, Jenny Cheshire argues that in Britain and the United States, conventional uses of English treat men and women unequally, rather than simply differently, and that this leads to stereotyping. She then outlines research into the relationship between language and gender that has led to conscious attempts to change discriminatory and stereotyping language. In the last article in this section, Deborah Tannen, in a chapter excerpted from *You Just Don't Understand: Women and Men in Conversation* (New York: Ballantine, 1990), argues that men and women have equally valid, albeit different, linguistic systems that often lead to misunderstanding. She then explores some of ways men and women respond to events in different manners, causing misunderstanding. A clearer understanding of the different ways in which men and women communicate should better enable the teacher to avoid gender-linked misunderstandings with students.

Most of the articles in this section have interesting and helpful bibliographies and provide a good starting point for further exploration into these topics. Those of you who are interested in exploring some of these topics still further will find the following bibliography of books and videotapes interesting.

Regional and Social Dialects

Allen, Harold B., and Michael D. Linn (eds.). *Dialect and Language Variation* (New York: Academic, 1986). A collection of articles on a wide range of topics in both regional and social dialects. Some pedagogically oriented articles.

Shuy, Roger W. *Discovering American Dialects* (Urbana, Ill.: NCTE, 1967). A practical introduction to dialects for both the student and teacher with exercises to show students how to collect dialect material.

Wolfram, Walt. *Dialects and American English* (Englewood Cliffs, N. J.: Prentice-Hall, 1991). An excellent survey that should be helpful to either the beginner or expert. Includes discussions of both regional and social dialects and some education-related topics.

Ethnic Dialects

The three items above contain discussions of ethnic dialects. Also useful are the following:

Baugh, John. *Black Street Speech: Its History, Structure, and Survival* (Austin: University of Texas Press, 1983).

Ornstein-Galicia, Jacob (ed.). *Form and Function in Chicano English* (Rowley, Mass.: Newbury, 1984). A collection of essays that examine of Chicano English as a system in its own right.

Peñalosa, Fernando. *Chicano Sociolinguistics: A Brief Introduction* (Rowley, Mass.: Newbury, 1980).

Gender Dialects

Besides reading further in Deborah Tannen's *You Just Don't Understand,* interested readers might also consult the following books and videotapes:

August, Eugene A. "Real Men Don't or Anti-Male Bias in English," *University of Dayton Review,* vol. 18, no. 2 (Spring 1986–87), pp. 115–124. An examination of how the English language stereotypes males.

Thorne, Barrie, Cheris Kramerae, and Nancy Henely (eds.). *Language, Gender and Society* (Rowley, Mass.: Newbury, 1983). Includes an excellent annotated bibliography.

Two excellent tapes to view are:

American Tongues. This video was produced and directed by Louis Alverez (New York: The Center for New American Media, 1987). It is a survey of regional and social dialects of American English with a discussion of the principles of sociolinguistics.

The Story of English. This seven-part video was coproduced by BBC-TV and MacNeil-Lehrer-Gannett Productions (PBS series, 1986). While this series provides a comprehensive survey of English worldwide and thorough history of the language, Part Seven, "Black on White," which probes the origins of and developments of Black English, is especially useful.

A

LANGUAGE AND THE
CONSTRUCTION OF REALITY

Thought and Word

Lev Semenovich Vygotsky

II*

The discovery that word meanings evolve leads the study of thought and speech out of a blind alley. Word meanings are dynamic rather than static formations. They change as the child develops; they change also with the various ways in which thought functions.

If word meanings change in their inner nature, then the relation of thought to word also changes. To understand the dynamics of that relation, we must supplement the genetic approach of our main study by functional analysis and examine the role of word meaning in the process of thought.

Let us consider the process of verbal thinking from the first dim stirring of a thought to its formulation. What we want to show now is not how meanings develop over long periods of time, but the way they function in the live process of verbal thought. On the basis of such a functional analysis, we shall be able to show also that each stage in the development of word meaning has its own particular relation between thought and speech. Since functional problems are most readily solved by examining the highest form of a given activity, we shall, for a while, put aside the problem of development and consider the relations between thought and word in the mature mind.

As soon as we start approaching these relations, the most complex and grand panorama opens before our eyes. Its intricate architectonics surpasses the richest imagination of research schemas. The words of Lev Tolstoy proved to be correct: "The relation of word to thought, and the creation of new concepts is a complex, delicate, and enigmatic process unfolding in our soul" (Tolstoy, 1903, p. 143).

*Note: Part I of this article has been omitted here.

The leading idea in the following discussion can be reduced to this formula: The relation of thought to word is not a thing but a process, a continual movement back and forth from thought to word and from word to thought. In that process, the relation of thought to word undergoes changes that themselves may be regarded as development in the functional sense. Thought is not merely expressed in words; it comes into existence through them. Every thought tends to connect something with something else, to establish a relation between things. Every thought moves, grows and develops, fulfills a function, solves a problem. This flow of thought occurs as an inner movement through a series of planes. An analysis of the interaction of thought and word must begin with an investigation of the different phases and planes a thought traverses before it is embodied in words.

The first thing such a study reveals is the need to distinguish between two planes of speech. Both the inner, meaningful, semantic aspect of speech and the external, phonetic aspect, though forming a true unity, have their own laws of movement. The unity of speech is a complex, not a homogeneous, unity. A number of facts in the linguistic development of the child indicate independent movement in the phonetic and the semantic spheres. We shall point out two of the most important of these facts.

In mastering external speech, the child starts from one word, then connects two or three words; a little later, he advances from simple sentences to more complicated ones, and finally to coherent speech made up of series of such sentences; in other words, he proceeds from a part to the whole. In regard to meaning, on the other hand, the first word of the child is a whole sentence. Semantically, the child starts from the whole, from a meaningful complex, and only later begins to master the separate semantic units, the meanings of words, and to divide his formerly undifferentiated thought into those units. The external and the semantic aspects of speech develop in opposite directions—one from the particular to the whole, from word to sentence, and the other from the whole to the particular, from sentence to word.

This in itself suffices to show how important it is to distinguish between the vocal and the semantic aspects of speech. Since they move in opposite directions, their development does not coincide; but that does not mean that they are independent of each other. On the contrary, their difference is the first stage of a close union. In fact, our example reveals their inner relatedness as clearly as it does their distinction. A child's thought, precisely because it is born as a dim, amorphous whole, must find expression in a single word. As his thought becomes more differentiated, the child is less apt to express it in single words, but constructs a composite whole. Conversely, progress in speech to the differentiated whole of a sentence helps the child's thoughts to progress from a homogeneous whole to well-defined parts. Thought and word are not cut from one pattern. In a sense, there are more differences than likenesses between them. The structure of speech does not simply mirror the structure of thought; that is why words cannot be put on by thought like a ready-made garment. Thought undergoes many changes as it turns into speech. It does not merely find expression in speech; it finds its reality and form. The semantic and the phonetic developmental processes are essentially one, precisely because of their opposite directions.

The second, equally important, fact emerges at a later period of development. Piaget demonstrated that the child uses subordinate clauses with *because, although,* etc., long before he grasps the structures of meaning corresponding to these syntactic forms. Grammar precedes logic. Here, too, as in our previous example, the discrepancy does not exclude union, but is, in fact, necessary for union.

In adults, the divergence between the semantic and the phonetic aspects of speech is even more striking. Modern, psychologically oriented linguistics is familiar with this phenomenon, especially in regard to grammatical and psychological subject and predicate. For example, in the sentence "The clock fell," emphasis and meaning may change in different situations. Suppose I notice that the clock has stopped and ask how this happened. The answer is, "The clock fell." Grammatical and psychological subject coincide: "The clock" is the first idea in my consciousness; "fell" is what is said about the clock. But if I hear a crash in the next room and inquire what happened, and get the same answer, subject and predicate are psychologically reversed. I knew something had fallen—that is what we are talking about. "The clock" completes the idea. The sentence could be changed to "What has fallen is the clock"; then the grammatical and the psychological subjects would coincide. In the prologue to his play *Duke Ernst von Schwaben,* Uhland says, "Grim scenes will pass before you." Psychologically, "will pass" is the subject. The spectator knows he will see events unfold; the additional idea, the predicate, is "grim scenes." Uhland meant, "What will pass before your eyes is a tragedy."

Analysis shows that any part of a sentence may become a psychological predicate, the carrier of topical emphasis. The grammatical category, according to Hermann Paul, is a petrified form of the psychological one.[1] To revive it, one makes a logical emphasis that reveals its semantic meaning. Paul shows that entirely different meanings may lie hidden behind one and the same grammatical structure. Accord between syntactical organization and psychological organization is not as prevalent as we tend to assume—rather, it is a requirement that is seldom met. Not only the subject and predicate, but grammatical gender, number, case, tense, degree, etc., have their psychological doubles. A spontaneous utterance, wrong from the point of view of grammar, may have charm and esthetic value. Alexander Pushkin's lines

---

[1]Hermann Paul (1846-1921), German liguist. See his *Principals of the History of Language,* College Park, MD: McGrath, 1970.

As rose lips without a smile,
Without error in the grammar
I Russian language will despise. . . .

bear a more serious message than is usually assumed. Absolute correctness is
achieved only in mathematics. It seems that Descartes was the first who recognized in mathematics a form of thought that, although originating in language,
goes beyond it. Our daily speech constantly fluctuates between the ideals of
mathematical harmony and imaginative harmony.

We shall illustrate the interdependence of the semantic and the grammatical
aspects of language by citing two examples that show that changes in formal
structure can entail far-reaching changes in meaning.

In translating the fable "The Grasshopper and the Ant," Krylov substituted a
dragonfly for La Fontaine's grasshopper. In French, *grasshopper* is feminine and
therefore well suited to symbolize a lighthearted, carefree attitude. The nuance
would be lost in a literal translation, since in Russian *grasshopper* is masculine.
When he settled for *dragonfly,* which is feminine in Russian, Krylov disregarded the literal meaning in favor of the grammatical form required to render La
Fontaine's thought.

Tiutchev did the same in his translation of Heine's poem about a fir and a
palm. In German *fir* is masculine and *palm* feminine, and the poem suggests the
love of a man for a woman. In Russian, both trees are feminine. To retain the
implication, Tiutchev replaced the fir by a masculine cedar. Lermontov, in his
more literal translation of the same poem, deprived it of these poetic overtones
and gave it an essentially different meaning, more abstract and generalized.
One grammatical detail may, on occasion, change the whole purport of what is
said.

Behind words, there is the independent grammar of thought, the syntax of
word meanings. The simplest utterance, far from reflecting a constant, rigid correspondence between sound and meaning, is really a process. Verbal expressions
cannot emerge fully formed, but must develop gradually. This complex process
of transition from meaning to sound must itself be developed and perfected. The
child must learn to distinguish between semantics and phonetics and understand
the nature of the difference. At first, he uses verbal forms and meanings without
being conscious of them as separate. The word, to the child, is an integral part of
the object it denotes. Such a conception seems to be characteristic of primitive
linguistic consciousness. Wilhelm von Humboldt retells the anecdotal story
about the rustic who said he wasn't surprised that savants with all their instruments could figure out the size of stars and their course—what baffled him was
how they found out their names. Simple experiments show that preschool children "explain" the names of objects by their attributes. According to them, an
animal is called "cow" because it has horns, "calf" because its horns are still
small, "dog" because it is small and has no horns; an object is called "car"
because it is not an animal. When asked whether one could interchange the

names of objects, for instance, call a cow "ink," and ink "cow," children will answer no, "because ink is used for writing, and the cow gives milk." An exchange of names would mean an exchange of characteristic features, so inseparable is the connection between them in the child's mind. In one experiment, the children were told that in a game a dog would be called "cow." Here is a typical sample of questions and answers:

"Does a cow have horns?"

"Yes."

"But don't you remember that the cow is really a dog? Come now, does a dog have horns?"

"Sure, if it is a cow, if it's called cow, it has horns. That kind of dog has got to have little horns."

We can see how difficult it is for children to separate the name of an object from its attributes, which cling to the name when it is transferred like possessions following their owner.

The fusion of the two planes of speech, semantic and vocal, begins to break down as the child grows older, and the distance between them gradually increases. Each stage in the development of word meanings has its own specific interrelation of the two planes. A child's ability to communicate through language is directly related to the differentiation of word meanings in his speech and consciousness.

To understand this, we must remember a basic characteristic of the structure of word meanings. In the semantic structure of a word, we distinguish between referent and meaning; correspondingly, we distinguish a word's nominative function from its significative function. When we compare these structural and functional relations at the earliest, middle, and advanced stages of development, we find the following genetic regularity: In the beginning, only the nominative function exists; and semantically, only the objective reference; signification independent of naming, and meaning independent of reference, appear later and develop along the paths we have attempted to trace and describe.

Only when this development is completed does the child become fully able to formulate his own thought and to understand the speech of others. Until then, his usage of words coincides with that of adults in its objective reference, but not in its meaning.

IV*

Our experiments convinced us that inner speech must be regarded, not as speech minus sound, but as an entirely separate speech function. Its main characteristic trait is its peculiar syntax. Compared with external speech, inner speech appears disconnected and incomplete.

*Note: Part III of this article has been omitted here.

It is not a new observation. All students of inner speech, even those who approached it from behavioristic standpoint, have noted this trait. But they usually did not venture to explore it. Even purely phenotypical analysis remained incomplete. The method of genetic analysis permits us to go beyond a mere description. Watson hypothesized that the abbreviated character of soundless speech stems from the same mechanism that produces "shortcuts" in the acquisition of sensory-motor skills. We think, however, that even if recorded in full with the help of some supersensitive phonograph, the inner speech would remain abbreviated and incoherent. The only way to investigate such speech is to trace its development from its very origin as a social function to its mature form, which is as an instrument of individual thought.

Observing the evolution of the child's egocentric speech step by step, we may discover that it becomes more and more peculiar and ultimately becomes inner speech. We applied the genetic method and found that as egocentric speech develops, it shows a tendency toward an altogether specific form of abbreviation, namely: omitting the subject of a sentence and all words connected with it, while preserving the predicate. This tendency toward predication appears in all our experiments with such regularity that we must assume it to be the basic form of syntax of inner speech.

It may help us to understand this tendency if we recall certain situations in which external speech shows a similar structure. Pure predication occurs in external speech in two cases: either as an answer or when the subject of the sentence is known beforehand to all concerned. The answer to "Would you like a cup of tea?" is never "No, I don't want a cup of tea," but a simple "No." Obviously, such a sentence is possible only because its subject is tacitly understood by both parties. To "Has your brother read this book?" no one ever replies, "Yes, my brother has read this book." The answer is a short "Yes," or "Yes, he has." Now let us imagine that several people are waiting for a bus. No one will say, on seeing the bus approach, "The bus for which we are waiting is coming." The sentence is likely to be an abbreviated "Coming," or some such expression, because the subject is plain from the situation. Quite frequently, shortened sentences cause confusion. The listener may relate the sentence to a subject foremost in his own mind, not the one meant by the speaker. If the thoughts of two people coincide, perfect understanding can be achieved through the use of mere predicates, but if they are thinking about different things they are bound to misunderstand each other.

Very good examples of the condensation of external speech and its reduction to predicates are found in the novels of Tolstoy, who quite often dealt with the psychology of understanding: "No one heard clearly what he said, but Kitty understood him. She understood because her mind incessantly watched for his needs" (*Anna Karenina,* part V, chapter 18). We might say that her thoughts, following the thoughts of the dying man, contained the subject to which his word, understood by no one else, referred. But perhaps the most striking example is the declaration of love between Kitty and Levin by means of initial letters (*Anna Karenina,* part IV, chapter 13):

> "I have long wished to ask you something."
>
> "Please do."
>
> "This," he said, and wrote the initial letters: *W y a: i c n b, d y m t o n.* These letters meant: "When you answered: it can not be, did you mean then or never?" It seemed impossible that she would be able to understand the complicated sentence.
>
> "I understand," she said, blushing.
>
> "What word is that?" he asked, pointing to the *n* which stood for "never."
>
> "The word is 'never,'" she said, "but that is not true." He quickly erased what he had written, handed her the chalk, and rose. She wrote: *I c n a o t.*
>
> His face brightened suddenly: he had understood. It meant: "I could not answer otherwise then."
>
> She wrote the initial letters: *s t y m f a f w h.* This meant: "So that you might forget and forgive what happened."
>
> He seized the chalk with tense, trembling fingers, broke it, and wrote the initial letters of the following: "I have nothing to forget and forgive. I never ceased loving you."
>
> "I understand," she whispered. He sat down and wrote a long sentence. She understood it all and, without asking him whether she was right, took the chalk and answered at once.
>
> For a long time he could not make out what she had written, and he kept looking up into her eyes. His mind was dazed with happiness. He was quite unable to fill in the words she had meant; but in her lovely, radiantly happy eyes he read all that he needed to know. And he wrote down three letters. Before he had finished writing, she was already reading under his hand, and she finished the sentence herself and wrote the answer, "Yes." Everything had been said in their conversation: that she loved him, and would tell her father and mother that he would call in the morning.

This example has an extraordinary psychological interest because, like the whole episode between Kitty and Levin, it was taken by Tolstoy from his own life. In just this way, Tolstoy told his future wife of his love for her. These examples show clearly that when the thoughts of the speakers are the same, the role of speech is reduced to a minimum. Tolstoy points out elsewhere that between people who live in close psychological contact, such communication by means of abbreviated speech is the rule rather than the exception: "Now Levin was used to expressing his thought fully without troubling to put it into exact words: He knew that his wife, in such moments filled with love, as this one, would understand what he wanted to say from a mere hint, and she did" (*Anna Karenina,* part VI, chapter 3).

Lev Jakubinsky and Evgeni Polivanov absolutely correctly emphasized that shared apperception by communicating parties is a necessary precondition of normal dialogue. If we were to communicate in an absolutely formal manner, we would use many more words than we usually use to convey our thoughts. In a word, it is natural that we talk by hints.

A simplified syntax, condensation, and a greatly reduced number of words characterize the tendency to predication that appears in external speech when the partners know what is going on. In complete contrast to this kind of understanding are the comical mix-ups resulting from people's thoughts going in different directions. The confusion to which this may lead is well rendered in this little poem of Pushkin:

Before the judge who's deaf two deaf men bow.
One deaf man cries: "He led away my cow."
"Beg pardon," says the other in reply,
"That meadow was my father's land in days gone by."
The judge decides: "For you to fight each other is a shame.
Nor one nor t'other, but the girl's to blame."

Kitty's conversation with Levin and the judgment of the deaf are extreme cases, the two poles, in fact, of external speech. One exemplifies the mutual understanding that can be achieved through utterly abbreviated speech when the subject is the same in two minds; the other, the total misunderstanding, even with full speech, when people's thoughts wander in different directions. It is not only the deaf who cannot understand one another, but any two people who give a different meaning to the same word or who hold divergent views. As Tolstoy noted, those who are accustomed to solitary, independent thinking do not easily grasp another's thought and are very partial to their own; but people in close contact apprehend one another's complicated meanings by "laconic and clear" communication in the fewest words.

REFERENCE

Tolstoy, L.* 1903. *Pedagogicheskie stali [Pedagogical Writings],* Moscow: Kushnerev.

---

*There is no reference made in the reference section as to which translation of *Anna Karenina* was used.

The Relation of Habitual Thought and Behavior to Language

Benjamin Lee Whorf

Human beings do not live in the objective world alone, nor alone in the world of social activity as ordinarily understood, but are very much at the mercy of the particular language which has become the medium of expression for their society. It is quite an illusion to imagine that one adjusts to reality essentially without the use of language and that language is merely an incidental means of solving specific problems of communication or reflection. The fact of the matter is that the "real world" is to a large extent unconsciously built up on the language habits of the group. . . . We see and hear and otherwise experience very largely as we do because the language habits of our community predispose certain choices of interpretation.

—Edward Sapir

There will probably be general assent to the proposition that an accepted pattern of using words is often prior to certain lines of thinking and forms of behavior, but he who assents often sees in such a statement nothing more than a platitudinous recognition of the hypnotic power of philosophical and learned terminology on the one hand or of catchwords, slogans, and rallying-cries on the other. To see only thus far is to miss the point of one of the important interconnections which Sapir saw between language, culture, and psychology, and succinctly expressed in the introductory quotation. It is not so much in these special uses of language as in its constant ways of arranging data and its most ordinary everyday analysis of phenomena that we need to recognize the influence it has on other activities, cultural and personal.

THE NAME OF THE SITUATION AS AFFECTING BEHAVIOR

I came in touch with an aspect of this problem before I had studied under Dr. Sapir, and in a field usually considered remote from linguistics. It was in the course of my professional work for a fire insurance company, in which I undertook the task of analyzing many hundreds of reports of circumstances surrounding the start of fires, and in some cases, of explosions. My analysis was directed toward purely physical conditions, such as defective wiring, presence or lack of air spaces between metal flues and woodwork, etc., and the results were presented in these terms. Indeed it was undertaken with no thought that any other significances would or could be revealed. But in due course it became evident that not only a physical situation *qua* physics, but the meaning of that situation to people, was sometimes a factor, through the behavior of the people, in the start of the fire. And this factor of meaning was clearest when it was a *linguistic meaning,* residing in the name or the linguistic description commonly applied to the situation. Thus around a storage of what are called "gasoline drums" behavior will tend to a certain type, that is, great care will be exercised; while around a storage of what are called "empty gasoline drums" it will tend to be different— careless, with little repression of smoking or of tossing cigarette stubs about. Yet the "empty" drums are perhaps the more dangerous, since they contain explosive vapor. Physically the situation is hazardous, but the linguistic analysis according to regular analogy must employ the word "empty," which inevitably suggests lack of hazard. The word "empty" is used in two linguistic patterns: (1) as a virtual synonym for "null and void, negative, inert," (2) applied in analysis of physical situations without regard to, e.g., vapor, liquid vestiges, or stray rubbish, in the container. The situation is named in one pattern (2) and the name is then "acted out" or "lived up to" in another (1); this being a general formula for the linguistic conditioning of behavior into hazardous forms.

In a wood distillation plant the metal stills were insulated with a composition prepared from limestone and called at the plant "spun limestone." No attempt was made to protect this covering from excessive heat or the contact of flame. After a period of use the fire below one of the stills spread to the "limestone," which to everyone's great surprise burned vigorously. Exposure to acetic acid fumes from the stills had converted part of the limestone (calcium carbonate) to calcium acetate. This when heated in a fire decomposes, forming inflammable acetone. Behavior that tolerated fire close to the covering was induced by use of the name "limestone," which because it ends in "stone" implies noncombustibility.

A huge iron kettle of boiling varnish was observed to be overheated, nearing the temperature at which it would ignite. The operator moved it off the fire and ran it on its wheels to a distance, but did not cover it. In a minute or so the varnish ignited. Here the linguistic influence is more complex; it is due to the metaphorical objectifying (of which more later) of "cause" as contact or the spatial juxtaposition of "things"—to analyzing the situation as "on" versus "off" the fire. In reality the stage when the external fire was the main factor had passed; the overheating was now an internal process of convection in the varnish from the intensely heated kettle, and still continued when "off" the fire.An electric glow heater on the wall was little used, and for one workman had the meaning of a convenient coat-hanger. At night a watchman entered and snapped a switch, which action he verbalized as "turning on the light." No light appeared, and this result he verbalized as "light is burned out." He could not see the glow of the heater because of the old coat hung on it. Soon the heater ignited the coat, which set fire to the building.

A tannery discharged waste water containing animal matter into an outdoor settling basin partly roofed with wood and partly open. This situation is one that ordinarily would be verbalized as "pool of water." A workman had occasion to light a blow-torch nearby, and threw his match into the water. But the decomposing waste matter was evolving gas under the wood cover, so that the setup was the reverse of "watery." An instant flare of flame ignited the woodwork, and the fire quickly spread into the adjoining building.

A drying room for hides was arranged with a blower at one end to make a current of air along the room and thence outdoors through a vent at the other end. Fire started at a hot bearing on the blower, which blew the flames directly into the hides and fanned them along the room, destroying the entire stock. This hazardous setup followed naturally from the term "blower" with its linguistic equivalence to "that which blows," implying that its function necessarily is to "blow." Also its function is verbalized as "blowing air for drying," overlooking that it can blow other things, e.g., flames and sparks. In reality a blower simply makes a current of air and can exhaust as well as blow. It should have been installed at the vent end to *draw* the air over the hides, then through the hazard (its own casing and bearings) and thence outdoors.

Beside a coal-fired melting pot for lead reclaiming was dumped a pile of "scrap lead"—a misleading verbalization, for it consisted of the lead sheets of old radio condensers, which still had paraffin paper between them. Soon the paraffin blazed up and fired the roof, half of which was burned off.

Such examples, which could be greatly multiplied, will suffice to show how the cue to a certain line of behavior is often given by the analogies of the linguistic formula in which the situation is spoken of, and by which to some degree it is analyzed, classified, and allotted its place in that world which is "to a large extent unconsciously built up on the language habits of the group." And we always assume that the linguistic analysis made by our group reflects reality better than it does.

GRAMMATICAL PATTERNS AS INTERPRETATIONS OF EXPERIENCE

The linguistic material in the above examples is limited to single words, phrases, and patterns of limited range. One cannot study the behavioral compulsiveness of such material without suspecting a much more far-reaching compulsion from large-scale patterning of grammatical categories, such as plurality, gender and similar classifications (animate, inanimate, etc.), tenses, voices, and other verb forms, classifications of the type of "parts of speech," and the matter of whether a given experience is denoted by a unit morpheme, an inflected word, or a syntactical combination. A category such as number (singular vs. plural) is an attempted interpretation of a whole large order of experience, virtually of the world or of nature; it attempts to say how experience is to be segmented, what experience is to be called "one" and what "several." But the difficulty of appraising such a far-reaching influence is great because of its background character, because of the difficulty of standing aside from our own language, which is a habit and a cultural *non est disputandum,* and scrutinizing it objectively. And if we take a very dissimilar language, this language becomes a part of nature, and we even do to it what we have already done to nature. We tend to think in our own language in order to examine the exotic language. Or we find the task of unraveling the purely morphological intricacies so gigantic that it seems to absorb all else. Yet the problem, though difficult, is feasible; and the best approach is through an exotic language, for in its study we are at long last pushed willy-nilly out of our ruts. Then we find that the exotic language is a mirror held up to our own.

In my study of the Hopi language, what I now see as an opportunity to work on this problem was first thrust upon me before I was clearly aware of the problem. The seemingly endless task of describing the morphology did finally end. Yet it was evident, especially in the light of Sapir's lectures on Navaho, that the description of the *language* was far from complete. I knew for example the morphological formation of plurals, but not how to use plurals. It was evident that the category of plural in Hopi was not the same thing as in English, French, or German. Certain things that were plural in these languages were singular in Hopi. The phase of investigation which now began consumed nearly two more years.

The work began to assume the character of a comparison between Hopi and western European languages. It also became evident that even the grammar of Hopi bore a relation to Hopi culture, and the grammar of European tongues to our own "Western" or "European" culture. And it appeared that the interrelation brought in those large subsummations of experience by language, such as our own terms "time," "space," "substance," and "matter." Since with respect to the traits compared there is little difference between English, French, German, or other European languages with the *possible* (but doubtful) exception of Balto-Slavic and non-Indo-European, I have lumped these languages into one group called SAE, or "Standard Average European."

That portion of the whole investigation here to be reported may be summed up in two questions: (1) Are our own concepts of "time," "space," and "matter" given in substantially the same form by experience to all men, or are they in part conditioned by the structure of particular languages? (2) Are there traceable affinities between (a) cultural and behavioral norms and (b) large-scale linguistic patterns? I should be the last to pretend that there is anything so definite as "a correlation" between culture and language, and especially between ethnological rubrics such as "agricultural," "hunting," etc., and linguistic ones like "inflected," "synthetic," or "isolating."[1] When I began the study the problem was by no

---

[1]We have plenty of evidence that this is not the case. Consider only the Hopi and the Ute, with languages that on the overt morphological and lexical level are as similar as, say, English and German. The idea of "correlation" between language and culture, in the generally accepted sense of correlation, is certainly a mistaken one.

means so clearly formulated and I had little notion that the answers would turn out as they did.

PLURALITY AND NUMERATION IN SAE AND HOPI

In our language, that is SAE, plurality and cardinal numbers are applied in two ways: to real plurals and imaginary plurals. Or more exactly if less tersely: perceptible spatial aggregates and metaphorical aggregates. We say "ten men" and also "ten days." Ten men either are or could be objectively perceived as ten, ten in one group-perception[2]—ten men on a street corner, for instance. But "ten days" cannot be objectively experienced. We experience only one day, to-day; the other nine (or even all ten) are something conjured up from memory or imagination. If "ten days" be regarded as a group it must be as an "imaginary," mentally constructed group. Whence comes this mental pattern? Just as in the case of the fire-causing errors, from the fact that our language confuses the two different situations, has but one pattern for both. When we speak of ten steps forward, ten strokes on a bell, or any similarly described cyclic sequence, "times" of any sort, we are doing the same thing as with "days." *Cyclicity* brings the response of imaginary plurals. But a likeness of cyclicity to aggregates is not unmistakably given by experience prior to language, or it would be found in all languages, and it is not.

Our *awareness* of time and cyclicity does contain something immediate and subjective—the basic sense of "becoming later and later." But in the habitual thought of us SAE people this is covered under something quite different, which though mental should not be called subjective. I call it *objectified,* or imaginary, because it is patterned on the *outer* world. It is this that reflects our linguistic usage. Our tongue makes no distinction between numbers counted on discrete entities and numbers that are simply counting itself. Habitual thought then assumes that in the latter case the numbers are just as much counted on *something* as in the former. This is objectification. Concepts of time lose contact with the subjective experience of "becoming later" and are objectified as counted *quantities,* especially as lengths, made up of units as a length can be visible marked off into inches. A "length of time" is envisioned as a row of similar units, like a row of bottles.

In Hopi there is a different linguistic situation. Plurals and cardinals are used only for entities that form or can form an objective group. There are no imaginary plurals, but instead ordinals used with singulars. Such an expression as "ten

---

[2]As we say, "ten at the *same time,* " showing that in our language and thought we restate the fact of group-perception in terms of a concept "time," the large linguistic component of which will appear in the course of this paper.

days" is not used. The equivalent statement is an operational one that reaches one day by a suitable count. "They stayed ten days" becomes "they stayed until the eleventh day" or "they left after the tenth day." "Ten days is greater than nine days" becomes "the tenth day is later than the ninth." Our "length of time" is not regarded as a length but as a relation between two events in lateness. Instead of our linguistically promoted objectification of that datum of consciousness we call "time," the Hopi language has not laid down any pattern that would cloak the subjective "becoming later" that is the essence of time.

NOUNS OF PHYSICAL QUANTITY IN SAE AND HOPI

We have two kinds of noun denoting physical things; individual nouns, and mass nouns, e.g., water, milk, wood, granite, sand, flour, meat. Individual nouns denote bodies with definite outlines: a tree, a stick, a man, a hill. Mass nouns denote homogeneous continua without implied boundaries. The distinction is marked by linguistic form; e.g., mass nouns lack plurals,[3] in English drop articles, and in French take the partitive article *du, de la, des*. The distinction is more widespread in language than in the observable appearance of things. Rather few natural occurrences present themselves as unbounded extents; air of course, and often water, rain, snow, sand, rock, dirt, grass. We do not encounter butter, meat, cloth, iron, glass, or most "materials" in such kind of manifestation, but in bodies small or large with definite outlines. The distinction is somewhat forced upon our description of events by an unavoidable pattern in language. It is so inconvenient in a great many cases that we need some way of individualizing the mass noun by further linguistic devices. This is partly done by names of body-types: stick of wood, piece of cloth, pane of glass, cake of soap; also, and even more, by introducing names of containers though their contents be the real issue: glass of water, cup of coffee, dish of food, bag of flour, bottle of beer. These very common container-formulas, in which "of" has an obvious, visually perceptible meaning ("contents"), influence our feeling about the less obvious type-body formulas: stick of wood, lump of dough, etc. The formulas are very similar: individual noun plus a similar relator (English "of"). In the obvious case this relator denotes contents. In the inobvious one it *suggests* contents. Hence the lumps, chunks, blocks, pieces, etc., seem to contain something, a "stuff," "substance," or "matter" that answers to the water, coffee, or flour in the container formulas. So with SAE people the philosophic "substance" and "matter" are also the naïve idea they are instantly acceptable, "common sense." It is

---

[3]It is no exception to this rule of lacking a plural that a mass noun may sometimes coincide in lexeme with an individual noun that of course has a plural; e.g., "stone" (no pl.) with "a stone" (pl. "stones"). The plural form denoting varieties, e.g., "wines" is of course a different sort of thing from the true plural; it is a curious outgrowth from the SAE mass nouns, leading to still another sort of imaginary aggregates, which will have to be omitted from this paper.

so through linguistic habit. Our language patterns often require us to name a physical thing by a binomial that splits the reference into a formless item plus a form.

Hopi is again different. It has a formally distinguished class of nouns. But this class contains no formal sub-class of mass nouns. All nouns have an individual sense and both singular and plural forms. Nouns translating most nearly our mass nouns still refer to vague bodies or vaguely bounded extents. They imply indefiniteness, but not lack, of outline and size. In specific statements "water" means one certain mass or quantity of water, not what we call "the substance water." Generality of statement is conveyed through the verb or predicator, not the noun. Since nouns are individual already they are not individualized either by type-bodies or names of containers, if there is no special need to emphasize shape or container. The noun itself implies a suitable type-body or container. One says, not "a glass of water" but kə·yi "a water," not "a pool of water" but pa·hə,[4] not "a dish of corn-flour" but ŋəmni "a (quantity of) corn-flour," not "a piece of meat" but sikʷi "a meat." The language has neither need for nor analogies on which to build the concept of existence as a duality of formless item and form. It deals with formlessness through other symbols than nouns.

PHASES OF CYCLES IN SAE AND HOPI

Such terms as summer, winter, September, morning, noon, sunset, are with us nouns, and have little formal linguistic difference from other nouns. They can be subjects or objects, and we say "at" sunset or "in" winter just as we say at a corner or in an orchard.[5] They are pluralized and numerated like nouns of physical objects, as we have seen. Our thought about the referents of such words hence becomes objectified. Without objectification it would be a subjective experience of real time, i.e. of the consciousness of "becoming later and later"—simply a cyclic phase similar to an earlier phase in that ever-later-becoming duration. Only by imagination can such a cyclic phase be set beside another and another in the manner of a spatial (i.e. visually perceived) configuration. But such is the power of linguistic analogy that we do so objectify cyclic phasing. We do it even by saying "a phase" and "phases" instead of, e.g., "phasing." And the pattern of individual and mass nouns, with the resulting binomial formula of formless item plus form, is so general that it is implicit for all nouns, and hence our very generalized formless items like "substance," "matter," by which we can fill

---

[4]Hopi has two words for water-quantities; kə·yi and pa·hə. The difference is something like that between "stone" and "rock" in English, pa·hə implying greater size and "wildness;" flowing water, whether or not outdoors or in nature, is pa•hə, so is "moisture." But unlike "stone" and "rock," the difference is essential, not pertaining to a connotative margin, and the two can hardly ever be interchanged.

[5]To be sure there are a few minor differences from other nouns, in English for instance in the use of the articles.

out the binomial for an enormously wide range of nouns. But even these are not quite generalized enough to take in our phase nouns. So for the phase nouns we have made a formless item, "time." We have made it by using "a time," i.e. an occasion or a phase, in the pattern of a mass noun, just as from "a summer" we make "summer" in the pattern of a mass noun. Thus with our binomial formula we can say and think "a moment of time," "a second of time," "a year of time." Let me again point out that the pattern is simply that of "a bottle of milk" or "a piece of cheese." Thus we are assisted to imagine that "a summer" actually contains or consists of such-and-such a quantity of "time."

In Hopi however all phase terms, like summer, morning, etc., are not nouns but a kind of adverb, to use the nearest SAE analogy. They are a formal part of speech by themselves, distinct from nouns, verbs, and even other Hopi "adverbs." Such a word is not a case form or a locative pattern, like "des Abends" or "in the morning." It contains no morpheme like one of "in the house" or "at the tree."[6] It means "when it is morning" or "while morning-phase is occurring." These "temporals" are not used as subjects or objects, or at all like nouns. One does not say "it's a hot summer" or "summer is hot;" summer is not hot, summer is only *when* conditions are hot, *when* heat occurs. One does not say *"this* summer," but "summer now" or "summer recently." There is no objectification, as a region, an extent, a quantity, of the subjective duration-feeling. Nothing is suggested about time except the perpetual "getting later" of it. And so there is no basis here for a formless item answering to our "time."

TEMPORAL FORMS OF VERBS IN SAE AND HOPI

The three-tense system of SAE verbs colors all our thinking about time. This system is amalgamated with that larger scheme of objectification of the subjective experience of duration already noted in other patterns—in the binomial formula applicable to nouns in general, in temporal nouns, in plurality and numeration. This objectification enables us in imagination to "stand time units in a row." Imagination of time as like a row harmonizes with a system of *three* tenses; whereas a system of *two,* an earlier and a later, would seem to correspond better to the feeling of duration as it is experienced. For if we inspect consciousness we find no past, present, future, but a unity embracing complexity. *Everything* is in consciousness, and everything in consciousness *is,* and is together. There is in it a sensuous and a non-sensuous. We may call the sensuous—what we are seeing, hearing, touching—the "present" while in the non-sensuous the vast image-world of memory is being labelled "the past" and

---

[6]"Year" and certain combinations of "year" with name of season, rarely season names alone, can occur with a locative morpheme "at," but this is exceptional. It appears like historical detritus of an earlier different patterning, or the effect of English analogy, or both.

another realm of belief, intuition, and uncertainty "the future;" yet sensation, memory, foresight, all are in consciousness together—one is not "yet to be" nor another "once but no more." Where real time comes in is that all this in consciousness is "getting later," changing certain relations in an irreversible manner. In this "latering" or "durating" there seems to me to be a paramount contrast between the newest, latest instant at the focus of attention and the rest—the earlier. Languages by the score get along well with two tense-like forms answering to this paramount relation of later to earlier. We can of course *construct and contemplate in thought* a system of past, present, future, in the objectified configuration of points on a line. This is what our general objectification tendency leads us to do and our tense system confirms.

In English the present tense seems the one least in harmony with the paramount temporal relation. It is as if pressed into various and not wholly congruous duties. One duty is to stand as objectified middle term between objectified past and objectified future, in narration, discussion, argument, logic, philosophy. Another is to denote inclusion in the sensuous field: "I *see* him." Another is for nomic, i.e. customarily or generally valid, statements: "We *see* with our eyes." These varied uses introduce confusions of thought, of which for the most part we are unaware.

Hopi, as we might expect, is different here too. Verbs have no "tenses" like ours, but have validity-forms ("assertions"), aspects, and clause-linkage forms (modes), that yield even greater precision of speech. The validity-forms denote that the speaker (not the subject) reports the situation (answering to our past and present) or that he expects it (answering to our future)[7] or that he makes a nomic statement (answering to our nomic present). The aspects denote different degrees of duration and different kinds of tendency "during duration." As yet we have noted nothing to indicate whether an event is sooner or later than another when both are *reported.* But need for this does not arise until we have two verbs, i.e. two clauses. In that case the "modes" denote relations between the clauses, including relations of later to earlier and of simultaneity. Then there are many detached words that express similar relations, supplementing the modes and aspects. The duties of our three-tense system and its tripartite linear objectified "time" are distributed among various verb categories, all different from our tenses; and there is no more basis for an objectified time in Hopi verbs than in other Hopi patterns; although this does not in the least hinder the verb forms and other patterns from being closely adjusted to the pertinent realities of actual situations.

---

[7]The expective and reportive assertions contrast according to the "paramount relation." The expective expresses anticipation existing *earlier* than objective fact, and coinciding with objective fact *later* than the status quo of the speaker, this status quo, including all the subsummation of the past therein, being expressed by the reportive. Our notion "future" seems to represent at once the earlier (anticipation) and the later (afterwards, what will be), as Hopi shows. This paradox may hint of how elusive the mystery of real time is, and how artificially it is expressed by a linear relation of past-present-future.

DURATION, INTENSITY, AND TENDENCY IN SAE AND HOPI

To fit discourse to manifold actual situations all languages need to express durations, intensities, and tendencies. It is characteristic of SAE and perhaps of many other language-types to express them metaphorically. The metaphors are those of spatial extension, i.e. of size, number (plurality), position, shape, and motion. We express duration by long, short, great, much, quick, slow, etc.; intensity by large, great, much, heavy, light, high, low, sharp, faint, etc.; tendency by more, increase, grow, turn, get, approach, go, come, rise, fall, stop, smooth, even, rapid, slow, and so on through an almost inexhaustible list of metaphors that we hardly recognize as such since they are virtually the only linguistic media available. The non-metaphorical terms in this field, like early, late, soon, lasting, intense, very, tending, are a mere handful, quite inadequate to the needs.

It is clear how this condition "fits in." It is part of our whole scheme of *objectifying*—imaginatively spatializing qualities and potentials that are quite non-spatial (so far as any spatially-perceptive senses can tell us). Noun-meaning (with us) proceeds from physical bodies to referents of far other sort. Since physical bodies and their outlines in *perceived space* are denoted by size and shape terms and reckoned by cardinal numbers and plurals, these patterns of denotation and reckoning extend to the symbols of non-spatial meanings, and so suggest an *imaginary space.* Physical shapes move, stop, rise, sink, approach, etc., in perceived space; why not these other referents in their imaginary space? This has gone so far that we can hardly refer to the simplest non-spatial situation without constant resort to physical metaphors. I "grasp" the "thread" of another's arguments, but if its "level" is "over my head" my attention may "wander" and "lose touch" with the "drift" of it, so that when he "comes" to his "point" we differ "widely," our "views" being indeed so "far apart" that the "things" he says "appear" "much" too arbitrary, or even "a lot" of nonsense!

The absence of such metaphor from Hopi speech is striking. Use of space terms when there is no space involved is *not there*—as if on it had been laid the taboo teetotal! The reason is clear when we know that Hopi has abundant conjugational and lexical means of expressing duration, intensity, and tendency directly as such, and that major grammatical patterns do not, as with us, provide analogies for an imaginary space. The many verb "aspects" express duration and tendency of manifestations, while some of the "voices" express intensity, tendency, and duration of causes or forces producing manifestations. Then a special part of speech, the "tensors," a huge class of words, denotes only intensity, tendency, duration, and sequence. The function of the tensors is to express intensities, "strengths," and how they continue or vary, their rate-of-change; so that the broad concept of intensity, when considered as necessarily always varying and/or continuing, includes also tendency and duration. Tensors convey distinctions of degree, rate, constancy, repetition, increase and decrease of intensity, immediate sequence, interruption or sequence after an interval, etc., also *qualities* of strengths, such as we should express metaphorically as smooth, even, hard, rough. A striking feature is their lack of resemblance to the terms of real space and movement that to us "mean the same." There is not even more than a trace of apparent derivation from space terms.[8] So while Hopi in its nouns seems highly concrete, here in the tensors it becomes abstract almost beyond our power to follow.

HABITUAL THOUGHT IN SAE AND HOPI

The comparison now to be made between the habitual thought worlds of SAE and Hopi speakers is of course incomplete. It is possible only to touch upon certain dominant contrasts that appear to stem from the linguistic differences already noted. By "habitual thought" and "thought world" I mean more than simply language, i.e. than the linguistic patterns themselves. I include all the analogical and suggestive value of the patterns (e.g., our "imaginary space" and its distant implications), and all the give-and-take between language and the culture as a whole, wherein is a vast amount that is not linguistic yet shows the shaping influence of language. In brief, this "thought world" is the microcosm that each man carries about within himself, by which he measures and understands what he can of the macrocosm.

The SAE microcosm has analyzed reality largely in terms of what it calls "things" (bodies and quasi-bodies) plus modes of extensional but formless existence that it calls "substances" or "matter." It tends to see existence through a binomial formula that expresses any existent as a spatial form plus a spatial formless continuum related to the form as contents is related to the outlines of its container. Non-spatial existents are imaginatively spatialized and charged with similar implications of form and continuum.

The Hopi microcosm seems to have analyzed reality largely in terms of *events* (or better "eventing"), referred to in two ways, objective and subjective. Objectively, and only if perceptible physical experience, events are expressed mainly as outlines, colors, movements, and other perceptive reports. Subjectively, for both the physical and non-physical, events are considered the expression of invisible intensity-factors, on which depend their stability and persistence, or their fugitiveness and proclivities. It implies that existents do not "become later and later" all in the same way; but some do so by growing, like plants, some by diffusing and vanishing, some by a procession of metamor-

---

[8]One such trace is that the tensor "long in duration," while quite different from the adjective "long" of space, seems to contain the same root as the adjective "large" of space. Another is that "somewhere" of space used with certain tensors means "at some indefinite time." Possibly however this is not the case and it is only the tensor that gives the time element, so that "somewhere" still refers to space and that under these conditions indefinite space means simply general applicability regardless of either time or space. Another trace is that in the temporal (cycle word) "afternoon" the element meaning "after" is derived from the verb "to separate." There are other such traces, but they are few and exceptional, and obviously not like our own spatial metaphorizing.

phoses, some by enduring in one shape till affected by violent forces. In the nature of each existent able to manifest as a definite whole is the power of its own mode of duration; its growth, decline, stability, cyclicity, or creativeness. Everything is thus already "prepared" for the way it now manifests by earlier phases, and what it will be later, partly has been, and partly is in act of being so "prepared." An emphasis and importance rests on this preparing or being prepared aspect of the world that may to the Hopi correspond to that "quality of reality" that "matter" or "stuff" has for us.

HABITUAL BEHAVIOR FEATURES OF HOPI CULTURE

Our behavior, and that of Hopi, can be seen to be coordinated in many ways to the linguistically-conditioned microcosm. As in my fire case-book, people act about situations in ways which are like the ways they talk about them. A characteristic of Hopi behavior is the emphasis on preparation. This includes announcing and getting ready for events well beforehand, elaborate precautions to insure persistence of desired conditions, and stress on good will as the preparer of right results. Consider the analogies of the day-counting pattern alone. Time is mainly reckoned "by day" (talk, -tala) or "by night" (tok), which words are not nouns but tensors, the first formed on a root "light, day," the second on a root "sleep." The count is by *ordinals*. This is not the pattern of counting a number of different men or things, even though they appear successively, for even then they *could* gather into an assemblage. It is the pattern of counting successive reappearances of the *same* man or thing, incapable of forming an assemblage. The analogy is not to behave about day-cyclicity as to several men ("several days"), which is what *we* tend to do, but to behave as to the successive visits of the *same man*. One does not alter several men by working upon just one, but one can prepare and so alter the later visits of the same man by working to affect the visit he is making now. This is the way the Hopi deal with the future—by working within a present situation which is expected to carry impresses, both obvious and occult, forward into the future event of interest. One might say that Hopi society understands our proverb "Well begun is half done," but not our "Tomorrow is another day." This may explain much in Hopi character.

This Hopi preparing behavior may be roughly divided into announcing, outer preparing, inner preparing, covert participation, and persistence. Announcing, or preparative publicity, is an important function in the hands of a special official, the Crier Chief. Outer preparing is preparation involving much visible activity, not all necessarily directly useful within our understanding. It includes ordinary practising, rehearsing, getting ready, introductory formalities, preparing of special food, etc. (all of these to a degree that may seem over-elaborate to us), intensive sustained muscular activity like running, racing, dancing, which is thought to increase the intensity of development of events (such as growth of crops), mimetic and other magic, preparations based on esoteric theory involving perhaps occult instruments like prayer sticks, prayer feathers, and prayer meal, and finally the great cyclic ceremonies and dances, which have the significance of preparing rain and crops. From one of the verbs meaning "prepare" is derived the noun for "harvest" or "crop:" na'twani "the prepared" or the "in preparation."[9]

Inner preparing is use of prayer and meditation, and at lesser intensity good wishes and good will, to further desired results. Hopi attitudes stress the power of desire and thought. With their "microcosm" it is utterly natural that they should. Desire and thought are the earliest, and therefore the most important, most critical and crucial, stage of preparing. Moreover, to the Hopi, one's desires and thoughts influence not only his own actions, but all nature. This too is wholly natural. Consciousness itself is aware of work, of the feel of effort and energy, in desire and thinking. Experience more basic than language tells us that if energy is expended effects are produced. *We* tend to believe that our bodies can stop up this energy, prevent it from affecting other things until we will our *bodies* to overt action. But this may be only because we have our own linguistic basis for a theory that formless items like "matter" are things in themselves, malleable only by similar things, by more matter, and hence insulated from the powers of life and thought. It is no more unnatural to think that thought contacts everything and pervades the universe than to think, as we all do, that light kindled outdoors does this. And it is not unnatural to suppose that thought, like any other force, leaves everywhere traces of effect. Now when *we* think of a certain actual rose-bush, we do not suppose that our thought goes to that actual bush, and engages with it, like a searchlight turned upon it. What then do we suppose our consciousness is dealing with when we are thinking of that rose-bush? Probably we think it is dealing with a "mental image" which is not the rose-bush but a mental surrogate of it. But why should it be *natural* to think that our thought deals with a surrogate and not with the real rose-bush? Quite possibly because we are dimly aware that we carry about with us a whole imaginary space, full of mental surrogates. To us, mental surrogates are old familiar fare. Along with the images of imaginary space, which we perhaps secretly know to be imaginary only, we tuck the thought-of actually existing rose-bush, which may be quite another story, perhaps just because we have that very convenient "place" for it. The Hopi thought-world has no imaginary space. The corollary to this is that it may not locate thought dealing with real space anywhere but in real space, nor insulate real space from the effects of thought. A Hopi would naturally suppose that his thought (or he himself) traffics with the actual rose-bush—or more likely, corn-plant—that he is thinking about. The thought then should leave some trace of itself with the plant in the field. If it is a good thought, one about health and growth, it is good for the plant; if a bad thought, the reverse.

---

[9]The Hopi verbs of preparing naturally do not correspond neatly to our "prepare;" so that na'twani could also be rendered "the practised-upon," "the tried-for," and otherwise.

The Hopi emphasize the intensity-factor of thought. Thought to be most effective should be vivid in consciousness, definite, steady, sustained, charged with strongly-felt good intentions. They render the idea in English as "concentrating," "holding it in your heart," "putting your mind on it," "earnestly hoping." Thought power is the force behind ceremonies, prayer-sticks, ritual smoking, etc. The prayer-pipe is regarded as an aid to "concentrating" (so said my informant). Its name, na'twanpi, means "instrument of preparing."

Covert participation is mental collaboration from people who do not take part in the actual affair, be it a job of work, hunt, race, or ceremony, but direct their thought and good will toward the affair's success. Announcements often seek to enlist the support of such mental helpers as well as of overt participants, and contain exhortations to the people to aid with their active good will.[10] A similarity to our concepts of a sympathetic audience or the cheering section at a football game should not obscure the fact that it is primarily the power of directed thought, and not merely sympathy or encouragement, that is expected of covert participants. In fact these latter get in their deadliest work before, not during, the game! A corollary to the power of thought is the power of wrong thought for evil; hence one purpose of covert participation is to obtain the mass force of many good wishers to offset the harmful thought of ill wishers. Such attitudes greatly favor cooperation and community spirit. Not that the Hopi community is not full of rivalries and colliding interests. Against the tendency to social disintegration in such a small, isolated group, the theory of "preparing" by the power of thought, logically leading to the great power of the combined, intensified and harmonized thought of the whole community, must help vastly toward the rather remarkable degree of cooperation that in spite of much private bickering the Hopi village displays in all the important cultural activities.

Hopi "preparing" activities again show a result of their linguistic thought background in an emphasis on persistence and constant insistent repetition. A sense of the cumulative value of innumerable small moments is dulled by an objectified, spatialized view of time like ours, enhanced by a way of thinking close to the subjective awareness of duration, of the ceaseless "latering" of events. To us, for whom time is a motion on a space, unvarying repetition seems to scatter its force along a row of units of that space, and be wasted. To the Hopi, for whom time is not a motion but a "getting later" of everything that has ever been done, unvarying repetition is not wasted but accumulated. It is storing

[10]See, e.g., Ernest Beaglehole, *Notes on Hopi Economic Life* (Yale University Publications in Anthropology, No. 15, 1937), especially the reference to the announcement of a rabbit hunt, and on p. 30, description of the activities in connection with the cleaning of Toreva Spring—announcing various preparing activities, and finally, preparing the continuity of the good results already obtained and the continued flow of the spring.

up an invisible change that holds over into later events.[11] As we have seen, it is as if the return of the day were felt as the return of the same person, a little older but with all the impresses of yesterday, not as "another day," i.e. like an entirely different person. This principle joined with that of thought-power and with traits of general Pueblo culture is expressed in the theory of the Hopi ceremonial dance for furthering rain and crops, as well as in its short, piston-like tread, repeated thousands of times, hour after hour.

SOME IMPRESSES OF LINGUISTIC HABIT IN WESTERN CIVILIZATION

It is harder to do justice in few words to the linguistically-conditioned features of our own culture than in the case of the Hopi, because of both vast scope and difficulty of objectivity—because of our deeply ingrained familiarity with the attitudes to be analyzed. I wish merely to sketch certain characteristics adjusted to our linguistic binomialism of form plus formless item or "substance," to our metaphoricalness, our imaginary space, and our objectified time. These, as we have seen, are linguistic.

From the form-plus-substance dichotomy the philosophical views most tradi-tionally characteristic of the "Western world" have derived huge support. Here belong materialism, psycho-physical parallelism, physics—at least in its tradi-tional Newtonian form—and dualistic views of the universe in general. Indeed here belongs almost everything that is "hard, practical common sense." Monistic, holistic, and relativistic views of reality appeal to philosophers and some scientists, but they are badly handicapped for appealing to the "common sense" of the Western average man. This is not because nature herself refutes them (if she did, philosophers could have discovered this much) but because they must be talked about in what amounts to a new language. "Common sense," as its name shows, and "practicality" as its name does not show, are largely matters of talking so that one is readily understood. It is sometimes stat-ed that Newtonian space, time, and matter are sensed by everyone intuitively, whereupon relativity is cited as showing how mathematical analysis can prove intuition wrong. This, besides being unfair to intuition, is an attempt to answer offhand question (1) put at the outset of this paper, to answer which this research was undertaken. Presentation of the findings now nears its end, and I think the answer is clear. The offhand answer, laying the blame upon intuition for our

---

[11]This notion of storing up power, which seems implied by much Hopi behavior, has an analogue in physics, acceleration. It might be said that the linguistic background of Hopi thought equips it to recognize naturally that force manifests not as motion or velocity, but as cumulation or acceleration. Our linguistic background tends to hinder in us this same recognition, for having legitimately con-ceived force to be that which produces change, we then think of change by our linguistic *metaphori-cal* analogue, motion, instead of by a pure motionless changingness concept, i.e. accumulation or acceleration. Hence it comes to our naive feeling as a shock to find from physical experiments that it is not possible to define force by motion, that motion and speed, as also "being at rest," are wholly relative, and that force can be measured only by acceleration.

slowness in discovering mysteries of the cosmos, such as relativity, is the wrong one The right answer is: Newtonian space, time, and matter are no intuitions. They are recepts from culture and language. That is where Newton got them.

Our objectified view of time is however favorable to historicity and to everything connected with the keeping of records, while the Hopi view is unfavorable thereto. The latter is too subtle, complex, and ever-developing, supplying no ready-made answer to the question of when "one" event ends and "another" begins. When it is implicit that everything that ever happened still is, but is in a necessarily different form from what memory or record reports, there is less incentive to study the past. As for the present, the incentive would be not to record it but to treat it as "preparing." But *our* objectified time puts before imagination something like a ribbon or scroll marked off into equal blank spaces, suggesting that each be filled with an entry. Writing has no doubt helped toward our linguistic treatment of time, even as the linguistic treatment has guided the uses of writing. Through this give-and-take between language and the whole culture we get, for instance:

1 Records, diaries, book-keeping, accounting, mathematics stimulated by accounting;

2 Interest in exact sequence, dating, calendars, chronology, clocks, time wages, time graphs, time as used in physics;

3 Annals, histories, the historical attitude, interest in the past, archaeology, attitudes of introjection towards past periods, e.g., classicism, romanticism.

Just as we conceive our objectified time as extending in the future like the way it extends in the past, so we set down our estimates of the future in the same shape as our records of the past, producing programs, schedules, budgets. The formal equality of the space-like units by which we measure and conceive time leads us to consider the "formless item" or "substance" of time to be homogeneous and in ratio to the number of units. Hence our pro-rata allocation of value to time, lending itself to the building up of a commercial structure based on time-prorata values: time wages (time work constantly supersedes piece work), rent, credit, interest, depreciation charges, and insurance premiums. No doubt this vast system once built would continue to run under any sort of linguistic treatment of time; but that it should have been built at all, reaching the magnitude and particular form it has in the Western world, is a fact decidedly in consonance with the patterns of the SAE languages. Whether such a civilization as ours would be possible with widely different linguistic handling of time is a large question—in our civilization our linguistic patterns and the fitting of our behavior to the temporal order are what they are, and they are in accord. We are of course stimulated to use calendars, clocks, and watches, and to try to measure time ever more precisely; this aids science, and science in turn, following these well-worn cultural grooves, gives back to culture an ever-growing store of applications, habits, and values, with which culture again directs science. But what lies outside this spiral? Science is beginning to find that there is something in the cosmos that is not in accord with the concepts we have formed in mounting the spiral. It is trying to frame a *new language* by which to adjust itself to a wider universe.

It is clear how the emphasis on "saving time" which goes with all the above and is very obvious objectification of time, leads to a high valuation of "speed," which shows itself a great deal in our behavior.

Still another behavioral effect is that the character of monotony and regularity possessed by our image of time as an evenly scaled limitless tape measure persuades us to behave as if that monotony were more true of events than it really is. That is, it helps to routinize us. We tend to select and favor whatever bears out this view, to "play up to" the routine aspects of existence. One phase of this is behavior evincing a false sense of security or an assumption that all will always go smoothly, and a lack in foreseeing and protecting ourselves against hazards. Our technique of harnessing energy does well in routine performance, and it is along routine lines that we chiefly strive to improve it—we are, for example, relatively uninterested in stopping the energy from causing accidents, fires, and explosions, which it is doing constantly and on a wide scale. Such indifference to the unexpectedness of life would be disastrous to a society as small, isolated, and precariously poised as the Hopi society is, or rather once was.

Thus our linguistically-determined thought world not only collaborates with our cultural idols and ideals, but engages even our unconscious personal reactions in its patterns and gives them certain typical characters. One such character, as we have seen, is *carelessness,* as in reckless driving or throwing cigarette stubs into waste paper. Another of different sort is *gesturing* when we talk. Very many of the gestures made by English-speaking people at least, and probably by all SAE speakers, serve to illustrate by a movement in space, not a real spatial reference but one of the non-spatial references that our language handles by metaphors of imaginary space. That is, we are more apt to make a grasping gesture when we speak of grasping an elusive idea than when we speak of grasping a doorknob. The gesture seeks to make a metaphorical and hence somewhat unclear reference more clear. But if a language refers to non-spatials without implying a spatial analogy, the reference is not made any clearer by gesture. The Hopi gesture very little, perhaps not at all in the sense we understand as gesture.

It would seem as if kinesthesia, or the sensing of muscular movement, though arising prior to language, should be made more highly conscious by linguistic use of imaginary space and metaphorical images of motion. Kinesthesia is marked in two facets of European culture: art and sport. European sculpture, an art in which Europe excels, is strongly kinesthetic, conveying great sense of the body's motions; European painting likewise. The dance in our culture expresses delight in motion rather than symbolism or ceremonial, and our music is greatly influenced by our dance forms. Our sports are strongly imbued with this element of the "poetry of motion." Hopi races and games seem to emphasize rather the virtues of endurance and sustained intensity. Hopi dancing is highly symbolic and is performed with great intensity and earnestness, but has not much movement or swing.

Synesthesia, or suggestion by certain sense receptions of characters belonging to another sense, as of light and color by sounds and *vice versa,* should be made more conscious by a linguistic metaphorical system that refers to non-spatial experiences by terms for spatial ones, though undoubtedly it arises from a deeper source. Probably in the first instance metaphor arises from synesthesia and not the reverse, yet metaphor need not become firmly rooted in linguistic pattern, as Hopi shows. Non-spatial experience has one well-organized sense, *hearing*—for smell and taste are but little organized. Non-spatial consciousness is a realm chiefly of thought, feeling, and *sound.* Spatial consciousness is a realm of light, color, sight, and touch, and presents shapes and dimensions. Our metaphorical system, by naming non-spatial experiences after spatial ones, imputes to sounds, smells, tastes, emotions, and thoughts qualities like the colors, luminosities, shapes, angles, textures, and motions of spatial experience. And to some extent the reverse transference occurs; for after much talking about tones as high, low, sharp, dull, heavy, brilliant, slow, the talker finds it easy to think of some factors in spatial experience as like factors of tone. Thus we speak of "tones" of color, a gray "monotone," a "loud" necktie, a "taste" in dress: all spatial metaphor in reverse. Now European art is distinctive in the way it seeks deliberately to play with synesthesia. Music tries to suggest scenes, color, movement, geometric design; painting and sculpture are often consciously guided by the analogies of music's rhythm; colors are conjoined with feeling for the analogy to concords and discords. The European theatre and opera seek a synthesis of many arts. It may be that in this way our metaphorical language that is in some sense a confusion of thought is producing, through art, a result of far-reaching value—a deeper esthetic sense leading toward a more direct apprehension of underlying unity behind the phenomena so variously reported by our sense channels.

HISTORICAL IMPLICATIONS

How does such a network of language, culture, and behavior come about historically? Which was first, the language patterns or the cultural norms? In main they have grown up together, constantly influencing each other. But in this partnership the nature of the language is the factor that limits free plasticity and rigidifies channels of development in the more autocratic way. This is because a language is a system, not just an assemblage of norms. Large systemic outlines can change to something really new only very slowly, while many other cultural innovations are made with comparative quickness. Language thus represents the mass mind; it is affected by inventions and innovations, but affected little and slowly, whereas *to* inventors and innovators it legislates with the decree immediate.

The growth of the SAE language-culture complex dates from ancient times. Much of its metaphorical reference to the non-spatial by the spatial was already fixed in the ancient tongues, and more especially in Latin. It is indeed a marked trait of Latin. If we compare, say Hebrew, we find that while Hebrew has some allusion to not-space as space, Latin has more. Latin terms for non-spatials, like *educo, religio, principia, comprehendo,* are usually metaphorized physical references: lead out, tying back, etc. This is not true of all languages—it is quite untrue of Hopi. The fact that in Latin the direction of development happened to be from spatial to non-spatial (partly because of secondary stimulation to abstract thinking when the intellectually crude Romans encountered Greek culture) and that later tongues were strongly stimulated to mimic Latin, seems a likely reason for a belief which still lingers on among linguists that this is the natural direction of semantic change in all languages, and for the persistent notion in Western learned circles (in strong contrast to Eastern ones) that objective experience is prior to subjective. Philosophies make out a weighty case for the reverse, and certainly the direction of development is sometimes the reverse. Thus the Hopi word for "heart" can be shown to be a late formation within Hopi from a root meaning think or remember. Or consider what has happened to the word "radio" in such a sentence as "he bought a new radio," as compared to its prior meaning "science of wireless telephony."

In the middle ages the patterns already formed in Latin began to interweave with the increased mechanical invention, industry, trade, and scholastic and scientific thought. The need for measurement in industry and trade, the stores and bulks of "stuffs" in various containers, the type-bodies in which various goods were handled, standardizing of measure and weight units, invention of clocks and measurement of "time," keeping of records, accounts, chronicles, histories, growth of mathematics and the partnership of mathematics and science, all cooperated to bring our thought and language world into its present form.

In Hopi history, could we read it, we should find a different type of language and a different set of cultural and environmental influences working together. A peaceful agricultural society isolated by geographic features and nomad enemies in a land of scanty rainfall, arid agriculture that could be made successful only by the utmost perseverance (hence the value of persistence and repetition), necessity for collaboration (hence emphasis on the psychology of teamwork and on mental factors in general), corn and rain as primary criteria of value, need of extensive *preparations* and precautions to assure crops in the poor soil and precarious climate, keen realization of dependence upon nature favoring prayer and a religious attitude toward the forces of nature, especially prayer and religion directed toward the ever-needed blessing, rain—these things interacted with Hopi linguistic patterns to mold them, to be molded again by them, and so little by little to shape the Hopi world-outlook.

To sum up the matter, our first question asked in the beginning (p. 82) is answered thus: Concepts of "time" and "matter" are not given in substantially the same form by experience to all men but depend upon the nature of the language or languages through the use of which they have been developed. They do not depend so much upon *any one system* (e.g., tense, or nouns) within the grammar as upon the ways of analyzing and reporting experience which have become fixed in the language as integrated "fashions of speaking" and which cut across the typical grammatical classifications, so that such a "fashion" may include lexical, morphological, syntactic, and otherwise systemically diverse means coordinated in a certain frame of consistency. Our own "time" differs markedly from Hopi "duration." It is conceived as like a space of strictly limited dimensions, or sometimes as like a motion upon such a space, and employed as an intellectual tool accordingly. Hopi "duration" seems to be inconceivable in terms of space or motion, being the mode in which life differs from form, and consciousness *in toto* from the spatial elements of consciousness. Certain ideas born of our own time-concept, such as that of absolute simultaneity, would be either very difficult to express or impossible and devoid of meaning under the Hopi conception, and would be replaced by operational concepts. Our "matter" is the physical sub-type of "substance" or "stuff," which is conceived as the formless extensional item that must be joined with form before there can be real existence. In Hopi there seems to be nothing corresponding to it; there are no formless extensional items; existence may or may not have form, but what it also has, with or without form, is intensity and duration, these being non-extensional and at bottom the same.

But what about our concept of "space," which was also included in our first question? There is no such striking difference between Hopi and SAE about space as about time, and probably the apprehension of space is given in substantially the same form by experience irrespective of language. The experiments of the Gestalt psychologists with visual perception appear to establish this as a fact. But the *concept of space* will vary somewhat with language, because as an intellectual tool[12] it is so closely linked with the concomitant employment of other intellectual tools, of the order of "time" and "matter," which are linguistically conditioned. We see things with our eyes in the same space forms as the Hopi, but our idea of space has also the property of acting as a surrogate of non-spatial relationships like time, intensity, tendency, and as a void to be filled with imagined formless items, one of which may even be called "space." Space as sensed by the Hopi would not be connected mentally with such surrogates, but would be comparatively "pure," unmixed with extraneous notions.

As for our second question (p. 82): There are connections but not correlations or diagnostic correspondences between cultural norms and linguistic patterns. Although it would be impossible to infer the existence of Crier Chiefs from the

---

[12]Here belong "Newtonian" and "Euclidean" space, etc.

lack of tenses in Hopi, or vice versa, there is a relation between a language and the rest of the culture of the society which uses it. There are cases where the "fashions of speaking" are closely integrated with the whole general culture, whether or not this be universally true, and there are connections within this integration, between the kind of linguistic analyses employed and various behavioral reactions and also the shapes taken by various cultural developments. Thus the importance of Crier Chiefs does have a connection, not with tenselessness itself, but with a system of thought in which categories different from our tenses are natural. These connections are to be found not so much by focusing attention on the typical rubrics of linguistic, ethnographic, or sociological description as by examining the culture and the language (always and only when the two have been together historically for a considerable time) as a whole in which concatenations that run across these departmental lines may be expected to exist, and if they do exist, eventually to be discoverable by study.

The Relationship Between Language and Thought

Edward Finegan and Niko Besnier

From the moment that children begin to utter their first words, language and thought appear to go hand in hand. That this should be so is not surprising, given that one of the functions of language is to express thought. But the exact nature of the relationship between language and thought is far from straightforward. In this section, we will address the question: To what extent does the language that we speak shape the way we think?

When children are young, the boundary between language and thought is shadowy. When we observe children at play, we find that they often talk to themselves. A five-year-old working on a jigsaw puzzle might be heard saying the following:

> Okay, the blue one. Goes here. Now, this one. This one fits here. The rabbit is here. It goes here. Another blue one, here it goes. And where does this one go?

This sort of verbal activity of children is referred to as *egocentric speech* (or self-directed speech). Children produce it whether or not they have an audience, and they produce it more frequently when the tasks that they face increase in complexity. So, for example, when children are asked to work on difficult jigsaw puzzles, they produce more egocentric speech than when working on easier ones.

Egocentric speech thus resembles adults' thoughts in more than one way:

Egocentric speech and thought are self-directed.
Egocentric speech and thought become more intense during problem-solving tasks.

In fact, many adults revert to egocentric speech when they have to make difficult arithmetic calculations, for example. It is likely that egocentric speech in children and thought in adults are related, although the exact nature of the relationship is not clear. The great Russian psychologist Lev Vygotsky suggested that egocentric speech is a precursor of thought; as children grow older, egocentric speech gradually becomes internalized and turns into thought in the young adult. The process of internalization begins very early, according to Vygotsky, and this accounts for the fact that young children can think, albeit in more limited ways than adults. Whether or not egocentric speech and language are related so directly, there is nevertheless some connection between the development of thought and the development of language in children.

But how tight is the "fit" between language and thought? In particular, to what extent are our thoughts shaped by the way we express ourselves in our native language? Note that Vygotsky's proposal to treat thought as internalized egocentric speech does not necessarily mean that thinking is subservient to what can be expressed in the adult's native language. Once egocentric speech becomes internalized and turns into thought, speech and thought do not necessarily remain similar.

As everyone who has tried to learn a foreign language knows, certain things can be expressed more conveniently in some languages than in others. While one language may have a special word to refer exclusively to a particular object or notion, in another language this object can be described only by using a whole phrase or sentence. For example, in Tuvaluan, a language spoken by the Polynesian inhabitants of a group of islands in the Central Pacific, there are different words to refer to many different types of coconut, which need to be described at great length in English. Here are a few examples:

pii: drinking coconut, with little flesh and much water, at a stage when the water is maximally sweet
mukomuko: young coconut with some flesh in it, before it has become too solid
uto: coconut at the stage when its husk can be chewed on and its water is still sweet
motomoto: same as *mukomuko,* but with firmer flesh
niu: coconut ripe enough for its flesh to be grated
uttanu: mature coconut whose sprout has already pierced through the husk and whose water has turned into an edible spongious solid kernel

Similarly, French speakers often note that English has more words for sounds *(crash, splash, roar)* than French has. The question then arises: Do these differences between languages mean that people from different cultures think differently or perceive the world differently?

In the first part of the century, three great scholars—Franz Boas (known as the "father of American anthropology"), Edward Sapir, and Benjamin Whorf— advanced a theory that the way people think is determined by the structure of their native language. Their proposal is usually referred to as the *Sapir-Whorf hypothesis* (or the theory of linguistic determinism or linguistic relativity). Marveling at the intricacies of the structure of American Indian languages (which the average Euro-American had previously considered "primitive" and "inferior"), Boas, Sapir, and Whorf maintained that we are mental prisoners of the structure of the language that we speak natively.

For example, Whorf noticed that in the Hopi language tense (such as past and present) is not a grammatical category as it is in English. Instead, every Hopi statement has to be marked as to whether it is a statement of unchangeable truth *(Water is fluid),* the report of an event that the speaker has witnessed *(I arrived yesterday),* or a hypothesis *(I assume that he'll be here tomorrow).* These categories are marked in the same way that tense is marked in English verbs *(talk* versus *talked).* Whorf maintained that the difference between the structure of Hopi and the structure of English explains certain differences in the cultural character of Hopi society and of Euro-American society. The Hopi, according to Whorf, are typically suspicious of hypotheses and conjectures and are very sensitive to the source of information. Euro-Americans, in contrast, pay much more attention to the passing of time than the Hopi do. According to the Sapir-Whorf hypothesis, these differences in the thought patterns of members of the two cultures are a direct consequence of the grammatical structures of Hopi and English.

While the Sapir-Whorf hypothesis is an attractive one, there are some problems with it. First of all, if thought were determined by language, it would be difficult to imagine how people from different cultural backgrounds could communicate at all. Second, many people in the world are bilingual or multilingual from a very early age. Would we want to say that these people have different "thought compartments" in their brains, each one associated with a different language? Obviously not. Third, the fact that a particular category does not exist in a language does not mean that native speakers of that language cannot understand (and, hence, think about) the category: the grammatical system marking the source of information in Hopi can be explained in English (as demonstrated in the previous paragraph) even though it does not exist in English grammar. Finally, the lexicons and grammars of all languages share many universal patterns, even though at first glance the languages of the world differ so strikingly from one another. Sapir and Whorf overestimated the variability in the structure of languages.

Today, few scholars take the Sapir-Whorf hypothesis literally. Many linguists take the position that language may have some influence on thought but thought may also influence the structure of language. So the interaction between thought and language is a two-way street rather than an absolute cause-and-effect relationship. Language and thought do appear to be closely connected in various ways. Their interaction is a complex one about which we still have much to learn.

REFERENCES

Sapir, Edward. 1921. *Language: An Introduction to the Study of Speech* (New York: Harcourt, Brace & World).

Vygotsky, Lev S. 1978. *Mind in Society: The Development of Higher Psychological Processes,* ed. Michael Cole, et al. (Cambridge, MA: Harvard University Press).

Whorf, Benjamin L. 1956. *Language, Thought, and Reality: Selected Writings of Benjamin L. Whorf,* ed. John B. Carroll (Cambridge, MA: MIT Press).

B

DIALECTS, LANGUAGE VARIATION, AND SCHOOLING

Varieties of American English

Walt Wolfram

"I knowed you wasn't Oklahomy folks. You talk queer kinda — That ain't no blame, you understan'."

"Ever'body says words different," said Ivy. "Arkansas folks says 'em different from Oklahomy folks says 'em different. And we seen a lady from Massachusetts, an' she said 'em differentest of all. Couldn' hardly make out what she was sayin'."

From John Steinbeck, Grapes of Wrath, quoted in Marckwardt 1958:131

It takes little linguistic sophistication to recognize that there exist a number of varieties of American English. For as long as it has been spoken in the New World, variation in the English language of this continent has been a topic for comment. During the earliest periods, the difference between the English developing in the colonies and that spoken in England was the main focus of attention. In later periods, the distinct varieties of English spoken in various regions throughout the continent became the center of interest. And more recently, the social correlates of language diversity have become the object of considerable commentary. While the focus of attention on English varieties certainly shifts from time to time, the interest itself appears to be constant, affecting both professional scholars of the English language and lay observers.

For our concern here, there are both advantages and disadvantages to the widespread recognition of variation in American English. On the one hand, this recognition indicates a natural curiosity about the ways in which varieties of English might differ from each other. It is inevitable, for example, that a visitor from Chicago traveling along the coasts of South Carolina will note some aspect of language difference between the varieties spoken in these respective locales.

A student of the English language who addresses these sorts of topics has only to stimulate this basic curiosity. More than one DIALECTOLOGIST has succumbed to temptation to become an instant social success by answering the person who approaches him with the query "Can you tell where I'm from just by hearing me talk?" As we shall see later in our discussion, this is sometimes a question considerably more complex than the inquirer may anticipate, involving a number of dimensions.

On the other hand, the widespread recognition of variation in American English can give rise to a number of misconceptions about the nature of this diversity. Stereotypes and prejudices about language differences manifest themselves in folk notions about speech. A professional scholar of language variety in American English has to confront many misconceptions which have arisen out of this tradition of recognizing diversity. Popular myths concerning the supposed unsystematic, illogical, linguistically inferior status of nonmainstream varieties have been highly cultivated over the past several centuries, and the re-education of students to accept the systematic but different nature of these varieties requires a massive effort. (Although we shall not take up this issue again here, these premises must be kept in mind as we wind our way through the complexities of linguistic diversity in American English.)

Typically, differentiation in the varieties of American English has been recognized on several levels of language organization. First of all, there are differences in the vocabulary or LEXICON of the language. Differences on this level are probably most widely recognized, and there is a long tradition of noting these differences which goes back to the earliest travelers in the New World. In fact, some literary scholars in London were sufficiently conscious of new words arriving from this continent in the 1750s to suggest that a glossary of these items would soon be in order. This popular interest has persisted to the present day, and travelers who come from a visit to New England talking about how *tonic* is used, where one might refer to *soda pop* or *pop* in other regions, indicate a recognition on this level.

Another fairly obvious level of recognized differences concerns the pronunciation or PHONOLOGY of the language. A person who notices how a New Yorker says *chocolate* or how a person in the South pronounces *time* is recognizing a difference in the organization of the phonological system. A further level of organization on which differences between varieties are realized is the SYNTAX—the combinations of items as they are placed in sentences. Observations of different negative patterns such as *He didn't do nothing* in one variety as opposed to *He didn't do anything,* or different verb patterns such as *He was a-singin' and a-laughin',* exemplify this level of differentiation.

Finally, there may be differences in language use, i.e., differences in how language forms are used in the context of speaking as opposed to differences in the forms themselves. Thus a Northerner who is familiar with the respect terms *sir* or *ma'am* might comment on the different set of social relationships and occasions in which these forms are used in some Southern areas.

A TRADITION OF STUDY

There is a long-standing tradition for collecting data on variation in American English. Some of the earliest collections were concerned with aspects of American English which set it apart from British varieties, particularly in vocabulary. Works such as Pickering's *A Vocabulary, Or Collection of Words and Phrases which have been supposed to be peculiar to the United States of America, to which is prefixed an essay on the present state of the English language in the United States* (1816) or Bartlett's *Dictionary of Americanisms* (1848) demonstrate such a concern motivating the collection of data. Although some early observers were impressionistic in their descriptions of differences, others were apparently quite meticulous in the collection of Americanisms, noting the setting, speakers, and context of usage for particular items which were recorded (Heath 1976b).

Differences between British and American English were not ignored in later concerns with language variation, but there was an increasing trend to focus on diversity within American English varieties themselves. Largely in connection with the study of settlement patterns, data on geographical distribution came into prominence. Thus, the American Dialect Society was formed in 1889 for "the investigation of English dialects in America with regard to pronunciation, grammar, vocabulary, phraseology, and geographical distribution." The initial hope of this society was to provide a body of data from which a DIALECT dictionary or a series of linguistic maps might be derived. Although a considerable amount of data on varieties of English was published in the society's original journal, *Dialect Notes*, it was not until 1928 that a large-scale systematic study of DIALECT GEOGRAPHY was undertaken, entitled *The Linguistic Atlas of the United States and Canada*. The primary purpose of the Linguistic Atlas was to trace the settlement history of the United States as reflected in the existent dialect patterning, although other objectives were also included, such as differences based on social levels, between spoken and written language, and so forth. The resultant works provided scores of articles on thousands of linguistic forms which could be differentiated across various sectors of American English, and the compilation of DIALECT ATLASES is still going on (Figure 2). Armed with a questionnaire designed to elicit particular items of phonology, syntax, and lexicon, fieldworkers could spend up to ten or twelve hours with one subject obtaining various forms. The fieldworker sought out locally rooted persons who were native speakers of English, some well-educated, others less so. Before addressing the specific questions from the manual prepared for fieldworkers (containing approximately 800 items designed to check points of pronunciation, grammar, and vocabulary), the fieldworker usually began the interview with broad ques-

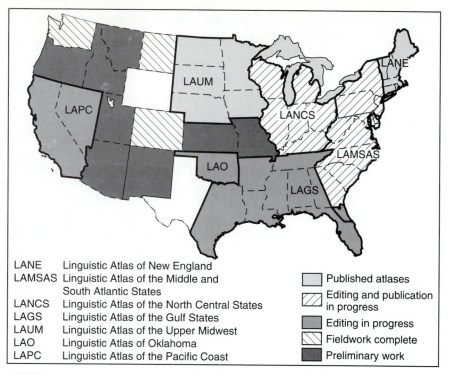

LANE   Linguistic Atlas of New England
LAMSAS Linguistic Atlas of the Middle and
                 South Atlantic States
LANCS   Linguistic Atlas of the North Central States
LAGS   Linguistic Atlas of the Gulf States
LAUM   Linguistic Atlas of the Upper Midwest
LAO   Linguistic Atlas of Oklahoma
LAPC   Linguistic Atlas of the Pacific Coast

☐ Published atlases
⊟ Editing and publication in progress
▨ Editing in progress
⧅ Fieldwork complete
■ Preliminary work

FIGURE 2
Progress of the American atlases. (*Based on McDavid 1979a: 87.*)

tions on topics of general knowledge, for example, "Tell me about the house you grew up in" (McDavid, O'Cain, and Dorrill 1978). Figure 3 provides excerpts from the fieldnotes of Raven McDavid, completed in 1946 on the basis of an interview in Charleston, South Carolina with a white female, age 69. An artist and author, she was a member of the highest social class and had been drilled by her family on "correctness." She knew many archaic terms and pronunciations; she insisted on using these. The thought of a grammatical error in her speech was inconceivable to her; in her words, "Grandmother would turn over in her grave if she heard me say *ain't.*"

REGIONAL VARIATION

Historically, probably more attention has been given to geographically correlated variation in American English than to any other type. The correlation of varieties of American English with geographical location is, of course, a reflection of underlying historical patterns which have led to a present-day pattern of regional variation. In some cases, regional variation can be traced to different patterns of settlement history where the migration of the early settlers is still reflected in the language. Some of the original differences may, of course, reflect

Pronunciation

What are the two parts of an egg? One is the white; the other is ——
Variants: yok, yelk, yulk, yilk, yoke
Response: yulk; "heard": yelk

What color would you say the yolk of the egg is?
Variants: yellow, yallow, yillow, yollow, yeller
Response: yellow; "heard from grandmother, old-fashioned": yillow, yollow: "new
       way": yallow

When your skin and eyeballs turn yellow, you're getting ——
Variants: yellow jaundice, janders, yellow janders, jaundice
Response: jaundice, jandice "I say either"

Grammar

I wanted to hang something out in the barn, so I just took a nail and ——
Variants: drive, druv, driv, drove, droove
Response: drove a nail

The nail didn't get in far enough; you'd say, "It's got to be —— further."
Variants: driv, drove, droven, driven
Response: driven

A schoolboy might say of a scolding teacher, "Why is she blaming me,
I —— wrong."
Variants: ain't done nothing wrong, haven't done anything wrong
Response: I haven't done anything wrong. [Field worker noted informant never used
       double negatives except quotatively, e.g. "I never had no head for machin-
       ery."]

Vocabulary

Where did you keep your hogs and pigs? Did this have shelter or was it open?
Variants: hog pen, pig pen, hog lot, hog crawl, pig sty
Response: hog pen, pig pen; "old fashioned or obsolete": crawl, hog crawl, cattle
       crawl

harmonica (with reeds and blown, as distinct from a Jews' harp)
The thing you put in your mouth and work back and forth and blow on it. Do you
remember any other names for it?
Variants: harp, breath harp, French harp, mouth organ, mouth harp, harmonica
Response: mouth organ

FIGURE 3
Samples from a dialect atlas worksheet. Included here are sample questions designed to
elicit certain points of pronunciation, grammar, and vocabulary; these questions were contained in the manual used by each fieldworker. Listed below the question are possible variants of each item provided in the manual for the fieldworkers' reference. Included in the
response is not only the actual response given, but also variants the informants mentioned
as having "heard," extraneous comments volunteered by the informant, and comments
noted by the fieldworker from other portions of the interview which related to this item.
(*Data provided by the editorial staff of the* Linguistic Atlas of the Middle and South Atlantic
States, *University of South Carolina.*)

the fact that settlers came from different regions of England where diversity was already existent; others may reflect the influences of another language where the settlers came from a non-English-speaking country. Patterns of population movement within the United States are also reflected in regional differences. Thus, a major shift in the White population has been from east to west, a pattern which is revealed in a number of language differences which parallel this movement.

When considering the regional aspects of variation in American English, the role of physical geography cannot be overlooked, since it, too, has exerted its historical influence on language differences. Although transportational obstacles are not generally considered to be a serious handicap with modern technological advances, separation of areas by rivers, mountains, and other natural boundaries has inhibited the spread of language in the past, because it restricted the mobility necessary for the diffusion of linguistic forms from one location to another.

Traditionally, the geographical distribution of differences in American English was traced by plotting particular linguistic items on maps. It was possible to draw ISOGLOSSES on a map (i.e., lines separating areas which used a particular item from those that did not). Major regional areas were defined, then, on the basis of a number of isoglosses which clustered in approximately the same way (i.e., an ISOGLOSS BUNDLE). An example of one type of map delimiting major regional varieties of American English based on the collection of Linguistic Atlas data, is seen in Figure 4.

While such a map might be useful in an approximative way, some qualification is necessary. Lines on a map such as this make it appear that the varieties are discrete entities exclusively possessing the territories in the area demarked by the lines. A careful examination of the isoglosses used to determine these areas would reveal that most often they do not coincide in a precise way. Thus, arbitrary decisions may be made in determining varieties. In most cases, differences between varieties are not discrete, but relative in terms of a continuum of differences. Furthermore, some of the differences between varieties may be quantitative rather than qualitative. That is, two or more varieties may share a particular feature, but its relative incidence in one variety is greater than that in another. And there is often a transitional area between varieties where forms may be in considerable fluctuation.

When we examine the nature of regional variation, we find that it is most frequently the result of the spread of language changes through geographical space over time. By analogy, this is likened to the effect of a pebble which is dropped in a pool of water. A particular change takes place at a given point in time and space and spreads from that point in successive waves or stages. The most concentrated existence of the linguistic item will be in the area where it was first introduced, and the outer periphery of the diffusion will evidence less concentration, since the change was later coming to that area. The outer boundaries, however, are not static but dynamic in nature, constantly undergoing change which

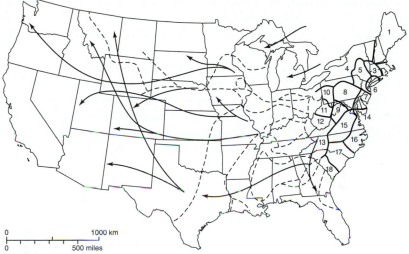

FIGURE 4
Dialect areas of the USA. Atlantic Seaboard areas (heavy lines) and tentative dialect areas elsewhere (dotted lines). Arrows indicate directions of migrations. (*Adapted from Francis 1958: 580–581*)

THE NORTH
1. Northeastern New England
2. Southeastern New England
3. Southwestern New England
4. Inland North (western Vermont, Upstate New York and derivatives)
5. The Hudson Valley
6. Metropolitan New York

THE MIDLAND
North Midland
7. Delaware Valley (Philadelphia)
8. Susquehanna Valley
10. Upper Ohio Valley (Pittsburgh)
11. Northern West Virginia

South Midland
9. Upper Potomac and Shenandoah
12. Southern West Virginia and Eastern Kentucky
13. Western Carolina and Eastern Tennessee

THE SOUTH
14. Delmarva (Eastern Shore)
15. The Virginia Piedmont
16. Northeastern North Carolina (Albemarle Sound and Neuse Valley)
17. Cape Fear and Peedee Valleys
18. The South Carolina Low Country (Charleston)

makes the rigorous delimitation of geographically related boundaries a relative rather than absolute thing. Finally, there are other social factors which complicate the examination of differences in simple terms of geographical space. Variables such as social status, speaking style, ethnicity, and so forth might clearly transcend the simple geographical distribution of items. Recently, sociolinguists, students of language who focus on the social and cultural parameters of language differences, have attempted to reorient some of the theoretical and methodological aspects of the study of language variation. They consider linguistic variation to be essential in solving issues fundamental to the construction of an adequate linguistic model for describing a language, since variation is endemic to all languages. Methodologically, sociolinguists focus on the language of everyday conversation and go into the field to do their work armed with tape recorders to record conversation.

For the most part, data on social status as a variable in linguistic diversity come from the analysis of relatively spontaneous conversation. In this approach, particular variants are tabulated in relation to the number of times these variants might have occurred in actual conversation. For example, if we are tabulating an Appalachian English form such as *a*-prefixing, we count the number of times the *a*-prefix occurs in relation to the number of times it might have occurred. This is illustrated in the following passage, where the *a*-forms are in bold type and the cases where it might have occurred are italicized.

> He was a retired Army man, and, we went up 'ere and John supposedly had a sack to put the coon in if we caught one. We's *gonna* try to bring it back alive, so we tromped through the woods 'til along about six o'clock in the morning. The dogs treed up a big hollow chestnut oak, and we proceeded to cut the thing down. It's about three or four inches all the way around. About four foot through the stump. We tied the dogs and cut the thing down. Well, we cut it down and turned one dog loose, and he went down in that thing, way down in the old hollow of the tree and it forked, and we couldn't get up in there so he backed out and he tied 'im. And we's **a-gonna** chop the coon out if it was in there, I's a kinda halfway thought maybe it just treed a possum or something. Well, I chopped in and lo and behold, right on top of the dang coon. Eighteen pounder, Jack Stern says, kitten coon. I run in with the axe handle down in behind him to keep him from getting out or backing down in the tree. He reached, fooled around and got him by the hind legs and pulled that thing out it looked big as a sheep to me. Turned 'im loose, he said "kitten, Hell." We had an old carbide light and he turned that over and the lights were . . . that's all the light we had. And, we had to hunt it then and the dogs took right after the coon right down the holler and the dogs caught it and Jack beat us all down there. Went down there and he's **a-holding** three dogs in one hand and the coon in the other hand. And they's all **a-trying** to bite the coon and the coon **a-trying** to bite Jack and the dogs, and Jack pulled out a sack and it wasn't a dang thing but an old pillow case that Maggie had used, his wife, it was about wore out. So we fumbled around 'ere and finally got that coon in that sack and he aimed to close the top of it and the coon just tore the thing in half, in two, and down the holler he went again. With that sack on him, half of it and we caught that thing, and you know, E. F. Wurst finally pulled off his coveralls and we put that thing down in one of the legs of his coveralls and tied that coon up. He's *tearing* up everything we could get, we couldn't hold him he's so stout. And I brought that thing home and kept 'im about a month, fed 'im apples and stuff to eat so we could eat 'em. Well, I did I killed him and tried eat that thing, I'd just soon eat a tomcat or a polecat, I wouldn't make much difference. And, that's about the best coon hunt I believe I was on.

Wolfram and Christian 1976: 181

This passage, taken from the conversation of a retired coal miner who was a native of southeastern West Virginia, shows six constructions where the *a*-form might have been used, and in four of them it actually appears. Thus, we end up with a percentage (for this passage 67 percent) figure showing the incidence of a particular variant in relation to its potential usage. This approach to data is considerably different from the traditional Linguistic Atlas approach in which particular items were elicited in interviews based on a questionnaire.

If the multiple dimensions of diversity in American English are to be understood, it will be necessary to record, describe, and analyze language variation as it co-occurs with as many of these dimensions as possible. Sociolinguists, in examining language differences, also provide some explanations of patterned behavioral differences between groups of Americans. Different types of studies highlight particular factors, such as sex or age of speaker, functions of speaking, or ethnic membership of speaker and audience. However, it is ultimately the interaction of a number of variables which accounts for the observed diversity in language structure and use. In the following sections, we shall isolate some of the more essential social factors which must be recognized in explaining diversity in American English. It should be kept in mind that the discussion of these factors separately is an artifice of our description, and that ultimately these factors intersect with each other to account for the varieties of American English.

SOCIAL STATUS

In a society where social status is an obvious aspect of its structure, it can be expected that there are essential dimensions of language variation which correlate with status differentiation. Naturally, this does not operate independently of other considerations, including the regional variation just discussed. We can speak of social varieties of American English as long as we realize that they do not exist in isolation from other factors. As it turns out, there are some aspects of variation in American English which may have social significance only within a given regional context, while others have a much broader geographical range. Thus, the absence of an upgliding vowel in an item like *time* (i.e., *tahm*) may not be particularly significant in some Southern contexts, whereas its use in some Northern urban context might hold considerable social significance. On the other hand, the absence of a third person singular *-s* form in *He go* for *He goes* may be socially significant regardless of the particular locale.

Socially diagnostic items of American English may be either prestigious or stigmatized. Socially prestigious items are those used by high status groups as linguistic manifestations of social status, whereas socially stigmatized items are those associated typically with low status groups. In some varieties of American English, a slight raising quality of the vowel in items like *pass* or *fact* appears to have a prestige function. On the other hand, the pronunciation of *th* as a STOP in *that* (i.e., *dat*) or *the (duh),* or the use of the so-called double negative, such as *They don't do nothing,* may be a socially stigmatized rule. The absence of a prestige feature does not necessarily imply that its alternative is stigmatized, nor vice versa. For example, the pronunciation of the vowel in *pass* or *fact* without a raised quality is not necessarily socially stigmatized; by the same token, the pronunciation of *th* in *that* or *the* or the use of a single negative in *They don't do anything* is not necessarily prestigious. To determine the particular social significance of a linguistic item at a given point in time does not, of course, mean that it will necessarily stay that way. The social significance may change over time, for one reason or another. Thus, the absence of postvocalic *r* in New York speech (e.g., *fouh* for *four*) was socially prestigious at one time, but has since reversed its social significance for a younger generation of New Yorkers.

Among the varieties of American English, there are many more differences where the dimension of social diagnosis contrasts stigmatized and nonstigmatized variants as opposed to prestige versus nonprestige variants. This appears to match the observation that Americans tend to react more in terms of negative responses to socially stigmatized linguistic items than they do positively to socially prestigious items. On an informal level, mainstream or standard varieties of English might most practically be defined in terms of the absence of various socially stigmatized items as opposed to the presence of prestige items. While this might be an oversimplification, it does capture the relative importance of the stigmatized/nonstigmatized dimension compared with the prestige/nonprestige dimension.

The reactions that people have to socially significant items in American English have been classified into three main types (from Labov 1964: 102). First of all, there are social indicators, items which may objectively correlate with social status differences, but have little effect on a listener's assessment of an individual's status. One of the important clues to the existence of social indicators is their lack of sensitivity to style shifts in the language that take place in response to interlocutors, topics, situations, and so forth. If speakers are aware (on a conscious or an unconscious level) of a socially significant item, they will vary its frequency of usage as a part of their style shifting. That is, in a more formal occasion, they may use a prestige variant more frequently or a stigmatized variant less frequently. In the case of social indicators, however, this does not take place because of the relative unawareness that a particular form correlates with social status.

There are other features which show both social and stylistic variation; furthermore, they have a regular effect on a listener's reaction to a person in terms of social status. These have been called social markers. The sensitivity that these linguistic variables show to the stylistic parameter (i.e., more frequent use of a prestige variant in a more formal style) indicates that these forms are recognized on some level, whether conscious or unconscious. There appear to be many more social markers in American English than social indicators.

Finally, there are social stereotypes. Not only are these socially significant variants recognized on some conscious level, but they become the topics of overt comments from members of the community, or those who fulfill roles with respect to the perpetuation of the language norms in the society. Items such as *ain't,* the pronunciation of *dese, dem,* and *dose* for *these, them,* and *those* respectively, and the use of negatives such as *They don't do nothing* all appear to exemplify social stereotypes. There are few Americans, including those who may regularly use them, who have not heard comments about the social stigma which these items carry.

Socially diagnostic items in American English do not differ only with respect to the relative awareness that is indicated toward them. They may differ also with respect to how they correlate with social status. There are some items which may correlate with more finely differentiated social groupings, while there are others which reveal a more discrete break between fewer social status groups. For example, consider the distribution of two variables for the Black speech community in Detroit. In the case of postvocalic *r* absence in items such as *fouh* or *fathuh* for *four* and *father* respectively, we find a gradual increase in the relative frequency of "*r*-lessness." On the other hand, in the case of the grammatical absence of third person singular present tense -*s* forms, such as *he go* for *he goes,* we find a sharp demarcation between the middle classes and the working classes. The contrast between the correlation of these two socially significant rules for the Black speech community in Detroit is given in Figures 5*a* and 5*b.*

The picture indicated in these two types of correlation is probably reflective of the status system in America which makes it difficult to classify in any simplistic way. There are aspects of the social status system which appear to reflect a continuum much more than a discretely defined social class—GRADIENT STRATIFICATION, but there are other aspects of the social status structure which reveal a sharp demarcation between groups on the basis of status—SHARP STRATIFICATION. We may hypothesize that the sharper, more rigid the social boundaries in a society are, the sharper the stratification of linguistic features will be.

ETHNICITY

Without a doubt, the most emotionally laden topic in the discussion of variation in American English is that of the relation between ethnicity and language differences. The essential debate here concerns whether varieties of American English correlate in a unique way with America's different ethnic groups, be they Black, Indian, Jewish, Italian, or any other group. Issues surrounding language and ethnicity have become highly charged for both lay and professional observers of language. For the layman, the possibility of distinct ethnic varieties has sometimes been associated with the supposed physical or mental attributes of the particular ethnic group. If, for example, it were admitted that some Black and White Americans spoke differently, then it might be a reflection of some

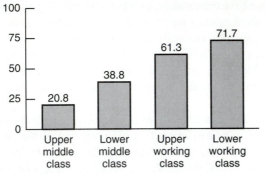

FIGURE 5a
Postvocalic *r* absence: an example of gradient stratification. (*Adapted from Wolfram 1969: 110.*)

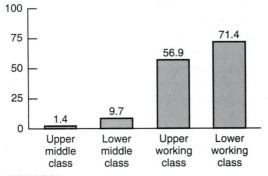

FIGURE 5b
Third person singular *-s* absence: an example of sharp stratification. (*Adapted from Wolfram 1969: 136.*)

inherent or physical difference between the two groups. For the professional student of language, the dispute concerning ethnic varieties of English centers around the historical origin of the varieties used in the United States and the dynamics of social patterns that affect speech. Language scholars take as axiomatic that the speech variety acquired by a given ethnic group has no relation to the physical or mental characteristics of that group. The supposed physical or mental basis of such a correlation is readily disproved by those situations where a person from one ethnic group is isolated from that ethnic group. In these types of situations, we find the individual speaking indistinguishably from those of the immediate social group. Thus, a Black who is socialized in an exclusively White group will speak as the others of that group, or a White American socialized in an exclusively Black cultural context will adopt the language of that group.

In recent years, the most hotly debated issue on ethnicity and language is that of Black–White speech relationship. In Northern urban areas, it is quite apparent that working class Blacks often use a variety of English which is considerably different from their White counterparts. The issue is, however, more hotly contested when comparable (or at least as comparable as American society will allow) socio-economic groups of Blacks and Whites are considered in the rural South, since most working class varieties of Black speech have had their origin in rural Southern varieties.

While some data must still be subjected to further analysis, recent studies indicate that even in the rural South, where the varieties are much more similar, there exist linguistic structures which distinguish Black and White working class speakers. For example, we have not been able to find consistent usage of the form *be* among White speakers in sentences such as *Sometime my ears be itching* or *She usually be here* meaning "something happens or is true at various times." This form is, however, fairly common among working class Black speakers. Some of the differences are more subtle. Thus, both Southern Whites and Blacks may have the absence of *be* in a structure such as *You ugly* where the absence of the form corresponds to Standard English *are,* but typically only Blacks will extend its absence to correspond to Standard English *is* as in *He ugly.* Perhaps the most important differences are found in the combinations of structures which make up the varieties, rather than any one structure in particular. Reinforcement of our analysis revealing Black–White speech differences comes from various identification tasks in which listeners are asked to identify the ethnicity of a speaker from an audio-recording. In most structured research of this type, the accuracy of ethnic identification is well over 80 percent.

In most instances, the extent to which ethnicity correlates with language diversity is a function of the social distance between particular ethnic groups. With increased assimilation of ethnic members into the larger culture, we may expect the factor of ethnicity to be of minimal significance, but with ethnic isolation of one type or another, we may expect this variable to be of major significance. In reality, ethnic isolation occurs in varying degrees, depending on the social role of particular ethnic groups in American society. We may expect, for example, that a relatively homogeneous Jewish community will reveal some linguistic differences when compared with other groups, but we would predict that the differences will not be nearly as striking as that revealed for the Black community because of the relative social roles of these ethnic groups. Where an ethnic group speaks another language, the influence of this language may be exerted in differentiating the variety. The influence of German on the English of southeastern Pennsylvania is well attested in structures such as *The soup is all.* Similarly, the English spoken by some Indian groups in the Southwest may be influenced both directly and indirectly by the indigenous Indian language. With this added dimension, the factor of ethnicity and language variation in American English can indeed become very complex.

SEX

Although we may not typically think of varieties of American English being differentiated on the basis of sex, it can be demonstrated that particular aspects of language selection and usage are related to the sex of the speaker and/or hearer. If asked, for example, to guess the sex of a speaker who utters a sentence such as *Oh my, you shouldn't have done that, but you are a dear,* or *What an adorable package,* most of us would identify the speaker as a female. This is because the selection of vocabulary items in certain domains typically correlates with the sex of the speaker. In the first sentence, a difference in the type of expletives used by men and women is demonstrated, whereas the second case illustrates a disparity in descriptive adjectives. Similar types of differences might have been illustrated with reference to color terms, where it has been demonstrated that fine color distinctions such as *beige, lavender, mauve,* and so forth are more common to women than to men.

All the distinctions cited above relate to systematic differences in the selection of vocabulary items used by men and women. It is much more difficult to establish similar types of differences with respect to syntax and phonology. Some recent studies have suggested that certain types of syntactic patterns might be used more frequently by women than men (e.g., certain types of positive imperatives such as *Do come for dinner!* or tag questions such as *John is here, isn't he?*), but these claims have been disputed strongly by others.

Although sex differences cutting across the different varieties of American English may be difficult to establish for syntax and phonology, sex has been shown to be an important variable intersecting with other social variables such as region and social status. Various studies have, for example, indicated that males realize a higher incidence of socially stigmatized features than females of comparable socio-economic classes. Thus, working class females who use *-in'* for *-ing* (e.g., *sittin'/sitting*) would typically not be expected to use it as frequently as their male counterparts. Similarly, females who use socially stigmatized multiple negation (e.g., *He didn't do nothing*) would not be expected to use it as frequently as their male counterparts. The tendency of males to use more stigmatized variants in their speech is probably best seen as a reflection of different behavioral roles for men and women. There are clearly positive, if covert, values of masculinity and toughness associated with nonstandard speech for men (e.g., compare the stereotypic notions of how masculine heroes such as football players talk) which are not matched for women. Conversely, we expect females to have a higher incidence of prestige features than their male counterparts of comparable social status. Thus, if a particular vowel quality of the *a* in *bat* takes on a prestige value, we would expect its higher incidence among middle class women than men. The sensitivity of women to prestige norms makes them prime candidates for linguistic change, and studies of linguistic change occurring across the United States indicate that females are often responsible for the initial adoption of new prestige variants in a given locale.

AGE

Two aspects of age differences can be cited to account for some types of diversity in the varieties of American English. First we have changes taking place in American English which differentiate successive generations. In this case, a change taking place in one generation of speakers in a particular locale would typically not affect the older speakers of that region whose language system had been firmly stabilized. Thus, older residents of Appalachia might use an *a-* prefix on verb forms such as *He was a-singin' and a-dancin'* or pronounce *fire* and *tire* something like *far* and *tar* respectively, whereas the current generation of speakers in Appalachia is not nearly as inclined to use these forms. This is a function of a language change taking place in which these particular items are being lost or changed. From this perspective, different generations within a population may be viewed as a reflection of American English varieties at different time periods. The difference between the English brought from England by the original English-speaking settlers and a given variety of English today is thus a summation of the changes exhibited by the successive generations of speakers.

The social significance of particular features can also change over time. Thus, there is little social significance for the absence of *r* in words like *York* (Yohk) or *four* (fouh) exhibited by New Yorkers over 50, whereas the absence of *r* may be socially stigmatized for speakers under 50. It is interesting to note, in this regard, that one of our shibboleths of nonstandard grammar, the "double" or multiple negative (e.g., *There wasn't nobody nowhere*) was once the common and only acceptable way of forming certain negative structures in the English language.

The other aspect of age differences relates to the life cycle of a particular individual. Within this cycle, there are certain behavioral patterns that are considered appropriate for various stages of life, and these include aspects of speech. For example, certain vocabulary items, identified popularly as "teenage slang," may be quite appropriate for one age group, but would be quite inappropriate for other age groups. Terms such as *gig* for *job, wheels* for *car,* or *bread* for *money* are associated with the teenage and early adult stage of life, but they would seem quite inappropriate for a middle-aged person. For the most part, these vocabulary items have a rapid life cycle, so that the expressions of today's youth will not be carried over by the next generation of youth. Though the particular items will change, the selection of a "slang" unique to the next generation of youth will be perpetuated.

The most obtrusive aspects of age-graded language differences in American English are probably found in certain vocabulary items, but there are also other differences. For example, socially stigmatized variants are used more frequently by adolescents than adults. During the adolescent period, the influence of peers on speech is also maximized, and children learn the variety of their local peers as opposed to the variety of their adults. It is quite typical to see a parent who moves from one region to another retain the variety of the original locale while the children adopt the new variety quickly. Aspects of this assimilation, which appears to be optimal from the ages of 5 to 12, are probably related to the acquisitional process as well as the influence of peers in forming the particular variety a child speaks.

FORMAL AND INFORMAL STYLES

Most of us are well aware of the fact that written language style is expected to be somewhat different from that of spoken English, or that we talk to a casual acquaintance quite differently from how we speak to a respected authority. Style is obviously a dimension that intersects with other variables in accounting for diversity in American English.

One of the essential dimensions for viewing style in American English is formality—how formal or informal a particular style is. This dimension can be approached most clearly by defining formality in terms of the amount of attention paid to speech. The more attention paid to speech, the more formal the style. Formal styles are thus defined as those situations where speech is the primary focus, whereas informal styles are defined in terms of those situations where there is the least amount of audio-monitoring of speech.

In many cases, the relative usage of particular features of American English is clearly related to style, regardless of the social or regional variety used. For example, the use of *-in'* for *-ing* (e.g., *swimming, hunting*), which is found to some extent among all regional and social varieties of English, is typically used more frequently in more informal styles. Similarly, the use of *d* for *th (this, the)* will be more frequent in more informal styles, where the lessened attention to speech will allow the greater usage of stigmatized variants. We can expect that a stigmatized variant will show decreased usage, and a prestige variant will show increased usage, as we move from informal to more formal styles. Some variants, such as taboo terms and certain socially stereotyped stigmatized features, may be totally absent from the more formal styles, while they persist in the informal styles.

The dimension of style appears to differ in its significance at various periods in the life cycle of an individual, although it is present to some extent at all periods. There is, however, less stylistic differentiation in the earliest stages of adolescence and the older stages of the life cycle. The reduced stylistic variation in the earliest stages is due to the acquisitional process, in which the sensitivity to the social significance of various styles usually precedes a full stylistic repertoire. During the later periods of life, adults have typically resigned themselves to their particular status and role in American society, and adaptation to particular situations becomes less variable. This is manifested in language by the reduction in the range of stylistic fluctuation. On the other hand, stylistic variation appears to be at its maximum during those periods in the life cycle when adults are establishing their own status and role in American society.

Stylistic variation also intersects with other social variables such as class. Intermediate social classes, such as the lower middle class, may be expected to show more stylistic variation than the upper middle class, which already "has it made," and the working class which basically has little contact with the upper middle class. The lower middle class, however, typically strives to emulate the middle class reference group with which it has contact, but by which it is not completely accepted. This creates a type of LINGUISTIC INSECURITY which results in the lower middle class sometimes using higher frequency levels of prestige features than the middle class itself when speech is in primary focus.

ON THE LINGUISTIC RELATIONSHIP BETWEEN VARIETIES OF ENGLISH

In the previous sections, we have attempted to set forth some of the regional and social parameters that are considered in accounting for the varieties of American English. At this point, we now want to turn to the nature of the linguistic relations among these varieties. As a preface to this discussion, it is necessary to recognize that there exists a large core of structures which is common to all varieties of English. The clear majority of syntactical, lexical, and phonological patterns are common to all varieties of American English. Granted this common base, however, we still want to know the nature and extent to which varieties differ from each other. We take as our underlying premise that the varieties of English will show structured, systematic relations to each other. While our notion of patterning may take us beyond some of the traditional notions of systematic patterning in linguistics, it can be demonstrated that there are sometimes intricate and subtle aspects of patterning to be found among the varieties of American English.

Differences between varieties may be either qualitative or quantitative in nature. In qualitative differences, linguistic forms found in one variety are categorically absent in another variety. For example, the use of so-called "distributive *be*" mentioned earlier (e.g., *He usually be upstairs*) as a characteristic of a Vernacular Black variety is a structure which is completely absent from the systems of many other varieties of English. Hence, we may speak of "distributive *be*" as a form which demonstrates qualitative differences among the varieties of English.

One of the most significant contributions of studies over the past decade has been the discovery that social varieties of English are often differentiated from each other not only by discrete sets of features, but also by variations in the frequencies with which certain forms or rules occur. This finding is in some ways at variance with popular perceptions of how the varieties of English are differentiated, since it is commonly held that certain low status groups always use particular socially stigmatized linguistic forms and high status groups never do. As it turns out, such "categorical" assessments do not match the actual language situation. In many cases, varieties of English are more typically differentiated by the extent to which a certain rule applies rather than the qualitative absence or presence of a rule. For example, consider the example of pronominal apposition in a structure such as *My mother, she went to the store*. While such a construction is often thought of as restricted to lower status groups, its actual distribution among four different social classes in Detroit can be seen in Table 1. In each case, the percentage figure indicates how frequently the appositive pronoun form is used in relation to how frequently it might have been used.

While the use of this form does differentiate different social groups of speakers, the differences are on a quantitative, not a qualitative scale. Out of the thirty-six speakers used in the tabulations presented in Table 1, no speaker reveals the incidence of pronominal apposition in every case where it might have been used, and only one speaker reveals the complete absence of this form.

Similar types of observations can be made with respect to phonological systems. Popular perceptions might attribute the *in'* of unstressed *-ing* forms (e.g., *swimming, laughing*) to lower status groups as an exclusive pattern and the *-ing* pronunciation to higher status groups as an exclusive pattern. Again, the careful examination of the actual incidence of the *-in'* pronunciation reveals a pattern of relative rather than absolute difference, as indicated in the frequency distribution of four social classes of Detroit speakers in Table 2.

Again we find a pattern of differentiation among social classes which is relative in nature. In fact all of the speakers in the sample cited here have some incidence of the *-in'* pronunciation.

That we observe variation between alternate forms, such as *-ing* and *-in'* does not necessarily mean that the fluctuation is completely random or haphazard. Although we cannot predict which form might be used in a given instance, there are factors which increase the likelihood that certain variants will occur. For example, the various social factors cited previously can all be important influences which affect the relative frequency of particular forms. Not all of the systematic effects on the variability of forms, however, can be accounted for by

TABLE 1
RELATIVE FREQUENCY OF PRONOMINAL APPOSITION USAGE IN FOUR SOCIAL STATUS GROUPS OF DETROIT SPEAKERS

	Upper middle class	Lower middle class	Upper working class	Lower working class
Percentage of pronominal apposition	4.5	13.6	25.4	23.8

Source: Adapted from Wolfram 1969.

TABLE 2
RELATIVE FREQUENCY OF *-IN'* **FORMS FOR FOUR SOCIAL GROUPS OF DETROIT SPEAKERS**

	Upper middle class	Lower middle class	Upper working class	Lower working class
Percentage of *-in'* forms	19.4	39.1	50.5	78.9

simply appealing to social factors. There are also aspects of the linguistic system itself which may systematically influence the likelihood of forms occurring. Particular types of linguistic context, such as surrounding structures or forms, may influence the relative frequency with which these forms occur.

The systematic effect of linguistic factors on the relative frequency of particular forms can best be understood by way of illustration. Consider the case of word-final CONSONANT CLUSTER reduction as it affects sound sequences such as *st, nd, ld, kt,* and so forth. In this rule, items such as *west, wind, cold,* and *act* may be reduced to *wes', win', col',* and *ac',* respectively. It is observed that the incidence of this reduction is quite variable, but certain linguistic factors influence the relative frequency of the reduction. These linguistic factors include whether the following word begins with a consonant as opposed to a vowel and the way in which the cluster has been formed. With reference to the following environment, we find that a following word which begins with a consonant will greatly increase the likelihood that the reduction process will take place. Thus, for example, we find reduction more frequent in a context such as *west coast* or *cold cuts* than in a context such as *west end* or *cold apple.* While some reduction may be found in both contexts, it is clearly favored when the following word begins with a consonant.

As mentioned above, we also find that reduction is influenced by the way in which the cluster is formed. To understand this relationship, we must note that some clusters are an inherent part of the word base, as in items like *guest* or *wild.* There are, however, other cases where a cluster is formed only through the addition of an *-ed* suffix, which is primarily formed phonetically through the addition of *t* or *d.* When the *-ed* suffix is added to an item such as *guess,* the form *guessed* is pronounced the same as *guest,* so that it now ends in an *st* cluster. Or, an item like *called* actually ends in an *ld* cluster as it is pronounced something like *calld.* In these cases, the cluster is formed because of the *-ed* addition, since neither *call* nor *guess* has a basic word form which ends in a cluster. When the degree of variation for base word clusters is compared with those formed through the addition of *-ed,* it is found that the former case clearly favors consonant cluster reduction. That is, we are more likely to find word-final consonant cluster reduction in an item such as *guest* or *wild* than in one like *guessed* or *called.* Again, we note that fluctuation can be observed in both types of clusters, so that the favoring effect of base word clusters on reduction is simply a matter of relative frequency.

When we compare different linguistic effects on the relative frequency of a variable reduction pattern such as word-final consonant clusters, we find that some will have a greater effect than others. In a sense, this is like the effect that social variables (e.g., class, sex, age, etc.) have on linguistic items where several different social factors influence the relative frequency of a form, but some social variables are more influential than others. Thus, the following linguistic context of a consonant versus a vowel may have a greater influence than the effects of a base word cluster versus a cluster formed through the addition of -ed.

In many cases, the linguistic constraints on variation can be found to operate across different social variables, such as class, sex, and age. The regular effect of the linguistic constraints mentioned above for consonant cluster reduction can be seen in Table 3 which compares this process in different regional and social variables of English.

As we see in Table 3, all the varieties of American English represented here are systematically influenced by the following environment and the formation of the cluster. While the different groups reveal the same linguistic constraints,

TABLE 3
PERCENTAGE OF CONSONANT CLUSTER REDUCTION IN DIFFERENT REGIONAL AND SOCIAL VARIETIES OF ENGLISH

Language variety	Not -ed, followed by consonant (e.g., west/coast)	-ed, followed by consonant (e.g., guessed/fast)	Not -ed, followed by vowel (e.g., west/end)	-ed, followed by vowel (e.g., guessed/it)
Middle class White Detroit speech	66	36	12	3
Working class Black Detroit speech	97	76	72	34
Working class White New York City adolescent speech	67	23	19	3
Working class White adolescent rural Georgia–Florida speech	56	16	25	10
Working class Black Adolescent rural Georgia–Florida speech	88	50	72	36
Southeastern West Virginia speech	74	67	17	5

however, the relative effect of their influence may differ. For two of these groups (Working class Black and Working class White adolescent rural Georgia–Florida speech) the effect of the formation of the cluster is more important than the following environment, but for the others the following environment has a greater effect.

To understand the nature of differentiation among different varieties of English, it is necessary to appreciate the quantitative dimensions of some of these differences as indicated above. The actual relationships of the forms that differentiate varieties are not nearly as simple as the categorical judgments people are sometimes prone to make, but are highly structured in some rather subtle ways. The systematic nature of the social and linguistic influences on fluctuating forms indicates one aspect of this detailed patterning.

IMPLICATIONAL RELATIONS BETWEEN THE VARIETIES OF ENGLISH

In the preceding discussion, we have focused on the systematic aspects of the quantitative dimension of language differences in the varieties of English. This is not, however, the only way in which the relations between varieties of language may be viewed. Another way of looking at the relationship between varieties of English is through the consideration of various combinations of language structures. Varieties of English do not distribute themselves randomly in terms of the forms that may differentiate one variety from another. Instead, there are IMPLICATIONAL RELATIONS that hold between various forms in particular varieties.

An implicational relation in language variation holds when the presence of a particular linguistic characteristic in any variety of a language implies the presence of another characteristic in that same variety. When a form B is always present whenever a form A is present, we say that "A *implies* B."

As an example of an implicational relation, we can consider the case of COPULA deletion as it is called, i.e., the absence of a form of the verb *to be* in the present tense in such items as *You ugly* (cf. *You are ugly*) and *He ugly* (cf. *He is ugly, He's ugly*). Varieties of American English differ in the amount of copula deletion they show, and the absence of *is* implies the absence of *are*. In other words, if a variety of English shows absence of *is* in such sentences, it is sure to show also the absence of *are,* but not vice versa. This is another way of saying that some varieties of American English drop the *are* in such sentences, but do not drop the *is.*

Linguists represent implicational relations of this kind in charts where they generally use "1" to mean presence of a characteristic, "0" absence of a characteristic, and "X" variable presence of a characteristic. Table 4 represents the implicational relation of *is* and *are* deletion in some varieties of American English. It shows that there are varieties of English (many Standard English

TABLE 4
IMPLICATIONAL RELATIONSHIP BETWEEN *IS* AND *ARE* ABSENCE

Language variety	*is* deletion	*are* deletion
Many standard varieties	0	0
Some Southern White varieties	0	1
Varieties of Vernacular Black English	1	1

varieties) which have neither *is* nor *are* deletion, that there are also varieties (Black English Vernacular) which have both *is* and *are* deletion, and that there are still other varieties (some Southern White varieties) which only have *are* deletion. Since we do not find a variety where *is* deletion is observed independent of *are* deletion we conclude that *is* copula deletion implies *are* copula deletion, but not the converse. Although we might extend the implicational table considerably beyond the one given here to represent many more details of copula deletion as it operates in a number of nonmainstream varieties of English, the basic relationship we have demonstrated here would still hold.

As we might expect, the implicational relationships that hold between the varieties of American English can sometimes be considerably more complex than our simplified illustrative case. To give a somewhat more extended picture, we can examine the case of so-called "double" or multiple negation as it is found in some varieties of English. We are essentially concerned with the syntactic pattern in English where a negative element is exhibited at more than one point in a sentence which contains an indefinite item of some type, such as a sentence like *He didn't do nothing because he was so lazy.* As it turns out, there are several different types of patterns which can potentially involve this type of negation. For our purposes we can identify four different types: (a) the realization of the negative element on all indefinites following the main verb (e.g., sentences like *He didn't do nothing because he was so lazy*), (b) the realization of a negative on an indefinite before the main verb and the placement of a negative within the main verb phrase (e.g., *Nobody can't do it because they're so dumb*), (c) the inversion of a negative of an auxiliary within the main verb phrase and an indefinite before the verb (e.g., *Can't nobody do it 'cause it's too hard*), and (d) the application of the negative element from one clause into the main verb phrase of another clause (e.g., *There wasn't much I couldn't do,* meaning something like 'There wasn't much I could do'). In Table 5 the three implicational symbols are used to indicate: the categorical operation of multiple negation, i.e., it is used in all cases where it might be used (1), the variable use of multiple negation, i.e., the rule may or may not apply to those cases where it could potentially apply (X), and the absence of the multiple negation, i.e., it categorically does not apply (0). Various varieties of American English are delimited in terms of the combinations of these rule applications, as indicated in the rows in Table 5.

TABLE 5
IMPLICATIONAL ARRAY FOR DIFFERENT TYPES OF MULTIPLE NEGATION IN
DIFFERENT VARIETIES OF ENGLISH

	Multiple negative type			
English variety	*d*	*c*	*b*	*a*
Standard English	0	0	0	0
Some Northern White nonmainstream varieties	0	0	0	X
Other Northern White nonmainstream varieties	0	0	X	X
Some Southern White nonmainstream varieties	0	X	X	X
Some varieties spoken in Appalachia	X	X	X	X
Some varieties of Black English Vernacular	X	X	X	1

One can see in Table 5 the detailed implicational relationships of the different negative types as typified in some representative varieties of English. If a variety has type *d* negation, then it will also have *c, b,* and *a;* if a variety has type *c,* then it will have both *b* and *a;* and if it has *b,* then it will necessarily have *a.* However, a variety will not have *d* but not *c,* or *b* but not *a,* and so forth.

The examination of implicational relations between various structures demonstrates two important dimensions with respect to language relationships. First of all, it gives a systematic basis for looking at the orderly relationships between varieties. Given the systematic implicational relationships, it is possible to determine the relative distance among different varieties of a language with respect to a given set of structures. For example, we may determine in Table 5 that the multiple negative structure in some Southern White varieties is considerably closer to that of Black English Vernacular than White Northern versions of this rule. By the same token, both Southern White varieties and Black English Vernacular are more distant from Standard English than White Northern nonmainstream varieties.

The second dimension added by implicational analysis relates to language change. Language change is an ongoing, dynamic process which takes place in a systematic way. One way of observing various stages in the process of change and which steps have preceded or will follow particular stages is to look at implicational relationships. For example, consider the case of the *h* in words such as *hit* for *it* and *hain't* for *ain't,* forms still found to some extent among speakers of American English in Appalachia and the Ozarks. At one point, *h* was found categorically for these items in both stressed and unstressed syllables. The presence of *h,* then, apparently became variable (i.e. sometimes it occurred and sometimes it didn't) in unstressed syllables while being categorically retained in stressed syllables. Next, the *h* was variably lost in both stressed and unstressed syllables, but more frequently in unstressed syllables where the change first started. If, however, it was variably lost in stressed syllables, it implied that it was lost in unstressed syllables as well, while the converse did not exist. Through time, the *h* was completely lost in unstressed syllables, while still retained variably in stressed syllables. And finally, it was lost in both stressed and unstressed syllables categorically. The stages of this change are summarized in Table 6. In this table 1 stands for categorical presence of *h* in *it* and *ain't*, X for variable presence, and 0 for categorical loss of the *h*.

Among American English varieties today, stages 3, 4, and 5 are still represented in some nonmainstream varieties and 5 is the Standard English usage where the loss of the *h* is complete. Ultimately, we would expect the varieties at stages 3 and 4 to carry through the change to stage 5, although we cannot predict how quickly this might take place. As found in this example, different varieties of American English may be seen to a certain extent as a reflection of ongoing language change at different stages in its progression. Based on the systematic nature of the implicational relations among forms, we can understand what steps have preceded and what steps are likely to follow in the dynamics of the change. With respect to some changes, a given variety may be ahead of others, whereas with others it may be at an earlier stage. For this reason, we should resist the temptation to say that a variety spoken in some relatively isolated region such as the Appalachian or Ozark mountain range is simply a reflection of an earlier stage of English. While there are certainly retentions of older forms to be found in these areas, there are also aspects of these varieties which are more advanced in their language change than those of the surrounding mainstream varieties.

Dialect variation in American English is extensive, and is conditioned by—at

TABLE 6
STAGES FOR LANGUAGE CHANGE IN THE LOSS OF *h* IN *hit* AND *hain't* IN AMERICAN ENGLISH

		Unstressed syllables	Stressed syllables
Stage 1.	Earliest stage of English, before undergoing change	1	1
Stage 2.	Earlier stage of English, at start of *h* loss	X	1
Stage 3.	Stages in full progress, still exhibited by some older speakers in Appalachia	X	X
Stage 4.	Change progressing toward completion, exhibited by some speakers in Appalachia	0	X
Stage 5.	Completed change, exhibited by most speakers of English outside of Appalachia and Ozarks and some younger speakers in Appalachia and Ozarks	0	0

least—the variables of the speaker's regional provenience, social status, ethnicity, age, and sex. Cutting across and intersecting with these variables are the dimensions of formality of style and occasion of use of the language. The research of dialectologists and sociolinguists has established some of the basic facts of variation in American English, but we are far from having an adequate picture of the present diversity or an adequate understanding of how the diversity is changing.

FURTHER READING

The regional aspects of diversity in American English are presented in the publications of the dialect geographers. Shuy 1967 and Reed 1977 provide summaries of this work intended for popular audiences. McDavid 1958 is an excellent account of the American dialect situation as known at that time, and McDavid 1979a, b provide articles which reflect the history of dialect geography in the United States. Originally conceived in 1929 as a comprehensive Linguistic Atlas of the United States, the atlas work has developed into a series of autonomous but interrelated projects. The results of investigations in different sections of the USA are available as follows: New England: Kurath et al. 1939P43, reprinted 1972; the Upper Midwest: Allen 1973P6; the Middle and South Atlantic states: Kurath et al. 1979; the North-Central states: Marckwardt et al. 1976P8; California and Nevada: Reed et al. forthcoming; Oklahoma: Van Riper et al. forthcoming; the Gulf states: Pederson et al. forthcoming. Work on many of the regional projects continues; for example, the Linguistic Atlas of the Middle and South Atlantic States, the largest and most comprehensive of the regional atlases, contains more than one million words and phrases, and is being prepared for publication in a tabular format. Interpretive summaries are available for some of the regional surveys; for example, Kurath 1949, Atwood 1953, and Kurath and McDavid 1961 for New England and the Middle and South Atlantic states, and Bright 1971 for California and Nevada. *The Dictionary of American Regional English (DARE),* forthcoming, edited by Cassidy, will provide regional identification of thousands of lexical items, with examples of their uses from spoken and written sources.

The social aspects of diversity in American English are presented in several studies carried out in metropolitan areas in the 1960s and early 1970s. Labov's *The Social Stratification of English in New York City* (1966) was the pioneering work, followed by Shuy, Wolfram, and Riley 1967 and Wolfram 1969. Discussions of the language use in urban centers and the methodology of sociolinguists studying social variation in language appear in Labov 1972a, b.

Shopen 1980 provides an introduction to selected aspects of dialect diversity by actively involving the reader in the analysis of data. Traugott and Pratt 1980 is an introduction to linguistics with emphasis on the uses of linguistic analysis for studying literature; Chapter 8, "Varieties of English: regional, social, and ethnic," is the best coverage of literary dialect available. Wolfram and Fasold 1974 emphasizes the social dimensions of diversity, with a fairly comprehensive discussion of specific socially diagnostic structures. The collection of papers in Shores 1972, particularly Section I, looks at the regional and ethnic dimensions of variation through specific examples. Another collection, from a different perspective, is Williamson and Burke 1971. Brewer and Brandes 1976 provide discussions of issues related to controversies surrounding dialects.

Research on language variation by sex of speaker or addressee is presented in the collection of papers by Thorne and Henley 1975 (2d ed. Thorne, Henley, and Kramarae 1980), which includes an extensive bibliography. Jespersen 1922, Chapter 13, provides the only extensive treatment of sex differences in language use in early general works on language. The most comprehensive and widely quoted articles are Key 1972 and Lakoff 1973a; both have been expanded into books, Key 1975 and Lakoff 1975, and both have been widely quoted (and sometimes loosely interpreted) in journalistic and popular treatments of sexism in language (e.g., Miller and Swift 1976). A popular source on sex differences in conversational interaction is Parlee 1979. A newsletter, *Women and Language,* produced by the Stanford University Department of Linguistics, links a network of scholars working on widely varying aspects of women's language.

REFERENCES

Allen, Harold B. 1973–1976. *Linguistics Atlas of the Upper Midwest,* 3 vols. Minneapolis: University of Minnesota Press.

Atwood, E. Bagby. 1953. *A Survey of Verb Forms in the Eastern United States.* Ann Arbor: University of Michigan Press.

Bartlett, John R. 1848. *Dictionary of Americanisms.* New York: Bartlett and Welford.

Brewer, Jeutonne, and Paul Brandes, eds. 1976. *Dialect Clash in America: Issues and Answers.* Metuchen, NJ: Scarecrow.

Bright, Elizabeth. 1971. *A Word Geography of California and Nevada.* Berkeley and Los Angeles: University of California Press.

Cassidy, Frederick G., ed. Forthcoming. *Dictionary of American Regional English.* Cambridge, MA: Belknap.

Francis, W. Nelson. 1958. *The Structure of American English.* New York: Roland.

Heath, Shirley Brice. 1976a. Colonial language status achievement: Mexico, Peru, and the United States. In *Language in Sociology.* A. Verdoodt and R. Kjolseth, eds. Louvain, Belgium: Peeters, pp. 49–91.

———. 1976b. Early American attitudes toward variation in speech: A view from social history and sociolinguistics. *Forum Lecture,* LSA Institute.

Jespersen, Otto. 1922. *Language: Its Nature, Development, and Origin.* London: Allen and Unwin.

Key, Mary Ritchie. 1972. Linguistic behavior of male and female. *Linguistics* 88: 15–31.

———. 1975. *Male/Female Language.* Metuchen, NJ: Scarecrow.

Kurath, Hans. 1939–1943. *Linguistics Atlas of New England,* 3 vols. (reprint). New York: AMS, 1972.

——. 1949. *A Word Geography of the Eastern United States.* Ann Arbor: University of Michigan Press.

Kurath, Hans, and Raven I. McDavid, Jr. 1961. *The Pronunciation of English in the Atlantic States.* Ann Arbor: University of Michigan Press.

Kurath, Hans, et al. 1979. *Linguistic Atlas of the Middle and Atlantic States.* Chicago: University of Chicago Press.

Labov, William. 1964. Stages in the acquisition of Standard English: In *Social Dialects and Language Learning.* R. W. Shuy, ed. Champaign, IL: National Council of Teachers of English, pp. 71–103.

——. 1966. *The Social Stratification of English in New York City.* Washington, DC: Center for Applied Linguistics.

——. 1972. *Language in the Inner City: Studies in the Black English Vernacular.* Philadelphia: University of Pennsylvania Press.

Lakoff, Robin. 1973. Language and woman's place. *Language in Society* 2: 45–79.

——. 1975. *Language and Woman's Place.* New York: HarperCollins.

Marckwardt, Albert H. 1958. *American English.* London and New York: Oxford University Press.

Marckwardt, Albert H., et al. 1976–1978. *Linguistic Atlas of the North-Central States. Cultural Anthropology Series* 38: 200–208.

McDavid, Raven I., Jr., 1979a. *Dialects in Culture.* W. Kretzschmar, ed. Tuscaloosa, AL: University of Alabama Press.

——. 1979b. *Varieties of American English.* Anwar Dil, ed. Stanford: Stanford University Press.

McDavid, Raven I., Jr., Raymond K. O'Cain, and George T. Dorrill. 1978. The Linguistic Atlas of the Middle and South Atlantic States. *Special Libraries Association Geography and Map Division.* Bulletin 113: 17–23.

Miller, Casey, and Kate Swift. 1976. *Words and Women.* New York: Doubleday Anchor.

Parlee, Mary Brown. 1979. Conversational Politics. *Psychology Today* 12: 48–56.

Pederson, et al. Forthcoming. *Linguistics Atlas of the Gulf States.*

Pickering, John. 1816. *A Vocabulary, or Collection of Words and Phrases which Have Been Supposed to Be Peculiar to The United States of America.* Also in *The Beginnings of American English: Essays and Comments.* M. M. Mathews, ed. Chicago: University of Chicago Press, 1931.

Reed, Carroll E. 1977. *Dialects of American English.* Amherst, MA: University of Massachusetts Press.

Reed, David W., et al. Forthcoming. *Linguistic Atlas of California and Nevada.*

Shopen, Timothy. 1980. *Standards and Dialects in English.* Cambridge, MA: Winthrop.

Shores, David. 1972. *Contemporary English: Change and Variation.* Philadelphia: Lippincott.

Shuy, Roger. 1967. *Discovering American Dialects.* Champaign, IL: National Council of Teachers of English.

Shuy, Roger, Walt Wolfram, and William K. Riley. 1967. *A Study of Social Dialects in Detroit.* Report on project 6-1347. Washington, DC: Office of Education.

Thorne, Barrie, and Nancy Henley, eds. 1975. *Language and Sex: Differences and Dominance.* Rowley, MA: Newbury House.

Thorne, Barrie, Nancy Henley, and Sheris Kramarae. 1980. *Language and Sex: Differences and Dominance,* 2d ed. Rowley, MA: Newbury House.

Traugott, Elizabeth, and Mary L. Pratt. 1980. *Linguistics and Its Uses in Literary Analysis: An Introduction.* New York: Harcourt, Brace, Jovanovich.

Van Riper, William Robert, et al. Forthcoming. *Linguistic Atlas of Oklahoma.*

Williamson, Juanita, and Virginia Burke, eds. 1971. *A Various Language.* New York: Holt, Rinehart, and Winston.

Wolfram, Walt. 1969. *A Sociolinguistic Description of Detroit Negro Speech.* Urban Linguistic Series No. 5. Arlington, VA.: Center for Applied Linguistics.

Wolfram, Walt, and Donna Christian. 1976. *Appalachian Speech.* Arlington, VA: Center for Applied Linguistics.

Wolfram, Walt, and Ralph W. Fasold. 1974. *Social Dialects in American English.* Englewood Cliffs, NJ: Prentice-Hall.

"What Go Round Come Round": *King* in Perspective

Geneva Smitherman

That teacher, he too mean. He be hollin at us and stuff.
Browny, he real little, he six, and he smart cause he know how to read.

Two of the plaintiff children in *King*

The children are the future and the hope of black America. Therefore, it is fitting and proper to begin with the words of those children who brought the federal lawsuit in the nationally prominent but widely misunderstood case of *Martin Luther King Junior Elementary School Children v. Ann Arbor School District Board.* Although this case has come to be known as the "Black English Case," it was as much a case about black children as about black English. As Judge Charles W. Joiner himself said, "It is a straightforward effort to require the court to intervene on the children's behalf to require the defendant School District Board to take appropriate action to teach them to read in the standard English of the school, the commercial world, the arts, science and professions. This action is a cry for judicial help in opening the doors to the establishment. . . . It is an action to keep another generation from becoming functionally illiterate" (473 F. Supp. 1371, E.D. Mich. 1979).

The precedent established by the *King* decision represents the first test of the applicability of 1703(f), the language provision of the 1974 Equal Educational Opportunity Act, to black English speakers. The case suggests new possibilities for educational and social policies in our struggle to save children and develop future leadership. As the plaintiff children's chief consultant and expert witness during the two years of litigation, I shall provide an analysis of *King* and its implications for public policy and black community development in light of the stark reality of white racism and class contradictions among blacks in the United States.

BACKGROUND

Briefly, the background facts of the case are as follows. On July 28, 1977, Attorneys Gabe Kaimowitz and Kenneth Lewis of Michigan Legal Services filed suit in eastern District Court located in Detroit, Michigan on behalf of fifteen black, economically deprived children residing in a low-income housing project on Green Road in Ann Arbor, Michigan. By the time the case came to trial in the summer of 1979, one family with four children had moved out of the school district, leaving eleven plaintiff children to litigate the case.

Initially, the plaintiffs' action was directed against the State of Michigan, the Ann Arbor School District, and officials at Martin Luther King Junior Elementary School, where black children comprised 13 percent of the school population of predominantly white, upper-class children. The allegation was that the defendants had failed to properly educate the children, who were thus in danger of becoming functionally illiterate. Specifically, plaintiffs charged that school officials had improperly placed the children in learning disability and speech pathology classes; that they had suspended, disciplined, and repeatedly retained the children at grade level without taking into account their social, economic, and cultural differences; and that they had failed to overcome language barriers preventing the children from learning standard English and learning to read. Actions taken by school officials, such as labeling the children "handicapped" and providing them with museum trips and other types of "cultural exposure," had failed to solve the academic problems of the children. The attitude of school officials was that the school had done its job, and that perhaps the children were uneducable. Yet close scrutiny of the academic records and psychological and speech-language evaluations failed to uncover any inherent limitation in the children's cognitive or language capacities. Further, the children's mothers were not persuaded that the academic and behavioral problems were due to slowness or mental retardation. The mothers' intuition was corroborated by professional judgment: their children were normal, intelligent kids who could learn if properly taught.

THE TRIAL

During the pretrial stages of *King,* Judge Joiner tried to settle the case out of court, perhaps wary of the precedent that would be set. The "Friends of *King,*" as we, the children's advocates, came to call ourselves, prepared a reading program which the officials rejected.[1] The Complaint was revised and amended several times to comply with Joiner's orders. For the course of future litigation in this area, the most critical revision was that all claims relative to economic, social, and cultural factors were dismissed. Joiner contended that there is no constitutional provision guaranteeing the right to educational services to overcome unsatisfactory academic performance based on cultural, social, or economic background. To put it more pointedly, the U.S. Constitution can provide protection on the basis of being black, but not on the basis of being poor.

In Judge Joiner's reasoning, it was necessary to focus the issues in *King* on a decidedly narrow set of arguments. He dismissed all of the plaintiffs' claims except one which forced the lawsuit to be tried solely on 1703(f), which reads in part: "No state shall deny equal educational opportunity to an individual on account of his or her race, color, sex, or national origin, by . . . the failure to overcome language barriers that impede equal participation by its students in its instructional programs." Restricting the case to the issue of language barriers, Joiner instructed plaintiffs to specify the nature of the barriers, the lack of appropriate action to overcome them, and the resulting denial of educational opportunity based on race. What began as much more than a "Black English Case" would now focus narrowly on language issues, and its outcome would depend on the interpretation of a single sentence. For the plaintiffs and their "friends of *King*," it was clear that the trial would depend on expert testimony. During the four-week trial, a biracial team[2] of expert witnesses in the fields of psychology, education, linguistics, and reading testified on behalf of the plaintiff children. The members of this team advised the court of the extensive research in their respective fields, the relationship of this knowledge to language barriers, and the obligation of schools to overcome these barriers.

Significantly, the defendant school board called no expert witnesses. Its attorney simply relied on cross-examination of the plaintiffs' experts—a strategy

---

[1]Since their children's low reading level was among the parents' chief concerns, one of Joiner's early attempts at mediation was to suggest that we draft a program targeted at reading. Philosophically, the program stressed inservice training, schoolwide involvement, community input, youth-training-youth, and the integration of multicultural material in all school subjects, at all grade levels, and for *all* children at King School. Pedagogically, emphasis was on a multidisciplinary approach to their teaching of reading, on the use of language experience and black cultural approach, and on oral and written activities aimed at developing communicative competence. The defendants objected, contending that the program was too broad in scope, that it did not address the specific, individual cases of the fifteen plaintiff children, and finally, that they had already been using some of the suggested approaches and materials with the plaintiff children, but nothing seemed to work.

[2]In addition to myself, the biracial team of experts included: Richard Bailey, University of Michigan; J. L. Dillard, Northern Louisiana State University; Ronald Edmonds, Harvard Graduate School of Education; Daniel N. Fader, University of Michigan; Kenneth Haskins, Roxbury Community College; Milford Jeremiah, Morgan State University; William Labov, University of Pennsylvania; Jerrie Scott, University of Florida; and Gary Simpkins, Watts Health Foundation.

consistent with the community's self-righteous posture. Ann Arbor prides itself on being a liberal community, and ranks among the country's top six public school systems in academic achievement. It is also the home of the prestigious University of Michigan and a multi-million dollar research program that has included the study of race, language, teaching, and learning. Indicative of its presumed enlightenment, Ann Arbor had decided to promote racial and economic integration by opting in the 1960s for scattered-site, low-income housing; poor blacks live in the same neighborhood and attend the same school as affluent whites and blacks. The Ann Arbor defendants, reflecting a blame-the-victim methodology, contended that their school district could not possibly have failed to practice equal educational opportunity. Although apparently confident about being vindicated, the school district nevertheless employed the expensive Detroit law firm that had successfully defended Detroit's suburbs before the U.S. Supreme Court in the *Bradley v. Milliken* school desegregation case.[3]

The trial proceedings established that the school district had failed to recognize the existence and legitimacy of the children's language, black English. This failure of the teachers to recognize the language as legitimate and the corresponding negative attitudes toward the children's language led to negative expectations of the children which turned into self-fulfilling prophecies. One critical consequence was that the children were not being taught to read. On July 12, 1979, Judge Charles W. Joiner, a resident of Ann Arbor himself, issued what he later described as a "rather conservative" ruling: on the basis of failing to overcome language barriers, the Ann Arbor School District had violated the children's right to equal educational opportunity. *Though black English was not found to be a barrier per se, the institutional response to it was a barrier.* In short, this ruling affirmed the obligation of school districts to educate black children and served to establish, within a legal framework, what has been well documented in academic scholarship: black English is a systematic, rule-governed language system developed by black Americans as they struggled to combine the cultures of Africa and the United States. The district was given thirty days to devise a remedy.

The intent of the Equal Educational Opportunity Act (EEOA) is fairly clear. Initiated by President Nixon and passed by Congress at the height of the antibus-

---

[3]In 1970, the NAACP, acting on behalf of one white parent and several black parents, filed a federal suit against the Detroit School District and the State of Michigan (Milliken was governor). The claim was that black children had been deliberately segregated and were receiving an inferior education. In his historic 1971 decision, Judge Stephen Roth ruled that Detroit schools had been intentionally segregated, and he ordered cross-district busing between Detroit and its predominantly white suburbs. At that time, Detroit's schools were 65 percent black. In his decision, Roth indicated that following the 1967 "civil disturbance," Detroit had suffered the most rapid exodus of whites of any northern city school system. In 1974 the Supreme Court overturned the Roth decision on cross-district busing and thus sounded the death knell for integrating Detroit's schools, which today are 86 percent black.

ing crusades, the EEOA shifted the policy emphasis from desegregation to quality education, and thus, in classic U.S. fashion, attempted to reconcile the two contradictory forces of white racism and black aspirations. Therefore, much of the impetus behind the new legislation was related to racial issues. Because bilingual legislation had already been in existence for four years, however, the inclusion of 1703(f) within the EEOA raises the question of whom this obscure language provision was originally designed to protect. In fact, once Joiner had ruled this a language case, the Ann Arbor School District immediately filed a motion to dismiss on the grounds that 1703(f) did not apply to black English speakers but only to those with foreign language backgrounds. Had this reasoning prevailed, of course, there would have been no case, since this was the only remaining claim of the plaintiffs that Joiner had allowed to stand. Emphasizing former HEW Secretary Elliott Richardson's interpretation that the statute protected the "legal right of any child [with] a language handicap" (118 Congressional Record 8928, 1972), Joiner denied Ann Arbor's motion and issued the following ruling that represented our first victory in the case:

> The President's [Nixon's] list of persons covered by his proposal is only merely illustrative but could well include students whose "language barrier" results from the use of some type of nonstandard English. . . . The statutory language places no limitations on the character or source of the language barrier except that it must be serious enough to impede equal participation by . . . students in . . . instructional programs. Barring any more legislative guidance to the contrary, 1703(f) applies to language barriers encountered by students who speak German (451 F. Supp. 1332, E.D. Mich. 1978).

The court's ruling in this regard meant that the case would not have to be based on the theoretical problem of differentiating a language from a dialect, nor consequently, on specifically determining whether black English is a language or a dialect. Yet it was an issue that really was not—and, in fact, cannot be—dismissed, for the lack of theoretical clarity and intellectual consensus on the question presented serious difficulties formulating our legal arguments and pedagogical remedies. Further, this confusion serves to account, in part, for the broad misinterpretations of *King* and the continuing ambivalence about black English in the lay community.

LANGUAGE OR DIALECT

In categorizing linguistic phenomena, a commonly applied test is that of mutual intelligibility. If speech data from Community A can be understood by Community B, and vice versa, with relative ease, requiring only slight adjustment on the part of each group of speakers, we can generally conclude that the two sets of speech data derive from the same source, that is, they are variations of the same language. Since there is an overlap between Africanized (black) English and Euro-American (white) English, mutual comprehension exists between blacks and whites, suggesting that black English is a dialect. There are also areas of significant linguistic differentiation between the two speech communities, however, which can lead to a lack of understanding and confusion, and can contribute to the conceptualization of black English as a language. (See Dillard 1972; Fasold and Shuy 1970; Labov 1971; Smitherman 1977, 1980; Valdman 1977.)

A few examples will serve to more fully illuminate the nature of the language-dialect controversy. An often-cited characteristic of black English, strikingly distinguishing it from standard white English, is the use of *be* as a full verb form, as in the opening quotation "He be hollin at us and stuff." This use of the verb "to be" derives from an aspectual verb system that is also found in African Pidgin English, and in the Gullah Creole spoken by blacks living on the Sea Islands along the southeastern seaboard of the United States. Its use conveys the speaker's meaning with reference to the qualitative character and distribution of an action over time. In the case of "He be hollin at us," the speaker indicates habitual action. The standard English verb system of past, present, and future tenses cannot accommodate this type of construction, while the black English usage has captured all three tenses simultaneously. The closest standard English equivalent would be: he is always (or constantly) hollering at us; he frequently (or often) hollers at us; or, he sometimes (or occasionally) hollers at us. Other examples of aspectual *be* collected from taped interviews with the plaintiff children are: *When school is out dis time, uhma be going to summer school; They be hitting on peoples;* and *I like the way he be psyching people out.* Black English also allows for sentences without any form of the copula, as in *He real little; He six; My momma name Annie; She my teacher;* and *They always fighting.*

In black English, possession does not require the inflectional *z* (written as *s* preceded or followed by an apostrophe), but rather, is indicated by juxtaposition, as in these examples from the children: *She took him to his grandmother house; Popeye girlfriend;* and *My daddy name John.* Consider the potential for linguistic confusion to the nonblack English speaker that can result from the co-occurrence of two or more features of black English within a single statement, as in the following item from the "Black Language Test" (Smitherman 1975): *"She the girl momma."* Does this mean that she is the mother of the girl in question; that she is a very young girl who is the mother of a child; or, that she is a girl being pointed out to somebody's mother?

It is not only in phonology (sound) and morpho-syntax (grammar and structure) that critical differences between the black and white speech communities occur. Intelligibility can be affected by the lack of familiarity with the rhetorical and semantic strategies of black English. For example, Muhammad Ali, hero and rapper par excellence to virtually the entire black English-speaking community, nearly caused an international diplomatic disaster by using the rules of "talkin black" when he said: "There are two bad white men in the world, the

Russian white man and the American white man. They are the two baddest men in the history of the world." Although the Tanzanians, to whom Ali was speaking at the time, apparently understood his meaning perfectly well, the standard white English-speaking world did not. He was castigated for using a term interpreted in the Websterian tradition as evil, wicked, negative, or not good. In the semantics of inversion used by the descendants of African slaves, however, "bad" can mean powerful, omnipotent, spiritually or physically tough, outstanding, wonderful, and with emphasis, very good. For this feature of language use in black English, Dalby (1969; 1972) cites linguistic parallels in Mandingo and several other African languages. His work remains the most rigorous treatment of the lexico-semantic system of black language from a diachronic perspective. (See also Dillard 1977; and Major 1970.)

I have deliberately chosen the example of Muhammad Ali because the contrasting black and white American interpretations of his verbal showmanship place the language-dialect controversy in bold relief. Although Ali's language appears to be English—and fairly standard English at that—the correct interpretation of his meaning requires the listener to have access to sociocultural data outside the realm of standard English. Ali represents the bad man of words in the black oral tradition. Through boastful talk, pungent rhymes, verbal repartee, and clever "signifyin" (indirect language used to tease, admonish, or disparage), the rapper establishes himself or herself (but more generally himself) as a cultural hero solely on the basis of oral performance. Preachers, politicians, and other black leaders reflect this tradition. A clever rapper can talk himself out of a jam, and in sessions of ritual insult such as "playing the dozens" (talking about somebody's momma or other kinfolk), tension is relieved and fights often avoided. Those who are verbally adept at the art of "selling woof (wolf) tickets" (boasting) often do not have to prove anything by action. It is believed that the African concept of *Nommo,* word power, can indeed "psych your opponent out." Thus, when Ali engages in the art of black braggadocio, the louder and badder he talks, the more blacks applaud him, but the more whites, lacking cultural experience in this tradition, censure him. Ali symbolizes a cultural value manifested in black language behavior, suggesting that we are dealing with more than surface dialect differences.

The black English language-dialect controversy reflects a fundamental contradiction within linguistics itself as to how language is to be defined, conceptualized, and studied. The classic dichotomy between *langue* and *parole* (loosely, speech and language) is evident in the differences between Chomskyian theoretical linguistics and Hymesian "socially constituted" linguistics. Chomsky (1966, 1972) abstracts language from social context and focuses on its structure— sound patterns, grammatical structure, and vocabulary. Hymes (1974) more broadly conceptualizes language within the framework of culture and society, and focuses on the use and users of language: their history, culture, values, world views, and social structure are considered basic to understanding a given language. The former is the more popular view of language and that taken by Judge Joiner when he demanded that we identify language barriers without reference to the children's cultural characteristics, which he deemed "irrelevant to a cause of action under the language barrier statute" (463 F. Supp. 1027 at 1030, E.D. Mich. 1978).

Elsewhere (Smitherman 1979), I detail the relationship of this general controversy in linguistics to study and research on black English. The point is that the semantics within which one formulates a general theory of language can determine whether one views the issue as black language or as black dialect. If one considers only words, grammar, and sounds as the essence of language, then black speech data might tend to look more like a dialect of English. If one also considers the history and social rules that govern the use, production, and interpretation of the words, grammar, and sounds, then black speech data more nearly resemble a different language. Applying this to *King,* if black English is a dialect, then the language barriers are mere surface differences that do not impede communication between teacher and student, nor between student and material written in standard English. If the barriers are not in language per se, we must look elsewhere for impediments to the children's access to equal educational opportunity. In this case they were found in attitudes of teachers and other school personnel toward language. On the other hand, if we are dealing with a language, then the barriers reside not only in attitudes, but also in actual linguistic interferences that hamper communication. Since linguistics cannot offer the definitive word on language-dialect differentiation, it ultimately comes down to who has the power to define; or as Max Weinreich once put it, the difference between a language and a dialect is who's got the army (1931).

With the *King* case clearly, if narrowly, focused on the language issue, Joiner outlined four areas to be covered in our final amended complaint. We were to identify the language barriers confronting the plaintiff children, specify how these barriers had impeded the equal participation of the children in the instructional program of King School, set forth the appropriate action that defendants had allegedly failed to take, and identify the connection between the defendants' failure to take appropriate action and the race of the plaintiff children.

The several versions of the complaint had consistently highlighted structural and nonstructural interference phenomena as constituting the basis of the language barriers confronting the plaintiff children at King School. These, we argued, represented essentially a languages-in-contact interaction (Weinreich 1963). Structural interferences derive from the structural differences between two languages—a mismatch of linguistic structures on the levels of phonology, lexico-semantics, and/or morpho-syntax. Nonstructural interference phenomena refer to differing attitudes and conflicting values about the two speech systems and the individuals who use them. The analysis of Muhammad Ali's speaking style illustrates both structural and nonstructural interference phenomena in operation. These phenomena are actually inextricable, though they are often expressed as a dichotomy to create an analytically convenient, if artificial, schema that readily lends itself to empiricism.

Because the language-dialect conflict remains unresolved, there is no consensus among language scholars as to whether there are both structural and nonstructural interferences between black and standard/white English ("What go round come round"). Some black psychologists (Simpkins 1976; Simpkins, Holt, and Simpkins 1976; Williams 1972; Williams, Rivers, and Brantley 1975; Wilson 1971) contend that the points of mismatch between standard and black English constitute cognitive barriers to meaning for black English-speaking children; that is, they have to translate standard English input data. Such mismatches seem to occur on the larger level of rhetorical patterning and discourse rather than being simple points of interference, as suggested in the contrast between "He look for me last night" and "He looked for me last night." This is not the cognitive-linguistic deficit argument espoused by Deutsch (1963), Bereiter and Engelmann (1966), and others, but a postulation that the two different speech communities employ differing thought patterns and conceptions of reality and that these differences are reflected in different styles of discourse. Cooper (1980), for example, suggests that standard English speakers employ a more impersonal style with greater distance from the material of their discourse.

Although the evidence is not definitive, the best available data and expert judgment, particularly from black psychologists, seem to suggest that black English speakers have language-based problems, and only those who master code-switching make it through the educational system successfully. With inconclusive research data at this point, coupled with the inadequacy of current language models to account for differences in discourse structure, the "friends of *King*" were unsuccessful in persuading the court that structural linguistic barriers existed. Although Joiner conceded that "there was initially a type of language difference," he reasoned that "it did not pose a communication obstruction" in teacher-student interaction (473 F. Supp. 1371, E.D. Mich. 1979).

ATTITUDES ABOUT LANGUAGE

Research on sociolinguists in the education process has been most fruitful and convincing in uncovering underlying attitudes about language. Specifying the nature of these nonstructural barriers proved to be our most powerful legal strategy. In the educational context, negative linguistic attitudes are reflected in the institutional policies and practices that become educationally dysfunctional for black English-speaking children. Research on language attitudes consistently indicates that teachers believe black English-speaking youngsters are nonverbal and possess limited vocabularies. They are perceived to be slow learners or uneducable; their speech is unsystematic and needs constant correction and improvement (Esselman 1978; Shuy and Fasold 1973; Williams 1972; Williams,

Whitehead, and Miller 1971). These beliefs, though linguistically untenable, are essentially those held about black English speakers.

Myths and misconceptions about language and negative attitudes toward language diversity are fostered in the school and perpetuated in the general populace of the public school experience (Pooley 1974). Schools and teachers are seen as guardians of the national tongue. Condemned as immoral, ignorant, and inferior are all those who depart from the idealized norm of standard English which, as Pooley's research (1969) so powerfully demonstrates, teachers themselves preach but do not practice. It was this type of mental set that led King School teachers to correct constantly, to the point of verbal badgering, some of the plaintiff children's speech, thereby causing them to become truly nonverbal; to exclude them from regular classes in order to take speech remediation for a nonexistent pathology; to give them remedial work since "that's the best they can do"; and to suspend them from class for trivial and inconsequential acts of so-called misbehavior.

The use, or rather misuse, of standardized tests is a prime example of institutional policy detrimental to the educational success of black English-speaking children. Intelligence tests and other diagnostic and assessment tools used in the schools have been normed on white, middle-class, standard English speakers and are obviously linguistically and culturally biased against poor black children. For example, standard speech articulation and language assessment tests measure forms and distinctions that do not exist in black language. One set calls for the distinction between "Ruth" and "roof," which in black English are pronounced the same. Examples of this feature of black English in the speech data from the King School children include: "maf" ("math") work; "birfday" ("birthday"); "bof" ("both"). Another set of test items calls for the singular/plural distinction to be made by changing the verb form, as in the task requiring children to match pictures with the examiner's spoken sentences: "The cat is playing" vs. "The cats are playing." In black English, each sentence would be expressed without the verb and without the morphemic indication of plural. Plurality is generally realized by context in black English. Examples from the plaintiff children include "Two captain," "a few cartoon," and "two year." In sum, what we were able to show is that these linguistically biased instruments of educational institutions cannot possibly validate the problems nor the promise of a black English-speaking student (Bliss and Allen 1978; Green 1975; Taylor 1971; Williams 1972; Williams, Rivers, and Brantley 1975).

This impressive array of social science research on attitudinal language barriers led the court to conclude that "if a barrier exists because of language used by the children in this case, it exists . . . because in the process of attempting to teach the students how to speak standard English the students are made somehow to feel inferior and are thereby turned off from the learning process" (473 F. Supp. 1371, E.D. Mich, 1979).

Since black English is viewed negatively by standard English-speaking teachers, it is not difficult to reconstruct the process whereby this language barrier impeded the educational success of the plaintiff children. King School teachers denied that the plaintiff children even spoke black English, contending that "they talk like everybody else." In contradiction, however, were their own formal commentaries on the children's school records indicating the use of black English forms, test data showing low verbal ability in standard English, and the taped samples of the children's speech, excerpts of which were cited in the final amended complaint and detailed during the trial. Because teachers did not even acknowledge the existence, much less the legitimacy, of the plaintiff children's language, they obviously failed to "take it into account" in teaching standard English. It is not, then, black language in and of itself that constitutes the barrier, but negative institutional policies and classroom practices relative to black English that were, and are, key causes of black children's reading problems. Since reading is crucial to academic achievement in all school subjects, the inability to read at grade level prevents equal participation in the educational programs of the school.

THE DECISION

What, then, was the appropriate action the defendant school board had failed to take? It had not instituted policies to assist King School teachers and personnel to handle the linguistic and educational needs of the plaintiff children. As Joiner indicated: "The court cannot find that the defendant School Board has taken steps (1) to help the teachers understand the problem; (2) to help provide them with knowledge about the children's use of a 'black English' language system; and (3) to suggest ways and means of using that knowledge in teaching the students to read" (473 F. Supp. 1371, E.D. Mich. 1979).

In his opinion, Joiner refers to the crucial data from social science research on effective schools for poor black children (Brookover and Beady 1978; Edmonds 1979; Weber 1971; Edmonds and Fredericksen 1978). This research has established that appropriate action by schools can result in educational achievement despite pupil characteristics. Educational climate is the critical variable, not the race or class of the children.

Finally, the relationship between the district's lack of appropriate action and race lies in the manner in which black English has developed and is maintained as a unique speech system. The speech patterns of black Americans developed from an African linguistic and cultural base which was transformed by their experience in the United States, and reinforced and sustained by racial oppression and segregation, on the one hand, and by the response to racism, in the form of ethnic solidarity, on the other. The institutionalization of racism in America, through both *de facto* and *de jure* mechanisms, has meant exclusion of blacks from participation in the dominant culture, and has resulted in the continuance of two separate societies and two distinct, if not entirely separate, languages.

Blacks, however, have been differentially affected by white racism, and that has created class distinctions within the black community. Differing degrees of competence in standard English is one way these distinctions are manifest. Not all black children suffer from language barriers. Indeed, at King, the only black children having great difficulty were those from the Green Road Housing Project, who were both black and poor. The other black children attending King were from middle-class, professional families. Though these middle-class children spoke black English, they were also competent in standard English: they were skilled at code-switching and, hence, "bilingual." This is precisely the case among those blacks who have successfully negotiated the educational system and become middle class. Thus, it may be said that a black speaker's ability to code-switch is a behavioral manifestation of the interaction of race and class. Not being adequate code-switchers, the economically deprived plaintiff children experienced language-based problems in school. The language barriers for the Green Road children were thereby directly related to racial, as well as economic discrimination, but Joiner had ruled out the latter as a consideration.

Put more succinctly, negative language attitudes are directed toward the "blackness" of black English; the attitudes and the language itself are the consequences of the historical operations of racism in the United States. To the extent that the district failed to take appropriate action, such failure was connected to the race of the plaintiff children by virtue of their speaking black English, and the barriers created are therefore directly related to race. This, in turn, obligates the district to take appropriate action under the Equal Educational Opportunity Act of 1974 to eliminate the discrimination. Such action would consist of an educational plan designed to help teachers identify black-English speakers to help these children learn to read standard English.

The educational plan approved by Joiner, however, falls far short of the mark. As Attorney Kenneth Lewis noted, the plan "amounts to no more than yet another shot in the arm of teacher inservice programs [which] only travels halfway to a full solution to overcome language barriers impeding learning" (Lewis 1980). Clearly, a teacher inservice program is desirable and needed to alter teacher attitudes toward black English. Programs of this nature are not uncommon, particularly among school districts undergoing desegregation. Yet such programs are pitifully inadequate as a remedy to eliminate barriers to equal educational opportunity. Inservice training should simply be a component of a more comprehensive education remediation plan that would have as its central theme the teaching of reading and other communication skills. In sum, with no assessment of teacher behavior and actual classroom practice, the Ann Arbor approach is premised on the theory that benefits will accrue to the children after teachers are properly trained and thereby develop new attitudes. This remedy is too slow and too limited for the immediate educational crisis facing poor black youth in schools in the United States.

Based on the procedural strategy and the outcome of *King,* there are several additional approaches to the formulation of public policy that would address this crisis. First, judicial processes are critical in shaping educational policy and practice. Joiner was reluctant to tread these waters, and partly for that reason. Ann Arbor's education plan is woefully inadequate. Despite the lament that the courts are too involved in the management of social institutions, the judiciary can promote the just and humane administration of large social bureaucracies that seem incapable of righting themselves. As the custodian and protector of values, the judiciary should be more involved, not less, in social management. The public school, more so than any other institution, directly involves and affects every citizen of the United States. Education is everybody's business— including the judge's.

Second, we need a school effectiveness policy monitored and enforced by the courts and by appropriate citizens' bodies. Accountability must be demanded and delivered. Race and class cannot be used to justify miseducation. There is now an overwhelming body of data to demonstrate that, as Edmonds put it, "some schools work, and more can" (1979). Further, schools must be willing to adopt policies to overcome cultural and economic handicaps. This is a basis for future litigation since this claim was dismissed early on in *King*. An argument could be made that culture and class are handicaps just as are physical infirmities. As Kaimowitz (1981) later put it, "Economic, social, and cultural factors, as well as the racial factors . . . and the language factor, must be taken into account."

Third, there should be a national moratorium on tests—standardized, employment, and other such assessment instruments. All evidence points to the cultural and linguistic biases of such tests. *King*, along with *Larry P. v. Riles* No. C-712270 RFP (N.C. Cal. October 1979), attests to the inadequacy of tests for evaluating and diagnosing black children. These rulings reinforce the call for such a moratorium, already issued by a number of professional and concerned citizens' groups.

Fourth, one outcome of Joiner's ruling was clearly to give legalistic legitimacy to a speech form spoken at times by 80–90 percent of the black community in the United States (Dillard 1972; Smitherman 1977). As a corollary to *King* and coincident with the goals of the Bilingual Education Act, we need a national public policy on language that asserts the legitimacy of languages and dialects other than standard English. As recommended by the Task Force on Language Policy and National Development (in press), a parallel tactic might be the development of awareness campaigns on black English conducted in communities throughout the country.

Fifth, just as *King* reaffirms the viability and appropriateness of black English, it also demands that students gain competence in standard English. As sociolinguists have maintained, effective speakers, writers, and readers have a highly developed level of communicative competence, that is, using language forms in socially appropriate contexts. Such competence allows one to manipulate a variety of speech forms, adapted to various audiences, media of communication, intention, and other social variables. There is not simply one form of standard English, but varieties of standard English—formal, informal, and colloquial. Similarly, there are varieties of black English conducive to communicating in various social situations; black church language, proverbs, and street raps are examples. The recognition of black English alongside standard English reinforces the call for a curriculum policy that would mandate and facilitate teaching of communicative competence.

Sixth, because of the distortions of *King* perpetrated by the media, a potential weapon for black child advocacy has been grossly misunderstood. There were over three hundred newspaper and magazine articles and editorials (Bailey 1981) along with numerous television and radio broadcasts. Yet media sensationalism prevented the issues from being clearly and fully delineated. There was a persistent attempt to discredit the plaintiffs' mothers and to exonerate the school district, and survey results indicate that many people received negative views of black English from media coverage of *King* (Wilks 1981). Black and other nonmainstream communities have traditionally been the victims of biased media coverage. Communities must rally to force the media to adhere to a standard of ethics and to establish media clearinghouses to counter the dissemination of inaccurate and distorted information (Task Force on Media and Information Dissemination 1981).

Seventh, in some circles it has become fashionable to disavow the need for and utility of academic research. *King,* however, reaffirms the need for more, not less, research, of the kind that is responsive to the needs of black and other similarly dispossessed communities. Joiner also commented in his ruling on the value of research in informing the court (473 F. Supp. 1371, E.D. Mich. 1979).

He noted the efficacy of the personal appearance and involvement of experts as advocates for the children. Research efforts of this kind should be encouraged, and blacks should be involved from the beginning. Creative ways must be found to encourage the allocation of funds for research on black children and youth. At the very least, blacks should vigorously monitor all such research to insure that only projects with policy implications for improving the education of black children and youth receive top priority.

To complete our analysis of *King,* I shall briefly examine the issues of black double-consciousness and class contradictions which were raised during the legal proceedings. "Double-consciousness" was first described by Du Bois when he said:

> After the Egyptian and Indian, the Greek and Roman, the Teuton and Mongolian, the Negro is a sort of seventh son, born with a veil, and gifted with second-sight in this American world—a world which yields him no true self-consciousness, but only lets him see himself through the revelation of the other world. It is a peculiar sensation, this double-consciousness, this sense of always looking at one's self through the eyes of others. . . . One ever feels his twoness—an American, a Negro: two souls, two

warring ideals in one dark body. . . . The history of the American Negro is the history of the strife—this longing to attain self-conscious manhood, to merge his double self into a better and truer self. In this merging, he wishes neither of the older selves to be lost (Du Bois 1903/1961, 44).

With respect to black speech, I describe the manifestation of double-consciousness in language as "linguistic push-pull": the push toward Americanization of black English counterbalanced by the pull of its Africanization (Smitherman 1977). Both linguistic forms have been necessary for black survival in white America—standard English in attempts to gain access to the social and economic mainstream, black English for community solidarity, deception, and "puttin on ole massa." In "If Black English Isn't a Language, Then Tell Me What Is?" (*New York Times* July 29, 1979), written shortly after the *King* trial, Baldwin spoke eloquently of the role of black English in the black experience: "There was a moment, in time, and in this place, when my brother, or my mother, or my father, or my sister, had to convey to me, for example, the danger in which I was standing from the white man standing just behind me, and to convey this with a speed, and in a language, that the white man could not possibly understand, and that, indeed, he cannot understand, until today."

With the beginnings of education for blacks in the late nineteenth century, linguistic push-pull became more pervasive in the Afro-American community. As Woodson (1936/1969) tells us, that education has always been away from—not toward—black culture, language, and community. Relating his critique specifically to language, Woodson (1933/1969) noted that: "In the study of language in school, pupils were made to scoff at the Negro dialect as some peculiar possession of the Negro which they should despise rather than directed to study the background of this language as a broken down African tongue—in short to understand their own linguistic history, which is certainly more important for them than the study of French Phonetics, or Historical Spanish Grammar" (1933/1969, 19).

This ambivalence about a dimension of blackness so close to personal identity explains the mixed reactions of blacks to *King*. Despite the decidedly forward advancement in black pride during the 1960s, there continues to be a lingering self-consciousness about the value of black culture and black language, even among those who speak it most frequently and who, in their more culturally chauvinistic moments, decry "nigguhs who talk all proper and white."

This linguistic push-pull also serves to account, in part, for the paucity of research on black speech by contemporary black scholars. Seeing the value and distinctive African character of black English, white researchers have produced a sizable body of data attesting to the systematicity, use, and functions of black English. Not all of this research has been to our betterment. In particular, blacks have decried treatments such as Folb's *Runnin' Down Some Lines* (1980) and Jackson's *Get Your Ass in the Water and Swim Like Me* (1974) because they focus on the sensational words and phrases in black speech. Black language is, after all, more than "jive-ass" lingo of ghetto teenagers or the "pussy-coppin" raps of prisoners. The "more than" awaits the treatment of black scholars who can continue in the black intellectual tradition of Frederick Douglass, W. E. B. Du Bois, Carter G. Woodson, and Lorenzo Turner. All wrote positively about— and in Turner's case, thoroughly analyzed—black English long before post-1960 white scholars. In fact, Turner's *Africanisms in the Gullah Dialect* (1949) was quoted, while still in manuscript form, by white anthropologist Herskovits in *Myth of the Negro Past* (1941), surely one of the rare instances in which a white scholar acknowledges an intellectual debt to a black scholar.

Black teachers and educators are often more negative toward black English-speaking children than are white educators. This reaction of educators and other black leaders to *King* serves to remind the black community that our class contradictions were never resolved in the 1960s era of black progress ("What go round come round"). Briefly, their fear is that black speech will prevent blacks from getting a share of the rapidly shrinking pie—a threat, as Baldwin indicated in his keynote speech to the National Invitational Symposium on Black English and the Education of Black Children and Youth, that is no longer in the power of the United States to give, as the Third World continues to cut off America's historically free and ready access to resources (Baldwin 1981). Several editorials by noted black columnist Rowan (*Detroit News,* July 11, 1979) are representative of the disturbing reaction of many members of the black middle class. Stating that *King* was one of the "silliest and potentially most destructive" cases to affect the education of black children, he argued that this approach would "consign millions of ghetto children to a linguistic separation [as if it doesn't already exist!] which would guarantee that they will never make it in the larger U.S. society." Note that it is not high unemployment, or the shifting balance in world economic power, or the crises caused by a highly advanced, technological capitalist society in the United States but "linguistic separation," mind you, that will keep black children and youth from making it in the United States.

The language, education, and other public policies typically proposed by black middle-class leadership will not serve the needs of the black underclass. Their programs only ensure that a few blacks slide past the gatekeepers. Limited by an analysis based solely on race, without considering issues of class, they are unable to propose solutions that address the broader structural crises that affect all groups in United States society, but affect poor blacks with disproportionate severity. While *King* reminds us that standard English is a *sine qua non* of survival in our complex society, the harsh reality is that if all blacks commanded the language of textbooks and technocracy, the system, as it is presently constructed, could not accommodate all of us. Further, if our society could solve the problem of black unemployment—and that's a big if—it would only shift the burden to some other group. It would do nothing to address the fundamental cause of unemployment.

There are no spoils to the victors in *King*. Though the ruling set a legal precedent establishing that black English falls within the parameters of the statutory language of 1703(f), it is an acknowledged reformist strategy. But it is a tool now available to other communities for manipulating the legal system to obtain a measure of redress from our continuing oppression.

The fate of black children as victims of miseducation continues to be the bottom line in the "Black English Case." *King* gives us yet another weapon in our struggle to save the children and develop future leadership. The case began with a claim of institutional mismanagement of education for children from the Green Road Housing Project. It ended with a claim of institutional mismanagement of the children's language. For those who know that language is identity, the issue is the same: *the children's language is them is they mommas and kinfolk and community and black culture and the black experience made manifest in verbal form.*

REFERENCES

Bailey, R. 1981. "Press Coverage of the Black English Case." In Geneva Smitherman, ed. *Black English and the Education of Black Children and Youth: Proceedings of the National Invitational Symposium on the King Decision.* Detroit: Center for Black Studies, Wayne State University.

Baldwin, J. 1981. "Black English: A Dishonest Argument." In Geneva Smitherman, ed. *Black English and the Education of Black Children and Youth: Proceedings of the National Invitational Symposium on the King Decision,* edited by Geneva Smitherman. Detroit: Center for Black Studies, Wayne State University.

Bereiter, C., and S. Engelmann. 1966. *Teaching Disadvantaged Children in the Preschool.* Englewood Cliffs, N.J.: Prentice-Hall.

Bliss, L., and D. Allen. 1978. Language Screening and Assessment Test for Preschool Children of Diverse Backgrounds. (Interim report to National Institute of Health. Research Project NIH-NINCDS-76-03) Detroit: Wayne State University.

Brookover, W. B., and C. Beady. 1978. *School Social Climate and Student Achievement.* New York: Praeger.

Chomsky, Noam. 1966. *Cartesian Linguistics.* New York: HarperCollins.

———. 1972. *Language and Mind.* New York: Harcourt Brace Jovanovich.

Cooper, G. 1980. "Black Language and Holistic Cognitive Style." Paper presented at the Association for the Study of Afro-American Life and History Conference, New Orleans, October.

Dalby, David. 1969. *Black through White: Patterns of Communication in Africa and the New World.* Bloomington: Indiana University Press.

———. 1972. "The African Element in American English." In T. Cochman, ed. *Rappin' and Stylin' Out: Communication in Urban Black America.* Urbana, IL: University of Illinois Press.

Deutsch, M. 1963. "The Disadvantaged Child and the Learning Process." In A. Passow, ed. *Education in Depressed Areas.* New York: Columbia University Press.

Dillard, J. L. 1972. *Black English: Its History and Usage.* New York: Random House.

———. 1977. *Lexicon of Black English.* New York: Seabury.

Du Bois, W. E. B. 1903. *The Souls of Black Folk.* Chicago: A. C. McClurg. Reprint. New York: Fawcett, 1961.

Edmonds, Ronald, and J. R. Fredericksen. 1978. "Search for Effective Schools: The Identification and Analysis of City Schools That Are Instructionally Effective for Poor Children." Cambridge, MA: Center for Urban Studies, Harvard University. Photocopy.

Edmonds, R. 1981. "Educational Policy and the Urban Poor: Search for Effective Schools." In Geneva Smitherman, ed. *Black English and the Education of Black Children and Youth: Proceedings of the National Invitational Symposium on the King Decision.* Detroit: Center for Black Studies, Wayne State University.

———. 1979. "Some Schools Work and More Can." *Social Policy* 9: 28–32.

Esselman, B. 1978. "An Investigation of Third and Fourth Grade Reading Teachers' Perceptions as Related to Those Who Speak Black Dialect in the School District of the City of Highland Park, Michigan." (Ph.D. diss., Wayne State University). *Dissertation Abstracts International* 39: 1320A.

Fasold, Ralph W., and Roger Shuy, eds. 1970. *Teaching Standard English in the Inner City.* Washington, DC: Center for Applied Linguistics.

Folb, Edith A. 1980. *Runnin' Down Some Lines.* Cambridge, MA: Harvard University Press.

Green, R. L. 1975. "Tips on Educational Testing: What Teachers and Parents Should Know." *Phi Delta Kappan* (October): 89–93.

Herskovits, M. 1941. *Myth of the Negro Past.* Boston: Beacon Press.

Hymes, D. 1974. *Foundations in Sociolinguistics.* Philadelphia: University of Pennsylvania Press.

Jackson, B. 1974. *Get Your Ass in the Water and Swim Like Me.* Cambridge, MA: Harvard University Press.

Kaimowitz, G. 1981. "Commentary on the *King* Case." In Geneva Smitherman, ed. *Black English and the Education of Black Children and Youth: Proceedings of the National Invitational Symposium on the King Decision.* Detroit: Center for Black Studies, Wayne State University.

Labov, W. 1971. "The Notion of Systems." In D. Hymes, ed. *Pidginization and Creolization of Languages.* New York: Cambridge University Press.

Lewis, Kenneth. 1980. "Analysis of the *King* Case." Detroit. Photocopy.

Major, Clarence. 1970. *Dictionary of Afro-American Slang.* New York: International Publishers.

Pooley, Robert C. 1969. "The Oral Usage of English Teachers." In V. McDavid, ed. *Language and Teaching: Essays in Honor of W. Wilbur Hatfield.* Chicago: Chicago State College.

———. 1974. *The Teaching of English Usage.* Urbana, IL: National Council of Teachers of English.

Shuy, Roger, and Ralph W. Fasold. 1973. *Language Attitudes: Current Trends and Prospects.* Washington, DC: Georgetown University Press.

Simpkins, G. 1976. "Cross-Cultural Approach to Reading." (Ph.D. diss., University of Massachusetts-Amherst) *Dissertation Abstracts International* 37: 5669A.

Simpkins, Gary, G. Holt, and C. Simpkins. 1976. *Bridge: A Cross-Culture Reading Program.* Boston: Houghton Mifflin.

Smitherman, Geneva. 1975. "Black Language Test." Detroit: Center for Black Studies, Wayne State University. Photocopy.

————. 1977. *Talkin and Testifyin: The Language of Black America.* Boston: Houghton Mifflin.

————. 1980. "White English in Blackface, or Who Do I Be?" In L. Michaels and C. Ricks, eds. *The State of the Language.* Berkeley and Los Angeles: University of California Press.

————. 1981. *Black English and the Education of Black Children and Youth: Proceedings of the National Invitational Symposium on the King Decision.* Detroit: Center for Black Studies, Wayne State University.

Taylor, O. 1971. "Recent Developments in Sociolinguistics: Some Implications for ASHA." *American Speech and Hearing Association Journal* 13: 340–347. Task Force on Language Policy and National Development. In Geneva Smitherman, ed. *Black English and the Education of Black Children and Youth: Proceedings of the National Invitational Symposium on the King Decision.* Detroit: Center for Black Studies, Wayne State University, 1981.

Turner, Lorenzo Dow. 1949. *Africanisms in the Gullah Dialect.* Chicago: University of Chicago Press.

Valdman, A. 1977. *Creole and Pidgin Linguistics.* Bloomington, IN: University of Indiana Press.

Weber, G. 1971. *Inner-City Children Can be Taught to Read: Four Successful Schools.* Washington, DC: Council for Basic Education.

Weinreich, M. 1931. "Tsveyshprakhikayt: Mutershpracht un tsveyte shprakh." *Yivo-Bleter* 1: 301–316.

Weinrich, U. 1963. *Languages in Contact.* The Hague, Netherlands: Mouton.

Wilks, M. 1981. "Black English and the Media." In Geneva Smitherman, ed. *Black English and the Education of Black Children and Youth: Proceedings of the National Invitational Symposium on the King Decision.* Detroit: Center for Black Studies, Wayne State University.

Williams, F., J. Whitehead, and L. Miller. 1971. *Attitudinal Correlates of Children's Speech Characteristics.* Austin: Center for Communication Research, University of Texas.

Williams, R. L. 1972. *The BITCH 100: A Culture-Specific Test.* St. Louis: Washington University.

Williams, R. L., L. W. Rivers, and M. Brantley. 1975. "The Effects of Language on the Test Performance of Black Children; Developing Cultural Specific Assessment Devices: An Empirical Rationale; Disentangling the Confusion Surrounding Slang, Nonstandard English, Black English and Ebonics." In *Ebonics: The True Language of Black Folks.* R. Williams, ed. St. Louis: Institute of Black Studies.

Wilson, R. 1971. "A Comparison of Learning Styles in African Tribal Groups with Afro-American Learning Situations and the Channels of Cultural Connection: An Analysis of Documentary Material." (Ph.D. diss., Wayne State University). *Dissertation Abstracts International,* 32/5A: 2497.

Woodson, Carter G. 1933. *The Mis-Education of the American Negro.* New York: AMS Press. Reprint. Washington, DC: Associated Publishers, 1969.

————. 1936. "The Education of the American Negro." In Carter G. Woodson, ed. *The African Background Outlined or Handbook for the Study of the Negro.* Washington, DC: Negro Universities Press. Reprint. New York: New American Library, 1969.

Recognizing Black English
in the Classroom

William Labov

The Ann Arbor decision must be considered an important step in the effort to achieve racial integration of American society. In recognizing Black English as a linguistic system, Judge Charles Joiner, Jr. acted to bring teachers and Black children closer together, arguing that teachers should have a better knowledge of the resources children bring to school. He also brought together linguists and educators: an immediate consequence of the Ann Arbor decision is that linguists must do a better job of making their research findings available to those who need them. This presentation is intended as an effort to organize our present knowledge of Black English in a form that will be useful to designers of reading programs.[1]

Research on Black English was begun by Black scholars particularly conscious of Black people's African heritage and the resemblance between the language used in the Caribbean and the Black speech forms of the United States. Lorenzo Turner's research on the African elements in Gullah (1949) and Beryl Bailey's description of Jamaican Creole English (1966) provide an excellent foundation for the study of inner-city Black dialects. This type of research began in the mid 1960's, a time when violent protests throughout the country called attention to high levels of unemployment and a low degree of educational success in the cities. My own work in Harlem, funded by the Office of Education, was concerned with the issue of reading failure. The biracial team of researchers addressed two main questions:

1 How great were the difference between the linguistic systems used by Black and white youth in the inner-cities?

2 Do language differences contribute to the reading problems of Black children in inner-city schools?

If the Ann Arbor case had emerged at that time, the court would have found very little agreement among linguists. There were violent controversies between

---

[1]The analysis of Black English presented here rests on the work of many other people besides my own. The research in New York City was a joint effort, and I am greatly indebted to my colleagues Paul Cohen, Clarence Robins, and John Lewis at every stage of field work and analysis. The work of Walt Wolfram and Ralph Fasold forms an essential part of our present knowledge of Black English, though I have not provided all the references identifying their contributions. My debt to John Baugh, John Rickford, and other scholars from the Black community appears throughout: the most creative work of the last decade comes from participant-observers who have drawn upon their entire social experience to solve linguistic problems. Finally, I must acknowledge my debt to Beryl Bailey, William Stewart, and Joey Dillard, who never stopped insisting on the importance of parallels between Black English and the creoles of the Caribbean, until even the most backward members of the linguistic community were at last convinced, including myself.

traditional dialectologists and students of Caribbean creoles, particularly on the historical origins of the dialects spoken in the United States. The dialectologists argued that Blacks spoke regional dialects no different from white speakers of the same southern region. Those familiar with the creoles of the Caribbean argued that Black English was a creole language with an underlying structure very different from other dialects and quite similar to the Caribbean English-based creoles. Dialectologists traced features of Black English to British dialect patterns: creolists maintained that those features were derived from a general American creole with Caribbean roots and ultimately from African grammar and semantics.

On the second question, the causes of reading failure, there was even less agreement. Most psychologists endorsed the verbal deprivation theory: that the language of Black children was impoverished as a result of deficiencies in their early environment (Deutsch, Katz, & Jensen; 1968). An alternative view developed, partly as a result of the alleged failure of enrichment programs, that lack of educational success was attributable to genetic defects in certain children (Jensen, 1969). Linguists and anthropologists as a whole disagreed with both of these views. They argued that Black children had very rich verbal resources which remained untapped because of ignorance on the part of children and teachers.

One might have expected the Ann Arbor Black English trial to become a battleground for these opposing points of view. One would think that the defense could find psychologists and linguists who would argue that there was no such thing as Black English, or that it was only a regional dialect, or that it was just the bad English of non-standard speakers. But this did not happen. There were no witnesses for the defense. The plaintiffs presented Joiner with a consistent testimony that appeared to represent the consensus of all scholars involved in the study of Black English and its educational implications. Although there was disagreement, the defense attorneys, who did a tremendous amount of research on the question, could not find anyone who would support a significantly different position.

How did such a remarkable consensus come about? Three distinct streams of events leading to this result can be identified. First, having weighed the evidence advanced by the other side, linguists and dialectologists achieved a certain consensus by the time of the trial. Second, the existence of Black English became recognized as a social fact, partly through the legitimization of the Black experience and of the term *Black,* and partly through the publication of such books as Dillard's *Black English* (1972). Third, a new generation of young Black linguists entered the field in the 1970's: John Baugh, Mary Hoover, John Rickford, Milford Jeremiah, Jerrie Scott, Geneva Smitherman, Arthur Spears, Anna Vaughn-Cooke, and many others. Their research has deepened our knowledge of Black English and its educational implications. For all these reasons, the testimony given at the trial carried far more weight than if the proceedings had taken place ten years earlier.

Judge Joiner's summary of the evidence (1979) was a model of clarity in its treatment of the general character of Black English, the relationship between Black English and other kinds of English, and the historical origins of this language variant. He saw clearly that Black English is a distinct linguistic system but that it is not a foreign language, that it has many features in common with southern dialects since most Blacks lived in the South for several centuries, and that it has distinct marks of an Afro-Caribbean ancestry, reflecting the earlier origins of the Black community. Joiner concluded that the law must therefore recognize a distinct linguistic form historically derived, in part, from Black people's heritage of slavery and segregation.

Joiner was not as clear on the details of these linguistic differences, on how Black English interferes with reading, or on what can be done to overcome any such interference. The opinion lists the twelve features of Black English that figured most prominently in the testimony. As it now stands, this list is not likely to be very useful to teachers who want to know if the children in their school use Black English, or to curriculum writers who want to take it into account in building reading programs. Yet the testimony did include many of the elements that we need for these purposes. The aim of this paper is to recognize the descriptions of Black English presented at the trial into a form that will be more useful to teachers and educators.

With the trial over, Black English grammar is seldom discussed. A great deal of attention has been paid to the teachers' attitudes toward the use of Black English in their classrooms, and to children's attitudes toward the use of standard English. Judge Joiner himself concluded:

> If a barrier exists because of the language used by the children in this case, it exists not because the teachers and students cannot understand each other, but because in the process of attempting to teach the children how to speak standard English the students are made somehow to feel inferior and are thereby turned off from the learning process. (1979, p. 6)

This was not the trial's original orientation. At first the judge had ruled out consideration of cultural and political factors, and insisted on an exact description of the *linguistic* barriers in question.[2] My own testimony was accordingly aimed at the grammatical description of the language used by Ann Arbor Black children, showing that it was the same as the Black English vernacular used in New York, Washington, Chicago and Los Angeles. I then presented evidence showing structural interference with the use of the alphabet and other steps in reading.

---

[2]Because the Judge's preliminary intructions to the plaintiffs seemed to convey a very narrow notion of linguistic description, the plaintiffs did not include in their presentation the problem of barriers caused by differences in the use of language: the area named by Hymes the "ethnography of communication." It is likely that cultural and linguistic conflicts contribute not only to educational failure, but also to behavioral differences in areas such as ways of showing attention, of turn-taking, and of showing respect and deference to adults.

The defense lawyers appeared to have read most of my written work, including unpublished galleys. They asked how I could reconcile my testimony with the earlier conclusion (Labov, Cohen, Robins, & Lewis, 1968; Labov & Robins, 1969) that structural differences between Black English and standard English could not in themselves account for massive reading failure. We had concluded that the principle problem was a cultural and political conflict in the classroom and that Black English had become a symbol of this conflict.

I responded to the defense's query with three main points. First, we know more about the structural differences between Black English and standard American English than we did ten years ago due largely to research conducted by Black linguists in the 1970's. Second, there is no reason to think that educational programs informed by popular attitudes alone can make major improvements in the teaching of reading. Teachers need to incorporate concrete information on the features of Black English into their daily lesson plans. Finally, the contradiction is only apparent since negative attitudes can be changed by providing people with scientific evidence of the language's validity.

Judge Joiner's opinion indicates that he may not have accepted this point of view. He did accept an educational program, initiated by the Ann Arbor Board of Education, designed to change general attitudes. No reading curriculum has yet been established using information on Black English.[3]

The gap between general discussion and concrete practice has not gone unnoticed. At a symposium on the outcome of the trial held in February, 1980, Benjamin Alexander, President of Chicago State University, argued that Black English was obviously a myth, since no one had been able to describe it to his satisfaction. At the conference held by the NIE in June, 1980, a teacher at the King School agreed that her attitude towards Black English may have been improved by the new training program, but said that she had not yet had instruction on what to do when faced with a child who had not learned to read.

This paper will apply our present linguistic knowledge to the teaching of reading. It will present not merely a list of Black English features, but a coherent view of its linguistic system that is accessible to non-linguists. I will then indicate how this system may interfere with the business of learning to read standard English, and where in a reading method this information may be taken into account.

---

[3]Only one educational program was presented by the plaintiffs to show how knowledge of Black language and culture could be used in reading programs: BRIDGE, written by Gary Simpkins, Grace Holt, and Charlotte Simkins, and published by Houghton Mifflin. Simpkins testified on the cognitive difficulties of Black youth who had to translate the standard English semantic system into their own framework as well as decode the alphabet. BRIDGE avoids this problem by a smooth transition between tapes and reading texts in BEV, an intermediate form, and standard English. The content draws on Black culture and folklore throughout. BRIDGE is written for adolescent youth who are returning to the problem of learning to read, while the focus in the Ann Arbor Black English case was more on younger children in their first approach to reading. The same general problems, however, are addressed in both.

1. TERMINOLOGY

Throughout the trial, the term "Black English" was used to refer to the vernacular system that was the home language of children living in the Green Road housing project, and to the system used by the majority of American Black people in their casual conversation (Joiner, 1979, p. 12). It is normally used in quotes by the judge, who notes at the outset two equivalent terms: "Black vernacular" and "Black dialect." *Black English* will undoubtedly remain the most commonly used term following Dillard's book (1972) of that title.

For more precise discussions, I prefer to apply the term *Black English* to the entire range of linguistic forms used by Black Americans. The term *Black English Vernacular* or BEV will be used to refer to the grammar used by children growing up in the Black community and by adults in the most intimate in-group settings.[4] *Standard Black English* refers to the speech forms used by educated Black speakers in formal and public situations. It contains phonological variation from standard forms, but the same standard English syntax. There are, of course, many intermediate forms, but no intermediate system has been identified clearly enough to deserve a separate name:

BLACK ENGLISH

Standard Black English  Black English Vernacular
[SBE]   [BEV]

This paper focuses on the Black English Vernacular, since it is the home language in the Ann Arbor case, and the linguistic system the great majority of Black children bring to their first reading experiences. This vernacular is not known perfectly to six- or seven-year-olds; there is considerable language learning that continues into late adolescence (Labov et al., 1968). Furthermore, there are many individuals in the Black community who are influenced by other dialects as they grow up. The most consistent vernacular is found among adolescents who are centrally located in their peer groups (Labov, 1972, Ch. 7) or among adults who live and work within the Black community (Baugh, 1979). It is not always possible for teachers to recognize these differences in social and linguistic status, with the result that classroom observations are often blurred (Garvey & McFarlane, 1968).

In this discussion, I will present some of the features that distinguish BEV from intermediate forms. Even though studies show that inner-city teachers can assume that the majority of their Black students participate in the BEV linguistic and cultural system, and that their approach to reading is profoundly influenced

---

[4]Research in the 1960's was concentrated primarily among Black youth in the inner cities, and it is their use of BEV that is reported. Baugh's research in Pacoima, California (1979) demonstrated that adults who lived and worked in the Black community used exactly the same linguistic system in peer group and family contexts.

by it, it is important that teachers recognize intermediate forms. I will also suggest a number of strategies for applying our knowledge of BEV to the teaching of reading: these will apply equally well to children who use BEV in its most consistent form and those whose system is shifted some distance towards classroom English.

Educators are often presented with stereotypic descriptions of BEV far-removed from linguistic systems used in everyday life. Media coverage of the Ann Arbor Black English case described BEV with examples never used by anyone anywhere, such as, "He am so big an cause he so, he think everybody do what him say" (*U.S. News & World Report,* 3/31/80, p. 64).[5] More often, educators are exposed to stereotypes that preserve only those forms of BEV that most differ from classroom English, eliminating all variation as the result of "borrowing" or "code-switching." This is sometimes a hold-over from the earlier days of controversy, when creolists were interested only in isolating those forms that resembled the Caribbean creoles. Sometimes these stereotypes are proffered by people who have never studied tape recordings of the language as it is spoken. But in any case, BEV is a full-fledged linguistic system, with the range of inherent variation that all such systems have. BEV has some obligatory rules where other dialects have optional rules, some variable rules where the others have obligatory ones, and some rules that don't exist in any other dialects.

Many educators have borrowed Robert L. Williams' term "Ebonics" to refer to both the linguistic and cultural systems particular to Black Americans. The term is not widely used by linguists, but discussions of Ebonics programs refer to many of the linguistic features presented at the Black English trial. There is considerable convergence between proponents of Ebonics and those who prefer the concepts Black English and Black English vernacular.

Finally a word must be said about the question of *language* vs. *dialect.* "Is BEV a separate language?" The answer is that linguistics does not make a technical distinction between languages and dialects; the difference is more political than linguistic. It is therefore factually correct to say that Black people have a language of their own. But if it appears that BEV is closer to classroom English than, say, Hawaiian creole English or Jamaican English, then I would prefer to say that BEV differs much more from regional dialects of the North than from Hawaiian creole English or Jamaican English, and in its tense and aspect system, is quite distinct from the dialects spoken by white Southerners.

2. THE TENSE AND ASPECT SYSTEM OF BEV

Much of the Ann Arbor Black English trial testimony made reference to the *aspect* system of BEV, and newspaper accounts have usually featured one exam-

---

[5]One exception to this was the series of newspaper stories generated by Geneva Smitherman in Detroit before the trial. These included accurate descriptions of the BEV tense and aspect system.

ple of habitual *be,* as in *She be sick.* This is the most prominent and the most frequent of the BEV aspects: Geneva Smitherman's texts of conversations with the Green Road children recorded seventeen examples of habitual *be.* Tito B. alone used the aspect eight times over the course of a short interview. His statement, *When it be raining, I be taking it to school* is a good example of the habitual *be.*

Habitual *be* is especially important because it does not exist in any other American dialect.[6] It also exemplifies the positive side of BEV grammar. Its survival in the classroom demonstrates better than any other aspect how BEV makes useful distinctions that aren't made as easily in classroom English. Tito B.'s sentence (1) cannot be accurately translated as (2), but requires the expanded version (3) to convey the same meaning in classroom style:

1 They be hitting on peoples.
2 They are hitting people.
3 They go around hitting people all the time.

Of all linguistic categories, the concept of *aspect* is the hardest to understand, and linguists disagree more about aspect than anything else. The meaning of *tense* is easier to comprehend for it situates an event at a point in time. Aspect communicates the *shape* of the event in time: Did it happen all at once (punctual), at many separate times (iterative or habitual), or was it spread out in time (durative)? Was it just beginning (inceptive) or was it finished and done with (perfective)? These are not clear and distinct ideas, but rather (as the term "aspect" implies) they represent ways of looking at things. Aspect is seldom found in pure form; it is often combined with questions of causation (is the event relevant to the present?) and reality (was it really so?). Finally, it is often combined with tense, so that we speak of a "tense-aspect system." Given all these complications, it isn't surprising that there is so little agreement on the meaning of general English aspects. There are almost as many theories to explain the contrast of (4) and (5) as there are linguists to argue about them.

4 They hit people.
5 They have hit people.

Since there is so little agreement about this topic in other languages, we should avoid dogmatism about the meanings of BEV aspects.

Before considering the meanings, we should look at the forms that these meanings hang on. Aspect can be expressed by independent adverbs like *already* or *really,* but the grammatical system we are interested in depends on short, one-syllable words placed before the verb. They usually don't carry stress, and as

---

[6]Rickford (1974) shows how the *doz be* forms of Gullah shift gradually to the invariant *be,* with the same "habitual meaning," responding to the overt stigmatization of the *doz.* He considers an alternative origin in the Anglo-Irish *does be,* but rejects this since Anglo-Irish dialects do not generally delete the first word.

will be shown, in BEV the tendency for unstressed words to wear down or even disappear in speech is even greater than in other dialects. This tendency is triggered by the reduction of a short vowel in these monosyllables (*is, was, had, will,* etc.) to the obscure shwa. This reduction does not occur if the vowel is long. It is no accident that the BEV tense and aspect system is built on three words with long vowels: *be, do,* and *go.* In building on these three root words, BEV makes use of a single ending, the one inflection that does not tend to disappear in spontaneous speech. In other dialects, these auxiliary words preceding the verb are often reduced to single consonants like the future *'ll,* the present *'s* or *'re,* the past perfect or conditional *'d* or the present perfect *'ve.* In BEV, these single consonants /l,s,z,r,d,v/ are more often missing than present. But final /n/ does not disappear entirely: if it is not heard as a consonant, it is heard as a nasal quality of the preceding vowel. The basic BEV aspect system is made up of six words:

be	do	go
been	done	gon'

Notice that although the vowel quality changes when we add the *-n,* it does not disappear even in fast speech.

The three root words carry the same basic meanings as other dialects of English. *Be* refers to existence, *do* to action, and *go* to movement. But in the auxiliary, they have become specialized: *be,* as we have seen, indicates a special kind of habitual or repeated state; *do* has lost its content, and is used to emphasize other actions or carry the negative particle *n't,* as in other dialects; and *go* takes on a sense of movement towards confrontation, as in the standard English *go and.*

When we add the *n,* a new set of meanings emerge that move the action away from the immediate present. *Be + n* has developed a complex meaning in BEV unknown in any other dialect or language.[7]

6 I *been* know your name.

7 I *been* own that coat.

In psychological terms, the speaker in example (6) is saying that he or she first got to know the other person's name, and in example (7) that he or she got the coat a long time ago. Both speakers stress that their respective situations remain true right up to the present.

When *n* is added to *do,* the meaning is *perfective:* the event referred to is completely and recently done, or really and truly done:

---

[7] The *been* with this meaning is always stressed and shows a low-pitch accent. Rickford (1975) reports a series of experiments showing dramatic differences in the interpretation of the sentence "She *been* married." Ninety-two percent of his Black subjects answered "yes" to the question, "Is she still married?" and only 32 percent of the whites.

8 You don't have it 'cause you done used it in your younger age.
9 I done forgot my hat! I done forgot my hat!

(Labov et al., 1968, p. 265)

The addition of *n* to *go* produces the future, as in many other dialects. In the following example, the contrast between *done* and *gone* is particularly clear.

10 After you knock the guy down, he done got the works.
11 You know he gon' try to sneak you.

(Labov et al., 1968, p. 265)

The richness of the BEV tense and aspect system is most clearly apparent when we look at combinations of these elements. To begin with, *be* is combined with *done* to yield *be done,* as in:

12 I'll be done put—struck so many holes in him he'll wish he wouldna said it.

(Labov et al., 1968, p. 266)

This combination is normally translated as a future perfect, equivalent to *will have* (and is often preceded by *'ll*). But there are sentences where this translation cannot be made and where in fact there is no straightforward translation into other dialects:

13 I'll be done killed that dude if he lays a hand on my child again.

(Baugh, 1979, p. 154)

What is the speaker's meaning? The statement was made with utmost seriousness by a man who had just witnessed his son being manhandled by a swimming pool aide. Normally, the English future perfect is the future form of the present perfect: it refers to the relevance of some future event for something else to follow. This is true of (12): the effect of sticking so many holes in the other person is that he will regret what he did. But in (13), we see a true perfect: the *be done* is attached to the result of the event. Instead of translating (13) into the nonsensical,

14 I will have killed that dude if he lays a hand on my child again.

we would have to translate the perfective sense as something like "I will really and truly have to kill. . . ." In trying to understand the cognitive differences between BEV and other dialects, considerable attention must be given to sentences like (13) which have no direct translation.

It almost must be stressed that *done* is combined with *been* in a variety of ways to express events that have been completely accomplished in the past and are separated from the present.

A final use of the *n* suffix is the most familiar: it is in the progressive aspect that BEV shares with all other dialects of English. Here the *n* is usually combined with a short vowel, and variably with various forms of the verb to *be*, including the invariant *be* meaning "habitual." The meaning of *He's workin'* as opposed to *he works* is the same as in other dialects: it is a "durative," referring to extended activity that is actually carried out, usually simultaneously with some other event. With the habitual *be* in *he be workin'*, the progressive is freed from association with any particular time. BEV speakers rarely use the *-ing* and use *in'* close to 100 percent of the time. The *-ing* appears primarily in writing and cannot be really considered a part of the vernacular language.

This symmetrical system of *do, be, go,* plus *n* is not all there is to the BEV tense and aspect system. The past tense *-ed* is firmly entrenched in the underlying grammar, though it is so often deleted after consonants that some speakers have trouble identifying it on the printed page (see sec. 3). In the auxiliary *had,* the final *d* appears again as a past tense marker. It is acquired early and is often used as the past perfect marker, meaning as in standard English, "occurred before the last event mentioned," and to denote other past tense meanings as well. In addition to *be,* there is an auxiliary *steady,* which is often combined with *be:*

15 Them fools steady hustlin' everybody they see.
16 Her mouth is steady runnin.'
17 Ricky Bell be steady steppin' in them number nines.

(Baugh, 1980)

Though *be* refers to habitual action, *steady* refers to much more. Baugh defines its scope as covering actions that are "persistent, consistent and continuous." In other words, *steady* has a lawful character: whenever this event could take place, it did.

We should also note the alternative form of the future:

18 I'm a do it.

This form is found only in BEV and apparently is a semantic equivalent of *gon'.* Fickett (1970) has argued that the *I'ma* form (which occurs only with the first person singular) is semantically distinct from *gon'* and it means "immediate future." The evidence is not all in on this: it is one of the many areas in the semantics of BEV that needs further work.

A near neighbor of these aspects is a special BEV use of *come* as in

19 He come tellin' me I don't love my parents.

Spears (1980) demonstrates that this is a "camouflaged" modal. It often looks like the standard English *come*. But the BEV speaker can also say "He come comin . . ." or "He come goin' . . ." The camouflaged modal *come* is a member of the BEV grammatical system that signals moral indignation: "He had the nerve to present himself doing this."

There are many similarities between these BEV forms and grammatical forms found in other dialects, and in creoles of the Caribbean and the Pacific.[8] Most of the BEV meanings, however, are unique combinations of semantic elements. There is every reason to think that BEV, like all other living languages, continues to develop its resources and enrich the cognitive system of its speakers.

To sum up, we can present the special features of the BEV tense and aspect system as:

be	"habitual," applied to events that are generally so
been	"remote present perfect," conditions that were so a long time ago, and are still so
done	"perfective," events that are completely and/or really so
be done	"future perfective," events in the future that are completely, really so
been done	"past perfective," events in the past that are accomplished and really so
steady	"persistently, consistently, and continuously so"
gon'	"future and less really so"

The organization and symmetry of this system should now be evident. With the exceptions of the invariant *be* and *gon'*, these are seldom heard in the classroom and rarely in the Black English of radio and television. Even in intimate vernacular settings, many of them are rare: it is only when highly particular contexts arise that they are needed and used. If the tense and aspect system of BEV doesn't appear in the speech and writing of the classroom, how can it affect reading? The answer to this question will be easier if we look first at other features of BEV that have a more obvious connection with reading.

3. ENGLISH INFLECTIONS IN BEV

So far, we have looked at the special BEV system of conveying grammatical meaning by invariant words placed before the verb. Now we will look at the other end: how does BEV use the system of modifying meaning by putting inflections—usually single consonants—at the ends of words?

We have already noticed that many final consonants tend to disappear in BEV speech. This happens not only in the auxiliary, but at the ends of all words. The variable process of consonant deletion as it affects words and grammatical

---

[8]The perfective particle *done* is also used by white speakers throughout the Southern states. It remains to be shown whether the semantics of their use is the same as the semantics of the BEV *done*. The combination *done* is not used by white speakers.

endings (the plural, the possessive, the past tense) has been studied in some detail. BEV is often described as a series of absences; to most people it looks like an over-simplified language "without grammar." It is said that BEV has no plural, no past tense, and no possessive, and that these categories are foreign to Black children. But a careful examination reveals that this view is highly exaggerated.[9]

We can first observe that some English inflections are present *more* often in BEV than in other dialects. One of these is the plural. While standard English has no plural inflection in words like *deer, sheep,* and *fish,* the corresponding BEV plurals are regular: *deers, sheeps,* and *fishes.*[10] Another example is the absolute possessive, as in:

20 This is mines.

BEV has generalized the possessive inflection found in *John's, yours,* and *hers.*

The past tense category is also quite secure. BEV speakers use the strong verb forms *gave, told,* and *left,* in the same way as all other dialects. In fact, it is even more regular, since the historical present seems to be used less by BEV speakers than by others.

The problem with the past tense is related to regular verbs ending in *-ed,* where the signal of the past tense is confined to a single consonant, /t/ or /d/. This signal is sometimes present, sometimes absent. But we have ample evidence that it is firmly located in the underlying grammatical structure representing the linguistic knowledge of the speakers. First, it is always present more often that the /t/ or /d/ in consonant clusters that do not signal the past tense, like *fist* or *old.* Second, when *-ed* follows a /t/ or a /d/ as in *wanted,* and a vowel breaks up the cluster, the final *-ed* is always present. Third, the past tense *-ed* is dropped less often before a vowel, and more often in difficult consonantal combinations like *mixed batter.* Fourth, the *ed* never occurs where it is not wanted: we never find the past tense used for the present, as in *He walked home these days.* For these and many other reasons, it is certain that present-day BEV has the grammatical suffix *-ed* and speakers have knowledge of it that they can draw on in reading standard English primers.

The rate of deletion may be so high, however, that BEV speakers may not recognize the *-ed* on the printed page as a carrier past tense of meaning. To determine the presence of this ability, we devised reading tests including such sentences as:

21 Last month I read five books.
22 When he passed by, he read the poster.

---

[9]The plural [s] suffix is often absent from "nouns of measure" when they are preceded by a number: *three cent, five year,* and so on. This is not peculiar to BEV: many other dialects show more systematic use of this feature, such as the north of England dialect of Leeds.

[10]Jane Torrey (1972) found this in her research among second graders in Harlem.

The task here is to transfer the past tense signal in the first half of the sentence to the unique homograph *read,* which demonstrates the form of the vowel, /riyd/ vs. /red/, whether the reader had the past tense in mind. For BEV speakers who had reached the fourth or fifth grade reading level, there was almost 100 percent success in transferring the past tense meaning from the adverb *last month;* but with the past tense *-ed* in *passed,* the results were not much better than chance (Labov, 1972, p. 30ff).

The case of the auxiliary and verb *to be* is parallel. The finite forms *is* and *are* are sometimes present in their full form, sometimes in contracted form, and sometimes entirely missing. There is now ample evidence indicating that in present-day BEV, the dropping of the copula is simply an extension of the contraction process found in other dialects and in BEV (Labov, 1972, Ch. 3). Here, too, the full verb forms are available and are freely used by BEV speakers; in fact, young children use more full forms than adults. It is the contracted forms, or single consonants fused with the preceding word, that can cause problems. Young children find it very hard to connect chains like these:

$$\text{/ay aem/} \longleftrightarrow \text{/ay am/} \longleftrightarrow \text{/aym/} \longleftrightarrow \text{/ay/}$$

Several investigators have found that children in the second grade lack the ability to analyze *I'm* into *I am,* though all the facts surrounding them would suggest that connection.[11] Many BEV speakers of this age will respond:

23 You're not George Baker!

   Yes I'm am!

Finally we come to the class of English inflections representing the maximum distance between BEV and classroom English. Although the third singular *-s* of *he works hard* is occasionally present in the speech and writing of BEV speakers, studies show that it is not present in the underlying linguistic knowledge that children bring to school. For each of the four points raised in the above discussion of *-ed,* the answers are the opposite for third singular *-s*. There is no general process of dropping final *s* in other words. It does not appear more often after /s/ or /z/, when a vowel appears between the stem and the consonant. When third singular *-s* does appear, there is no effect on the surrounding consonants or vowels; there is not even a reverse effect. It often appears in the wrong context, from the point of view of classroom English, as in

24 He can goes out.   (Labov et al., 1968, p. 166)

For these reasons and many others, we believe that the task of acquiring consistent use of third singular *-s* is harder for BEV speakers than is learning to use *-ed* consistently. Furthermore, the problem is harder for BEV speakers than for

---

[11]William Stewart (1968) pointed this out in an early article and Torrey's work in Harlem found experimental confirmation.

Spanish speakers. Though Spanish has no mark on the third singular, the notion of agreement between subject and verb is fundamental to Spanish grammar. In BEV, it is not simply third singular -*s* that is absent. The general machinery of number agreement between subject and verb is barely represented in the grammar. The irregular alterations *have/has, do/does*, and *was/were* are represented in BEV by invariant *have, do*, and *was*. It is only in the finite forms of the verb *to be* that we find some agreement between subject and verb.

We discussed the absolute form of the possessive as an example of a grammatical category that is fully represented, even over-represented, in BEV. The opposite is the case when the possessive -*s* relates two noun phrases. In the great majority of cases, the possessive -*s* is absent for BEV speakers, and demonstrates many of the traits of third singular -*s*. In some cases, the choice seems to be categorical: *whose book* is not heard and is very hard to reproduce in repetition tests.

Thus a portrait of BEV inflections can be drawn of three distinct situations: features entirely absent from the underlying grammar of BEV, features present in the grammar but variably deleted to a point hard to retrieve, and features that are generalized beyond the point of the standard language:

Absent	Variable	Generalized
Subject-verb agreement: 3rd singular [s]	Regular tense [ed]	Regular plural [s]
Possessive [s]: noun adjuncts	Contracted copula [s] & [r]	Possessive [s] : absolute form

4. LOSS OF INFORMATION AT THE ENDS OF WORDS

In most of the language families of the world, words gradually become worn away at their ends. There are many reasons for this. While a principle of least effort is certainly involved, it is also true that the distribution of information must also be taken into account. The first sound or letters of a word are the most useful in helping the listener determine the meaning of the word; the last few sounds or letters may be completely predictable. For example, if a one-syllable word begins *des-*, there is only one way to finish it: with a *k*. Even if the /k/ was not pronounced, the word would have to be *desk*.

This tendency to lose information at the ends of words may be encouraged by the fact that the ends of words do not carry as much information as the beginnings, but it is not limited to cases where the information is not needed. In the course of linguistic history, sound changes in languages like Chinese and French have produced thousands of homonyms, words that have exactly the same sound, though they were once quite different. For languages that carry their grammatical information in the form of single consonants at the ends of words, this leads to a great deal of unhappiness in the grammatical system. English has lost most of its inflections through this wearing away process.

The Black English vernacular loses information at the ends of words in a more extreme fashion than other dialects.[12] But those who grow up speaking BEV, like speakers of other dialects, have many indirect ways to learn about the shapes of words. They do not necessarily pick the form of the word they hear most often as the base of their mental dictionary. If they are exposed to older speakers who have an underlying knowledge of the form of a particular word that includes all of the sounds in the standard dictionary entry, they will sometimes pronounce these full forms, particularly when the next word begins with a vowel. In some cases, where a stop consonant is sandwiched between two *s*'s, as in *wasps, tests,* or *desks,* the stop may never be pronounced. Still, the *t* in *tests* can be discovered if a *t* reappears in the word *testing.* When young children are first learning to read, they may not yet have put together all the bits of information they need to arrive at the final solution—the shape of the word in the grown-up dictionary. Just as some think that *I* has an extra sound /m/, they may also assume that *desk* has only three sounds, or that *old* has two or only one.

Because the tendency to delete final /r/, /l/, /t/, /d/, /v/, and other consonants is more extreme in BEV than in other dialects, the relation between the spelling forms and the spoken language can be much harder to figure out for children learning to read and write the standard language. The following list contains some of the words that can be heard the same way. Each word stands for a member of a class of words: all the words that rhyme with it.

(a) The Deletion of Final t or d Can Give:

In simple words:

cold = coal	mist = miss	tent = ten
field = feel	paste = pace	pant = pan
world = whirl	must = muss	wand = wan

In the regular past tense:

rolled = roll	missed = miss	fanned = fan
healed = heal	faced = face	penned = pen

In the past tense of irregular verbs:

told = toll	lost = loss	went = when
held = hell	bent = Ben	meant = men

---

[12]The wearing away of inflections is a slow evolutionary process in most languages, but in the formation of pidgins and creoles it is much faster. The long history of BEV seems to be dominated by the reverse of this evolution, as inflections are replaced under the influence of the standard language. But the existence of this long-term decreolization does not end the normal process of wearing away in rapid and spontaneous speech. Grammatical particles like [ed] that have been replaced are still frequently deleted—even more drastically than in other dialects, since the earlier tradition without [ed] is not entirely eliminated from the scene.

With the general merger of /i/ & /e/ before /n/:

```
penned = pinned = pen = pin
send = sinned = sin
```

(b) The Deletion of l and r Can Give:

With the Southern deletion of the glide after back vowels

```
told = toll = tore = toe
sold = soul = sore = so
```

With the more common Northern pronunciation:

```
sore = Saul = saw
cord = called = cawed
```

and generally:

```
guard = God          tool = too
par = pa             jewel = Jew
```

with the tensing of /e/ before /l/:

```
held = hell = hail
sailed = sail = sell
```

With the monophthongization of /ay/:

```
wired = wide = why       wild = wowed = wow
fire = far = fa          piled = Powell = pow
mire = mar = ma          tiled = towel
```

The examples are not intended to suggest that all of these words are the same for all speakers of BEV. With the exception of a few cases (like *pen* and *pin*), identity is variable. But the frequency of deletion can be very high, and the experience of the learned does not yield enough information to keep these words apart.

The differences between the spoken and written form can cause problems at each step in the reading process. When the child reads a word correctly, the teacher may not recognize this success unless he or she can also recognize the equivalent sets of pronunciations outlined above. As early as 1965, these patterns were presented to the National College Teachers of English to illustrate some of the special problems confronting a speaker of BEV learning to read (Labov, 1967). It was then proposed that teachers who conduct oral reading practice begin to make clear distinctions between mistakes in reading and differences in pronunciation. Since that time, the principle has been widely accepted, but we do not know to what extent it has affected classroom practice.

It is now possible to put forward a more concrete program for reading curricula incorporating these special properties of BEV. A great deal of reading research is devoted to the fundamental problem of the acquisition of the alphabet. We are not only concerned here with the learning of the alphabetic principle, but also with its use as a general tool in decoding the printed page. In the Harlem study of 1965-1968, it was shown that many young people were effectively illiterate. Researchers found, for example, twelve-year-olds who scored at the first or second grade level on the Metropolitan Reading Test. Yet surprisingly enough, every one of them had mastered the alphabet. Early mastery of the alphabet was apparent in the patterns of reading mistakes on reading tests and standardized tests as well. When someone did not recognize a word, and had to guess, the guess almost always had the same first consonant as the printed form, and the same first vowel. But the rest of the guess showed no relation to the letters on the page. A typical example shows (25a) read as (25b):

25 a I sold my soul to the devil.
   b I saw my sour to the deaf.

The sentence has not been read and understood. But in attempting to decode its meaning, the reader hasn't neglected the alphabet. The alphabet has been used for as long as it could be trusted: for the first several letters. The weak connection between the last letters on the page and the form of the word as it is perceived and grasped by the reader has led to this loss of confidence. The same pattern appears clearly when we analyze reading errors. For seventeen pre-adolescent youth in the Harlem study, ages ten through thirteen, we considered all those misread words whose pronunciation had some relation to the letters on the printed page. The number of letters read correctly in each position were:

		Letters read correctly						
	N	1st	2nd	3rd	4th	5th	6th	7th
3-letter words	11	8	4	6				
4-letter words	77	65	55	45	31			
5-letter words	46	45	30	34	25	24		
6-letter words	26	26	19	20	19	15	10	
7-letter words	11	11	10	9	10	10	8	3

The problem is not the mastery of the alphabet itself, but one of acquiring the confidence to use it consistently. The weak correlation between the spelling forms on the printed page and the forms of the words as they are spoken has apparently led many Black youth to limit their use of the alphabet to the first few letters—or more accurately, to lose all confidence in the value of the alphabet for the last few letters.

Preliminary results of reading research by J. Baron point in the same direction. Eleven Black and eleven white children were matched for their ability to read regular words (34 correct out of 51). On exception words, Black children scored better, averaging 30.3 correct out of 51, than white children, who averaged 27.6. But on nonsense words, which require alphabetic skills, the results were reversed: 30.9 correct out of 51 for Blacks, as against 32.5 correct for whites. Other tests confirm the small but significant tendency of Black readers to use the alphabet less than whites. If we were to distinguish the use of the alphabet at the ends of words from its use at the beginnings of words, this difference might well be magnified.

Though there are many unanswered questions on how the structure of BEV interacts with the business of learning to read, there are a number of clear findings that can be applied to reading curricula. But before considering strategies for putting this knowledge to use, we should complete our look at the whole picture. It isn't hard to see how the sound patterns of BEV affect reading. But what about the more abstract semantics of section 1? Forms like *be done* and *been done* do not appear very often in the classroom—neither in writing nor in speech. Is there any way in which the BEV aspect system enters into the process of learning to read standard English? The next section will show that this underlying semantic system may not be as far away from the classroom as it first appears.

5. AMBIGUITIES OF TENSE AND ASPECT

The child who comes to school speaking BEV meets classroom English in two main forms: the teacher's speech and the printed words on the page. We've looked at some evidence about the result of interaction with the second: the full forms of words are hard to decipher, even when there is reason to think that adult speakers of BEV have the same full forms. It is also hard for children who speak BEV to make use of the final consonants that represent inflections, even when there is reason to believe that their own underlying grammars include this information.

There is no hard evidence on children's ability to interpret the speech of the teacher. But there are many indications that some of the speech signals of classroom English will be missed, and no reason to believe that children who speak BEV will automatically understand and absorb the standard system of tense and aspect.

We have seen that BEV-speaking children do use contractions like *We'll* and *They're* and *They'd*. But contractions are less common in BEV than in white dialects since they alternate with zero forms as well as with full forms. Among young children, full forms are more common than among older children and, as we have noted, contractions are often misinterpreted as in *Yes I'm am*. The *'ve* in *I've* or *they've* is particularly rare, and there is strong reason to doubt that the underlying grammar has a *have* auxiliary in the present perfect.

It is not generally realized that the full forms of auxiliaries are widely used in

BEV. Typical BEV forms are shown below as (a) rather than as (b), which represents forms more common in white dialects:

26 a. I had come over.
 b. I'd come over.

27 a. We will have succeeded . . .
 b. We'll have succeeded . . .

28 a. We have said it . . .
 b. We've said it . . .

The past perfect of (26a) is very common among young Black children, and the uncontracted form is normal in the most vernacular speech. The *will have* of (27a) is formal; but the informal shift is to the simple future or to the complex *be done* (28a) is again formal. The informal alternate, however, is not (28b) but rather the past tense *We said it.* In a word, there are many contradictions that are common currency for white children but not for Black children.

This disparity results in multiple ambiguity in the contact situation. The BEV-speaking child's problem shows up in this input-output diagram:

Teacher's production	Heard as	Interpreted as
They will be there → They'll be there		Future
	They be there	Habitual *be*
They would be there → They'd be there		Conditional
They have been there → They've been there		Present perfect
	They been there	Remote present perfect
They had been there → They'd been there		Past perfect

Here are two situations where the grammatical information of classroom English may be neutralized, and open to a three-way interpretation by the listener. The multiple ambiguities shown here are only some of the problems resulting from structural mismatch in the learning situation. It might be argued that context will usually make the teacher's intention less ambiguous. But this can be said for any part of language. We do not know how many misunderstandings are needed to produce cognitive confusion of a more permanent sort. Nonetheless, it is reasonable for the teacher to be aware of potential confusions and try to avoid them.

When the forms on the left are found on the printed page, the students' problems are much more evident. The contracted forms are hard for BEV readers to interpret and relate to their full forms or zero forms. The readers we are most concerned with interpret words one at a time—with some of the bizarre results exemplified by (25b) above. Any steps promoting the shift to reading meaning-ful sentences will be a major step forward in reading. Any mismatch on the printed page between the readers' grammatical knowledge and the letters to be read can only delay that process.

For all dialects, there are homonyms in speech that must be rendered unam-biguous if they are going to be correctly connected to the printed page. To be helpful, teachers must know what words sound the same and what connections have to be made. Two other sets of homonyms in BEV illustrate the principle.

It was noted at the outset that BEV grammar does not rely on words with short, reducible vowels so much as on words with long vowels that never disap-pear. Two long nasal vowels do a great deal of work for BEV:

(a) long nasal *e:*

> They haven't = They ain't = They 'e'
> They aren't = They ain't = They 'e'
> They didn't = They ain't = They 'e'

Most people realize that *ain't* can correspond to standard *haven't, hasn't, amn't, isn't* and *aren't.* But few people realize that BEV can also use *ain't* where other dialects use *didn't.*

(b) long nasal *o:*

> They are going to = They gon' = They 'o'
> They do not = They don' = They 'o'
> They will not = They won' = They 'o'

Here we have two future forms and one present tense form, all expressed by the same vowel. Such drastic reductions can create problems in working out the relationship between the colloquial forms and the full forms of classroom English.

6. FIVE STRATEGIES FOR TEACHING READING TO SPEAKERS OF BEV

This last section will outline five strategies for bringing our knowledge of BEV grammar into the day-to-day teaching of reading. It is not intended as a series of suggestions of how to teach reading: that is the business of teachers and educa-tors who know the full range of problems and practices involved. These princi-ples are put forward as a means of making linguistic knowledge available to those who design reading curricula. My aim here is to put into practice the letter and spirit of the Ann Arbor Black English decision, so that knowledge of the Black English Vernacular can be taken into account in the teaching of reading.

Strategy 1: Recognize Reading Errors   Teachers should be ready to distinguish between mistakes in reading and features of pronunciation typical of BEV. This strategy rests on the fundamental principle put before the National College Teachers of English in 1965, that the teaching of reading should distinguish true reading errors from differences in the ways that words are pronounced. The underlying concept is generally recognized: that reading is a way of deriving meaning from the printed page. But discussions of the trial have focused far more attention on the way children speak or are allowed to speak in the classroom. Arguments about "Black English in the classroom" have little to do with the Ann Arbor decision, and distract from the main task at hand: helping children learn to read.

Oral reading is not used to the same extent in every classroom. When children do read aloud, however, corrections by the teacher have considerable impact: they affect both readers and listeners at the same time. Certainly teachers should know enough about the constants and variables of BEV pronunciation to be able to decide whether the reader has misunderstood the message on the printed page. Thus, in

29 When I passed by, I read the posters.

we can use the pronunciation of *read* to draw such a conclusion, but not the pronunciation of *passed,* since the final /st/ cluster is variable. In

30 He lost his tests and hers too.

we cannot tell from the presence or absence of the /t/ in *lost* or *tests* whether those words have been read correctly, since the first is variable and the second always absent in BEV pronunciation; but we can judge from the /s/ in *hers,* because *her* and *hers* are never confused in BEV.

It is generally agreed that success in reading is the critical first step in the acquisition of basic skills, and all programs must be weighed against this priority. If educators should decide that training in standard English pronunciation is an essential step in reading, that should be undertaken as a separate program. But the bulk of current research indicates that success in reading is not dependent on pronunciation. Practice in imitating the teacher's pronunciation will not necessarily add to children's underlying knowledge of the language, since it has been shown that such superposed dialects do not develop systematic knowledge. Strategies 4 and 5 below may be more effective in this respect.

Strategy 2: Pay Attention to the Ends of Words   Evidence has been brought forward showing that the loss of information at the ends of words is a critical factor in the use of the alphabet by BEV speakers. Yet reading programs pay far more attention to the use of the alphabet for decoding letters at the beginnings of words. I have reviewed a number of phonics texts in current use, and found that the majority devote only a small fraction of their lesson plans to final consonants, and that only one gave roughly equal time to beginnings and ends of words.

This idea does not apply only to reading programs that rely heavily on phonics. No matter how the curriculum is designed, some means should be found to focus the BEV reader's attention on the *d* in *child* and the *ed* in walked at an early age. Some reading teachers avoid paying too much attention to the ends of words because of the danger of reading reversals: getting *saw* instead of *was*. It seems to me that this is usually a minor problem compared to the major difficulties documented in section 4 above, and it should not be allowed to dictate the fundamental strategies used in teaching of reading.

I have tried to show that the potential knowledge is often present. If the task of the educator is to build on that knowledge, the means must be found to make it available to the reading process. One such means is presented as Strategy 3.

Strategy 3: Introduce Words in the Most Favorable Contexts   The most common way to introduce a new word is in citation form: that is, in isolation, or at the end of a short presentative sentence:

31 This is a *desk*.

This method has the advantage of focusing attention of the word, with full final stress, and minimizing confusion with other information. Yet for BEV speakers this is not the best way to introduce a word into the reading process. It has been shown that BEV differs from other dialects in that consonant cluster simplification is relatively high before pause, and lowest before a following vowel. For a speaker of BEV, the full form of the word will be recognized more fully in the context

32 There is a *desk* in this room.

This principle applies most obviously to spoken interaction, as when an adult is introducing a word for the first time, or reading a new lesson, or even correcting a mis-reading. But we have reason to think that it also affects individual and silent reading in the course of the complex feedback between decoding, recognition, and encoding.

This is one case where differences between dialects are most relevant to teaching strategies. For some white dialects, like that found in Philadelphia, consonant clusters are preserved most often in final position. In these cases citation form of instruction works very well. But for other dialects (New York City, BEV, Puerto Rican English) final position behaves like a following consonant. Here, a following vowel helps bring out the form of the word more clearly.

Adopting this strategy would not favor Black children at the expense of the others. For every speaker of English, final consonants are pronounced far more often before a following vowel than before the next word that begins with a consonant, and the advantage of final position is, at best, not very large.

Strategy 4: Use the Full Forms of Words   This principle follows from all that has been said about the role of contracted forms in BEV. Contractions are not alien to BEV and are frequently used in speech. But for many young speakers of BEV, they are not easily analyzed as distinct from the word they are attached to, or related to the verb phrase. It would therefore be best to avoid the use of such contractions in reading texts and in the first steps of learning to read. Some textbook writers would interpret this alteration as a step backward, since they feel that

33 This is Rex. He is my dog.

is stiff and traditional. They would tend to replace it with the more relaxed and colloquial

34 This is Rex. He's my dog.

Although this second form is less stilted, it does not automatically help speakers of BEV. For them, the first form is likely to be more clear and natural. A more extreme kind of problem is created by

35 This is Rex. He's my brother's dog.

which introduces the possessive 's sandwiched between two noun phrases, and is especially hard for BEV speakers to recognize and use. It might be easier for them to apprehend

36 The name of this dog is Rex. He is my brother's.

which does not involve any letters that are hard to recognize.

The choice of sentence forms is not based on difficulty in understanding the basic message. BEV speakers will not necessarily misunderstand *He's my brother's dog.* But it will not be easy for them to interpret the two *'s* signals. If they ignore them, it will be one more step towards the loss of confidence in the alphabet we have already witnessed.

It might be argued that sooner or later all children must learn to read sentences like (34) and (35). This is certainly so. But the strategies suggested here are designed to facilitate the first steps in reading and to avoid any conflict of BEV and classroom English. The next strategy looks toward further reading steps and toward bridging the distances between linguistic systems.

Strategy 5: Relate Full Forms to Contracted Forms   Here we enter an area that goes beyond the first steps in the teaching of reading. The central principle involved is to make use of the child's own knowledge of language by developing the relation between the various forms that he or she uses in everyday speech, especially those that are closest to classroom English. Thus the relation between full, contracted and deleted forms of the copula:

37 a. He is on my side of the room.
    b. He's on my side of the room.
    c. He on my side of the room.

is implicit in the child's production of language but not necessarily available to him for further advances in reading. One of the most extreme examples of such expansion and contraction is found in the English periphrastic future, where the child's competence may include such forms as:

38 a. I am going to do it.
    b. I'm going to do it.
    c. I'm goin' to do it.
    d. I'm gonna do it.
    e. I'm gon' do it.
    f. I'm 'on' do it.
    g. I'm 'o' do it.
    h. I'm a do it.

The child may recognize the relationship between any two of these. But faced with the contrast between (38a) and (38g) or (38h), most people will not see much relationship at all.

There are many ways in which this relationship can be developed within the reading program or in the more general teaching of English. At each step, specific linguistic information is needed, and this information has to be made available to those curriculum designers who are prepared to use it. Even if linguists were better at communicating their own knowledge of grammar to other scholars and to the general public, their suggestions alone are likely to be wide of the mark. This communication is submitted to educators as part of one effort to put our linguistic knowledge to use in the critical problem of improving the teaching of reading to American children.

REFERENCES

Bailey, Beryl. 1965. *Jamican creole syntax.* London: Cambridge University Press.
Baugh, John. 1979. Linguistic style-shifting in Black English. Ph.D. dissertation. University of Pennsylvania.
———. 1980. Steady: Progressive aspect in Black English. Mimeographed.
Deutsch, Martin, Irwin Katz, and Arthur Jensen. 1968. *Social class, race and psychological development.* New York: Holt, Rinehart & Winston.
Dillard, J. L. 1972. *Black English.* New York: Random House.
Fickett, Joan. *Aspects of morphemics, syntax and semology of an inner-city dialect.* West Rush, NY: Meadowbrook.
Garvey, Catherine, and Paul T. McFarlane. 1968. A preliminary study of standard English speech patterns in the Baltimore city public schools. Report No. 16. Baltimore: Johns Hopkins University.

Jensen, Arthur. 1969. How much can we boost IQ and scholastic achievement? *Harvard Educational Review, 39.*

Joiner, Charles W. 1979. Memorandum opinion and order in Civil Action 7-71861. *Martin Luther King Junior Elementary School Children, et al. vs. Ann Arbor School District Board,* July 12.

Labov, William. 1967. Some sources of reading problems for speakers of non-standard Negro English. In A. Frazier (Ed.), *New directions in elementary English.* Champaign, Ill.: National College Teachers of English.

———. 1972. *Language in the inner city.* Philadelphia: University of Pennsylvania Press.

Labov, William, and Clarence Robins. 1969. A note on the relation of peer-group status to reading failure in urban ghettos. *Teachers College Record, 70* (5).

Labov, William, P. Cohen, C. Robins, and J. Lewis. 1968. A study of the non-standard English of Negro and Puerto Rican Speakers in New York City. *Cooperative Research Report 3288.* 2 vols. Philadelphia: U.S. Regional Survey.

Rickford, John. 1974. The insights of the mesolect. In D. DeCamp and I. Hancock (Eds.), *Pidgins and creoles: Current trends and prospects.* Washington, D.C.: Georgetown University Press.

———. 1975. Carrying a new wave into syntax: The case of Black English *been.* In R. Fasold and R. Shuy (Eds.), *Analyzing variation in language.* Washington, D.C.: Georgetown University Press.

Spears, Arthur. 1980. Come: a modal-like form in Black English. Paper read at the Winter meeting of the Linguistic Society of America, Los Angeles.

Stewart, William. 1968. Continuity and change in American Negro dialects. *The Florida FL Reporter 6*: 14–16, 18, 304.

Torrey, Jane. 1972. *The language of Black children in the early grades.* New London: Connecticut College. [ERIC ED 067 690]

Turner, Lorenzo. 1949. *Africanisms in the Gullah dialect.* Chicago: University of Chicago Press.

Black Talking on the Streets

Roger D. Abrahams

Deny the Negro the culture of the land? O.K. He'll brew his own culture—on the street corner. Lock him out from the seats of higher learning? He pays it no nevermind—he'll dream up his own professional doubletalk, from the professions that are available to him . . . These boys I ran with at The Corner, breathing half-comic prayers at the Tree of Hope, they were the new sophisticates of the race, the jivers, the sweettalkers, the jawblockers. They spouted at each other like soldiers sharpening their bayonets—what they were sharpening, in all this verbal horseplay, was their wits, the only weapons they had. Their sophistication didn't come out of moldy books and dicty colleges. It came from opening their eyes wide and gunning the world hard. . . .

They were the genius of the people, always on their toes, never missing a trick, asking

*no favors and taking no guff, not looking for trouble but solid ready for it. Spawned in a
social vacuum and hung up in mid-air, they were beginning to build their own culture.
Their language was a declaration of independence.*

Mezzrow & Wolfe 1969: 193–4

*Black is . . . Being so nasty and filthy you cook in all the big downtown restaurants . . .
Exploited by the news/Tortured by the blues/breaking the rules/and paying your
dues . . . Realizing 'they' all look alike too! . . . Playing the 'dozens!'*

From a Black cocktail napkin

Blacks do indeed speak differently than whites. Here I do not refer to the phonological and morphological differences much discussed in the literature of Black
English, but rather to the ways in which Blacks use talk as part of their daily
lives. Whether or not it is sufficient basis for an argument of *cultural* differences
(as Mezzrow implies above), it seems clear that Afro-Americans in the United
States do constitute a separate *speech community*. That is, they differ from other
groups in the varieties of speech they employ and in the ways they use these
varieties in carrying out the ritual (predictable) dimension of their personal interactions. Or, to put it in Hymes' terms for speech community, they 'share rules
for the conduct and interpretation of speech, and rules for the interpretation of at
least one linguistic variety' (Hymes 1972: 54).

We recognize, then, this sense of community in Black speaking in a great
many ways—not least of which is the kind and intensity of talk about talk which
one encounters in conversations and the special in-group names given by the
speakers to ways of talking. Such Black terms for speech events constitute one
important dimension of their system of speaking, and focus on speech use in
very different ways from the usages of Euro-American discourse. This is not to
say that there are not parallel terms or analogous practices in standard American
English. Rather, the range, the intensity, the proliferation of terms, and the
importance of such events are, as a whole, quite different from the configuration
of communicative systems found elsewhere.

The existence of this distinct speaking community is recognized by Blacks
(as well as whites) in their lore about themselves. One hears discussions not only
about how *bad* or *country* some Blacks talk, but also how *lame* and uninformed
whites are at communicating with each other. The Black ability to use words art-
fully and playfully is often encountered as an explanation of how and why
Blacks outwit whites in certain conflict situations. There is thus a ground-level
recognition of speaking differences among Blacks that gives the idea of a distinct speaking community a sense of analytic reality. Furthermore, analysis is
carried on by the Black speakers themselves in discussions about the effectiveness or ineffectiveness of someone's abilities at using speech on some level of
performance.

Perhaps the clearest indication of the distinctiveness of the Black speech community lies in the use of speech in the pursuit of public *playing,* and a parallel use of silence or other verbal restrictions in the more private sectors of the community. That is, attitudes toward work and play differ in Afro- and Euro-American communities. In Black communities, work is essentially a private matter, something learned in the home as part of the respectable and cooperative ideals of home life. Play, on the other hand, is inappropriate for the most part in the home, but rather is regarded as a public kind of phenomenon. Playing, in fact, is an important way in which one distinguishes oneself in public, and engaging in witty verbal exchanges is one important way of playing. (In the Euro-American system, on the other hand, play tends to be regarded as something appropriate for an adult to do in private—certainly something you don't usually want to get caught at, unless you're a member of a team. Work is the way in which one distinguishes oneself, and is therefore properly a public activity.) Thus, one crucial distinction to be made with regard to defining the Black speaking community is between house talk, especially 'around moms,' and street talk. Because active verbal performance in the street is one of the main means of asserting one's presence and place, there are a greater number of terms for street talk than for house talk. In the house, communications often are defined in terms of a Momma's imposed set of restrictions; especially when the speaking is defined as playful (Abrahams 1973). Here the restrictions may be on the subject of discussion, the vocabulary used, the amount of noise generally permitted to emanate from the residents of the house, and the communication relationships pursued in that ambience. There are, of course, numerous modes of talk, especially in the area of conversation, which are shared in both worlds. But the distinctions between the two are dramatic, for in the street world certain kinds of play are regarded as a norm—and valued as such—which are out of place for the most part in the house.

In general women—and especially female heads of households and older women—speak differently than men. Women are expected to be more restrained in their talk, less loud, less public, and much less abandoned. Parents attempt to instill this in the girls in their family by attempting to get them never to talk loudly or curse, not even when involved in street encounters. As Louise Meriwhether explains it in her autobiography. 'Daddy even didn't want me to say darn. He was always telling me: "It's darn today, damn tomorrow, and next week it'll be goddamn. You're going to grow up to be a lady, and ladies don't curse"' (1970: 28). But the problem is more than cursing. Any kind of public talk may not be respectably ladylike. The house is the locus of a woman's sense of respectability, and it is by respectability canons that a woman is judged by her community and especially her peers (Wilson 1969). Communication is regarded as properly restricted there, to the point that silence from children (especially in the presence of Momma) is highly valued.

The major difference between the house and the street worlds, beyond the relative privacy and restriction, lies in the kind of relationships pursued and the varieties of communication used. The house world is populated in the main by members of the family. The home is regarded as the place to keep the family together. Here (and in the church) is therefore where Momma asserts her respectability most fully. In the street world, on the other hand, male friendships are established and kept up, and this is done by maintaining the possibility of *playing* (with all that comes to mean) at all times. This essay deals primarily with the communication events most characteristic of street behaviors, under-standing that street includes all areas regarded as public.[1]

Elliot Liebow's study, *Tally's Corner,* describes how one friendship circle operates. His description is characteristic of other such groups.

> On the streetcorner, each man has his own network of . . . personal relationships and each man's network defines for him the members of his personal community. His personal community, then, is not a bounded area but rather a web-like arrangement of man-man and man-woman relationships in which he is selectively attached in a partic-ular way to a definite number of discrete persons. . . .
>
> At the edges of this network are those persons with whom his relationship is affec-tively neutral, such as area residents whom he has 'seen around' but does not know except to nod or say 'hi' to as they pass in the street. . . .
>
> In toward the center are those persons he knows and likes most, those with whom he is 'up tight'; his 'walking buddies,' 'good' or 'best' friends, girl friends, and some-times real or putative kinsmen. These are the people with whom he is in more or less daily, face-to-face contact, and whom he turns to for emergency aid, comfort or sup-port in time of need or crisis. He gives them and receives from them goods and ser-vices in the name of friendship, ostensibly keeping no reckoning. Routinely, he seeks them out and is sought out by them. They serve his need to be with others of his kind, and to be recognized as a discrete, distinctive personality, and he in turn serves them the same way. They are both his audience and his fellow actors.

(1967: 161–3)

Liebow's use of the metaphor of performance is appropriate here because friend-ship is not only defined by whom one may call upon for aid, but more important, with whom one may *play.*

In such a person-centered society a man establishes his reputation. A man with a *big rep* is so judged, in part, by the number of people he is able to call friend and therefore call upon for such goods and services as well as joke with.

---

[1]I do this recognizing that I am continuing to commit an error of my past studies of Black com-munication styles, justly pointed out by Valentine (1972), by treating primarily Black male behavior patterns. I have done this because there are more data on this street dimension of Black culture. But I hope to redress this lack in future studies in which the more private and less performance-centered dimensions of talking Black will be discussed. (For preliminary attempts in the United States and the British West Indies, see Abrahams 1970a,b,c.)

Both are implied in the word *play*. Because a reputation is so person-centered, it needs to be constantly guarded. As Rap Brown put it: 'Once I established my reputation, cats respected it . . . If I went out of my neighborhood, though, it was another story. I'd be on someone else's turf and would have to make it or take it over there' (H. R. Brown 1969: 15). This is echoed in Piri Thomas' comment, 'In Harlem you always lived on the edge of losing rep. All it takes is a one-time loss of heart' (1967:58).

This personalistic, reputation-centered approach has been noted by numerous ethnographers. Somewhat complicating the matter, Herbert Gans has noted this feature as a general characteristic of lower-class socialization, which he calls an 'action seeking' style of life; but the manner in which Blacks set up the action and the modes of performance differ from that of any other ethnic enclave. (For an indication that these differences are perceived and maximized on the street level, see Suttles' [1968: 65ff.] description of lower-class Italian-American reactions to Black performance style.)

In such a street world, one must dramatize oneself constantly, and one is therefore always looking for opportunities to do so. Perhaps the most important means one has to do so in the Black world—and especially in the cities—is through verbal performances. In this expressive life style, performance and especially talk become the major means for establishing friendships—a process Rainwater describes as 'a single adaptation in lower-class Negro society, which has as its primary goal the maintenance of reciprocity between members on the basis of a symbolic exchange of selves, *an entertainment of each by the other*' (1970: 378, my italics).

There is ample testimony to the importance of learning to talk well to operate successfully outside the home environment (a move Claude Brown repeatedly calls 'coming out of the house'—'cutting loose from . . . parents' [1966; see esp. pp. 166ff.]). Not only do the ethnographic studies carried out by myself, Kochman, Kernan, Hannerz, Rainwater, the Milners, and others underline this feature of Black life style, but such an in-group commentator as Malcolm X describes how crucial it was to learn to talk right to establish his *rep* wherever he went, especially in Harlem when he was operating as a pimp–waiter (1965). Rap Brown devotes a whole chapter to his street education which emphasizes the relationship between learning to talk well and the development of his reputation:

> I used to hang out in the bars just to hear the old men 'talking shit.' By the time I was nine, I could talk Shine and the Titanic, Signifying Monkey three different ways, and Piss-Pot Peet for two hours without stopping. Sometimes I wonder why I even bothered to go to school. Practically everything I know I learned on the corner. . . .
>
> The street is where young bloods get their education. I learned how to talk on the street, not from reading about Dick and Jane going to school and all that simple shit. The teacher would test our vocabulary every week, but we knew the vocabulary we needed. They'd give us arithmetic to exercise our minds. Here, we exercised our minds by playing the Dozens. . . .

> There'd be sometimes 40 or 50 dudes standing around and the winner was deter-
> mined by the way they responded to what was said. If you fell all over each other
> laughing, then you knew you'd scored. It was a bad scene for a dude that was getting
> humiliated. I seldom was. That's why they called me Rap, cause I could rap.

(H. R. Brown 1969: 25–7, 30; for similar accounts see Abrahams 1970a, chapter 2)

It would be easy to conclude from such accounts that this attitude and verbal
practice are characteristic only of Black enclaves in the big cities. To do so
would be to be misled by the urban terms that Brown uses. In fact, the focus on
using (among other techniques) verbal abilities as a means of establishing and
maintaining reputation is a widely observed Afro-American characteristic which
extends to Black communities outside the United States (e.g., Wilson 1969;
Abrahams & Bauman 1971). But most important for the present argument, verbal *playing* has been reported from a number of non-urban communities (e.g.,
Ferris 1972; Lewis 1964; Friedland & Nelkin 1971) as part of a complex in
which males find meeting places where they can pursue their male expressive
behaviors—in spite of it being judged as *bad* by both the respectables and, when
pressed to it, themselves.

Although much described in the literature, these behaviors are all too often
judged from a Euro-American perspective which sees them as 'idling' or 'killing
time' without recognizing the system by which they operate. Street-level terms
are *hanging* (Keiser 1969), *hanging out, taking care of business.*[2]

Even those who do not accord much significance to expressive phenomena in
their analyses of Black culture acknowledge the importance of a certain range of
talking in these interactive settings. For instance, Hylan Lewis in his *Blackways
of Kent* reports that in the Piedmont community which he studied there was
much 'public idling' which he associated with male behavior. He noted 'specific
idling places, informal idling cliques, a range of conventional idling behavior,
and certain days and periods when idling is expected' (1964: 68).

The importance of talk in such situations is nowhere so clearly reflected as in
the large number of terms describing the varieties of such talk. In fact, these
terms are a good index not only to the importance of talk but to the range of
speech events whereby such public friend-groups celebrate themselves while

---

[2]The term *business* in the sense of personal concerns is a focal term in Afro-American communities. Though this is not the appropriate place to fully explore the semantic field of the Black uses of
the term, there are some features which are important to point out. *Business* essentially means
'name' maintenance. Thus, if a woman uses the term, it is liable to be in protection of her sense of
respectability, warning others that her doings are 'nobody's business but my own.' On the other
hand, when a man says 'I'ma *t.c.b.* [take care of business]' he is generally referring to leaving to see
others, to maintain his connections, his friendship (or loveship) networks. *T.c.b.* generally is taken
to mean 'I'm going to see a man about something which (I want you to think) is important'; but it
also can refer to pursuing a sexual conquest or to the sexual act itself. For an important early commentary on the special Afro-American use of the term see F. L. Olmsted, *A Journey in the Seaboard
States* (1856: 206).

getting the action going. The street world is thought of as the public world and therefore one in which playing is appropriate. This does not mean that in verbal interactions on the street only play is found, but rather that it seems to operate as a norm—or at least a constant incipiency—and other events are distinguished from it. This may account for the great number of ground-level distinctions made with regard to verbal *playing* or *signifying.*

Play is a difficult phenomenon to describe in any culture. On the one hand play relies on the distinction between it and the 'real' or the 'serious.' On the other, for such play to operate successfully, there must be a recognizable relationship between it and the real world. One of these vital connections is that for play to operate successfully, there must be a sense of threat arising from the 'real' and 'serious' world of behavior. The threat of incursions from the real world must be constant. That is, in the most successful kinds of play, the most constant message must be the deeply ambivalent one: this is play—this is *not* play. With joking activity (which accounts for most *playing* in the street world) this paradoxical message is very commonly carried out by the use of the same aggressive, hostile formulaic devices found in use in real arguments—i.e., the same curses, boasts, devices of vilification and degradation, etc. This is precisely what one finds in the Black street world—so much so that the passer-by often has a hard time discerning whether joking or a real argument is taking place. Indeed, it becomes an important part of the show on many occasions to keep even the other participants wondering whether one is still playing.

This blurring of the line between play and seriousness is often observable in the terms which are used to describe the communicative event. *Cursing,* for instance, may be either a device of *playing,* or used very seriously, as are *mounting, charging, getting on someone's case,* and many others. The very same words that constitute a *put-down* or a *put-on* in one situation may be used as playful *woofing* or *talking shit* in another. This is why it is important to be at home, on your *own turf,* when you begin to use these devices. One can suddenly find that one has *gone too deep,* and that what one thought to be jokes are being taken very seriously indeed. But it also means that if one wants to test someone on one's own turf, one can use these devices with an outsider without giving clear cues as to whether one is being serious or not. Or in the most extreme circumstances, one can use them to start a real fight. This is why neither the witty, aggressive, traditional devices nor even the generic terms for them can be used as the primary basis of a taxonomy (even though they are the data which originally indicated that a ground-level taxonomy exists).

Only the most extreme forms of play are regarded as appropriate only on the street. The range of joking called (among other things) *talking smart* may occur wherever women and men find themselves in courtship-level conversation— though the smart talk is as often used to fend off a courting move as it is to encourage or continue it. *Talking smart,* however, is primarily regarded as street talk because it involves the kind of display of wit which is most useful and appropriate in public places. Nevertheless, it is a style of talk carried on between the participants without any need for an audience, and is often reported as occurring just between two people who find themselves in some situation of contention. That these *are* reported in anecdotal form, however, indicates the close relationship between such *smart talking* and *talking shit*. A good display of wit is too valuable to waste it only on a two-person conversation. It must be repeated to a larger audience later, one which can admire the witty verbal control.

There are, in this recognition of distinctions within the Black speaking community, three basic kinds of street-talk events: those intended primarily to pass on information, those in which interpersonal manipulation or argumentation involving a display of wit is going on, and those in which play is the primary component of the interaction. This distinction is keyed as much by proxemic and kinesic elements as by verbal means. The more informational, the more private the interaction. The more wit is involved, the more the possibility of onlooker involvement. When men are talking in public and primarily with other men (i.e., *to* them, with messages meant primarily for their ears), the major indication of what range of speaking event is going on is given by how their bodies are stationed. The most casual kind of grouping in which *talking shit* or *woofing* is probably taking place is a group standing or sitting shoulder-to-shoulder, in either a line or semicircle, where the passing action may be observed without disturbing the state of talk. As the discussion gets *deeper* (the more intensively stylized and aggressive or the more personal), the participants get closer to each other, stationing themselves so that you can make eye contact with whoever is talking. The instigators of talk will maintain their mobility, for they will be dramatizing their talk with action. A good talker will somewhat immobilize the others around him. The more one commands attention, the longer his talk is countenanced. He must receive constant verbal and kinesic support from the others. (For interesting pictures, see Keiser 1969: *passim;* Friedland & Nelkin 1971.) This support is indicated in a number of verbal and kinesic ways—one of which is the bending at the waist and knees. The deeper the bending, the greater the supportive intensification, it would seem. In all adult interactions, but especially public ones, participation must be actively indicated constantly. As one commentator noted: 'Unlike a white audience, careful to suppress enthusiasm, the black man and woman were silent [and still] only when they were negative and suspicious' (Keegan 1971: 7).

The older the members of the group talking, the less low-level kinesic activity will go on among the non-talking members. But with adolescents who are just perfecting the style of their *pimp walk* (see Johnson 1971: 19 and Ellis & Newman 1971: 302 for descriptions) there is a need to *style* constantly. As Kenneth R. Johnson describes this grouping technique:

> When talking in a group, the participants (say four or five young Black males) will often adopt a kind of stationary 'pimp strut' . . . while [they] are talking, they stand

with their hands halfway in their pockets, and they move in the rhythmic, fluid dance-type way (without actually walking) to punctuate their remarks. The arm that is free will swing, point, turn and gesture as conversation proceeds . . . This kind of behavior always accompanies a light or humorous conversation, or a conversation about masculine exploits. It never accompanies a serious discussion about more general topics (planning something, difficulties with parents, political issues, etc.).

(1971: 19)

If two (or more) people are seen engaging in close talk, facing each other and maintaining eye contact, the assumption is that something *deep* is going on, either one is *running something down* to the other—passing on valid information on which he is supposed to act—or that one is *running a game* on the other, *hyping* or *shucking* him—passing on invalid information. If two are arguing and engaging in talking smart, they will face each other but be farther apart and more mobile than when getting the *run down* on something.

If two (or more) are in a casual state of talk they will signify this by looking outward. This is even true when two friends meet on the street and shake hands. If they are not *hipping* someone to something that is *happening,* they will gaze away even while still shaking or just holding hands. The more other-person-centered the talk becomes (of the 'have you heard about so-and-so' sort concerning mutual friends or acquaintances), the closer the two will come, and the more their bodies will face each other, especially if the news of the other's *business* is concerned with a life-change (moving, any sort of conflict or confinement).

These kinesic and proxemic observations might be used to describe street behaviors of any age. But, as noted above, there are differences in the amount of movement within a group depending on how recently the young men have learned to *walk their walk* and *talk their talk,* to *style* their actions to make themselves appear *cool* (under control through stylistic moves) and *hip* (informed).

Performing by *styling* is thus one of the means of adapting oneself to the street world, of developing a public persona through which one can begin to establish and maintain one's *rep.* Naturally, as a young man learns how to *style,* he is much more self-conscious of how he is coming over to the others, and he therefore constantly looks for openings in which he can demonstrate his styling abilities. At first he does this almost formularistically—by imitation of those whom he has observed and admired. Later, when he has lived with *styling* devices, he will be less self-conscious and more able to take the styling for granted and thus be more message-oriented in his stylized communications.

Though it is in walking and dressing well that such a young man asserts his style most immediately, it is often in learning to *talk shit,* to effectively play with words by *talking that talk,* that his street image will be most firmly established. (This is especially true of the *pimp* or *cat* approach to the streets. The alternative gorilla approach of using one's strength is explored in Abrahams 1970a: 85–96 and in Firestone 1964, and is commented upon in Hannerz 1969:

115 and Milner & Milner 1972: 319–20. For somewhat different taxonomies of available social roles 'on the street,' see Ellis & Newman 1971 and Strong 1940.) This is what Rap Brown seems to have meant when he stressed the origin of his name in his ability to contest effectively with words, and how central this was to his *high rep.*

Because *styling* is so important during this period of life, the Black community tends to view certain performances as being age-specific to adolescence. That is, there are a number of speech events which continue to be played throughout life when men congregate, but because they are more self-consciously stylized during adolescence, their names and the self-conscious dimension of their performance may be rejected. Thus, among the older members of the community, the names for these practices may become pejorative; certainly their practice becomes less habitual, more restricted. But the same patterns of interaction may be observed throughout a man's life as long as he identifies with his peer group and engages in congregations on the street or some other equally public place.

Whenever men get together to engage in talk, this may lead to an increasingly stylized set of behaviors which, as they become more stylized, will be progressively more aggressive, more contest-oriented, and more centered on witty style and delivery. This progression, too, is taken note of in Black terms for self-conscious interactions, being referred to in a number of ways like *going deep, getting heavy, really getting into it,* or *getting to it.* The heavier or deeper the performance, the more attention the interchange will attract, and the more responding movement (a kind of dancing with) and answering verbal response (continuatives of the *right on* variety) will arise.

In this realm there seem to be important age-differentials in what speaking events arise most often in such states of talk. Among the younger adolescents, the devices used are not only more formulaic but also shorter. The older the group, the more time is given the performer to develop his point; thus, jokes, toasts (long narrative often heroic verses), and personal experience narrations emerge more often with older performers.

Hannerz describes such differences in regard to these aggressive verbal practices, focussing on the fuzzy semantic boundaries of the in-group descriptive terms *joning* and *joking.*

> Verbal contests occur among young males as well as among adult counterparts. . . . This is the phenomenon which has become most known [in the literature] as 'the dozens,' but it is also known as 'sounding' and under some other local names. The term most often used in Washington, D.C., is *'joning'.* . . .
>
> Joning is an exchange of insults. . . . The boundaries of the concept are a little fuzzy; there is some tendency to view joning as any exchange of insults of a more or less jocular type in sociable interaction among children and adolescents. Joning is definitely associated with joking. For smaller boys it seems to shade imperceptibly into the category of 'cracking jokes,' and when joning occurs in a peer group sociable session it is often preceded and followed by other kinds of jokes. These are also

exchanged in a manner resembling a contest, and some of them have a form and content somewhat similar to jones. . . .

The exchanges can occur between two boys who are alone, and it is even possible for them to jone on some third absent person, usually one of their peers, but the typical situation involves a group of boys: while a series of exchanges may engage one pair of boys after another, most members of the crowd function as audience, inciters, and judges—laughing, commenting upon the 'scoring,' and urging the participants on. . . .

As the boys become men they gradually cease to amuse themselves with joning. Although verbal aggression continues, it becomes less patterned; the insults contain hardly any references to mothers any more, and if a man, often by chance rather than intentionally, should say anything which could be construed as an abuse of another's mother, the latter might simply say, 'I don't play that game no more.'

(1969: 129–30)

Just what the difference is between this and adult joking behaviors is not quite clear from either the literature or my own observations, except that, as noted, the younger men use more formulaic devices, and are therefore less improvisational in their contest techniques than adults. Ferris's (1972) argument with regard to his Mississippi informants suggests that the older one gets, the less fictional and the more personal stories may get.

There is, however, a tendency to identify all such adolescent *playing* with the specific practice of *playing the dozens.* This leads to a use of the same terms for all aggressive play on a more particular level as synonyms for the dozens. But, as Rap Brown pointed out above, these same groups may want to distinguish between different kinds of *playing: cracking* on the other person, on the other person's family, or on yourself. Another important distinction is the use of boasts in the same context.

There are, then, terminological distinctions made by the participants in the public street world of the Black speaking community which suggest the existence of a native taxonomy of ways of speaking. Thus, in my original formulation, I worked out the distinctions on the level of the terms—as they were distinguished by some speakers at some time. But it became clear that these distinctions are acted on even in those Black communities that do not have a contrast-set of terms. Therefore, the taxonomy must be described with regard to the distinctions in speaker-to-speaker relationships and strategies. However, because these terms do provide some sense of the distinction, one ground-level term will be given for each taxonomic slot—and the terms will be surveyed and discussed in an appendix.

I regard this taxonomy as an underlying record of some of the most important distinctions in Black life, felt, acted upon, and judged if not always named by agrarian and post-agrarian Black communities in the United States. Interactions which are named in one community but not in another are nevertheless practiced in both. Further, many of the names for these ways of speaking change constantly from time to time and place to place, but the patterned interactions and the relations between the types of situated speech remain essentially constant (at least as far back as our data will take us).

Fig. 6 presents the relationships between the major ways of speaking on the street, emphasizing the continuities between patterns of interaction and persuasion from casual conversation to stylized playing with words in the aggressive, contest situation characteristic of *playing the dozens* and *woofing*. There are a number of techniques of manipulation used in both serious and playful aggressive contexts, like *mounting, bragging,* and others. These will be discussed in the appendix of terms.

The taxonomy is divided in three parts from talk in which information is the focus, to the most stylized, in which more concern is shown for the artful patterning of the utterance than the message. With the former the style is buried in favor of the message; the interaction to be effective must seem relatively spontaneous. With the latter, the message is subordinated or disavowed (since it is all just play) while the intensity and effectiveness of presentation become most important. Between these are interactions in which stylized devices are introduced—and call attention to themselves—but in which message remains as important as style.

FIGURE 6

Conversation on the streets; ways of speaking between equals				
Informational; content focus. *Running it down*	Aggressive, witty performance talk. *Signifying*			
	Serious, clever conflict talk. 'Me-and-you and no one else' focus. *Talking smart*		Non-serious contest talk. 'Any of us here' focus. *Talking shit*	
	Overly aggressive talk. *Putting down*	Convertly aggressive, manipulative talk. *Putting on*	Non-directive. *Playing*	Directive. *Sounding*

Going deep; talking baad

Conversational (apparently spontaneous)	Arises in conversational context, yet judged in performance (stylistic) terms	Performance interaction, yet built on model of conversational back-and-forth

The greater the use of wit or special information and energy, the *heavier* the interaction is judged to be, and the more the onlooker is entertained. This is as true of *hipping* or the *put-on* and *put-down* as it is in *woofing,* for such interactions will either draw onlookers or they will become performance pieces in later retellings.

In other words, not only are these distinctions made, but more important, exceptional scenes in which such talking is featured become topics for further talk. And there are numerous ground-level ways in which the effectiveness and usefulness of talk are discussed. Again, the *deeper* the interaction is judged to be, the more a recounting is liable to occur. These scenes may be of all three types, those in which *heavy* information is being passed on (*rifting*), where someone is showing his *smarts,* or where a remarkable capping session has occurred.

Less noticed is that the aggressive and competitive interactions in Black talk have been those concerned with the discussion and dissemination of information. Only Labov and his associates have analyzed the importance of such talk in street talk, specifically with regard to the concept terms of *rifting* and being *on the square,* local terms for what Dillard has referred to as *fancy talk.*

Rifting is, as Labov *et al.* (1968: 152) describe it, a 'form of display, of both knowledge and verbal style.' The more knowledge one has of a subject, the more he is regarded as being *heavy in the head.* Thus, it is not just verbal style which is the mark of the street man-of-words; in certain situations when a potential peer is put *on the square,* expressions of knowledge are equally important. The style of rifting, like that of sermonizing and other formal and oratorical situations involves

> a style of speech—an elevated high flown delivery which incorporates a great many learned Latinate words, spelling out the uncontracted form of function words with characteristic level and sustained intonation pattern that lays extra stress and length on the last stressed word. The occult knowledge which is delivered in this way is described as 'heavy'—it is *heavy knowledge, heavy stuff,* or *heavy shit;* and too heavy for outsiders to understand. Heavy or secret knowledge is learned by rote; adepts are examined in a speech event known as 'putting someone on the square.'
>
> (Labov *et al.* 1968: 136)

Hannerz discusses the place of such *heavy* informational talking in the range of other more playful types.

> All prestige accrued from being a good talker does not have to do with the strictly utilitarian [manipulative] aspect. A man with good stories well told and with a good repartee in arguments is certain to be appreciated for his entertainment value, and those men who can talk about the high and the mighty, people and places, and the state of the world, may stake claims to a reputation of being heavy 'upstairs.'
>
> (1969: 85)

He later discusses two men from the neighborhood in which he worked who were known for this weightiness of knowledge, causing their friends and neighbors to regard them as 'intellectuals' (p. 106).

That this is a Black role-type is noted by many Black writers. For instance, George Cain in his remarkable *Blueschild Baby* observes:

> J. B., the storyteller . . . found in all civilizations, preserver of unwritten histories, keeper of legends and oral tradition. Daily he holds forth, as at an African marketplace. Surrounded by black faces reflecting the moods of his narrations, he translates what is in the white mind and media into the idiom of his audience. Every corner has its J.B., that funny nigger who makes a crowd dance with laughter at themselves and their shortcomings . . .
>
> Many dismiss him as bullshit, unable to see his role or contribution, but like all black people, they're respectful of knowledge so don't protest too vehemently. . . . On the absence of truth-telling media James and those like him evolved. Street-corner philosophers with all the technique of gifted actors, they hold the most difficult audience in the world.

(1970: 29–30)

Often this performance of knowledge is commented upon in a metalingual and metacritical way, leading to further routines by the *heavy* talker on his streetcorner training. Typical of such speeches is one reported briefly from a Florida conservative Black politician, Norman E. Jones: 'His education, he once said, consists of "Ph.D.'s" from "the University of Beale Street, the University of Harlem and many other universities throughout the nation—generally called the street where people exist"' (Hooker 1972: 4; for a longer routine, see Killens 1972: 157).

However, such *heavy* displays are more likely to occur while *playing,* for in the *hanging* situation such *playing* is a constant possibility. It is in this range of situations, also, that there is the greatest number of terms, and they change most frequently. These terms (given in the appendix) sometimes indicate more particularity in distinguishing techniques of wit and argumentation that might have been used to make the taxonomic chart deeper in the realm of playing. For instance, some communities make a distinction between the *clean* and the *dirty dozens.* By this they mean, in the case of the former, that the joke is directly aimed at one of the others in the interacting group, while the latter directs them at some member of the other's family. Further, there are a number of such *clean* techniques, such as *bragging* or *boasting,* in which the main reference is the speaker, or *charging* and *mounting* in which the other is the target; or the general *capping* remark, which may be a witticism which only indirectly downs the other.

Beyond these distinctions, there are terms (and much discussion) which may refer to such intensification of verbal performances—though they may have reference to nonverbal presentational effects. These are terms like *styling, having the flash* (Woodley 1971: 11), *styling out,* or *showing out,* which point out dramatically foregrounded presentational techniques; but more often they are concerned more with clothing and hair style than verbal display.

Similarly, if an interaction is regarded as a dramatic success, comment will occur with regard to how someone really got *on someone's case* or *charged all over him.* (Sale 1971: 90, 104, has the Blackstone Rangers refer to *getting shot through the grease.*) But if such a strategy fails, the instigator is liable to be accused of being *lame, running off at the mouth, or talking off the wall shit* (not knowing what he is talking about). Since this arises in comment on the informational content of a person's argument, he also may be accused of wanting to appear to be serious but being interpreted as *playing.* In such a context, any of the terms for *signifying* may be used negatively, like *talking shit* (now with an emphasis on the last word) or *woofing.* Older terms are *spouting* and *muckty muck* (Major 1970) and *boogerbooing* or *beating your gums* (Hurston 1942).

Similarly, terms like *jiving* and *shucking* may be used to call someone at a *lame* use of speech. Or if someone begins to *go deep* in an inappropriate context (not with close enough friends, or using techniques of a younger age-set), he may be called on it with an 'I don't play that shit' kind of remark, or 'I laugh, joke, and smoke, but I don't play' (see Abrahams 1970b). On the other hand, if the thrust of the remarks does hit home but they are regarded as inappropriate—an attempt to start a fight—the response will be the slightly different 'You better not play that shit with *me.*'

In such situations, there are a number of disavowal techniques, reclassifying the remarks into the category of *playing,* like 'Man, I was only bullshitting.' This strategy of trying to get out of an uneasy verbal situation in certain cases is engineered by the other as part of his strategy of a *put-down.* In such a case, the speaker seeking an out will have to do the more extreme act of verbal subjugation termed *copping a plea, gripping* (Kochman 1970; Sale 1971: 43), or the most recently encountered *eating cheese* and *cowdown* (Woodley 1972: 143). This most often occurs when someone (or a group) has really gotten *on your case,* or more extremely if you are suspected of wrongdoing, being put *on the square* (Labov *et al.* 1968).

Perhaps the most important dimension of the discussion on the judgment criteria used with regard to these situated ways of speaking is that one of the best things that can be said of the street talker is that he *comes on baad.* This obvious inversion of the term seems certainly to arise in opposition to the household respectability perspective. It is the expression of this opposition between the two 'worlds' of Black life that presents the largest problem in the description and analysis of an Afro-American world order—the problem of accounting for this high valuation of *baadness.* We know that these values are the opposite of the private respectable world and operate them primarily in the public realm. Furthermore, the recent studies of child rearing and language learning carried on by Young and by Ward indicate that a certain amount of this *baadness* is encouraged among the precocious within the home, with even the baby's first movements being positively interpreted as aggression (Young 1970; Ward 1971). The ramifications of this establishment of the contrarieties between these worlds and the accompanying ambivalent attitude toward public display are only now being noticed and analyzed. But in this area of investigation, I am convinced, lies one of the key dimensions of those role and behavior configurations that will enable us to designate not only the patterns of characteristics of the Black speaking community, but the integrity and uniqueness of Black culture in general.

APPENDIX: THE TERMS

Since the existence of this taxonomy, and the importance of verbal wit in understanding the street world, arose because of the use of terms for ways of speaking in some Black communities, it might be useful to review what these terms are and what speaking strategies and relationships they have been used to name. I will do this in sections, by key terms.

There are certain basic semantic problems involved in such a presentation, however. This is not only because of the number of terms involved, but because the same terms are used in different Black communities at different times to designate different types of speech events. Yet it seems important to present what data are available to demonstrate these problems and to indicate that there is an historical dimension to this taxonomy of ways of speaking.

SIGNIFYING

An example of how semantically confusing such a presentation can become can be seen in Kernan's discussion and review of the scholarship concerning the term *signifying*. In *Deep Down in the Jungle*, reporting on Black folklore in one black neighborhood in Philadelphia, I had heard the term used for a wide variety of verbal techniques united by the single strategy of verbal manipulation through indirection. The examples I reported there, which were quoted by Kerman, were

> [an] ability to talk with great innuendo, to carp, cajole, wheedle and lie . . . in other instances, to talk around a subject . . . [or] making fun of a person or situation. Also it can denote speaking with the hands and eyes . . . Thus it is signifying to stir up a fight between neighbors by telling stories; it is signifying to make fun of the police by parodying his motion behind his back; it is signifying to ask for a piece of cake by saying 'my brother needs a piece of that cake.'

> (Abrahams 1970b: 51–2)

Kernan then notes, agreeing that for most of her Oakland informants 'some element of indirection was criterial to *signifying*,' nevertheless 'many would label the parodying of the policeman's motions *marking* and the request for cake *shucking*' (Kernan 1971: 88). It is impossible to judge from her data whether these acts might be both *signifying* (as the general term), and *marking* or *shucking* as kinds of *signifying,* or whether contrast existed among these three terms on the same taxonomic level. For my Philadelphia informants, at least, the former was the case (though the most common term at that time for *shucking* was *jiving,* or, among the older people, *jitterbugging* or *bugging*).

But the labelling problem is even more complicated in Kernan's description of *signifying;* she notes that for Thomas Kochman's Chicago informants, *signifying* and *sounding* are used interchangeably, while most of her Oakland informants 'referred to the direct taunts which Kochman suggests are the formal features of signifying, when its function is to arouse emotions in the absence of directive intent [as in a verbal duelling game] as *sounding* or *woofing'* (1971: 89). But, she goes on, using herself as an informant: 'As a child in the Chicago area, my age group treated *signifying* and *sounding* as contrasting terms. . . . *Signifying* . . . was a fairly standard tactic . . . employed in *sounding* (as a verbal insult game). That is, the speech event *sounding* could involve either direct insults *sounds* or *signifying,* indirect insults . . .' (pp. 89–90). However, with my Philadelphia informants, *sounding* and *woofing* were commonly used to refer just to the game of mother-rapping, *playing the dozens.* On the other hand, Rap Brown seems to insist on a basic distinction between *playing the dozens* and *signifying,* in which it is clear that the latter means, for him and his peers, what my Philadelphia informants called *mounting* and what Blacks in many parts of the country last year were calling *charging, cracking,* or *harping.* 'Signifying is more humane [than *playing the dozens*]. Instead of coming down on somebody's mother, you come down on them' (H.R. Brown 1969: 27). He further complicates matters by equating signifying with any kind of intensifying verbal activity (exclusive of the *dozens*), and not just putting someone down, by noting:

> before you can signify you got to be able to rap. . . . Signifying allowed you a choice—you could either make a cat feel good or bad. If you had just destroyed someone or if they were down already, signifying was also a way of expressing your own feelings. . . . Signifying at its best can be heard when the brothers are exchanging tales.

> (pp. 27–30)

Brown here seems to be setting up some kind of range and hierarchy of speaking events running from the most general term, *talking shit,* anyone's talk from the most casual to the most stylized and witty, to *rapping* or semi-public, spontaneously witty talk, to *playing the dozens* and *signifying,* openly competitive, public, witty, hyperbolic, highly stylized talk (including tales). But the place of *signifying* in this speech map would not be validated by Kernan's (1971) or Kochman's (1970) data, nor mine (see also Mezzrow & Wolfe 1969; Anderson 1959; Milner & Milner 1972; Eddington 1967; Hurston 1935 for more specific uses of the term).

These difficulties are more apparent than real, especially to the ethnographer of speaking. Clearly what we have here are terms which are used on more than one level in a taxonomy of ways of speaking, and which are used in different places and times to describe related but different speaking activities. Further, what I hope I have shown in the taxonomy is that with *signifying* we have a term not only for a way of speaking but for a rhetorical strategy that may be characteristic of a number of other designated events.

RAPPING

There are numerous terms to be found for casual talk, such as *beating the gums*, *gum beating*, *jawblock* (Mezzrow & Wolfe 1969). But none of these are place-specific to talk in public. With many informants in the last ten years there has been the feeling that the term *rapping* was the appropriate one for this public (street) talking—a perspective seemingly shared by Kochman when he noted that 'Rapping [is] used . . . to mean ordinary conversation' (Kochman 1970: 146; see also Keiser 1969: 72; Milner & Milner 1972: 306; Claerbaut 1972: 77; Woodley 1972: 144). But when asked whether terms like *sounding* or *shucking* were a kind of *rapping*, informants' responses are usually an initial giggle and then an 'I guess so.' I think that the reason my informants laughed when I asked them whether such terms are kinds of *rapping* was that while on the one hand rapping means 'just talking,' on the other hand in its most common uses it refers to interactions somewhat less public than the larger *playing* contest activities. That is, *rapping* in its more pointed uses is something generally carried on in person-to-person exchanges, ones in which the participants don't know each other well; it is often therefore a kind of *out of the house* talking which is primarily manipulative.

Kochman, in his full study of the semantic field of the term *rap*, indicates that he has observed three common uses:

1 When *running something down,* providing information to someone.

2 *Rapping* to a woman—'a colorful way of asking for some pussy,' used at the beginning of a relationship only, most used by *pimp-talkers, jivers,* the most fluent and lively men-of-words. This use I have therefore included under the concept term of *running a game* (a placing recognized or accepted by every one of my informants).

3 As the verbal dimensions of a *con,* when *whupping the game* (Kochman 1970: 147).

TO HIP

Running something *down*, as discussed in the body of the paper, refers to *straight*, valid-information-centered conversations, and may be distinguished from ones in which either *game* is being *run* or *played*. That is, *running it down* commonly means giving advice to someone in a situation in which a decision has to be made, or *hipping* someone to what's happening, letting him know of some possible activity or of the doings of others. 'Running it down is the term used by ghetto dwellers when they intend to communicate information, either in the form of an explanation, narrative, giving advice, and the like; . . . running it down has simply an informative function, telling somebody something that he doesn't already know' (Kochman 1970: 154–5, with quotations from King 1965, Claude Brown 1966, and Iceberg Slim 1967). 'Run it down: to tell the whole truth of whatever is in question' (Major 1970: 98; see also Killens 1972: 24, 41; Claerbaut 1972: 78; Milner & Milner 1972: 301, *to run down game*). Once one has had it *run down* to him, he is *down, in the know* (cf. Thomas 1967: 210, 243; Milner & Milner 1972: 299).

The earlier term, and one which is still widely in use, is to *hip*—'to inform a person of something he should know; to put [someone] wise' or *to be hipped* (to)—'informed; hep, knowledge; wise to' (Wentworth & Flexner 1960: 258; see also Gold 1960: 146; Milner & Milner 1972: 302; Claerbaut 1972: 68).

The basic distinction here is between the contest-focussed message of *running it down, hipping* someone to something, or *hitting on* a given subject, and the style-focussed message of *signifying,* styling which is foregrounded by the devices of making a point by indirection and wit. This is not to say that *running it down* has no style, or *signifying* has no content, but that their primary focus differs in this regard. Note that *signifying* here is designated only with regard to its street uses (see Kernan 1971: 87ff. for a discussion of sex-specific differences).

TALKING SHIT

Most *signifying* arising in the street world is of a sort in which the participants in the interaction engage in talk to elicit more talk—to get some *action* going. Witty remarks will be made calling for a response in kind. Though such exchanges often sound like arguments to outsiders, there is no rhetorical intent to create a status distinction.

There are many terms which have been employed for this kind of *signifying* play, *talking shit* seeming to be the most common today. Older terms, some of which are still in use, are *woofing* (though in most communities this refers to more particular events like *playing the dozens* or *sounding*), *telling lies, shaglag,* and *bookooing.* Hurston uses all four terms on this level in her works:

> Woofing is a sort of aimless talking. A man half seriously flirts with a girl, half seriously threatens to fight or brags of his prowess in love, battle or financial matters. The term comes from the purposeless barking of dogs at night.

> (Hurston 1935: 305)

She makes it plain, however, in her numerous *woofing* scenes, that 'aimless talk-ing' means an active display of wits.

The term most widely used now is *talking shit,* at least according to students from all over the country. That it is not just a student term is testified by Killens' use of it (Killens 1972: 26, 40), by the Milners (1972: 309), and by Major's ref-erence to the expression and by Friedland and Nelkin's reporting of the term from a migratory labor camp in connection with a man-of-words and his abilities to joke and rhyme on people effectively (Friedland & Nelkin 1971: 152).

On the other hand, there are types of behavior in which the talker does seek to establish dominance or to *signify* to evade a situation in which he is already dominated. A distinction is made between *putting down* or *low-rating* in which witty devices are used to establish dominance, and *copping a plea,* in which an already dominated person attempts to establish equilibrium by admitting his sub-ordinated status. (Kochman 1970 and Rainwater 1970 both report this term, as well as the less extremely deferential *gripping;* see also Major 1970: 41.) Thomas, discussing the strategy, notes: 'Mom was asking us to cop a plea to the white man . . . A—accept, B—behave, C—care.' The term also means *to rat on,* inform on (Thomas 1967: 134, 243). The most recently reported term (from Texas) for this is *eating cheese.* These terms are of recent usage in this sense, but may inhabit the same semantic field as *tomming, jeffing* (cf. Kochman 1970; Eddington 1967) or *playing Uncle Tom*—though in present usage the *tomming* of slaves tends to be regarded as closer to *shucking* in that it uses deference as a means of achieving some sense of dominance, and is therefore one type of *putting on* behavior. In the absence of actual reportings of such behavior labeled as *tomming,* however, I would not so categorize it; it should be noted, however, that the Marster-John stories (Abrahams 1970a) represent similar accommodative strategies in narrative form to *tomming* (cf. Kochman 1970: 149).

Putting on involves the entire range of strategies for verbal manipulation to establish control. Essentially the term refers to 'play-acting for real,' using any of the devices of playing but in a situation in which eventually a psychological dominance is sought by the speaker, even if the person (or persons) being *put-on* doesn't recognize this. *Putting on* therefore involves a use of any of the strate-gies in one or another of its manifestations. As *running a game* or *whupping game* (cf. Kochman 1970; Milner & Milner 1972: 301; Claerbaut 1972: 65, 78, 86) it will actively involve all three—deference, dominance, and parity. With other *put-on* styles, the range is not so wide. *Putting on,* in any case, emphasizes the dominance strategy, and would have been regarded as a special kind of *put-down* except that my informants in both Philadelphia and Austin insist that a *put-on* is not a *put-down* but something quite distinct.

The difference is primarily in regard to where the speaker stands in regard to those he wishes to dominate. With a *put-down,* the dominance is already appar-ently felt, the speaker ratifying the relationship with each *put-down.* With a *put-*

on, the dominance is not yet established; thus the speaker needs a less tendentious mode of asserting control, using a wide number of artful talking techniques. That there is a strong relationship between the two is indicated by the recognition by street talkers that some of the techniques of *putting* someone *on* can also be used to *put* them *down.*

PUT-DOWN

There seems to be a basic distinction between the *put-down* style that relies on sharpness of perception and verbal focus and one in which the speaker gets louder and louder. This distinction is noted by communities most commonly when *loud-talking* is regarded as an inappropriate way to achieve a put-down. Hurston (1934) defines *loud talk me* in her glossary as 'making your side appear right by making more noise than the others,' but her use of the term in the novel is pejorative (p. 158). On the other hand, Heard gives us a *loud-talking* scene, using the term in which our response is intended to be ambivalent. In this use of the technique by a pimp, he uses a proverb, 'Talk loud and draw a big crowd' (1968: 227; this use of the term differs from its employment in the *put-on;* see below).

 Mounting, downing (Abrahams 1970a; Eddington 1967: 198), and *ranking* are the same terms as used in one form of *playing the dozens;* the relationship is hardly fortuitous, for the same verbal devices are used in the *put-down* for serious purposes and in the *dozens* for play. In this serious interpersonal context, when the *mounting* is extended and one person is strongly *put down,* that has been called *getting on his case* or *charging*—though *downing* is not the only technique used in such situations.

PUT-ON

Loud-talking (or *louding*) (in a different meaning than above) and *marking* are two special techniques of achieving a *put-on.* Both involve a performance not overtly directed to the object of the remark. *Louding* is where the speaker is talking to others (or himself) loud enough so that the person referred to can hear— but when that person reacts, the speaker can reply to the effect 'Oh, I wasn't talking to you.' To be pulled off most effectively, the 'overheard' remark must refer to the overhearer in some oblique way. (Kernan 1971 gives an extended description, pp. 129–37, as do Labov *et al.* 1968: *passim,* but esp. pp. 14ff. and 27ff.) Mezzrow & Wolfe (1969) report the practice, perhaps in a more formal game context, as *snagging.* My informants agree that this is a way of *putting* someone *on,* but many argue that it may be a *put-down* as well. Kernan's examples would seem to argue the same way.

 Marking, on the other hand, in its largest sense is simply the Black term for dramatic imitation or aping. It is not always used pejoratively. However, when the imitation is addressed to others than the person imitated, and especially when it is done in his presence but without his recognition, this is regarded as a *put-on* device. (*Marking* in the larger sense of imitation can be found in any verbal interaction as an intensifying device, especially in jokes and *getting on* someone's *case*. Kernan surveys the technique and its uses [1971: 137–43]). In the case where *marking* is used as a *put-on* device, it too can turn into a *put-down*.

With *running a game* we are in a domain of street performance in which verbal manipulation is central (see Killens 1972: *passim,* but esp. pp. 22ff.; also Milner & Milner 1972: 301; Claerbaut 1972: 65, 78, 86). Here the speaker uses as many techniques as possible to convince his target audience of the validity of his credentials, so that he may exploit them for sexual favors, money, or simply to enhance his reputation. With professional men of words, the *pimps, jivers, mackmen,* etc., *running* some sort of *game* is a constant preoccupation. Other men share in this to the extent that they have the ability to use their words to assert and maintain their *rep.*

There are many terms for running a game, all more or less synonymous. One term commonly used for this domain is *talking bullshit.* Claude Brown describes his persuasive powers of performance using this term:

> When Dad tried to talk to me, it never work out . . . It was easier for me [to get hit] than trying to listen to all that stupid shit he was telling me with a serious face. Sometimes I would bullshit him by looking serious and saying something that made him think he was saying something real smart. I had a special way of bullshitting everyone I knew, and that was how I bullshitted Dad.

> (1966: 45)

Kochman's discussion of *rapping* describes that term as the most casual dimension of the *gaming* complex of terms (see also Suttles 1968: 159; Milner & Milner 1972: 306; Claerbaut 1972: 76). *Jiving* and *shucking* seem to refer to more intensive *rapping,* with an accompanying growth in the amount of purposeful deception involved in such talking. Both of these are complicated terms historically and semantically. *Jive* and *jiving* used to mean simply the argot of the young Blacks on the street (see, e.g., Hurston 1942) and *jive-talk* was still used in this sense until recently. But because of the types who had greatest command over this style of talking, *jive* and *bulljive* came to be used in more and more pejorative contexts, as they are today (Strong 1940; Major 1970; Grange 1968; Rainwater 1970; Gold 1960; Claerbaut 1972; Milner & Milner 1972). The negative features fastened upon are an overstress on *styling* (obviously *styling* which doesn't come off) or too much emphasis on dominance at the expense of the parity strategy implied in *rapping.* Mezzrow and Wolfe make a distinction between *jive* and *high-jive,* the latter involving the use of 'fancy-talk,' a variety more commonly found in the semi-private courtship situation: 'High-jive: intellectual patter, the smoothest and most elaborate line. Highjiver: smooth character with a very fancy and intellectual line of talk.' (1969: 306)[3]

Shucking and *jiving* are often used as one term. *Shucking* is also used to refer to any kind of name-establishing *bullshit,* though not so strongly focussed on knowledge of the in-group terms as *jiving* (see Abrahams 1970b, though the etymology for *shucking* there is faulty, as it is in Gold—the base reference of the term almost certainly goes back to a corn-shuck, either in regard to the practice of the corn-shucking performance gathering or to the expression 'lighting a shuck,' i.e., using a burning shuck for light for some peer-grouping activity [cf. Hurston 1934: 206]; Rainwater 1970: 284; Kochman 1970; Cain 1970; Milner & Milner 1972: 307; Claerbaut 1972: 79; Killens 1972: 25, 141).

Shucking, where it is used, refers to the artful means by which one person can get around another by whatever means he can devise. It therefore involves more devious means than *rapping,* especially as Kochman explores the two terms:

> *Shucking, jiving, shucking and jiving* or S-ing and J-ing, when referring to language behavior practiced by blacks when interacting with one another on the peer-group level, is descriptive of the talk and gestures appropriate to 'putting someone on' by creating a false impression, conveying false information, and the like. The terms seem to cover a range from simply telling a lie, to bullshitting, to subtly playing with someone's mind.
>
> (1970: 154)

This use of *shucking and jiving* differs in white-Black interactions only in the actual techniques used, not in the motives or intensity.

More intense and indicating deceit are terms like *hyping* and *conning,* but these are less often used in reference to in-group street-talking activity, and more in commentary on effective talking by some of their members in interactions outside the group (Mezzrow & Wolfe 1969: 306).

HOORAWING

Hoorawing, an active contest of wits in which everyone may join, is the most volatile of all the categories for ways of speaking. It is known by a number of terms even within the same community. *Hoorawing* or *talking hooraw shit* seem to be the oldest terms here according to my older informants in both Philadelphia and Texas. Other names are *signifying* (Kochman 1970; Rainwater 1970), *joning* (Hannerz 1969; Rainwater 1970), *screaming, ranking, cracking,*

---

[3]Puckett and Dillard discuss the uses of these traditions of eloquence (Puckett 1926: 38 ff; Dillard 1972: 245–259), and I survey the West Indian literature and the possible African backgrounds (Abrahams 1970c). Hannerz discusses the uses of such talk on the streets, as do Mezzrow and Wolfe, though the latters' interpretation seems wrong-headed (Hannerz 1969: 85; Mezzrow & Wolfe 1969: 195).

snapping, sounding (Thomas 1967; Labov *et al.* 1968; Abrahams 1970b), *woofing* (Abrahams 1970b), and *telling lies*. The practice is commonly carried on in trading short formulaic items, but among adults often includes the longer narrative items like *jokes, toasts,* or *stories.* Hurston's books, especially *Mules and Men* (1935), eloquently describe this practice and with many texts. The importance of this kind of verbal play is discussed throughout the literature (see especially Hannerz 1969; Labov *et al.* 1968; Rainwater 1970; Abrahams 1970a,b; Kochman 1970). The larger term for this kind of play is *cutting contest* (see, for instance, Mezzrow & Wolfe 1969: 1971) and, by extension, a friend with whom one can play, *a cutting buddy, cutting man,* or *cutty* (Abrahams 1970b).

As Rap Brown pointed out, a distinction is often made between verbal contests involving insults to members of the families of the other contestants and those which aggrandize or deprecate in other ways. Explicitly or implicitly, there are further distinctions made in the playing of the clean dozens: to devices which are *lies* about oneself (whether they are aggrandizing of self doesn't seem to matter—if they are exaggerations they may be termed *bragging,* even if the content is about how poor or hungry or thin you are); to devices which wittily discuss the shortcomings of others, sometimes referred to as *mounting;* and simply witty remarks which build upon the word-play of others, *capping.* (Abrahams 1970d; Eddington 1967:198; Claerbaut 1972:60; Mezzrow & Wolfe 1969:304 define it as 'having the last word, go one better, outdo,' but their use of the term indicates a speaking frame of reference primarily.)

Boasting seems to mean intensive talk about oneself in a contest situation, whether one is emphasizing one's strengths or shortcomings. Thus, there may be exchanges based on how quick one is, how strong, or how hungry, lazy, tired, or whatever. (The same witticisms may be used to discuss someone else, in which case they are noncompetitive devices simply used to flavor conversational discussions.) These self-aggrandizing devices are also called *lies,* though that term is generally used for stories, jokes, and tall tales.

Dick Gregory, in his book *Nigger,* shows how important it was in learning how to cope with the realities of street life (and how he developed his comic sense) to learn a repertoire of these self-degrading *boasts,* by which he could capitalize on an underclassed position, building it into a strength (Gregory 1964:40–2). The technique emerges in many other works by Black authors.

More commonly, such *hoorawing* takes the form of *mounting,* attacking the other(s) by denigrating them. This may be done either by boasting at the same time or just *putting* the other *down.*[4]

[4]I want to thank John Szwed and Robert Farris Thompson, Tony Terry and Robert Wilson, for talking some of the matters out. To the editors I am even further indebted—and far beyond matters editorial—for they both helped in the conceptualization and rendering of the paper at times when despair had settled in. Beverly Stoeltje's discussion of women *talking smart* clarified my ideas in this area. Marilyn Sandlin, too, bore up under the despair and the frenzy, typing the (too) many drafts. Barbara Babcock-Abrahams not only drew the chart many times, but helped with many other finishing touches.

REFERENCES

Abrahams, R.D. (1970a). *Positively Black.* Englewood Cliffs, N.J.

———. (1970b). *Deep down in the jungle.* rev. ed. Chicago.

———. (1970c). Traditions of eloquence in the West Indies. *Journal of Inter-American Studies and World Affairs* 12: 505–527.

———. (1970d). Rapping and capping: Black talk as art. In J. Szwed (ed.). *Black Americans.* New York: 145–153.

———. (1973). *Toward a Black rhetoric: Being a survey of Afro-American communication styles and role-relationships.* Texas Working Papers in Sociolinguistics no. 15.

Abrahams, R.D., and R. Bauman. (1971). Sense and nonsense in St. Vincent: Speech behavior and decorum in a Caribbean community. *American Anthropologist* 73(3): 262–272.

Anderson, A. (1959). *Lover man.* New York.

Brown, C. (1965). *Manchild in the promised land.* New York.

Brown, H.R. (1969). *Die Nigger die!* New York.

Cain, G. (1970). *Blueschild baby.* New York.

Claerbaut, D. (1972). *Black jargon in White America.* Grand Rapids, MI.

Dillard, J. (1972). *Black English.* New York.

Eddington, N. (1967). The urban plantation: The ethnography of oral tradition in a Negro community. Ph.D. dissertation, University of California at Berkeley.

Ellis, H., and S. Newman. 1971. 'Gowster,' 'Ivy-Leaguer,' 'Hustler,' 'Conservative,' 'Mackman,' and 'Continental': A functional analysis of six ghetto roles. In E.G. Leacock (ed.), *The culture of poverty: A critique.* New York: 299–314.

Ferris, W. (1972). Black prose narrative in the Mississippi Delta: An overview. *Journal of American Folklore* 85: 140–151.

Firestone, H. (1964). Cats, kicks and color. In H.S. Becker (ed.), *The other side.* New York. 281–297.

Friedland, W., and D. Nelkin. (1971). *Migrant.* New York.

Gold, R. (1960). *A jazz lexicon.* New York.

Grange, K. (1968). Black slang. *Current Slang* III(2).

Gregory, D., with R. Lipsyte. (1964). *Nigger.* New York.

Hannerz, U. (1969). *Soulside.* New York.

Heard, N. (1968). *Howard street.* New York.

Hooker, R. (1972). Florida Black supports Wallace. *Race Relations Reporter* (December): 4.

Hurston, Z. (1934). *Jonah's gourd vine.* Philadelphia.

———. (1935). *Mules and men.* Philadelphia.

———. (1942). Story in Harlem slang *American Mercury* (July): 84–96.

Hymes, D. (1972). Models of the interaction of language and social life. In J.J. Gumperz and D. Hymes (eds.), *Directions in sociolinguistics.* New York. 35–71.

Iceberg, Slim. (1967). *Pimp: The story of my life.* Los Angeles.

Johnson, K.R. (1971). Black kinesics—some non-verbal patterns in Black culture. *Florida F/L Reporter* 9: 17–21, 57.

Keegan, F. (1971). *Blacktown, U.S.A.* Boston.

Keiser, R. (1969). *The vice-lords: warriors of the streets.* New York.

Kernan, C. (1971). *Language behavior in a Black urban community.* Berkeley, CA.

Killens, J. (1972). *Cotillion.* New York.

King, W., Jr. (1965). The game. *Liberator* 5:20–25.

Kochman, T. (1970). Toward an ethnography of Black American speech beha Szwed and N. Whitten (eds.), *Afro-American anthropology: Contemporar tives.* New York. 145–162.

Labov, W., P. Cohen, C. Robins, and J. Lewis. (1968). *A study of the no English of Negro and Puerto Rican speakers in New York City,* vol. II. New

Lewis, H. (1964). *Blackways of Kent.* New Haven, CT.

Liebow, E. (1967). *Tally's corner.* Boston.

Major, C. (1970). *Dictionary of Afro-American slang.* New York.

Malcolm X with Haley, A. (1965). *The autobiography of Malcolm X.* New Yor

Meriwether, L. (1970). *Daddy was a numbers runner.* New York.

Mezzrow, M., and B. Wolfe. (1969). *Really the blues.* New York.

Milner, C., and R. Milner. (1972). *Black players.* Boston.

Olmsted, F.L. (1856). *A journey in the seaboard states.* New York.

Puckett, N. (1926). *Folk beliefs of the Southern Negro.* Chapel Hill, NC.

Rainwater, L. (1970). *Behind ghetto walls.* Chicago.

Sale, R.T. (1971). *The Blackstone rangers.* New York.

Strong, S. (1940). Social types in the Negro community of Chicago. Ph.D. University of Chicago.

Suttles, G. (1968). *The social order of the slums.* Chicago.

Thomas, P. (1967). *Down these mean streets.* New York.

Valentine, C. (1972). *Black studies and anthropology: Scholarly and politica Afro-American culture.* Reading, MA.

Ward, M. (1971). *Them children: A study in language learning.* New York.

Wentworth, H., and Flexner, S. (1960). *Dictionary of American slang.* New

Whitten, N., and Szwed, J. (1970). *Afro-American anthropology: Contempo tives.* New York.

Wilson, P. (1969). Reputation and respectability: Suggestions for Caribbe *Man*: 4. 70–84.

Woodley, R. (1972). *Dealer: portrait of a cocaine merchant.* New York.

Young, V. (1970). Family and childhood in a Southern Negro commu *Anthropologist* 72:269–288.

Chicano English:
The Anguish of Definition

John Baugh

The Chicano English community is highly diversified, to sa other varieties of Hispanic English in the United States. Like English (BVE), Chicano (vernacular) English is a nonstandard

REFERENCES

Abrahams, R.D. (1970a). *Positively Black.* Englewood Cliffs, N.J.

———. (1970b). *Deep down in the jungle.* rev. ed. Chicago.

———. (1970c). Traditions of eloquence in the West Indies. *Journal of Inter-American Studies and World Affairs* 12: 505–527.

———. (1970d). Rapping and capping: Black talk as art. In J. Szwed (ed.). *Black Americans.* New York: 145–153.

———. (1973). *Toward a Black rhetoric: Being a survey of Afro-American communication styles and role-relationships.* Texas Working Papers in Sociolinguistics no. 15.

Abrahams, R.D., and R. Bauman. (1971). Sense and nonsense in St. Vincent: Speech behavior and decorum in a Caribbean community. *American Anthropologist* 73(3): 262–272.

Anderson, A. (1959). *Lover man.* New York.

Brown, C. (1965). *Manchild in the promised land.* New York.

Brown, H.R. (1969). *Die Nigger die!* New York.

Cain, G. (1970). *Blueschild baby.* New York.

Claerbaut, D. (1972). *Black jargon in White America.* Grand Rapids, MI.

Dillard, J. (1972). *Black English.* New York.

Eddington, N. (1967). The urban plantation: The ethnography of oral tradition in a Negro community. Ph.D. dissertation, University of California at Berkeley.

Ellis, H., and S. Newman. 1971. 'Gowster,' 'Ivy-Leaguer,' 'Hustler,' 'Conservative,' 'Mackman,' and 'Continental': A functional analysis of six ghetto roles. In E.G. Leacock (ed.), *The culture of poverty: A critique.* New York: 299–314.

Ferris, W. (1972). Black prose narrative in the Mississippi Delta: An overview. *Journal of American Folklore* 85: 140–151.

Firestone, H. (1964). Cats, kicks and color. In H.S. Becker (ed.), *The other side.* New York. 281–297.

Friedland, W., and D. Nelkin. (1971). *Migrant.* New York.

Gold, R. (1960). *A jazz lexicon.* New York.

Grange, K. (1968). Black slang. *Current Slang* III(2).

Gregory, D., with R. Lipsyte. (1964). *Nigger.* New York.

Hannerz, U. (1969). *Soulside.* New York.

Heard, N. (1968). *Howard street.* New York.

Hooker, R. (1972). Florida Black supports Wallace. *Race Relations Reporter* (December): 4.

Hurston, Z. (1934). *Jonah's gourd vine.* Philadelphia.

———. (1935). *Mules and men.* Philadelphia.

———. (1942). Story in Harlem slang *American Mercury* (July): 84–96.

Hymes, D. (1972). Models of the interaction of language and social life. In J.J. Gumperz and D. Hymes (eds.), *Directions in sociolinguistics.* New York. 35–71.

Iceberg, Slim. (1967). *Pimp: The story of my life.* Los Angeles.

Johnson, K.R. (1971). Black kinesics—some non-verbal patterns in Black culture. *Florida F/L Reporter* 9: 17–21, 57.

Keegan, F. (1971). *Blacktown, U.S.A.* Boston.

Keiser, R. (1969). *The vice-lords: warriors of the streets.* New York.

Kernan, C. (1971). *Language behavior in a Black urban community.* Berkeley, CA.

Killens, J. (1972). *Cotillion.* New York.

King, W., Jr. (1965). The game. *Liberator* 5:20–25.

Kochman, T. (1970). Toward an ethnography of Black American speech behavior. Szwed and N. Whitten (eds.), *Afro-American anthropology: Contemporary perspectives.* New York. 145–162.

Labov, W., P. Cohen, C. Robins, and J. Lewis. (1968). *A study of the non-standard English of Negro and Puerto Rican speakers in New York City,* vol. II. New York.

Lewis, H. (1964). *Blackways of Kent.* New Haven, CT.

Liebow, E. (1967). *Tally's corner.* Boston.

Major, C. (1970). *Dictionary of Afro-American slang.* New York.

Malcolm X with Haley, A. (1965). *The autobiography of Malcolm X.* New York.

Meriwhether, L. (1970). *Daddy was a numbers runner.* New York.

Mezzrow, M., and B. Wolfe. (1969). *Really the blues.* New York.

Milner, C., and R. Milner. (1972). *Black players.* Boston.

Olmsted, F.L. (1856). *A journey in the seaboard states.* New York.

Puckett, N. (1926). *Folk beliefs of the Southern Negro.* Chapel Hill, NC.

Rainwater, L. (1970). *Behind ghetto walls.* Chicago.

Sale, R.T. (1971). *The Blackstone rangers.* New York.

Strong, S. (1940). Social types in the Negro community of Chicago. Ph.D. dissertation, University of Chicago.

Suttles, G. (1968). *The social order of the slums.* Chicago.

Thomas, P. (1967). *Down these mean streets.* New York.

Valentine, C. (1972). *Black studies and anthropology: Scholarly and political interests in Afro-American culture.* Reading, MA.

Ward, M. (1971). *Them children: A study in language learning.* New York.

Wentworth, H., and Flexner, S. (1960). *Dictionary of American slang.* New York.

Whitten, N., and Szwed, J. (1970). *Afro-American anthropology: Contemporary perspectives.* New York.

Wilson, P. (1969). Reputation and respectability: Suggestions for Caribbean ethnology. *Man*: 4. 70–84.

Woodley, R. (1972). *Dealer: portrait of a cocaine merchant.* New York.

Young, V. (1970). Family and childhood in a Southern Negro community. *American Anthropologist* 72:269–288.

Chicano English:
The Anguish of Definition

John Baugh

The Chicano English community is highly diversified, to say nothing of other varieties of Hispanic English in the United States. Like Black Vernacular English (BVE), Chicano (vernacular) English is a nonstandard dialect, but the

lectual patter, the smoothest and most elaborate line. Highjiver: smooth character with a very fancy and intellectual line of talk.' (1969: 306)[3]

Shucking and *jiving* are often used as one term. *Shucking* is also used to refer
to any kind of name-establishing *bullshit,* though not so strongly focussed on
knowledge of the in-group terms as *jiving* (see Abrahams 1970b, though the etymology for *shucking* there is faulty, as it is in Gold—the base reference of the
term almost certainly goes back to a corn-shuck, either in regard to the practice
of the corn-shucking performance gathering or to the expression 'lighting a
shuck,' i.e., using a burning shuck for light for some peer-grouping activity [cf.
Hurston 1934: 206]; Rainwater 1970: 284; Kochman 1970; Cain 1970; Milner &
Milner 1972: 307; Claerbaut 1972: 79; Killens 1972: 25, 141).

Shucking, where it is used, refers to the artful means by which one person can
get around another by whatever means he can devise. It therefore involves more
devious means than *rapping,* especially as Kochman explores the two terms:

> *Shucking, jiving, shucking and jiving* or S-ing and J-ing, when referring to language
> behavior practiced by blacks when interacting with one another on the peer-group
> level, is descriptive of the talk and gestures appropriate to 'putting someone on' by
> creating a false impression, conveying false information, and the like. The terms seem
> to cover a range from simply telling a lie, to bullshitting, to subtly playing with some-
> one's mind.
>
> (1970: 154)

This use of *shucking and jiving* differs in white-Black interactions only in the
actual techniques used, not in the motives or intensity.

More intense and indicating deceit are terms like *hyping* and *conning,* but
these are less often used in reference to in-group street-talking activity, and
more in commentary on effective talking by some of their members in interactions outside the group (Mezzrow & Wolfe 1969: 306).

HOORAWING

Hoorawing, an active contest of wits in which everyone may join, is the most
volatile of all the categories for ways of speaking. It is known by a number of
terms even within the same community. *Hoorawing* or *talking hooraw shit* seem
to be the oldest terms here according to my older informants in both
Philadelphia and Texas. Other names are *signifying* (Kochman 1970; Rainwater
1970), *joning* (Hannerz 1969; Rainwater 1970), *screaming, ranking, cracking,*

---

[3]Puckett and Dillard discuss the uses of these traditions of eloquence (Puckett 1926: 38 ff;
Dillard 1972: 245–259), and I survey the West Indian literature and the possible African backgrounds (Abrahams 1970c). Hannerz discusses the uses of such talk on the streets, as do Mezzrow
and Wolfe, though the latters' interpretation seems wrong-headed (Hannerz 1969: 85; Mezzrow &
Wolfe 1969: 195).

snapping, sounding (Thomas 1967; Labov *et al.* 1968; Abrahams 1970b), *woofing* (Abrahams 1970b), and *telling lies.* The practice is commonly carried on in trading short formulaic items, but among adults often includes the longer narrative items like *jokes, toasts,* or *stories.* Hurston's books, especially *Mules and Men* (1935), eloquently describe this practice and with many texts. The importance of this kind of verbal play is discussed throughout the literature (see especially Hannerz 1969; Labov *et al.* 1968; Rainwater 1970; Abrahams 1970a,b; Kochman 1970). The larger term for this kind of play is *cutting contest* (see, for instance, Mezzrow & Wolfe 1969: 1971) and, by extension, a friend with whom one can play, a *cutting buddy, cutting man,* or *cutty* (Abrahams 1970b).

As Rap Brown pointed out, a distinction is often made between verbal contests involving insults to members of the families of the other contestants and those which aggrandize or deprecate in other ways. Explicitly or implicitly, there are further distinctions made in the playing of the clean dozens: to devices which are *lies* about oneself (whether they are aggrandizing of self doesn't seem to matter—if they are exaggerations they may be termed *bragging,* even if the content is about how poor or hungry or thin you are); to devices which wittily discuss the shortcomings of others, sometimes referred to as *mounting;* and simply witty remarks which build upon the word-play of others, *capping.* (Abrahams 1970d; Eddington 1967:198; Claerbaut 1972:60; Mezzrow & Wolfe 1969:304 define it as 'having the last word, go one better, outdo,' but their use of the term indicates a speaking frame of reference primarily.)

Boasting seems to mean intensive talk about oneself in a contest situation, whether one is emphasizing one's strengths or shortcomings. Thus, there may be exchanges based on how quick one is, how strong, or how hungry, lazy, tired, or whatever. (The same witticisms may be used to discuss someone else, in which case they are noncompetitive devices simply used to flavor conversational discussions.) These self-aggrandizing devices are also called *lies,* though that term is generally used for stories, jokes, and tall tales.

Dick Gregory, in his book *Nigger,* shows how important it was in learning how to cope with the realities of street life (and how he developed his comic sense) to learn a repertoire of these self-degrading *boasts,* by which he could capitalize on an underclassed position, building it into a strength (Gregory 1964:40–2). The technique emerges in many other works by Black authors.

More commonly, such *hoorawing* takes the form of *mounting,* attacking the other(s) by denigrating them. This may be done either by boasting at the same time or just *putting* the other *down.*[4]

---

[4]I want to thank John Szwed and Robert Farris Thompson, Tony Terry and Robert Wilson, for talking some of the matters out. To the editors I am even further indebted—and far beyond matters editorial—for they both helped in the conceptualization and rendering of the paper at times when despair had settled in. Beverly Stoeltje's discussion of women *talking smart* clarified my ideas in this area. Marilyn Sandlin, too, bore up under the despair and the frenzy, typing the (too) many drafts. Barbara Babcock-Abrahams not only drew the chart many times, but helped with many other finishing touches.

REFERENCES

Abrahams, R.D. (1970a). *Positively Black.* Englewood Cliffs, N.J.

———. (1970b). *Deep down in the jungle.* rev. ed. Chicago.

———. (1970c). Traditions of eloquence in the West Indies. *Journal of Inter-American Studies and World Affairs* 12: 505–527.

———. (1970d). Rapping and capping: Black talk as art. In J. Szwed (ed.). *Black Americans.* New York: 145–153.

———. (1973). *Toward a Black rhetoric: Being a survey of Afro-American communication styles and role-relationships.* Texas Working Papers in Sociolinguistics no. 15.

Abrahams, R.D., and R. Bauman. (1971). Sense and nonsense in St. Vincent: Speech behavior and decorum in a Caribbean community. *American Anthropologist* 73(3): 262–272.

Anderson, A. (1959). *Lover man.* New York.

Brown, C. (1965). *Manchild in the promised land.* New York.

Brown, H.R. (1969). *Die Nigger die!* New York.

Cain, G. (1970). *Blueschild baby.* New York.

Claerbaut, D. (1972). *Black jargon in White America.* Grand Rapids, MI.

Dillard, J. (1972). *Black English.* New York.

Eddington, N. (1967). The urban plantation: The ethnography of oral tradition in a Negro community. Ph.D. dissertation, University of California at Berkeley.

Ellis, H., and S. Newman. 1971. 'Gowster,' 'Ivy-Leaguer,' 'Hustler,' 'Conservative,' 'Mackman,' and 'Continental': A functional analysis of six ghetto roles. In E.G. Leacock (ed.), *The culture of poverty: A critique.* New York: 299–314.

Ferris, W. (1972). Black prose narrative in the Mississippi Delta: An overview. *Journal of American Folklore* 85: 140–151.

Firestone, H. (1964). Cats, kicks and color. In H.S. Becker (ed.), *The other side.* New York. 281–297.

Friedland, W., and D. Nelkin. (1971). *Migrant.* New York.

Gold, R. (1960). *A jazz lexicon.* New York.

Grange, K. (1968). Black slang. *Current Slang* III(2).

Gregory, D., with R. Lipsyte. (1964). *Nigger.* New York.

Hannerz, U. (1969). *Soulside.* New York.

Heard, N. (1968). *Howard street.* New York.

Hooker, R. (1972). Florida Black supports Wallace. *Race Relations Reporter* (December): 4.

Hurston, Z. (1934). *Jonah's gourd vine.* Philadelphia.

———. (1935). *Mules and men.* Philadelphia.

———. (1942). Story in Harlem slang *American Mercury* (July): 84–96.

Hymes, D. (1972). Models of the interaction of language and social life. In J.J. Gumperz and D. Hymes (eds.), *Directions in sociolinguistics.* New York. 35–71.

Iceberg, Slim. (1967). *Pimp: The story of my life.* Los Angeles.

Johnson, K.R. (1971). Black kinesics—some non-verbal patterns in Black culture. *Florida F/L Reporter* 9: 17–21, 57.

Keegan, F. (1971). *Blacktown, U.S.A.* Boston.

Keiser, R. (1969). *The vice-lords: warriors of the streets.* New York.

Kernan, C. (1971). *Language behavior in a Black urban community.* Berkeley, CA.

Killens, J. (1972). *Cotillion.* New York.

King, W., Jr. (1965). The game. *Liberator* 5:20–25.

Kochman, T. (1970). Toward an ethnography of Black American speech behavior. In J. Szwed and N. Whitten (eds.), *Afro-American anthropology: Contemporary perspectives.* New York. 145–162.

Labov, W., P. Cohen, C. Robins, and J. Lewis. (1968). *A study of the non-standard English of Negro and Puerto Rican speakers in New York City,* vol. II. New York.

Lewis, H. (1964). *Blackways of Kent.* New Haven, CT.

Liebow, E. (1967). *Tally's corner.* Boston.

Major, C. (1970). *Dictionary of Afro-American slang.* New York.

Malcolm X with Haley, A. (1965). *The autobiography of Malcolm X.* New York.

Meriwhether, L. (1970). *Daddy was a numbers runner.* New York.

Mezzrow, M., and B. Wolfe. (1969). *Really the blues.* New York.

Milner, C., and R. Milner. (1972). *Black players.* Boston.

Olmsted, F.L. (1856). *A journey in the seaboard states.* New York.

Puckett, N. (1926). *Folk beliefs of the Southern Negro.* Chapel Hill, NC.

Rainwater, L. (1970). *Behind ghetto walls.* Chicago.

Sale, R.T. (1971). *The Blackstone rangers.* New York.

Strong, S. (1940). Social types in the Negro community of Chicago. Ph.D. dissertation, University of Chicago.

Suttles, G. (1968). *The social order of the slums.* Chicago.

Thomas, P. (1967). *Down these mean streets.* New York.

Valentine, C. (1972). *Black studies and anthropology: Scholarly and political interests in Afro-American culture.* Reading, MA.

Ward, M. (1971). *Them children: A study in language learning.* New York.

Wentworth, H., and Flexner, S. (1960). *Dictionary of American slang.* New York.

Whitten, N., and Szwed, J. (1970). *Afro-American anthropology: Contemporary perspectives.* New York.

Wilson, P. (1969). Reputation and respectability: Suggestions for Caribbean ethnology. *Man*: 4. 70–84.

Woodley, R. (1972). *Dealer: portrait of a cocaine merchant.* New York.

Young, V. (1970). Family and childhood in a Southern Negro community. *American Anthropologist* 72:269–288.

Chicano English:
The Anguish of Definition

John Baugh

The Chicano English community is highly diversified, to say nothing of the other varieties of Hispanic English in the United States. Like Black Vernacular English (BVE), Chicano (vernacular) English is a nonstandard dialect, but this is where the similarity ends. Most of my research on English dialects has looked at nonstandard black speech. The research trends and precedents that have been established for BVE can in turn help future studies of Chicano English. At this stage let it suffice to say that Chicano English is a more complex phenomena, in purely linguistic terms, due to the combined population of monolingual Chicano English and bilingual Chicano English speakers. Black English by contrast consists of a spectrum of dialects within a monolingual paradigm.

As we shall see momentarily, this is an intricate phenomena, because of several linguistic and social factors. My title is drawn from the fact that the Chicano English community is dynamic, and it will continue to be so in the face of continued migration from Mexico. Four general topics will illustrate the point: we will first review the history of Chicano English dialect. Next we will turn to the nature of contemporary (i.e., synchronic) linguistic variation, which, again, is more complex than the corresponding variation in BVE. These observations are going to set the stage to consider the dynamic nature of the Chicano English population, and the added dimension of group loyalties, which are reinforced by language and dialect use. In the final analysis we shall observe that Chomsky's notion of "linguistic competence" must also be taken into account in any adequate definition.

Those who are familiar with BVE research will observe that I have retraced the major themes that grew out of the early sociolinguistic research trends for Black English. By outlining the same topics for future Chicano English research, we can perhaps avoid some of the mistakes that have been made in the past. Black English research has given rise to other productive studies of language around the world. By comparison, Chicano English research has been sorely neglected. As with previous research on nonstandard dialects in the United States, the ultimate practical value will be felt in pedagogical terms, when more Chicanos have an opportunity to gain competitive insights from our observations and suggestions. It is my hope that my brief remarks point out the scope and magnitude of the issue.

THE EVOLUTION OF CHICANO ENGLISH

The majority of the American population has very little idea of the richness of the Mexican heritage in the United States. I will not be providing a detailed survey of that contribution here, but it should be noted that the major urbanization of the Southwestern United States was established by Spanish-speaking people, and the names of several major cities in the Southwest stand as a testament to that early settlement. Chicano English is therefore quite old when compared to other ethnic varieties of English that came to the U.S. with the waves of European immigrants. However, like the blacks, Native Americans, and Orientals, the actual history of Chicanos, and their culture, has been distorted through time and reinforced by stereotypes. García (1981) illustrates the history of Chicano English in terms of the generation in which a family came to reside in the United States. Paraphrasing her observation, there are some Chicanos who do not speak Spanish. These individuals are typically members of third-generation families, where their grandparents were among the first Chicanos to move to the U.S. There are, of course, many exceptions across each generation; many tend to be balanced bilinguals, or they may be dominant in English with some Spanish borrowings. The more recent arrivals, by contrast, shift emphasis in the direction of Spanish, such that there is a population of first-generation arrivals that know little or no English at all.

Concentrating for the moment on English, we would expect to find a continuum, similar to that described by Bickerton (1973) for varieties of Guyanese English, spanning between nonstandard Chicano English and impeccable Standard. The variety of Standard English could be influenced by regional or national norms; thus, standard Chicano English in Texas may sound different from standard Chicano English in California. Although some have argued that the history of Black English has also resulted in a continuum, Chicano English evolves within a stable bilingual situation, whereas BVE has been tied to a pidgin/creole history. This is due to the fact that black slaves were separated from others who spoke their native tongue upon capture, presumably to eliminate communication and the potential for uprisings. Spanish speakers, on the other hand, have gained exposure to English in much the same way as have other non-English immigrants. The native language, in this case Spanish, is preserved in the barrio while the younger generations come to learn English through increased exposure. As an individual, or perhaps a family, gains wealth and education, there is increased emphasis on using standard varieties of English.

In this respect the history of Chicano English is like every other nonstandard variety of English in the United States. Insiders know that there are negative stereotypes about their speech outside of their community, and this results in several responses. Some call for making the United States a bilingual nation, pointing to the size and continued growth of the Spanish-speaking population. Others, with equally good intentions, say that we must teach English to everyone as soon as possible so that they can "melt into the pot." If there is a fact that history has shown us, and that is echoed in the dialect diversity that exists today, it is that some immigrants have melted at a faster rate than have others, and this has historically followed strong racial and ethnic boundaries.

The history of Chicano English, then, is highly diversified, where various Chicanos speak more than one style of English. Up to this point I have not focused on the bilingual dimension, but it is very relevant. This is where the question of linguistic competence first appears; some speakers of Spanish will borrow English words, but for my purpose here I will not include them within the Chicano English community because of their lack of proficiency. In the remainder of the paper I will be referring to Chicano English as any variety of English spoken by a Chicano who can conduct conversations in English exclusively. This definition will therefore include Chicanos who are not competent in Spanish, but borrow elements of Spanish in their English usage. These distinctions will become clear in the next section where we look at the variable nature of modern Chicano English.

VARIATION ALONG TWO LINGUISTIC CONTINUA

The main reason why it will be difficult to define Chicano English, in terms of a traditional fixed definition, lies in the variable nature of the styles of English and Spanish that are used. The Black English situation serves, once again, to illustrate the complexity of the task. In Figure 7, we see the entire Black English population. The vernacular community, that is, the most nonstandard speakers, are comprised of those black Americans who have minimal contact with whites. They primarily interact with other members of the vernacular black culture in their living, working, and recreational situations. This is represented by the decreasing progression from 3–to–0 in Figure 7. Other blacks, included in the right three quadrants of the figure have contacts with nonblacks (primarily whites) in some combination of the preceding social domains. In this case the dialect is distributed along a continuum, although it would be wrong to suggest that all black Americans are part of the same speech community. It would likewise be misleading to suggest that all Chicanos are members of the Chicano English community.

If we extend the same interactional criteria to the Chicano community, we get a very different picture due to the vital bilingual influence. While Black English experiences linguistic change within an English grammatical system, the con-

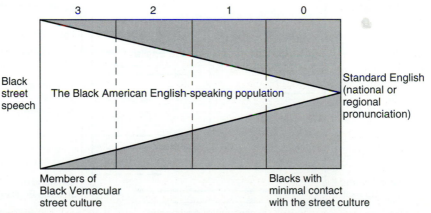

FIGURE 7
The Black American English speech community. The combination of social domains (that is, Living, Working, and Recreational Situations) where blacks primarily interact with other members of the street culture.

stant influx of monolingual Spanish speakers replenishes a bilingual cycle, the same cycle that has faced every generation of Hispanics to come to the United States. Thus, if a Chicano has limited exposure to non-Chicano English speakers, then it is quite possible, even likely, that the speaker will need to command fluent Spanish. There is, nevertheless, a small population that has limited contact with non-Chicanos, but limited proficiency in Spanish. Figure 8 outlines the bilingual foundations of Chicano English, and, with slight modification, can be extended to other Hispanic and bilingual communities in the United States.

Here we must contend with two linguistic continua. Even though our interest is focused on Chicano English, it does not exist in linguistic isolation. The center line of Figure 8 represents the balanced bilinguals. These people are fluent in both languages. Often they are second or third generation immigrants who have been exposed to Spanish at an early age. There are thousands of exceptions, however, among the older populations, even first generation immigrants, who made tremendous personal sacrifices to learn English. The vertical parameters at the left and right of the figure correspond to monolingual speakers of Spanish and English respectively. In both cases speakers may control more or less standard varieties, that is, monolinguals and bilinguals alike will control styles of one or both languages that fall somewhere on the scale between the standard and nonstandard vernacular. At the extremes, then, we find the monolinguals, with the center line representing a continuum of balanced bilinguals. The limitation in this illustration is that an individual balanced bilingual may know a nonstandard variety of one language while controlling a more standard variety of the other; this will rely very much on personal experience and several other factors. Generally speaking, we find that educated speakers tend toward the standard in

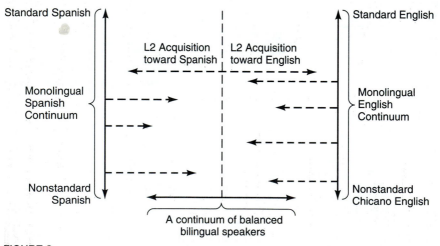

FIGURE 8
Spanish/English bilingualism in the United States.

both languages, due in large measure to their formal training. Others, primarily among the less educated populations, may speak nonstandard varieties of both languages.

Having considered the extremes, including monolinguals or balanced bilinguals, there are vast numbers of others who are in the process of learning a second language, be it English or Spanish, who are not yet balanced bilinguals, but they are moving in that direction as a result of formal training or increased personal exposure to L2. These individuals have marginal competence in L2, and they may produce utterances that are identical, in surface forms, to that of a balanced bilingual who is "code-switching." In other words, a balanced bilingual may produce the following sentence:

They can go, y tu tambien, if we have enough money.

However, the same sentence could be produced by an English speaker with marginal Spanish competence. Similarly, a balanced bilingual might produce the following sentence:

Her suegros are from Tennessee y los van a traer y quieren llevarlos a una corrida de toros. (Valdés, 1976)

which would more readily be understood by another bilingual speaker.

The main point that Figure 8 illustrates is the fluid nature of the bilingual/monolingual exposure that faces Chicanos. This of course brings the anguish of definition to mind once again. Peñalosa (1980) provides detailed discussion of Chicano English in his book on Chicano sociolinguistics. He observes a disproportionate amount of research on Spanish, while Chicano English has been neglected by comparison. A critical aspect of any adequate definition must establish the thresholds of fluency that delineate members of the Chicano English community. Scholars may in turn decide to divide performance ability and perceptive competence, because most people tend to comprehend L2 long before they become fluent speakers of it.

As Shuy (1980) observed, minority scholars have often encountered frustrations when they bring their deep personal concerns to social science. In linguistics it has often been necessary to examine idealized data to develop formal theories, but the consequence of this tradition is to examine language as one would a series of still photographs. The variable nature of Chicano English defies this kind of idealized categorization. It would be much more appropriate to think of Chicano English as part of a linguistic circulatory system. To the best of my knowledge it seems that speakers of Chicano (vernacular) English engage in several different linguistic styles depending on what a given situation calls for. In the case of balanced bilinguals we might expect code-switching to occur (see Poplack, 1979). On other occasions, the balanced bilingual and monolingual English speakers may style-shift within English exclusively. Thus, when Chicano students attend public schools they may use one style of English with their teachers, and another with their peers on the playground. Similar analogies can be found for the adult populations as well.

Because the Chicano English community includes nonstandard vernacular dialects along with Standard English as spoken by Chicanos, we should expect the variation that is presented in Figure 8 to be stable for quite some time. However, if past practice is a fair indication of what we should expect for the future, it will be important to make clear distinctions between the special problems that face speakers of Chicano English; that is, as opposed to the problems of Native American bilinguals, or Black English bidialectals. In the face of shrinking educational budgets, there may be a tendency to continue the past practice of simply placing all minorities in the same "language arts" basket; namely, consisting of those populations who do not speak Standard English. As we shall see below, the shared plight of poverty should not imply that various minority groups will be able to use the same language arts strategies to compete on an equal footing with their Standard English counterparts.

DYNAMIC AND FIXED MINORITY POPULATIONS

One need only look at the migratory patterns of minority groups to appreciate their linguistic differences. The Native Americans have seen their mother tongues dwindle, for several well-known historical reasons. Black Americans, on the other hand, are the only American minority where non-English immigrants (i.e., captured slaves) were separated from others who spoke their native African language. This unique linguistic history has given rise to the contemporary bidialectal systems between black street speech (or rural vernacular speech), and more standard varieties of American English. Both of these groups contrast with the situation affecting Chicanos and the varieties of English they speak.

Black speech patterns are changing within an English grammatical system, and there are no longer large numbers of new black minorities, with the possible exception of new Haitians, that will not know some dialect of English as their native language. Hispanics who speak English will encounter a greater range of diversity, because, unlike Native American bilingualism, Spanish is a language with a long-standing written tradition, in the well-known sense of Western culture. And, like all other languages that are spoken in advanced industrial societies, there are some dialects of Spanish that are associated with poor and/or social elites. Chicano English, then, when viewed as the varieties of English spoken by Chicanos, regardless of their different linguistic and social experience, is broad indeed.

Another dimension of the Black English situation that does hold some analogies lies in the need to distinguish nonstandard varieties of vernacular Chicano English from the more standard styles of Chicano English, namely, those that are indistinguishable for Anglo Standard English. Gonzalez (1974) observes that many middle-class Chicano families in the U.S. stress the learning of Standard English. However, personal attitudes and spontaneous group loyalties can be embraced or denied by different ways of speaking. If the Chicano English situation reflects the black English pattern, and this should be established empirically, then we would expect individual speakers to shift their manner of speaking depending on several factors. These factors would include the immediate participants in the speech event, the location of the conversation, and the topic(s) under discussion. It would be wrong to suggest that any individual has a fixed style of speech, and others stratify above or below that particular point. Rather, different people will control various ranges of styles; for Chicanos this could include stylistic ranges in English or English and Spanish, depending on the degree of bilingual proficiency.

Even when an individual is a competent bilingual, or a competent bidialectal, having the ability to use various styles at will, it is often difficult to predict how speakers will respond to different speaking contexts. This can be attributed, at least in part, to the competing values that are conveyed through this spontaneous linguistic selection. For example, imagine a situation where a young Chicano is talking to his teacher. If some of his friends walk by, there may be a noticeable shift in the phonology in the direction of vernacular Chicano English. This type of shifting conveys group loyalties, and the pride of individuals is often linked closely with their native colloquial dialects. In the following section we conclude our discussion with the most perplexing definitional problem of all: How do we establish the factors that influence dialect loyalties and related linguistic behavior?

DIALECT LOYALTY

Every group that has migrated to the United States from some foreign land, especially those where English is not the native language, have experienced a period of transition. Again, this alludes to the well-known melting pot myth. The simple fact of the matter is that white immigrants have always melted at a faster rate. Race has always been a larger social barrier than that of a foreign accent, but a foreign accent or nonstandard dialect can reinforce social borders, especially when race is a factor. It is largely for this reason, and the social isolation that has existed among various groups in America, that long standing stereotypes are perpetuated.

The question of dialect loyalty has therefore caused scattered responses, because some members of these groups made every effort to adopt American behavior, including language, as soon as they possibly could. Others, by choice or social exclusion, developed subcultural norms that were shared among intimates of their minority. When poverty and the pervasive lack of educational and economic opportunities are taken into account, those who feel that they are in a "good" social position try to avoid contact with those groups that they feel are less fortunate. The minority group, recognizing these competing norms, is faced with a paradox. Some have become highly educated, mastering the same norms and behaviors as the social elites. The opposite, of course, holds true for those who reject all things associated with the dominant culture. So, the individual members of the minority group, be they black or brown, may find that their group loyalties are tested as they are judged in two societies.

The competitive nature of American society rewards cultural homogeneity; this is simply a historical fact and is not intended as a value judgment. Nevertheless, when the language of family and friends is linked with a stigmatized dialect, one that is judged negatively by others who are in a relative position of social power, then it is possible for the individual speaker to feel a sense of frustration. This will continue to be the case in the Hispanic community as more and more people come to develop different strategies for their personal survival.

The terms *Uncle Tom* and *Tio Taco* have sprung from the vernacular communities in response to the fact that some members of the racial group have abandoned, or at least are perceived as having abandoned, the masses of less fortunate people who remain in the ghetto/barrio. The fact of the matter is that loyalties are capricious commodities. As Goffman (1959) observes, a single individual may behave in the presence of close friends in ways that are very different from circumstances where there are no friends to judge that behavior. While I have no solution for resolving this paradox, which I consider to be natural, it has a direct impact on Chicano English.

In this paper I have tried to outline some of the considerations that scholars and interested laypersons will want to take into account as studies of Chicano English grow and mature. We have witnessed several major advances in sociolinguistics in the past twenty years, and the number of interested students, educators, and parents has grown tremendously in that time. My main objective has been to outline some of the potential problems that will affect an adequate definition. I base these observations, in part, on mistakes that were made in the early descriptions of Black English; they tended to be quite simplistic, and, by extension, unrealistic. The fact of the matter is that languages, to say nothing of languages in change under social pressure, are not static. If I have provided any useful information at all it lies in the recognition that vernacular Chicano English, like other nonstandard dialects of American English, is a dynamic and everchanging linguistic system. Since so much of this research will serve as the foundation of educational and social policies, we must take care not to treat all Chicanos or Hispanics as if they have been stamped out of a single casting. It is my sincere hope that our combined efforts will give rise to precise analyses of these dialects, and that these studies ultimately serve the needs of the entire Chicano population.

REFERENCES

Bickerton, Derek. 1973. "The Nature of a Creole Continuum." *Language* 5(49): 640–669.

Chomsky, Noam. 1965. *Aspects of the Theory of Syntax*. Cambridge, MA: M.I.T. Press.

García, Maryellen. 1981. "Spanish-English Bilingualism in the Southwest." In Bruce Cronnell (ed.), *The Writing Needs of Linguistically Different Students*. Los Alamitos, CA: SWRL Educational Research and Development.

Goffman, Erving. 1959. *The Presentation of Self in Everyday Life*. New York: Doubleday-Anchor.

González, Gustavo. 1974. "The Acquisition of Questions in Texas Spanish." In Garland O. Bills (ed.), *Southwest Areal Linguistics*. San Diego, CA: Institute for Cultural Pluralism, San Diego State University, pp. 251–266.

Peñalosa, Fernando. 1980. *Chicano Sociolinguistics: A Brief Introduction*. Rowley, MA: Newbury House.

Poplack, Shana. 1979. "Sometimes I'll Starta Sentence in Spanish Termino en Español: Toward a Typology of Code-Switching." New York: Center for Puerto Rican Studies, City University of New York. Working Paper 4.

Shuy, Roger. 1980. "Foreword." In Fernando Peñalosa, *Chicano Sociolinguistics: A Brief Introduction*. Rowley, MA: Newbury House.

Valdés, G. 1976. "Code-Switching Patterns: A Case Study of Spanish/English Alternation." In G. D. Keller, R. V. Teschner, and S. Viera (eds.), *Bilingualism in the Bicentennial and Beyond*. New York: Bilingual Press/Editorial Bilingue, pp. 58–85.

American Indian English and Its Implications for Bilingual Education

William L. Leap

This paper is concerned with some aspects of language pluralism found within the membership of contemporary American Indian tribes and communities. It also deals with some of the consequences of that pluralism, with which educational policy and bilingual theory are concerned.

1 At the present time, we estimate that some 206 different languages and language dialects are being spoken in Indian country. The results of a survey by Wallace Chafe, published in 1962, provide a sense of the range of fluency which may be subsumed under this figure: 49 of these languages have fewer than 10 speakers, all over 50 years of age; 6 of these languages have more than 10,000 speakers within all generational groupings in each community. Fluency in the remaining 151 languages may fall at any point between those two extremes. Fluency is not, as some suspect, an open-and-shut, yes-no matter. And, of course, social and cultural factors will also affect the placement for each group—as in the instance where a person knows how to carry out his/her religious responsibilities in the native language, but does not use the language for any purpose outside of that context.

Levels of English language fluency within the tribes and communities may be similarly wide ranging. It is not uncommon to find, within any given community, persons who speak virtually no English at all. Usually, if such statements can be made for such a highly heterogeneous population, the younger members of the tribe tend to be the more fluent in English and/or rely on English more frequently as the medium of conversation and discussion. The increase in locally available schooling opportunities, which replaces the older practice of off-reservation, boarding school instruction; the creation of federal work-incentive programs which encourages Indians to seek employment in the off-reservation, urban context; the availability of Sesame Street and other English-dominated media packages; and other such factors have all had a hand in shaping the distribution of English fluency within each tribal and community context. Thus the differences in levels of English facility from one tribe to the next can be traced in part to the differences in impact which one or more of these factors may have had on any particular locale.

Still, some generalities about the English of Indian people can be drawn. One of these, as described in the Havinghurst report (see Fuchs and Havinghurst 1972:206–212) and in subsequent studies, has to do with the priority which Indian people place on having their children acquire English language skills. A second, as reported in the U.S. Civil Rights Commission's *Southwest Indian Report* (1973) and elsewhere, refers to the continuing perception by many non-Indians of the inadequacy of the English language skills of Indians. The BIA, for example, continues to treat the strengthening of its students' English skills as one of its highest educational priorities, since, by their report,

> . . . [M]ost Indian children entering BIA schools continue to be tribal speakers first and speakers of English as a second language second [and] . . . are closer to tribal lifeways than students enrolled in the public schools.

(Benham 1977:31)

These data may seem to be contradictory—e.g. how can there be an increase in English fluency, high levels of interest in maintaining English fluency, and still be reported inadequacy of English fluency, all within the same population? The answer lies in part in the level of generalization which must be used to talk about the common problems of the memberships of over 400 politically autonomous and culturally separate Indian tribes. It lies also in the persisting stereotypes of unsocialized Indian behavior reinforced by the media, the textbooks, and other social institutions. Indians have been portrayed as 'poor unfortunates' for so long that it may be difficult for people to see anything other than poverty and misfortune even when they are confronted with facts to the contrary. Witness, for example, the assumption in the passage just cited, that BIA students tend to be closer to tribal lifestyles than Indian students in public schools—when, as of latest count, well over 70 percent of all Indian children are enrolled in public schools, regardless of where they reside. The procedures used for testing levels of language proficiency, which often base their conclusions on nothing more than the results of vocabulary identification tasks, certainly make their contribution. But the contradictions also refer us to some facts about the nature of the English spoken by persons in many Indian communities.

One hundred years ago, familiarity, to say nothing of fluency, with English was a novel thing in most Indian communities in the west. See, for example, DuBois' comment that: 'for the period 1846–1880, Spanish was the vehicle for communicative interaction with Anglo-Americans . . . particularly with the Mescalero' (1977:191). By the beginnings of this century, the prime mandate of the Indian school had become defined around developing speaking, reading, and writing skills in English. Any carryover of native language arts instruction, as had been the case in Choctaw and Cherokee schools, for example, was eliminated by federal fiat. School classrooms and dormitories were set up in the off-reservation contexts, specifically to encourage the use of non-Indian codes. Persons from differing tribal backgrounds were often placed in the same classroom and dormitory, to prevent continued reliance on the student's ancestral language as the means for conversation. Schooling policies, in addition, forbade the use of Indian languages for any public purpose, and punished students who violated the restriction. This added significantly to the pressure to use English as the exclusive means of student communication.

What emerged from this context, as we currently understand it, was a set of English language 'codes' based, to certain extents, on the speaking knowledge which the students had already mastered—the skills in ancestral language expression. As reflected in student term papers and examination essays from Haskell Indian school in 1916 (see Malancon and Malancon 1977 for discussion), sentence constructions, details of spelling (and therefore, pronunciation as well), and vocabulary usage began to show direct Indian language influence, almost as if the students were forming English expressions with non-English grammars. The students obtained a kind of English fluency in this fashion, yet the fluency remained distinct from the sense of fluency defined and expected by Standard English speakers. Tribally distinctive English codes emerged—each formed off the grammar of the particular Indian language. They all utilized a common core of English vocabulary words, with various lexical items from the speaker's Indian language (i.e. Indian loan words) enriching the potential for expression of each code, something which was highly appropriate given the nature of the sentence formation process underlying each code.

The students who went through this process of 'creative construction' are among the grandparents and great-grandparents of today's tribal and community membership. Their children (persons in today's parental generation) learned both their Indian language and their parents' 'Indian English' at home. The schools continued to construct their language arts curriculum in terms of the language needs of Standard English speakers. This, in turn, bypassed the specific language arts needs which the students brought with them into the classroom. And it also did something else. For the curriculum to have impact on the level of the students' English fluency, instruction would have to make direct inroads into the Indian language grammar underlying that fluency. Growth (i.e. standardization) of English skills resulted in a weakening and ultimately a loss of Indian language skills in many instances. Maintenance of Indian language fluency required resistance and rejection of Standard English influence in the grammar, and this Standard English convention in their speech.

Consider now the contemporary consequences of this situation. Students in the present generation encounter the local variety of Indian English, influenced by the ancestral language tradition of the community, as the first language in the home. They may also be exposed to the ancestral language of their community, depending on the situation within the home and the tribe. Yet even if this does not occur, since the English being learned shows ancestral language influence, the children are able to become passively fluent in their Indian language (i.e. receptively, though not necessarily productively competent) through the acquisition of their locally appropriate, Indian English code. This helps explain why so many nonspeakers in the contemporary Indian communities can understand what parents and grandparents say to them in their native/ancestral tongue, even though they are not able to respond to the speaker in the same linguistic terms. The children's English may in fact allow them to be predisposed to learning (or relearning) Indian language fluency, something which will greatly assist them in later life if, for example, they decide to become active members of tribal government and/or to participate more extensively in the tribe's ceremonial life.

The less positive sides of Indian English fluency may emerge within school-related contexts in a variety of ways. Fluency in the local Indian English code may, for example, lead a student to use sentences such as (1)–(5) in written compositions.

1 Two womens was out there fighting.
2 Since the church close down, we been goin to mass in Pajarito.
3 You do not record none of your wills or any of your transactions with BIA.
4 Any fiestas which we might have are given early in the summer.
5 The individual pick out their own cattle.

Each of these sentences reflects a construction type common to the spoken English at one community in the United States Southwest, but quite inappropriate as far as written (or spoken standard) English expression is concerned. Similarly, Indian English fluency may lead the student to interpret material on the printed page in terms quite different from those intended by the writer; familiar 'problems' in reading comprehension reported in the literature on

Indian schooling can often be traced to such causes. Other examples could be suggested; the point is clear. Without adequate control over the kinds of basic English skills expected and assumed by educational authorities, impediments to educational progress can be predicted. The record on leaving school, test-score placements, and other signs of the so-called 'under-achievement' of the Indian student all bear out the validity of this prediction.

2 The impact of the Indian student's English language skills on his/her educational progress has long been recognized by schooling authorities and by language planners and researchers. As Fuchs and Havinghurst noted in the summary volume of the National Study of Indian Education (1977:208ff.), two solutions—intensive programs of ESL instruction, and programs offering (transitional) bilingual education—have come to be relied upon to bring about the necessary strengthening of English language skills which effective classroom performance appears to require. Until the 1970s, however, the nature of the English language 'problem' toward which these remedial strategies were to be directed was presented in the literature in terms of a subtractive (or outright deficiency) model—identifying what Standard English conventions were not present in Indian English speech; or in terms of a contrastive model—identifying what problem areas in English fluency might be present within the English of a given Indian community. To my knowledge, it was not until 1971 that serious attempts to describe and account for the linguistic and sociolinguistic details actually present in any variety of American Indian English were initiated.

My own study of the varieties of English spoken at Isleta pueblo, New Mexico, began during this period as an outgrowth of dissertation-related studies of Isletan Tiwa, the ancestral language of that community. The first suggestion that Isletan English might have a logic independent of that of Standard English came with the conclusion of an analysis of the surface-level phonology of the English of several adult speakers. While English vocabulary was being employed in their speech, the words and phrases were pronounced in terms of Tiwa, and not English, phonological constraints. (See Leap 1973 for discussion.)

This was not, then, a case of Isletan Tiwa interference with an otherwise intact English phonological pattern: if anything, Isletan phonology has preempted the English pattern, not just selected portions of it. Elaboration of this comment is provided in Leap (1977c) and in Stout's (1977) analysis of the Keresan English of Santa Ana, New Mexico.

The phonological analysis also highlighted a series of Isletan English sentence constructions which seems to be directly influenced by Tiwa grammatical constraint. Additional papers (Leap 1974b and 1974c) reviewed several of these constructions to show how Tiwa grammatical rule was taking precedence over English grammatical rule in Isletan English sentence formation. The creative synthesis of Tiwa and English syntax present in this English code continued to be the topic of subsequent analysis. Instances appeared such as in the contrastive use of single vs. double negation in the code, where Tiwa semantic rules were being directly replicated in Isletan English. Cases also appeared, as in the formation of sentences with cognate object constructions, where both a Tiwa and an English language explanation could be used to account for the particulars of the derivation. These implied that criteria for selecting between the explanations needed to be developed in the analysis, possibly replicating the decision-making which the Isletan English speaker has to carry out when initiating the act of derivation. (For discussion, see Leap 1977d.)

Constructions also appeared where the source could not be traced either to Isletan Tiwa grammar or to the grammatical component of Standard English: the use of uninflected *be* in Isletan English shows some decided parallels to the use of *be* in Black English vernacular, for example. Analysis showed, in fact, that a close association between this aspect of the deep structure of these two nonstandard codes could be established, provided Fasold's definition of distributive *be* were brought into closer harmony with the absence of tense-specification reflected in his own data but not highlighted in his discussion of theme. (See Leap 1975 for the details.)

While some of the affinities between Isletan and other varieties of nonstandard English were beginning to be explored through such interdialectal comparisons, the limitations of using typological characteristics of one nonstandard code when describing or interpreting the features of a second also were becoming clear. In a recent paper (Leap 1977a), I show how the absence of tensemarking on Isletan English verbs may reflect any number of grammatical constraints. Thus to assume that tenseless verbs in Isletan English are derived through phonological simplification, as is the case in some Black English dialects, is as inappropriate as it is premature.

The uniqueness of the Isletan English code was beginning to be highlighted in the interdialectal comparisons. Speaker assessments of a set of Isletan English sentences, following the elicitation technique outlined in Fasold (1969), proved to be markedly distinct from those given by speakers of Anglo and Spanish American English varieties common to the communities immediately adjacent to the Isletan reservation. (See Leap 1977e, for further discussion.) Arguments that Indian English codes merely represent some variant of regionally appropriate American English are seriously weakened by these findings.

Intertribal comparisons of Indian English forms yielded similarly useful perspectives on the uniqueness of Isletan English. I had been advised on numerous occasions that Indian people in the southwest and elsewhere could place a person's tribal background merely by listening to the way he/she spoke English. (See, in particular, the anecdote reported in Leap 1974a.) Comparison of these specifics of word-final consonant cluster reduction in Isletan and Cheyenne English (Leap 1977b); Penfield's (1975, 1977) several papers on the continuing autonomy of four Indian English varieties—Navajo, Ute, Mojave, and Hopi, within the same classroom; Stout's continuing analysis of syntactic details and their sociolinguistic correlates within the English of elementary students at Laguna pueblo, New Mexico (much of which is summarized in Stout 1978), and Miller's (1976) study of English language acquisition among children on the Pima reservation, have provided ample evidence to support the language-specific nature of each community's Indian English variety. A study of the English of school children from San Juan and Laguna pueblos, New Mexico, currently ongoing at the Center for Applied Linguistics under support from the National Institute of Education promises to add additional support to these claims, especially where the impact of Indian English fluency on school performance is concerned. Natalie Kuhlman's work on Papago and Pima English (Kuhlman and Longoni 1975, Kalectaca and Kuhlman 1977) achieves the same end, in spite of her continuing reliance on subtractive/deficiency models in her descriptions.

In the light of these studies, my argument (Leap 1973, passim) that there are as many different kinds of American Indian English as there are American Indian language traditions becomes readily understandable. Descriptive data, comparative insights, tribal opinion, and speaker assessments of grammaticality and sentence acceptability all combine to support the claim. The arguments of Mary Jane Cook (1973, passim) and others who continue to interpret the English of Indian people in the southwest strictly in terms of shared, area-wide phenomena must be dismissed in the light of this conclusion.

3 The argument that there are as many kinds of Indian English as there are Indian language traditions—that is, a minimum of 206 different Indian English varieties, carries with it some particular implications for the interests of this year's Georgetown University Round Table, and I want to explore several of those implications in the following paragraphs.

Taken uncritically, the claim might seem to imply that speakers of Indian English are also speakers of their appropriate ancestral languages. Such is not always the case, as the argument and statistics in the first section of this paper have already suggested. I am personally aware of instances in Indian country where the control over ancestral language grammar contained in the knowledge of the local Indian English code is the only reflex of Indian language skill which the community membership (or a significant portion of that membership) now possesses. At some phase in the transmission of language skills within the community, Indian English must have begun to be acquired autonomously—i.e. successful acquisition was not dependent on the presence of an existing Indian language grammar or Indian language speaking skill. We might, for this reason, want to view Indian English as some kind of creole if, in the strict sense of the term, its predecessor was some sort of pidgin. Then, we would want—as Stout and Erting (1977) have done for uninflected *be* in Isletan English—to interpret the English language dynamics in the community in terms of a postcreole model. Doing this would detract from the more critical point: the grammar being transmitted autonomously is a whole grammar, whatever its origin—that is, it is systematic enough to be learnable, and complete enough to be learned in the same (or comparable) form by various segments of the community membership, through reliance on the same range of cognitive skills which all human beings employ in the natural language acquisition process. While the codes may have had their original basis in some process of relexification or other form of 'creative construction', such processes do not appear to be necessary for their successful maintenance or their successful transmission.

The complexity faced by language arts programs in American Indian schools can, I believe, best be interpreted in these very terms. Given the diversity in range and level of language fluency which may occur within any Indian speech community, the local classroom may contain, at minimum: (1) students who have learned Indian English and have little, or no, control over their ancestral language; (2) students who speak both their ancestral language and some variety of English; and (3) students fluent in their ancestral language but showing minimal fluency in English. Schooling authorities tend to view the language condition of their students through a much more unified perspective—building the language profile around greater or lesser degrees of evidenced English fluency. The BIA continues to estimate the number of speakers of Indian languages in its schools by extrapolating from the number of students who speak English as a second language—see the statistics reported in Fuchs and Havinghurst 1972:207–208, or the conclusions of the survey of bilingual education needs of Indian children, carried out by the National Indian Training and Research Center (1975). Here lies the basis for the oft-reported divergence between institutional and parental expectations where the student-general need for strengthening English language skills exists, while the parents (and students) express concern about unaddressed, student-specific Indian language fluency. And even when native language instruction is included in the school curriculum, the justification advanced for doing so emphasizes a promised growth in student English facility, rather than the strengthening of student native language arts.

The school-based perspective on student language needs has some serious consequences for interests in ancestral language maintenance as well. For, regardless of the level of ancestral language fluency which the student brings into the first grade classroom, the general pattern in Indian country shows a marked reduction in (if not elimination of) that fluency by the time the student completes the sixth grade. The causes for this reduction extend far beyond the failure of school to include ancestral language instruction in the curriculum. As argued in an earlier section of this paper, by focusing attention only on English language questions, and by attempting to rework the students' existing control of English into a more standardized format, the school is literally undermining student fluency in his/her ancestral language—the grammar underlying his locally appropriate English code and the grammar underlying his ancestral fluency being, in essence, one and the same.

Under current practice, and I would include here the various transitional bilingual programs funded under the Bilingual Education Act (Title VII, ESEA), a successful program of English language instruction in any Indian school virtually guarantees native language genocide. This will continue to be the case, until educational policy and classroom practice cease treating the Indian English question as something totally autonomous from the remaining portions of the Indian student's verbal repertoire.

4 What kind of educational strategy is appropriate for students with fluency in some variety of American Indian English?

It is not appropriate merely to ignore the differences in structure and usage convention which distinguish the student's Indian English grammar from that of the standard code. To present the students with exercises highlighting the differences between the past tense forms of *lay* and *lie,* when the student may not ever use *laid* or *lay* (or, more generally, the {-d} morpheme or verbal ablaut) to mark past tense expression for these verbs (if, in fact, he/she defines tense/aspect distinctions in temporal terms at all) is both an inefficient and irresponsible use of the student's schooling experience—to say nothing about the previously noted impact such instruction could have on the Indian language skills he/she already controls.

Still, speaking situations outside the home community and tribal context often require some evidence of Standard English expression as a precondition for effective mobility within their context. Educational programs which fail to provide Indian students with opportunities to gain stronger control over Standard English conventions are therefore equally inefficient and equally irresponsible.

The school's task is to find an educational strategy which will integrate Standard English into the student's verbal repertoire without detracting from the native language skills already evidenced within that repertoire, or allowing Standard English to supersede the English usage patterns already familiar to the student. The school also needs to help the student distinguish between sentence variants, so that he/she can select the sentence form most appropriate to any given speaking situation. And, because the student's existing English fluency is, to a large part, governed by the grammar of her/his ancestral language, it will also be necessary for the school to provide instruction in Indian as well as English language arts. The more secure the student is in the language skills she/he already controls, the more prepared she/he will be to integrate new speaking tasks into the scope of his verbal repertoire.

In effect, what is being called for here is a program of bilingual education, if by that term is meant an education strategy which starts with the students' existing language skills—in this case, those subsumed under the phrase 'Indian English,' and then directs those skills toward the building of language fluencies deemed appropriate by the membership of the home community as well as by persons in the surrounding society. Such an educational strategy is highly appropriate for schooling programs in Indian country, regardless of specific locale; it is often said that Indian people have their feet in 'two worlds.' If so, it is only fitting that their children gain control over the verbal codes basic to mobility and movement within each sphere.

But a problem remains: the kinds of language needs described here are not viewed as appropriate for bilingual services under current HEW practice. The Lau Remedies, the provisions of the Bilingual Education Act (Title VII, ESEA), and other federal programs facilitating the development of bilingual/bicultural instruction in the nation's schools define student eligibility for federally supported bilingual services in terms of the presence of 'limited English-speaking ability'. LESA, when used in reference to an individual, refers to someone who has difficulty speaking and understanding instruction in the English language because his/her dominant language—i.e. the language most relied upon for communication in the home—is other than English; and whose educational progress can be shown to be impeded as a result of that difficulty.

As this discussion has shown, the Indian English-speaking student may experience the same kinds of difficulties in speaking and/or in understanding English language instruction in the classroom, and may find his/her educational progress impeded as a result of those difficulties—even though the language relied upon for communication in the home is Indian English, and not the student's ancestral tongue. As a result, Indian participation in the Title VII network has never been extensive—in FY 1976, for example, of the $135 million disbursed for basic program support under this Act, only $3.25 million, approximately 2.5 percent of the available monies, were awarded to LEAs serving Indian students—even though Indian students could benefit equally well from Title VII services currently made available to non-Indian LEAs whose students show closer conformity to the description of language need defined in the Title VII regulations.

There has been, in recent months, much discussion about the need to rewrite the Title VII act so that it could become more sensitive to the language needs of the nation's linguistic minorities. In the present case, a simple change in the definition of limited English-speaking ability will allow for greater Indian eligibility for Title VII support without requiring extensive changes in the original mandate and purpose of this legislation: Section 703(a)(1)(B) should be revised to allow LESA to refer to 'individuals who come from environments where a language other than English has had measurable or demonstrable impact on their level of English proficiency'. Following that passage with the remainder of section 703(a)(1) as presently worded will allow Indian students to become eligible for Title VII services provided the students are speakers of their community's Indian English code. Such will clearly be the case for students in many Indian communities, whether they are fluent in their ancestral language or not. The change suggested here would facilitate the introduction of bilingual instruction into the schooling programs serving these communities, and remove the language barrier which so often impedes the progress of the 'monolingual-English-speaking Indian' through the American education system. And I am pleased to report that Resident Commissioner Baltasar Corrada has included it in the proposed reauthorization of the Bilingual Education Act which he introduced to the 95th Congress; and that Senators Dominici and Hart have included the same definition in the text of the comparable legislation introduced in the U.S. Senate.

NOTE

I want to thank Rosario Gingras, Lance Potter, Paul Murphy, and Angui Madera for their help in preparing this statement, and to dedicate the paper to Rudy Troike, former director of the Center for Applied Linguistics, under whose tutelage many of the insights being explored here were originally conceived.

REFERENCES

Benham, William J., Jr. 1977. *Education in the Bureau of Indian Affairs.* Research and Evaluation Report Series No. 52. Washington, DC: Bureau of Indian Affairs, Office of Indian Education Programs.

Chafe, Wallace. 1962. Estimates regarding the present speakers of North American Indian languages. *IJAL* 28:162–171.

Cook, Mary Jane. 1973. Problems of Southwestern speakers in learning English. In: *Bilingualism in the Southwest.* Edited by Paul Turner. Tucson: University of Arizona Press, pp. 175–198.

DuBois, Betty Lou. 1977. Spanish, English and the Mescalero Apache. In: *Studies in Southwestern Indian English.* William L. Leap. San Antonio: Trinity University Press, pp. 175–198.

Fasold, Ralph. 1969. Tense and the verb *be* in Black English. *Language.* 45:763–776.

Fuchs, Estelle, and Robert J. Havinghurst. 1972. *To live on this earth: American Indian education.* New York: Doubleday.

Kalectaca, Milo, and Natalie Kuhlman. 1977. *Sacaton School District language assessment project.* San Diego: National Training Resource Center. Multilith.

Kuhlman, Natalie, and Robert Longoni. 1975. Indian English and its implications for education. In: *Southwest languages and linguistics in educational perspective.* Edited by Gina C. Harvey and M. F. Heiser. San Diego: Institute for Cultural Pluralism, pp. 333–348.

Leap, William L. 1973. Language pluralism in a Southwestern pueblo: Some comments on Isletan English. In: *Bilingualism in the Southwest.* Edited by Paul Turner. Tucson: University of Arizona Press, pp. 275–293.

———. 1974a. Ethnics, emics, and the 'new' ideology: The Identity Potential of Indian English. In *Social and Cultural Identity.* Edited by Thomas Fitzgerald. Athens, GA: University of Georgia Press, pp. 51–62.

———. 1974b. Grammatical structure in native American English: The Evidence from

218 SECTION 2: LANGUAGE AND CULTURE

Isleta. In *Southwest Areal Linguistics.* Edited by Garland Bills. San Diego: Institute for Cultural Pluralism, pp. 175–188.

———. 1974c. On grammaticality in native American English: The evidence from Isleta. *International Journal of the Sociology of Language* 2:79–89.

———. 1975. 'To be' in Isletan English: A study in accountability. Presented at the International Conference on Pidgins and Creoles, Honolulu.

———. 1976. How Isletan, Isletan English? Presented at the annual meeting of the Southwestern Anthropological Association, San Francisco.

———. 1977a. A note on subject-verb agreement in Isletan English. In *Studies in Southwestern Indian English.* Edited by William Leap. San Antonio: Trinity University Press, pp. 121–130.

———. 1977b. On consonant simplification in Isletan English and elsewhere. In: *Studies in Southwestern Indian English.* Edited by William Leap. San Antonio: Trinity University Press, pp. 45–54.

———. 1977c. The study of American Indian English: An introduction to the issues. In *Studies in Southwestern Indian English.* Edited by William Leap. San Antonio: Trinity University Press, pp. 3–20.

———. 1977d. Two examples of Isletan English syntax. In: *Studies in Southwestern Indian English.* Edited by William Leap. San Antonio: Trinity University Press, pp. 65–78.

Malancon, Richard, and Mary Jo Malancon. 1977. Indian English at Haskell Institute, 1916. In: *Studies in Southwestern Indian English.* Edited by William Leap. San Antonio: Trinity University Press, pp. 141–154.

Miller, Mary Rita. 1977. *Children of the Salt River: First and second language acquisition among Pima children.* Bloomington: Indiana University Language Science Monographs, vol. 16.

National Indian Training and Research Center. 1976. *Bilingual education needs of Indian children: a survey.* Research and Evaluation Report No. 36. Washington, DC: Bureau of Indian Affairs, Office of Indian Education.

Penfield, Susan. 1975. A grant proposal. Suggestions for dealing with Mojave English. In: *Southwest Languages and Linguistics in Educational Perspective.* Edited by Gina Harvey and M. F. Heiser. San Antonio: Trinity University Press, pp. 335–364.

———. 1977. Some examples of Southwestern Indian English compared. In: *Studies in Southwest Indian English.* Edited by William Leap. San Antonio: Trinity University Press, pp. 23–44.

Stout, Steven O. 1977. A comment on selective control in English expression at Santa Ana. In: *Studies in Southwestern Indian English.* Edited by William Leap. San Antonio: Trinity University Press, pp. 55–64.

———. 1978. *Aspects of the Indian English of Laguna Elementary School, New Mexico.* Unpublished doctoral dissertation, The American University, Washington, DC.

Stout, Steven O., and Carol Erting. 1977. Uninflected BE in Isletan English: Implicational scaling and the relationship of Isletan English to other ethnically identifiable varieties of English. In: *Studies in Southwestern Indian English.* Edited by William Leap. San Antonio, Trinity University Press, pp. 101–120.

U.S. Civil Rights Commission. 1973. *The Southwest Indian report.* Washington, DC.: Government Printing Office.

AUTHOR'S POSTSCRIPT

This paper was written in the spring of 1978 and contains in its final paragraphs some comments about possible (as of that writing) changes in the wording of the Bilingual Education Act (Title VII, ESEA). It is worth noting that the definition of eligibility for Title VII services *was* modified by the Congress later that summer to allow:

> individuals who are American Indian and Alaskan Native students and who come from environments where a language other than English has had a significant impact on their level of English language proficiency . . .

to be eligible to receive bilingual instruction through Title VII support programs *whether these students are speakers of their ancestral languages or not.* A larger number of schools serving American Indian students had already begun to receive Title VII funding after 1976, due in large part to the outreach services provided to schools and to tribal governments through the network of Title VII Resource Centers. The introduction of new eligibility criteria intensified this trend. By 1979, more than twice the amount of the allocation for American Indian projects in 1976 was needed to support Title VII services in American Indian education. Since that time, funding for American Indian projects has remained between eight and ten percent of the total appropriation for support of basic projects during each fiscal year.

(January 1, 1985)

The Relationship Between Language and Sex in English

Jenny Cheshire

Many sociolinguistic studies have shown how social divisions between speakers, such as age, socio-economic class or sex, are reflected in their language. In some tribal societies where men and women lead relatively separate lives, there are often clear phonological, lexical or syntactic differences in their speech: this was true, for example, of many AmerIndian and Australasian languages. Where the sexes are less segregated, as in modern Western societies, language differences are more subtle (for examples, see Trudgill, 1974a; Chapter 4). More recently, research on language and sex has gone beyond the analysis of sex-differentiated varieties of language, to investigate the way that language reflects and helps to maintain social attitudes towards women and men.

In Britain and the USA, for example, it has been shown that our conventional use of English treats men and women unequally, rather than simply differently. This paper will briefly collate some of the more important research findings in this area, and will discuss their implications. It will also document some examples of changes in the use of English, which reflect an increased social awareness of the way in which English discriminates against women. These changes result in part from the dissemination of research findings (Miller and Swift, 1977 and 1981, for example, are written for the general reader rather than for a purely academic audience), but they can also be seen as a natural result of the changing position of women in British and American society, and of growing interest and support for some of the issues raised by the feminist movement.

The first two sections of this paper discuss research into sexism in English, and the way in which our use of language maintains stereotyped images of the sexes. They also discuss some of the implications of the research findings, and describe some efforts that have been made, by both individuals and group organizations, to avoid discriminatory language themselves and to encourage others to avoid it also. The following two sections point out some potential applications of research into two other aspects of language and sex: the analysis of sex differences in language use, and the evaluation of men's and women's speech.

SEXISM IN ENGLISH

A great deal of research into sexism in English has focussed on the third person singular pronoun forms, which force speakers to specify the sex of the person to whom the pronoun refers. As Conklin (1974) points out, this means, among other things, that it is possible to write a recommendation for a job that avoids discrimination on the grounds of race, nationality, or religion; but it is not possible to avoid discrimination on the grounds of sex, since it is difficult to avoid using pronouns.

Several attempts have been made to introduce a neutral third person singular pronoun into English, one *(thon)* dating from as far back as 1859. This early proposal is, in fact, the one that has had the greatest impact; it was listed in Funk and Wagnell's New Standard Dictionary in 1913, and it was still sufficiently recognized in 1959 to be included in the second edition of Webster's International Dictionary. Other proposals have had more limited success. *Co* is used in some communes in the USA, particularly in Virginia and Missouri, and it is routinely used in the magazine "Communities". It has also been used in a book on radical therapy, published by Harper and Row in 1973 (see Miller and Swift, 1977, p. 130). Some recent novels have used *na* (Arnold, 1973) and *person* or *per* (Piercy, 1979) and a supervisors' guide issued by a division of American Management Associations uses *hir* (Killian, 1979). Other suggestions include *e, tey, hesh, po, re, xe* and *jhe,* but none of these has been widely accepted, perhaps, as Lakoff (1973) suggests, because of the difficulty of artificially introducing a new item into a closed linguistic system. A solution that might meet with more success is to extend the function of an item that is already in the system. The plural pronoun *they,* in fact, has been used in spoken English for centuries in phrases such as "everyone must do their best" (see Bodine, 1975). Prescriptive grammarians argue against this on the grounds that *they* is inaccurate in terms of number, and recommend *he* instead as a "sex-indefinite" pronoun. This, of course, is equally inaccurate, in terms of sex, but their insistence has meant that *he* is the form that is now generally used as a "neutral" pronoun in formal written English.

One important application of work on language and sex has been the experimental demonstration that "neutral" *he* is interpreted as referring not to both males and females, but to males only (see, for example, Martyna, 1978; Moulton *et al.,* 1978). Mackay (1979) found that this form occurs so often in university textbooks that educated Americans must be exposed to more than ten million occurrences during their lifetimes, which means that this cannot be dismissed as a trivial phenomenon. Furthermore, it is not only the intended "neutral" pronoun that is misinterpreted: generic *man,* in phrases such as *stone-age man* or *no man is an island,* is also interpreted as a masculine noun, by both children and adults (see Nilsen, 1973; Harrison, 1975; Schneider and Hacker, 1973). The main implication of these findings is that the use of these terms excludes women from our thinking and our culture. Most school and university textbooks, in fact, do exclude women and women's achievements, as Hoffmann (1981) points out. Another important implication is that the use of "false generics" in surveys, and of male-orientated thinking generally, may lead to inaccurate results in many areas of research. Goot and Reid (1975) suggest that most of the received wisdom about the political attitudes of women is inaccurate, because it stems from ambiguous questionnaires that ask about "the ordinary man", or "the man with high ideals". And Delamont (1980) points out that political scientists often talk of "democracies" that deny the vote to women and that cannot, therefore, be democracies. It seems probable that culturally conditioned sexist thinking has affected our "knowledge" in other areas of enquiry also (for some attempts to remedy this, see Roberts, 1981; Spender, forthcoming).

"Thinking male" is not confined to academic research, however. The following quotations, from everyday life, show that it is not only nouns of masculine gender that are assumed to have male reference. (They also, incidentally, provide examples of the way in which women are often considered to be the possessions of men.)

> My ambition is to have a show in London with the same sort of reputation that the Crazy Gang had. It would be glamorous, spicy, but above all a family show. People would bring their wives, mothers, and children.
>
> Ken Dodd, in *Woman* magazine

What causes most distress to the residents is the kerbcrawlers, molesting their women-folk.

James Hill, MP, on *This Week in Westminster,* Radio 4

Lack of a neutral singular pronoun and the use of "generic" nouns of masculine gender are the most obvious examples of sexism in English; there are many other linguistic features, however, that reflect the social status of women (for examples, see Lakoff, 1973; Miller and Swift, 1971; 1981).

Recognition of the existence and of the implications of these features has led to conscious attempts to eliminate them from the language. These moves originated in the USA, but awareness of the issues is now spreading to Britain. Several American publishing companies issue guidelines for their authors and editors that suggest ways of avoiding sexist language. Scott, Foresman and Co., for example, issued "Guidelines for improving the image of women in textbooks" in 1972, and McGraw-Hill's "Guidelines for equal treatment of the sexes in McGraw-Hill book publications" has been widely distributed since 1974 to individual writers as well as to government agencies, schools and universities, and the media. In Britain, the Women in the Publishing Industry Group drew up the "Non-sexist code of practice for book publishing" in 1976, and the British Edition of "The handbook of non-sexist writing" (Miller and Swift, 1981) contains examples of writing that is unintentionally sexist, from *The Sunday Times* and *The Observer,* and suggests ways of avoiding offending forms.

Some writers make a conscious effort to avoid sexism: Aitchison (1981), for example, uses both *she* and *he* as "sex-indefinite" pronouns in order, as she writes in the Preface, "to help conquer the all-pervading sexism which exists in the English language". Use of the written form *s/he* is becoming quite widespread, and the order of the nouns and pronouns in phrases like "he and she", "men and women", "mother and father" is sometimes purposely reversed. The reference book "Baby and Child" (Leach, 1977) uses *she* as a "neutral" pronoun throughout.[1] This is an important step, for the book is widely used, and although it is ultimately, of course, as sexist as using only *he,* it should attract the attention of readers who might otherwise not have been aware of the issue. Books on childcare appear to be leading the attack on the use of "neutral" *he.* Dr Spock has promised to alternate *she* and *he* in the next edition of his popular "Baby and Child Care", and Salk has already done so in his standard reference book for parents (Salk, 1974).

Professional organizations are also taking steps to encourage change in the language. The American Anthropological Association, for example, passed a resolution in 1973 urging its members to "become aware in their writing and

---

[1] In the 1979 and 1982 editions, however, Leach reverts to using *he* to refer to babies that may be either male or female, on the grounds that most readers prefer this. *She* remains in the text of most charts on the book, and in the captions to illustrations.

teaching that their wide use of the term 'man' as generic for the species is conceptually confusing" (reported in Miller and Swift, 1977, p. 129). The American Library Association resolved in 1975 to avoid using sexist language in all future publications and official documents, and to change existing publications when they were revised. And in 1976, library cataloguers in the USA initiated a campaign to revise the use of sexist language in subject headings and in catalogue descriptions.

Several religious bodies are also changing the language used in their publications. In the USA, the General Synod of the United Church of Christ announced in 1973 that it would eliminate sex and race discrimination in all areas of its teaching, and it has, since then, been revising all its printed materials, including hymn books, service procedures and journals, to ensure that the language used is deliberately inclusive. The Jewish prayerbook "Gates of Prayer", was also revised in 1975, and it acknowledges in the Introduction to the Revised Edition a similar commitment to equality of the sexes. The revisions include substitutions such as "God of all generations" for "God of our fathers", and additions such as "God of our mothers, God of Sarah, Rebekah, Leah . . ." as a parallel to "God of our fathers, God of Abraham, Isaac and Jacob . . . ." And the influential inter-denominational *Journal of Ecumenical Studies* devoted an editorial to "linguistic sexism" in 1974 (Volume XI, no. 2, Spring edition).

Although religious bodies in Britain are not renowned for equality in the treatment of the sexes (witness, for example, the refusal until last year to admit women into the Ministry, and the persistence of all-male choirs in the Anglican church), an initiative has come from the Methodist movement. The revised version of the Methodist Hymn Book, which is due to be published in 1983, omits some hymns that are considered to be blatantly sexist ("Rise up, O men of God", for example, has been excluded), and contains adapted versions of others. In many cases the adapted hymns are historically more accurate than the original versions: "O God our help in ages past", for example, contained the lines

Time, like an ever-rolling stream
Bears all its sons away

but the revised version, which substitutes "Bears mortal flesh away" for the second line, above, bears more resemblance to the wording of the psalm on which the hymn is based. The Methodist Hymn Book also makes some attempt to avoid male personification of God, by addressing the Deity directly as *Thou,* rather than indirectly as *He.* It continues, however, to use masculine imagery, referring to God as a father, king, shepherd and lord. Research into the language of religion has shown how the predominance of masculine imagery in religion results from the orientation of Western culture. Female imagery that was present in the Hebrew scriptures, for example, was often changed to masculine imagery during the process of translation (see Miller and Swift, 1977, Chapter 5; Spender, 1980, pp. 165–171). And until about AD200, Christian writers portrayed God as androgynous or feminine more often than as masculine (see Pagels, 1976). The use of masculine pronouns to refer to God must have some effect on the way that our culture conceptualizes a deity; and the effect will inevitably be greater for children, as the following "letter to God" from "Sylvia" suggests:

Dear God, Are boys better than girls? I know you are one but try to be fair.

From Marshall and Hample, 1966

Children are particularly susceptible, of course, to discriminatory language. Although the majority of the school books used in Britain still contain sexist language, some teachers and educators are now pointing out the social implications to their colleagues and their pupils. The 1980 Special Issue of the Journal *Women in Education,* for example, provides a checklist designed to be used by teachers for assessing the language used in school books. It warns that few books will be free of sexism, but gives suggestions for overcoming its effects, such as through class discussions or projects involving writing to publishers. There are also books designed for use in the classroom that point out the way in which the position of women in society is reflected in language. Though most of these are primarily concerned with sexual stereotyping, some also deal with sexism in English (see, for example, Adams and Laurikietis, 1976, 3, Unit 1:3).

The changes in the use of English that have been discussed in this section are relatively minor when seen in isolation, but together they reflect an increasing awareness of the way in which language often discriminates against women, and of the need to change the way that we use language, if we are to change the way that society views women.

THE LINGUISTIC MAINTENANCE OF SEXUAL STEREOTYPES

It is sometimes difficult to separate linguistic features that are sexist from linguistic features that help to maintain sexual stereotypes. For example, the choice of *he* as the sex-indefinite pronoun is sexist because it excludes women, but it also perpetuates the idea that women are of secondary importance.

Sometimes language is used to make sexual divisions, but simply as one aspect of a more general sexual discrimination. Several schools, for example, use gender differences between pupils as a convenient way of dividing the class. Teachers list girls and boys separately in their registers; they may also play one gender off against the other, hoping to encourage the class to finish their work quickly (see Delamont, 1980). Language is involved here, but it is not the only way that a sexual division is enforced: girls and boys may be made to sit separately in assembly, and even to enter school by separate doors (again, see Delamont, 1980). This is not sexual stereotyping, but it prepares the way for it by encouraging children to strongly identify with their own sex and to view the opposite sex as completely distinct from themselves. Although language plays a part in this, it is not the language that needs to be changed, but the divisive practices of the schools.

Sometimes, however, language is more directly involved in making unnecessary gender distinctions. Some universities list male students with their surname and initials (as in *J. A. Smith*) but list female students with their full name and marital status *(Mrs Jane A. Smith)* (see Acker, 1980); and most make the same distinction in their lists of academic staff.

There are several cases, though, where language clearly reflects stereotyped sex-roles. Research in this area has been able to point to those features of language that need to be changed. For example, some "pairs" of words like *to mother* and *to father* are parallel in form (both are verbs derived from nouns) but not in meaning. As Lakoff (1973) points out, the phrase "she mothered the child" implies a psychological as well as a biological relationship, reflecting the fact that traditionally it is the mother who is responsible for the upbringing of children, whereas "he fathered the child" implies only a limited biological act. Some writers have made conscious efforts to dispel the stereotypes implied by pairs of this kind; Dodson (1975a) and Parke (1981) use *to father* as a semantic parallel to the verb *to mother* in their books "How to Father" and "Fathering", and Dodson introduces a neutral term in a second book entitled "How to Parent" (Dodson, 1975b).

Dictionary definitions often reveal the existence of sexual stereotypes and, of course, perpetuate them. The Concise Oxford Dictionary (1976), for example, defines *manly* in terms of virtues said to be possessed by men: "having a man's virtues, courage, frankness, etc." But if *manly* is used to describe a woman, qualities rather than virtues are involved: "(of woman) having a man's qualities". *Womanly,* in contrast, is defined not in terms of inherent virtues but in terms of unspecified qualities that are considered suitable for women (one wonders by whom!): "(of woman or her feelings, conduct, etc.) having or showing the qualities befitting a woman". The Shorter Oxford English Dictionary (1973), which gives fuller definitions, adds independence and uprightness to the list of manly virtues, and gives gentleness and devotion as examples of qualities of women.

One application of the analysis of language and sexual stereotyping has been to avoid these kinds of definitions in the compilation of the *American Heritage School Dictionary.* This uses examples that assign to women virtues that traditionally have been attributed to men (for example, "she has *brains* and courage"). Similarly, characteristics that are usually considered to be feminine are attributed to men, in sentences such as "tears *welled* up in his eyes" or "striving to attain *mastery* over his emotions". Job stereotyping is also corrected, by using sentences like "he *teaches* kindergarten" and "he *studies* typing at night" (see Graham, 1975). The dictionary is designed to be used by schoolchildren, which means that it will play an important role in educating the next generation towards a less sexually divisive society. Another result of work in this area has been the publication of *The Feminist English Dictionary* (Todasco *et al.,* 1973), which takes material from established dictionaries to show how their definitions embody sexual stereotypes.

Work on sexual stereotyping in children's books has led to attempts to correct it. Research has shown that the vast majority of children's books portray stereotyped sex roles; what is more, they do not merely fail to prepare children for a more egalitarian society, but they even fail to depict life as it is at present (see Hoffman, 1981). The reading schemes that are used most commonly in British schools have twice as many male characters as female characters, and show the male characters taking part in a wider variety of roles and activities than the female characters (see Lobban, 1974; 1975). Furthermore, the books that are read most widely by children are frequently the ones that are the most guilty of stereotyping: *Little Women,* for example, is among the five books most often read by children over ten (see Whitehead *et al.,* 1977); and some of the worst offenders have been specifically recommended by the Schools Council and by literary critics (see Hoffmann, 1981). School textbooks also perpetuate outdated stereotypes: junior science books, for example, show experiments conducted by boys, while girls look on (see Austerfield and Turner, 1972), and textbooks on other subjects usually portray stereotyped sex roles, or else omit women entirely (again, see Hoffmann, 1981).

In Britain the Equal Opportunities Commission (1979, 1980) and the National Council for Civil Liberties (1978) have published practical suggestions for avoiding inadvertent sex discrimination in schools, that include a discussion of stereotyping in children's books. Some writers of children's fiction have purposely made girls the central figures of their books (for example, Lindgren, 1971; Garner, 1979; Sutcliff, 1967); others portray girls as tough and daring, as well as compassionate (Bawden, 1967; Kemp, 1977), and boys as sensitive and caring, but still tough (Southall, 1971; Byars, 1976). Other writers attempt to dispel outdated stereotypes by using as characters a working mother (Gripe, 1973), a politically active mother (Avery, 1978), a mother active in the Women's Movement (Perl, 1978), and even a mother who is a pirate (Mahy, 1972). A useful list of children's books which are free of sex bias (and also of class and race bias) can be found in Dixon (1977). Collections of fairy stories that avoid sexual stereotyping have also been published, some in their original form (Phelps, 1981), others specially written (Williams, 1979) or rewritten (Merseyside Women's Liberation Movement, n.d.). Lists of books that are free of sexual stereotyping are provided by a number of publishers and organizations (for details, see Hoffmann, 1981; and *Women in Education, Special Issue, 1980*), and checklists and guidelines for assessing the sexist content of children's books are produced by the Centre for Urban Educational Studies, the Equal Opportunities Commission, the National Union of Teachers and several other organizations. Discussion material for use in schools is also available, on fiction (see, for example, Cadogan and Craig, 1976; Whyatt, 1980), on women's issues (for example, Fyson and Greenhill, 1979), and also on ways of avoiding sexism and sexual stereotyping in teaching history, science and other school subjects (for example, O'Faolain and Martines, 1979; Snail *et al.,* 1981). Excellent annotated bibliographies and resource lists can be found, again, in the Special Issue of *Women in Education* (1980) and also in Spender and Sarah (1980).

In the USA the problem of sexual stereotyping in education has been taken seriously for a very long time. Not only have writers and professional organizations taken steps to correct stereotyping, but government funds have been set aside for intervention programmes for teachers, both as in-service and pre-service training courses (for details, see Ekstrom, 1979).

Language also maintains (and exaggerates) sexual stereotypes in advertising. The advertisement below, used in the early 70s in the USA by Parker Pens, is a good example:

> You might as well give her a gorgeous pen to keep her checkbook unbalanced with. A sleek and shining pen will make her feel prettier. Which is more important to any girl than solving mathematical mysteries.

> Quoted in Komisar, 1971

Nowadays stereotyping tends to be more subtle, and often results from the pictures rather than the wording of the advertisements (for examples, see Goffmann, 1979). Language is still sometimes involved, though, as in the current advertisements for TWA airlines, which have the words "Fly me" accompanying photographs of pretty air hostesses. In both the USA and Britain, stickers can be obtained with the messages "This ad insults women" or "This exploits women", and these have been used on advertisements in public places. In Britain the Women's Monitoring Network studies the representation of women in advertising and in the press generally, and relays its findings to offending companies.

Advertisements portray male stereotypes as well as female stereotypes, of course. In the USA some advertising companies are beginning to reverse traditional stereotypes in an attempt to correct them (for examples, see Komisar, 1971). In Britain a few advertisers appear to be aware of the issue: a recent television commercial for Sony, for example, plays on stereotyping by saying that since women may have been offended by their commercials, this one will deal only with the technical details that women are interested in. And a current television commercial for British Rail makes a half-hearted attempt to avoid stereotyping by addressing "Business men and business ladies"—half-hearted because the choice of the word "ladies" rather than "women" gives the phrase an ironic air (for discussion of the different connotations of *lady* and *woman,* see Lakoff, 1973). These advertisements, of course, reinforce traditional stereotypes by making fun of the issue, but they may nevertheless attract the attention of people who had not thought about stereotyping before. And, as Komisar (1971) suggests, the images of men and women that appear in advertisements are so exaggerated and ludicrous that they may influence people to stop acting out sexual stereotypes.

Sex-role stereotyping also exists in job descriptions. Job titles have been officially revised, first in the USA, and then in Britain to comply with the Sex Discrimination Act of 1975: air hostesses, to give one example, are now officially referred to as flight attendants. Changing the titles of jobs will help to avoid sex-role stereotyping, but the language that is used in job descriptions needs to be changed also. The third person singular pronoun often indicates which sex employers have in mind: a recent advertisement in *The Guardian* (18th December, 1981), for instance, read "Our clients . . . are looking for a Secretary who can use her initiative". Careers Guides often perpetuate stereotyping in the same way: the "Daily Telegraph Careers A-Z" guide, which is aimed at school leavers, writes under "Accountant": "he may work in public practice" (p. 7).

Some books designed to counteract sexual stereotyping in schools contain examples of this, and suggestions for discussion. Adams and Laurikietis (1976, 1) for example, has a useful chapter on "Your choice of career". At least one Careers guide makes a conscious effort to dispel sexual stereotyping in career possibilities: "Equal Opportunities: a careers guide" (Miller, 1978) uses the feminine third person singular pronoun throughout, and explains in the introduction that its aim is to "chivvy girls off the tramlines" and "encourage girls to widen their career choice and speed their progress towards equality in the job market".

Language, as a social phenomenon, inevitably reflects social attitudes towards women and men. But it also influences and to some extent moulds the views of its speakers, as Kress and Hodge (1979) point out. This means that the changes in language use that have been outlined in this section should lead to changes in the way that society treats men and women, which, in turn, will lead to further changes in language. Language change and social change, in other words, are mutually reinforcing.

THE FORMAL ANALYSIS OF LINGUISTIC DIFFERENCES IN MALE AND FEMALE SPEECH

Sociolinguistic surveys of American and British English usually include the sex of speakers as a sociological variable. Where linguistic features can occur in both a standard English and a non-standard form, the surveys have found that female speakers tend to use more of the standard English forms than male speakers. This is true for both phonological and morphosyntactic features (see, for example, Labov, 1966; Trudgill, 1974b). One reason may be that women are more conscious of the social significance of different linguistic features, so that they use more of the socially prestigious speech forms; another reason is, perhaps, that non-standard working-class speech has masculine connotations of "roughness" and "toughness" in Western society, so that men choose to use more non-standard forms (see Trudgill, 1974a). Conklin (1974) suggests that women are simply more sensitive to the constraints of different social contexts, so that they are less likely than men to use their most relaxed speech style (where the maximum use of nonstandard forms would occur) when talking to a linguistic investigator, particularly if, as has usually been the case, the investigator is male. In fact, some recent studies where the investigator was female found that differences in the use of non-standard forms depended not only on the sex of speakers but also on the degree to which they were integrated into the local culture (see Milroy, 1980; Cheshire, 1982a). Trudgill (1972) found that covert prestige is attached to non-standard features by younger working-class speakers of *both* sexes, and suggested that this reflects adherence to a subculture that is distinct from the mainstream value system of our society.

The analysis of sex differences in language has been useful within linguistics, by helping to explain some of the social mechanisms that are involved in language change (see, for example, Trudgill, 1972; Milroy, 1980). But it also has important implications for education. Children who speak non-standard English are at a disadvantage at school, because their variety of English is not the same as the variety used by the teachers and in school reading books. They have to choose, perhaps at an unconscious level, whether to use the standard English forms that are linked with mainstream culture and the school, or the non-standard English forms that symbolize solidarity with the vernacular culture. It is sometimes thought that boys are more likely than girls to reject standard English and the values of the school, because "female" values and female teachers predominate there (see, for example, Shuy, 1969). In fact, however, girls who are integrated into the peer group vernacular culture are equally likely to reject the language and the values of the school (see Cheshire, 1982b), and any attempt at teaching standard English should take this into consideration.

Research has also shown that some linguistic features function differently for female and male speakers (see Milroy, 1980; Cheshire, 1982a). One example of this is the non-standard past tense verb form *come,* which occurs in sentences such as "I come here last night". Adolescent boys in the town of Reading, in Berkshire, invariably use this non-standard form in both formal and informal speech; adolescent girls, on the other hand, use the form intermittently, varying it with the standard English past tense form *came.* We would expect, therefore, that boys will have more difficulty in replacing the non-standard form with the standard form, in their school writing. This kind of differentiation, then, also needs to be given careful consideration by educationists and teachers.

Some researchers have carried the analysis of sex differences in language a stage further, by looking at female and male roles in conversations. It has been suggested, for example, that in conversations between men and women, it is women who initiate the conversation and encourage men to speak, while men control the topics. It has also been claimed that men interrupt more often than women (see Zimmerman and West, 1975; Acker, 1980). As yet there is no valid empirical confirmation, but if these differences do exist, the knowledge could have some useful social applications, perhaps in counselling or therapy, or even, as Kramer *et al.* (1978) suggest, as an unobtrusive measure of sexual inequality.

EVALUATION OF SPEECH

Sex differences in the evaluation of speech have been analysed from the point of view of the hearer (in other words, analysing the way in which men and women evaluate speech) and from the point of view of the speaker (focussing on the way in which judges evaluate men's speech and women's speech). Elyan *et al.* (1978) found clear differences in the way that women and men evaluate speech. Women rated speakers who used Received Pronunciation more highly than men, in terms of status, intelligence, independence and egoism; and they gave lower ratings than men to speakers with regional accents. These findings have implications for education, for they imply that female teachers might form different stereotyped views of their pupils than male teachers. The way that children speak is thought to affect teachers' evaluation of their academic potential (see Seligman, Tucker and Lambert, 1972) and this, in turn, can affect academic success (Rosenthal and Jacobson, 1968). There could be serious consequences in other areas, too: in trial by jury, for example, in job interviews, and in politics.

As Smith (1979) points out, it is difficult to analyse how women's and men's speech is evaluated, because judges may be reacting to the sex of speakers, rather than to their language. It has been suggested that women's speech is characterized by a number of linguistic features, such as a more frequent use of tag questions, fillers, intensifiers and "empty" adjectives (for example, *divine* or *lovely*) (see Lakoff, 1973), but this has not been confirmed by empirical studies. It is now thought that the linguistic characteristics described by Lakoff typify a more general "powerless" variety of speech, used by speakers who have little social prestige (see Lind and O'Barr, 1979), and, therefore, associated more often with women than with men. Lind and O'Barr set up simulated legal hearings, and found that jurors of both sexes rated witnesses using the "powerless" variety of speech as less competent, trustworthy, convincing, socially attractive and socially dynamic than witnesses who did not use this variety, irrespective of their sex. Although these findings do not bear directly on sex differences in language use, they do show that using certain linguistic features can affect the way in which speakers of both sexes are evaluated, and are relevant in all areas where language plays a central role. Those speakers who have low social prestige may reveal this in their speech, and be evaluated negatively in job interviews, legal proceedings and other important social situations. Thus, although the initial impetus for this research came from an interest in sexual inequality, the results have wider implications that could affect all sections of society that are treated unequally.

CONCLUSION

Changes that take place in society are reflected in language, though language change tends to lag behind social change. Sex roles in the USA and in Britain have been changing during the course of this century, and we would normally expect these social changes to be accompanied by gradual changes in language. We have seen, however, that research into the relationship between language and sex has led to conscious attempts to change discriminatory and stereotyping language. These practical applications are accelerating the rate at which language is changing and this should, in turn, accelerate the rate at which society is changing.

We have also seen that research in this area has implications for education and for legal proceedings and job interviews. It has potential applications for many other areas also: in the field of language pathology, for example, where it seems that sex-role stereotyping could account for some language disorders in male speakers (see Kramer, 1974).

The main application of work on the relationship between language and sex has, of course, been in attempts to change our use of discriminatory language, in order to remove sexual inequality from society. It has wider applications also, however, that have been only briefly mentioned here: it helps our general understanding of the way in which language reflects and maintains social divisions, and of the way in which our thinking is often unconsciously moulded by our language. An understanding of this will help to eliminate not only sexual inequality, but inequality in all areas of social life.

REFERENCES

Acker, S. (1980). Women, the other academics. *British Journal of Sociology of Education,* **1,** (1), 81–91.

Adams, C., and R. Laurikietis. (1976). *The gender trap: A closer look at sex roles*, Book 1: Education and work. Book 2: Sex and Marriage. Book 3: Messages and Images. Virago, London.

Aitchison, J. (1981). *Language change: Progress or decay?* Fontana, London.

Arnold J. (1973). *The Cook and the Carpenter*, Daughters, Houston, Texas.

Austerfield, V., and J. Turner. (1972). What are little girls made of? *Spare Rib,* 3 September.

Avery, G. (1978). *Huck and her time machine*, Armada, London.

Bawden, N. (1967). *A handful of thieves*, Gollancz, London.

Bodine, A. (1975). Androcentrism in prescriptive grammar: Singular 'they', sex-indefinite 'he', and 'he or she.' *Language in Society,* **4** (1), 129–146.

Byars, B. (1976). *The Midnight Fox*, Penguin, Harmondsworth.

Cadogan, M., and P. Craig. (1976). *You're a brick, Angela: A new look at girls' fiction 1839–1975*, Gollancz, London.

Cheshire, J. (1982a). *Variation in an English dialect: A sociolinguistic study*, Cambridge University Press, London.

———. (1982b). Dialect features and linguistic conflict in schools. *Educational Review,* **34** (1), 53–67.

Conklin, N. (1974). Toward a feminist analysis of linguistic behaviour. *University of Michigan Papers in Womens Studies,* **1** (1), 51–73.

Daily Telegraph Careers A–Z, (1981). William Collins, London.

Delamont, S. (1980). *The Sociology of Women,* George Allen and Unwin, London.

Dixon, B. (1977). *Catching them young: Sex, race and class in children's fiction,* (Vol. 1), Pluto Press, London.

Dodson, F. (1975a). *How to parent,* Star books, London.

———. (1975b). *How to father,* New American Library, New York.

Ekstrom, R. B. (1979). Intervention strategies to reduce sex-role stereotyping in education. In *Sex-role stereotyping: Collected papers,* (O. Hartnett, G. Boden and M. Fuller, eds.), Tavistock Publications, London.

Elyan, O., et al. (1978). R.P. accented female speech: The voice of perceived androgyny? In *Sociolinguistic patterns in British English,* (P. Trudgill, ed.), Edward Arnold, London.

Equal Opportunities Commission, (1979). *Do you provide equal educational opportunities?*

———. (1980). *Ending sex-stereotyping in schools.*

Fyson, N. L. and S. Greenhill. (1979). *People talking,* Macmillan Educational, London.

Garner, A. (1979). *The Stone Book,* Armada, London.

Goffman, E. (1979). *Gender advertisements,* Harvard University Press, Cambridge, Mass.

Goot, M., and E. Reid. (1975). *Women and voting studies,* Sage, London.

Graham, A. (1975). The making of a nonsexist dictionary. In *Language and sex: Difference and dominance,* (B. Thorne and N. Henley, eds.), Newbury House Publishers, Rowley, Mass.

Gripe, M. (1973). *The Night Daddy,* Chatto and Windus, London.

Guttenag, M., and H. Bray. (1976). *Undoing sex-stereotypes: Research and resources for educators,* McGraw-Hill, New York.

Harrison, L. (1975). Cro-magnon woman—in eclipse. *The Science Teacher,* April 1975, pp. 8–11.

Hoffman, M. (1981). Children's reading and social values. In *Language in School and Community,* (N. Mercer, ed.), Edward Arnold, London.

Kemp, G. (1977). *The turbulent term of Tyke Tiler,* Faber, London.

Kidd, V. (1971). A study of the images produced through the use of the male pronoun as the generic. *Moments in Contemporary Rhetoric and Communication,* **1** (1), 25–30.

Killian, R. A. (1979). *Managers must lead!* AMACOM, USA.

Komisar, L. (1971). The image of woman in advertising. In *Woman in sexist society,* (V. Gornick and B. K. Moran, eds.), Basic Books, New York.

Kramer, C. (1974). Women's speech: separate but unequal? *Quarterly Journal of Speech,* **60** (February), 14–24. Reprinted in Thorne and Henley, 1975.

Kramer, C., B. Thorne, and N. Henley. (1978). Perspectives on language and communication. *Signs: Journal of Women in Culture and Society,* **3** (3), 638–651.

Kress, G., and R. Hodge. (1979). *Language as ideology,* Routledge and Kegan Paul, London.

Labov, W. (1966). *The social stratification of English in New York City*, Center for Applied Linguistics, Washington, D.C.

Lakoff, R. (1973). Language and woman's place. *Language in Society,* **2** (1), 45–79.

Leach, P. (1977). *Baby and Child*, Michael Joseph, London.

Lind, E. A., and W. M. O'Barr. (1979). The social significance of speech in the court-room. In *Language and social psychology* (H. Giles and R. N. St. Clair, eds.), Blackwell, Oxford.

Lindgren, A. (1971). *Pippi Longstocking*, Oxford University Press, Oxford.

Lobban, G. (1974). Presentation of sex-roles in reading schemes. *Forum for the Discussion of New Trends in Education,* **16** (2), Spring, pp. 57–60.

———. (1975). Sex-roles in reading schemes. *Educational Review,* **27** (3), 202–209.

Mahy, M. (1972). *The Man whose mother was a pirate*, Dent, London.

Marshall, E., and S. Hample. (1966). *Children's letters to God*, Pocket Books, New York.

Martyna, W. (1978). What does "he" mean? Use of the generic masculine. *Journal of Communication,* **28** (1), 131–138.

Mackay, D. G. (1979). On the goals, principles and procedures for prescriptive grammar: Singular *they. Language and Society* **9,** 349–367.

Mackay, D. G., and D. Fulkerson. (1979). On the comprehension and production of pronouns. *Journal of Verbal Learning and Verbal Behaviour.*

Merseyside Women's Liberation Movement. (n.d.). *Once and Future Tales* (Snow White, Red Riding Hood, The Prince and the Swineherd). Available from 53, Sandown Road, Liverpool.

Miller, R. (1978). *Equal opportunities: A careers guide*, Penguin, Harmondsworth.

Miller, C., and Swift, K. (1977). *Words and Women*, Gollancz, London.

———. (1981). *The handbook of non-sexist writing for writers, editors and speakers*, The Women's Press, London.

Milroy, L. (1980). *Language and social networks.* Blackwell, Oxford.

Moulton, J., G. M. Robinson, and C. Elias. (1978). Sex bias in language use: "Neutral" pronouns that aren't. *American Psychologist,* **33** (11), 1032–1036.

National Council for Civil Liberties. (1978). *Sex discrimination in schools: How to fight it.*

Nilsen, A. P. (1973). Grammatical gender and its relationship to the equal treatment of males and females in children's books. Unpublished Ph.D. Thesis, University of Iowa.

O'Faolain, J., and L. Martines. (1979). *Not in God's image: Women in history*, Virago, London.

Pagels, E. H. (1976). What became of God the mother? Conflicting images of God in early Christianity. *Signs: Journal of Women in Culture and Society,* **2** (2), 293–303.

Parke, R. (1981). *Fathering*, Fontana, London.

Perl, L. (1978). *That crazy April*, Armada, London.

Phelps, E. J. (1981). *The maid of the North and other folk tales' heroines*, Holt, Rinehart and Winston, New York.

Piercy, M. (1979). *Woman on the edge of time*, The Women's Press, London.

Roberts, H. (1981). *Doing feminist research*, Routledge and Kegan Paul, London.

Rosenthal, R., and L. Jacobson. (1968). *Pygmalion in the classroom*, Holt, Rinehart and Winston, New York.

Salk, L. (1974). *Preparing for parenthood*, David McKay, New York.

Schneider J. W., and S. L. Hacker. (1973). Sex role imagery and the use of the generic 'man' in introductory texts: a case in the sociology of sociology. *The American Sociologist,* **8** (1), 12–18.

Seligman, C. R., G. R. Tucker, and W. E. Lambert. (1972). The effects of speech style and other attributes on teachers' attitudes towards pupils. *Language in Society,* **1** (1), 131–142.

Shuy, R. (1969). Sociolinguistic research at the Center for Applied Linguistics: The correlation of language and sex. *Giornata Internazionali di Sociolinguistica,* Palazzo Baldassini, Rome.

Smith, P. (1979). Sex markers in speech. In *Social markers in speech* (K. P. Scherer and H. Giles, eds.), Cambridge University Press, Cambridge.

Snail, M., A. Kelly, and J. Whyte. (1980). *Girls into science and technology,* available from 91 Didsbury Park, Manchester 20.

Southall, I. (1971). *Josh,* Penguin, Harmondsworth.

Spender, D. (1980). *Man made language,* Routledge and Kegan Paul, London.

——. (forthcoming). *Men's studies modified: The impact of feminism on the academic disciplines,* Pergamon, Oxford.

Spender, D., and E. Sarah. (eds) (1980). *Learning to lose: Sexism and education,* The Women's Press, London.

Sutcliff, R. (1967). *The chief's daughter,* Hamish Hamilton, London.

Thorne, B., and N. Henley. (eds.) (1975). *Language and sex: Difference and dominance,* Newbury House Publishers, Rowley, Mass.

Todasco et al. (1973). *An intelligent woman's guide to dirty words: English words and phrases reflecting sexist attitudes towards women in patriarchal society, arranged according to usage and idea,* Vol. I of *The Feminist English Dictionary,* Feminist Writers Workshop, Loop Center YWCA, Chicago.

Trudgill, P. (1972). Sex, covert prestige and linguistic change in the urban British English of Norwich. *Language in Society,* **1,** (1), 179–195.

——. (1974a). *Sociolinguistics,* Penguin, Harmondsworth.

——. (1974b). *The social differentiation of English in Norwich,* Cambridge University Press, London.

Whitehead F., et al. (1977). *Children and their books,* Macmillan Education, London, for the Schools Council.

Whyatt, B. (1980). *Myths and legends for young feminists, and for old feminists the original version,* available from B. Whyatt, 90, Plane Avenue, Wigan, Lancs. WN5 9PT.

Williams, J. (1979). *The practical princess and other liberating fairy tales,* Chatto and Windus, London.

Women in Education, Special Issue 1980. Autumn, no. 20: Women and Education Newsletter Group: 14, St. Brendan's Road, Withington, Manchester 20.

Zimmerman, D. H., and C. West. (1975). Sex roles, interruptions and silences in conversations. In *Language and sex: Difference and dominance* (B. Thorne and N. Henley, eds.), Newbury House Publishers, Rowley, Mass.

Asymmetries: Women and Men Talking at Cross-Purposes

Deborah Tannen

Eve had a lump removed from her breast. Shortly after the operation, talking to her sister, she said that she found it upsetting to have been cut into, and that looking at the stitches was distressing because they left a seam that had changed the contour of her breast. Her sister said, "I know. When I had my operation I felt the same way." Eve made the same observation to her friend Karen, who said, "I know. It's like your body has been violated." But when she told her husband, Mark, how she felt, he said, "You can have plastic surgery to cover up the scar and restore the shape of your breast."

Eve had been comforted by her sister and her friend, but she was not comforted by Mark's comment. Quite the contrary, it upset her more. Not only didn't she hear what she wanted, that he understood her feelings, but, far worse, she felt he was asking her to undergo more surgery just when she was telling him how much this operation had upset her. "I'm not having any more surgery!" she protested. "I'm sorry you don't like the way it looks." Mark was hurt and puzzled. "I don't care," he protested. "It doesn't bother me at all." She asked, "Then why are you telling me to have plastic surgery?" He answered, "Because you were saying *you* were upset about the way it looked."

Eve felt like a heel: Mark had been wonderfully supportive and concerned throughout her surgery. How could she snap at him because of what he said—"just words"—when what he had done was unassailable? And yet she had perceived in his words metamessages that cut to the core of their relationship. It was self-evident to him that his comment was a reaction to her complaint, but she heard it as an independent complaint of his. He thought he was reassuring her that she needn't feel bad about her scar because there was something she could *do* about it. She heard his suggestion that she do something about the scar as evidence that *he* was bothered by it. Furthermore, whereas she wanted reassurance that it was normal to feel bad in her situation, his telling her that the problem could easily be fixed implied she had no right to feel bad about it.

Eve wanted the gift of understanding, but Mark gave her the gift of advice. He was taking the role of problem solver, whereas she simply wanted confirmation for her feelings.

A similar misunderstanding arose between a husband and wife following a car accident in which she had been seriously injured. Because she hated being in the hospital, the wife asked to come home early. But once home, she suffered pain from having to move around more. Her husband said, "Why didn't you stay in the hospital where you would have been more comfortable?" This hurt her because it seemed to imply that he did not want her home. She didn't think of his suggestion that she should have stayed in the hospital as a response to her complaints about the pain she was suffering; she thought of it as an independent expression of his preference not to have her at home.

"THEY'RE MY TROUBLES—NOT YOURS"

If women are often frustrated because men do not respond to their troubles by offering matching troubles, men are often frustrated because women do. Some men not only take no comfort in such a response, they take offense. For example, a woman told me that when her companion talks about a personal concern—for example, his feelings about growing older—she responds, "I know how you feel; I feel the same way." To her surprise and chagrin, he gets annoyed; he feels she is trying to take something away from him by denying the uniqueness of his experience.

A similar miscommunication was responsible for the following interchange, which began as a conversation and ended as an argument:

*He:*I'm really tired. I didn't sleep well last night.
*She:*I didn't sleep well either. I never do.
He: Why are you trying to belittle me?
*She:*I'm not! I'm just trying to show that I understand!

This woman was not only hurt by her husband's reaction; she was mystified by it. How could he think she was belittling him? By "belittle me," he meant "belittle my experience." He was filtering her attempts to establish connection through his concern with preserving independence and avoiding being put down.

"I'LL FIX IT FOR YOU"

Women and men are both often frustrated by the other's way of responding to their expression of troubles. And they are further hurt by the other's frustration. If women resent men's tendency to offer solutions to problems, men complain about women's refusal to take action to solve the problems they complain about. Since many men see themselves as problem solvers, a complaint or a trouble is a challenge to their ability to think of a solution, just as a woman presenting a broken bicycle or stalling car poses a challenge to their ingenuity in fixing it. But whereas many women appreciate help in fixing mechanical equipment, few are inclined to appreciate help in "fixing" emotional troubles.

The idea that men are problem solvers was reinforced by the contrasting responses of a husband and wife to the same question on a radio talk show. The couple, Barbara and William Christopher, were discussing their life with an autistic child. The host asked if there weren't times when they felt sorry for themselves and wondered, "Why me?" Both said no, but they said it in different ways. The wife deflected attention from herself: She said that the real sufferer was her child. The husband said, "Life is problem solving. This is just one more problem to solve."

This explains why men are frustrated when their sincere attempts to help a woman solve her problems are met not with gratitude but with disapproval. One man reported being ready to tear his hair out over a girlfriend who continually told him about problems she was having at work but refused to take any of the advice he offered. Another man defended himself against his girlfriend's objection that he changed the subject as soon as she recounted something that was bothering her: "What's the point of talking about it any more?" he said. "You can't do anything about it." Yet another man commented that women seem to wallow in their problems, wanting to talk about them forever, whereas he and other men want to get them out and be done with them, either by finding a solution or by laughing them off.

Trying to solve a problem or fix a trouble focuses on the message level of talk. But for most women who habitually report problems at work or in friendships, the message is not the main point of complaining. It's the metamessage that counts: Telling about a problem is a bid for an expression of understanding ("I know how you feel") or a similar complaint ("I felt the same way when something similar happened to me"). In other words, troubles talk is intended to reinforce rapport by sending the metamessage "We're the same; you're not alone." Women are frustrated when they not only don't get this reinforcement but, quite the opposite, feel distanced by the advice, which seems to send the metamessage "We're not the same. You have the problems; I have the solutions."

Furthermore, mutual understanding is symmetrical, and this symmetry contributes to a sense of community. But giving advice is asymmetrical. It frames the advice giver as more knowledgeable, more reasonable, more in control—in a word, one-up. And this contributes to the distancing effect.

The assumption that giving advice can be oneupmanship underlies an observation that appeared in a book review. In commenting on Alice Adams's *After You've Gone,* reviewer Ron Carlson explained that the title story is a letter from a woman to a man who has left her for a younger woman. According to Carlson, the woman informs her former lover about her life "and then steps up and clobbers him with sage advice. Here is clearly a superior woman. . . ." Although we do not know the intention of the woman who wrote the story, we see clearly that the man who reviewed it regards giving advice as a form of attack and sees one who gives advice as taking a superior position.

PARALLEL TRACKS

These differences seem to go far back in our growing up. A sixteen-year-old girl told me she tends to hang around with boys rather than girls. To test my ideas, I asked her whether boys and girls both talk about problems. Yes, she assured me, they both do. Do they do it the same way? I asked. Oh, no, she said. The girls go on and on. The boys raise the issue, one of them comes up with a solution, and then they close the discussion.

Women's and men's frustrations with each other's ways of dealing with troubles talk amount to applying interpretations based on one system to talk that is produced according to a different system. Boys and men do not respond to each other the way women respond to each other in troubles talk. The roots of the very different way that men respond to talk about troubles became clear to me when I compared the transcript of a pair of tenth-grade boys talking to each other to the transcripts of girls' coversations from videotapes of best friends talking, recorded as part of a research project by psychologist Bruce Dorval.

Examining the videotaped conversations, I found that the boys and girls, who expressed deep concerns to each other, did it in different ways—ways that explain the differences that come up in daily conversations between women and men. The pairs of girls at both the sixth grade and tenth grade talked at length about one girl's problems. The other girl pressed her to elaborate, said, "I know," and gave supporting evidence. The following brief excerpts from the transcripts show the dramatic difference between the girls and boys.

The tenth-grade girls are talking about Nancy's problems with her boyfriend and her mother. It emerges that Nancy and Sally were both part of a group excursion to another state. Nancy suddenly left the group and returned home early at her mother's insistence. Nancy was upset about having to leave early. Sally reinforces Nancy's feelings by letting her know that her sudden departure was also upsetting to her friends:

> *Nancy:* God, it was *bad*. I couldn't believe she made me go home.
> *Sally:* I thought it was kind of weird though, I mean, one minute we were going out and the next minute Nancy's going, "Excuse me, gotta be going."[Both laugh] I didn't know what was going on, and Judy comes up to me and she whispers (the whole place knows), "Do you know that Nancy's going home?" And I go, "What?"[Both laugh] "Nancy's going home." I go, *"Why?"* She goes, "Her mom's making her." I go [makes a face], "Ah." She comes back and goes, "Nancy's left." Well, I said, "WELL, that was a fine thing TO DO, she didn't even come and say goodbye." And she starts boiling all over me. I go [mimicking yelling], *"All right!!"* She was upset, Judy. I was like "God"—

Sally's way of responding to her friend's troubles is to confirm Nancy's feelings of distress that her mother made her leave the trip early, by letting her know that her leaving upset her friends. In contrast, examining the transcript of a conversation between boys of the same age shows how differently they respond to each other's expressions of troubles.

The tenth-grade boys also express deep feelings. Theirs too is troubles talk, but it is troubles talk with a difference. They don't concentrate on the troubles of one, pursuing, exploring, and elaborating. Instead, each one talks about his own troubles and dismisses the other's as insignificant.

In the first excerpt from these boys' conversation, Richard says he feels bad because his friend Mary has no date for an upcoming dance, and Todd dismisses his concern:

> *Richard:* God, I'm going to feel so bad for her if she stays home.
> *Todd:* She's not going to stay home, it's ridiculous. Why doesn't she just ask somebody?

Yet Todd himself is upset because he has no date for the same dance. He explains that he doesn't want to ask Anita, and Richard, in turn, scoffs at his distress:

> *Todd:* I felt so bad when she came over and started talking to me last night.
> *Richard:* Why?
> *Todd:* I don't know. I felt uncomfortable, I guess.
> *Richard:* **I'll never understand that.** [Laugh]

Far from trying to show that he understands, Richard states flatly that he doesn't, as shown in boldface type.

Richard then tells Todd that he is afraid he has a drinking problem. Todd responds by changing the subject to something that is bothering him, his feelings of alienation:

> *Richard:* When I took Anne home last night she told me off.
> *Todd:* Really?
>
> . . .
>
> *Richard:* You see when she found out what happened last Thursday night between Sam and me?
> *Todd:* Mhm.
> *Richard:* She knew about that. And she just said—and then she started talking about drinking. You know? . . . And then she said, you know, "You, how you hurt everybody when you do it. You're always cranky." And she just said, "I don't like it. You hurt Sam. You hurt Todd. You hurt Mary. You hurt Lois."
>
> . . .
>
> I mean, when she told me, you know I guess I was kind of stunned.[Pause] I didn't really drink that much.
> *Todd:* **Are you still talking to Mary, a lot, I mean?**
> *Richard:* Am I still talking to Mary?
> *Todd:* Yeah, 'cause that's why—that's why I was mad Friday.

Richard: Why?

Todd: Because.

Richard: 'Cause why?

Todd: 'Cause I didn't know why you all just wa- I mean I just went back upstairs for things, then y'all never came back. I was going, "Fine. I don't care." I said, "He's going to start this again."

As the lines printed in boldface show, when Richard says that he is upset because Anne told him he behaved badly when he was drunk, Todd responds by bringing up his own concern: He feels left out, and he was hurt when Richard disappeared from a party with his friend Mary.

Throughout the conversation, Todd expresses distress over feeling alienated and left out. Richard responds by trying to argue Todd out of the way he feels. When Todd says he felt out of place at a party the night before, Richard argues:

Richard: **How could you feel out of place? You knew Lois, and you knew Sam.**

Todd: I don't know. I just felt really out of place and then last night again at the party, I mean, Sam was just running around, he knew everyone from the sorority. There was about five.

Richard: **Oh, no, he didn't.**

Todd: He knew a lot of people. He was—I don't know.

Richard: **Just Lois. He didn't know everybody.**

. . .

Todd: I just felt really out of place that day, all over the place. I used to feel, I mean—

Richard: Why?

Todd: I don't know. I don't even feel right in school anymore.

Richard: I don't know, last night, I mean—

Todd: I think I know what Ron Cameron and them feels like now.[Laugh]

Richard: [Laugh] **No, I don't think you feel as bad as Ron Cameron feels**

Todd: I'm kidding.

Richard: Mm-mm. **Why should you? You know more people—**

Todd: I can't talk to anyone anymore.

Richard: **You know more people than me.**

By telling Todd that his feelings are unjustified and incomprehensible, Richard is not implying that he doesn't care. He clearly means to comfort his friend, to make him feel better. He's implying, "You shouldn't feel bad because your problems aren't so bad."

MATCHING TROUBLES

The very different way that women respond to the telling of troubles is dramatized in a short story, "New Haven," by Alice Mattison. Eleanor tells Patsy that she has fallen in love with a married man. Patsy responds by first displaying understanding and then offering a matching revelation about a similar experience:

"Well," says Patsy. "I know how you feel."

"You do?"

"In a way, I do. Well, I should tell you. I've been sleeping with a married man for two years."

Patsy then tells Eleanor about her affair and how she feels about it. After they discuss Patsy's affair, however, Patsy says:

"But you were telling me about this man and I cut you off. I'm sorry. See? I'm getting self-centered."

"It's OK." But she is pleased again.

The conversation then returns to Eleanor's incipient affair. Thus Patsy responds first by confirming Eleanor's feelings and matching her experience, reinforcing their similarity, and then by encouraging Eleanor to tell more. Within the frame of Patsy's similar predicament, the potential asymmetry inherent in revealing personal problems is avoided, and the friendship is brought into balance.

What made Eleanor's conversation with Patsy so pleasing to Eleanor was that they shared a sense of how to talk about troubles, and this reinforced their friendship. Though Eleanor raised the matter of her affair, she did not elaborate on it until Patsy pressed her to do so. In another story by the same author, "The Knitting," a woman named Beth is staying with her sister in order to visit her sister's daughter Stephanie in a psychiatric hospital. While there, Beth receives a disturbing telephone call from her boyfriend, Alec. Having been thus reminded of her troubles, she wants to talk about them, but she refrains, because her sister doesn't ask. She feels required, instead, to focus on her sister's problem, the reason for her visit:

> She'd like to talk about her muted half-quarrels with Alec of the last weeks, but her sister does not ask about the phone call. Then Beth thinks they should talk about Stephanie.

The women in these stories are balancing a delicate system by which troubles talk is used to confirm their feelings and create a sense of community.

When women confront men's ways of talking to them, they judge them by the standards of women's conversational styles. Women show concern by following up someone else's statement of trouble by questioning her about it. When men change the subject, women think they are showing a lack of sympathy—a failure of intimacy. But the failure to ask probing questions could just as well be a way of respecting the other's need for independence. When Eleanor tells Patsy that she is in love with Peter, Patsy asks, "Are you sleeping with him?" This exploration of Eleanor's topic could well strike many men—and some women—as intrusive, though Eleanor takes it as a show of interest that nourishes their friendship.

Women tend to show understanding of another woman's feelings. When men try to reassure women by telling them that their situation is not so bleak, the women hear their feelings being belittled or discounted. Again, they encounter a failure of intimacy just when they were bidding to reinforce it. Trying to trigger a symmetrical communication, they end up in an asymmetrical one.

A DIFFERENT SYMMETRY

The conversation between Richard and Todd shows that although the boys' responses are asymmetrical if looked at separately—each dismisses the other's concerns—they are symmetrical when looked at together: Todd responds to Richard's concern about his drinking in exactly the same way that Richard responds to Todd's feeling of alienation, by denying it is a problem:

> *Richard:* Hey, man, I just don't feel—I mean, after what Anne said last night, I just don't feel like doing that.
> *Todd:* **I don't think it was that way. You yourself knew it was no big problem.**
> *Richard:* Oh, Anne—Sam told Anne that I fell down the levee.
> *Todd:* **It's a lie.**
> *Richard:* I didn't fall. I slipped, slid. I caught myself.
> *Todd:* **Don't worry about it.**
> *Richard:* But I do, kind of. I feel funny in front of Sam. I don't want to do it in front of you.
> *Todd:* **It doesn't matter 'cause sometimes you're funny when you're off your butt.**

Todd denies that Richard was so drunk he was staggering ("It's a lie") and then says that even if he was out of control, it wasn't bad; it was funny.

In interpreting this conversation between tenth-grade boys, I initially saw their mutual reassurances and dismissals, and their mutual revelations of troubles, in terms of connection and sameness. But another perspective is possible. Their conversation may be touching precisely because it was based on asymmetries of status—or, more precisely, a deflecting of such asymmetries. When Todd tells his troubles, he puts himself in a potentially one-down position and invites Richard to take a one-up position by disclaiming troubles and asymmetrically offering advice or sympathy. By offering troubles of his own, Richard declines to take the superior position and restores their symmetrical footing, sending the metamessage "We're just a couple of guys trying to make it in a world that's tough on both of us, and both of us are about equally competent to deal with it."

From this perspective, responding as a woman might—for example by saying, "I can see how you feel; you must feel awful; so would I if it happened to me"—would have a totally different meaning for boys, since they would be inclined to interpret it through the lens of status. Such a response would send a metamessage like "Yes, I know, you incompetent jerk, I know how awful you must feel. If I were as incompetent as you, I'd feel the same way. But, lucky for you, I'm not, and I can help you out here, because I'm far too talented to be upset by a problem like that." In other words, refraining from expressing sympathy is generous, insofar as sympathy potentially condescends.

Women are often unhappy with the reactions they get from men when they try to start troubles talk, and men are often unhappy because they are accused of responding in the wrong way when they are trying to be helpful. But Richard and Todd seem satisfied with each other's ways of reacting to their troubles. And their ways make sense. When men and women talk to each other, the problem is that each expects a different kind of response. The men's approach seeks to assuage feelings indirectly by attacking their cause. Since women expect to have their feelings supported, the men's approach makes them feel that they themselves are being attacked.

"DON'T ASK"

Talking about troubles is just one of many conversational tasks that women and men view differently, and that consequently cause trouble in talk between them. Another is asking for information. And this difference too is traceable to the asymmetries of status and connection.

A man and a woman were standing beside the information booth at the Washington Folk Life Festival, a sprawling complex of booths and displays. "You ask," the man was saying to the woman. "I don't ask."

Sitting in the front seat of the car beside Harold, Sybil is fuming. They have been driving around for half an hour looking for a street he is sure is close by. Sybil is angry not because Harold does not know the way, but because he insists on trying to find it himself rather than stopping and asking someone. Her anger stems from viewing his behavior through the lens of her own: If she were driving, she would have asked directions as soon as she realized she didn't know which way to go, and they'd now be comfortably ensconced in their friends' living room instead of driving in circles, as the hour gets later and later. Since asking directions does not make Sybil uncomfortable, refusing to ask makes no sense to her. But in Harold's world, driving around until he finds his way is the reasonable thing to do, since asking for help makes him uncomfortable. He's avoiding that discomfort and trying to maintain his sense of himself as a self-sufficient person.

Why do many men resist asking for directions and other kinds of information? And, it is just as reasonable to ask, why is it that many women don't? By the paradox of independence and intimacy, there are two simultaneous and different metamessages implied in asking for and giving information. Many men tend to focus on one, many women on the other.

When you offer information, the information itself is the message. But the fact that you have the information, and the person you are speaking to doesn't, also sends a metamessage of superiority. If relations are inherently hierarchical, then the one who has more information is framed as higher up on the ladder, by virtue of being more knowledgeable and competent. From this perspective, finding one's own way is an essential part of the independence that men perceive to be a prerequisite for self-respect. If self-respect is bought at the cost of a few extra minutes of travel time, it is well worth the price.

Because they are implicit, metamessages are hard to talk about. When Sybil begs to know why Harold won't just ask someone for directions, he answers in terms of the message, the information: He says there's no point in asking, because anyone he asks may not know and may give him wrong directions. This is theoretically reasonable. There are many countries, such as, for example, Mexico, where it is standard procedure for people to make up directions rather than refuse to give requested information. But this explanation frustrates Sybil, because it doesn't make sense to her. Although she realizes that someone might give faulty directions, she believes this is relatively unlikely, and surely it cannot happen every time. Even if it did happen, they would be in no worse shape than they are in now anyway.

Part of the reason for their different approaches is that Sybil believes that a person who doesn't know the answer will say so, because it is easy to say, "I don't know." But Harold believes that saying "I don't know" is humiliating, so people might well take a wild guess. Because of their different assumptions, and the invisibility of framing, Harold and Sybil can never get to the bottom of this difference; they can only get more frustrated with each other. Keeping talk on the message level is common, because it is the level we are most clearly aware of. But it is unlikely to resolve confusion since our true motivations lie elsewhere.

To the extent that giving information, directions, or help is of use to another, it reinforces bonds between people. But to the extent that it is asymmetrical, it creates hierarchy: Insofar as giving information frames one as the expert, superior in knowledge, and the other as uninformed, inferior in knowledge, it is a move in the negotiation of status.

It is easy to see that there are many situations where those who give information are higher in status. For example, parents explain things to children and answer their questions, just as teachers give information to students. An awareness of this dynamic underlies one requirement for proper behavior at Japanese dinner entertainment, according to anthropologist Harumi Befu. In order to help the highest-status member of the party to dominate the conversation, others at the dinner are expected to ask him questions that they know he can answer with authority.

Because of this potential for asymmetry, some men resist receiving information from others, especially women, and some women are cautious about stating information that they know, especially to men. For example, a man with whom I discussed these dynamics later told me that my perspective clarified a comment made by his wife. They had gotten into their car and were about to go to a destination that she knew well but he did not know at all. Consciously resisting an impulse to just drive off and find his own way, he began by asking his wife if she had any advice about the best way to get there. She told him the way, then added, "But I don't know. That's how I would go, but there might be a better way." Her comment was a move to redress the imbalance of power created by her knowing something he didn't know. She was also saving face in advance, in case he decided not to take her advice. Furthermore, she was reframing her directions as "just a suggestion" rather than "giving instructions."

"I'LL FIX IT IF IT KILLS ME"

The asymmetry implied in having and giving information is also found in having and demonstrating the skill to fix things—an orientation that we saw in men's approaches to troubles talk. To further explore the framing involved in fixing things, I will present a small encounter of my own.

Unable to remove the tiny lid that covers the battery compartment for the light meter on my camera, I took the camera to a photography store and asked for help. The camera salesman tried to unscrew the lid, first with a dime and then with a special instrument. When this failed, he declared the lid hopelessly stuck. He explained the reason (it was screwed in with the threads out of alignment) and then explained in detail how I could take pictures without a light meter by matching the light conditions to shutter settings in accordance with the chart included in rolls of film. Even though I knew there wasn't a chance in the world I would adopt his system, I listened politely, feigning interest, and assiduously wrote down his examples, based on an ASA of 100, since he got confused trying to give examples based on an ASA of 64. He further explained that this method was actually superior to using a light meter. In this way, he minimized the significance of not being able to help by freeing the battery lid; he framed himself as possessing useful knowledge and having solved my problem even though he couldn't fix my camera. This man wanted to help me—which I sincerely appreciated—but he also wanted to demonstrate that he had the information and skill required to help, even though he didn't.

There is a kind of social contract operating here. Many women not only feel comfortable seeking help, but feel honor-bound to seek it, accept it, and display gratitude in exchange. For their part, many men feel honor-bound to fulfill the request for help whether or not it is convenient for them to do so. A man told me about a time when a neighbor asked him if he could fix her car, which was intermittently stalling out. He spent more time than he could spare looking at her car, and concluded that he did not have the equipment needed to do the repair. He felt bad about not having succeeded in solving her problem. As if sensing this, she told him the next day, and the next, that her car was much better now, even though he knew he had done nothing to improve its performance. There is a balance between seeking help and showing appreciation. Women and men seem equally bound by the requirements of this arrangement: She was bound to show appreciation even though he hadn't helped, and he was bound to invest time and effort that he really couldn't spare, in trying to help.

Another example of the social contract of asking for help and showing appreciation occurred on a street corner in New York City. A woman emerged from the subway at Twenty-third Street and Park Avenue South, and was temporarily confused about which direction to walk in to reach Madison Avenue. She knew that Madison was west of Park, so with a little effort she could have figured out which way to go. But without planning or thinking, she asked the first person to appear before her. He replied that Madison did not come down that far south. Now, she knew this to be false. Furthermore, by this time she had oriented herself. But instead of saying, "Yes, it does," or "Never mind, I don't need your help," she found a way to play out the scene as one in which he helped her. She asked, "Which way is west?" and, on being told, replied, "Thank you. I'll just walk west."

From the point of view of getting directions, this encounter was absurd from start to finish. The woman didn't really need help, and the man wasn't in a position to give it. But getting directions really wasn't the main point. She had used the commonplace ritual of asking directions of a stranger not only—and not mostly—to find her way on emerging from the subway, but to reinforce her connection to the mass of people in the big city by making fleeting contact with one of them. Asking for help was simply an automatic way for her to do this.

"I'LL HELP YOU IF IT KILLS YOU"

Martha bought a computer and needed to learn to use it. After studying the manual and making some progress, she still had many questions, so she went to the store where she had bought it and asked for help. The man assigned to help her made her feel like the stupidest person in the world. He used technical language in explaining things, and each time she had to ask what a word meant she felt more incompetent, an impression reinforced by the tone of voice he used in his answer, a tone that sent the metamessage "This is obvious; everyone knows this." He explained things so quickly, she couldn't possibly remember them. When she went home, she discovered she couldn't recall what he had demonstrated, even in cases where she had followed his explanation at the time.

Still confused, and dreading the interaction, Martha returned to the store a week later, determined to stay until she got the information she needed. But this time a woman was assigned to help her. And the experience of getting help was utterly transformed. The woman avoided using technical terms for the most part, and if she did use one, she asked whether Martha knew what it meant and explained simply and clearly if she didn't. When the woman answered questions, her tone never implied that everyone should know this. And when showing how to do something, she had Martha do it, rather than demonstrating while Martha watched. The different style of this "teacher" made Martha feel like a different "student": a competent rather than stupid one, not humiliated by her ignorance.

Surely not all men give information in a way that confuses and humiliates their students. There are many gifted teachers who also happen to be men. And not all women give information in a way that makes it easy for students to understand. But many women report experiences similar to Martha's, especially in dealing with computers, automobiles, and other mechanical equipment; they claim that they feel more comfortable having women explain things to them. The different meanings that giving help entails may explain why. If women are focusing on connections, they will be motivated to minimize the difference in expertise and to be as comprehensible as possible. Since their goal is to maintain the appearance of similarity and equal status, sharing knowledge helps even the score. Their tone of voice sends metamessages of support rather than disdain, although "support" itself can be experienced as condescension.

If a man focuses on the negotiation of status and feels someone must have the upper hand, he may feel more comfortable when he has it. His attunement to the fact that having more information, knowledge, or skill puts him in a one-up position comes through in his way of talking. And if sometimes men seem intentionally to explain in a way that makes what they are explaining difficult to understand, it may be because their pleasant feeling of knowing more is reinforced when the student *does not* understand. The comfortable margin of superiority diminishes with every bit of knowledge the student gains. Or it may simply be that they are more concerned with displaying their superior knowledge and skill than with making sure that the knowledge is shared.

A colleague familiar with my ideas remarked that he'd seen evidence of this difference at an academic conference. A woman delivering a paper kept stopping and asking the audience, "Are you with me so far?" My colleague surmised that her main concern seemed to be that the audience understand what she was saying. When he gave his paper, his main concern was that he not be put down by members of the audience—and as far as he could tell, a similar preoccupation was motivating the other men presenting papers as well. From this point of view, if covering one's tracks to avoid attack entails obscuring one's point, it is a price worth paying.

This is not to say that women have no desire to feel knowledgeable or powerful. Indeed, the act of asking others whether they are able to follow your argument can be seen to frame you as superior. But it seems that having information, expertise, or skill at manipulating objects is not the primary measure of power for most women. Rather, they feel their power enhanced if they can be of help. Even more, if they are focusing on connection rather than independence and self-reliance, they feel stronger when the community is strong.

"TRUST ME"

A woman told me that she was incredulous when her husband dredged up an offense from years before. She had been unable to get their VCR to record movies aired on HBO. Her husband had looked at the VCR and declared it incapable of performing this function. Rather than accepting his judgment, she asked their neighbor, Harry, to take a look at it, since he had once fixed her VCR in the past. Harry's conclusion was the same as that of her husband, who was, however, incensed that his wife had not trusted his expertise. When he brought it up years later, the wife exclaimed in disbelief, "You still remember that? Harry is dead!" The incident, though insignificant to the wife, cut to the core of the husband's self-respect, because it called into question his knowledge and skill at managing the mechanical world.

Trust in a man's skill is also at issue between Felicia and Stan, another couple. Stan is angered when Felicia gasps in fear while he is driving. "I've never had an accident!" he protests. "Why can't you trust my driving?" Felicia cannot get him to see her point of view—that she does not distrust *his* driving in particular but is frightened of driving in general. Most of all, she cannot understand why the small matter of involuntarily sucking in her breath should spark such a strong reaction.

"BE NICE"

Having expertise and skill can reinforce both women's and men's sense of themselves. But the stance of expert is more fundamental to our notion of masculinity than to our concept of femininity. Women, according to convention, are more inclined to be givers of praise than givers of information. That women are expected to praise is reflected in a poster that was displayed in every United States post office branch inviting customers to send criticism, suggestions, questions, and compliments. Three of these four linguistic acts were represented by sketches of men; only compliments were represented by a sketch of a woman with a big smile on her face, a gesture of approval on her fingers, and a halo around her head. The halo is especially interesting. It shows that the act of complimenting frames the speaker as "nice."

Giving praise, like giving information, is also inherently asymmetrical. It too frames the speaker as one-up, in a position to judge someone else's performance. Women can also be framed as one-up by their classic helping activities as mothers, social workers, nurses, counselors, and psychologists. But in many of these roles—especially mothers and nurses—they may also be seen as doing others' bidding.

OVERLAPPING MOTIVATIONS

When acting as helpers, women and men typically perform different kinds of tasks. But even the same task can be approached with eyes on different goals, and this difference is likely to result in misjudgments of others' intentions. The end of my camera story underlines this. At a family gathering, I brought the camera to my brother-in-law, who has a reputation in the family for mechanical ability. He took it to his workshop and returned an hour and a half later, having fixed it. Delighted and grateful, I commented to his daughter, "I knew he would enjoy the challenge." "Especially," she pointed out, "when it involves helping someone." I felt then that I had mistaken his displayed concern with the mechanics of the recalcitrant battery cover as reflecting his ultimate concern. But fixing the camera was a way of showing concern for me, of helping me with his effort. If women directly offer help, my brother-in-law was indirectly offering help, through the mediation of my camera.

A colleague who heard my analysis of this experience thought I had missed an aspect of my broken-camera episode. He pointed out that many men get a sense of pleasure from fixing things because it reinforces their feeling of being in control, self-sufficient, and able to dominate the world of objects. (This is the essence of Evelyn Fox Keller's thesis that the conception of science as dominating and controlling nature is essentially masculine in spirit.) He told me of an incident in which a toy plastic merry-go-round, ordered for his little boy, arrived in pieces, having come apart during shipping. His wife gave the toy to her uncle, renowned in the family as a fixer and helper. Her uncle worked for several hours and repaired the toy—even though it was probably not worth more than a few dollars. The uncle brought this up again the next time he saw them, and said he would have stayed up all night rather than admit he couldn't put it together. My colleague was convinced that the motivation to gain dominion over the plastic object had been stronger than the motivation to help his sister and nephew, though both had been present.

Furthermore, this man pointed out that he, and many other men, take special pleasure in showing their strength over the world of objects for the benefit of attractive women, because the thanks and admiration they receive is an added source of pleasure and satisfaction. His interpretation of my revised analysis was that my niece and I, both women, would be inclined to see the helping aspect of an act as the "real" or main motive, whereas he still was inclined to see the pleasure of demonstrating skill, succeeding where the camera expert had failed, and whacking the recalcitrant battery lid into line as the main ones.

The element of negotiating status that characterizes many men's desire to show they are knowledgeable and skillful does not negate the connection implied in helping. These elements coexist and feed each other. But women's and men's tendencies to place different relative weights on status versus connection result in asymmetrical roles. Attuned to the metamessage of connection, many women are comfortable both receiving help and giving it, though surely there are many women who are comfortable only in the role of giver of help and support. Many men, sensitive to the dynamic of status, the need to help women, and the need to be self-reliant, are comfortable in the role of giving information and help but not in receiving it.

THE VIEW FROM A DIFFERENT MOUNTAIN

In a story by Alice Mattison, "The Colorful Alphabet," a man named Joseph invites another man, Gordon, to visit his family in the country, because Gordon's wife has just left him. During the visit, they all climb a mountain. On the way down, they stop to rest, and Gordon realizes that he left his beloved old knapsack on the mountaintop. Joseph volunteers to climb back up to get it, because Gordon is not used to climbing and his feet are sore. Joseph's wife goes with him, but she is too tired to climb all the way to the top, and he leaves her on the path to complete the mission himself. When he finds her again, he is empty-handed: The bag wasn't there. He says then that he knew it wouldn't be, because he had seen a man carrying the bag pass them when they all stopped to rest. He explains why he didn't just say that he had seen someone go by with the bag: "I couldn't tell him I'd seen it and hadn't been smart enough to get it back for him." Instead, he says, "I had to *do* something."

Exhausted and frustrated, the wife is not so much angry as incredulous. She can't understand how he could have preferred reclimbing the mountain (and making her reclimb it too) to admitting that he had seen someone carrying Gordon's bag. "I would never have done that," she says, but she speaks "more in wonder than anger." She explains, "I'd have just blurted it out. I'd have been upset about making the mistake—but not about people *knowing*. That part's not a big deal to me." Her husband says, "Oh, is it ever a big deal to me."

This story supports the view of men's style that I have been proposing. Joseph wanted to help Gordon, and he did not want to let it be known that he had done something he thought stupid. His impulse to do something to solve the problem was stronger than his impulse not to climb a mountain twice. But what struck me most strongly about the story was the wife's reflections on the experience. She thinks:

> It was one of the occasional moments when I'm certain I haven't imagined him: I would never have done what he'd done, wouldn't have dreamt it or invented it— Joseph was, simply, *not me*.

This excerpt reflects what may be the subtlest yet deepest source of frustration and puzzlement arising from the different ways that women and men approach the world. We feel we know how the world is, and we look to others to reinforce that conviction. When we see others acting as if the world were an entirely different place from the one we inhabit, we are shaken.

We look to our closest relationships as a source of confirmation and reassurance. When those closest to us respond to events differently than we do, when they seem to see the same scene as part of a different play, when they say things that we could not imagine saying in the same circumstances, the ground on which we stand seems to tremble and our footing is suddenly unsure. Being able to understand why this happens—*why* and *how* our partners and friends, though like us in many ways, are *not* us, and different in other ways—is a crucial step toward feeling that our feet are planted on firm ground.

THREE

LANGUAGE AND THE TEACHING OF READING AND WRITING

In our present educational system, reading and writing are important to the learning that takes place in every academic discipline, and as teachers in that system, it is important for us to understand the way that skills in reading and writing are acquired. This section investigates how the human mind goes about learning and then focuses on the learning necessary for reading and writing. The section is divided into three parts ("Literacy," "Language and the Reading Process," and "Language and the Writing Process"), and it builds on what we have learned about language in former sections. We know from Vygotsky and Moskowitz that children acquire language by experiencing its use in meaningful situations, and reading, and writing and literacy theorists demonstrate in this section how that is also true for older children, adolescents, and even adults.

LITERACY

James Paul Gee begins the section on literacy by clarifying distinctions between "acquisition," the unconscious inductive development of facility in language, and "learning," conscious learning that takes place through deductive learning from rules and drill. He then provides an explanation of why minority students and children of uneducated parents have a harder time in school. He urges that all students have opportunities with acquisition of language skills, especially those whose home discourse is very different than that of schools. As teachers, we usually want to make a difference for all students and often feel frustrated with our limited success with minority and low-income students. Gee's article and that of Nan Elsasser and Vera John-Steiner give us insight into the dynamics that make it harder for these students to learn and give us practical suggestions for working with them. Elsasser and John-Steiner refer to Vygotsky and Paolo Freire, reiterating what becomes a recurring theme in this collection, that language and the language skills of reading and writing are best learned when students are active learners making meaningful interactions with language. They propose situations in which students learn literacy skills by working both in speaking and in writing with "issues of significance to their lives." You have already had references to Vygotsky's books, but there is much in what Freire has written, and in what has been written about him, that will be of interest to prospective and practicing teachers who are interested in issues of literacy. Freire does not write for beginners in literacy study, but Ira Shor's edited collection is both accessible and very practical. Michael Rose's book is on literacy issues at the college level.

Freire, Paolo. *Pedagogy of the Oppressed* (New York: Continuum, 1970).
Freire, Paolo. *The Politics of Education* (South Hadley, Mass.: Bergin and Garvey, 1985).
Rose, Michael. *Lives on the Boundary* (New York: Penguin, 1989).
Schor, Ira. (ed.), *Freire for the Classroom: A Sourcebook for Liberatory Teaching* (Portsmouth, N.H.: Boynton/Cook of Heinemann, 1987).

LANGUAGE AND THE READING PROCESS

Reading is a skill that is often used to measure progress in school. Therefore, understanding how reading happens is important to each and every teacher. Helene Anthony, David Pearson, and Taffy Raphael contribute a review of past and current research on reading comprehension, discuss the light shed on the current phonics/whole language debate, and provide implications for teaching. As we consider how important prior knowledge and interest are in the reading process, we return to an organizing theme in this section: Reading and other language activities go best when they have significance in the reader's life. Margaret Early and Bonnie Ericson review and elucidate much of what Anthony, Pearson, and Raphael say, and though they focus on literature, they give teachers practical suggestions to help students in any secondary class to grow in reading ability. Yetta Goodman presents miscue analysis, a way to analyze the reading difficulties of students. She illustrates the procedure by her experience with "Frankie" and shows how dialect difference can affect reading. It is important to note that all of these authors say something in common: Students learn to read by reading and by learning to guess and predict, and they learn best by reading material that is interesting and significant to their lives.

If you have further interest in research on reading and its implications for teaching, Frank Smith's work will be of interest. His book *Understanding Reading* is a challenging text and appropriate for graduate students and practicing teachers. Those who want a less technical understanding of reading research that supports a whole language approach might prefer his book *Reading Without Nonsense.* Kenneth Goodman's book on miscue analysis will offer more information for someone whose interest was peaked by Goodman's article.

Goodman, Kenneth S. *Miscue Analysis: Applications to Reading Instruction* (Urbana, Ill.: ERIC, 1981).

Smith, Frank. *Understanding Reading,* 4th ed. (Hillsdale, N.J.: Erlbaum, 1988).

Smith, Frank. *Reading Without Nonsense,* 2d ed. (New York: Teachers College Press, 1985).

LANGUAGE AND THE WRITING PROCESS

Six articles comprise the subsection "Language and the Writing Process." In the first, Donald Murray, a man who has contributed much to our understanding of writing and teaching writing, has set forth some assumptions that he has about writing: that writing is thinking, that writing is a process, that effective teaching is responsive, that writing is an interaction of the global and the particular, and that there is no one way to write. Steven Zemelman and Harvey Daniels expand on Murray's basic assumptions in their contribution to this text. They look at the historical roots of the whole language movement and the place of the writing process in it; they then show how the writing process can be implemented in the classroom. There are three books listed below that are both engaging and useful for teachers; Nancie Atwell's book is particularly relevant to junior high or middle school teachers, Tom Romano's to high school teachers, and Murray's to college writing instructors.

Atwell, Nancie. *In the Middle: Writing, Reading, and Learning with Adolescents* (Portsmouth, N.H.: Boynton/Cook of Heinemann, 1987).

Romano, Tom. *Clearing the Way: Working with Teenage Writers* (Portsmouth, N.H.: Boynton/Cook of Heinemann, 1987).

Murray, Donald. *A Writer Teaches Writing,* 2d ed. (Boston: Houghton Mifflin, 1985).

Studying the development of language ability can be a complex task though most state licensure agencies and both NCATE and NCTE deem it important for prospective teachers of at least the language arts. Thus James Collins's article, "The Development of Writing during the School Years," presents a challenge to us as teachers. Collins argues that a linear model of the development of writing abilities does not take into consideration societal and instructional influences. He argues that a functional conception of writing development is important if teachers are to understand the societal or cultural influences on writing development. Not included, but of particular significance in considering adolescent language development, is Richard Beach and Susan Hynds's edited collection of readings, *Developing Discourse Practices in Adolescence and Adulthood* (Norwood, N.J.: Ablex, 1991).

The next two articles in this section, "Spelling and Grammar Logs" by

Richard Van de Weghe and "Developing Correctness in Student Writing: Alternatives to the Error Hunt" by Lois Matz Rosen, give the teacher useful ways to work on "correctness" in writing while focusing students on the audience, purpose, and content. Finally Linda Miller Cleary's article, "A Profile of Carlos: Strengths of a Nonstandard Dialect Writer," provides teachers with a view of the complexity of writing problems that face basic writers and of instructional strategies to use with these writers. Mina Shaugnessy's book *Errors and Expectations: A Guide for the Teachers of Basic Writing* (New York: Oxford University Press, 1977) is important additional reading for teachers who work with basic writers.

A

LITERACY

What Is Literacy?

James Paul Gee

It is a piece of folk wisdom that part of what linguists do is define words. In over a decade as a linguist, however, no one, until now, has asked me to define a word. So my first try: what does "literacy" mean? It won't surprise you that we have to define some other words first. So let me begin by giving a technical meaning to an old term which, unfortunately, already has a variety of other meanings. The term is "discourse." I will use the word as a count term ("a discourse," "discourses," "many discourses"), not as a mass term ("discourse," "much discourse"). By "a discourse" I will mean:

> a socially accepted association among ways of using language, of thinking, and of acting that can be used to identify oneself as a member of a socially meaningful group or "social network."

Think of discourse as an "identity kit" which comes complete with the appropriate costume and instructions on how to act and talk so as to take on a particular role that others will recognize. Let me give an example: Being "trained" as a linguist meant that I learned to speak, think and act like a linguist, and to recognize others when they do so. Now actually matters are not that simple: the larger discourse of linguistics contains many subdiscourses, different socially accepted ways of being a linguist. But the master discourse is not just the sum of its parts, it is something also over and above them. Every act of speaking, writing and behaving a linguist does as a linguist is meaningful only against the background of the whole social institution of linguistics, and that institution is made up of concrete things like people, books and buildings; abstract things like bodies of knowledge, values, norms and beliefs; mixtures of concrete and abstract things like universities, journals and publishers; as well as a shared history and shared stories. Some other examples of discourses: being an American or a Russian, being a man or a woman, being a member of a certain socio-economic class, being a factory worker or a boardroom executive, being a doctor or a hospital patient, being a teacher, an administrator, or a student, being a member of a sewing circle, a club, a street gang, a lunchtime social gathering, or a regular at a local watering hole.

There are a number of important points that one can make about discourses, none of which, for some reason, are very popular to Americans, though they seem to be commonplace in European social theory (Belsey, 1980; Eagleton, 1983; Jameson, 1981; Macdonnel, 1986; Thompson, 1984):

1 Discourses are inherently "ideological." They crucially involve a set of values and viewpoints in terms of which one must speak and act, at least while being in the discourse; otherwise one doesn't count as being in it.

2 Discourses are resistant to internal criticism and self-scrutiny since uttering viewpoints that seriously undermine them defines one as being outside them. The discourse itself defines what counts as acceptable criticism. Of course, one can criticize a particular discourse from the viewpoint of another one (e.g., psychology criticizing linguistics). But what one cannot do is stand outside all discourse and criticize any one or all of them—that would be like trying to repair a jet in flight by stepping outside it.

3 Discourse-defined positions from which to speak and behave are not, however, just defined internal to a discourse, but also as standpoints taken up by the discourse in its relation to other, ultimately opposing, discourses. The discourse of managers in an industry is partly defined as a set of views, norms and standpoints defined by their opposition to analogous points in the discourse of workers (Macdonell, 1986: 1-7). The discourse we identify with being a feminist is radically changed if all male discourses disappear.

4 Any discourse concerns itself with certain objects and puts forward certain concepts, viewpoints and values at the expense of others. In doing so it will marginalize viewpoints and values central to other discourses (Macdonell, 1986: 1-7). In fact, a discourse can call for one to accept values in conflict with other discourses one is a member of—for example, the discourse used in literature departments used to marginalize popular literature and women's writings. Further, women readers of Hemingway, for instance, when acting as "acceptable readers" by the standards of the discourse of literary criticism, might find themselves complicit with values which conflict with those of various other discourses they belong to as women (Culler, 1982: 43-64).

5 Finally, discourses are intimately related to the distribution of social power and hierarchical structure in society. Control over certain discourses can lead to the acquisition of social goods (money, power, status) in a society. These discourses empower those groups who have the least conflicts with their other discourses when they use them. For example, many academic, legalistic and bureaucratic discourses in our society contain a moral subdiscourse that sees "right" as what is derivable from general abstract principles. This can conflict to a degree with a discourse about morality that appears to be more often associated with women than men in terms of which "wrong" is seen as the disruption of social networks, and "right" as the repair of those networks (Gilligan, 1982). Or, to take another example, the discourse of literary criticism was a standard route to success as a professor of literature. Since it conflicted less with the other discourses of white, middle class men than it did with those of women, men were empowered by it. Women were not, as they were often at cross-purposes when engaging in it. Let us call discourses that lead to social goods in a society "dominant discourses" and let us refer to those groups that have the fewest conflicts when using them as "dominant groups." Obviously these are both matters of degree and change to a certain extent in different contexts.

It is sometimes helpful to say that it is not individuals who speak and act, but rather historically and socially defined discourses speak to each other through individuals. The individual instantiates, gives body to, a discourse every time he acts or speaks and thus carries it, and ultimately changes it, through time. Americans tend to be very focused on the individual, and thus often miss the fact that the individual is simply the meeting point of many, sometimes conflicting, socially and historically defined discourses.

The crucial question is: how does one come by the discourses that he controls? And here it is necessary, before answering the question, to make an important distinction, a distinction that does not exist in non-technical parlance, but one which is important to a linguist: a distinction between "acquisition" and "learning" (Krashen, 1982, 1985; Krashen & Terrell, 1983). I will distinguish these two as follows:

Acquisition is a process of acquiring something subconsciously by exposure to models and a process of trial and error, without a process of formal teaching. It happens in natural settings which are meaningful and functional in the sense that the acquirer knows that he needs to acquire the thing he is exposed to in order to function and the acquirer in fact wants to so function. This is how most people come to control their first language.

Learning is a process that involves conscious knowledge gained through teaching, though not necessarily from someone officially designated a teacher. This teaching involves explanation and analysis, that is, breaking down the thing to be learned into its analytic parts. It inherently involves attaining, along with the matter being taught, some degree of meta-knowledge about the matter.

Much of what we come by in life, after our initial enculturation, involves a mixture of acquisition and learning. However, the balance between the two can be quite different in different cases and different at different stages in the process. For instance, I initially learned to drive a car by instruction, but thereafter acquired, rather than learned, most of what I know. Some cultures highly value acquisition and so tend simply to expose children to adults modeling some activity and eventually the child picks it up, picks it up as a gestalt, rather than as a series of analytic bits (Scollon & Scollon, 1981; Heath, 1983). Other cultural groups highly value teaching and thus break down what is to be mastered into sequential steps and analytic parts and engage in explicit explanation. There is an up side and a down side to both that can be expressed as follows: "we are better at what we acquire, but we consciously know more about what we have learned." For most of us, playing a musical instrument, or dancing, or using a second language are skills we attained by some mixture of acquisition and learning. But it is a safe bet that, over the same amount of time, people are better at these activities if acquisition predominated during that time. The point can be made using second language as the example: most people aren't very good at attaining a second language in any very functional way through formal instruction in a classroom. That's why teaching grammar is not a very good way of getting people to control a language. However, people who have acquired a second language in a natural setting don't thereby make good linguists, and some good linguists can't speak the languages they learned in a classroom. What is said here about second languages is true, I believe, of all of what I will later refer to as "secondary discourses": acquisition is good for performance, learning is good for meta-level knowledge (cf. Scribner & Cole, 1981). Acquisition and learning are thus, too, differential sources of power: Acquirers usually beat learners at performance, learners usually beat acquirers at talking about it, that is, at explication, explanation, analysis and criticism.

Now what has this got to do with literacy? First, let me point out that it renders the common sense understanding of literacy very problematic. Take the notion of a "reading class." I don't know if they are still prevalent, but when I was in grammar school we had a special time set aside each day for "reading class" where we would learn to read. Reading is at the very least the ability to interpret print (surely not just the ability to call out the names of letters), but an interpretation of print is just a viewpoint on a set of symbols, and viewpoints are always embedded in a discourse. Thus, while many different discourses use reading, even in opposing ways, and while there could well be classes devoted to these discourses, reading outside such a discourse or class would be truly "in a vacuum," much like our repairman above trying to repair the jet in flight by jumping out the door. Learning to read is always learning some aspect of some discourse. One can trivialize this insight to a certain degree by trivializing the notion of interpretation (of printed words), until one gets to reading as calling out the names of letters. Analogously, one can deepen the insight by taking successively deeper views of what interpretation means. But, there is also the problem with "reading class" that it stresses learning and not acquisition. To the extent that reading as both decoding and interpretation is a performance, learning stresses the production of poor performers. If we wanted to stress acquisition, we would have to expose children to reading, and this would always be to expose them to a discourse whose name would never be "Reading" (at least until the student went to the university and earned a degree called "Reading"). To the extent that it is important to have meta-level skills in regard to language, reading class as a place of learning rather than of acquisition might facilitate this, but it is arguable that a reading class would hardly be the best place to do this. While reading classes like mine might not be around any more, it encapsulated the common sense notion of literacy as "the ability to read and write" (intransitively), a notion that is nowhere near as coherent as it at first sounds.

Now I will approach a more positive connection between a viable notion of literacy and the concepts we have dealt with above. All humans, barring serious disorder, get one form of discourse free, so to speak, and this through acquisition. This is our socio-culturally determined ways of using our native language in face-to-face communication with intimates (intimates are people with whom we share a great deal of knowledge because of a great deal of contact and similar experiences). This is sometimes referred to as "the oral mode" (Gee, 1986b)—it is the birth right of every human and comes through the process of primary socialization within the family as this is defined within a given culture. Some small, so-called "primitive," cultures function almost like extended families (though never completely so) in that this type of discourse is usable in a very wide array of social contacts. This is due to the fact that these cultures are small enough to function as a "society of intimates" (Givon, 1979). In modern technological and urban societies which function as a "society of strangers," the oral mode is more narrowly useful. Let us refer then to this oral mode, developed in the primary process of enculturation, as the "primary discourse." It is important to realize that even among speakers of English there are socio-culturally different primary discourses. For example, lower socio-economic black children use English to make sense of their experience differently than do middle class children; they have a different primary discourse (Gee, 1985; 1986a; Michaels, 1981; 1985). And this is not due merely to the fact that they have a different dialect of English. So-called "Black Vernacular English" is, on structural grounds, only trivially different from standard English by the norms of linguists accustomed to dialect differences around the world (Labov, 1972). Rather, these children use language, behavior, values and beliefs to give a different shape to their experience.

Beyond the primary discourse, however, are other discourses which crucially involve social institutions beyond the family (or the primary socialization group as defined by the culture), no matter how much they also involve the family. These institutions all share the factor that they require one to communicate with non-intimates (or to treat intimates as if they were not intimates). Let us refer to these as "secondary institutions" (such as schools, workplaces, stores, government offices, businesses, churches, etc.). Discourses beyond the primary discourse are developed in association with and by having access to and practice with these secondary institutions. Thus, we will refer to them as "secondary discourses." These secondary discourses all build on, and extend, the uses of language we acquired as part of our primary discourse, and they should be more or less compatible with the primary discourses of different social groups. It is, of course, a great advantage when the secondary discourse is compatible with your primary one. But all these secondary discourses involve uses of language, either written or oral, or both, that go beyond our primary discourse no matter what group we belong to. Let's call those uses of language in secondary discourses which go beyond the uses of language stemming from our primary discourse "secondary uses of language." Telling your mother you love her is a primary use of language, telling your teacher you don't have your homework is a secondary use. It can be noted, however, that sometimes people must fall back on their primary uses of language in inappropriate circumstances when they fail to control the requisite secondary use.

Now we can get to what I believe is a useful definition of literacy:

Literacy is control of secondary uses of language (i.e., uses of language in secondary discourses).

Thus, there are as many applications of the word "literacy" as there are secondary discourses, which is many. We can define various types of literacy as follows:

Dominant literacy is control of a secondary use of language used in what I called above a "dominant discourse."

Powerful literacy is control of a secondary use of language used in a secondary discourse that can serve as a meta-discourse to critique the primary discourse or other secondary discourses, including dominant discourses.

What do I mean by "control" in the above definitions? I mean some degree of being able to "use," to "function" with, so "control" is a matter of degree. "Mastery" I define as "full and effortless control." In these terms I will state a principle having to do with acquisition which I believe is true:

Any discourse (primary or secondary) is for most people most of the time only mastered through acquisition, not learning. Thus, literacy is mastered through acquisition, not learning, that is, it requires exposure to models in natural, meaningful, and functional settings, and teaching is not liable to be very successful—it may even initially get in the way. Time spent on learning and not acquisition is time not well spent if the goal is mastery in performance.

There is also a principle having to do with learning that I think true:

One cannot critique one discourse with another one (which is the only way to seriously criticize and thus change a discourse) unless one has meta-level knowledge in both discourses. And this meta-knowledge is best developed through learning, though often learning applied to a discourse one has to a certain extent already acquired. Thus, powerful literacy, as defined above, almost always involves learning, and not just acquisition.

The point is that acquisition and learning are means to quite different goals, though in our culture we very often confuse these means and thus don't get what we thought and hoped we would.

Let me just briefly mention some practical connections of the above remarks. Mainstream middle class children often look like they are learning literacy (of various sorts) in school. But, in fact, I believe much research shows they are acquiring these literacies through experiences in the home both before and during school, as well as by the opportunities school gives them to practice what they are acquiring (Wells, 1985; 1986a, b). The learning they are doing, provided it is tied to good teaching, is giving them not the literacies, but meta-level cognitive and linguistic skills that they can use to critique various discourses throughout their lives. However, we all know that teaching is not by any means always that good—though it should be one of our goals to see to it that it is. Children from non-mainstream homes often do not get the opportunities to acquire dominant secondary discourses, for example those connected with the school, prior to school in their homes, due to the lack of access their parents have to these secondary discourses. Thus, when coming to school, they cannot practice what they haven't yet got, and they are exposed mostly to a process of learning and not acquisition. Since little acquisition thereby goes on, they often cannot use this learning-teaching to develop meta-level skills since this requires some degree of acquisition of secondary discourses to use in the critical process. Further, research pretty clearly shows that many school-based secondary discourses conflict with the values and viewpoints in some non-mainstream children's primary discourses and other community-based secondary discourses (e.g., stemming from religious institutions) (Heath, 1983; Cook-Gumperz, 1986; Gumperz, 1982).

While the above remarks may all seem rather theoretical, they do in fact lead to some obvious practical suggestions for directions future research and intervention efforts ought to take. As far as I can see some of these are as follows:

1 Settings which focus on acquisition, not learning, should be stressed if the goal is to help non-mainstream children attain mastery of literacies. This is certainly not liable to be a traditional classroom setting (let alone my "reading class"), but rather natural and functional environments, which may or may not happen to be inside a school.

2 We should realize that teaching and learning are connected with the development of meta-level cognitive and linguistic skills. They will work better if we explicitly realize this and build this realization into our curricula. Further, they must be ordered and integrated with acquisition in viable ways if they are to have any effect other than obstruction.

3 Mainstream children are actually using much of the teaching-learning they get not to learn but to acquire, by practicing developing skills. We should thus honor this practice effect directly and build on it, rather than leave it as a surreptitious and indirect by-product of teaching-learning.

4 Learning should lead to the ability for all children—mainstream and non-mainstream—to critique their primary discourses and secondary discourses, including dominant secondary discourses. This requires exposing children to a variety of alternative primary discourses and secondary ones (not necessarily so that they acquire them, but so that they learn about them). It also requires realizing explicitly that this is what good teaching and learning is good at. We rarely realize that this is where we fail mainstream children just as much as non-mainstream ones.

5 We must take seriously that no matter how good our schools become, both as environments where acquisition can go on (so involving meaningful and functional settings) and where learning can go on, the non-mainstream child will always have more conflicts in using and thus mastering dominant secondary discourses, since they conflict more seriously with his primary discourse and community-based secondary ones. This is precisely what it means (by my definitions above) to be "non-mainstream." This does not mean we should give up. It also does not mean merely that research and intervention efforts must have sensitivity to these conflicts built into them, though it certainly does mean this. It requires, I believe, that we must also stress research and intervention efforts that facilitate the development of wider and more humane concepts of mastery and its connections to gate-keeping. We must remember that conflicts, while they do very often detract from standard sorts of full mastery, can give rise to new sorts of mastery. This is commonplace in the realm of art. We must make it commonplace in society at large.

REFERENCES

Belsey, C. (1980). *Critical Practice.* London: Methuen.

Cook-Gumperz, J., Ed. (1986). *The Social Construction of Literacy.* Cambridge, England: Cambridge University Press.

Culler, J. (1982). *On Deconstruction: Theory and Criticism after Structuralism.* Ithaca, NY: Cornell University Press.

Eagleton, T. (1983). *Literary Theory: An Introduction.* Minneapolis: University of Minnesota Press.

Gee, J. P. (1985). The narrativization of experience in the oral mode, *Journal of Education, 167,* 9–35.

———. (1986a). Units in the production of discourse, *Discourse Processes, 9,* 391–422.

———. (1986b). Orality and literacy: From the *Savage Mind* to *Ways with Words, TESOL Quarterly, 20,* 719–746.

Gilligan, C. (1982). *In a Different Voice.* Cambridge, MA: Harvard University Press.

Givon, T. (1979). *On Understanding Grammar.* New York: Academic Press.

Gumperz, J. J., Ed. (1982). *Language and Social Identity.* Cambridge, England: Cambridge University Press.

Heath, S. B. (1983). *Ways with Words: Language, Life, and Work in Communities and Classrooms.* Cambridge, England: Cambridge University Press.

Jameson, F. (1981). *The Political Unconscious: Narrative as a Socially Symbolic Act.* Ithaca, NY: Cornell University Press.

Krashen, S. (1982). *Principles and Practice in Second Language Acquisition.* Hayward, CA: Alemany Press.

———. (1985). *Inquiries and Insights.* Hayward, CA: Alemany Press.

Krashen, S., and T. Terrell. (1983). *The Natural Approach: Language Acquisition in the Classroom.* Hayward, CA: Alemany Press.

Labov, W. (1972). *Language in the Inner City.* Philadelphia: University of Pennsylvania Press.

Macdonell, D. (1986). *Theories of Discourse: An Introduction.* Oxford: Basil Blackwell.

Michaels, S. (1981). "Sharing time": Children's narrative styles and differential access to literacy, *Language in Society, 10,* 423–442.

———. (1985). Hearing the connections in children's oral and written discourse, *Journal of Education, 167,* 36–56.

Scollon, R., and S. B. K. Scollon. (1981). *Narrative, Literacy, and Face in Interethnic Communication.* Norwood, NJ: Ablex.

Scribner, S., and M. Cole. (1981). *The Psychology of Literacy.* Cambridge, MA: Harvard University Press.

Thompson, J. B. (1984). *Studies in the Theory of Ideology.* Berkeley and Los Angeles: University of California Press.

Wells, G. (1985). "Preschool literacy-related activities and success in school," in D. R. Olson, N. Torrance, and A. Hildyard, eds. *Literacy, Language, and Learning.* Cambridge, England: Cambridge University Press.

———. (1986a). "The language experience of five-year-old children at home and at school," in J. Cook-Gumperz, ed. *The Social Construction of Literacy.* Cambridge, England: Cambridge University Press.

———. (1986b). *The Meaning Makers: Children Learning Language and Using Language to Learn.* New York: Heinemann.

An Interactionist Approach to Advancing Literacy

Nan Elsasser and Vera John-Steiner

Today millions of people throughout the world who have historically been excluded from institutions that control their lives are claiming their right to an education. Central to their assertion is the recognition that oral communication is inadequate to meet the requirements of the modern world and that written communication is necessary for social and economic well-being. Because of their demands, teachers are now more frequently confronted with students who demonstrate competence in oral communication but who produce written work that is often incoherent. The history of the last decades shows that traditional approaches to teaching writing do not work. As a result educators are being forced to look beyond the age-old debates centered on motor skills and "good" grammar and to raise more significant questions concerning literacy. For example, the first issue of *Basic Writing,* a journal devoted to developing theory and strategies to help students master basic writing skills, addressed itself to these questions: "How do we teach [the student] to judge the degree of common ground he can assume? how far he must go in spelling out his meanings in detail? how many cues of place, sequence and reference he must build in?" (D'Eloia, 1975, p. 11).

Answers to these questions are basic to a theory of written speech, but another set of questions must be answered first—questions regarding the cognitive and social dynamics that produce incoherent writing. In the works of L. S. Vygotsky and Paulo Freire we have found a set of theoretical assumptions from which to develop an analysis of these issues. We believe these works are critical to an understanding of the mental and social processes involved in producing accomplished writing. In addition, they provide the bases of strategies designed to aid learners by expanding their awareness and control of these processes.

Each of these theorists conceived of the use of words both as an historically shaped process and as one that in this century has become increasingly necessary for more and more people. Vygotsky ([1934] 1962) described the developmental course of language and the different phases in the interweaving of language and thought. A central theme of his analysis is the concept of internalization: children engaged in the process of acquiring language are viewed as active learners able to unite the diverse strands of their experience to form critical, human consciousnesses. Vygotsky's theory is interactionist in its assumptions and relies upon dialectical concepts as essential tools for analysis of human development. Particularly significant for our theory of the advancement of literacy is Vygotsky's concept of the multiple transformations required to "unfold" inner speech. In the course of their development, young speakers engage in meaningful interactions with members of their community; through this interaction, telegrammatic inner language unfolds to become the basis of competent oral communication.

As we will describe later, a different and more complex set of transformations is necessary to attain competence in written communication. Yet most people have very limited opportunities to develop personally and socially relevant written communication skills. Lacking these opportunities, it is unrealistic to expect that learners will be motivated to perfect their skills beyond the most elementary levels of literacy. However, rapid social changes during the twentieth century, including the rise of technology and an urban style of life, have created a need for more widespread literacy. This combination of social need and lack of individual motivation calls for the development of powerful teaching strategies to advance the rudimentary writing skills of students who spend a limited time in the classroom.

Although many attempts have been made to provide literacy programs for populations previously excluded from their countries' economic and educational institutions, most of these attempts have failed. In our opinion, the lack of success has been due in part to the absence of a meaningful analysis of the social realities of poverty and rural life.[1] To meet this need, Freire has developed programs based upon his political understanding of and sensitivity to living conditions that give individuals a profound sense of powerlessness.

In many oppressive societies poor people respond to their feeling of powerlessness through silent forms of resistance (Freire, 1973).[2] One commentator has noted that poor people practice silence "because they have been forced by circumstances to reject as dangerous a 'thrusting' orientation to life" (Greenberg, 1969, p. 79). Children are taught that "silence is safest, so volunteer nothing; that the teacher is the state and tell them only what they want to hear; that the law and learning are white man's law and learning" (Cobb, 1965, p. 106). This silent opposition, the result of their apparent inability to intervene and transform their reality, is often misinterpreted by people who have not been subjected to such oppression. Frustrated, impatient educators who observe this silence often conclude that poor people do not care about the education of their children. Educators and social scientists fail to consider that oppressed peoples have developed their stances toward dominant social groups in response to particular historical experiences.

The silence through which poor people communicate with strangers and officials contrasts sharply with the intensity of daily verbal communication among community people. Labov, in particular, has described this contrast and its educational implication for young black children in urban ghettoes (Labov, 1972, pp. 201–240). These latter exchanges take place within a shared life context that makes certain kinds of verbal elaborations and written explanations unnecessary. Anyone who has ever asked for directions in an isolated rural community has probably experienced bewilderment similar to that of Polly Greenberg, an activist educator working in Mississippi. Greenberg recounts her misadventures

---

[1]The failure of such programs also stems from their sociohistorical contexts. A student's sense of personal power and control emerges largely as a result of the increasing movement of his or her social group towards self-determination. In the absence of such movement, educational intervention is most often futile.

[2]Freire calls this resistance "the culture of silence" by which he means the form of passive protest used by the oppressed when confronting individuals of the oppressing classes. Freire's sense of the term is not to be confused with the idea as it is used by verbal deprivationists who believe that oppressed peoples, owing to some inner shortcomings—either cultural or psychological or genetic— do not possess linguistic skills at any but the most minimal level.

in trying for the third time to locate a day-care center of the Child Development Group of Mississippi.

> The directions were "turn right at the puddle"—but it had dried up—"turn left at the dairy farm"—it was a weathered heap of grayboards without visible cows and I didn't know it was a dairy farm—"go a ways"—it was ten miles—"and left at the high embankment where the hogs are"—the whole road was beautiful, high, wild, vine-swarming embankments and the hogs weren't there that day.
>
> Greenberg, 1969, p. 241

According to Freire's analysis, it is very difficult to sustain dialogues with people who are not members of one's own social and economic community. True communication demands equality between speakers, and this often requires an alteration in current social relationships. Similarly, the increasing urgency with which oppressed people are now claiming the right and the need to be taught more complex literacy skills reflects a change in their perception, if not the reality, of their social roles and status. Educators genuinely interested in making communication skills available to all members of a society must understand the educational impact of such social transformations.

TURNING THOUGHTS INSIDE OUT

Mastery of written communication requires a difficult but critical shift in the consciousness of the learner, a shift of attention from an immediate audience that shares the learner's experiences and frame of reference to a larger, abstract, and unfamiliar audience. This necessary change in perspective is illustrated by the Schoolboys of Barbiana (1970). The authors decided to footnote all references to people, places, and institutions that might be unfamiliar to readers. However, they did not supply a footnote for Don Borghi, a local priest. When one of the English translators asked the young men why, they replied, "But everyone knows Don Borghi!" (p. 86).

We have found in Vygotsky's theory of thought and language, specifically in his examination of inner speech and its elaboration into written speech, a powerful explanation of why students' writings are often context-bound. He argues that to communicate well in writing a person must unfold and elaborate for an unknown audience an idea that may very well be represented in her or his mind by a single word or short phrase. To write, one must proceed from the "maximally compact inner speech through which experiences are stored to the maximally detailed written speech requiring what might be called deliberate semantics—deliberate structuring of the web of meaning" (Vygotsky, [1934] 1962, p. 100). The mastery of such transformations is determined by the internal cognitive processes from which writing derived and the social context in which it is produced.

Vygotsky recognizes written speech as "a separate linguistic function, differing from oral speech in both structure and mode of functioning'' (Vygotsky, [1934] 1962, p. 98). The key difference between these two forms of communication is the high level of abstraction and elaboration required for minimally comprehensible written speech. The audience for writing most likely does not share the writer's physical or emotional context and, therefore, cannot provide any immediate feedback about the success of the communication effort. The writer lacks the immediate clues of audience response—facial expressions, sounds, pitch, and intonation—all of which are characteristic of oral dialogue. Furthermore, written communication is a system of second-order symbolism: signs replace the sounds of words, which, in turn, are signs for objects and relations present in the real world (Vygotsky, 1978). In oral speech every sentence is prompted by an immediate, obvious motive; in the written monologue "the motives are more abstract, more intellectualized, further removed from immediate needs'' (Vygotsky, [1934] 1962, p. 99).

For our purpose the most exciting and significant part of Vygotsky's theory of writing is his description of the internal processes that characterize the production of the written word. Vygotsky says that the original mental source of writing is "inner speech,'' which evolved from a child's egocentric speech and is further abbreviated and personalized. Vygotsky distinguishes four features of inner speech, which is the language of self-direction and intrapersonal communication. One feature is *heavy predication.* Because the speaker always knows the subject of thought, the referent is likely to be either missing completely or vaguely developed. In the following description of a movie, a junior-high-school student has directly transferred inner speech to paper: "He was talking trash. Boy was triing to tell him to get away from her. He said do you want a knuckles sandwich. He say I am waiting for a chile burger. Then he wint to a liquor store. . . .''[3] *Semantic shortcuts* appear because "a single word is so saturated with sense that many words would be required to explain it in external speech'' (Vygotsky, [1934] 1962, p. 148). Effective written communication requires the transformation of the predicative idiomatic structure of inner speech into syntactically and semantically elaborated forms.[4] When this cognitive act fails to occur, writing may look like the two student samples below:

The many advantages and disadvantages of inflation and desire to see some of the Northern Colorado, the rush hour, Nursing School at UNM, and tutoring is a big step to want a student to attend UNM to try a smaller college where the population is lower in New Mexico, or a college with more educational advancement.

---

[3]Courtesy of Dean Brodkey, Director, English Tutorial Program, University of New Mexico. This example and the two following are from students enrolled in his program.

[4]Throughout this essay we are using the term *elaborated* in Vygotsky's sense as a form of speech (usually written) that is fully deployed and maximally decontextualized because it does not rely on the more usual verbal and visual communicative cues.

Well, I agree with the electricity that people are using more of it. But I think people are overdoing how they should use less energy. They don't think electric is just for fun using it but it's hard to get it.

In *agglutination,* according to Vygotsky, "several words are merged into one word, and the new word not only expresses a rather complex idea but designates all the separate elements contained in that idea." This may be what is occurring when words like *importation, undevplored* (underdeveloped and explored) or *bass* (band and jazz)[5] appear in students' writing. The final feature, *the combination and unity of the senses of different words,* is "a process governed by different laws from those governing combinations of meanings. . . . The senses of different words flow into one another—literally 'influence' one another—so that the earlier ones are contained in, and modify, the later one" (Vygotsky, [1934] 1962, p. 147).

In his description of inner speech, Vygotsky recognizes that, as in all aspects of human cognition, an individual changes and develops with age and experience. Language is extraordinarily important in the growing cognitive sophistication of children, as well as in their increasing social affectiveness, because language is the means by which children (and adults) systematize their perceptions. Through words human beings formulate generalizations, abstractions, and other forms of mediated thinking. Yet these words, the fragile bridges upon which our thoughts must travel, are sociohistorically determined and therefore shaped, limited, or expanded through individual and collective experience.

For educators the challenge, then, is to develop a teaching methodology that expands this experience, that allows people previously excluded to master the written word. As we have shown, Vygotsky and Freire provide a reasonable and fecund explanation of why millions of people have difficulty in learning to write organized prose. But their theories not only provide explanation, they also suggest strategies through which silent speakers can become potent writers. Through Vygotsky's work we can begin to appreciate the nature and complexity of the cognitive changes that are required to expand basic literacy to advanced literacy. And Freire leads us to further understand the dynamics of this intellectual process:

> Knowing, whatever its level, is not the act by which a Subject transformed into an object docilely and passively accepts the contents other give or impose on him or her. Knowledge, on the contrary, necessitates the curious presence of Subjects confronted with the world. It requires their transforming action on reality. It demands a constant searching. It implies invention and reinvention. . . . In the learning process the only

[5]These examples are from: The English Tutorial Program, University of New Mexico; D'Eloia, 1975, p. 11; and courtesy of Chris Behling (Behling & Elsasser, 1976), respectively.

person who really *learns* is s/he who appropriates what is learned, who apprehends and thereby reinvents that learning; s/he who is able to apply the appropriate learning to concrete existential situations. On the other hand, the person who is filled by another with "content" whose meaning s/he is not aware of, which contradicts his or her way of being in the world, cannot learn because s/he is not challenged.

Freire, 1973, p. 101

THE HISTORICAL BASIS OF COGNITIVE CHANGE

No one has yet scientifically documented the specific relationship between historical change and the expansion of intellectual and cognitive skills among oppressed peoples. The full analysis of this relationship is a challenge beyond the scope of this essay. However, in the absence of systematic data we have drawn upon the anecdotal accounts of observers in very diverse social settings to examine the historical basis of cognitive change. In addition, we have relied upon Alexander R. Luria (1976), who detailed some of the psychological changes that took place in the Soviet Union during thirty years of profound social and economic transformation.

Shortly after the Russian Revolution, Vygotsky and his student, Luria, visited remote rural areas of Uzbekistan and Kirghizia. They were impressed by the difference in attitudes between those individuals still personally untouched by the social transformations under way and those who, as a result of experiences on collective farms and in literacy courses, were already becoming "Subjects" in Freire's sense. The people lacking new social and educational experiences were reluctant to enter into dialogue, to participate in discussion as critical beings. When invited to ask the visitors questions about life beyond the village, they responded:

> I can't imagine what to ask about . . . to ask you need knowledge and all we do is hoe weeds in the field.
> I don't know how to obtain knowledge . . . where would I find the questions. For questions you need knowledge. You can ask questions when you have understanding but my head is empty.

Luria, 1976, pp. 137–138

But the peasants who had participated in the transforming process of the revolution had many questions about their collective lives:

> How can life be made better? Why is the life of a worker better than that of a peasant? How can I acquire knowledge more readily? Also: Why are city workers more skilled than peasants?
> Well, what could I do to make our kolkhozniks [members of collective farms] bet-

ter people? . . . And then I'm interested in how the world exists, where things come from, how the rich become rich and why the poor are poor.

Luria, 1976, pp. 141–142.

This type of change has been observed in varied contexts where people have begun to transform their sociolinguistic reality—in Chile, Brazil, Guinea-Bissau, Cuba, Mississippi, and the Navajo Nation.[6] When people are convinced that they can shape their social reality and that they are no longer isolated and powerless, they begin to participate in dialogue with a larger world, first orally and then through writing.

This development is not linear; it involves multiple transformations that are complex and dialectical. One transformation brings to individuals a growing sense of control as they change from "objects" into "Subjects." A peasant who had always toiled in the fields expressed the significance of this realization by stating, "I work and in working I transform the world" (Freire, 1973, p. 48). A second transformation reflects the consequences of these altered relationships that are of particular significance in people's cognitive and motivational approaches. Instead of denying their right to engage in dialogue with others as equals, they affirm their responsibility as creators and transformers of their culture: "Every people has its own culture, and no people has less than others. Our culture is a gift that we bring to you" (Schoolboys of Barbiana, 1970, p. 109). Third, the desire and need for educationally transmitted knowledge become of vital concern as a result of social and personal changes. Although in many instances schools and educational institutions have failed to meet the legitimate aspirations of oppressed groups, parents and students alike recognize that formal education offers skills that they need to transform themselves and their relationships with the dominant society:

> I would like to see the younger Indian people to get a good education so they can compete against the palefaces. . . . I don't want my kids to go far away to take up a career which won't be of benefit to the Navajos. I prefer that they stay around here . . . and become the Indian leaders of tomorrow.

Norris, 1970, p. 18

Or, as a young woman replied when asked why she spent her summer vacation attending a "freedom school," "I want to become a part of history also" (Holt, 1963, p. 322).

In spite of the belief, widely held in America, that education in and of itself can transform both people's sense of power and the existing social and economic hierarchies, educational intervention without actual social change is, in fact,

---

[6]For information on these programs see: Freire, 1970b and 1973 (Brazil and Chile); Darcy de Oliveira and Darcy de Oliveira, 1976 (Guinea-Bissau); Holt, 1965 and Greenberg, 1969 (Mississippi); and Norris, 1970 (Ramah, Navajo Nation).

ineffective. This is particularly true in poor and Third World communities where parents and children have traditionally felt marginal or excluded. Testimonies by a Mississippi subsistence farmer and a Navajo parent illustrate some reactions to such programs:

> They [the school] leaves me out; so I stay out, all the way out. They got no use for me cause they says I ain't got sense. I got no use fer them, neither, cause they ain't got sense enough to treat peoples human.
>
> Greenberg, 1969, p. 100

> If a student learns in school, then he grows away from what he had learned to value at home. I don't know what parents think about these problems. They're bewildered.
>
> Norris, 1970, p. 15

As long as children sense the powerlessness of their community, the impact of educators' best efforts lasts but a short time. Effective education requires the recognition and utilization of the potential in all human beings to participate actively in their own learning. Therefore educational success depends upon a change in the social environment—a break with the past alienation and marginality. Thus educational reform is an essential component but not in and of itself a cause of changes in educational engagement.

Although they lived in different times and worked in different hemispheres, Vygotsky and Freire shared approaches that emphasized the crucial intertwining of social and educational change. While Vygotsky focused on the psychological dynamics, Freire concentrated on developing appropriate pedagogical strategies.

THE DIALOGUE IN EDUCATION

During periods of rapid social change many individuals envision new futures for themselves. However, for people to benefit fully from new possibilities, meaningful educational programs must be created. The ultimate success of these programs depends on two factors. First, mutual respect and understanding must flow between educators and students—between representatives of the larger outside world and the poor with whom they are working. Second, the curriculum must be built upon the "here and now" of the learners (Freire, 1970b). Educational programs that are directed by distant bureaucracies without regard for local interests, resources, or needs produce boredom, frustration, and apathy. In Chile, for example, literacy workers using Freire's methods found that "the peasants became interested in the discussion only when the codification related directly to their felt needs. Any deviation . . . produced silence and indifference" (Freire, 1970b, p. 109).

Freire explains such silence and indifference in this way: "For the act of communication to be successful, there must be accord between the reciprocally communicating Subjects. That is, the verbal expressions of one of the Subjects must be perceptible within a frame of reference that is meaningful to the other Subject'' (Freire, 1973, p. 138). This entails more than avoiding or explaining "big" words; often the same word or sign has entirely different meanings to different peoples in different contexts. This type of semantic confusion is illustrated by Greenberg's account, described earlier in this essay, of her attempt to locate an isolated day-care center in Mississippi.

Even in classes grounded in the here and now, where there is mutual respect between teachers and students, academic progress is not guaranteed. Chilean educators, for example, found that their adult students were sometimes unable to perceive relationships between their felt needs and the causes of those needs (Freire, 1970b). One explanation for these learning difficulties is found in Luria's work in Uzbekistan and Kirghizia. The tasks Luria and Vygotsky presented included defining abstract concepts—What is the sun? How would you explain it to a blind man? What is freedom?—and generic classification. Nonliterate adults in these communities had great difficulty handling some of these tasks. For example, under the category "tool," peasants often grouped such diverse possessions as a donkey, firewood, an axe, cocoons, and a skull cap. When asked to solve problems requiring logical reasoning skills, individuals had to go beyond the insights gained from practical experience. Decontextualized thought is required to solve such problems and to recognize the connections between felt needs and external conditions. The necessary cognitive operations function within a closed system of logical formulation and are detached from the here and now. But it was just such a mode of cognition with which the peasants Luria studied and many other peoples were unfamiliar.

These kinds of cognitive skills are often both acquired and required in school. From their work in West Africa, Cole and Scribner (1974) have documented the cumulative effects of schooling on the acquisition of logical forms of thought. To interpret their findings, they use Luria's argument that "higher mental functions are complex, organized, *functional* systems" triggered by the task at hand (Luria, 1976, pp. 23 ff.). As Vygotsky originally described these functional learning systems, both the elements in these systems and their working relationships are formed during the course of an individual's development and are dependent upon the child's social experiences.

Most contemporary education, however, fails to trigger the growth of new functional systems because it follows what Freire has called "the banking concept," which "anesthetizes and inhibits creative power" (Freire, 1970b). The student is only expected to internalize existing knowledge; frequently this means internalizing the objectives of the dominant groups in society. By contrast, meaningful knowledge builds upon the human potential for active learning and is linked to praxis. When teachers and learners are partners in dialogue, a different conception of the processes of knowledge acquisition emerges:

Insofar as language is impossible without thought and language and thought are impossible without the word to which they refer, the human word is more than vocabulary—it is word-and-action. The cognitive dimensions of the literacy process must include the relationships of men with their world. These relationships are the source of the dialectic between the products men achieve in transforming the words and the conditioning which these products in turn exercise on men.

Freire, 1970a, p. 12

In no intellectual endeavor are these skills more essential than in the acquisition of mastery of written speech. To move beyond oral speech to writing, students must make an additional leap: they have to acquire a new code that demands further abstraction, semantic expansion, and syntactic elaboration.

Many literacy workers have emphasized the complexities of learning to communicate through an abstract sign system that lacks the cues of oral speech. Freire, however, has demonstrated that literacy can itself be the focal point for transformations of consciousness. When socially significant, "generative" words are employed in literacy programs, they permit learners to reflect on their experiences, to critically examine it. In this way teaching adults to read and write is no longer an inconsequential matter of *ba, be, bi, bo, bu* or of memorizing alienated words, but a difficult apprenticeship in "naming the world" (Freire, 1970a, p. 11). And such naming is liberating:

> In some areas of Chile undergoing agrarian reform the peasants participating in the literacy programs wrote words with their tools on the dirt roads where they were working. . . . "These men are sowers of the word," said a sociologist. . . . Indeed, they were not only sowing words, but discussing ideas, and coming to understand their role in the world better and better.

Freire, 1970a, p. 22

Through this type of education, learners and educators participate together in an ever-widening context; no longer are students limited to their immediate experience. As the circle of communication expands both for teachers and students, the role and structure of the linguistic sign are stretched and transformed. In this process, "it is not merely the content of a word that changes, but the way in which reality is generalized and reflected in a word" (Vygotsky, [1934] 1962, pp. 121–122). This transformation, however, does not take place in isolation; as Freire insightfully reminds us: "Just as there is no such thing as an isolated human being there is also no such thing as isolated thinking. Any act of thinking requires a Subject who thinks, an object thought about which mediates the thinking Subjects and the communication between the latter, manifested by linguistic signs" (Freire, 1973, pp. 136–137).

FROM LITERACY TO WRITING: A PILOT STUDY

Literacy is valued as a source of other skills and strategies necessary to achieve critical reconstruction of social and personal realities. The aim of the best literacy programs has been "to challenge the myths of our society, to perceive more clearly its realities and to find alternatives, and, ultimately, new directions for action'' (Holt, 1965, p. 103). Basic literacy, however, is not sufficient to achieve these far-reaching ends. People must reach a level of mastery of language skills from which they can critically examine and theoretically elaborate their political and cultural experiences. Simultaneously literacy must be adequately developed so as to provide increasing numbers of women and men with access to technological and vocational skills and information (Darcy de Oliveira & Darcy de Oliveira, 1976).

To date, many advanced-literacy programs have lacked the coherence and direction that only a clearly defined and articulated theoretical framework can provide. Some basic-literacy programs, both in the United States and abroad, have been constructed implicitly or explicitly on some of the principles of Vygotsky and Freire. We believe that Freire's methods and Vygotsky's hypotheses concerning the transformation of inner speech to written speech can be not only powerful tools in basic-literacy programs, but also a framework for promoting more advanced writing skills.

Using the theories of Freire and Vygotsky, Elsasser, Behling, and others developed a pilot program for advanced literacy within the context of an open-admissions policy at two New Mexico universities.[7] Compared to more usual methods, the results of this approach have been impressive (Behling & Elsasser, 1976; Elsasser, 1976). The commonly used anthology-based curricula assume that students' cognitive structures are such that mere exposure to well-formulated literary models is contagious and effective. The behavioristically based curricula, on the other hand, assume that writing skills should be broken down into specialized tasks to be taught individually and sequentially. In contrast to these two approaches, the experimental courses of the Elsasser-Behling pilot study assume an intricate interaction among teachers, learners, and social change, which in turn provides a dynamic of continuity and change that enhances the development of written communication. At the beginning of the course, teachers explain this interaction to the students in detail. They also discuss Vygotsky's analysis of the elaboration of thoughts to increasingly more decontextualized forms of communication—from intimate verbal speech through more formal verbal communication to fully elaborated written speech. Thus, the learners gain an appreciation of both the difficulties and the advantages of expressing their thoughts through the written word. Several specific exercises that built upon the original explanation demonstrate the process of decontextualizing and elaborating one's thoughts. Before students attempt written exposition, Behling and Elsasser's initial exercises offer them an opportunity to become aware of the skills required in writing for an audience that does not share the writer's frame of reference.

---

[7]The students involved were predominantly Chicano and Native American. Their communities' powerlessness vis-à-vis the institutions of the larger society is parallel in many ways to the oppression of peasants and workers in other nations.

The need for one such skill, elaboration, can be illustrated by displaying several pictures that express a similar theme, each with some markedly distinguishable features. The pictures should depict familiar aspects of the learner's environment, such as local landscapes; those used at the University of Albuquerque showed mountains and mesas. Each learner is asked to select one picture and to list a series of words that describes the picture in such a way that other members of the class can easily identify it. In his work, Freire observed that simply projecting familiar representations on a board or slide aids learners to "effect an operation basic to the act of knowing: they gain distance from the knowable object . . . the aim of decodification is to arrive at the critical level of knowledge, beginning with the learner's experience of the situation in the 'real' context" (Freire, 1970a, p. 15).

When learners at the University of Albuquerque shared their lists and attempted to find each other's choices, everyone became more aware of differences among kinds of words. Some words denoting objective, physical attributes (crags, shadows, peaks) were immediately mutually descriptive; other words indicating subjective reactions to the visual stimulus (spacious, inviolate, freedom, proud) were personally descriptive. Through dialogue, especially when different individuals had divergent reactions to the same representation, participants learned what types of further explanation would allow another to comprehend personally descriptive attributes. The need for elaboration in all forms of communication, particularly in writing, thus became apparent.

A second method demonstrates to learners the abbreviated nature of intrapersonal communication and the amount of detail required to flesh it out. This method relies on a common, everyday task like grocery shopping. Each learner is asked to prepare two sets of instructions—one for himself or herself and one for an unknown other person. One's personal set is usually a cryptic, minimal reminder, as these lists from three students demonstrate:

Student A	Student B	Student C
Milk	Soap	Milk
Eggs	Meat	Meat
Bread	Chips	Eggs
Soap	Beer	Potatoes
T.P.	Bread	Ice cream
		Vitamins

The participants discussed what additional kinds of information might be helpful if the task were assigned to someone else: for instance, size, grade, brand, type, price limitations. After the discussion some students immediately prepared elaborated shopping lists which would have been sufficient for any surrogate shopper:

Student A	Student B

Cream and homogenized
  milk, one-half gallon
1 dozen grade A large eggs
Roman Meal bread—large loaf
Toni soap
Toilet tissue—individually wrapped Scott
	2 bars of soap
	            1 package of hamburger meat
	1 package of potato chips
	2 six-packs of Budweiser
	1 loaf of bread

Some simply repeated the lists written for themselves.

In the ensuing conversation students added other hints, including explanations of what foods could be purchased with food stamps and which store was closest to the buyer's home. These comments, in turn, provided the basis for further elaboration suited to an even more removed audience. What if the buyer didn't know about food stamps? Was not familiar with supermarkets? Did not know your neighborhood? In this process students gained a heightened awareness of the need for full description and explanation. Thus an initially simple task stimulated the kind of dialogue that Freire considers crucial to the transformation of the individual's understanding of communicative exchanges. The assignment following this discussion was to write an essay on grocery shopping, incorporating the material discussed.

A third type of exercise used in this program emphasized our everyday reliance in oral speech on verbal and visual cues and aided learners in decontextualizing their explanations. Each member of the class received a geometric design and attempted to give other members of the group verbal instructions for reproducing the design. The instructions had to be sufficiently clear so that, without seeing the original, the listeners could construct reasonable facsimiles of the design. Some students performed facing the class, interacting verbally and visually; others transmitted the instructions with their backs to the group, forfeiting all verbal and visual response. The other students' reproductions immediately indicated the relative adequacy of the explanations. Initially the learners who interacted with their audience performed significantly better than those denied any response, but variations of the task were repeated until every member of the group was cognizant of the audience's needs and what information had to be provided to meet those needs.

This theoretically based program for advanced literacy proceeds sequentially to encourage and guide the unfolding of conceptual knowledge. Through a process of oral discussion in which ideas are continually broadened and fleshed out, constant attention to the types of elaboration required for an unknown other are emphasized. Immediate feedback from both the instructor and the students' peers indicates the success or failure of the written effort. This methodological continuity can lead from the initial tasks to more extended forms of writing traditionally required in composition courses. Among the communicative efforts emphasized within this theoretical framework are definition of an abstract concept, persuasion based on an imagined audience's values, narration of a personal experience, and a letter to an editor. Exercises in written communication can require increasing decontextualization for a removed and impersonal audience. Each assignment can be preceded by a discussion of several topics: what is or is not shared knowledge; the information needs of the intended audience; the particularities of the writer's experience; and the linguistic prejudices of the projected audience. Group discussion of these facts helps learners make their thoughts explicit. It also produces an understanding of the sources of thoughts and the ways in which thoughts change in the process of critical examination and analysis.

COGNITIVE AND SOCIAL DYNAMICS OF WRITING

The literacy programs we are advocating differ fundamentally from remedial instruction based on behaviorism or nativism. We believe that a more effective approach uses as its basis Vygotsky's interactionist assumption relating the biological substrata of behavior to changing social conditions. He wrote:

> In order to study development in children, one must begin with an understanding of the dialectical unity of two principally different lines (the biological and the cultural); to adequately study this process, then, an experimenter must study both components and the laws which govern their *interlacement* at each stage of the child's development.

Vygotsky, 1978, p. 5

Vygotsky's "exploration of these interactions is based on a view that regards the human organism as one of great plasticity and the environment as historically and culturally shifting contexts into which children are born and which they, too, eventually will come to change" (John-Steiner & Souberman, 1978, p. 5).

The model we have presented and are committed to developing further evolves from the theories of both Freire and Vygotsky. They argue that language is developed, extended, and modified through the constant interaction of individuals and their social context. Written speech is an act of knowing "the existence of two interrelated contexts. One is the context of authentic dialogue between learners and educators as equally knowing subjects . . . the second is the real, concrete context of facts, the social reality in which men exist" (Freire, 1970a, p. 14). Education designed for active, engaged learners provides an opportunity to understand the nature of the written word, the possibilities for its effective communication, and the difficulties in its production. Above all, such education offers learners a range of strategies that enables them to externalize their thoughts through writing. To develop these strategies we must direct our attention not only to written products but to the cognitive underpinnings of those products. Vygotsky's theory of the structure of language and its transformation into communicatively effective written and oral speech suggests many programmatic possibilities. Short-term improvement in literacy skills can be achieved by motivating students and by reinforcing their written work. But only programs that build upon cognitive processes can help individuals meet the long-term objective of using their literacy as a tool of personal growth and social transformation.

Although most educators now acknowledge the social nature of language, they do not recognize it in their programs. The critical role of dialogue, highlighted by both Freire and Vygotsky, can be put into effect by the conscious and productive reliance upon groups in which learners confront and work through—orally and in writing—issues of significance to their lives.

REFERENCES

Behling, C., and N. Elsasser. (March 1976). *Role taking in writing.* Workshop conducted at the TESOL Convention, New York.

Cobb, C. (1965). Notes on teaching in Mississippi. In L. Holt (Ed.), *The summer that didn't end.* New York: Morrow.

Cole, M., and S. Scribner. (1974). *Culture and thought.* New York: Wiley.

Darcy de Oliveira, R., and M. Darcy de Oliveira. (1976). *Guinea-Bissau: Reinventing education* (Document 11/12). Geneva: Institute of Cultural Action.

D'Eloia, S. (1975). Teaching standard written English. *Basic Writing,* 1, 5–14.

Elsasser, N. (1976). *Turning our thoughts inside out.* Unpublished manuscript, University of New Mexico, Albuquerque, NM.

Freire, P. (1970a). *Cultural action for freedom* (Monograph Series No. 1). Cambridge, MA: Harvard Educational Review & Center for Study of Development and Social Change.

———. (1970b). *Pedagogy of the oppressed.* New York: Seabury.

———. (1973). *Education for critical consciousness.* New York: Seabury.

Greenberg, P. (1969). *The devil has slippery shoes.* London: Macmillan.

Holt, L. (Ed.), (1965). *The summer that didn't end.* New York: Morrow.

John-Steiner, V., and L. Leacock. (1978). The structure of failure. In D. Wilkerson (Ed.), *Educating children of the poor.* Westport, CT: Mediax.

John-Steiner, V., and E. Souberman. (1978). The dialectic of cognitive growth (Introductory Essay). In L. S. Vygotsky, *Mind in society: The development of higher psychological processes* (M. Cole, V. John-Steiner, S. Scribner, and E. Souberman, Eds.). Cambridge, MA: Harvard University Press.

Labov, W. (1972). The logic of nonstandard English. In *Language in the inner city.* Philadelphia: University of Pennsylvania Press.

Laurence, P. (1975). Error's endless train: Why students don't perceive errors. *Basic Writing,* 1, 23–42.

Luria, A. R. (1976). *Cognitive development: Its cultural and social foundations.* Cambridge, MA: Harvard University Press.

Norris, R. (1970). *A Navajo community develops its own high school curriculum.* Unpublished manuscript, University of New Mexico, Albuquerque, NM.

Schoolboys of Barbiana. (1970). *Letter to a teacher.* New York: Random House.

Vygotsky, L. S. (1962). *Language and thought.* (Originally published, 1934). Cambridge, MA: MIT Press.

———. (1978). *Mind in society: The development of higher psychological processes.* (M. Cole, V. John-Steiner, S. Scribner, and E. Souberman, Eds.). Cambridge, MA: Harvard University Press.

B

LANGUAGE AND THE READING PROCESS

Reading Comprehension: A Selected Review

Helene M. Anthony, P. David Pearson, and Taffy E. Raphael

Research in reading comprehension has received more attention in the past fifteen years than in the previous six decades. In the foreword to *Becoming a Nation of Readers: The Report of the Commission on Reading,* Robert Glaser suggests that the research now available on the reading process can help to identify teaching practices that are effective and to differentiate effective strategies from those that are less useful (Anderson, Heibert, Scott and Wilkinson, 1985). This chapter will summarize selected research in the area of reading comprehension and describe ways in which these findings should, could, can, and do influence instructional practice. First, we discuss reasons for the reemerging interest in comprehension research. Then we describe the research bases that form our knowledge of the development of the comprehension process, summarizing both descriptive studies and instructional intervention studies.

THE EMERGENCE OF READING COMPREHENSION RESEARCH

The growing number of books concerned with reading comprehension (e.g., Cooper, 1986; Duffy, Roehler and Mason, 1984; Garner, 1987; McNeil, 1987; Oransanu, 1985; Pearson, 1984a; Spiro, Bruce, and Brewer, 1980) and chapters within more general scholarly works in cognition (e.g., Mandl, Stein and Trabasso, 1984) and education (e.g., Wittrock, 1985) attest to the importance ascribed to the processes of reading comprehension.

　　To what can this increased interest be traced? Our interest in comprehension processes actually can be traced back to the turn of the century when scholars such as Huey (1908), Cattell (1886), and Thorndike (1917) considered reading as a process worthy of intensive and extensive research. This was a period of time during which Gestalt psychology, with its emphasis on holistic mental processes, was popular first in Europe and later in the United States. Such a milieu invited study of reading comprehension research as a unified mental event. The research from this era substantiates exactly this view: research studied holistic mental processes such as the perception of print (Cattell, 1886) and the influence of mental set, or prior knowledge (Huey, 1908).

This early research forged the beginning threads of current reading comprehension research. In fact, reading Huey's (1908) *Psychology and Pedagogy of Reading* may cause modern researchers some embarrassment because we seem to have progressed little beyond his level of understanding. The snail's pace of advances from 1915 to 1970 reflects the continuing influence of the behavioral tradition that dominated psychology during that time. Behaviorism emphasized the study of *observable* behavior or events. Since the reading process was considered to be primarily a *mental* event, it was viewed as a phenomenon outside the scope of experimental psychology. Only those aspects of reading that were observable (not the process itself) became the focus of reading research. Research in reading began to assume a "product orientation," with attention given to accuracy in oral reading and performance on tests of reading skills. These tests portrayed reading comprehension as a large set of discrete, remediable subskills. A result of the close tie to such testing was an undue emphasis on phonics. However, regardless of which was the cause and which the effect, the fact is that these movements complemented one another. While the assessment of the processes of reading comprehension was quite difficult, the assessment of phonic skills such as knowledge of letter sounds, blending skills, auditory perception and discrimination was relatively simple. The comprehension process was treated as a "byproduct," since many assumed that comprehension automatically followed once students had "broken the code," and could "listen to what they themselves said."

Fortunately for those of us currently concerned with reading comprehension, the field of psychology that had banned reading comprehension as a field of study heralded its return. Only this time, it was cognitive psychology rather than behaviorism that held the day (Pearson, 1986). Reading, considered to be one form of problem solving, began to be studied by psychologists, linguists, and anthropologists, in addition to reading educators. New models of reading blossomed during this period. Gough (1972) and LaBerge and Samuels (1974) proposed bottom-up models emphasizing the flow of information from the text, to visual memory, to auditory memory, to the building of acoustic representations into words to semantic memory and, finally—comprehension. Smith (1971, 1978) and Goodman (1976), on the other hand, developed top-down oriented models that emphasized the influence of internally developed hypotheses about the possible meaning of a text segment, a higher level process, on the lower level processes (e.g., word recognition). Inevitably, other researchers (Rumelhart, 1977; Stanovich, 1980) constructed interactive models which allow the flow of information to switch from bottom-up to top-down depending on the characteristics of the text, context, and reader. Further, the nature of assessment in reading came into question, with researchers arguing for an interactive approach that better reflects our knowledge of the reading process (Pearson and Valencia, 1987; Lipson and Wixson, 1986). It is this view of reading which guides the research report in this review.

Many definitions of reading comprehension have been suggested (for an extensive treatment of definitions, see Johnston, 1983). The definition we have adopted for purposes of discussing reading comprehension research reflects an interactive view of reading in which "reading is the process of constructing meaning through the dynamic interaction among the reader's existing knowledge, the information suggested by the written language, and the context of the reading situation." This definition was proposed by Wixson and Peters (1983) and developed for the Michigan State Board of Education in conjunction with the Michigan Reading Association. It is representative of current trends away from a decoding-only emphasis in which the reader's task is to derive meaning from text and toward a conceptualization of reading as an interactive process in which the reader brings to the task a wealth of knowledge and experiences. Reading comprehension involves interpreting text and constructing meaning in light of this background knowledge, and within a social context that helps to determine the reader's goals, purposes, and expectations.

THE DEVELOPMENT OF COMPREHENSION PROCESSES: RESEARCH BASES

Since reading is an interactive process, it is important to understand those interacting factors that contribute to learners' development of effective reading strategies and desire to read. In other words, it is important to understand the context in which reading occurs. While we recognize the difficulty of considering in isolation factors that exist as part of a broad context, for purposes of this chapter, we examine the development of reading comprehension processes in terms of three primary influences: learner characteristics, text characteristics, and the social context in which learning to read occurs. Our decision to treat each separately reflects our desire to give each a complete hearing rather than any claim that they are operationally separate entities. The following sections present selected research on the characteristics of learner, the text, and the social context, respectively. Research discussed includes both descriptive studies and intervention studies designed to change current features of the learners, the text, or social contexts.

Learner Characteristics

Learner characteristics involve such factors as background knowledge, metacognitive knowledge, social-cultural background, ability, vocabulary knowledge, motivation, SES, gender, and developmental level. Some of these are amenable to change through instruction; others are not. In this section we examine the research in three areas particularly relevant to instructional issues and responsive to interventions designed to enhance responses to reading comprehension: background knowledge, vocabulary knowledge and metacognitive knowledge.

Background Knowledge   One of the most well-studied learners' characteristics is background knowledge; not surprisingly, the dominant theme in this work is its effect upon reading comprehension. This research results from such developments in cognitive psychology as the advancement of schema theory contributing to the changing conceptions in research and practice in reading (Anderson and Pearson, 1984). Schema theory is based on the notion that an individual's stored knowledge, what we frequently call long-term memory, is the systematic personal organizational of that individual's total experiences. How we make sense of incoming information is influenced by what we already know. For example, most adults have a well-developed schema for restaurant. There are waiters or waitresses that take your order for food which you get from a menu, and when you've finished eating you pay for your meal. If someone began describing what happened while eating lunch with a friend, you would connect what you were hearing with what you already know about going to a restaurant. As you listened, you would fill the "slots" in your restaurant schema.

Several studies have shown that one's schemata, or background knowledge, influences how one interprets and remembers text. Anderson, Reynolds, Schallert, and Goetz (1977) wrote two passages that were potentially ambiguous for the reader. The majority of subjects in a pilot group interpreted the first passage as being about a prison break and the second, about a card game. Then, thirty male wrestling students and thirty female music students read the two passages. A majority of the wrestling students (64%) interpreted the first passage as a wrestling match, rather than a prison break, and a majority of the music students (74%) perceived the second passage to be friends getting together to play music, rather than a card game. Yet each group's interpretation of the other passage was the same as that of the pilot group.

One source of background knowledge that influences comprehension is the set of experiences derived from one's own cultural background. To demonstrate the power of such background knowledge, Steffensen, Joag-Dev, and Anderson (1979) asked college students from the United States and from India to read about an American and an Indian wedding ceremony. The students not only were able to recall their native passage more quickly, but they were able to recall more of the elements rated as important by other students who had the same cultural background. Similar cultural findings have been demonstrated for religion (Lipson, 1982) and national culture (Pritzhard, 1987).

Two important studies have demonstrated the role that background knowledge plays in children's comprehension. In the first, Pearson, Hansen, and Gordon (1979) examined how greater knowledge about spiders provided an advantage to one group of second graders. Although these students did not differ from a second group of second graders in their reading ability, they were more successful in answering comprehension questions, particularly inferential questions, after each group read the same selection about spiders. Marr and Gormley (1982) provided further evidence of the power of background knowledge in a study of fourth-grade students. Instead of varying the amount of knowledge across groups of students, they had the same students read passages that were equivalent in readability level, but that differed in topic familiarity. Students read passages on familiar topics (i.e., baseball, the mosquito, and apples) and unfamiliar topics (i.e., curling, aphids, and papaya). Topic familiarity influenced students' ability to draw inferences and elaborate upon the texts that they read. In fact, prior knowledge was a better predictor of this ability than a measure of reading ability. Similar results were found in studies by Langer (1984), Langer and Nicolich (1981), and Lipson (1983).

Learners must not only possess background knowledge, but they must also be able to apply the knowledge relevant to the text they are reading. Bransford and his colleagues (Bransford and Johnson, 1972; Bransford and McCarrell, 1974) cleverly demonstrated this necessity using passages purposely written in an ambiguous fashion. In a now classic demonstration of the importance of accessing appropriate background knowledge, adult readers were read a paragraph which began,

> The procedure is really quite simple. First you arrange the items into different groups. Of course one pile may be sufficient depending on how much there is to do. If you have to go somewhere else due to lack of facilities that is the next step. . . .
>
> Bransford, 1979, p. 134

Then the readers were asked to rate the comprehensibility and to recall the passage. The passage was rated as having low comprehensibility and recall of the passage was quite poor. Yet, only the rare adult does not have the background knowledge to understand a paragraph on this topic, washing clothes. Thus, it can be seen that to have background knowledge is not sufficient; readers must access appropriate and relevant knowledge to successfully comprehend text.

The studies presented thus far underscore the importance of background knowledge. There is also instructional research that demonstrates the effects on reading comprehension of activating and enhancing learners' background knowledge. Several parallel lines of research have provided the basis for a variety of instruction used to enhance background knowledge. These instructional recommendations can be thought of as: (1) general frameworks for planning activities throughout the comprehension process, (2) specific strategies designed to be used to enhance background knowledge before students engage in reading their text, and (3) student strategies for independently accessing background knowledge and using it appropriately as they read the text.

One of the major implications of the studies of background knowledge is the importance of helping students access relevant information that they may already possess, or to help students build knowledge if they have little or no relevant amount prior to reading a selection. Suggested frameworks for lessons focusing on comprehension instruction suggest that prior to reading, teachers engage in activities designed to help students access or develop appropriate background knowledge. Also, prior to reading a text, teachers ask students to apply their knowledge as they generate predictions about the content of the upcoming reading material. After reading sections of the text or, if reasonable, the entire selection, the frameworks encourage guided reading by questioning students or having students engage in such activities as question asking and summarizing to ensure that students understand the central theme of the story or the major elements of an informational text. Finally, once meaning has been assured, these frameworks provide opportunity to extend or apply concepts learned to new situations.

For example, Au and her colleagues (Au, 1979; Wong and Au, 1985; Au and Kawakami, 1986) have developed two frameworks, one each for narrative and expository selections. Experience-Text-Relationship (ETR) directs teachers to tap into students' *experiences* prior to reading, examine the *text* to ensure students' comprehension of central ideas, and then build *relationships* between information in the text and the students' knowledge base. Similarly, Concept-Text-Application (CTA) encourages building background knowledge before reading expository text. However, the C phase focuses specifically on building concepts of ideas central to the texts' theme (e.g., the concept, monster, might be discussed prior to reading about the Loch Ness monster) rather than tapping into relevant personal experiences. Then, like the ETR sequence, students are directed to discuss ideas from the *text* to ensure that the meaning is clear, finally, applying concepts from the text to a new situation (e.g., differences between scientific discoveries and fantasies). Other frameworks, such as Stauffer's (1969) Directed-Reading-Thinking-Activity (DRTA), stress the importance of using predictions during prereading to promote students' monitoring of their comprehension during the guided phase of the lesson.

While these frameworks provide a set of general guidelines for constructing the overall reading comprehension lesson, a related area of research has provided specific instructional strategies to use within these more general lesson frameworks. For example, Langer (1982, 1984) has developed a three-phase PreReading Plan (PReP) that not only builds students' knowledge about central concepts, but also provides teachers with a tool for evaluating the level of their students' knowledge. Initially, the teacher presents students with a word, phrase or picture related to the central idea of the to-be-read text. Students are encouraged to share any associations with the selected topic that come to mind. Second, students are asked to explain their associations. For example, the teacher may ask, "Why did the word handicap make you think of wheelchair? Where did that idea come from?" During this phase students are able to listen to their peers' explanations for their associations. This discussion serves the dual purpose of informing the teacher about the sophistication of the students' knowledge base, and allowing students to activate relevant background knowledge, correct misconceptions, and/or enrich current background knowledge. Third, students are given another chance to make associations with the original concept before going on to reading the selection.

Hansen and Pearson's (1983) Inference Training is a questioning technique in which students are encouraged to use their background knowledge to make predictions about what might happen in the text to be read. A prior knowledge question invites students to think of relevant personal experiences (e.g., "Have you ever been embarrassed? Tell us about it."). Following a discussion of personal experiences, students are asked to predict how a story character may behave in a similar situation (e.g., "In our story today, Billy is embarrassed when his friends sing happy birthday to him. What do you think he will do?"). Both Inference Training and PReP specify procedures useful during the prereading phases of a comprehension lesson. Other prereading activities focus on the development of specific vocabulary knowledge or concepts related to upcoming selections.

Vocabulary Knowledge   It is well-documented that there is a strong relationship between measures of vocabulary knowledge and reading comprehension level (see Anderson and Freebody, 1981, for a review). What has not been clear is the nature of this relationship. Attempts to raise reading comprehension through instruction in vocabulary have had disappointing results (Ahlfors, 1980; Evans, 1981; Pany and Jenkins, 1978). As discussed in the previous section, we know that background knowledge contributes to reading comprehension. Some have argued, therefore, that the relationship between vocabulary and comprehension is due to the fact that knowledge of vocabulary is actually a measure of background knowledge and should not be thought of as a separate influential factor in reading comprehension (Johnston, 1983). However, more recent intervention studies in vocabulary instruction have succeeded in enhancing students' comprehension (Beck, Perfetti, and McKeowen, 1982; Kameenui, Carnine, and Freschi, 1982; McKeowen, Beck, Omanson, and Perfetti, 1983; McKeowen, Beck, Omanson, and Pople, 1985; Stahl, 1983; Stevens, 1982; Wixson, 1986).

Results of these studies suggest that there are particular characteristics of effective vocabulary instruction. First, instruction should teach the key words for the passages to be read rather than general lists of vocabulary words. In addition, instruction should stress the relationship between the word and the reader's background of experiences, thereby improving both word meanings and background knowledge. Finally, only a few words should be taught for each lesson each week and they should be learned thoroughly.

Metacognitive Knowledge   In addition to possessing knowledge about the world, learners also possess metacognitive knowledge about the reading process. The term, metacognition, has come to be associated with one's understanding and appropriate use of cognitive processes and strategies. These metacognitive processes can be thought of as *knowledge of self, knowledge of the task, and self-monitoring* (Flavell, 1979; Garner, 1987; McNeil, 1987), or of knowing "that" (declarative knowledge), knowing "how" (procedural knowledge) and knowing "when and why" (conditional knowledge) (Paris, Lipson, and Wixson, 1983). For example, declarative knowledge would include one's knowledge about the task of reading—knowing *that* reading is a process, *that* background is useful, *that* different materials should be read at different rates if meeting different purposes. Procedural knowledge would include knowing how to run through the steps in a summary writing routine or how to search ahead in the text for clues about the meaning of a word.

Conditional knowledge, knowing when and why, is particularly relevant since that is the context-based, flexible application of learned strategic knowledge. For example, students reflect conditional knowledge when they are able to select an appropriate study strategy when given a goal and a set of materials. Effective use of conditional knowledge depends on knowing oneself as a learner (e.g., "I know I never can remember all these categories of animals if I only read this once. I'd better plan to do something to help me remember this."), having a range of available strategies (e.g., "I could make a list of all the animals and say them to myself to test if I remember them. No . . . maybe instead I'll put the animals the book describes into groups. I know that groups are easier to remember than single things."), and knowing when to apply the strategy selected.

Metacognitive knowledge appears to develop through both experience and through instruction. Myers and Paris (1978) interviewed lower and upper elementary good and poor readers and found that the younger and less able readers had limited understanding of the reading process as compared to older and more capable readers. For example, they did not know that reading silently is faster than reading aloud, or that retelling a story is more efficiently done at gist level rather than at verbatim level. Younger and less able readers have also been described as less likely to detect anomalous information as incomprehensible (Bransford, Stein, Shelton, and Owings; 1981) even if there is evidence that they are monitoring their reading (i.e., hesitation, repetition) (Paris and Myers, 1981). It appears that poorer readers concentrate on decoding goals and not comprehension goals.

In a series of studies, Garner and her colleagues (1980, 1981, 1981–82, 1983) found that younger readers and poor comprehenders, in contrast to more mature or successful readers, were more likely to miss inconsistencies that had been deliberately inserted in the text. They continued to read despite the lack of comprehensibility. In addition, they were not likely to possess effective strategies for remediating comprehension failure. In one study, sixth grade "tutors" instructed fourth graders to reread an entire passage when the younger children could not answer a comprehension question, rather than instructing them to *strategically* look back in the article for the appropriate information. In summary, *poorer readers have little awareness of the purpose of reading, do not notice blocks to comprehension,* and *do not employ effective fix-up strategies.*

In one line of research designed to enhance students' awareness of strategic reading, and the mental activities that underlie skilled reading, Duffy and Roehler and their colleagues argue for process-into-content instruction. That is, they are departing from reading instruction that focuses only on the **content** of a piece of text, i.e., traditional comprehension questions, in favor of instruction that teaches students how to make use of knowledge about the reading **process** to make sense of text (Roehler, Duffy and Meloth, 1986). In a series of studies, they have observed reading lessons, evaluating teachers' talk in terms of the explicitness with which they provide instruction in the reading process, for example, giving students information about when and where a particular strategy, such as using context clues, will be used and how this strategy is a **means** to the end of comprehension of content. They then examine the students' awareness of these purposes and procedures through interviews following lessons, and the impact of such an awareness on students' comprehension through various comprehension tests. These data support the idea that when teachers talk **explicitly** about the processes of reading, students' awareness of when to use and how to use strategies increases (Duffy, Roehler, Meloth, Vavrus, Book, Putnam, and Wesselman, 1986; Duffy, Roehler, Savin, Rackliffe, Book, Meloth, Vavrus, Wesselman, Putnam, and Bassiri, 1987).

Another instructional program designed to enhance students' metacomprehension, or comprehension monitoring, is Palincsar and Brown's reciprocal teaching (1984, 1986). Reciprocal teaching is based upon the premise that the social setting of the instructional situation dramatically affects the development of cognitive strategies (e.g., reading comprehension). Students are taught four strategies to help them detect and fix comprehension difficulties: summarizing, question asking, clarifying, and predicting. Each reading session begins with a discussion to activate relevant background knowledge and, depending upon student independence, some strategy modeling by the teachers. Then, after each segment of text is read by the students, one student, acting in a quasiteaching role, uses the four strategies with help from peers and the teacher. When summarizing, the student describes in a simple sentence what just happened in the text. In question asking, the student asks his or her peers to answer a question about a main idea from the text. In clarification, the student identifies parts of the text which are unclear, for example, a word whose meaning is unknown, or the use of a referent which is confusing. Predicting requires the student to make an inference about what might happen in the next segment of text. The reciprocal teaching procedure is embedded in ongoing content area lessons such as science or social studies. The goal of instruction, therefore, is to help students internalize the four comprehension-monitoring strategies within the context of reading and remembering classroom materials so that they can use these strategies when reading independently. Indeed, numerous studies with a variety of age-groups have shown this instructional program to dramatically increase students' reading comprehension (for a review, see Brown and Palincsar, 1985). In addition, it is an effect that is maintained over time.

Another approach to enhancing students' metacognitive knowledge is to engage students in rather explicit instruction in strategy use using a curriculum designed specifically for that purpose. Paris and his colleagues (Paris, 1986; Paris, Cross, and Lipson, 1984), also interested in the fact that poorer readers have difficulty detecting comprehension problems and lack the strategies needed to remedy comprehension failures, developed Informed Strategies for Learning (ISL). The program, which includes 16 different lessons aimed at developing students' metacognitive knowledge in reading, uses metaphors to make abstract strategies concrete. For example, to underscore the importance of evaluating a reading task before beginning to read, the metaphor, "Be a reading detective," is used. The metaphor conjures up images of a detective collecting relevant information and trying to discover motives to solve a particular case. Similarly, a good reader gets a sense of both the purpose for reading and the difficulty of a reading task to determine the best prereading approach. Although the ISL instructional intervention did not improve students' performance on traditional standardized reading tests, students did improve on cloze tests and error detection tests.

In summary, there are many options open to enhancing reading comprehension through attention to developing readers' background knowledge, building conceptual knowledge through vocabulary instruction, and enhancing metacognitive knowledge through instruction that focuses on purposive learning of strategies as well as an understanding of conditions under which application of learned strategies would improve comprehension. Such knowledge is applied to acquiring information and building knowledge from text, and it is to characteristics of the texts to be read that we now turn.

Text Characteristics

The learner's role is central to constructing meaning from text; but other factors have important influences too. Fundamental to the interactive view of reading is that comprehension results from the joint construction of meaning between the author of the text and the reader. Research that has examined the nature of the text has focused on a number of variables, including types of materials used for reading instruction (e.g., basal readers), narrative text structures and related instructional strategies, expository text structures (e.g., Meyer, 1975; Stein and Glenn, 1979; Mandler and Johnson, 1977), the degree to which such texts are written and structured in ways that are sensitive to readers' background knowledge and expectations, and instructional interventions for enhancing learning from text. In this selection, we focus on these issues as we discuss narrative and expository text.

Meyer and Rice (1984) use the term *text structure* to refer to the way ideas in a text are interrelated to convey a message. One way to think about these interrelationships is to think about the questions that the text was designed to answer. For example, information a reader expects to find in a story includes where the story is taking place, who the main characters are, what the problem is that the main characters have to solve, etc. In contrast, information one might expect to find presented in a science text may be explanations of particular processes. This information invites questions such as, What is being explained? Who or what is involved? What are the steps? Although any given text is usually a combination of different text structures, research suggests that knowledge of the different text structures can be used by the reader to aid comprehension (e.g., Raphael and Kirschner, 1985; Armbruster, Anderson, and Ostertaj, 1987; Taylor, 1982; Meyer, Brandt and Bluth, 1980).

Narrative Text   Narrative text, or stories, are the basis for reading instruction, particularly in the case of the basal reader. The structure of a story is frequently referred to as story grammar, but researchers have coined story schema, story map, story frames, and other phrases to communicate the same idea. It has been found that individuals with better knowledge of story grammar tend to be better comprehenders of narrative text (Fitzgerald, 1984; Mandler and Johnson, 1977). Knowledge of story structure helps these readers to understand and remember stories; they are able to anticipate what information is to come, aiding comprehension, and they have an organizational structure for connecting pieces of information together, thus aiding recall.

Several studies have attempted to influence students' reading comprehension through instruction in the elements in a story and their order. For example, Fitzgerald and Spiegel (1983)—also, Spiegel and Fitzgerald (1986)—provided fourth graders, who were poor comprehenders and had low knowledge of story grammar, with direct instruction in the Setting (who, where, when), the Beginning (event or problem), the Simple Reaction (thoughts or response to the Beginning), the Goal (decision), the Attempt, (efforts to reach the Goal), the Outcome (results of the Attempt), and the Ending (long range consequences) of a story. Each element of the story was pointed out to students in a well-formed example. Then teacher and students discussed additional examples as well as non-examples for each story part. This instruction succeeded in enhancing students' knowledge of story structure and increasing their reading comprehension.

Gordon and Braun (1983) instructed fifth-grade students in a story schema similar to that used by Spiegel and Fitzgerald, composed of setting, theme, plot (with five subparts) and resolution. The focus of the instruction was to familiarize students with **schema-related** questions, such as, "What does the main character do?" Students were then encouraged to use their knowledge of these schema-related questions to generate story-specific questions in reading unfamiliar texts, and in composing their own narratives. Similarly, Singer and Donlan (1982) taught high-school students a set of story grammar-based questions which aided their comprehension of complex short stories.

Basal texts are used in most American classrooms to teach students to read (Anderson, Osborn, and Tierney, 1984; Winograd, Wixson, and Lipson, in press). Although comprised mostly of narrative text, basal reader selections have not been found to follow the story grammars mentioned above. In several studies, basal reader selections were rewritten to conform to story grammar and to improve coherence through linkage words that explicitly stated relationships (Beck, McKeowen, Omanson, and Pople, 1984; Brennan, Bridge, and Winograd, 1986). The rewritten selections, although slightly more difficult than the original passages according to readability formulas, were, in fact, easier for students to comprehend.

Expository Text   Research in expository text structures began with descriptive studies of the different types of text structures used to convey information. Much of this work extended that of rhetoriticians who identified such rhetorical structures as invention, arrangement, and style (Meyer and Rice, 1984). For example, Meyer (1975) described the set of expository text structures as including antecedent/consequent, response, comparison, collection, and description.

A second line of descriptive research that extended the work delineating the structures used in informational writing was research on the relationship between such "pure" structures and those actually identifiable in basal and content area materials. Schallert and Tierney (1982) examined social studies materials and found that most texts used a combination of structures within a given selection, rather than the pure forms identified. Similarly, Gallagher and Pearson (1982) found that basal readers tended to use a "pure" form of expository organization while the content area textbook selections almost always had a combination of forms. In addition, students' recall was higher for the pure form than for the mixed format. Anderson and Armbruster (1984), after analyzing content area textbooks, concluded that these materials are frequently "inconsiderate," that is, they are lacking in terms of using a clear discourse structure, explicitly stating relationships among ideas, addressing one purpose at a time, and having the text fit the knowledge base of the reader.

In spite of the lack of pure structures in existing content area materials, research findings from several studies suggest that skilled reading comprehenders were, in fact, aware of the different structures and appeared to use these as conventions for aiding memory for text read (Englert and Hiebert, 1984; McGee, 1982; Meyer, Brandt, and Bluth 1980; Richgels, McGee, Lomax, and Sheard, 1987; Taylor, 1980, 1982). For example, Meyer et al. (1980) found that ninth graders who had knowledge of and used the author's top-level structure recalled more information, including more important information, than those students who did not use the text organization. In a study of sixth-grade students using three different measures of structure awareness and two different measures of recall, Richgels et al. (1987) reached the same conclusions. Students who possessed knowledge of the structures that authors used were better able to understand and remember texts that were well-organized. The researchers also found that sixth-grade students were more likely to have knowledge of the comparison/contrast structure than the collection or problem/solution structure. Causation was the structure for which students had the least awareness.

A third line of research on expository text structures involved extending the above findings to intervention studies. Despite the fact that students are better able to recall narrative than expository text (Taylor and Berkowitz, 1981), until recently, students have been expected to be able to comprehend informational text, usually content area textbooks, by virtue of receiving reading instruction in predominantly narrative text. Unfortunately, the studies of students' awareness of organizational structures of expository texts suggest that these structures may be unfamiliar to the students, contributing to comprehension difficulties as they enter the upper elementary and middle school grades where the ability to read informational text independently is frequently assumed. On the other hand, since pure structures rarely appear in existing content area materials, researchers questioned the effect of teaching students about text structures. In fact, several studies have now examined the effects of such instruction on students' recall of informational text (Armbruster, Anderson, and Ostertaj, 1987; Berkowitz, 1986; Flood, Lapp, and Farnan, 1986; McGee and Richgels, 1985; Raphael, Englert, and Kirschner, 1986; Taylor, 1982; Taylor and Beach, 1984).

While students representing a range of age groups participate in these studies and a variety of techniques are used, overall, students are learning to identify major categories and supporting information. For example, Taylor (1982) looked at fifth-grade students' free recalls of expository passages with clear headings and subheadings, comparing students who received instruction in writing hierarchical summaries with students receiving instruction in answering questions. The students who learned to write summaries had greater free recall of expository text and greater sensitivity to text organization. Taylor and Beach (1984) reported similar results with middle-grade subjects.

Using naturally occurring text typical of content area textbook selections, Berkowitz (1986) taught students to generate maps related to content area texts. Maps are graphic representations of the superordinate and subordinate ideas in the passage. The title of the passage is placed in the center of the paper and 4–6 important categories of information are placed in a clockwise direction around the title. Under each category heading are important ideas for that category, such as, definitions, examples, and details. Each category has a box drawn around it and then it is connected by a line to the title. Berkowitz found that sixth-grade students who learned to use text organization via map construction performed better on immediate and delayed free recalls of expository text than did students who answered questions, reread text, or studied maps constructed by the researcher, and concluded that map construction helped students read and remember content area texts. An important finding from this study, however, is that improving free recall is dependent upon **active** study strategies. Students who studied maps that they did not construct were not significantly different on their free recalls from students who were not exposed to the text's organization. Furthermore, the free recalls of students in the map construction group were only affected when they actually constructed a map on paper; mental mapping was not enough.

Instruction in specific text structures, such as problem/solution and comparison/contrast, has also resulted in improved comprehension of expository text. Raphael and Kirschner (1985) instructed middle school students in comprehending social studies material written in a compare/contrast structure. They provided students with a list of four questions specific to this particular text structure: (a) What is being compared or contrasted? (b) On what are they being compared or contrasted? (c) How are they alike? and (d) How are they different? Initially students were presented with brief, clearly written paragraphs found in social studies texts (e.g., colonists' and native Americans' view of land). Students used the guiding questions to identify important information and supporting details and also were taught how to use key words and phrases to locate relevant information.

This instructional program was extended by Raphael, Kirschner, and Englert (1986) to aid in both composing and comprehending the additional text structures of problem/solution and explanation. The results of this and other studies (Flood, Lapp and Farnan, 1986; McGee and Richgels, 1985) suggest that having students become authors of expository text themselves is one vehicle for internalizing the question guides. Students who were writers themselves learned the importance of text structure questions and the key words and phrases used to signal to readers the organization of their text. For example, Armbruster, Anderson, and Ostertag (1987) taught fifth-grade students a schematic representation, or frame, of the problem/solution text structure and specific guidelines for writing summaries for a problem/solution text. After instruction, students were more sensitive to social studies selections using the problem/solution text structure and they recalled about 50% more of the top-level ideas on an independently read passage than did students with traditional question-answering instruction.

Instruction in text structure can assist students in the use of other strategies described above. For example, one of the important strategies used in reciprocal teaching (cf. p. 14) is generating predictions about upcoming information in text.

Readers with knowledge of different text structures are advantaged when asked to predict. Assume that readers are learning about how materials can be substituted for one another. They have just read how a rhinestone is **similar** to a diamond in particular ways. Their knowledge of the comparison/contrast text structure can help them predict that the next segment will tell how these two substances are different. They might even make an hypothesis about the particular attribute to be discussed, generating a question such as, "What characteristics do you think a rhinestone and a diamond could be contrasted on?" Instruction in text organization gives teachers and students a shared language that can be used to discuss comprehension processes.

In summary, there are a variety of texts with which readers interact. Current basal instructional materials fall short in their ability to prepare students to cope with the range of potential materials to comprehend within and outside of school. More attention needs to be directed at enhancing both the quality and the range of text used in elementary and middle schools. However, attention to learner characteristics and to enhancing the reading materials used during comprehension instruction is not sufficient to change current practice. A better understanding of the third influence on comprehension must develop—understanding the social context in which learning to read occurs.

The Social Context

Where does meaning reside? This question initially was debated in terms of whether meaning existed in a given text with the readers' task defined as decoding the printed symbols to obtain the intended meaning, or whether meaning existed in the mind of the reader who read to interpret the author's words in light of his or her own background and experience. Recently, there has been an increased focus on the contribution of the social context in which the reader and text exist. The social context has been defined in terms of the social/historical milieu in which learning occurs (Gavelek, 1986); the philosophical beliefs of the teacher (DeFord, 1986); the cultural background of the students (Au and Kawakami, 1986; Heath, 1982); the participation structures guiding students' involvement in comprehension lessons (Au and Mason, 1982), and so forth. In this section we focus on two of these areas that have a major impact on reading instruction: the students' cultural background and the instructional context most frequently used to teach reading—the basal reading program.

Cultural Knowledge   One way in which the influence of cultural knowledge on one's comprehension of text can be demonstrated concerns the relationship between cultural and background knowledge (e.g., the example of the American and Indian students who read about each culture's wedding ceremonies). However, the broader influences of cultural rules or norms on school learning in general, and reading in particular, have been demonstrated by researchers with anthropological and/or linguistic orientations. Of concern is the student's sociolinguistic competence, for example, knowing who talks when, to whom, and how. Frequently, speech interactions in classrooms are the avenues through which students not only learn, but also communicate competency in terms of knowledge of content. Therefore, operating under different "rules" may mean that certain students are (1) denied access to learning and (2) are not perceived to know as much as they know. Several studies have shown that children's home environments and classroom environments may, in fact, run by such different rules that they are culturally incongruent.

Phillips (1972) investigated the poor academic performance of Indian children on the Warm Springs Indian Reservation in Oregon. Teachers reported that Indian children were reluctant to participate in class and, in fact, did so less and less often as time in school increased. Phillips found that Indian children, when compared with non-Indian children, rarely spoke in whole-class or small-group lessons led by the teacher. However, they initiated individual contact with the teacher when working independently, as frequently, or more frequently, than non-Indian children. In addition, when students were working in small student-run groups, Phillips report that the Indian children "become most fully involved in what they are doing, concentrating completely on their work until it is completed, talking a great deal to one another within the group, and competing, with explicit remarks to that effect, with the other groups" (Phillips, 1972, p. 379). Indian students' willingness to participate, specifically, to participate verbally, and subsequent learning from school lessons, appeared directly related to the way the interaction was organized and who controlled it. The preferred opportunities were those in which students worked in groups, rather than as an individual speaker to an audience, and those in which the student him or herself determined participation.

By studying how Indian children acquire skills in their community, Phillips discovered that they first, observe successful performance, then, participate in an activity with supervision, and finally, engage in **private** self-testing. The procedure of "learning through public mistakes" that is adopted in the classroom runs counter to this. That is, the norms for Indian children for determining when participation is appropriate at home and in the community are different from those interactions that are expected in many classroom activities.

Heath (1982) also gathered detailed descriptions about language use in different contexts. She looked at the use of questions in the black, working-class community of "Trackton," and in the homes of classroom teachers. The teachers' questions at home with their own children were very similar to the teachers' questions at school. Both of these were different from the questions that parents used in Trackton. Most Trackton caregivers had other adults around while they were at home with their children, so children were not sought out as conversational partners. Children were not seen as information-givers or question-answerers. When questions were asked of children, they tended to be of the analogy variety, for example, "What's that like?" In the teachers' homes, where it was common for the adult to be alone with the preschooler, questions dominated. The most common type of question asked was one in which the questioner has the information being requested of the child, for example, "Where's Missy's nose?" Heath suggests that these different experiences with language use help explain the Trackton students' lack of participation in classroom interactions.

One of the most influential of the cultural congruence studies has probably been the Kamehameha Early Education Project (KEEP). Au and Jordan (1981), concerned about the poor academic performance of native Hawaiian children, studied and documented differential interaction patterns between the children's conversation at home and reading instruction at school. Reading lessons were redesigned so as to allow children to make use of the "talk-story" pattern they were accustomed to. That is, during the telling of a story, students' contributions could overlap, as in "talk-story," rather than proceed by the one-at-a-time turn-taking that was part of their previous instruction. Direct comprehension instruction conducted in this manner resulted in significant gains in students' reading comprehension.

Sociolinguistic studies can be helpful in explaining the learning difficulties that some students experience. If cultural incongruity results in poor academic performance by a particular group of students, changes in the instructional environment are in order. However, the types of changes needed are not self-evident. In the case of the Indian children studied by Phillips, she reported that some teachers, particularly in the lower elementary grades, did adapt their teaching to accommodate the preferences of the Indian children. For example, teachers had students work on group projects rather than reading text and asking and answering questions, or giving students the opportunity to ask the teacher questions privately rather than in front of the class. While this instructional modification seems laudable and a step in the right direction, Phillips also raises the point that "by doing so, they, teachers, are avoiding teaching the Indian children how to communicate in precisely the contexts in which they are least able but most need to learn if they are to `do well in school'" (Phillips, 1972, p. 383). Despite the lack of consensus concerning application of the research, the picture that emerges from the sociolinguistic studies is one which is commensurate with the interactional view of reading. Reading performance is clearly influenced by a variety of factors, and performance at any one point in time, whether in a reading group which runs by unfamiliar rules or in a testing situation, should not be equated with an individual's potential for reading comprehension.

Instructional Context: Basal Reading Programs   Basal reading programs constitute the most frequent setting in which students learn to read. The basal reading programs typically used consist of the students' basal reader, usually a collection of selections dominated by narrative text, a teacher's manual which provides the teacher with specific procedures for instruction from introduction of new vocabulary (often as many as 20 words per story) to the set of questions to ask throughout the text to the skills that should be taught following reading of the story, workbooks which provide students with tasks designed to give them independent practice in their reading skills, and accompanying materials such as flashcards, charts, and filmstrips.

It has been well-documented that teachers adhere rather firmly to the teaching of reading as it is prescribed in the basal reader series (Durkin, 1984; Osborn, 1984; Shannon, 1983). In addition, it has been suggested that the reading activities delineated in these basal reader series, while they may be **related** to teaching comprehension, do not necessarily **teach** comprehension (Durkin 1978–79, 1981). Durkin found that fewer than 50 of the 17,997 minutes of observations of reading lessons contained any comprehension instruction. The most commonly observed behavior was assessment followed by giving and helping with assigned worksheets. Allington (1983) found that students in different ability-based reading groups receive slightly **different** instruction. Unfortunately, students in low-ability reading groups experience even less comprehension instruction than students in the higher groups. They usually read orally while the higher groups read silently, and the focus is on word identification rather than sense-making.

When examining the basal manuals themselves, Durkin (1981) noted that the length of a directive which might be classified as **instructive** was sometimes only a single sentence, for example, "Remind students that the main idea is the most important idea in the paragraph." Durkin did find one difference between teachers' instruction and basal manuals; manuals were more prone to suggest application activities than teachers were to employ them. That is, the manuals suggested that teachers guide students to complete an example of an exercise for a given skill. However, it is important to note that when teachers did use application activities it was usually in lieu of, not in addition to, instruction. Students were given a chance to show that they can perform a skill correctly instead of instruction about what the skill is and how one applies it. In addition, Durkin found that manuals rarely offer any suggestions for what to do when students failed; instead, more application opportunities were provided.

Beck and McKeown (1981, 1987) analyzed comprehension instruction in basal manuals from a somewhat different perspective from Durkin. Guided by the concept of story grammars, they examined the support features of the guided reading lesson (suggestions for before, during, and after reading the selection) and found them to be problematic. First, pre-reading suggestions for building background knowledge frequently focused students' attention on aspects of the selection that were not central to understanding the story. In addition, after-reading questions often represented a randomly accumulated quiz of unrelated details rather than a carefully planned sequence of questions designed to elucidate the casual connections between major story elements and events.

Similar research has been conducted on content area materials, with similar results. Armbruster and Gudbrandsen (1986) found that teachers' manuals for social studies programs were as negligent as basal reader manuals in teaching comprehension of informational text. Not surprisingly, Neilsen, Rennie, and Connel (1982) found little comprehension instruction occurring in elementary social studies lessons.

In addition to problems in the materials and corresponding instruction using basal and content area texts, other research has documented problems with accompanying workbooks and the effects of using such materials. Osborn (1984a) found students' workbooks to be lacking in their contribution to developing skill in reading comprehension. For example, none of the workbooks in the six basal series she examined required students to "integrate their own reactions into their workbook responses" (p. 109), rather focusing on specific practice in particular subskills. There were also few instances of workbook tasks that require students to read a connected piece of text and apply the comprehension concepts they have been taught. In a related study, Anderson, Brubaker, Alleman-Brooks, and Duffy (1985) found little understanding on the part of first graders as to why they were doing their seatwork assignments. For the most part, they interpreted these activities as ends in themselves; the goal was to get finished. In addition, students who experienced difficulty with the independent tasks rarely received informative feedback from the teacher on how to address these problems. It seems reasonable, then, to begin to question the value of reading seatwork, an integral part of basal reading programs.

Given these problems in the materials and current instructional practices, it is reasonable to ask whether instructional alternatives exist. Instructional research of the past decade has provided a great deal of support and suggestions related to improved comprehension instruction, with suggestions for alternative instructional models, guidelines for teacher/student dialogue, and a focus on developing independent readers.

Explicit Instruction Model   Based on both the reading process research and the intervention studies cited in the previous sections, and the descriptive studies of current classroom reading instruction, the view of reading comprehension instruction is shifting. It is not merely a call for more instruction (one way to apply Durkin's findings), but a call for **different** instruction. One current instructional model focuses on the importance of teachers being *explicit* in their comprehension instruction (see Anderson, in press, for a review of the explicit instruction model). This model centers around the **transfer of control** of the reading process from the teacher (the experienced reader) to the student (the naive reader), whether the student is a kindergartner or first grader learning to read his/her first primer, a fourth grader learning to comprehend content area textbooks, or a high school student learning to analyze literature. Pearson (1985) refers to this as the "gradual release of responsibility" for a task. The goal of instruction, then, is to set the stage and bring about this transfer of control of comprehension processes, not merely to assess students' comprehension ability.

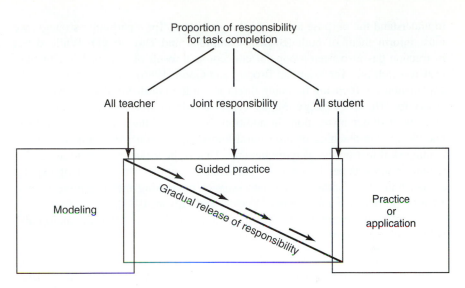

FIGURE 9
Proportion of responsibility for task completion.

Several concepts are key to this view of instruction. They are: explicit explanation, modeling, and scaffolding. Many of the instructional methods for the intervention studies mentioned in previous sections have some or all of the instructional characteristics to be discussed here. When appropriate, specific programs will be described as illustrations. An often-cited and helpful graphic of this framework is found in Pearson and Gallagher (1983, p. 337) and is reproduced in Figure 9.

The diagonal line on the graph represents the transition from total teacher responsibility (the far left) to total student responsibility (the far right). When the teacher is taking all or most of the responsibility for task completion, he or she is explaining or modeling the desired application of some strategy. When the student is taking all or most of the responsibility, he or she is independently applying that strategy. In between those two points comes the gradual release of responsibility from teacher to student.

Explicit Explanation Duffy, Roehler, and their colleagues' work (for example, Duffy and Roehler, 1987a; Duffy and Roehler, 1987b; Duffy, Roehler, and Hermann, 1988; Roehler and Duffy, 1986) has helped focus attention on the effects of teachers' explanations on students' metacognitive knowledge about the skills being taught in reading lessons. Included as part of an **explicit** explanation is (1) why the strategy should be learned, (2) **what** the strategy is, (3) **how** to use the strategy, (4) **when** and **where** the strategy is to be used, and (5) **how** to **evaluate** use of the strategy (Baumann and Schmitt, 1986; Duffy, Roehler, Meloth, and Vavrus, 1984; Hare and Winograd, in press). This is based on the assumption that students learn what they are taught; thus, if we wish them to understand the purpose as well as the procedures for a particular strategy, we must inform them of both (Brown, Campione and Day, 1981). While direct instruction has also been a popular concept as a result of the teacher effectiveness research (see for example, Brophy and Good, 1986) proponents of explicit explanation are focusing on being direct about the **conditional** knowledge necessary for effective strategy use, as well as the declarative and procedural components of direct instruction. In addition, because of the focus on conditional knowledge, the teaching of procedural knowledge, the usual fare of traditional reading skill instruction, is more flexible. That is, how one chooses to use a particular strategy depends upon the particular situation. This model of explicit explanation, then, addresses the necessity of possessing metacognitive knowledge for proficient reading (Paris, Wixson, and Lipson, 1983).

The following example of a lesson teaching students to "find the main idea" is illustrative of an explicit explanation:

> Finding the main idea means summarizing what you've read, deciding what's important in the piece of text. It's a helpful thing to learn to do because it can let you know if you're having trouble understanding the author. Sometimes we read on and on, and then find out that we aren't sure what we've read; we're not really comprehending or understanding what the author is trying to say. Taking the time to find the main idea, maybe after every paragraph when we're reading something with a lot of words that seem new, or maybe after every page, will help us discover problems so we can fix them.

After the above explanation, students would be introduced to **how** to find the main idea, not as an inflexible series of steps, but as a series of alternative ways to finding the main idea. The emphasis on the flexible use of strategies is what differentiates this model from the usual skill instruction. Students learn not only a flexible procedure but they understand why and when to use it. Additionally, students learn to evaluate the success of the strategy in terms of improving their comprehension of text.

Modeling   Teacher **modeling** of thinking processes is part of the explicit explanation model described above. Decisions made by the reader concerning strategy use are usually invisible and it is the task of the teacher to make these invisible processes visible for students. Duffy and Roehler refer to this as mental modeling while Palincsar and Brown speak of the teacher as a cognitive model. In neither case is the teacher merely modeling a correct answer, for example, "The main idea for this selection is . . .", or, "A good clarification question is. . . ." Rather, the teacher makes observable for students the thinking that leads to an answer or idea. When modeling "finding the main idea" the teacher might say,

> I want to be sure I have an idea about what I've read so far before I go on. Otherwise I might have trouble understanding what the author is trying to tell me later on. So I'm

going to summarize what I've read, or, state the main idea. One word that was repeated a lot in this piece of text was snakes so I know this was telling me something about snakes. Usually, when I think about snakes I think of snake **bites** but that was never mentioned here. Instead, the author described a lot of different places, sandy deserts, then mountains, then jungles. And the author mentioned the snakes that live there. So I think the main idea is that snakes live in a lot of different places. Places that are really dry and really cold or really hot and rainy. Yuck, I wonder if there are snakes in Michigan?

Similarly, in the Cognitive Strategy in Writing (CSIW) Project of the Institute for Research on Teaching (Englert, Raphael, Anderson, Anthony, Fear, and Gregg, in press) students learned to use informational text structures to guide their composing and comprehending of text. As part of the instruction, teachers developed "think-aloud" strategies to introduce students to different strategies related to text generation. One area in which thinking aloud played an important part was introducing students to strategies for selecting topics. The following think-aloud illustrates the instruction that occurred:

> I thought about some of the things that I did over Christmas vacation like opening presents, playing some games, cooking. I decided that I knew enough about all of these. Then I remembered how much we went cross country skiing and how good I got at it. I think I can explain it to someone else, and that it is something that other people would want to know about.

Scaffolding   Recently, there has been increased emphasis on the importance of developing *independent* readers, readers able to apply strategies learned across a variety of contexts. The term, scaffolded instruction, has been coined to underscore the **temporary, adjustable,** and **supportive** aspects of instruction. Like a scaffold, the teacher's role early in acquisition of new concepts is to provide the appropriate amount of support needed by the learner to implement a skill or strategy. Over time, the teacher makes deliberate attempts to release task responsibility to the students, gradually reducing, adjusting, and eventually removing the support initially provided. Recall that studies of existing comprehension instruction (i.e., Durkin, 1978–79, 1981) revealed that teachers used basals and worksheets in such a way as to give students "massive doses of unguided practice" (Pearson, 1984b, p. 226). The notion of scaffolding is in direct contrast to this. Guided practice is a dynamic and interactive process between teacher and students. As such, it is the most unpredictable part of the explicit instruction model and the most difficult to explain (Pearson and Dole, 1987).

One of the clearest examples of scaffolded instruction is seen in reciprocal teaching. There are several key features of reciprocal teaching which contribute to this. First, students are reading existing text to comprehend an entire selection. The task is not broken into smaller pieces; rather, the teacher helps reduce the students' load through guiding the students' question asking, predicting, and so forth. Thus, the task is essentially identical to what students will do independently at some future point.

A second key feature is that each student in the group takes a turn at being "teacher" to use the strategies of summarizing, question asking, clarifying, and predicting. Thus, individual and group feedback occurs throughout the lesson in support of the students' application of learned strategies. Third, reciprocal teaching depends on dialogue around the students' strategy use (Palincsar, 1986). Through the dialogue the teacher assesses the student's understanding of and ability to use each strategy. Depending on the student's response, the teacher may ask another question, clarify the strategy by giving an example, partially perform the task for the student, and let him or her finish it, etc. For example, after the group has received explicit explanation for summarizing (presented as a "finding the main idea" task above), and the teacher has modeled his/her thinking about this strategy, the students are ready to use the strategy with guidance. If a student is playing teacher and is unable to summarize the piece of text just read about how humans living in space need life support systems, the teacher might ask specifically, "What kind of city is being described here? Is it like your neighborhood or is it like a city in the Old West, like we read about last week?" Or she may ask more generally, "Is there any word or words that you read several times in different sentences?" Gradually, the teacher leads the student to correctly summarize the text, providing prompts and referring back to the initial explanation when appropriate. This dialogue allows teacher to respond to individual differences in students' understanding for each of the strategies taught.

Similarly, through analyses of transcripts of small-group reading lessons, Roehler and Duffy (1986) found that the most successful explicit teachers use interactive or mediated instruction, an activity the researchers refer to as "responsive elaboration." In responsive elaboration, teachers engage in many specific activities, such as questioning, assessing student understanding, and elaborating and clarifying concepts (e.g., giving examples of analogies as well as further explanation). These teacher-student interactions, therefore, are very much like those observed in the dialogues of teachers using reciprocal teaching.

Some of the instructional interventions mentioned previously have made use of support materials as well as dialogue to help students internalize and use strategies effectively. Ogle (1986; 1987) has developed a worksheet for her K-W-L program (similar to Wong and Au's C-T-A program) to help students use effective strategies while reading a piece of informational text. For example, students prepare for reading by having a discussion and then filling in their "What I Know" and "What I Want To Learn" sections of their paper. The "What I Learned" section triggers students to take notes while reading or to summarize after reading, the ideas from the text. In the K-W-L PLUS version, students are helped to develop understanding of text organization. First, students categorize the information listed under their "What I Learned" section. For example, after reading about a particular animal a student may place a D next to all the statements that are descriptions or an L next to statements about location. These categories are then used to construct a map with the explanatory details listed under the category headings. In this way, the information on the worksheet assists or scaffolds students in constructing their map, which can then be used as an aid for writing a summary.

Thus, while current research suggests that there are severe limitations in terms of current materials used to teach students to read, we are fortunate to have a wealth of information about effective instruction that transcends the use of a particular set of instructional materials.

CONCLUDING REMARKS

In our review, we have attempted to provide insight from current research that identifies ways in which readers, text, and context interact and influence children's comprehension of text. What is clear is that while much is known about the comprehension process and important instructional features related to comprehension instruction, there still exist wide gaps between our current knowledge and ongoing practice. What is also clear is that teachers and teacher educators have the knowledge available to make large-scale reform in terms of both materials and instruction. Teachers who are knowledgeable about the research described in this review can make significant changes in the nature of reading comprehension instruction. In fact, there are a growing number of places where such change has occurred, for example, the Benchmark School in Media, Pennsylvania (Gaskins, in press; Samuels and Pearson, 1988); the Kamehameha Early Education Program in Honolulu, Hawaii (Tharp, 1982); and the Content Reading Instruction and Study Strategies program in Kalispell, Montana (Samuels and Pearson, 1988). Increased knowledge can also provide the support for those in influential positions such as curriculum adoption committees who wish to see better materials available for use in classrooms. Finally, teacher educators have both the power and the means to empower our teachers and, in turn, their students, to become independent readers and critical thinkers as they read a variety of materials, in a variety of contexts, and for a variety of purposes.

REFERENCES

Ahlfors, G. (1980). Learning word meanings: A comparison of three instructional procedures (Doctoral dissertation, University of Minnesota). *Dissertation Abstracts International, 40,* 5803–A.

Allington, R. L. (1983). The reading instruction provided readers of differing reading abilities. *Elementary School Journal, 83,* 548–559.

Anderson, L. M. (in press). Classroom instruction. In M. Reynolds (Ed.), *The knowledge base for the beginning teacher.* New York: Pergamon Press.

Anderson, L. M., N. Brubaker, J. Alleman-Brooks, and G. Duffy. (1985) A qualitative study of seatwork in first grade classrooms. *Elementary School Journal, 86*(2), 123–140.

Anderson, R. C. and D. P. Pearson. (1984). A schema-theoretic view of basic processes in reading comprehension. In P. D. Pearson (Ed.), *Handbook of reading research.* New York: Longman.

Anderson, R. C., and P. Freebody. (1981). Vocabulary knowledge. In J. T. Guthrie (Ed.), *Comprehension and teaching: Research reviews.* Newark, DE: International Reading Association.

Anderson, R. C., J. Osborn, and R. J. Tierney (Eds.). (1984). *Learning to read in American schools.* Hillsdale, NJ: Erlbaum.

Anderson, R. C., E. H. Hiebert, J. A. Scott, and I. A. Wilkinson. (1984). *Becoming a nation of readers: The report of the commission on reading.* Washington, D.C.: U.S. Department of Education, National Institution of Education.

Anderson, R. C., R. E. Reynolds, D. L. Schallert, and E. T. Goetz. (1977). Frameworks for comprehending discourse. *American Journal of Educational Research, 14,* 367–381.

Anderson, T. H., and B. B. Armbruster. (1984). Content area textbooks. In R. C. Anderson, J. Osborn, and R. J. Tierney (Eds.), *Learning to read in American schools.* Hillsdale, NJ: Erlbaum.

Armbruster, B. B. (1984). The problem of "inconsiderate text." In *Comprehension instruction: Perspectives and suggestions.* New York: Longman.

Armbruster, B. B., and B. Gunbrandsen. (1986). Reading comprehension instruction in social studies. *Reading Research Quarterly, 21,* 36–48.

Armbruster, B. B., T. H. Anderson, and J. Ostertaj. (1987). Does text structure/summarization instruction facilitate learning from expository text? *Reading Research Quarterly, 22,* 331–346.

Au, K. H. (1979). Using the experience-text-relationship with minority children. *The Reading Teacher, 32,* 677–679.

Au, K. H-P, and C. Jordan. (1981). Teaching reading to Hawaiian children: Finding a culturally appropriate solution. In H. T. Treuba, G. P. Guthrie, and K. H-P. Au (Eds.), *Culture and the bilingual classroom: Studies in classroom ethnography.* Rowley, MA: Newbury House.

Au, K. H., and A. J. Kawakami. (1986). Influence of the social organization of instruction on children's text comprehension ability: A Vygotskian perspective. In T. E. Raphael (Ed.), *The contexts of school based literacy.* New York: Random House.

Au, K. H., and J. M. Mason. (1981). Social organization factors in learning to read: The balance of rights hypothesis. *Reading Research Quarterly, 17,* 115–152.

Baumann, J. F., and M. C. Schmitt. (1986). The what, why, how, and when of comprehension instruction. *The Reading Teacher, 39,* 640–646.

Beck, I. L., and M. G. McKeowen. (1981). Developing questions that promote comprehension. *Language Arts, 58,* 913–918.

———. (1987). Getting the most from basal reading selections. *Elementary School Journal, 87,* 343–356.

Beck, I. L., M. G. McKeowen, R. C. Omanson, and M. T. Pople. (1984). Improving the comprehensibility of stories: The effects of revisions that improve coherence. *Reading Research Quarterly, 19,* 263–277.

Beck, I. L., C. A. Perfetti, and M. G. McKeowen. (1982). Effects of long-term vocabulary instruction on lexical access and reading comprehension. *Journal of Educational Psychology, 75,* 506–521.

Berkowitz, S. J. (1986). Effects of instruction in text organization on sixth-grade students' memory for expository reading. *Reading Research Quarterly, 21,* 161–178.

Bransford, J. D. (1979). *Human Cognition.* Belmont, CA: Wadsworth.

Bransford, J. D., and M. K. Johnson. (1972). Contextual prerequisites for understanding: Some investigations of comprehension and recall. *Journal of Verbal Learning and Verbal Behavior, 11,* 717–726.

Bransford, J. D., and N. S. McCarrell. (1974). A sketch of a cognitive approach to comprehension. In W. Weimer and D. Palermo (Eds.), *Cognition and the symbolic processes.* Hillsdale, NJ: Erlbaum.

Bransford, J. D., B. S. Stein, T. S. Shelton, and R. A. Owings. (1981). Cognition and adaptation: The importance of learning to learn. In J. Harvey (Ed.), *Cognition, social behavior, and the environment.* Hillsdale, NJ: Erlbaum.

Brennan, A. D., C. A. Bridge, and P. N. Winograd. (1986). The effects of structural variation on children's recall of basal reader stories. *Reading Research Quarterly, 21,* 91–104.

Brophy, J., and T. L. Good. (1986). Teacher behavior and student achievement. In M. C. Wittrock (Ed.), *Handbook of research on teaching.* New York: Macmillan.

Brown, A. L., and A. S. Palincsar. (1985). *Reciprocal teaching of comprehension strategies: A natural history of one program for enhancing learning* (Technical Report No. 334). Champaign, IL: University of Illinois, Center for the Study of Reading.

Brown, A. L., J. C. Campione, and J. D. Day. (1981). Learning to learn: On training students to learn from text. *Educational Researcher, 10*(2), 14–21.

Cattell, J. M. (1886). The time taken up by cerebral operations. *Mind, 11,* 220–242.

Cooper, J. D. (1986). *Improving reading comprehension.* Boston, MA: Houghton Mifflin.

DeFord, D. E. (1986). Classroom contexts for literacy learning. In T. E. Raphael (Ed.), *The contexts for school-based literacy.* New York: Random House.

Duffy, G. G., and L. R. Roehler. (1987a). Teaching reading skills as strategies. *Reading Teacher, 40,* 414–418.

———. (1987b). Improving reading instruction through the use of responsive elaboration. *Reading Teacher, 40,* 514–520.

Duffy, G. G., L. R. Roehler, and B. A. Hermann. (1988). Modeling mental processes helps poor readers become strategic readers. *Reading Teacher, 41,* 762–767.

Duffy, G. G., L. Roehler, and J. Mason. (1984). (Eds.). *Comprehension instruction: Perspectives and suggestions.* New York: Longman.

Duffy, G. G., L. R. Roehler, M. S. Meloth, and L. G. Vavrus. (1986). Conceptualizing instructional explanation. *Teaching and Teacher Education, 2,* 197–214.

Duffy, G. G., L. R. Roehler, M. S. Meloth, L. G. Vavrus, C. Book, J. Putnam, and R. Wesselman. (1986). The relationship between explicit verbal explanations during reading skill instruction and student awareness and achievement: A study of reading teacher effects. *Reading Research Quarterly, 21*(3), 237–322.

Duffy, G. G., L. R. Roehler, E. Sivan, G. Rackliffe, C. Book, M. S. Meloth, L. G. Vavrus, R. Wesselman, J. Putnam, and D. Bassiri. (1987). Effects of explaining the reasoning associated with using reading strategies. *Reading Research Quarterly, 22,* 347–368.

Durkin, D. (1978–1979). What classroom observations reveal about comprehension instruction. *Reading Research Quarterly, 14,* 481–533.

———. (1981). Reading comprehension instruction in five basal reader series. *Reading Research Quarterly, 16,* 515–544.

———. (1984). Is there a match between what elementary teachers do and what basal reader manuals recommend? *Reading Teacher, 37,* 334–344.

Englert, C. S., and E. H. Hiebert. (1984). Children's developing awareness of text structures in expository materials. *Journal of Educational Psychology, 76,* 65–75.

Englert, C. S., T. E. Raphael, L. M. Anderson, H. M. Anthony, K. Fear, and S. L. Gregg. (in press). Establishing a case for writing intervention: The what and why of expository writing. *Learning Disability Focus.*

Evans, B. (1981). Preteaching vocabulary from superordinate propositions. Paper presented at the meeting of the National Reading Conference, Dallas.

Fitzgerald, J. (1984). The relationship between reading ability and expectations for story structures. *Discourse Processes, 7,* 21–41.

Fitzgerald, J., and D. L. Spiegel. (1983). Enhancing children's reading comprehension through instruction in narrative structure. *Journal of Reading Behavior, 15,* 1–17.

Flavell, J. H. (1979). Metacognition and cognitive monitoring: A new area of cognitive-developmental inquiry. *American Psychologist, 34,* 906–911.

Flood, J., D. Lapp, and N. Farnan. (1986). A reading-writing procedure that teaches expository paragraph structure. *Reading Teacher, 39,* 556–562.

Gallagher, M. C., and P. D. Pearson. (1982). *An examination of expository texts in elementary instructional materials.* National Reading Conference, Clearwater, FL.

Garner, R. (1987). *Metacognition and reading comprehension.* Norwood, NJ: Ablex Publishing.

———. (1980). Monitoring of understanding: An investigation of good and poor readers' awareness of induced miscomprehension of text. *Journal of Reading Behavior, 12,* 159–162.

Garner, R., and C. Kraus, (1981–82). Good and poor comprehender differences in knowing and regulating reading behaviors. *Educational Research Quarterly, 16,* 569–582.

Garner, R., and R. Reis, (1981). Monitoring and resolving comprehension obstacles: An investigation of spontaneous lookbacks among upper-grade good and poor comprehenders. *Reading Research Quarterly, 16,* 569–582.

Garner, R., S. Wagoner, and T. Smith. (1983). Externalizing question-answering strategies of good and poor comprehenders. *Reading Research Quarterly, 18,* 439–447.

Gaskins, I. (in press). *Perspectives on the reading disabled.* Newark, DE: International Reading Association.

Gavelek, J. R. (1986). The social contexts of literacy and schooling: A developmental perspective. In T. E. Raphael (Ed.), *The contexts of school based literacy.* New York: Random House.

Goodman, K. S. (1976). Behind the eye: What happens in reading. In H. Singer and R. B. Ruddell (Eds.), *Theoretical models and processes of reading.* Newark, DE: International Reading Association.

Gordon, C. J., and C. Braun. (1983). Using story schemata as an aid to reading and writing. *Reading Teacher, 37,* 116–121.

Gough, P. B. (1972). One second of reading. In J. F. Kavanaugh and I. G. Mattingly (Eds.), *Language by ear and eye.* Cambridge, MA: MIT Press.

Hansen, J., and D. P. Pearson. (1983). An instructional study: Improving the inferential comprehension of good and poor fourth-grade readers. *Journal of Reading, 26,* 594–598.

Heath, S. B. (1982). Questioning at home and at school: A comparative study. In G. Spindler (Ed.), *Doing ethnography of schooling: Educational anthropology in action.* New York: Holt, Rinehart & Winston.

Huey, E. B. (1908). *The psychology and pedagogy of reading.* Cambridge: MIT Press. (reprinted, 1968).

Johnston, P. H. (1983). *Reading comprehension assessment: A cognitive basis.* Newark, DE.: International Reading Association.

Kaameenui, E. J., D. W. Carnine, and R. Freschi. (1982). Effects of text construction and instructional procedures for teaching word meanings on comprehension and recall. *Reading Research Quarterly, 17,* 367–388.

LaBerge, D., and S. J. Samuels. (1974). Toward a theory of automatic information processing in reading. *Cognitive Psychology, 6,* 293–323.

Langer, J. A. (1982). Facilitating text processing: The elaboration of prior knowledge. In J. A. Langer and M. Smith-Burke (Eds.), *Reader meets author/bridging the gap: A psycholinguistic and sociolinguistic perspective.* Newark, DE: International Reading Association.

———. (1984). Examining background knowledge and text comprehension. *Reading Research Quarterly, 19,* 468–481.

Langer, J. A., and M. Nicolich. (1981). Prior knowledge and its effects on comprehension. *Journal of Reading Behavior, 13,* 373–379.

Lipson, M. Y. (1982). Learning new information from text: The role of prior knowledge and reading ability. *Journal of Reading Behavior, 14,* 243–261.

———. (1983). The influence of religious affiliation on children's memory for text information. *Reading Research Quarterly, 18,* 448–457.

Lipson, M. Y., and K. K. Wixson. (1986). Reading disability research: An interactionist perspective. *Review of Educational Research, 56,* 11–136.

Mandl, H., N. L. Stein, and T. Trabasso. (Eds.) (1984). *Learning and comprehension of text.* Hillsdale, NJ: Erlbaum.

Mandler, J. M., and M. S. Johnson. (1977). Remembrance of things past: Story structure and recall. *Cognitive Psychology, 9,* 11–151.

Marr, M. B., and K. Gormley. (1982). Children's recall of familiar and unfamiliar text. *Reading Research Quarterly, 18*(1), 89–104.

McGee, L. M. (1982). Awareness of text structure: Effects on children's recall of expository text. *Reading Research Quarterly, 17,* 581–590.

McGee, L. M., and D. J. Richgels. (1985). Teaching expository text structure to elementary students. *Reading Teacher, 38,* 739–748.

McKeown, M. G., I. L. Beck, R. C. Omanson, and C. A. Perfetti. (1983). The effects of long-term vocabulary instruction on reading comprehension: A replication. *Journal of Reading Behavior, 15,* 3–18.

McKeown, M. G., I. L. Beck, R. C. Omanson, and M. T. Pople. (1985). Some effects of the nature and frequency of vocabulary instruction on the knowledge and use of words. *Reading Research Quarterly, 20,* 522–535.

McNeil, J. D. (1987). *Reading comprehension.* Glenview, IL: Scott, Foresman.

Meyer, B. J. F. (1975). *The organization of prose and its effect on memory.* Amsterdam: North Holland Publishing.

Meyer, B. J. F., and G. E. Rice. (1984). The structure of text. In P. D. Pearson (Ed.), *Handbook of reading research.* New York: Longman.

Meyer, B. J. F., D. M. Brandt, and G. J. Bluth. (1980). Use of top-level structure in text: Key for reading comprehension of ninth grade students. *Reading Research Quarterly, 16,* 72–103.

Myers, M., and S. G. Paris. (1978). Children's metacognitive knowledge about reading. *Journal of Educational Psychology, 70,* 680–690.

Neilsen, A. R., B. Rennie, and B. J. Connell. (1982). Allocation of instructional time to reading comprehension and study skills in intermediate grade social studies classrooms. In J. A. Niles and L. A. Harris (Eds.), *New inquiries in reading research and instruction. Thirty-first yearbook of the National Reading Conference.* Rochester, NY: National Reading Conference.

Ogle, D. M. (1986). K-W-L-: A teaching model that develops active reading of expository text. *Reading Teacher, 39,* 564–570.

———. (1987). K-W-L Plus: A strategy for comprehension and summarization. *Reading Teacher, 41,* 626–631.

Oransanu, J. (1985). *Reading comprehension: From research to practice.* Hillsdale, NJ: Erlbaum.

Osborn, J. (1984a). The purposes, uses and contents of workbooks and some guidelines for publishers. In R. C. Anderson, J. Osborn, and R. J. Tierney (Eds.), *Learning to read in American schools.* Hillsdale, NJ: Erlbaum.

———. (1984b). Workbooks that accompany basal reading programs. In G. Duffy, L. Roehler, and J. Mason (Eds.), *Comprehension instruction: Perspectives and suggestions.* New York: Longman.

Palincsar, A. S. (1986). The role of dialogue in scaffolded instruction. *Educational Psychologist, 21,* 73–98.

Palincsar, A. S., and A. L. Brown. (1984). Reciprocal teaching of comprehension-fostering and comprehension-monitoring activities. *Cognition and Instruction, 1,* 117–175.

———. (1986). Interactive teaching to promote independent learning from text. *Reading Teacher, 39,* 771–777.

Pany, D., and J. R. Jenkins. (1978). Learning word meanings: A comparison of instructional procedures and effects on measures of reading comprehension with learning disabled students. *Learning Disabled Quarterly, 1,* 21–32.

Paris, S. G. (1986). Teaching children to guide their reading and learning. In T. E. Raphael (Ed.), *The contexts of school-based literacy.* New York: Random House.

Paris, S. G., D. R. Cross, and M. Y. Lipson. (1984). Informed strategies for learning: A program to improve children's reading awareness and comprehension. *Journal of Educational Psychology, 76,* 1239–1252.

Paris, S. G., M. Y. Lipson, and K. K. Wixson. (1983). Becoming a strategic reader. *Contemporary Educational Psychology, 8,* 293–316.

Paris, S. G., and M. Myers. (1981). Comprehension monitoring, memory, and study strategies of good and poor readers. *Journal of Reading Behavior, 13,* 5–22.

Pearson, P. D. (1986). Twenty years of research in reading comprehension. In T. E. Raphael (Ed.), *The contexts of school-based literacy.* New York: Random House.

————. (Ed.) (1984a). *Handbook of reading research.* New York: Longman.

————. (1984b). Direct explicit teaching of reading comprehension. In G. G. Duffy, L. R. Roehler, and J. Mason (Eds.), *Comprehension instruction: Perspectives and suggestions.* New York: Longman.

————. (1985).Changing the face of comprehension instruction. *Reading Teacher, 38,* 724–738.

Pearson, P. D., and J. A. Dole. (1987). Explicit comprehension instruction: A review of research and a new conceptualization of instruction. *Elementary School Journal, 88,* 151–165.

Pearson, P. D., and M. C. Gallagher. (1983). The instruction of reading comprehension. *Contemporary Educational Psychology, 8,* 317–344.

Pearson, P. D., J. Hansen, and C. Gordon. (1979). The effect of background knowledge on young children's comprehension of explicit and implicit information. *Journal of Reading Behavior, 11,* 201–209.

Pearson, P. D., and S. Valencia. (1987). Assessment, accountability, and professional prerogative. In J. E. Readence and R. Scott Baldwin (Eds.), *Research in literacy: Merging perspectives.* Rochester, NY: National Reading Conference.

Phillips, S. U. (1972). Participant structures and communicative competence: Warm Springs children in community and classroom. In C. B. Cazden, U. P. John, and D. Hymes (Eds.), *Functions of language in the classroom.* New York: Teachers College Press.

Pritzhard, R. H. (1987). *The effects of cultural schemata on proficient readers' comprehension monitoring strategies and their comprehension of culturally familiar and unfamiliar passages.* Unpublished doctoral dissertation, Indiana University, Indiana.

Raphael, T. E., and B. M. Kirschner. (1985). *The effects of instruction in compare/contrast text structure on sixth-grade students' reading comprehension and writing products* (Research Series No. 161). East Lansing: Michigan State University, Institute for Research on Teaching.

Raphael, T. E., C. S. Englert, and B. W. Kirschner. (1986). *The impact of text structure instruction and social context on students' comprehension and production of expository text* (Research Series No. 177). East Lansing: Michigan State University, Institute for Research on Teaching.

Richgels, D. J., L. M. McGee, R. G. Lomax, and C. Sheard. (1987). Awareness of four text structures: Effects on recall of expository text. *Reading Research Quarterly, 22,* 177–196.

Roehler, L. R., and G. G. Duffy. (1986). Studying qualitative dimensions of instructional effectiveness. In J. V. Hoffman (Ed.), *Effective teaching of reading: Research and practice.* Newark, DE: International Reading Association.

Roehler, L. R., G. G. Duffy, and M. S. Meloth. (1986). What to be direct about in direct instruction in reading. In T. E. Raphael (Ed.), *Contexts of school-based literacy.* New York: Random House.

Rumelhart, D. E. (1977). Toward an interactive model of reading. In H. Singer and R. B. Ruddell (Eds.), *Theoretical models and processes of reading.* Newark, DE: International Reading Association.

Samuels, S. J., and P. D. Pearson. (1988). (Eds.), *Changing school reading programs,* Newark, DE: International Reading Association.

Santa, C. (1988). Changing teacher behavior in content reading through collaborative research. In S. J. Samuels and P. D. Pearson (Eds.), *Changing school reading programs: Principles' and case studies.* Newark, DE: International Reading Association.

Schallert, D., and R. Tierney. (1982). *Learning from expository text: The interaction of text structure with reader characteristics* (Grant NIE-G-79-0167). Washington, DC: National Institute of Education.

Shannon, P. (1983). The use of commercial reading materials in American elementary schools. *Reading Research Quarterly, 19,* 68–85.

Singer, H., and P. Donlan. (1982). Problem-solving schema with question generation for comprehension of complex short stories. *Reading Research Quarterly, 17,* 166–186.

Smith, F. (1971). *Understanding reading.* NY: Holt, Rinehart & Winston.

———. (1978). *Understanding reading: A psycholinguistic analysis of reading and learning to read.* New York: Holt, Reinhart & Winston.

Spiegel, D. L., and J. Fitzgerald. (1986). Improving reading comprehension through instruction about story parts. *Reading Teacher, 7,* 676–682.

Spiro, R. J., B. C. Bruce, and W. F. Brewer. (1980). (Eds.) *Theoretical issues in reading comprehension.* Hillsdale, NJ: Erlbaum.

Stahl, S. (1983). Differential word knowledge and reading comprehension. *Journal of Reading Behavior, 15,* 33–50.

Stanovich, K. E. (1980). Toward an interactive-compensatory model of individual differences in the development of reading fluency. *Reading Research Quarterly, 16,* 32–71.

Stauffer, R. (1969). *Reading as a thinking process.* New York: HarperCollins.

Steffensen, M. S., C. Joag-Dev, and R. C. Anderson. (1979). A cross-cultural perspective on reading comprehension. *Reading Research Quarterly, 15,* 10–29.

Stein, N. L., and C. G. Glenn. (1979). An analysis of story comprehension in elementary children. In R. O. Freedle (Ed.), *New directions in discourse processing.* Norwood, NJ: Ablex.

Stevens, K. C. (1982). Can we improve reading by teaching background information? *Journal of Reading, 25,* 326–329.

Taylor, B. (1980). Children's memory of text after reading. *Reading Research Quarterly, 15,* 399–411.

———. (1982). Text structure and children's comprehension and memory for expository material. *Journal of Educational Psychology, 74,* 323–340.

Taylor, B., and R. Beach. (1984). The effects of text structure instruction on middle grade students' comprehension and production of expository text. *Reading Research Quarterly, 19,* 134–146.

Taylor, B. M., and S. Berkowitz. (1980). Facilitating children's comprehension of content material. In M. L. Kamil and A. J. Moe (Eds.), *Perspectives on reading research and instruction. Twenty-ninth yearbook of the National Reading Conference.* Washington, DC: National Reading Conference.

Tharp, R. G. (1982). The effective instruction of comprehension: Results and description of the Kamehameha Early Education Program. *Reading Research Quarterly, 17,* 503–527.

Thorndike, E. L. (1917). Reading as reasoning: A study of mistakes in paragraph reading. *Journal of Educational Psychology, 8,* 323–332.

Winograd, P., and V. C. Hare. (in press). Direct instruction of reading comprehension strategies: The nature of teacher explanation. In E. Goetz, P. Alexander, and C.

Weinstein (Eds.), *Learning and study strategies: Issues in assessment, instruction and evaluation.* Hillsdale, NJ: Erlbaum.

Winograd, P., K. K. Wixson, and M. Y. Lipson. (in press). (Eds.), *Expanding perspectives on basal reading instruction.* New York: Teacher's College Press.

Wittrock, M. C. (Ed.). (1985). *Handbook of research on teaching.* New York: Macmillan.

Wixson, K. K. (1986). Vocabulary instruction and children's comprehension of basal stories. *Reading Research Quarterly, 21,* 317–329.

Wixson, K. K., and C. W. Peters. (1984). Reading redefined: A Michigan Reading Association position paper. *The Michigan Reading Journal, 17,* 4–7.

Wong, J. A., and K. H. Au. (1985). The Concept-Text-Application approach: Helping elementary students comprehend expository text. *Reading Teacher, 38,* 612–618.

The Act of Reading

Margaret Early and Bonnie O. Ericson

Reading used to be the primary channel for the intake of literature. Today, film and television challenge the primacy of reading in the lives of many adults. In school, however, reading remains the chief medium through which teachers and students engage literature. How students read is therefore a major concern for all teachers of literature.

About fifteen years ago, spurred by developments in cognitive psychology and studies of language acquisition, reading researchers shifted their attention from the results of reading instruction to the act of reading itself. They asked how readers at different levels comprehend texts of various kinds. Readers' answers to questions became less important to researchers than tracing the thought processes that led to these answers. Sometimes readers' answers, especially unexpected ones, gave researchers clues that they might pursue further or provided support for notions or theories about what happens when readers understand written messages. Painstaking and expensive, this new research in reading is more likely to yield detailed case studies than to amass solid statistical "proof." Naturally, many gaps need to be filled when studies concentrate on individuals' thought processes. Nevertheless, even at this stage, research examining the reading process has freshened teachers' understanding of how their students read literature even as it has affirmed inferences and intuitions stemming from their own experiences and from their knowledge of literary theory.

Teachers of literature find that the new research in reading supports many ideas they have long subscribed to. At the same time, it renews and refreshes, suggesting altered emphases, variations, even changes in direction. Nor is this surprising, since reading researchers and teachers of literature frequently hold ideas in common, although they label them differently. For example, where reading teachers talk about "structured overviews," teachers of literature may talk of "setting up points of connection" or "imaginative entry." Yet both groups are concerned with helping students bring what they already know (prior knowledge) to bear upon a new reading task.

As reading researchers learn more about how readers comprehend, they become more aware, too, of the writer's share in the act of reading. "Text" becomes an integral factor in the complex process of reading, and researchers ask how "considerate" the text is of the reader. Today's teachers, too, are careful to avoid statements about how well Johnny reads. Reads *what* is the issue. And under what conditions. Researchers have therefore added the issue of *context* to the study of readers and texts. In what kinds of classrooms, schools, communities and with what kinds of instruction are readers learning? How do teachers' explanations, directions, expectations affect how readers comprehend?

In this chapter, then, we organize our comments around three pivots of current reading research: reader, text, and context. This is not a review of that research, however; citations will be eclectic and sparse. Instead, we shall present research-based generalizations, widely accepted by scholars in reading in this decade, that influence how we teach literature.

1. Readers Make Meanings. To Do So They Use (1) Their Knowledge of the World and (2) the Cues Supplied by the Text.

Of all the new, or renewed, insights coming out of recent reading research, the impact of prior knowledge on comprehension is the one that speaks loudest to teachers of literature. More than other kinds of text, literature draws on the reader's prior knowledge: of people and places, of historical periods and cultures, of spoken and written language, of human nature, of story grammar and literary forms, to name but a few categories.

The concept of prior knowledge derives from schema theory, which hypothesizes that a person's knowledge of the world is stored in interconnected structures called schemata (Rumelhart 1980). Readers use their schemata in comprehending what they are reading, in making predictions during reading, and in remembering what they have read. What readers of *To Kill a Mockingbird* understand about the courtroom scenes depends to a large degree on what they know about—that is, their schema for—court trials. Similarly, readers of Steinbeck's *The Red Pony* rely on schemata for ranch life, parent-son relationships, and horses.

Schema theory hypothesizes two complementary processes: readers fit new information from the text into existing schemata (they "fill in the slots"), and they modify their existing schemata to accommodate information in the text that otherwise would not fit. How well readers manage these processes of assimilation and accommodation determines how closely their reconstruction of the text's meaning corresponds to that of other readers and perhaps to the meanings intended by the writer of the text. Thus the teacher's role is to activate students' prior knowledge of, say, a particular time and place or of how people act under certain circumstances. The teacher has two reasons for prereading discussions: first, to help students marshal their resources; second, to test out gaps in prior knowledge that might better be filled before reading than after confusion sets in.

[handwritten margin note: most important step in aiding learners comprehension]

A teacher in middle school, anticipating the reading of *My Brother Sam is Dead,* invited her students to talk about life in colonial America on the eve of the Revolution. She found that many of them peopled that era with cowboys, Indians, and gunfighters seen on television. Colonial New England was a long way from contemporary Kansas, and eighth-grade social studies had not modified existing schemata as much as the English teacher had assumed. She had, however, identified gaps she could fill with pictures, maps, a timeline, filmstrips, and films; with short, easy books she could recommend to individuals; and with essential information she herself could present. Even more important than knowledge of the setting in understanding this short novel is sensitivity to the feelings engendered by family relationships. The teacher focused attention on these feelings by introducing brief role-playing sessions. For some readers, this novel's chief value is its information on the American Revolution; for others, the novel provides a strong emotional and aesthetic experience. Most young readers would place themselves variously on Louise Rosenblatt's continuum from aesthetic to efferent if they were to define their purposes in her terms (Rosenblatt 1978, pp. 22–47).

[handwritten margin note: Prereading tools]

An important aspect of prior knowledge is the students' familiarity with language patterns and modes of discourse. Good readers anticipate words and phrases because they are familiar with how twentieth century language works, as well as with many of the ideas conveyed in that language. (Research into comprehension processes using *cloze* techniques—having students supply words systematically deleted from statements—confirms that skillful readers add to their prior knowledge as they read, picking up clues that lead them to make accurate predictions of what is coming next.) Texts from another century, however, may limit even good readers' ability to predict and thus slow down their rate of comprehension.

In addition to schemata for vocabulary and concepts, readers also have schemata, or sets of knowledge and expectations, for literary forms (Applebee 1978; Ericson 1985; Galda 1982; Mauro 1984) and for the role of the reader. For example, students' expectations for fiction develop from their earliest experiences with stories heard, seen on television, and read on their own. Similarly, they have expectations for poetry, some of them negative and erroneous.

Expectations for literary form and attitudes toward authors' purposes and the students' own purposes in reading influence the quality of comprehension.

Frank Smith's description of the reading process (1978) distinguishes two sources of information, visual and nonvisual. Visual information is what a reader's eye can see and send to the brain—the words printed on a page. Nonvisual information is what a reader already knows and relates to the material being read. If a reader has more of one type of information, less of the other is needed for comprehension—within limits. Too little of either visual or nonvisual information results in the breakdown of comprehension. (This is one explanation of the varying success the same student may have in reading contemporary and historical texts.)

We have all seen students struggle with sentences such as these from Edgar Allan Poe's "The Cask of Amontillado": "I must not only punish, but punish with impunity. A wrong is unredressed when retribution overtakes its redresser." With such sentences, difficulties in decoding the unfamiliar vocabulary may force students to attend primarily to visual information to such an extent that they are unable to use the nonvisual at the same time. What can the teacher do to prevent or remedy such bottlenecks? One tactic, of course, is to choose texts that match as closely as possible either students' present level of vocabulary development or their willingness to struggle for meaning. Another is to preteach essential vocabulary before assigning essential reading and to bolster students' perseverance through interest-inducing prereading activities. Even more effective over the long term will be carefully paced and invigorating instruction in vocabulary keyed to students' needs and interests. Both recent and long-familiar research studies have shown that excellent teaching of vocabulary can facilitate comprehension. Literature offers rich sources for vocabulary development, more so than do most other subjects in the curriculum, to the extent that the vocabulary is nontechnical and widely applicable.

2. The Best Way to Learn to Read Is by Reading

Reduced almost to a slogan, this finding from research on beginning reading is a powerful reminder to teachers of literature in the upper grades of the importance of wide reading. Like any slogan, this one oversimplifies, but its truth is self-evident when we examine profiles of students who demonstrated mastery of higher order reading skills on the National Assessment of Educational Progress (1981). These students were the ones who read widely, choosing books of fiction and nonfiction beyond those required in school.

The impact of prior knowledge on comprehension tells us why students learn to read by reading. To acquire sufficient prior knowledge to read new texts easily, students must read widely because only a fraction of knowledge about the world can come from other experiences in their short lives. Since prior knowledge includes familiarity with varying modes of discourse as well as with concepts and their labels, we realize why students who do not read (even though they have no trouble with decoding words) are severely handicapped when required to approach literature (especially that selected by others) through reading on their own.

The implications for teachers of literature are obvious. Particularly in the middle grades and early secondary years, the balance between in-common reading and individualized reading must favor the latter. In-common reading selected by the teacher and directed toward familiarizing students with literary concepts and forms and with developing literary sensibilities must be relatively brief. Personal reading, guided by a teacher who knows the student's reading abilities, attitudes, and interests, must occupy a large share of time in class and out of class. Organized around themes, such reading contributes to common goals and is by no means unstructured and random. What is being argued for here, of course, is the thematic unit, supported in research and theory for more than sixty years and still widely ignored by teachers, publishers, and curriculum makers.

Because children and adolescents learn to read by reading, a literature program that embraces wide reading is most likely to lead to goals long cherished by teachers. That students enjoy reading is prerequisite to establishing lifetime reading habits that include literature. But beyond acquiring a habit of turning to books, students who read widely go on learning how to interpret literary works reasonably. They may also learn to respond fully to a range of literature. Without the experience of reading widely throughout their school years, students are unlikely to reach any of these three interlocking goals.

3. To Make Meanings, Readers Need to Experience the Whole Text

This insight from research on beginning reading also has implications for teachers at later stages. To reading teachers in primary grades, it is an injunction against too much attention to isolated skills and too little attention to the holistic process that combines many skills and strategies. To literature teachers, who are also concerned with the way their students make meanings, this research finding says: Focus on the whole text whenever possible. It is more nearly possible to respect the wholeness of a short text than a long one. So, especially with immature readers of literature whatever their age or grade level, literature teachers prefer the *short* story, poem, or play. After an appropriate introduction, students can read a short selection independently all the way through for the pleasure of the first impact. They can then reread it in whole or in part as they examine why or how the author has made them respond as they did on first reading.

Not every literary text can be treated holistically. Sometimes, as we note below, teachers want to emphasize how predicting and self-questioning affect comprehension. They also want students to experience a long, intricate novel or a five-act Shakespearean drama. With longer works they make reasonable study assignments, introducing each part with prereading activities. But they come back regularly to shorter pieces. Teachers avoid asking too many questions directed to small sections of a whole text, except where necessary to demonstrate particular strategies.

4. Good Readers Understand How They Make Meanings and Are Aware of Breakdowns in the Process

Much recent research in reading has been concerned with monitoring comprehension. Good readers know when their reading makes sense and when it does not. When their understanding appears adequate, they simply read on, but when their understanding is unclear, they employ corrective strategies (Brown 1980; Olshavsky 1977; Wagoner 1983).

Comprehension monitoring is said to have two aspects. The first is awareness of adequacy of comprehension or assessment of inadequacy. When reading a Shakespearean sonnet, for instance, students may comment: "I don't get it," or "He couldn't mean *that,* " or "Oh, now I see what this is about." Assessment of comprehension assumes that readers have established, however unconsciously, a purpose for reading. If students elect to read *The Pearl* only to find out what happens to Kino, Juana, and Coyotito, they will be satisfied with understanding the story line, which they may accomplish quickly, paying scant attention to details. On the other hand, if their purpose is to understand the motivations of various characters or to examine the symbolic meaning of the pearl, their self-assessment will question their inferences and judgments.

The second aspect of monitoring comprehension, applying corrective strategies, should follow awareness that comprehension is inadequate. Research has identified the value of strategies such as rereading or looking back, reading ahead, using context to figure out word meanings, making inferences, referring to personal experience, and making predictions. Research documents our assumption that fluent readers use a greater variety of corrective strategies than poor readers do and tend to use them more often (Garner and Reis 1981; Olshavsky 1977).

Poor readers are often unaware of their lack of adequate understanding, or if they do recognize their failure to comprehend, they are unable to apply an appropriate corrective strategy. Such students cannot be told to "figure it out" because they do not know how to go about it. And teachers often have trouble describing how to "figure it out" because they themselves are so skilled in monitoring comprehension that they are unconscious of the process.

How teachers can facilitate appropriate comprehension-monitoring strategies (as well as other aspects of the reading process) has been the object of much recent research, which brings us to our next generalization.

5. Modeling, Direct Explanations, and Questioning Are Teaching Strategies That Improve Comprehension.

How can we teach students to monitor their comprehension? Research points to two strategies that many teachers tend to neglect. One is modeling the process; the other is explaining or describing what students should do. These strategies are also used to teach students how to make inferences, since failure to do so is frequently the cause of faulty comprehension.

From time to time teachers talk about their own misreading of words or phrases, speculate on why a particular miscue has occurred, and estimate the distortion in understanding that may result. Students, too, share their own miscues and thus raise their level of consciousness about this aspect of the reading process. Since it is easier to monitor miscues, that is a good place to begin, but monitoring the assimilation of ideas is more important. A teacher might begin by reading aloud a poem, short story, or essay, interrupting the text to insert his or her own interpretations and queries. (This must be a genuine first reading on the teacher's part.) Modeling the process, the teacher makes predictions and corrects them as new data are gathered from the text.

Good choices for introducing students to monitoring (and thinking aloud as they do so) are short stories that begin by withholding all the clues, or poems that compress much meaning into a few lines. Some teachers find May Sarton's *Poems to Solve* particularly effective for this type of demonstration; one of them is the widely anthologized "Southbound on the Freeway."

One suggestion from research is to model the inference process when answering questions (Gordon 1985; Roehler and Duffy 1984). The teacher defines what an inference is, then reads a portion of text, asks an inference question, gives the answer, and explains the reasoning involved. Gradually students take over the successive phases of the procedure. When given this type of instruction, students improve in their ability to draw inferences.

Another strategy is to teach students that answers to questions have different sources. Teachers classify inference questions as "think and search" (putting together information from several different places in the text) and "author and me" (combining what the reader knows with what the author tells) (Raphael 1984).

Questions have long been the staple of teachers' techniques for promoting comprehension. What is new in the research investigating teacher intervention in the comprehension process is that students are taught to ask their own questions. A reciprocal questioning strategy aimed at helping students to adopt a question approach to their reading is the ReQuest procedure (Manzo 1969). Working with individuals or small groups, the English teacher and students take turns asking each other questions following the reading of segments of a poem, short story, or essay. The teacher may ask, "What is the significance of the character's age?" or "What do you think will happen next?" or "What would you do now if you were she?" These questions require inferences based on details from the selection as well as from the reader's prior knowledge. Through teachers' modeling, students may be led to produce inference questions in class and when they read independently.

Questions may be presented in an "anticipation guide" in which students are asked to agree or disagree with four or five statements before reading a selection. For example, before reading Ray Bradbury's "The Flying Machine," students might ponder the following statements: (1) Two people could use the same invention in very different ways. (2) Advances in technology usually have more potential for good than harm. (3) Progress can be stopped. Discussion of students' responses before reading may inform the teacher as to their depth of knowledge, intensity of beliefs, and misconceptions. Discussion of the same statements after reading can strengthen students' ability to support inferences and analyze generalizations.

The success of modeling, direct explanations, and questioning depends to a significant degree on timing. Sensitive teachers plan *brief* demonstrations of processes; they know when a modeling session loses its audience. Likewise, they carefully time students' demonstrations of thinking aloud and their discussions of miscues and misapprehensions. Through experience, intuition, trial and error, teachers learn when to transfer responsibility for questioning from themselves to their students. They interrupt discussions from time to time to assess the significance of students' questions and the purpose of their own or textbook questions. They provide many examples of high level questions in discussion guides that they design themselves, borrow from others, and get their students to make.

All of these strategies for reading literature are necessary and planned for, not left to chance. But they must never be allowed to get in the way of the story. They are means to an end—the enjoyment of literature.

6. Good Readers Use Cues in the Text and Knowledge in Their Heads to Make Predictions. Predicting Strengthens Comprehending.

Literature teachers at every level have made creative use of this research finding. Primary grade teachers share lists of "predictable books" that they read aloud. As children catch on to the story line or to repetitive phrases, the teacher invites them to finish the sentence or to predict what will happen next. A middle school teacher might duplicate and cut up a "short short" story, giving students one segment at a time to read silently. In discussion at the end of each section, students speculate on what will happen next and point out the cues in the text that support the prediction. Science fiction, mysteries, and surprise-ending stories are good choices for this kind of exercise. The author's conclusions may or may not be predicted accurately. In either case, the readers retrace the author's steps, looking for planted clues (foreshadowing). They judge whether the author's conclusion is inevitable or the surprise ending fair.

With mature students at any grade level, teachers ask them to read carefully the first half or two-thirds of a story. The students are then invited to write an ending that uses the author's clues and is in keeping with the style. An instructor in freshman composition uses Kate Chopin's "The Story of an Hour" in this fashion and finds that it stimulates precise reading as it instructs students in the writer's craft.

7. Analysis of Inferences Supports Teaching Strategies That Focus on How to Read Literature

Inferences are at the very heart of the comprehension process and never more so than when readers are making meanings of literature. Authors can never state explicitly and entirely what characters look like or think or do, nor do they want to. Instead, they call on readers to elaborate on details, drawing upon their own experiences (that is, prior knowledge). Imaginative literature especially places demands on the reader's ability and willingness to draw inferences and thus to integrate information about characters and their motives, events and their sequence, about setting, conflict, and theme.

Several means of helping students to draw inferences have already been described in this essay, since so much of comprehending is inferring. Predicting, for instance, is a form of inferring. In addition to examining how (and if) students draw inferences and what teaching strategies affect the process, recent research has examined the nature of inferences. One study categorizes the inferences needed for comprehending narratives as (1) informational inferences (about characters, setting, things); (2) logical inferences (about motivations and causes); and (3) value inferences (readers' evaluations of aspects of a story). Logical inferences seem to be more difficult for readers than informational inferences.

Hillocks and Ludlow (1984) identify an order of increasing difficulty: (1) simple implied relationships (can be identified from cues close to each other in the text); (2) complex implied relationships (cues are scattered); (3) author's generalizations ("implied by the whole fabric of the literary work as it reflects some conception of the human situation as it exists outside the limits of the work" [p.12]); and (4) structural generalizations (inferences about how aspects of the work achieve their effect). The hierarchical order of these categories is affirmed by studies showing that students who are unable to draw type 2 inferences, for example, also fail with types 3 and 4.

Such categorizing is helpful to teachers. They can build that necessary platform of success with poor readers by pitching them questions that require them to put together details about character, setting, and things. As readers develop, teachers move gradually toward discussions requiring inferences from several sources of information within the text and drawn from the reader's prior knowledge.

Moreover, awareness of "levels of inferences" guides teachers in judging the difficulty of texts they select for in-common reading and the objectives they aim for in literature study with different members of their class.

8. Inferences Depend on Apprehension of Details

Research on the inferential dimension of the reading process, whether it is based on examination of readers or texts, underscores the importance of attending to or catching details. Generalizations are derived from details. How much emphasis, and what kind, teachers put on detail is a matter of crucial importance and complexity, but as yet research offers little guidance. Experience suggests, however, that teachers' strategies with respect to details must vary according to readers' achievement.

The naive teacher is likely to ask questions aimed only at details and to hit too many too fast. The teacher who is a sophisticated reader may aim first at the broad generalizations (inference types 3 and 4 in the Hillocks and Ludlow scheme), assuming that the students have assimilated the right details and have enough prior knowledge to recognize their significance. Both kinds of teacher may confuse or bore some of their students. With mature readers, it may be a good idea to begin with higher order inferences, referring only as necessary to the details that support them. With poor readers, the focus on details should be discriminating, but should precede asking for generalizations based on them.

Reading for details (facts) has received a bad press over the years, largely because some teachers quizzed students *only* on details and often on insignificant ones. These teachers stopped short of the reason for attending to details— that is, to use them for arriving at larger meanings. The reaction against this kind of poor teaching led many to discount the importance of details. The new attitude toward teaching higher order skills promises to reinstate the value of apprehending and assessing details. In literature as in other arts, details create the effect; we want students to realize both the effect and its sources.

9. The Range of Students' Reading Achievement Grows Wider at Each Successive Grade Level until Dropouts Occur

That students differ in their reading potential and achievement is no news to teachers. The new research, however, offers more detailed descriptions of these differences. As current and future research documents how differences among readers are affected by texts and contexts, especially by teaching strategies, teachers will know more about why and how to individualize instruction. In the meantime, they can act upon two well-established and gross research generaliza-

tions that are often overlooked in spite of pious respect for individual differences.

First, students in every class, even "homogeneous" ones, read at different
rates. (A very wide range of reading rates is often observed in gifted classes.)
Teachers can help students estimate their rates of reading and can then take them
into consideration when planning in-common reading and homework assignments. To prevent an experience with a novel from stretching beyond an optimal
two to three weeks, teachers abridge and skip some chapters, while still encouraging their best readers to absorb every word. Similarly, in assigning different
works to individuals and clusters, teachers can easily consider length; complexity is a more difficult criterion.

Second, cultural diversity, which is increasing in many schools, accounts
heavily for differences in comprehension. Students who read English as a second language constitute a large part of our school population. Their proficiency
in reading varies greatly. In spite of significant advances in the teaching of
beginning reading, many students, native as well as immigrant, arrive in junior
and senior high school with very limited comprehension skills and negative attitudes toward reading for nonutilitarian purposes.

For students of low reading ability, whatever the reason, the best approach to
literature may be through nonreading channels. But literature, because it is the
stuff of human experience, can be a highly motivating vehicle for learning how
to read. So teachers supplement listening and viewing with reading-based literature lessons. The best first step they can take is to broaden their view of what literature is (tolerate a little trash!). The second step is to think very carefully
about the variability of prior knowledge and its impact on comprehension.
Thinking should lead to creative prereading activities: previews or synopses
(advance organizers), semantic mapping or highlighting words and concepts,
interest-arousing questions, films, role playing, and improvising.

For all students, the ultimate goal must be: "I can read it myself—and I will."
The "it" of that goal statement represents literature of the widest diversity in
content and quality, appropriate to the reading levels of those who make the declaration.

BIBLIOGRAPHY

Applebee, A. N. 1978. *The Child's Concept of Story: Ages Two to Seventeen.* Chicago:
University of Chicago Press.

Brown, A. L. 1980. Metacognitive Development and Reading. In *Theoretical Issues in
Reading Comprehension,* ed. R. J. Spiro, B. C. Bruce, and W. F. Brewer. Hillsdale,
N.J.: Erlbaum.

Ericson, B. O. 1985. A Descriptive Study of the Individual and Group Responses of
Three Tenth-Grade Readers to Two Short Stories and Two Textbook Selections.
Dissertation Abstracts International 46, no. 2: 388-A.

Galda, L. 1982. Assuming the Spectator Stance: An Examination of the Responses of Three Young Readers. *Research in the Teaching of English* 16:1–20.

Garner, R., and R. Reis. 1981. Monitoring and Resolving Comprehension Obstacles: An Investigation of Spontaneous Lookbacks among Upper-Grade Good and Poor Comprehenders. *Reading Research Quarterly* 16:569–582.

Gordon, C. J. 1985. Modeling Inference Awareness Across the Curriculum. *Journal of Reading* 28:444-447.

Hillocks, G., and L. H. Ludlow. 1984. A Taxonomy of Skills in Reading and Interpreting Fiction. *American Educational Research Journal* 21:7-24.

Manzo, A. V. 1969. The ReQuest Procedure. *Journal of Reading* 13: 287–91.

Mauro, L. H. 1984. Personal Constructs and Response to Literature: Case Studies of Adolescents Reading about Death. *Dissertation Abstracts International* 44, no. 7:2073-A.

National Assessment of Educational Progress. 1981. *Three National Assessments of Reading: Changes in Performance, 1970–1980.* Report 11-R-01. Denver: Education Commission of the States.

Olshavsky, J. E. 1977. Reading as Problem Solving: An Investigation of Strategies. *Reading Research Quarterly* 12: 654–674.

Olson, M. W. 1985. Text Type and Reader Ability: The Effects on Paraphrase and Text-Based Inference Questions. *Journal of Reading Behavior* 17: 199–213.

Raphael, T. E. 1984. Teaching Learners about Sources of Information for Answering Comprehension Questions. *Journal of Reading* 27:303–311.

Roehler, L., and G. G. Duffy. 1984. Direct Explanation of Comprehension Processes. In *Comprehension Instruction,* ed. G.G. Duffy, L.R. Roehler, and J. Mason. New York: Longman.

Rosenblatt, L. 1978. *The Reader, the Text, the Poem.* Carbondale, Ill.: Southern Illinois University Press.

Rumelhart, D. E. 1980. Schemata: The Building Blocks of Cognition. In *Theoretical Issues in Reading Comprehension,* ed. R. J. Spiro, B. C. Bruce, and W. F. Brewer. Hillsdale, N.J.: Erlbaum.

Smith, F. 1978. *Understanding Reading.* 2d ed. New York: Holt, Rinehart and Winston.

Wagoner, S. A. 1983. Comprehension Monitoring: What It Is and What We Know About It. *Reading Research Quarterly* 18: 328–346.

Warren, W. H., D. Nicholas, and T. Trabasso. 1979. Event Chains and Inferences in Understanding Narratives. In *New Directions in Discourse Processing,* ed. R. Freedle. Norwood, N.J.: Ablex.

I Never Read Such A Long Story Before

Yetta Goodman

He came into the room. It was packed; to Frankie it seemed to be wall to wall teachers. He wondered if any of his own teachers were there, but he was too anxious to look around and study every face. There was a big man way over in the corner. He wondered if that was Mr. Bender, his English teacher. He didn't get along too well with Mr. Bender. Mr. Bender was always upset if you were even a little bit tardy.

He wondered what he was doing in this room. How could he help these teachers learn about reading? He didn't read too good himself. But Mr. Castillo had asked him if he would read a story for a bunch of teachers who were trying to learn about how kids read. Well, he knew he read lousy. He didn't read much anyway except for magazines at the drug store. But Mr. Castillo had said he could be a big help. He would do anything for Mr. Castillo. Mr. Castillo was the junior high counselor. He had known him since seventh grade. Mr. Castillo was always helping him get back into class. He liked the buzz group Mr. Castillo held two times a week. He never missed that if he could help it. They talked about important things like why they had problems with teachers, about girls, problems with parents, even being Mexican. He only missed the buzz group when he had to take Mama to the hospital. She went to that shrink every week. He wondered if the shrink spoke Spanish. How would the shrink understand Mama without knowing Spanish?

He got to the table. There was the lady Mr. Castillo had told him about. She was going to help the teachers learn about reading.

"Hi!" she said to him. "My name is Yetta Goodman."

He brushed his long straight black hair from his eyes and nodded a greeting.

"You're Francisco?" the lady asked.

"Yes" he answered, "my name is Francisco, but most people call me Frankie."

"What would you prefer I call you?" the lady asked.

"Frankie," he responded.

Frankie is an eighth grader in a Southern California junior high school. He lives alone with his mother. She is an out-patient from a psychiatric clinic; she speaks Spanish most of the time. Frankie's cumulative folder indicates that he does not do well in written language, either composition or spelling. His reading test score a month earlier had been 5.3.

His profile indicated that he was the kind of young man who would help the teachers of this workshop begin to focus on the reading process. Since I knew the student would be reading before a large group of teachers, I also asked Mr.

Castillo for an outgoing student, one with good self-confidence. I selected a story, "Anita's Gift," from a literature series for junior high students because there was some Spanish language in the story. In addition, although the story dealt with a Puerto Rican family, I hoped that the reader would be able to relate to the young man in the story, who is assuming responsibility and solving problems for the family.

I started the taping session immediately, expecting Frankie might be somewhat nervous.

"Frankie", I said, "All the teachers are here because we want to find out how people read when no one helps them. I'm going to ask you to read out loud, and I'll be taping your reading so we can listen to it after you've returned to your classes. When you finish your reading, I'll ask you to tell me everything you remember about the story. Remember that I won't help you. If you come to a problem as you read, work it out the best you can."

The tape recorder was started and Frankie began to read.

READING MISCUE ANALYSIS

So began a workshop in miscue analysis to help secondary teachers understand more about the reading process. Miscue analysis helps the reading teacher examine the reading process almost as a scientist might look through a microscope in order to examine biological phenomena. When students read orally, evaluating their miscues gives the teacher the opportunity to discover why students make miscues as they read and to infer something about the student's ability from the quality of miscues that a reader makes.[1]

A miscue is any unexpected response which is heard during oral reading. For example if the text says, *Where did those come from?,* and a reader reads, *Where did these come from?, these* is a miscue for the text word *those.*

Through miscues, teachers can see if readers are using language knowledge. In evaluating *these* as a miscue for *those,* it is obvious that the two words have a very high degree of graphic similarity (they both look very much alike) as well as a great deal of sound similarity. In addition, both words function the same way grammatically in the sentence in which they occur. This miscue produced what is essentially an "acceptable" sentence, since it only changed the meaning of the story in which it occurred minimally.[2]

In miscue analysis, every miscue which a student produces is analyzed using questions which provide information relating to the graphophonic, syntactic and semantic systems of language.

In this article I will use selections from Frankie's reading to provide evidence about the amount of language information he brings to his reading. At the

[1]Kenneth Goodman, editor, *Miscue Analysis,* Urbana: ERIC and NCTE, 1973.
[2]Yetta Goodman and C. Burke, *Reading Miscue Inventory: Manual,* Macmillan, 1972.

same time, I will suggest means by which proficient secondary students use language in reading and I will finally make suggestions for classroom teachers.

To learn about Frankie's pattern of reading strategies, I evaluated the first fifty consecutive miscues he made during his reading of the story "Anita's Gift".[3]

This evaluation provides a pattern of reading miscues. I asked the student to read something orally which he had never seen.[4] The following is a section of "Anita's Gift" showing how Frankie's miscues were marked on a copy of the story.

Frankie read directly from the printed text.*

He

There was no jumping around this morning and no whistling. They walked in silence.

d

and each step seem(ed) to Pablo to be bringing them near something serious and he wished

they were running the other way.

d

At last they reached the florist(s) corner. The door of the shop was open. A gray-haired

ⓒ *sitting*   *There*

man was setting cans of flowers on the sidewalk where Anita said they had been yester-
                                                            ∧

ⓒ *They*   ⓒ *and they*   *they*

day. The two stood behind him as he pushed the cans this way (and) that and arranged

                                  ⓒ *seem.* *Then*

blossoms in several of the cans. Would he never see them?

QUANTITY OF MISCUES

"Anita's Gift" is a story of approximately 1,550 words. In the total story Frankie made 7.8 miscues per hundred words (not including repeated identical

[3]Yetta Goodman and C. Burke, "Anita's Gift" *Reading Miscue Inventory: Readings for Taping,* Macmillan, 1973, pp. 43–49.
[4]Oral reading provides the opportunity to examine miscues, but it does pose limitations since the reader's understanding may be greater through silent reading. However, by giving the students a total story, article, or self-contained chapter to read, a continuous language context is available in which readers can become involved; thus providing a picture of what reading would look like when students read independently. Students are never aided during their reading because the purpose is to discover what strategies readers use when they do not have a teacher or other outside resources available to help them.

*Substitutions are marked over the word; omissions are circled; insertions are indicated with a ∧, corrections are shown by underlining the portion repeated and the mark ⓒ; ⓓ indicates a dialect-influenced miscue.

miscues).[5] Numbers of miscues can vary from one group of 100 words in a story to the next group of 100 words. Frankie's miscues within every 100 words in the story ranged from 3 to 14. The table below shows Frankie's miscues per hundred words calculated for every 400 words in the story. In the last section of the story Frankie made almost 9 miscues per hundred words while in the first quarter of the story his miscues were about six miscues per hundred words.

TABLE 8

	Number of miscues	Miscues per hundred words
First 400 words	25	6.3
Second 400 words	35	8.8
Third 400 words	29	7.3
Fourth 400 words	31	8.9
Total	120	7.8

Implications for Instruction

Frequency of miscues in and of itself is not an especially useful measure. Teachers should not be too quick to judge or evaluate a student's reading ability based on numbers of miscues. Students who are very adept at silent reading have learned to read quickly and often produce many miscues which show sophisticated language transformations. The grammatical structure, style of writing or concept load of any particular part of a story all are involved in the complex reasons which cause readers to produce miscues and which cause miscue numbers to vary from one part of a story to another.[6]

Using oral reading for evaluative purposes, however, can provide insight into which miscues do or do not interfere with the reader's ability to reconstruct the author's meaning. By looking at the *pattern* of miscues through such a screen, the teacher can begin to understand not only the reading process but the degree to which the student is proficiently comprehending.

GRAPHIC AND SOUND SIMILARITY

Through miscue analysis, we can evaluate the use readers make of the graphic and sound systems of language. The questions asked to evaluate these two aspects of language in reading are:

---

[5]Many reading evaluations suggest that miscues per hundred words can provide information about the ease or difficulty of a passage. My own research does not support such an assumption ("Reading Diagnosis: Qualitative or Quantitative?" *Reading Teacher,* Volume 26, Number 1, October, 1972, pp. 32–37.

[6]Interpretative or dramatic reading may call for carefully acted out oral reading; however this is a specialized kind of reading and is never used by most readers. Flawless surface reading focuses on careful pronunciation and away from the majority priority of reading—the reader's search for meaning.

To what degree do the two words (the text word and the miscue) look alike? To what degree do the two words sound alike?

In Frankie's case, 81% of the expected and observed responses of word substitutions looked very much alike. Such substitutions included:

Text	Miscue
then	when
the	he
voice	voices
they	then
the	their
though	thought

Ten percent of his substitution miscues showed no graphic similarity at all. Every one of these words, however, were either the same part of speech as the text word or produced grammatically acceptable sentences. These included:

Text	Miscue
of	at
a	the
and	that

High sound similarity between the text word and miscue was 57% while no sound similarity was 20%. Miscues with no sound similarity included words like the ones which produced no graphic similarity but also included words which had high graphic similarity but no sound similarity such as the substitution of *the* for *he* and *thought* for *though*. In all miscue analysis studies, virtually all readers, regardless of ability, produce more frequent miscues which look more like the text word than sound like the text word.

In other words, readers tend to pay more attention to the graphic system than to the sound system as they read. Proficient readers seldom produce substitution miscues which consistently show high sound and graphic similarity. Often substitution miscues which have very little look alike or sound alike qualities are the very best miscues. Examples of such miscues include *baby* for *child, home game* for *home opener, third floor* for *third level*.

Implication for Instruction

Some readers in junior high and high school are more concerned with the ways words look than they are with the meaning of what they are reading. This tends to be especially true of readers who have been considered problems for whatever reasons. Much remediation helps students concentrate on the way words look, on sounding out techniques or on syllabication rules. It seems that when students concentrate on the graphic system, they become less aware that reading is supposed to make sense. This interferes with their development as proficient readers. Secondary school students would benefit most from reading instruction which helps them concentrate on comprehending what they are reading rather than on careful surface accuracy. It is *not* important for a reader to be able to sound out carefully a word like *contented* which may appear six or seven times in a story. A reader needs to be encouraged to keep reading and decide what the word means from the cumulating context. Any reading instruction which does not emphasize comprehension and the use of context through which to build meanings as the main concern for readers, will short change the student and will help produce reading problems rather than eliminate them.

DIALECT

In the first 50 miscues Frankie produced in "Anita's Gift," four of the miscues were related to his dialect. One of the dialect miscues was the insertion of the modifier *the* prior to a proper name which is probably an influence from his knowledge of Spanish.

> *Text:*   . . . to go down to Ferris Center.
> *Frankie:* . . . to go down the stairs to *the* Ferris Center.

The other dialect miscues included reduction of consonant clusters in certain environments. These were the omissions of *ed* and *s* endings and *or* substituted for *nor*. In the miscues which occurred after the initial 50, Frankie produced eight more dialect related miscues which all involved the omission of the *ed*, the *s* on plural nouns or the possessive *s*. In all cases the sentences were read with intonation indicating that Frankie was comprehending what he was reading. His retelling of the story which followed his reading also confirmed a good understanding of the story. The dialect miscues never got in the way of his understanding tense changes or numbers in the story. All the Spanish words in the story like the names *Anita, Mamita, Pablo, Pablito, Don Antonio,* and one Spanish phrase, "y yo tengo, tambien" were read appropriately. Frankie shifted to Spanish phonology whenever he read those words although he had never had any formal teaching in Spanish.

Implication for Instruction

Dialect in and of itself does not seem to present a significant problem for readers.[7] It is only when a teacher focuses a reader's attention on producing some

---

[7] Kenneth Goodman, "Dialect Barriers to Reading Comprehension Revisited," *The Reading Teacher,* October, 1973.

standard dialect which may be artificial that the student focuses on surface features in reading and loses concern for comprehending. When a student produces features of his own dialect as he reads, he is providing evidence for the teacher that he is understanding so well that he is translating the written code into his own oral code. Reading instruction should *never* be the time to attempt to change a student's pronunciation.

USE OF THE GRAMMATICAL SYSTEM

Even ineffective readers' substitution miscues usually retain the same part of speech as the text word which is replaced. Seventy percent of Frankie's substitution miscues were the same part of speech as the word they replaced. This indicates that he was making use of the grammatical cueing system. Even then, half of the miscues which were not the same part of speech, were self-corrected.

Related to substitution of grammatical function is the reader's ability to produce acceptable sentences regardless of miscues.

Although Frankie's score indicated that he was predicting appropriate grammatical function rather successfully, the miscues did not always produce acceptable sentences. However, it is significant to explore which portion of the story produced the greatest number of unacceptable sentences. For this purpose, the first 25 miscues of Frankie's reading which occurred in the first 400 words of the story were scored separately from the second 25 miscues. Fifty-six percent of these miscues produced acceptable sentences. Sixteen percent were grammatically, but not semantically acceptable, and 28% showed weakness both grammatically and semantically. Sentences with miscues which showed weaknesses included:

Text: Then he saw them.
Frankie: When he saw . . . (no). Then he saw . . .Then he saw them (no wait) . . . Then he saw then.
Text: By this time Anita was clinging to Pablo crying against his sleeve.
Frankie: By the time Anita was climbing into Pablo's . . . clinging into Pablo's crying against his sleeve.
Text: How Pablo wished for Papa to tell them what to do.
Frankie: No Pablo wished for Papa to tell them what to do.

During the reading of the next 300 words, Frankie made 25 additional miscues but this time 92% showed both grammatical and semantic acceptability, and the remaining 8% were grammatically acceptable but not acceptable semantically. During the second 25 miscues, Frankie began to make miscues which resulted in sentences like the following:

Text: The flowers would wither and be thrown out and that would be all there would be to it.

Frankie: The flowers would wither and be thrown out. That would be all
there would be to it.
Text: . . . the flower man is a kind man and does not hate Puerto Ricans.
Frankie: . . . the flower man is a kind man that doesn't hate Puerto Ricans.

It is clear by examining the second 25 miscues and those even later in the
story that Frankie is learning to read by *reading;* he has developed control over
reading the syntactic structure of the author. He learned to predict and handle the
structure well enough that his miscues produced acceptable sentences. The sample of Frankie's reading provided at the beginning of this article occurred in the
third quarter of the story. By reading that section over again including Frankie's
miscues you can see how he was controlling syntactic structure.

Implications for Instruction

Such a dramatic change from the first 25 miscues of a story to the second 25
miscues is evidence that reading something one has never read before can be
an excellent self-teaching device. The ability to develop the necessary strategies
to handle the structure of the author as he began to move into the story indicates
that the best way for Frankie to learn about variability in language structure is
to have available a variety of language materials to read. The content of
the materials needs to be within the interest and concept level of the student,
but the greater the variety of types of writing materials, the more opportunity
students will have to expand their ability to handle varieties of material.
Students should be encouraged to read magazines, newspapers and various types
of books. By limiting students to a standard text and a few required stories
teachers are severely limiting the students' opportunities to become flexible
readers.

Frankie was able to verbalize for Mr. Castillo a level of awareness of his own
limitations. After he had finished his reading before the teachers, Mr. Castillo
drove Frankie back to school. On the way, Mr. Castillo said to Frankie, "You
did a pretty good job of that." Frankie replied, "No, I really messed it up." Mr.
Castillo said, "But you seemed to understand it." "Yes," said Frankie, "but I
found it sort of confusing because I'm not used to reading stuff where people
always keep interrupting each other. You know," he continued, "that story was
interesting and if I could find more things like that I might read them. *I never
read such a long story before.*"

Frankie was aware that there was something unusual about the grammatical
structure and that he wasn't used to reading materials which had a good deal of
dialogue. The experience of reading such materials provided him with the
opportunity to learn to read such materials. No direct or formal teaching was
necessary. The reader interacting with an author from whom he wishes to gain a
message or meaning can learn a lot about the language of the author. Relegating
readers to materials which have short words and sentences on the basis that this

is easy for students may actually get in the way of students developing the ability to handle various material. Short, simple sentences can cause older readers confusion because they expect more from written language. It also conditions students to predict a somewhat limited number of sentences and author styles. If the *concept* of the material is within the student's knowledge system and if the reader is *interested* in the subject matter he can often handle material which seems to be more sophisticated than his test scores might reveal. The reverse of this is also true. No matter what reading test scores indicate, if the material is beyond the knowledge and interest of the readers, they may not be able to comprehend what they are reading.

Frankie's comment about the length of "Anita's Gift" is a common one made by students who have been considered reading problems after they have read for a miscue analysis. Many students after completing a story have indicated, "Boy, that was really long, but I liked it," or "That's the first time I ever read a whole story by myself," or "I didn't know I could read something so long."

Often because students are having some difficulty with reading, it is assumed that skills materials which concentrate on words, sentences or sometimes paragraphs will be the easiest for such students to read. All readers should be provided with materials of some length (more than 400 words). When a story has length it can provide interesting content which may be relevant to the student. Longer written material can also provide the necessary context through which students can build concepts as well as become acquainted with stylistic differences. In a sense, reading longer materials is easier than reading words, sentences or paragraphs.

COMPREHENSION

The most significant aspect of reading is the comprehension which the reader gains. Miscue analysis provides two measures of comprehension. One is a score based on the degree to which the miscues produced by the readers change the meaning or intent of the author. After self-correction, 82% of Frankie's 50 miscues did *not* change the meaning or intent of the author. This score was substantiated by Frankie's retelling of the story after his reading, the second measure used in miscue analysis.

In an open-ended fashion, Frankie was asked to simply retell what he had read. He did a very adequate job of recalling the events and the characters, but more important, he was able to infer from the story aspects of characterization and theme. His retelling score was 90 out of a possible 100 points.

I asked Frankie why Pablo had to think about something to do (referring to something Frankie had said earlier about the main character). Frankie said, "Cause he was, well, at that time he was the man in the house." Here he suggested one theme in the story.

In another question-answer sequence Frankie states two more of the themes in the story.

YG: Was there some problem the story was trying to solve?

Frankie: It just proves that people are kind to other people not just to their own race.

YG: Was that what the author was trying to say?

Frankie: No, the author meant that you shouldn't get anything. The grandmother said in the story she (Anita) shouldn't pick up anything without paying for it.

After Frankie left the room, the teachers and I talked about his comprehension. Most of the teachers were surprised that a reader could make so many miscues and still retain so much of the meaning of the story, but Frankie's own teachers were the most surprised. They all regarded Frankie as a student who was unable to handle most reading tasks. One of them said, "I always considered that he was just a non-reader." Another said, "But he never gives any indications that he reads or understands anything that he reads in class. Maybe it's because I expect that kind of behavior from him."

Implications for Instruction

Generally, miscue analysis has shown that many of the students in junior high school and senior high who are diagnosed as being problem readers are able to do a lot better job of reading and thinking than they are given credit for. Students with whom I have worked who have profiles like Frankie's, when given an opportunity to read without interruption a whole story which has some relevance to them, are often able to comprehend and discuss significant issues from the story. Frequently, however, these students are defeated by the belief that they are bad readers. They may refuse to even make simple attempts at reading material unless they are working with someone they trust not to laugh or constantly correct their efforts.

Classroom time should be organized so that more actual reading takes place. Students should have the opportunity to read silently and independently in the classroom setting. If learning to read is a major priority in schools then it seems logical that opportunity should be provided for students to read. The material to be read should be interesting to the students so that class discussions related to their reading could be as meaningful and interesting as Mr. Castillo's discussions which Frankie never missed. This might not be too difficult a task if students were involved in the selection of a good deal of their own reading material. Teachers should become better acquainted with books written specifically for teenagers and dealing with their problems. These are becoming greater in number and more available for classroom use.[8]

---

[8]Virginia Reid, ed., *Reading Ladders for Human Relations.* American Council on Education, Washington, D.C., 1972.

In this article, I have attempted to provide some insights into the reading process through analyzing Frankie's reading. I have suggested some implications for teachers which have been based on more than a decade of miscue analysis. I wish to conclude with three suggestions which teachers should keep in mind during the teaching of reading.

1. Permit Your Students to Read   No one has learned to swim by practicing the skills of backstrokes, flutter kicks or treading water while staying on the edge of the swimming pool. Yet, in the teaching of reading we often do just that. Rather than let the readers into "the water," we keep them in skills books learning rules about letters, syllables or definitions of words rather than letting them into the book itself, permitting them to be immersed in the language which comes from the author as the readers try to reconstruct the written message.

2. Encourage Your Students to Guess or Predict   Readers' guesses or predictions are based on the cumulative information and syntactic structure they have been learning as they have been reading. Therefore, their guesses are more often than not appropriate to the material. Students have to realize that risk taking in reading is appropriate; that using context to decide what words mean is a proficient reading strategy and that they have the language sense to make appropriate guesses which can fit both the grammatical and semantic sense of what they are reading.

3. Focus Your Students' Attention on Meaning   Help your students understand that the only reason to read is for themselves. They have to have their own *purpose* to read and reading *must make sense to them*. If reading does not make sense, they have to find ways of doing something about it. They should be encouraged either to reread or to continue reading to gain meaning. But they must realize that the meaning is not in the teacher, but in the interaction between the reader and author. Students should be encouraged to ask themselves repeatedly, "Does this make sense to me?" Students should be encouraged to reject and to be intolerant of reading materials which do not make sense. It has always impressed me that when we adults can not make sense out of what we are reading, like a text on statistics or Chomsky's latest article on transformational-generative grammar, we have the right to say "This is badly written," "I really don't want to know that stuff," or "It's beyond me," but when students say they can't read something, the student is said to have a reading problem.

The lesson that should be learned from the many Frankies that exist in our schools is that much of what we do in the teaching of reading gets in the way of the student's learning.

We can cause problems by underestimating the students as well as by looking at reading as a careful, exact process.

Kids have a lot going for them. If teachers can turn their hard work toward supporting the language strengths kids already have, providing kids with a feeling of success, finding materials and planning classroom experiences which will turn kids on to reading, then reading will develop with much greater ease than it does at the present time.

C

LANGUAGE AND THE WRITING PROCESS

Assumptions

Donald M. Murray

I think it is important for teachers—and students—to know the assumptions and beliefs on which their teaching is based. Several key assumptions underlie this book.

WRITING IS THINKING

Meaning is not thought up and then written down. The act of writing is an act of thought. This is the principal reason writing should be taught in the academy, yet, ironically, it is this concept that is most often misunderstood by academicians. They give writing assignments based on the assumption that writing begins after the thinking is concluded, and they respond to those assignments as if the etiquette of language were more important than the thinking represented by language.

Writing is not superficial to the intellectual life but central to it; writing is one of the most disciplined ways of making meaning and one of the most effective methods we can use to monitor our own thinking.

We write to think—to be surprised by what appears on the page; to explore our world with language; to discover meaning that teaches us and that may be worth sharing with others. We do *not* know what we want to say before we say it; we write to know what we want to say.

WRITING IS A PROCESS

Writing is a craft before it is an art; writing may appear magic, but it is our responsibility to take our students backstage to watch the pigeons being tucked up the magician's sleeve. The process of writing can be studied and understood. We can re-create most of what a student or professional writer does to produce effective writing.

The process is not linear, but recursive. The writer passes through the process once, or many times, emphasizing different stages during each passage.

There is not one process, but many. The process varies with the personality or cognitive style of the writer, the experience of the writer, and the nature of the writing task.

EFFECTIVE TEACHING IS RESPONSIVE

We learn best—at least in the study of composition—when we are *not* told in the abstract what to do and then commanded to do it, but are encouraged to write and then have the opportunity to examine what we have done with an experienced writer, who can help us discover what worked and what needs work.

This method of instruction allows the student to learn how to read each draft so that future drafts—on this subject and others—may be improved. The student, when responsive teaching is effective, becomes the student's best teacher.

WRITING IS AN INTERACTION OF THE GLOBAL AND THE PARTICULAR

Traditional writing instruction usually works on the assumption that students need to learn the parts so they can eventually construct a meaningful whole. Traditionally, emphasis is first on vocabulary, spelling, usage, mechanics, and the conventions of manuscript presentation and later on organization, style, and appeals to an audience. Usually the subject is supplied by the instructor since the students do not know anything "substantial." It is logical, but it doesn't work for most students; the particulars are not abstractly significant to students who cannot understand their purpose or importance until they use them to make their own meaning.

Non-traditional composition teaching usually reverses the process and emphasizes personal content and personal voice first, working backwards from global concerns to the particulars of language and manuscript presentation. I voted with that caucus for many years, and if forced to choose between the two positions I would again. Writing is not, however, that simple.

Writing is a product of the interaction of the global and the particular. We use a word to catch a vague idea and it becomes less vague, and so we work back and forth from whole to part and part to whole, each influencing the other, each strand helping the writer weave a pattern of meaning.

THERE IS NO ONE WAY

We do not teach writing effectively if we try to make all students and all writing the same. We must seek, nurture, develop and reward difference. The rich diversity of our students is to our advantage. There is no single kind of person to teach, no one reason to write, no one message to deliver, no one way to write, no single standard of good writing.

Neither is there one way of teaching. I am delighted by the differences in teaching style and methods of the effective writing teachers with whom I work. I would hate it if they all taught as I do or if I were forced to teach as any of them do. Our individuality as students and teachers should be central to all that we do.

The world is complex and diverse, and writing can thrive in such ever-changing and ever-varying soil. We should not just accept diversity but also seek it and make use of it in our writing and our teaching.

I hope this book will help teachers take advantage of diversity and begin to see how to learn to teach less, so that their students can learn more. Our greatest challenge in developing the craft and the art of teaching is to learn how to allow learning, how to get out of the way of our students, so that we can run after them, supporting them when they need support, encouraging them when they've earned it, and kicking tail when they need to get going.

The title of this book, *A Writer Teaches Writing,* implies a personal book by a single writer, but I hope that each reader will become, through the experience of writing and teaching, the writer in the title; that each of us individually and differently will use the book and depart from it as we learn from our own pages and our own students.

This book is not the end for me, but another beginning. I have learned from writing it, and having written it I will learn how to depart from it. It is the sum of what I know today, but fortunately it is not the sum of what I will know at the end of the next semester or the next year or the next years of writing and teaching.

If you accept this profession—this calling, this vocation—you have apprenticed yourself to a lifetime of learning. Neither you nor your students will learn to write. You will use writing as a way of learning, a way of discovering and exploring, of finding what you may have to say and finding ways in which you may say it.

The same is true of teaching. Each semester your students are new, and you are new too. Together you will share the frustrations, the satisfactions, the difficulties, the failures, the successes, the despair, the joy of writing. And you will discover in your own way the secret that all effective composition teachers share: teaching writing is fun.

Defining the Process Paradigm

Steven Zemelman and Harvey Daniels

This new paradigm, which we conveniently call "process writing," isn't actually new, of course. One can look back into history and find teachers from almost any age employing methods that sound much like our modern process approach. The Roman rhetorician Marcus Fabius Quintillian advised that students should "practice composition and be constantly employed in that enterprise" and stated that their teachers shouldn't stress correctness so much as "boldness" and "exuberance." Go easy on the evaluation, Quintillian warned writing instructors in 91 A.D.: "Youthful minds sometimes give way beneath the weight of correction excessively severe, become despondent and grieve and in the end . . . in their fear of blundering everywhere, attempt nothing."

Closer to home, a number of nineteenth-century American educators struggled to teach language arts in ways that seem fully contemporary; in their time, of course, they were called romantics. Barrett Wendell, a professor of rhetoric at Harvard in the 1890s, wrote of his frustrations and his deepening appreciation of what it means to teach writing:

> Bewildering, depressing, maddening, debasing, I should have found this work years ago, but for the growing conviction, which strengthens as the years go by, that the meanest of these works [student papers] if we will only let ourselves see it truly, is a very marvelous thing. Careless, thoughtless, reckless as these [students] so often are, the most careless, the most thoughtless, the most reckless of all, has put before me an act of the creative imagination for which . . . one can find no lesser word than divine. All unknowing, and with the endless limitations of weakness and perversity, he has looked for himself into the great world of immaterial reality, which, just as he knows it, no other human being can ever know; and with these strange, lifeless conventions we call words he has made some image of what he has known in that world which is all his own; and that image begins by and by to arouse within me some conception of what life has meant to him.

> English Composition (New York: Charles Scribner's Sons, 1903), p. 304

Reading this heartfelt testimony a century later, we can almost hear Wendell's harder-boiled Harvard colleagues chuckling in the background at his naive idealism. But we know that Wendell was right about writing and about students. We recognize that Wendell's eagerness to care for his students, to see the world through their eyes, to appreciate their strengths, to exult in their tiniest steps of exploration, in a very real sense to love them, reflects one of the oldest, and certainly the best, elements of our profession's true ideals and traditions.

THE WHOLE LANGUAGE MOVEMENT

So even if today's enthusiasm for process writing superficially resembles a fad, it is vital to recognize its deep roots. This view of language learning is part of an old and evolving set of ideas that may eventually prevail over other models and more permanently guide our teaching of literacy. In recent years, the term *whole language* has come to designate this broader, historically evolving philosophy of language-arts instruction, of which the process approach to writing is only a part.

As Mark Clarke of the University of Denver explains, whole-language teaching means, first of all, that reading and writing teachers use "complete texts in communicative situations, as contrasted with focused skills practice or the use of 'phonics' or isolated language drill."

> Teachers in such classrooms emphasize the use of "real" texts (i.e., newspapers, children's books, school memos, notes to and from home, etc.) for the teaching of reading rather than basal readers or publisher packets or textbook series. They reason that children do better when they are attempting to understand something they have chosen to read, rather than when they are trying to make sense of a book which the teacher has chosen for them. Similarly, writing instruction is based on the children's attempts at communicating with someone else. The kids are encouraged to experiment with the language in order to get it to express what they want it to express. Relatively little isolated practice takes place in such traditional activities as spelling, word lists, grammar and punctuation exercises, etc. The rationale is that the acquisition of conventions of print and grammar (i.e., spelling, punctuation, handwriting, etc.) will be taught when the child is ready to attend to accuracy in the course of producing a meaningful text. Whole language teachers have a strong philosophical commitment to the idea that errors are a natural part of learning. It is through a focus on meaning and revision that conventions of print and grammar are learned. In whole language classrooms children are encouraged to experiment with reading and writing strategies in order to communicate with others through print.

Figure 10 shows some of the roots of the whole-language approach, the intellectual heritage, if you will, of this movement. As you can see, this is not the diagram of some transitory fad, but rather of a group of closely related yet evolving ideas across a broad historical span.

The roots of the whole-language movement emerge from four different fields: the language-arts curriculum, linguistics, educational philosophy, and social psychology. The *language-arts curriculum* has always had both programs and theories that stress having students use real language for real purposes as a means of acquiring and stretching linguistic abilities. Over the past fifty years, *linguistics* has described children's language acquisition, providing us with an increasingly clear and generative model of how human beings undertake the incredibly complex task of learning, mostly unconsciously and untaught, the thousands of abstract rules that make up the grammar of their native language. In *educational philosophy,* there has long been a school of thought that stresses education as an active, inductive, social, and democratic experience. And in *social psychology,* our growing knowledge of group processes, and the centrality of communication in those processes, has long invited us to recognize and use the classroom group itself as the most powerful tool for teaching and learning.

In reviewing the diagram in Figure 10, note that the process approach to writing—the kind of writing this book is about—is just one corner of the whole language or integrated language-arts movement. It connects with everything teachers and kids can do with reading, speaking, listening, and other elements of the

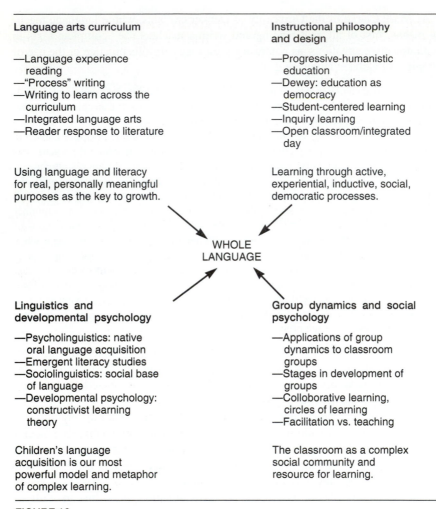

Language arts curriculum

—Language experience
  reading
—"Process" writing
—Writing to learn across the
  curriculum
—Integrated language arts
—Reader response to literature

Using language and literacy
for real, personally meaningful
purposes as the key to growth.

**Instructional philosophy
and design**

—Progressive-humanistic
  education
—Dewey: education as
  democracy
—Student-centered learning
—Inquiry learning
—Open classroom/integrated
  day

Learning through active,
experiential, inductive, social,
democratic processes.

WHOLE
LANGUAGE

**Linguistics and
developmental psychology**

—Psycholinguistics: native
  oral language acquisition
—Emergent literacy studies
—Sociolinguistics: social base
  of language
—Developmental psychology:
  constructivist learning
  theory

Children's language
acquisition is our most
powerful model and metaphor
of complex learning.

**Group dynamics and social
psychology**

—Applications of group
  dynamics to classroom
  groups
—Stages in development of
  groups
—Colloborative learning,
  circles of learning
—Facilitation vs. teaching

The classroom as a complex
social community and
resource for learning.

FIGURE 10
Origins of the whole language movement.

curriculum, but it is still only a part of the picture. We believe that this is how most teachers explore and take ownership of the larger model—by trying something from one corner and then growing out toward the others. Anyway, that's how it worked for us.

This set of ideas cycles in and out of education, repeatedly being pushed back by the traditional (Janet Emig calls them the "magical") approaches and then re-emerging. This may remind you of the often-used image in education of a pendulum swinging back and forth; indeed, this seems to be the standard metaphor for changes in our field. How impartial and content-free this pendulum image is, tempting us to believe that the fluctuations in educational practice are merely the results of some pointless, random, eternal variation. In fact, this is no impartial pendulum swinging; it is more like the battle front in a war that moves back and forth with assaults and retreats. This is a historical struggle of one set of ideas against another, continually being fought out in close relation to the social-political-economic issues outside of schools.

Process writing and whole language, when taught in their true, pure forms, are related to a specific set of educational ideas, ideas that are partisan, that are opposed to other ideas, and that contend with opposing models and paradigms. To refer to this continuing struggle as the vacillation of vacuous fads or the swinging of a pendulum cheapens the efforts of people who are working, often against much resistance, to put these ideas into practice and to show how they work. We believe that this struggle is crucially important. As we wrote on the final page of our last book:

> Teaching writing is connected with democracy, with teaching and enacting respect for human beings, helping them to respect themselves—as opposed to worshipping the American Star and Hero System. . . . Teaching writing—if it's done in a good way and not just to put kids through their paces—is about helping kids see that all of them are the heroes in this country. They grow up to be the people who make it run, keep it afloat, sustain its values, suffer its deprivations and self-destructiveness, pick up its always reviving struggle for connection, for community, for joy and creation.

We think the cycle is really more like a spiral. Each time this set of ideas comes back it gains strength and coherence from the new research and practice that connects with it, and each time it appears it exerts more influence on the schools before it is once again suppressed. Today, we don't parse or diagram sentences as much as we once did, even though grammar still holds a central place in most curricula; we don't stress having students recite memorized poems or chunks of literature; we don't spend so much time having them copy over passages from books in order to practice penmanship; we don't spend energy on elocution exercises. As each of these unproductive practices is dropped, and as more effective, growth-producing methods prove themselves, we see gradual progress toward a better understanding of how human beings actually learn and acquire new uses of language.

DEFINING PROCESS WRITING

Now, having provided some of the context into which the process approach to writing fits, we need to return to writing itself—to the upper left-hand corner of the diagram in Figure 10—and to the problem of more clearly defining what process writing is. As John Dewey pointed out fifty years ago, innovators always bear a greater burden of explanation than traditionalists: "It is easier to walk in the paths that have been beaten than it is, after taking a new point of view, to

TABLE 9
COMPARISON OF POLARITIES

Old/traditional view	New/process view
Writing is a product to be evaluated.	Writing is a process to be experienced.
There is one correct procedure for writing.	There are many processes for different situations, subjects, audiences, authors.
Writing is taught rather than learned.	Writing is predominantly learned rather than taught.
The process of writing is largely conscious.	Writing often engages unconscious processes.
The process of writing is essentially linear: planning precedes writing and revision follows drafting, etc.	Writing processes are varied and recursive.
Writers must be taught atomistically, mastering small parts and subskills before attempting whole pieces of writing.	Writers learn best from attempting whole texts.
Writing can be done swiftly and on order.	The rhythms and pace of writing can be quite slow, since the writer's actual task is to create meaning.
Writing is a silent and solitary activity.	Writing is essentially social and collaborative.

work out what is practically involved in the new point of view." We first need to identify the key points of contrast between the old and new paradigms. As a place to start, Table 9 is an abridged version of Janet Emig's helpful graphic comparison of the polarities, which appears in the *Encyclopedia of Educational Research.*

Emig's chart provides a quick, schematic comparison of the new model and the older one. It also raises a number of tricky and important implications: for example, if writing is mostly learned rather than taught, what are teachers supposed to do? Emig's "Process View" column carries a few hints about teaching, and fortunately, over the past two decades, a great deal of thinking, testing, and research have fleshed out these ideas into a full, working definition of the process model. The fifteen principles for teaching writing that we outlined in Chapter 1 embody the major implications of this research, and we can begin to fill in Emig's sketch by discussing these principles in more detail.

But first, a brief word about the body of research supporting these principles. After being the stepchild of the three R's throughout the educational history of this country, writing has in recent years finally attracted the attention of many skillful, well-funded researchers. The results of this burst of empirical investigation have strongly endorsed the new process paradigm, and generally lent very little credence to the traditional pedagogical approaches. These research findings have been so consistent and powerful that they have helped to legitimize the new model in official public discourse about education.

While our list of principles draws upon many valuable sources, we want especially to credit a recent book by George Hillocks, *Research on Written Composition.* Hillocks has compiled the results of all the research studies in composition done over the period 1963–83 into one invaluable resource for both teachers and policymakers. Further, Hillocks employed a statistical technique called *meta-analysis,* which allows the results of many differently designed research studies to be combined and compared, so that the effectiveness of different types of treatments can be looked at overall. The result is that Hillocks' book provides the best available summary of what works in teaching writing. The only drawback of this important resource for both teachers and policymakers is Hillocks' personal prejudice against the National Writing Project, which he wrongly categorizes as promoting low-level and ineffective teaching strategies. Readers who recognize that most NWP sites *do* practice "environmental" methods of writing instruction (the most effective approach, according to Hillocks) will be able to screen the text accordingly and enjoy its full benefit.

There are fifteen teaching concepts which should provide a sufficient definition of the process model of writing instruction. We want to caution as we offer this list that we are not implying "good" writing teachers must enact *all* of these ideas in their classrooms, or that you, the teacher-reader, should implement and master all of them. On the contrary, we've noticed that the very finest writing teachers we know have intuitively picked two or three or four methods on this list, ideas that somehow fit their own style of teaching, and then translated them in a highly personalized way for working with their own students. Even more on the contrary, we think a list like this can be dangerous if teachers or their supervisors view it as embodying all the necessary parts ("subskills") of ideal practice. To make this menu of possibilities into a checklist of requirements is to engage in an insidious kind of perfectionism.

The common thread in the list below is that in the supporting research summarized by Hillocks and others, *each of these fifteen practices is associated with growth in students' writing performance according to measures of overall quality or effectiveness.* Research shows that improvement in student writing performance is related to the following elements.

1 Teachers who understand and appreciate the basic linguistic competence that students bring with them to school, and who therefore have positive expectations for students' achievements in writing

Educators have long been familiar with the "Pygmalion in the Classroom" research by Rosenthal and Jacobsen and others, which shows the tremendous power of teachers' expectations to condition the outcomes of student learning.

We are now discovering the altogether unsurprising fact that teachers' expectations are also very powerful in writing instruction. As Perl and others have documented, kids seem to grow more rapidly as writers when their teachers take delight in what they can do with language, accept and appreciate the language kids bring to school, and think of their job as building upon a solid base. On the other hand, teachers who see students' language as crude, handicapping, underdeveloped, immature, incomplete, or stunted have far less success in nurturing successful writers. Obviously there is nothing startling about this finding—in a way, it simply recapitulates the old Peace Corps ad about the glass that's described as being either half full or half empty. Teachers who see student writers as half full stimulate more growth than those who see them as half empty.

2 Regular and substantial practice at writing

Kids who write a lot get better at it. Not much news about that—but lack of practice is probably the single greatest reason for American students' dismal performance in writing. Kids in our schools simply don't write enough to grow as writers. Statistics from the National Assessment of Educational Progress, from reports like Arthur Applebee's, and from various individual states dramatically demonstrate that students write surprisingly little. According to NAEP, the average high school student in the United States completes a substantial piece of writing (which NAEP defines as one paragraph or more) about once a month. Now, how could anyone build competence at an activity so complex and demanding as writing by practicing only nine or ten times a year? Clearly, one of the main challenges to all teachers is to devote more student time, more learning time, to actually doing writing. There are really only two main ways of doing this: by reallocating instructional time presently used for other activities (many of which, like spelling, usage, or punctuation, can more effectively be taught through increased time-on-writing); or by using writing as a tool or method of teaching other subject matter content in the curriculum. We believe that both approaches can and should be used by teachers, and much of this book is about how.

3 Instruction in the process of writing—learning how to work at a given writing task in appropriate phases, including prewriting, drafting, and revising

Perhaps the second most important finding of all this research—after the need for much more writing practice—is that students' writing improves when their teachers break the work into stages, instead of simply assigning topics and then grading the eventual products. In other words, teachers need to help students approach writing as a process, a series of steps or stages an author goes through to develop a piece of writing. Many students are unaware of this craftsmanlike view of writing; they believe that good writers magically spin a perfect product out of their heads in one try. Instead, teachers need to create the staged process in the classroom: first, to structure time and activities for prewriting to help students gather and organize material and prepare for writing; next, to structure time and space for drafting, providing good conditions and support for students as they generate first versions of a piece; then, to provide activities for revision, helping students to resee and rework their writing toward clearer and better-edited products; finally, to arrange for students' writing to reach a variety of audiences, outlets for the work that provide direction during the writing and feedback on the product. There is a great deal of research showing that when students internalize this process approach, learning to take time and effort with prewriting and revision, their writing grows much more than students who don't have such an awareness. But students will not begin using this staged approach simply because they are exhorted to, or because someone tells them about it. The teacher needs to institute the process in the classroom, structuring and sequencing activities so that students experience it firsthand and internalize the stages of the process.

4 The opportunity to write for real, personally significant purposes

Where students often select their own subjects for writing, their writing grows more than in programs where the teacher always sets the topic. This finding is supported by the classroom studies of Donald Graves and others who observe that, at least some of the time, students need to exercise complete responsibility for the writing process from beginning to end. In order to appreciate the depth of this idea, we need to acknowledge the high degree of dependence upon the teacher that is created by the usual approach to teaching writing. Traditionally, the teacher decides on the topic; says what form or mode the writing is supposed to take; announces a length for the piece (or minimum number of words or pages, at least); offers some guidance about the tone, style, vocabulary, and other matters; and then, after the student has cranked out a piece according to these specifications, the teacher reviews the result against preset criteria and even locates each mechanical error for the student. In other words, the teacher has made all the important choices and decisions in the "writing," and has even done the clerical work of proofreading the final copy. If this is supposed to be rigorous, traditional instruction, how come it doesn't demand very much work from the students in terms of thinking, judgment, or responsibility? The research shows, on the contrary, that when students take more responsibility—we might even say authorship— from the very start, defining their own subjects and developing them through their own choices and decisions, their investment in writing increases.

5 Experience in writing for a wide range of audiences, both inside and outside of school

One of the most important things skilled writers do is to anticipate and meet the needs of an unseen, and perhaps only partly known, audience. This complex and deeply embedded skill seems to develop not through listening to precepts offered by teachers, but by actually trying to communicate with a wide range of audiences and learning from the results. When students have opportunities to write for a variety of audiences other than the teacher, their writing seems to grow more than when their only outlet for the work is a teacher's in-box. We speculate that there are four reasons why using different audiences with kids is so powerful. For one thing, a real audience provides that little jolt of energy that comes with knowing that the work is real, and not just another school hurdle to jump through. Second, writing for real audiences gives the authors some vital practice in thinking about their readers, trying to guess what they know, believe, understand, respond to, what language they recognize, what tone may be most effective with them, and so on. Third, audiences provide real feedback, priceless information about how effective a piece of writing really was, how it struck someone. Finally, writing for a real audience exerts upon the writer natural pressure to edit. If kids in school are writing to a clearly defined audience, perhaps one outside of the classroom in the "real" world, they easily recognize the importance of polishing the product, of taking pride in the form of their work— not because they'll get in trouble with the teacher or get their mechanics grade lowered, but because they don't want anything to compromise the effectiveness of their writing as communication. And this, of course, is the same reason real writers have for careful editing.

6 Rich and continuous reading experience, including both published writing and the work of peers and teachers

One of the least surprising findings from recent research on writing is the correlation between reading widely and well, and writing well. We adults probably recognize intuitively that a lot of what we know about writing we've learned from our reading; we have internalized vocabulary, sentence patterns, discourse types, even the underlying structures of whole genres of writing simply through the osmotic process of reading. Kids who have many opportunities to absorb these patterns learn in a very important way about how to write. One direct and more narrow implication of this idea is that kids must have a chance to read examples or models of the kinds of writing they are expected to produce in school. Too often, we ask students to produce highly conventionalized genres or forms of writing—research papers being the leading example—without their ever having had the chance to read and internalize the implicit patterns that characterize the genre.

7 Exposure to models of writing in process and writers at work, including both classmates and skilled adult writers

Students need to see skilled writers at work, so that they can gain insight into the processes by which writing gets done. Unfortunately, many students have crippling misconceptions about writing. Many believe, for example, that "good" writers write it right the first time. They define good writers as those who work neatly and effortlessly, and make no mistakes. But students need to see the way it really is: that experienced writers develop a piece through stages and steps, that it usually isn't perfect at first, that writing doesn't get easier or neater as you get better at it. One key practice that helps students better understand mature writing is for the teacher to write with the students, and to talk about his mental processes with them. For many kids, their teacher may be the only adult they ever really see at work writing, using writing to get something important done for himself—so this modeling may be vitally important. Students can also learn much from studying early drafts from their classmates, teachers, or even famous writers so they can discover the various processes by which rough ideas are gradually revised and shaped into final works.

8 Collaborative activities that provide ideas for writing and guidance in revising drafts in progress

The research strongly shows that social activities integrated into the writing process—such as prewriting discussions, collaborative drafting, peer editing groups, reading work aloud to the whole class or subgroups—can lead to better writing. These findings reflect an idea we discussed earlier: that writing is in fact a highly social act, and that past instructional practices mistakenly conceiving it as a solitary activity have been counterproductive. Even if drafting is done in solitary fashion, most real writing is part of a dialogue, one voice in an ongoing conversation in some larger community. When that conversation is aborted by having students simply write, turn in the paper, and get it back with a grade, we cut them off from a major portion of the available learning experience.

9 One-to-one writing conferences with the teacher

A number of studies have shown that when the teacher takes time to conduct regular, individual conferences with students about their writing, this kind of feedback helps students grow. Conferences may be very short (two or three minutes, in some studies) and may be fairly widely spaced (once every two or three weeks, for example) and still have considerable impact. It seems clear that the direct, personal focusing that happens in a conference is what makes it one of the most powerful things a teacher can do to promote growth in writing. Most teachers have long acknowledged the value of this practice but found it difficult to manage—figuring out what to do with the other twenty-nine students while these one-to-one conferences are going on. Later, we explain how some teachers we know have solved the management problems and what they do in conferences.

10 Inquiry-oriented classroom activities that involve students with rich sets of data and social interaction, and that focus on specific modes or elements of writing

Hillocks' research has contributed a couple of new terms to the literature of writing and writing research; one of them is *environmental* instruction. Hillocks identified four main approaches to teaching writing: presentational, individualized, natural process, and environmental. In his meta-analysis of research studies, he found the following differences in performance between treatment and control groups measured in terms of fractions of a standard deviaton.

Mode of instruction experimental/control effects	
Presentational	.02
Individualized	.16
Natural process	.18
Environmental	.44

In the *presentational* approach, the teacher lectures and conducts whole-class discussions about characteristics of good writing, sets students to work implementing these precepts, and gives written feedback on the results. On average, this approach results in essentially no measurable growth in students' writing performance. In fact, it was found that if the focus of the teacher's presentations is grammatical terminology, students' writing actually tends to detriorate.

The next method, which Hillocks labels the *individualized* mode, uses the one-to-one teacher-student conference as its main instructional strategy. This model delivers about eight times the growth in student writing as the presentational approach. However, in Hillocks' meta-analysis, this change represents less than a fifth of a standard deviation, so this improvement is actually quite modest.

The next model, the *natural process* approach, is just about as effective as the individualized. It is characterized by free writing on topics of student interest followed by peer-group sharing and teacher comment, but little direct instruction. Although the essence of this model seems to be having the teacher stand aside and let the kids write, it is associated with a considerably higher level of growth in the overall quality of student writing than the traditional, presentational approach.

The final category of instruction is what Hillocks calls the *environmental*. This approach is more than twice as effective as either the individualized or the natural process models. In environmental instruction, the teacher re-enters the process not as a grammarian or rule giver, but as a structurer of time, materials, and activities. The environmental teacher organizes many of the factors in the classroom environment to provide rich and structured writing practice for students, focusing sequentially on specific aspects of the writing work at hand, and involving a wide range of social-collaborative processes to help move the work along. As we'll explain later, we call this sort of artful teaching "facilitation." And even though Hillocks incorrectly tries to assign this latter term and this special teacher role to the natural process mode, this book aims to show why facilitation is the key to doing environmental-mode writing instruction in the classroom.

11 Increased use of sentence-combining exercises, which replaces instruction in grammatical terminology

Probably the best-researched question in the history of composition instruction concerns the connection between the teaching of formal grammar—diagramming sentences, learning the names of the parts of speech, and the like—and skill at writing. The outcome of nearly a hundred years of study is essentially unanimous: there is no positive relationship between knowing formal grammar and writing well. As one article in a 1920 issue of *Elementary School Journal* matter-of-factly began, "We were shown a number of years ago that children who have studied formal grammar do not write any better or interpret literature any better than children who have not studied formal technical grammar." In fact, as Hillocks' more recent and more sophisticated study shows, focusing on grammar and mechanics in a writing class is the only approach that causes an average *worsening* in students' writing performance (about a third of a standard deviation in his meta-analysis). This doesn't mean that grammar is actually harmful, but simply that it is irrelevant to composition and steals instructional time from classroom activities more directly related to writing.

On the other hand, sentence combining, a type of exercise in which students combine several short "kernel" sentences into longer, more complex ones, is strongly associated with improved writing performance. Sentence combining works because it is a productive, not an analytic, activity; it works by helping students to tap into their oral language base, their latent knowledge of many complex sentence types, and then to practice transferring this oral knowledge to writing.

It is important that you, the reader, not confuse the messenger with the message here—especially since debates over the value of grammar are finally religious in nature. Both of us are quite fond of grammar and have a good deal of training in linguistics. We believe that the study of language is a vital element of a humanistic education. Indeed, if we were kings of the world, students would probably be studying a lot more grammar and descriptive linguistics than is currently the case: we'd have them learning about semantics and phonology and syntax, the origins and history of language, language change, social dialects and occupational jargons, attitudes toward language, and dozens of other fascinating subjects. But what we wouldn't do—based on what we've learned from the research and from our own work with real, live writers—is to expect grammatical terminology to help anyone learn how to write. So we wouldn't use writing time to teach grammatical terms or linguistic information.

12 Mechanics of writing taught in the context of students' own compositions, rather than in separate exercises and drills

The research confirms what most teachers have already learned through long and painful experience: there's often little transfer between what kids can do in a controlled drill situation and on actual pieces of writing. Spelling is perhaps the most familiar example. Students who have scored 100 percent on the weekly spelling test will promptly misspell half the words from the very same list on a book report or in-class essay. This reminds us that teaching kids how to manifest subskills on a ditto is no guarantee of any transfer to consistent, productive use in actual writing. The problem is that the cognitive task of getting correct answers on a one-skill test is totally different from the demands of a real writing situation, where an author must balance and attend to dozens of factors—content, audience, purpose, rhetoric, vocabulary, tone, mechanics of all kinds. Indeed, research offers little support for atomized drills in mechanics and instead points teachers toward addressing mechanics where they make the most sense: amid the texts kids create themselves.

13 Moderate marking of the surface structure errors in student papers, focusing on sets or patterns of related errors

Much research has been devoted to teacher marking of student papers in order to find the "right" way for teachers to handle the problem of errors. The standard, traditional approach is for the teacher to mark every error in every paper every student ever writes with a red pen. While this is viewed by the public, most principals, and many teachers as the only responsible and appropriate kind of teacher feedback, the research does not validate its effectiveness. In fact, students do not seem to be able to learn very well from such a flood of red ink. They often cannot see through the welter of undifferentiated marks to notice what the related sets or patterns of errors are; in other words, the feedback is not clear and focused. Many students also experience such wholesale marking of their papers as a personal rejection and become discouraged from paying any further attention to the paper at all. Instead, the research recommends that teachers focus students' attention on one or two related patterns of error at a time, making sure the problem is mastered before directing their attention to another category of errors.

14 Flexible and cumulative evaluation of writing that stresses revision. The teacher's written comments include a mixture of praise and criticism, with praise predominating

In some of the most effective writing programs recently studied, teachers separate evaluation from grading and hold off grading until late in the development of each assignment—or even until late in the term. This approach emerges from the insight that grades tend to kill off pieces of writing. Since students know that grades customarily mark the end of a piece of work in school, teachers who put grades on early drafts of writing often inadvertently terminate students' engagement with the work and cut off the possibility of revision. More effective teachers focus on giving students formative responses to early drafts, using this feedback to move students along into a process of revising.

One element of such responding is written comments on papers. The comparative value of different forms of these comments has been investigated. The conclusion: the most growth-inducing sort of comment is not all praise or all criticism, but a mixture of praise and criticism, with praise predominating. Of course this is a mixture that many skillful teachers have long since discovered for themselves: "I liked your story a lot because it was funny and full of details. I got a little bit confused in the middle where Abraham Lincoln and Janet Jackson were dancing on the roof, but then it all came together at the end, and the Easter Bunny's speech really summed things up nicely."

15 Writing as a tool of learning in all subjects across the curriculum

Students grow not so much by practicing writing as by using it, applying writing as a tool for learning both in and out of school. One of the dangers, ironically, of the process-writing movement is that we want to make more time in the instructional day for writing—which, at one level, of course, is welcome. But we mustn't focus on writing just because we want to do a better job with a neglected element of the official school curriculum. The larger reason for learning to write—the reason that ought to be reflected in the time we spend on writing with kids—is that writing helps people get important things done: thinking, exploring, relating, and making connections. In school, we have unlimited opportunities to embed writing activities into the work of other content areas—literature, science, history, music, art, everything. In schools where writing is used across the curriculum, students' writing performance grows strongly. That's because kids are being shown, in countless ways every day, how they can take power over writing and, through writing, think for themselves and express themselves.

This, then, is the list of observations and recommendations researchers are continuing to refine. However, as we know, educational research too often fails to influence classroom practice very much, or for very long. While this may seem to be another manifestation of the fad/pendulum phenomenon, we believe that the history of obstacles and frustrations offers a much better explanation of why this happens. In addition, researchers themselves are frequently quite unhelpful about translating their findings into usable classroom practices, and their lack of awareness of teachers' everyday working conditions hampers communication between the two groups. This book aims to improve the connection at the secondary level, using the tremendous resourcefulness of good teachers who have shared their ideas and strategies with us over the past ten years. In so doing, we hope to strengthen the cycle of progressive whole-language teaching, which forms the larger context for our effort, as it comes round once again in the ongoing battle for the soul of American schooling.

A NOTE ON PROPHETS AND PARADIGMS

The daughter of a friend of ours attends seventh grade at a fine local junior high school. Julianna's teacher has been through a couple of district-sponsored in-service programs on writing and has become a disciple of the writing-process approach. Among other things, this teacher enthusiastically pressures students to revise their writing, asking them to leave the trail of their revisions right in the work. "Don't worry about making it pretty," he says. "Let me see the scratch-outs, arrows, insertions, and other changes right on your paper." Julianna's personal composing process has comfortably accommodated the teacher's preferences. When she writes, Julianna still works, as she always has, in one essentially continuous and skillful draft. Then, when she's done, she looks back through the text for a few especially fine or sophisticated word choices. If she has written "gigantic," for example, she'll now erase it and write in "big." Then she crosses out "big" and writes "gigantic" above it. Once she's made a few more such "revisions," Julianna smudges up the corners of the paper and turns it in to her delighted teacher.

Sarah Freedman's research has uncovered similar instances. In a long-term ethnographic study of two California classrooms where peer response groups were being used, Freedman collected delightful transcripts of students in editing groups collaboratively subverting the teacher's instructions. The kids would negotiate ways of pretending to get the work done and to fake some peer feedback that the teacher would believe was genuine. The two teachers Freedman selected for the study were, like Julianna's teacher, highly respected veteran teachers reportedly dedicated to the new process paradigm. But both teachers admitted to Freedman their personal lack of belief in the strategy. Indeed, these teachers' management of the response groups—including inconsistent directions and the failure to provide systematic, staged training—dramatized how a teacher's halfhearted embrace of a half-understood idea can completely undermine a promising activity.

What Julianna and the students in California have done is to turn the new paradigm back into the old one: once again, students are grinding out disconnected writing to a teacher's specifications, rather than truly owning their words and work. This regression happens over and over when teachers don't implement and monitor their innovations deeply, congruently, thoughtfully, and self-critically. There's no power like the power of violated expectations among students: when teachers try something unexpected in the classroom, even when it may be pleasant and valuable, kids have limitless ways of channeling things right back into the old, familiar ways. If a teacher is just mimicking the surface features of an ill-understood strategy, subversion and regression are inevitable.

We've seen many other disturbing cases where blind or shallow allegiance to the process paradigm has created classrooms just as rigid and uncreative as any that adhere to the traditional approach. We've seen teachers exhausted and demoralized from trying to publish handmade books or class magazines on the frantic timetable dictated by Graves. We hear from teachers who blame themselves for not being able to meet the conferencing schedule set forth by Calkins. We meet teachers who have been made to feel guilty, apologetic, and untrendy because they still give their students occasional writing assignments or, Graves forbid, have a whole class write on the same topic at the same time.

As Nancie Atwell says in a reflective moment in her book *In the Middle,* "I realize that I am running just as tight a ship as I ever did, it's just a different kind of ship." When we teachers fall in love with our own innovations, it's important to ask ourselves: How different is this ship? How tight? And how tight can it be and really be different from the traditional one?

We think that the process model, which we've just generally endorsed, is an important step ahead for our field. However, like any paradigm, it opens the door to blind allegiance, to rigidity, to loyalty tests, even to oppression. Some of these problems have already begun to afflict the process approach to writing. The ideas of a few key theorists—Graves, Calkins, Murray—have ossified into doctrine for too many teachers. But in writing, as in everything else, the map is not the territory, and the prophets are not the paradigm.

If a new paradigm starts to restrict teachers' choices, to narrow the range of things you're allowed to try in the classroom, something has gone astray. If the paradigm asks you to blindly follow the dictates of some guru, then it's no better than blindly following the dictates of dumb tradition. Indeed, how can we ask students to be responsible for their own work if we won't take responsibility for our own teaching?

The same principle applies in full to this book: We offer many concrete, explicit suggestions and activities for teaching writing. It's a complex and sensitive art, and only through specifics can we exemplify and elucidate what we're trying to say. However, readers should not mistake these suggestions for The Method of teaching writing, nor will wise teachers try to do all the things we mention. We hope that, instead, teachers will be inspired by one or more of these ideas to go ahead and create their own new activities for teaching writing, that they'll choose one or two aspects of the craft at a time to explore in more depth, and that they'll fill in the many gaps and blind spots we've neglected.

This book is not about becoming anyone's disciple or being converted to a pedagogical religion. It's about expanding your choices, your repertoire, your flexibility. We believe that teachers should have the widest possible range of strategies from which to draw in working with the students they have. While we do believe that some ideas and techniques are better than others—and we will continue to make our preferences clear—we recognize that for almost any imaginable situation with real kids in real schools, there will usually be several good ways for a teacher to behave. You don't have to possess the "right" technique; you just need one that works.

The danger we face in our field today, and it's now a serious threat, is the idea that there is only one right way to handle a given kid, a given grade level, a given chunk of curriculum, a given element of writing. This is not just wrong; it is profoundly, dangerously, insidiously wrong. It makes a joke of any connection we assert between kids' authorship of writing and our hopes that schools can build freedom, democracy, or liberation. If there's only one right way to teach writing, then all that's left for teachers to do is decide which church to join and then follow the doctrine.

Orthodoxy is the enemy. Donald Graves said this loud and clear a few years back, and what happened? Most people just ignored his warning and elevated *him* to the pantheon. So we'll say it again. Orthodoxy is the enemy. This is *our* one orthodoxy, but we sincerely hope it's the only one.

REFERENCES

Applebee, Arthur N. 1981. *Writing in the Secondary School: English and the Content Areas.* Urbana, IL: National Council of Teachers of English.

Atwell, Nancie. 1987. *In the Middle: Writing, Reading, and Learning with Adolescents.* Portsmouth, NH: Boynton/Cook.

Calkins, Lucy McCormick. 1986. *The Art of Teaching Writing.* Portsmouth, NH: Heinemann.

Clarke, Mark. 1987. "Don't Blame the System: Constraints on Whole Language Reform." *Language Arts 64*: 384–396.

Emig, Janet. 1983. *The Web of Meaning: Essays on Writing, Thinking, Learning, and Teaching.* Portsmouth, NH:Boynton/Cook.

Emig, Janet. 1971. *The Composing Processes of Twelfth Graders.* Urbana, IL: National Council of Teachers of English.

Freedman, Sarah W. 1987. *Peer Response Groups in Two Ninth-Grade Classrooms.* Berkeley, CA: Center for the Study of Writing.

Graves, Donald H. 1983. *Writing: Teachers and Children at Work.* Portsmouth, NH: Heinemann.

Hillocks, George, Jr. 1986. *Research on Written Composition: New Directions for Teaching.* Urbana, IL: National Council of Teachers of English.

Murray, Donald. 1968. *A Writer Teaches Writing.* Boston: Houghton Mifflin.

Perl, Sondra. 1978. "Five Writers Writing: Case Studies of the Composing Processes of Unskilled College Writers." Ph.D. diss., New York University.

Perl, Sondra, and Nancy Wilson. 1986. *Through Teachers' Eyes: Portraits of Writing Teachers at Work.* Portsmouth, NH: Heinemann.

The Development of Writing Abilities During the School Years

James L. Collins

INTRODUCTION

My purpose here is to modify a rather conventional approach to understanding the development of writing abilities. This approach describes writing development in terms of a linear or hierarchical model, as a continuum consisting of identifiable, sequentially ordered stages. I argue that this conception is problematic on two related counts: it appropriately describes only one dimension of writing development, and it neglects societal and instructional influences on writing abilities. It emphasizes cognitive processes and tends to exclude social ones. In place of this conventional approach, I argue for one that includes a functional perspective on writing development during the school years. This latter approach rests on two major theoretical premises. Writing development is viewed as an interaction between cognitive processes involved in writing and educational and cultural contexts that influence these processes (Collins, 1981; Elsasser & John-Steiner, 1977; John-Steiner & Tatter, in press; Kroll, 1980). This influence, furthermore, is accomplished through the functions of writing in particular contexts (Britton, Burgess, Martin, McLeod, & Rosen, 1975; Scribner & Cole, 1978, 1981). In reasoning from these premises, I synthesize findings in research on writing development within what can be called a developmental-functional framework.

COGNITIVE DEVELOPMENT AND WRITING

The key concept in such a framework is that development in writing varies with the functions of writing. Writing development is a hybrid; it combines development in the sense of genetic maturity with development in the sense of learning from instruction and socialization. In the first sense, writing development resembles the learning of oral language or of a second language; the pattern of development shows emphasis on phonology and lexicon at early stages and on syntax and discourse at later ones (Shuy, 1981). In the second sense, writing development is less concerned with form and more with function. Here writers learn to write (or not to write) for socially and educationally determined purposes; the pattern of development becomes dominated particularly by school-sponsored functions of writing. As Bereiter puts the matter, "writing development, in a highly schooled society, is whatever the schools make it to be" (1980, p. 88).

If writing development varies with the functions of writing, we can expect a linear or hierarchical developmental model to most accurately describe an early stage in the growth of writing abilities, a stage where most children have no need for writing or any real sense of its usefulness (Vygotsky, 1934/1962). This does not mean that early writing serves no function; rather, it suggests that writing is functionally associated at first with other symbolic activities. Writing in these early, spontaneous occurrences does show sequential development (King & Rentel, 1979), and a functional association with other activities has been noted (Gundlach, 1981). These activities include gestures (Vygotsky, 1978) and symbolic play (Pellegrini, 1980; Vygotsky, 1978). The association between writing and drawing is particularly strong. Dyson (1982) concluded from her observations of kindergarten writers that writing is at first a form of graphic representation that is made meaningful through talk. Others, as well, have noted that writing by young children often occurs in conjunction with drawing (Graves,

1975; Gundlach and Moses, Note 1). An example of this early writing will illustrate how easily it conforms to a linear developmental model:

I was wawking thrue the wds,
Wan I saw a pritty brd. It
was bringing the babby brds
a wrm to eat. It was a
butifl day. The sky was
blue and clear. I was waring my
red shrt with the blue trimming
and my blue geandges.

The paragraph was spontaneously written by a first-grade girl. The writing was done on the back of a piece of paper, and on the front side she had first drawn the scene described in the writing. The writing is personal and concrete, expressive and narrative in form, and shows a high degree of implicit meaning. The writing leans on graphic representation and on spoken sounds that govern invented spellings in a regularly abstracted way (Chomsky, 1970; Read, 1971). Developmentally, the writing suggests Bruner's (1966) division of representation into three sequential modes (enactive, ikonic, and symbolic), since the writing combines graphic and written modes. The writing also suggests a linear model that places personal writing before social writing, as when Britton (1970, 1975) traces poetic and transactional writing to their roots in expressive writing (see also Emig's, 1971, similar distinctions among reflexive, extensive, and expressive writing). And, of course, the writing also suggests Piaget's (1926/1955) developmental scheme leading from egocentric to socialized speech. Each of these linear or hierarchical models places our writer at the early end of a developmental continuum, and since she is in first grade, such placement is appropriate.

When the same placement is attempted for older writers, however, it becomes problematic. Such an attempt is made when writing problems are attributed to the egocentricity of the apprentice writer (Moffett, 1968; Shaughnessy, 1977). This argument, particularly in its stronger forms—basic writers in college have not attained a concept-forming level of cognitive development (Lunsford, 1979); in matters of coherence, some adult writers are like young children (Brostoff, 1981)— assumes that writing development is a function of cognitive growth. Adult writers, that is, produce writing characterized by egocentric language and thought because they are somehow arrested at an early, egocentric stage of cognitive development. Such reasoning confuses description with explanation (Krauss & Glucksburg, 1977) and is inconsistent with research showing that fourth-grade writers decenter less while writing than while speaking (Kroll, 1978). Curiously, the egocentricity argument is usually supported with reference to Piaget (1926/1955), in spite of his view that particular social environments help children become more sociocentric (Ducksworth, 1979; Inhelder & Piaget, 1959).

LITERACY AND WRITING

An alternative formulation of the linear model of writing development argues that cognitive growth is a function of literacy. In reality this is the same "line of development" just discussed, only now the development of writing abilities proceeds in the reverse direction; writing ability pushes cognitive growth instead of cognition pushing growth in writing abilities. Research supporting this alternative formulation often is based on differences between spoken and written language. Spoken language is concrete and context-dependent; it requires shared reference and an interlocutor. Written language is more abstract and context-independent; reference is textual, thus permitting communication with an absent or unknown reader. Greenfield (1972) argues that these differences distinguish between characteristic modes of thought in oral and literate cultures. Many others (Elsasser & John-Steiner, 1977; Emig, 1978; Goody & Watt, 1976; Hartwell, 1980; Hirsch, 1977; Olson, 1977; Shaughnessy, 1977; see also the essays in Kroll & Vann, 1981) make these differences the basis of a developmental transition from speaking to writing or from dialogue to monologue.

Two parallel concerns characterize recent research investigating this transition. One is the role of instruction in what is perceived as a "natural" cognitive-developmental process. In Bereiter and Scardamalia (1982), for example, a dozen or so experiments reporting the effects of procedural facilitations, i.e., strategies designed to ease the cognitive demands of writing, are reviewed. Generally, they found that teaching that does not involve new knowledge or skills and that does not deal with the content of writing eases the cognitive burdens of writing and the oral-to-written transition for fourth- and sixth-grade writers. The second concern is with the functions of language and writing. In Olson and Torrance (1981), for example, problems in learning to read and write are investigated in respect to the realignment of the primary functions of language that accompanies the speaking-writing transition. These functions, the interpersonal in speech and the ideational in writing, create the demand for explicit and autonomous meaning in written language; thus, mastery of the ideational or logical functions of language results from the development of writing (and reading) abilities.

These concerns for the instructional and functional contexts of writing underscore the problematic nature of an understanding of writing development that is restricted to a linear model. Whether cognitive development promotes or results from literacy is not the real issue. A more meaningful approach to understanding writing development is to admit that cognitive processes and writing abilities develop together in particular educational and social settings. This approach asks that we take a contextualized perspective on writing development, including contexts that are rhetorical (purpose, topic, audience), educational (conditions associated with schooling), and societal (the sociocultural backgrounds of writers and audiences). Consideration of each of these contexts shows that development in writing varies with the functions of writing.

CONTEXTS OF WRITING

The meaning of that variation is illustrated at the rhetorical level by studies of syntactic maturity. These studies analyze student writing in respect to the T-unit (one main clause and other, dependent clauses attached to or embedded in it). Researchers have used mean number of words per T-unit, mean number of clauses per T-unit, and mean number of words per clause as the chief measures of syntactic maturity. The major findings in this research are that written syntactic complexity develops chronologically in the direction of increased complexity (Hunt, 1965, 1970; O'Donnell, Griffin, & Norris, 1967) and that data on syntactic maturity can be regarded as normative (Hunt, 1965; Mellon, 1969; O'Hare, 1973; Stotsky, 1975). Recent research, however, suggests that these findings might be misleading. Studies that show a connection between assigned purpose of discourse and syntactic complexity (Crowhurst & Piché, 1979; Rubin & Piché, 1979; San Jose, 1972; Smith & Swan, 1978) argue against a linear conception of syntactic maturity. Crowhurst and Piché, for example, found a greater difference in mean T-unit length between argument and narration at grade 10 than Hunt (1965) found between grades 8 and 12, suggesting that syntactic complexity varies with the functions of writing more than it varies with chronological age or grade.

Collins and Williamson (1981, in press) found evidence of a similar variation in what can be called *semantic complexity.* They examined a possible developmental transition from implicit spoken dialogue to explicit written monologue at two ability levels (measured by primary trait scoring) in each of three grade levels (4, 8, 12). Measures of dialogic features were personal and demonstrative exophoric references (Halliday & Hasan, 1976) and formulaic expressions (Ong, 1979). In the first study, purpose of writing and audience were held constant, and better writers showed a decrease in the proportion of dialogic features in their writing across grade levels; weaker writers, however, did not. In the second study, better writers adjusted the proportion of dialogic features in their writing appropriately according to assigned variations in purpose and audience. Weaker writers adjusted the same proportion for audience but not for purpose. Taken together, these studies suggest a strong developmental trend toward explicit expression of meaning in writing. That trend, however, varies with grade, ability, and assigned rhetorical contexts, especially purpose.

When we move from consideration of rhetorical context to consideration of the educational contexts of writing, we find that audience and function play an even larger role in the development of writing abilities (Britton et al., 1975). Britton et al.'s report consists of a comprehensive description of factors involved in the development of writing and of how these factors are addressed and neglected in school-sponsored writing in British schools (and a recent report by Applebee, 1981, extends many of the findings to American schools). Britton et al. identified audience and mode, in respect to function or purpose for writing, as the crucial dimensions in writing development. Each of these dimensions was seen as developing through processes of differentiation from the self outward. They described differentiation in the writer's sense of audience in terms of categories ranging from self to unknown general reader. In differentiation of function they described categories that range from expressive, personal, writing outward in two directions, toward the poetic or literary, and toward the transactional or nonliterary. In their analysis of more than 2,000 samples of writing across school disciplines and across ages 11 to 18, Britton and his colleagues found that 92% of school writing is done for a teacher audience, that 49% is done for the teacher in the role of examiner, and that these audiences increase generally with grade level. The results for the function categories are similar: 63% of the writing done in school is transactional, most of which (37%) shows an informative purpose, and this category increases with grade level. Britton et al. concluded that writing experiences in schools seriously neglect the full range of options available to writers. Schooling generally takes a restricted, and possibly restricting, view of writing development. That possibility is illustrated in the following example, written by an eighth-grade girl:

Propaganda is the spreading of invented
or real facts to support a particular
set of beliefs such as a political
ideology. In *Animal Farm,* George Orwell
is warning us about the dangers of
propaganda that is accepted without
criticism.

This example was written by the same writer whose first-grade writing was quoted earlier. Her writing no longer leans on drawing and experience. Or perhaps she has learned to be a good academic writer, one who writes about recently studied literature in a knowledgeable, abstract, formal, syntactically complex way, since such is a dominant purpose of writing in school. Britton's study suggests that these are one and the same: development in writing is limited to the functions of writing in school.

The Scribner and Cole studies (1978, 1981) of an indigenous writing system used by the Vai of Liberia suggest that the dominance of school-sponsored functions of writing may be culture-specific. This extends our consideration of contexts of writing development to the societal level. Among the Vai, the learning of literacy skills and schooling are separate activities, and the effects of literacy can be studied apart from the effects of schooling. The Scribner and Cole studies of these effects resulted in the conclusions that literacy involves quite particular skills and functions and that schooling develops abilities to generalize intellectual skills across various problem-solving situations. These conclusions contradict the theoretical assumption that writing (and reading) development is tied to cognitive growth either as cause or consequence. Writing development is tied to experiences with literate language. Cole and Scribner make this last point by emphasizing the functions of reading and writing. Functional analysis, that which examines the uses of literate language in and out of school, becomes more promising than developmental analysis by itself. Studying the ways that written language is perceived and used in particular school and social settings can inform our understanding of how and why writing ability develops for some students and not for others. Writing ability is tied to specific uses of writing in the home, school, and larger social settings.

A recent study by Kroll (in press) shows one form that analysis of the developmental influences of language in use can take. Kroll used data from two phases of a major longitudinal study of children's language development in Bristol, England. In the first phase, radio microphones had been used to record samples of spontaneous speech in the homes of 64 children selected to represent Bristol children in terms of gender, age, and social class. The one-half million recorded utterances were transcribed, coded and used to study the relationship among language development, socioeconomic background, and language interaction in the home. In the second phase, a subsample of 20 of the same children at age 7 was studied to determine factors that contribute to the acquisition of reading. (Wells, 1979, 1981).

Kroll used 18 of the 20 children in the reading project at age 9 as the principal subjects in his study, and he included 56 children, identified as typical writers by teachers of the same classes as this project group, as a comparison group. The antecedent factors Kroll examined for influence on writing development were oral language development, preschool knowledge of literacy, parental interest in literacy, socioeconomic background, and level of reading attainment. Kroll devised specific tasks to obtain four writing samples from each child during a 5-week period. The tasks were built around functions of writing: a personal experience (expressive purpose); a story based on a picture (narrative purpose); letters seeking a home for a puppy (persuasive purpose); and instructions to play a new game (explanatory purpose). Kroll analyzed the compositions written in response to these tasks for syntactic complexity measured by mean T-unit length, subordination measured as a mean number of clauses per T-unit, and vocabulary figured by Carroll's (1964) type/token ration. In addition, the overall quality of compositions was determined using holistic scoring (as described by Myers, 1980) for the expressive and narrative tasks, measures of context and appeals for the persuasive task, and a measure of informational adequacy (as in Kroll, 1978; Kroll & Lempers, 1981) for the explanatory task. Kroll's findings identified parental interest in literacy and preschool knowledge of literacy as powerful predictors of writing attainment at age 9. He interpreted these findings in terms of the insight process variables, such as parental interest in literacy, offer in clarifying the meaning of the status variable, socioeconomic background.

Correlational studies of out-of-school language and writing attainment are, of course, not the only way to study writing development from a functional perspective. Ethnographic methods, such as Cazden (in press) used to explore the applicability of Vygotsky's concept of a zone of proximal development, ethno-historical methods to study the functions of writing in society (Heath, 1981), and sociolinguistic methods to study styles and registers found in school and social contexts (Labov, 1975) are other approaches to a functional understanding of writing development. These examples are not meant to be exhaustive but rather to be representative of diverse methods that can be used to build that understanding.

Functional analysis adds a societal or cultural dimension to our understanding of writing development. The linear, cognitive model does not take into account the ways society distributes and uses literacy skills. We have suspected for some time that writing development is connected to societal contexts: socioeconomic status affects language development (Loban, 1976) and language performance (Bernstein, 1975; Hawkins, 1977); adult basic writers hold membership in residually oral subcultures (Farrell, 1977); writing ability is unevenly distributed along class lines (Hendrix, 1981). These theories can be examined with continued research into functional aspects of writing development.

In addition to implications for further research, the functional perspective has a major implication for the way educators conceive of writing development. The linear model is simply inadequate. Writing development does not have a fixed and uniform pattern; if we want to hold onto the notion of stages, then we have to view these stages as variable (Bereiter, 1980). And it might be better to reject the notion of stages entirely. We are all capable of "egocentric" writing, for example, when the task gets difficult enough (Rubin, 1981; Onore, Note 2). I have often suspected that another example of "regression to an early stage" is available in the charts and lines we use to represent models of writing processes and writing development; perhaps this is the same connection between writing and drawing that was noted in the first-grade sample I provided above. We need a flexible, functional conception of writing development rather than a fixed, linear one. Writing development is negotiated every time written language is used.

REFERENCE NOTES

1 Gundlach, R., and Moses, R. 1976. *Developmental issues in the study of children's written language.* Paper presented at the Boston University Conference on Language Development.
2 Onore, C. S. 1982. *Revision, learning and the myth of improvement.* Paper presented at the Conference on College Composition and Communication, San Francisco, March.

REFERENCES

Applebee, A. N. 1981. *Writing in the secondary school.* Urbana, IL: NCTE.
Bereiter, C. Development in writing. 1980. In L. W. Gregg and E. R. Steinberg (Eds.), *Cognitive processes in writing.* Hillsdale, NJ: Erlbaum.
Bereiter, C., and M. Scardamalia. 1982. From conversation to composition: The role of

instruction in a developmental process. In R. Glaser (Ed.), *Advances in instructional psychology* (Vol. 2). Hillsdale, NJ: Erlbaum.

Bernstein, B. 1975. *Class, codes and control* (Vol. 1). London: Routledge and Kegan Paul.

Britton, J. 1970. *Language and learning.* Baltimore, MD: Penguin.

———. 1975. Teaching writing. In A. Davies (Ed.), *Problems of language and learning.* London: Heinemann.

Britton, J., T. Burgess, N. Martin, A. McLeod, and H. Rosen. 1975. *The development of writing abilities, 11–18.* London: Macmillan Education.

Brostoff, A. 1981. Coherence: "Next to" is not "connected to." *College Composition and Communication, 32,* 278–294.

Bruner, J., R. Olver, P. Greenfield, J. Hornsby, H. Kemey, M. Maccoby, N. Modiano, F. Moser, D. Olson, M. Potter, L. Reisch, and A. Sonstroem, 1966. *Studies in cognitive growth.* New York: Wiley.

Carroll, J. B. 1964. *Language and thought.* Englewood Cliffs, NJ: Prentice-Hall.

Cazden, C. B. In press. Peekaboo as an instructional model: Discourse development at home and at school. In B. Bain (Ed.), *The sociogenesis of language and human conduct.* New York: Plenum.

Chomsky, C. 1970. Reading, writing, and phonology. *Harvard Educational Review, 40,* 287–309.

Collins, J. L. 1981. *Spoken language and the development of writing abilities.* Paper presented at the Conference on College Composition and Communication, Dallas. (ERIC Document Reproduction Service No. ED 199 729)

Collins, J. L., and M. M. Williamson. 1981. Spoken language and semantic abbreviation in writing. *Research in the Teaching of English, 15,* 23–35.

———. In press. Assigned rhetorical context and semantic abbreviation in writing. In R. Beach & L. Bridwell (Eds.), *New directions in composition research.* New York: Guilford.

Crowhurst, M., and G. L. Piché. 1979. Audience and mode of discourse effects on syntactic complexity in writing at two grade levels. *Research in the Teaching of English, 13,* 101–109.

Duckworth, E. 1979. Either we're too early and they can't learn it or we're too late and they know it already: The dilemma of "applying Piaget." *Harvard Educational Review, 49,* 297–312.

Dyson, A. H. In press. The role of oral language in early writing processes. *Research in the Teaching of English.*

Elsasser, N., and V. P. John-Steiner. 1977. An interactionist approach to advancing literacy. *Harvard Educational Review, 47,* 355–369.

Emig, J. 1971. *The composing processes of twelfth graders.* Urbana, IL: NCTE.

———. 1978. Hand, eye, brain: Some "basics" in the writing process. In C. Cooper and L. Odell (Eds.), *Research on composing: Points of departure,* Urbana, IL: NCTE.

Farrell, T. J. 1977. Literacy, the basics, and all that jazz. *College English, 38,* 443–459.

Goody, J., and I. Watt. 1976. The consequences of literacy. In J. Karabel and A. H. Halsey (Eds.), *Power and ideology in education.* New York: Oxford University Press.

Graves, D. 1975. An examination of the writing processes of seven year old children. *Research in the Teaching of English, 9,* 227–241.

Greenfield, P. M. 1972. Oral or written language: The consequences for cognitive development in Africa, the United States and England. *Language and Speech, 15,* 169–178.

Gundlach, R. A.. 1981. On the nature and development of children's writing. In C. H. Frederiksen and J. F. Dominic (Eds.), *Writing: The nature, development, and teaching of written communication.* (Vol. 2) Hillsdale, NJ: Erlbaum.

Halliday, M. A. K., and R. Hasan, 1976. *Cohesion in English.* London: Longman.

Hartwell, P. 1980. Dialect interference in writing: A critical view. *Research in the Teaching of English, 14,* 101–118.

Hawkins, P. R. 1977. *Social class, the nominal group and verbal strategies.* London: Routledge and Kegan Paul.

Heath, S. B. 1981. Toward an ethnohistory of writing in American Education. In M. F. Whiteman (Ed.), *Writing: The nature, development, and teaching of written communication* (Vol. 1). Hillsdale, NJ: Erlbaum.

Hendrix, R. 1981. The status and politics of writing instruction. In M. F. Whiteman (Ed.), *Writing: The nature, development, and teaching of written communication* (Vol. 1). Hillsdale, NJ: Erlbaum.

Hirsch, E. D., Jr. 1977. *The philosophy of composition.* Chicago: University of Chicago Press.

Hunt, K. W. 1965. *Grammatical structures written at three grade levels.* Research Report No. 3. Urbana, IL: NCTE.

———. 1970. Syntactic maturity in school children and adults. *Monographs of the Society for Research in Child Development, 35,* (1, Serial No. 134).

Inhelder, B., and J. Piaget. 1959. *The growth of logical thinking.* London: Routledge and Kegan Paul.

John-Steiner, V., and P. Tatter. In press. An interactionist model of language development. In B. Bain (Ed.), *The sociogenesis of language and human conduct.* New York: Plenum.

King, M. L., and V. Rentel. 1979. Toward a theory of early writing development. *Research in the Teaching of English, 13,* 243–253.

Krauss, R. M., and S. Glucksberg. 1977. Social and nonsocial speech. *Scientific American, 236,* 100–105.

Kroll, B. M. 1978. Cognitive egocentrism and the problem of audience awareness in written discourse. *Research in the Teaching of English, 12,* 269-281.

———. 1980. Developmental perspectives and the teaching of composition. *College English, 41,* 741-752.

———. In press. Antecedents of individual differences in children's writing attainment. In. B. M. Kroll and C. G. Wells (Eds.), *Explorations in the development of writing.* Chichester: John Wiley.

Kroll, B. M., and J. D. Lempers. 1981. Effect of mode of communication on the informational adequacy of children's explanations. *The Journal of Genetic Psychology, 138,* 27–35.

Kroll, B. M., and R. J. Vann. (Eds.). 1981. Exploring speaking-writing relationships: *Connections and contrasts.* Urbana, IL: NCTE.

Labov, W. 1975. *The study of nonstandard English.* Urbana, IL: NCTE.

Loban, W. 1976. *Language development: Kindergarten through grade twelve.* Research Report No. 18. Urbana, IL: NCTE.

Lunsford, A. 1979. Cognitive development and the basic writer. *College English, 41,* 39–46.

Mellon, J. C. 1969. *Transformational sentence-combining.* Research Report No. 10. Champaign, IL: NCTE.

Moffett, J. 1968. *Teaching the universe of discourse.* Boston: Houghton Mifflin.

Myers, M. 1980. *A procedure for writing assessment and holistic scoring.* Urbana, IL: NCTE.

O'Donnell, R. C., W. J. Griffin, and R. C. Norris. 1967. *Syntax of kindergarten and elementary school children: A transformational analysis.* Research Report No. 8. Urbana, IL: NCTE.

O'Hare, F. 1973. *Sentence combining: Improving student writing without formal grammar instruction.* Research Report No. 15. Urbana, IL: NCTE.

Olson, D. R. 1977. From utterance to text: The bias of language in speech and writing. *Harvard Educational Review, 47,* 257–281.

Olson, D. R., and N. Torrance. 1981. Learning to meet the requirements of written text: Language development in the school years. In C. H. Frederiksen and J. F. Dominic (Eds.), *Writing: The nature, development, and teaching of written communication* (Vol. 2). Hillsdale, NJ: Erlbaum.

Ong, W. J. 1979. Literacy and orality in our times. *Profession 79,* New York: Modern Language Association of America.

Pellegrini, A. 1980. The relationship between kindergartners' play and achievement in prereading, language, and writing. *Psychology in the Schools, 17,* 530–535.

Piaget, J. 1955.[The language and thought of the child] (M. Gabain, trans.). New York: New American Library. (Originally published, 1926)

Read, C. 1971. Pre-school children's knowledge of English phonology. *Harvard Educational Review, 41,* 1–34.

Rubin, D. In press. *Social cognitive dimensions of composing processes.* Durham, NC: Monographs of the Duke University Wiring Project.

Rubin, D. L., and G. L. Piché. 1979. Development in syntactic and strategic aspects of audience adaptation skills in written persuasive communication. *Research in the Teaching of English, 13,* 293–316.

San Jose, C. P. M., 1972. Grammatical structures in four modes of writing at fourth grade level. (Doctoral dissertation, Syracuse University, 1972). *Dissertation Abstracts International, 33,* 5411A. (University Microfilms No. 1, 73–9563)

Shaughnessy, M. P. 1977. *Errors and expectations: A guide for the teacher of basic writing.* New York: Oxford University Press.

Scribner, S., and M. Cole. 1978. Literacy without schooling: Testing for intellectual effects. *Harvard Educational Review, 48,* 448–461.

Scribner, S., and M. Cole. 1981. Unpackaging literacy. In M. F. Whiteman (Ed.), *Writing: The nature, development, and teaching of written communication* (Vol. 1). Hillsdale, NJ: Erlbaum.

Shuy, R. W. 1981. Toward a development theory of writing. In C. H. Frederiksen & J. F. Dominic (Eds.), *Writing: The nature, development, and teaching of written communication* (Vol. 2). Hillsdale, NJ: Erlbaum.

Smith, W. L., and M. B. Swan. 1978. Adjusting syntactic structures to varied levels of audience. *Journal of Experimental Education, 46,* 66–72.

Stotsky, S. L. 1975. Sentence-combining as a curricular activity: Its effect on written language development and reading comprehension. *Research in the Teaching of English, 9,* 30–71.

Vygotsky, L. S. 1962. [*Thought and language*] (E. Hanfmann & G. Vakar, Eds., and trans.). Cambridge, MA: MIT Press. (Originally published, 1934).

———. 1978. *Mind in society: The development of higher psychological processes.* (M.

Cole, V. John-Steiner, S. Scribner, & E. Souberman, Eds.). Cambridge, MA: Harvard University Press.

Wells, C. G. 1979. Describing children's linguistic development at home and at school. *British Educational Research Journal, 5,* 75–98.

———. 1981. *Learning through interaction: The study of language development.* Cambridge: Cambridge University Press.

Spelling and Grammar Logs

Richard VanDeWeghe

One problem writing teachers face is that of helping students with their spelling and their use of edited English while developing their writing. A related problem is that of individualizing instruction in both areas in efficient and effective ways that keep both spelling and grammar in their "places" in the writing process. A solution to both problems is the use of spelling and grammar logs, two individualized, self-paced approaches which help students become more proficient at spelling and at using edited English. I have used the logs with university students, and I have helped other teachers use them with their junior high, high school, and college students. The logs work well with all students, but particularly well with linguistically or dialectically different students for whom spelling and grammar are special concerns in their writing development.

The spelling log is a one-page student handout divided into four labeled columns, with student examples (see Figure 11). The spelling log is literally a log where students keep track of their misspellings during the copyediting stage of writing, or after others (teachers, parents, peers) have pointed out a misspelling.

FIGURE 11
Spelling log.

Correct Spelling	My Misspelling	Why the Word Confuses Me	Helps for Remembering the Correct Spelling
meant	ment	I spell it like I think it sounds.	It's the past of *mean.*
demonstrate	demenstrate	I use *e* instead of *o*.	A demo is used to demonstrate.
coarse	course	I get it mixed up with course as a class.	*a* = coarse is hard.

I came upon the idea of spelling logs in Lou Kelly's fine text, *From Dialogue to Discourse,*[1] where her "Guide to Correct Spelling" uses the same format but does not include the second column. My addition of this column provides a visual contrastive analysis which allows students to *see* graphemic differences between the two versions. The third column is also instructive: Students write, in their own words, why they're confused. Coming as it does after the contrastive analysis, this is generally an easy task. Its strengths are that students explore the reason(s) for a misspelling in a personal, and hence more meaningful, chronicle, and that it combines thinking about and writing out the reason(s) in a risk-free, exploration and discovery way. Similarly, because the fourth-column entry represents a personal attempt at finding a cognitive key to the confusion, it locks in long-term memory of an individualized aid to remembering the correct spelling. Students thus do more than simply list misspelled words, for they must also analyze the correct spelling-misspelling confusion and find a mnemonic aid for fixing the correct spelling in their minds.

While it is best if students complete columns three and four themselves, they sometimes have difficulty determining a reason for the confusion or finding some aid for remembering the correct spelling. In such instances, teachers or others can help. For example, I've often had an entire class brainstorm a fourth-column entry for a student who just couldn't come up with something. These sessions are lively and instructive for all, since we've found that the best mnemonic aids are those that are silly or sing-songy. One student, in fact, remarked that he was amazed how well he could remember the "stupid sayings" in his spelling log.

Students work well with the spelling log because it formalizes a spelling strategy that many people do informally or unconsciously. And because it calls on students to write their way to personal solutions, they retain the resultant learning more readily. Further, teachers can quickly and easily monitor students' use of the log by examining it periodically. This provides teachers an opportunity to spot patterns in spelling problems and then to develop specific strategies for dealing with them (for example, applying the *ei-ie* rule). The log works best for fair to somewhat poor spellers who spell correctly the greater percentage of words they write. For severely handicapped spellers (I once had a student who misspelled 85 percent of the words he wrote), I recommend Mina Shaughnessy's more systematic spelling analysis in her book, *Errors and Expectations.*[2]

Here are some student entries which illustrate their use of the spelling log. Student A recorded *angle* as a misspelling of *angel,* noted that "I get the *l* and the *e* mixed up," and then wrote his marvelous memory help: "Angels have *gel* in them." Student B noted "famialy or famaly" as the misspelling of *family;* he

---

[1]Lou Kelly, *From Dialogue to Discourse* (Glenview, Ill.: Scott Foresman, 1972), p. 323.
[2]Mina Shaughnessy, *Errors and Expectations* (New York: Oxford University Press, 1977), pp. 175–176.

said he was confused "because of the way [he says] it," and then devised his personal memory link in "*i* am in a fam*i*ly." Student C spelled *committee* as either "comitte" or "commity," noting that she "only hears one *t* or forgets the other *e*." Her mnemonic aid was simple and rhythmical: "2 *m*'s, 2 *t*'s, 2 *e*'s." Finally, student D wrote *holler* as "hollar," explaining that "That's how [she says] it," and then wrote that she could remember it by saying, "When you holl*er*, you *ger*."

While resembling the spelling log in form, function, and use, the grammar log[3] is a descriptive rather than prescriptive approach to helping students analyze how their personal grammar (spoken language and informal written language) differs from their written grammar (edited English conventions). I am using *grammar* here in its broadest lay sense to include syntax, punctuation, usage, and vocabulary. Divided into three columns, the grammar log is exemplified in Figure 12.

Students use the grammar log as they use the spelling log—to chart and analyze discrepancies between personal and written grammars. Unlike the spelling log entries, however, there are no "incorrect" entries (with the exception of punctuation) in the grammar log; the only judgments to be made are those of appropriateness. Thus, when students enter syntactic structures in their logs (for example, "I wonder how can I accomplish this?" versus "I wonder how I can accomplish this?"), they are actually recording linguistic styles more or less appropriate to social situations. Because the grammar log is descriptive, no value judgments are thus placed on students' personal grammars. In fact, when teachers explain to students the meanings of personal and written grammars, they need to emphasize that people have a variety of personal grammars, and

FIGURE 12
Grammar log.

Personal Grammar	Written Grammar	Reasons for Differences
my brothers house	my brother's house	I need to put in an apostrophe (') to show ownership.
We took the following items, a camera, a backpack, and a canteen.	We took the following items: a camera, a backpack, and a canteen.	I should use a colon (:) when I introduce a series of things.

[3] I first began working with the idea of grammar logs in an inservice project in language arts at Michigan State University, Department of English—Sturgis, Michigan, Middle School. The final report of that project is *Beyond Basics* (East Lansing: Michigan State University, 1977).

illustrate this fact by drawing examples from their own idiolects or dialects. Further, teachers need to emphasize that personal grammar is natural to the idea-generating nature of the drafting phrases of writing, and that the application of written grammar structures and conventions comes in the editing phase. This introduction thus maintains the students' right to their own language, and, if handled properly, shows them the "place" of their personal grammar in the total writing process when an edited English style is the desired goal.

While the contrastive analysis in columns one and two allows students to see the differences, arriving at reasons for the differences helps them to learn the "rules" we often teach, but in an individualized, situation-specific way. Their rules, assuming they're accurate, can be in their own words or they may be paraphrases of comments made by teachers or others. Merely copying a rule from a handbook is wasted rote transcription and is to be avoided. The important point is that the process of arriving at reasons for the differences, and the process of writing them out combine to promote genuine understanding of punctuation, grammar, and usage principles. And in the process, students often pick up common terms that identify features of edited English (for example, punctuation signals, grammatical markers).

Some examples: Student A's writing contained many features of black dialect. In his log, he noted in the personal grammar column the phrase "that he be a fine . . . "; in the written grammar column, he logged in "that will be a fine. . . ." Similarly, he noted that "I wonder did . . ." in his personal grammar was "I wonder if . . ." in his written grammar. His reason for both entries was simply the differences in the way he spoke and the way he should have written in the final draft of a college paper. Student B wrote that "they gained and unyielding critic" in her personal grammar became "they gained an unyielding critic" in her written grammar because she could *see* the differences that she couldn't *hear*. Student C, who noted that in her personal grammar she referred to an "older-held view," logged in "traditional view" at a peer's suggestion because "it was a better way to say it." Finally, Student D wrote that "there was fifteen students in class" was all right for his personal grammar, but "there were fifteen students" is more appropriate in his written grammar because "*was* is used with one thing and *were* is used with a few."

Spelling and grammar logs supplement a writing course. They should be seen as an opportunity for students to find solutions to problems they face in these two areas without distracting them from their natural writing processes. The logs also provide an opportunity for teachers to monitor students' development, discover patterns in spelling and grammar, and attend to incidental problems that do not form patterns. Used as an aid in copyediting, logs can, and do, develop genuine student understanding of correct spelling and appropriate grammar.

Developing Correctness in Student Writing: Alternatives to the Error-Hunt

Lois Matz Rosen

I don't understand why good students leave out possessives when I've taught it, reinforced it, quizzed it. . . . Yet even after all this, there are those errors in the title, in the very first sentence!

Do I read a paper and ignore all punctuation? What good is that for them?

I put 5X on their papers and they have to write it over five times. It's so stupid, obviously. But I can't reinforce this by doing nothing.

We spend hours at night with papers. It's not fun after a while and it gets to you. . . . I'm not sure the students get as much from it as the time I spend on it.

These comments by high school English teachers discussing the process of marking student papers reflect the dissatisfaction and frustration of many teachers over the problem of dealing with errors in student writing—the obvious mistakes in spelling, punctuation, capitalization, grammar, and usage that often pepper student papers and refuse to disappear despite the teacher's most diligent attention.

Traditionally, teachers have worked to eradicate error in two ways: (1) by teaching mechanical and grammatical correctness through drill exercises in grammar/usage texts, and (2) by pointing out all errors when marking student papers, perhaps also expecting students to make corrections when papers are returned. Although numerous research studies show that there is little or no transfer of learning from isolated drills to actual writing experiences and that the time-intensive practice of the teacher's "error-hunt" does not produce more mechanically perfect papers, this 100-year-old tradition still persists. (See Braddock et al., Haynes, Rosen for discussion of research in this area.) The presence of classroom sets of grammar/usage texts in almost any school attests to this approach to correctness as do the results of several recent studies into teachers' marking procedures.

THE ERROR-HUNT

Harris (1977) found that 66 percent of the corrections and annotations the high school teachers in her study made on student papers were on mechanics and usage. Searle and Dillon's study (1980) of the commenting done by nine teachers in grades four through six revealed that teachers in their study tried to correct all errors in spelling, usage, and punctuation, which led to a heavy emphasis on what the researchers characterized as "Form-Correction Response." The latest survey of writing instruction in the United States, Applebee's 1981 study, *Writing in the Secondary School: English and the Content Areas,* reflects the same pattern:

> The major vehicle for writing instruction, in all subject areas, was the teacher's comments and corrections of completed work. Errors in writing mechanics were the most common focus of these responses; comments concerned with the ideas the student was expressing were the least frequently reported. (pp. 90–91)

A study I completed in 1983 of patterns in responses by the high school English teachers quoted at the opening of this article showed similar results. Almost 50% of their combined responses (defined as any type of written feedback to the student including underlinings, symbols, phrases, corrections, suggestions, and comments) on their students' papers focused on mechanical and grammatical errors. Each of the six teachers in my study had a specific approach to dealing with errors on student papers.

One teacher admitted that she tried to find and mark 100% of the mistakes "because parents like it." This technique, coupled with her strong belief that students needed lots of feedback on their ideas, led to papers that averaged eight responses per page and often resulted in a returned paper so full of marks and remarks that it seems likely a student would have difficulty figuring out what was worth attending to. Another teacher concentrated on two or three types of errors for each writing assignment, told the students when making the assignment which ones she would look for, and then tried to find 100% of these errors on each paper. This technique cut down on the time she spent on marking papers, but she was not encouraged by any rapid improvement in correctness. A third teacher put a minus (−) sign in the margin beside each line that had an error in it in the belief that this was less punitive to students than pointing out the actual mistake. Because she worked with basic writers whose skills in this area were low, 90% of her responses on student papers were these minus signs. When papers were returned, a full class period was spent with students identifying and correcting their errors. Combine her marking emphasis with class time on error-correction, and one can see the strong focus on correctness that this method produced, a silent message to these basic writers about the importance of avoiding error when one writes.

Symbols to ease the marking burden were used by all teachers in my study: the standard "awks" and "frags" but idiosyncratic ones as well, such as one teacher's "T.E." for a "target error" that had to be "terminated" by the end of the year. Only one of the teachers in my study told me he preferred to dismiss the problem as one that would take care of itself. "I mark the errors that bother me when I see them; it's not much of a problem," he said. The other teachers, however, seemed to support the statement quoted earlier, "I just can't reinforce this by doing nothing."

The problem writing teachers face when dealing with mechanical/grammatical error in student writing is a more complex one than simply deciding whether or not to ignore it. The visual signposts, the surface features and grammatical structures of English that readers expect, are certainly an important part of any written communication. Numerous surface errors *do* distract the reader, and we are all aware that society places great value on correctness as an indication of writing ability. Nevertheless, anyone who has read through a perfectly correct but perfectly empty student paper can verify the primary importance of *what* the student says regardless of how correctly it is stated. The dilemma, then, becomes one of balance and proportion in the writing program. *Namely, how does a teacher focus on content in student writing and still ensure that progress is also being made toward mastery of the mechanical and grammatical structures of written English?*

Recent research and theory in writing instruction suggest that this dilemma can be resolved by abandoning the traditional approach to error outlined above and working with other methods that are proving to be highly effective in helping students at all levels develop competence in the mechanical/grammatical aspects of writing. Before I discuss these new approaches to correctness, let me first present several key assumptions about the nature of the composing process and the way it is learned that provide the underlying rationale for the methods which follow.

UNDERLYING ASSUMPTIONS

Writing is a complex process, recursive rather than linear in nature, involving thinking, planning, discovering what to say, drafting, and re-drafting. Writers who worry about mechanics while they are composing are not concentrating fully on what they have to say because it's difficult to do two things well at the same time, especially if neither task is yet completely under the writer's control. Therefore, any attention to correctness should be saved for "postwriting"—the final proofreading and polishing stages of a finished piece. Students should be told this; and teachers should not contradict this message by commenting on errors in early drafts, journals, or free writing unless they seriously interfere with meaning.

Learning to use the correct mechanical and grammatical forms of written language is a developmental process and as such is slow, unique to each child, and does not progress in an even uphill pattern. Weaver (1982) argues that "semantic and syntactic growth are normally accompanied by errors in language use" (p. 443). She demonstrates by tracing changing patterns in the kinds of sentence fragments students make from first through sixth grade. As the young writers in her study worked to express increasingly more complex ideas and to use more sophisticated sentence constructions, the kinds of fragments predominant in

early grades disappeared, only to be replaced by others. First graders, for example, produced numerous fragments that were explanatory clauses beginning with
because:

I want a car, because I'm old enouf.

By sixth grade, types of fragments had blossomed to include a wide variety of
subordinate clauses:

Finally one day *when the machine spanked a kid, Billy.* Billy turned around
and hit the machine.
I would like to have a raffle. *So we can have some money for a special pro. in
our room like roller-skating, skying* [skiing] *ice skating*

When students struggle to learn new skills, using dialogue or writing a persuasive essay, they need time to master the unfamiliar aspects of mechanics and
grammar that accompany them. To quote Weaver, "growth and error go hand in
hand" (p. 443), which suggests that writing teachers must have a certain tolerance for error, accepting it as a normal part of writing growth.

*The mechanical and grammatical skills of writing are learned when a writer
needs to use them for real purposes to produce writing that communicates a
message he or she wants someone else to receive.* A piece of writing should not
be seen as a "test" of the student's ability, or lack of it, to produce perfect prose,
but rather as a chance for a developing writer to use all his or her present language capabilities to their fullest extent in producing a genuine written communication.

*Responsibility for the correctness of any given piece of writing should fall main-
ly on the student, not the teacher.* Students learn to become accurate and self-
sufficient writers by searching for, finding, and correcting their own mistakes.
They may fail to achieve perfection, may miss many errors, in fact; but in the
end they learn much more from identifying and correcting whatever errors they
can find on their own papers and those of their peers than from the teacher's
painstaking proofreading which may identify errors they don't understand or,
worse yet, focus their attention on correctness instead of content. Copy editing is
one of the skills a competent writer must learn, and it is never too early to start
teaching independence in this area.

*Students learn to write by writing, and they learn to write correctly by writing,
revising, and proofreading their own work*—with some help or direction from
the teacher when necessary. They do not learn to write correctly by studying
about writing or doing isolated workbook exercises unrelated to their own writing. In *The Art of Teaching Writing,* Calkins urges teachers to trust the "incidental learning" that takes place when students are actively and frequently engaged

in writing (p. 199). They begin to read like writers and to view the world with a writer's eyes, not only for language and ideas but for the surface features of writing as well.

METHODS

The following approach to correctness, culled from the work of such master-teachers as Donald Graves, Lucy Calkins, Ronald Cramer, Mina Shaughnessy, or experimented with in my own work with developing writers, views correctness within a larger framework that puts composing at the center of writing instruction. It also changes the teacher's role from drill sergeant/error-hunter to coach/helper. If there is a common theme running through the methods below, it is that *revision is the key* to helping students master the mechanical and grammatical aspects of writing. When students view early drafts of their work as fluid, rather than fixed, they are free to concentrate on what they wish to say. Aspects of correctness can then be saved for final drafts with specific points of grammar and mechanics taught when necessary as students compose and revise their own writing. The techniques described below encourage students to work independently on correctness, show them how to become competent proofreaders, and at the same time suggest ways for a teacher to deal with the mechanical problems that appear on student papers. Although several of these methods were originally designed for elementary students, they are equally effective with secondary level and college students.

Let Students Write

The most important technique a teacher can use to guide students toward mechanically and grammatically correct writing is also the simplest: let them write. Let them write daily if possible and provide opportunities for them to experiment with all kinds of whole discourse from journals, letters, and personal essays to poems, short stories, and analytical prose. Mina Shaughnessy's work with adult basic writers at the City University of New York led her to observe that the single most important characteristic of these students was their lack of writing experience: ". . . the basic writing student is . . . likely to have written 350 words a semester. It would not be unusual for him to have written nothing at all" (p. 14).

Provide Time for All Stages of the Writing Process

A second fundamental method for increasing correctness is showing students that writing consists of several overlapping steps: pre-writing and planning, writing and revising, editing and proofreading, or, as Kirby and Liner put it so aptly for students, "getting started, getting it down, getting it right, checking it out" (p. 8). Teaching effective strategies for each of these stages increases students' confidence as writers and allows them to concentrate their full attention on correctness at the stage of writing when it matters most.

Use Editing Workshops

A third basic method for working with correctness is the use of editing workshops, classroom time regularly set aside for final editing and polishing of papers that have already been revised for content. Delegating specific classroom time for this task is valuable in two ways. It gives students a definite message about both the importance of correctness and the appropriate time in the writing process to focus on it. Second, many strategies for effective proofreading and mastery of mechanical/grammatical skills can be incorporated into this workshop time while still keeping the classroom focus on the students' own writing. Four different activities teachers and students can engage in during an editing workshop are recommended throughout the literature on teaching the composing process.

Modeling   Many students, even at the college level, don't know how to proofread effectively. When directed to "check your paper for errors," they quickly scan over their work, perhaps adding a comma here or there or changing a spelling that suddenly looks odd. In *Children's Writing and Language Growth,* Cramer recommends modeling the editing process by obtaining permission from one student writer in the class to make a transparency of his or her paper for editing by the whole class on the overhead projector. Once the class has had a chance to read the paper projected on the screen, the teacher opens discussion by focusing on the content of the paper. "What do you like about this paper?" or "What has the writer done well?" are good questions to ask at this point. Then the teacher directs the discussion to proofreading by asking, "Can anyone find something that needs to be changed?"—a neutral question, suggesting error-correction is a natural part of this stage in the writing process. As students identify and correct individual errors, the teacher corrects each on the transparency, giving a brief explanation of the reason for the correction, and also starts a list on the chalkboard of kinds of errors identified: spelling, capital letters, run-on sentences, etc. The teacher can point out errors the students don't identify and use this as an opportunity to discuss the error, or can stop when the class has corrected all the errors it can identify. The final step is for the students to apply this process to their own papers, using the list on the board as a guide for kinds of errors to look for.

If this write/model/apply process is followed regularly, students receive numerous short lessons on grammar and mechanics plus the constant opportunity to apply these lessons to their own papers. The middle school teachers I work with in the Flint, Michigan, Community Schools have been using this modeling strategy with their classes with good success. Students get involved, arguing points of grammar with each other and voluntarily checking the dictionary. One teacher tells of the gradual inching up of student chairs to the overhead projector as they group-edit and the enthusiasm with which students approach their own writing after the modeling session.

Mini-Conferences   While students are actively involved in editing their own writing, the teacher can give individual help with proofreading by holding mini conferences. In *Writing: Teachers and Children at Work,* Graves describes brief conferences focusing on proofreading held with the writer when the paper is essentially completed and moving toward a final draft. The teacher quickly scans the paper, looking for recurrent errors, and tells the writer what kinds of proofreading activities are needed. This can be done in two- or three-minute conferences at the teacher's desk, or the teacher can move up and down the aisles, leaning over shoulders, and concentrating more attention on students whose writing would benefit from more help with mechanics. The dialogue might go something like this. "OK, John, looks like you're ready for a final proofreading and polishing. First I'd like you to circle all the words you think might be misspelled and look them up in the dictionary. Then work on complete sentences. There are several places in your paper where you've got two sentences strung together." The teacher might ask John to work with him in identifying the first few run-ons and correcting them before telling John to do the same throughout the rest of his paper and then let the teacher see it again. There could be a brief lesson on possessives for one student, another on its, it's for someone else. Never lingering for more than a few minutes with each writer, the teacher identifies an area for proofreading, illustrates what he or she means, and gets the writer started working independently. The "eavesdroppers" on either side often learn as much as the student being worked with. "Can I help you with anything?" works well as an opening question from the teacher for it permits an immediate and accurate response to a student's need.

Peer Proofreading   Another valuable way to work toward correctness during editing workshop time is to have students work together when proofreading. Students always say it is much easier to correct someone else's work than it is to identify errors in their own, and this technique depends on that perception. If writing is not seen as a "test" of an individual student's writing ability but as a process that is growing and developing, this method permits for learning by both writer and editor. Proofreading thus becomes a collaborative learning experience. When I do this with my own students, both basic writers and average freshmen, I usually put students in pairs after each has had a chance to proofread his or her own paper. The only rule I impose is that no corrections are to be made on the writer's paper without the knowledge and consent of the author. This means both writers must confer over any error on either paper and both must agree on the correction. I also ask that the editor initial all corrections he or she finds, which gives me some sense of the mechanical skills both the writer and the proofreader bring to the paper. If the two writers can't agree on an error, I am called over to make a decision, giving me a chance to teach a mini-lesson as I resolve the problem. Students enjoy being editors for each other, and I find that it takes a great deal of pressure off each writer to make the work perfect on his or her own. Peer proofreading can also be handled in groups of three or four students, who are instructed to pass their papers around the group, each student correcting any errors found. It helps if the groups are structured so that each one has a student good at spelling and mechanics.

Mini-lessons   Brief ten-minute lessons on common mechanical problems can have immediate value when they are taught as part of an editing workshop. A short lecture at the beginning of a proofreading session can then be applied immediately to the students' own papers, reinforcing the new information through personal use rather than through a textbook exercise. Students can share problem sentences during these short sessions, ask specific questions from their own writing, and get help from the shared knowledge of the entire class. Teaching these skills and having students apply them while writing is in process produces much better results than teaching them from grammar/usage texts as isolated skills. By giving mini-lessons during editing workshops throughout the school term or year, a teacher could easily review almost all the kinds of mechanical errors students make and never need to rely on a textbook or drill exercises to reinforce the learning. If several students in a class share the same mechanical/grammatical problem, grouping these students for a mini-lesson during the editing workshop and then permitting them to work together to correct this error on their own papers can be highly effective.

Help Students Self-Edit

Several correction strategies are aimed at enhancing students' abilities to self-edit. Among the most useful are these.

Editing Checklists   These are lists of common errors that students can use as a guide when proofreading their own papers. Simple ones for young children who can ask questions about spelling and capital letters, while older writers can be instructed to check their writing for a dozen or more surface features such as run-ons and fragments, subject-verb agreement, possessives, etc.

Proofreading Strategies   Show students some methods to improve their own proofreading:

Running a blank sheet of paper slowly down the composition so the writer is forced to read one line at a time

Reading one sentence at a time from the bottom up to take each sentence out of context and thus focus on errors, not meaning

Circling all suspected spelling errors before consulting a dictionary

Reading aloud to oneself or a friend, or reading into a tape recorder and playing it back

Listing three of one's most frequent errors at the top of the paper, then reading the paper three times, each time focusing on one of these errors

An Editing Corner   Something as simple as an editing corner heaped with handbooks, dictionaries, a thesaurus, can also help students become responsible for their own mechanical/grammatical correctness. The walls around the editing corner can be decorated with a chart on how to proofread, a list of spelling demons, rules of punctuation or capitalization, examples of dialogue punctuated properly. One-page handouts with explanations and examples of common errors and ways to correct them can be filed in this corner along with displays of student writing taken through several drafts, including final proofreading. Students should be allowed free access to these materials as they write: they should be encouraged to use the corner to solve mechanical problems themselves.

Abandon the Error-Hunt

A fifth cluster of correctness strategies centers on marking techniques for the teacher, ones which differ significantly from the traditional "red-pencillitis" approach and are always preceded by classroom use of an editing workshop and self-editing strategies.

Benign Neglect   Students involved for the first time in the process approach to writing, those newly engaged in journal-writing, pre-writing exercises, multiple drafts, revision, and proofreading, can benefit from a period of teacher inattention to correctness when marking final drafts of papers. Especially if students' previous writing instruction focused heavily on form and correctness, they need time to re-center their attention on what they have to say as writers and to learn the various composing strategies that will make writing more pleasurable for both the writer and the reader of his or her paper. If students are generating a great deal of writing and are frequently engaged in editing workshop strategies, the teacher can safely focus written comments on content. This benign neglect gives students a chance to internalize writing and proofreading skills and to demonstrate what they *do* know before the teacher begins to identify and work on areas of weakness.

Selectivity   Rather than engage in intensive error-correction when responding to student writing, teachers are encouraged by recent writing researchers and theorists to adopt a more moderate approach to error. Research has never been able to show that circling all the errors—the error-hunt approach to marking—

makes a significant difference in writing quality; instead it discourages the student whose paper is full of mistakes and focuses students on errors instead of ideas. Students are more likely to grow as writers when the teacher's primary purpose in reading student papers is to respond to content. However, if attention to content and correctness are combined when marking papers, it is more helpful to select one or two *kinds* of errors the individual student is making than to point out every error in the paper. The teacher can identify a selected error, show an example or two on the student's paper, and either explain the correct form or direct the student to a handbook for further explanation.

Error-Analysis   A third method for working with student error, one that can be especially fruitful for the teacher, is to approach it from an analytic perspective. The composition teacher as error-analyst looks for patterns in the errors of an individual student, tries to discover how the student arrived at the mistake by analyzing the error (i.e., Is it lack of knowledge about a certain grammatical point? A mis-learned rule? A careless error? Overgeneralization of a particular rule? The influence of oral language?), and plans strategies accordingly. Kroll and Schafer, Bartholomae, and Shaughnessy have demonstrated the efficacy of error-analysis in helping teachers better understand the source of student error as an aid to planning more effective ways of dealing with it.

Publish Student Writing

The final basic strategy recommended for working toward correctness is publishing. Writers, professionals as well as students, need a reason for laboring over a draft until it is perfect; the urge to see oneself in print can be a powerful drive toward revision and proofreading. Watch what happens when a class publication is handed out. Each writer is likely to flip immediately to his or her own work for a minute of personal pleasure before browsing through the rest of the book. Writing teachers need to take advantage of this human need to be heard, to leave a physical imprint on the world, by offering numerous opportunities for sharing and publishing: bulletin boards in the class and the hall, "paper of the week" on the door, individual books, dittoed class books, a classroom anthology of one piece from each writer that sits on public display in the library, writing as gifts for parents, pen pals, contests to enter, a class newspaper.

RESEARCH INDICATIONS

As these methods for working toward correctness show, over the past decade writing teachers and theorists have developed a body of techniques that can be termed a process-oriented approach to correctness, methods that help students master the mechanical/grammatical aspects of writing itself or making correctness the central focus of the composition program. Relatively few studies document the effectiveness of this approach. Mainly the literature on how to teach writing deals with the process as a whole and shows its effectiveness in improving the quality of student writing in all dimensions, including surface level correctness. However, two studies suggest specifically that working with correctness within the writing process is more effective than the traditional skills approach.

Calkins, in "When Children Want to Punctuate: Basic Skills Belong in Context," reports on a 1980 study of teaching punctuation in the third grade. In one classroom the teacher taught language mechanics through daily drills and workbook exercises; her children rarely wrote. In another classroom the children wrote an hour a day three times a week with no formal instruction in punctuation. At the end of the year, the "writers" could not only define and explain many more marks of punctuation than the children who had been drilled in this (8.65 kinds as opposed to 3.85 kinds) but were also actively using these punctuation marks for real purposes in their own writing. Calkins notes that "When children need punctuation in order to be seen and heard, they become vacuum cleaners, sucking up odd bits from books, their classmates' papers, billboards, and magazines. They find punctuation everywhere, and make it their own" (p. 573).

The second piece of research documenting the fact that developing writers *do* learn mechanical and grammatical skills through the process of writing is a 1984 study by DiStefano and Killion with fourth, fifth, and sixth grade students. Students in the experimental group were taught by teachers trained in the process model of writing while the control group students were exposed to a skills approach. Using pre- and post-writing samples in September and May, the researchers showed that students in the process model group did significantly better than those in the skills group in organization, spelling, usage, and sentence structure, the latter three items ones that are usually associated with a skills approach. The students in the skills group did not do better than the process group on any of the three grade levels. The researchers conclude "that the writing-process model takes into account skills such as spelling and usage as well as organization of ideas" (p. 207).

CONCLUSIONS

Writing instruction has long been dominated by an emphasis on correctness. Increasingly, however, as our knowledge of the writing process and the way it is learned grows, we are coming to understand that correctness develops naturally when students are continuously engaged in composing and revising activities that are meaningful to them. When young writers need a better understanding of mechanical and grammatical matters to ensure more effective communication of their ideas, they learn what they need to know to prepare final drafts for readers. The methods described above are designed to support this learning of the mechanical and grammatical elements of written language while still keeping writers focused on the content of their writing.

In compiling these techniques, I do not suggest that teachers either ignore or replace grammar exercises and intensive marking with a heavy emphasis on editing workshops. Rather, I present these methods so that teachers will see them as evidence that skills *can* be learned in the context of writing and will, therefore, free students from the correctness focus in composition and permit them to find themselves as writers.

REFERENCES

Applebee, Arthur N. 1981. *Writing in the Secondary School: English and the Content Areas.* Urbana, Illinois: NCTE.

Bartholomae, David. 1980. "The Study of Error." *College Composition and Communication* 31 (October): 253–269.

Braddock, Richard, Richard Lloyd-Jones, and Lowell Schoer. 1963. *Research in Written Composition.* Urbana, Illinois: NCTE.

Calkins, Lucy McCormick. 1986. *The Art of Teaching Writing.* Portsmouth, New Hampshire: Heinemann.

———. "When Children Want to Punctuate: Basic Skills Belong in Context." 1980. *Language Arts* 57 (May): 567–573.

Cramer, Ronald L. 1978. *Children's Writing and Language Growth.* Columbus, Ohio: Charles E. Merrill.

DiStefano, Philip, and Joellen Killion. 1984. "Assessing Writing Skills Through a Process Approach." *English Education* 16 (December): 203–207.

Graves, Donald H. 1983. *Writing: Teachers and Children at Work.* New Hampshire: Heinemann.

Harris, Winifred Hall. 1977. "Teacher Response to Student Writing: A Study of the Response Patterns of High School English Teachers to Determine the Basis for Teacher Judgment of Student Writing." *Research in the Teaching of English* 11 (Fall): 175–185.

Haynes, Elizabeth. 1978. "Using Research in Preparing to Teach Writing." *English Journal* 67 (January): 82–88.

Kirby, Dan, and Tom Liner. 1981. *Inside Out: Developmental Strategies for Teaching Writing.* Montclair, New Jersey: Boynton/Cook.

Kroll, Barry M., and John C. Schafer. 1978. "Error-Analysis and the Teaching of Composition." *College Composition and Communication* 29 (October): 242–248.

Rosen, Lois Matz. 1983. "Responding to Student Writing: Case Studies of Six High School English Teachers." Dissertation, Michigan State University.

Searle, Dennis, and David Dillon. 1980. "The Message of Marking: Teacher Written Response to Student Writing at Intermediate Grade Levels." *Research in The Teaching of English* 14 (October): 233–242.

Schaughnessy, Mina P. 1977. *Errors and Expectations.* New York: Oxford University Press.

Weaver, Constance. 1982. "Welcoming Errors as Signs of Growth." *Language Arts* 59 (May): 438–444.

A Profile of Carlos: Strengths of a Nonstandard Dialect Writer

Linda Miller Cleary

The complex problems that the nonstandard dialect student faces in learning to write were of concern to me during my thirteen years of teaching. I finally turned this concern into a formal inquiry. In selecting participants I wanted diversity, and I found diversity . . . in the basic classes. In those classes there was a rich melange of Black, Hispanic, and working-class white students who had one thing in common: none spoke standard English. In eight schools, urban, suburban, and rural, the story was the same, and although I knew that tracking was a complex social phenomenon, it seemed at the moment of selection that "ability" tracking was based in a profound way on language.

Following an intensive study of thirteen basic writers, I selected Carlos Morales to show the predicament of the nonstandard dialect writer and to show teaching methods that will utilize their strengths and address their underlying problems. To permit anonymity for Carlos, I have changed his name and the names of his family, friends, and teachers.

I first saw Carlos when he entered the English office of his New England high school. Teachers greeted him warmly and joked with him before his English teacher/drama coach, Mr. O'Neil, brought him over to meet me. "Here's an eleventh grader you can learn from," the drama coach said. Carlos and I walked down the hall to the small room near the library where we would begin exploring Carlos' past experience with writing and his present process.

Carlos began his life in a large city and in a large family where his Puerto Rican mother spoke Spanish and where his eleven brothers and sisters taught him what he called "street talk," a dialect of English which shows Spanish language interference and Black English interference. In third grade Carlos went to a reform school where teachers tried to bring his language closer to standard English through years of remedial exercises. Later, Carlos moved to a New England town where he attended junior-high school and high school. In his eleventh-grade year I spent many hours with him and other basic writers to explore their experience with writing. As I worked with these students, it became clear that beneath their defensiveness, they believed their problem with writing to be a problem with their intellect. With Carlos, feeling stupid compounded his very real problems with writing, language, and reading.

During our in-depth interviews, Carlos described his past and present experience with writing. But it was only in analysis of his writing process through composing-aloud sessions and in classroom observation that I understood the full agony of the battle he was waging. Carlos would sit at a desk with books and papers spread around him and on his lap. He groaned, swore under his breath, and in moments of greater frustration, pounded his forehead with his palm, as if to force the clogged words and ideas onto the page. In both his own words and in my observations, threads emerged which wove an explanation of his struggle.

Carlos' struggle paralleled that of the thirteen basic writers. But he was unique among the participants because he had not given up the fight when I met him. Due to the good work and advocacy of some teachers, he was less defensive, and he was still trying. Many of his peers had already left school in frustration and failure.

CARLOS' VIEW OF HIMSELF AS A WRITER

Carlos' shifting view of himself as a student and a writer profoundly affected his work. Carlos felt good about himself during his early, inner-city school years. "When I was in first and second grade, I loved to read," he said. "In second I had Miss Banducci. She let me read a lot in the group. I would always sit right across from her, and I just go, 'Miss, can I read?' In third grade I had Miss Hirsch; she was my favorite; she still writes to me. I did a lotta math, spelling, learning big words, learning how to do script, learning how to write and all that. They didn't mind run-on sentences, but they got to that later."

Miss Hirsch was Carlos' first advocate; she was Carlos' connection with the world outside what he called the "training school." She wrote letters to him, took him to the movies, and visited him on his birthday and Christmas; his only other visit in three years was from his uncle. His positive relationship with Miss Hirsch was, perhaps, the reason he grew to trust teachers. In training school, he lost his positive perception of himself as a student and writer.

"I didn't like the school. I didn't like writing; I didn't know how to make a sentence. If I get it wrong, I got to rewrite it all over again. I didn't know how. The teacher said I was bad at making up stories, too short. I knew I'd be getting it wrong. No wonder I refused to write, but they still made me do other exercises and exercises. But it was always wrong, too. I wondered why I stopped. Now I realize why. I guess it's the way someone's looking at it, analyzed it. Before I like to write and see what I write cause nobody's gonna grade it. I just write and write, but I don't know I'm wrong so I write.

"When I got to training school, things that I did I know are wrong. Why should I write when everything always wrong? There was this one lady came there. She told me how to start writing again. She'd say, 'Write down what you can and what you know.' I like the way she helped me on things. She also taught me how to do apple trees. I got a plant that big, and then it died. She said, 'Write down on paper why it died.' I felt good cause I'd see what's happening, and I'd just write it down. She gave me a hundred. But she left the program. I stopped writing again."

While Carlos refused to write, other students his age were becoming fluent in getting their ideas into words—a skill that was still not automatic for Carlos in eleventh grade. In junior high, Carlos had a few teachers who gave him the opportunity to write and others kept him focused on word-level exercises. I asked him if he had received any help at home.

"It's hard for my mom, cause she has eleven kids. She never helped; my mother doesn't know how to do it. In junior high I try to do my writing at home, but I can't. I don't have a table in my room. When I write at home, my brothers and sisters and then my mom comes in the kitchen and cook and I have to leave. And so much noise, and the cat gets on the table. 'Get off cat; get away from my writing.' And then the TV comes on, and then my mom is cooking. But if I try to write, I smell the food, and I go taste it. I go back to my table, and I have grease all over my hands and get a messy paper. And the telephone rings. I don't write at home."

Carlos went to a high school where the faculty was sensitive to the difficulties of students whose first language was not standard English. Nevertheless, he had a wound that was not easily healed. "When I was a kid, I was dumb, too dumb. And I still am cause I'm way behind. Because I was supposed to be a senior this year, and I should have been higher, on my level, cause I'm in a lotta basic classes. I hate being in basic level, but I am gonna have to do it. They put me in ESL again, but I knew I was way above that. I know I got the capability to learn, nuttin is helping to bring it out. And I notice that my family's always in basic and low; I don't know why. My uncle wants me to graduate. I would be the first one in my family to graduate."

Although frequently validated by his teachers, Carlos went back and forth about how he felt about himself. His nagging feelings of inadequacy, his "hidden injuries of class" (Sennet and Cobb 1973) surfaced at every occasion.

Carlos had moments of doubt and moments when he would tell himself that he was all right. "Teachers got me in Upward Bound: that's why I have a tutor. I know that I'm getting smarter. But not in the speed I wanted to. To me I feel dumb, but to other people, I don't know. And I wonder, how the people look at me. Why am I going to graduate? And when I don't know so much. I wish that I went back to do better. In school I am dumb. I mean with the students, not to adults. Connie[a friend], she told me her problem, and I talked with her. Then she went to a counselor, and she came back, and the counselor told her the same thing. She was surprised I was smart."

In observing Carlos in his film class (his first class that wasn't designated as basic), I began to understand how painfully sensitive he was to peer opinion. "I knew as soon as I see the assignments paper coming that I wouldn't understand," Carlos told me later. "But I'm embarrassed to ask questions in front of the class, but I could ask Mr. Marsh. And the boy next to me was in basic, too, so he wouldn't think I'm stupid. But I could only ask the advanced girl spelling, cause I hear advanced kids asking spelling." Carlos' self-consciousness limits what might be useful peer interaction.

Carlos' perseverance was a tribute to his teachers' validating attitudes; by caring they provided the impetus Carlos needed to keep writing. The other basic students in my study hadn't been so lucky. Nevertheless, Carlos had three years of negative response to his work, and the negative view of himself as a writer and student that was reflected to him during those years was not without cost.

Smitherman reports, "Research on language attitudes consistently indicates that teachers believe black English-speaking youngsters are non-verbal and possess limited vocabulary. They are slow learners or ineducable. Their language is unsystematic and needs constant corrections and improvement" (Smitherman 1985, 50). Speakers of black English are not alone. Some teachers' attitudes towards speakers of low-prestige dialects are similar. Carlos and his low-prestige-dialect peers must be kept from interpreting their problems with writing as a problem with intellect. Conferencing with students to identify and acknowledge the presence of difficulties unrelated to intelligence may decrease the students' defensiveness and increase their willingness to begin to work on writing. Most important, teachers must trust in each student's ability to improve. Teachers must look beyond students' mistakes and find value in the ideas they are trying to express. When their ideas are taken seriously, they will find reason to write.

STRUGGLE DUE TO COGNITIVE OVERLOAD

The writing process is much more difficult for Carlos than for most other eleventh graders for a number of reasons. Too many concerns and too much to attend to during the writing process or "cognitive overload" complicate the process enormously.

"In writing," Carlos said, "You have to do a lot of thinking. It hurts my head. I worry about what to say, when it's due, about how long is it gonna take, how long they want it, idea they want, what's the paper gonna look like, [if] it get too short, how neat it's gonna be, is the sentence right, my tense is right, did I use the right word, I mean past tense all the time? I always forget that."

Most of Carlos' worries promoted a consciousness which should have improved his written expression. But together with concern about capitalization, spelling, language, punctuation, reading, and organization, Carlos had little room left in his conscious attention (that part of the mind that attends to writing while it is being done) for the actual writing process. And with that "overload" came frustration. Hayes and Flower (1980) show how cognitive overload can occur even for the skilled writers for whom much is already automatic.

When Carlos said aloud what he was thinking while he was writing, I better understood his frustration. He planned sentences and parts of sentences that he didn't write. He said things in standard English and then wrote them in his dialect, and he wrote things in standard English that he had said in dialect. He spelled the same words correctly and incorrectly even within the same sentence. He often practiced a sentence before actually writing it but then was interrupted during transcription by one of his many concerns and forgot what he was going to write. He made reading mistakes in the constant rereadings of his text which were necessary for going on, causing further writing mistakes. All this made for a stop-and-go process.

On the one hand his process was like that of a fourth grader, but on the other he was asked (and tried) to accomplish eleventh-grade writing. And indeed, there were signs of the eleventh-grade writer in his process. In a plan Carlos did for a research paper on Bette Davis, he showed some skill and creativity in organization, but he was unable to implement it in his writing. "I want to go back and tell about her movie and the roles she's played," Carlos said before putting pen to page, "and then gradually go back to how she started . . . the way she learned." But when Carlos began to write, he struggled with syntax, spelling, and synthesis of material from several books and couldn't carry out his plan. He pounded his head with his fist, said, "Oh, damn! Oh well," and slipped into a chronological presentation of her life. In this and in three other observed instances, Carlos began with rather sophisticated writing plans, and in each case he reverted to a more automatic, chronological organization because he had reached a state of overload. Groans and sighs and forehead drumming were outward symptoms of inner struggle with writing.

Writing must be broken into steps for Carlos and his peers until they become more fluent in writing. Carlos' tutor, Mary Sue, began to help him to plan before writing. She encouraged him to freewrite, to list, to cluster, and finally to reap the best from these ideas and to incorporate them into a plan. She often helped by allowing him to use his strong oral skills and by taking notes as he dictated a plan to her. She then announced that he was to write the first draft from the plan without stopping to think about any of his normal concerns. This was a time for Carlos to convey meaning. He began to enjoy that.

Careful assignment design allows nonstandard dialect students (1) to write about their experience, (2) to value that experience, and (3) to eliminate, for a time, their dependence on outside sources. Encouraging them to have a real audience and a purpose in writing, encouraging them to confer with peers about writing allows them to utilize their oral skills. Carlos' apple-plant teacher shows us how nonstandard dialect students can bring their strength to writing. "Write down what you can and what you know."

It was in the final steps of revision and editing that Carlos needed the most help; this will be covered in the next section. Most of all, nonstandard dialect writers need to write often, and not all of that writing needs to be evaluated. Gaining fluency is the first important step; time with pen and paper to work beyond the word-by-word struggle is imperative.

While keeping in mind Carlos' problems of overload and self-confidence, I would like to focus on perhaps the largest of his problems—language—to see how it further encumbers his writing process.

LANGUAGE

"My English is terrible. My English to me I understand what I am saying; to other people, they don't understand. I just don't wanna speak; don't know what words to use. My English crashes into Spanish. It mixed together. If I ever try to speak Spanish, Spanish people would say, 'Are you Spanish?' I say, 'Yes.' They say, 'You don't talk like you're Spanish; you don't know how to speak well.' My mother is always telling me I should be ashamed. I don't feel like I'm Spanish; I don't feel like anything. I just feel . . . like a plant."

An analysis of Carlos' composing-aloud sessions shows that language concerns were foremost on Carlos' mind during writing. Carlos often used English words with Spanish syntax; he followed the wrong rules. Subject/verb agreement and formation of plurals were constant problems for him, and yet his errors had a Spanish logic. Carlos wrote, "The Joad were able to sell some of their furnitures." His mistake, "The Joad," is understandable because the Spanish equivalent, *Los Joad* is plural but has no plural marker on the noun. Carlos should have used "furniture" as a collective noun, yet he used "furnitures" in accord with the plurality accorded *los muebles.* In his sentence, "There were enough job," Carlos confused job and work which use the same word in Spanish (*trabajo*/work; *trajajos*/jobs).

Carlos said, "I always put past tense into present. I still do that. It just comes to me as I'm writing to put it in present." The interaction of Black English, Spanish, and working-class English that he learned in the streets may explain the verb tenses that he identified as present tense because reduction of consonant clusters in Black English leads to omission of past tense markers. Carlos said, "To me I understand what I'm saying." (More Spanish syntax, but the meaning is clear.) He can't write acceptably without assistance, and his tutor has to help him "make it clearly." (The Spanish verb *hacer,* to do or to make, takes an adverb, whereas the English verb, "to make," requires an adjective.)

Though Carlos had spent hours of classroom time doing grammar exercises, he didn't call up those lessons when he wrote. The lessons, in fact, kept him from getting down to writing. Ironically, his strategy in editing was to correct on the basis of whether it sounded right to his already confused ear.

It is tempting to say that because of Carlos' Spanish background, language is more of a problem for him than for most basic writers, but in my investigations that wasn't the case. Working class English and black English were only troublesome for basic students because the language problems were so subtle. Teachers saw poor "grammar" and ignorance rather than use of dialect. Working with Carlos and other basic writers has made me see how social class can be perpetuated by our educational system. Nonstandard dialect students often work at the word/exercise level, thus preventing them from becoming fluent in written expression, from getting any joy from the process, or in practicing abstract thought.

It is in the last step of Mary Sue's new tutoring procedure that Carlos needs her most, for it is in editing that serious attention to language takes place. She stopped assigning him exercises to correct his errors and began to help him see the specific differences between his oral language and standard English. Carlos and Mary Sue began to keep a chart of these dialect differences. After each draft they looked for the nonstandard constructions together. They started with the most frequent mistakes and went from there, one problem at a time (Collins 1979). Van de Weghe (1983) has recently come out with a refinement of that process, "Grammar Logs," which helps students to take ownership of this process by logging errors and making sense of them following teacher feedback. He has the student set up three columns: (1) Personal Grammar, (2) Written Grammar, and (3) Reasons for Differences. Conscious understanding of how personal language is different from formal written language enables non-standard dialect students to be more aware that their problem is one of language and not of intellect.

READING PROBLEMS

Carlos' carefully hidden difficulty with reading kept him working with yet another handicap. He had difficulty reading his assignment sheets and material from books for research papers, and he struggled to read his own writing. Toward the end of my work with Carlos, his tutor, Mary Sue, said to me, "I think Carlos may have some trouble with reading." Carlos shielded the truth so cleverly that it took Mary Sue nearly eight months of daily work with Carlos to realize it.

At first, Carlos' stance with his tutor frustrated her. He made halfhearted attempts to read the complex assignment sheets and handouts on theory of film criticism and then simply refused. "In this film class I looked at a movie, so I know what to say. It's memory. I know examples from the movie. I never read the reading. I just ask friends." It was better to appear lazy or obstinate than illiterate. Carlos' subterfuge protected him, but again there was a toll. If he and other basic writers do not seek or permit help in reading, they will get none. His difficulty with reading makes getting material together for a paper difficult at best. It also means he has less experience with the written code he is trying to emulate. Finally, it intervenes in his writing process. Carlos said, "Sometimes I can't read my own writing. I leave out words. I have to read it over again." Struggling with reading during the actual composing process was a common occurrence for him.

Reading film-class handouts was frustrating and meaningless for Carlos. He needs to read . . . a lot. He needed to begin reading at a level he could understand in subjects that interested him. Carlos had neither the prior knowledge nor the reading skills to read academic articles about the theory of film criticism. But his interests in his heritage, jazz dance, and theatre were strengths that he could bring to reading. To some extent, ability to use standard constructions and to gain sentence sense, paragraph sense, and correct spelling comes through reading by a sort of osmosis.

Nonstandard dialect writers confront a complex construct of problems. So far we have considered the most concrete (problems with language, reading, and fluency) and have referred to the social problems of confidence, of teacher attitudes and expectations, of family circumstances, and of the well-entrenched, exercise-based remedial writing programs. Though the final problem to consider has been referred to, it must be stressed, as it is at once the most invisible and the most debilitating—lack of consciousness of the real problems in the nonstandard dialect speaker.

CONSCIOUSNESS AND THE NONSTANDARD DIALECT WRITER

Carlos was caught somewhere between feeling good about himself and bad about himself as a student and a writer, but he was becoming more conscious of his real problems in writing. His new ability to see himself as "behind" instead of "dumb" decreased both the defenses he used and the inadequacy he felt in writing. The interaction of defenses and consciousness in Carlos was revealing. With most people, defenses remain as barriers to consciousness of one's world and the way it affects them. Other basic students with whom I worked were defensive about their lack of success in school and, therefore, less willing to continue to work on writing. They must be shown the real reasons for their lack of progress. Statements such as "I don't care," "Writing is dumb," and more self-deprecatory postures such as "I guess I'm lazy," "I'm not smart in English," and even occasionally, "I'm dumb," kept these students from looking at the real reasons and left them with feelings of inadequacy. Because Carlos had support and advocacy of teachers, he defended himself less. As Carlos reflected on his writing, he came to some realizations. The oft-repeated, "Now I realize why," was one such indication that this happened. When I asked him whether he got help on his work at home, he realized for the first time that other students received help from their parents or older siblings. Suddenly he felt less reprehensible because he had a tutor. Before he said, "I have to have tutors in school, cause I can't do the work." After he said, "I didn't know other kids got help."

Other statements that Carlos made indicated a growing consciousness of what was going on in the world which had surrounded his writing. "My ideas are not dumb. It's my writing; I cannot put it into words." When I showed him how Spanish syntax interacted with his writing, he said, "I didn't know I had a Spanish grammar," and more worries about his intellect slipped away. Carlos' emerging consciousness of the reasons for his problems with his writing will be the greatest strength that he can bring to his work. It will increase his willingness to do it and to take the risks that permit future growth.

Carlos' perseverance in the face of his struggle with writing was remarkable. It was a by-product of increasing self-regard, purpose, and integrity, and it was a tribute to teachers like Ms. Hirsch, Mr. O'Neil, and Mary Sue. But time is running out for Carlos and other basic writers. We need to get down to the hard task of helping them to understand consciously what lies beneath their "basic writer" symptoms and make them writers.

University of Minnesota
Duluth, Minnesota 55812

REFERENCES

Collins, James L. 1979. "Dialect Variation and Writing: One Problem at a Time." *English Journal* 68.8: 48–51.

Hayes, John F., and Linda S. Flower. 1980. "The Dynamics of Composition: Making Plans and Juggling Constraints." *Cognitive Processes in Writing.* Ed. Lee W. Gregg and Erwin R. Steinberg. Hillsdale, NJ: Erlbaum Associates.

Sennett, Richard, and Jonathan Cobb. 1973. *Hidden Injuries of Class.* New York: Vintage.

Smitherman, Geneva. 1985. "'What Go Round Come Round': King in Perspective." *Tapping Potential: English and Language Arts for the Black Learner.* Ed. Charlotte K. Brooks. Urbana: NCTE.

Van de Weghe, Richard. 1982. "Grammar and Spelling Logs." *Non-Native and Non-Standard Dialect Students.* Ed. Candy Carter. Urbana: NCTE.

Note: For a further description of the problems encountered by Carlos and other nonstandard dialect writers, see Linda Miller Cleary. 1992. *From The Other Side of the Desk: Students Speak Out About Writing.*

THE NATURE OF LANGUAGE AND ITS CLASSROOM APPLICATIONS

In the past, spelling and vocabulary instruction have been directed by that small "grammar" book which students brought to English classes. Perhaps that grammar book should have commensurate stature with its weight and size, but it has held a mighty place in the language arts curriculum for many years. As we have come to a better understanding of language acquisition in the last forty years, it has become clearer and clearer that instruction in language must be studied in a broader perspective than that limited by the English "grammar." The study of usage, spelling, and vocabulary is best integrated with the study of the other language arts, again in meaningful contexts. This section of *Linguistics for Teachers* investigates the ways that humans acquire spelling, usage, syntax, semantics, and vocabulary and then indicates what methods teachers can use to move students along in acquisition.

PHONOLOGY AND THE TEACHING OF SPELLING

The first part of this section takes a look at phonology and then at its interaction with spelling. We begin with an article by Ben Crane, Edward Yeager, and Randal Whitman which looks at the sounds of the English language and the way they are generated. Hodges follows with an article that shows how sounds do and do not affect orthography, the spelling of words. Richard Hodges's article concludes with suggestions for spelling instruction, and Elizabeth Grubgeld follows with practical suggestions for working with problem spellers.

393

SYNTAX AND THE TEACHING OF GRAMMAR

The second part of this section examines the relationship between theories of syntax and the teaching of grammar. It begins by examining the two dominant theories of grammar in the twentieth century: structural grammar and transformational grammar. While the structural revolution in grammar has been replaced by the generative transformational grammar, the first article by Nelson Francis remains the best short description of this useful theory of grammar. A knowledge of it is helpful in teaching English as a second language and in explaining to students how grammar can be studied objectively, in a descriptive manner. The second article by Neil Smith and Deirdre Wilson, written with a generative transformational approach, explains the important role intuitions play in understanding the nature of grammar. This article is followed by Joan Klecan-Aker's empirical study of the syntactic pattern of sixth- and ninth-grade students. It is hoped that knowledge of where typical students are in their syntactic development will help future teachers understand what level can be expected of their students at their grade level. The next three articles work collectively. In the first, James Stalker points out that standard English usage is that which is maximally clear and socially appropriate and which falls in some appropriate register. In the next article, John Algeo discusses how "good English" is just what the users of the language decide is good or proper for that situation. Linda Miller Cleary and Nancy Lund debunk the seven myths that have provided the historical rationale for the extensive study of traditional grammar by showing that it does little to help students learn to read or write or to do better on the SAT tests. Elaine Chaika further shows that if grammar is to be studied, generative transformational grammar is the best model to use because it is the most interesting and will help the students develop their intuitions about English that hopefully will carry over into their writing. This section ends with the article by the late Robert Pooley who discusses what grammatical items are important to teach in elementary school and which will work themselves out by the time the students are in high school. He further discusses the nature of standard English and what usage items are important for senior high school students to know.

Most of the articles in this section have interesting and helpful bibliographies and provide a good starting point for further exploration into these topics. Those of you who are interested in exploring some of these topics still further will find the following books interesting:

Allen, Harold B. and Michael D. Linn. *Readings in Applied English Linguistics,* 3rd ed. (New York: Knopf, 1982). A collection of articles on a wide range of topics concerned with the teaching of English.

Baron, Dennis E. *Grammars and Good Taste: Reforming the American Language* (New Haven, Conn.: Yale University Press, 1982). An interesting and readable history of the attempts to reform English in the United States.

Baron, Dennis E. *Declining Grammar and Other Essays on the English Vocabulary*

(Urbana, Ill.: NCTE, 1989). A collection of essays that look at various attitudes toward the English language.

DeStefano, Johanna S. *Language: The Learner and the School* (New York: Wiley, 1978). An introduction to language and its effects on learning reading, writing, and spelling. Also discusses how the teacher's attitude toward a student's dialect has an effect on the student's learning.

Greenbaum, Sidney and Randolph Quirk. *A Student's Grammar of the English Language* (London: Longman, 1990). Shorter and revised version of *A Comprehensive Grammar of The English Language.* Makes an excellent reference book.

Pooley, Robert C. *The Teaching of English Usage* (Urbana, Ill.: NCTE, 1974). An older book, but an excellent discussion of the nature of proper usage, what items should be taught, and how they can be effectively taught.

Weaver, Constance. *Grammar for Teachers: Perspectives and Definitions* (Urbana, Ill.: NCTE, 1979). Looks at grammar as a psycholinguistic process and how it functions in relationship to the teaching of reading and writing.

SEMANTICS AND VOCABULARY

Prior to World War II, the study of semantics focused on the study of vocabulary, and that study held an important place in the secondary schools. Following the world wars, the frightening implications of "brainwashing" and propaganda made a place for the broader study of semantics in the secondary school curriculum. In their attention to "doublespeak," the National Council of Teachers of English has long supported the efforts of teachers to allow students to think critically about the language of international and national politicians and that of advertisements. This section begins with a review of semantic properties of morphemes (the parts, that is, building blocks, of words) and of words, and thus provides a view into the complexity of learning words and their meanings.

As Whorf has indicated, language plays a major role in the way we make sense of our world, both consciously and unconsciously, and as George Lakoff and Mark Johnson suggest, the metaphors common to our language make powerful contributions to the way we think and understand the world. Seth Katz provides us with an introduction to cognitive linguistics and additional understanding of how we build concepts of our world. Dwight Bolinger's seminal article, "Truth is a Linguistic Question," describes "verbal slight of hand" and the manipulation that is possible when readers don't understand how propaganda is used to mislead. Finally, Nancy McCracken gives us good ideas on how to permit our students to study language and its potential for manipulative use by those who are in a position to gain from it. Three books are important to further study in this area:

Bolinger, Dwight. *Language and the Loaded Weapon: The Use and Service of Language Today* (London: Longman, 1980).

Dieterich, Daniel. (ed.), *Teaching about Doublespeak* (Urbana, Ill.: NCTE, 1976).

Luts, William. (ed.), *Beyond Nineteen Eighty-Four: Doublespeak in a Post-Orwellian Age* (Urbana, Ill.: NCTE, 1989).

James Coomber and Howard Peet lead us to an important study of how to teach vocabulary in the classroom. They provide a rich review of research on the acquisition of vocabulary and its implication for instruction. Steven Grubaugh's article gives us a brief glimpse of how vocabulary can come alive in the classroom. More technical information about vocabulary acquisition is available in Coomber's and Peet's bibliography.

In the final article in this section, John Mayher draws on the work of Whorf, Vygotsky, Bruner, Lakeoff and Johnson, and others to talk about language education. The passages included in this volume come from his book *Uncommon Sense: Theoretical Practice in Language Education,* which is a critical analysis of what has been "common sense" in traditional language instruction. He advocates that teachers examine assumptions perpetuating unproductive classroom practices and replace the antiquated common-sense curriculum with an uncommon-sense curriculum based on recent research and theory in language. The section included in this anthology lends us a rationale for what has become an important theme throughout this section: Children learn about form and function of language fairly easily as long as they are using it for real purposes.

A

PHONOLOGY AND THE TEACHING OF SPELLING

Phonetics

Ben L. Crane, Edward Yeager, and Randal L. Whitman

An obvious way of beginning an analysis of spoken language is by studying its sounds; this study is called **phonetics.** We can take two basic approaches to phonetics: the acoustic approach, which looks at the physical properties of the sounds themselves; or the articulatory approach, which looks at sounds in terms of how they are produced, or articulated. The acoustic approach tells us that speech is a continuous flow of sound. Sophisticated sound-recording instruments reveal this continuity in speech as well as another fact: no speaker ever produces two utterances that sound exactly the same. In contrast, the articulatory approach looks at speech sounds as composed of segments.

Despite its distortion of reality, we begin with the articulatory approach for two reasons: people tend to perceive speech as segmented, and the articulatory approach gives us a way of talking about and classifying the sounds of speech. Thus, we begin this chapter by looking at how in general humans produce sounds and how we can classify sounds according to the way they are produced. Then we examine relationships among sounds and two acoustic characteristics of speech.

THE PRODUCTION OF SPEECH SOUNDS

Speech is an incredibly complex activity. It involves coordinated efforts of all the participating parts of the vocal tract (see Figure 13). One of the basic exercises in voice control is breath control, which involves training certain muscles involved in air expulsion, the first step in producing sounds. Air proceeds from the lungs through the **trachea** to the **larynx,** commonly called the **voice box,** which houses the **vocal cords.** If the cords are slightly tensed, the passage of air sets the vocal cords vibrating, which gives a basic sound quality to the air stream, which continues into the **pharynx,** where basic voice quality is estab-

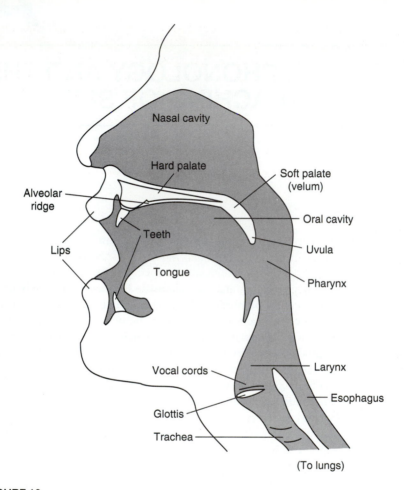

FIGURE 13
The vocal tract.

lished. Voice quality determines the unique characteristics of each speaker's voice, so that an individual often can be recognized by voice alone. Above the pharynx is the **uvula,** which is a movable flap that controls the passage of air through the nasal cavity. The uvula is always open when an individual breathes through the nose, but it is only open at certain times during the course of speech. For the most part, the **velum** (or **soft palate**) is closed in speech, and the air moves through the **oral cavity** (the mouth), the dimensions of which change according to the interaction of the tongue and lips. These changes result in what all speakers of a language recognize to be the sounds of their language. The study of these speech sounds is called *phonetics*.

Every language has a variety of sounds, and many of the sounds found in the languages of the world are not found in English. In this chapter, all discussion refers to American English. The English alphabet consists of twenty-six letters, but quite a few more than twenty-six sounds are used in speaking English. To discuss these sounds, a new alphabet of sounds, or a **phonetic alphabet,** is required. The phonetic symbols are enclosed in brackets to distinguish them from letters. Thus, [p] is a phonetic symbol indicating a particular sound. Although in many cases this phonetic alphabet corresponds to English spelling, many phonetic symbols have no direct correspondent in English spelling. Thus, it is important to remember that the phonetic alphabet describes only *sounds,* and each symbol represents only one sound.

CONSONANTS

The principal division of sounds is between vowels and consonants. Every language makes this distinction. **Vowels** are defined as those sounds produced with the oral cavity relatively open to the flow of air. **Consonants,** on the other hand, are sounds produced with a constriction or occlusion in the oral cavity.

The consonants may be grouped according to how the sounds are produced. English then has six groups of consonant sounds: stops, fricatives, affricates, nasals, liquids, and glides (see Table 10). The sounds within these groups can be further classified according to the place of articulation, that is, the position of the lips or tongue as the sounds are made.

1 If the lips are pressed together, the sound is a **bilabial.**

2 If the lower lip is pressed to the upper teeth, a **labiodental** is produced.

3 The tip of the tongue may be placed between the teeth, producing an **interdental.**

4 The tip or blade of the tongue may be placed against the alveolar ridge (the hard ridge behind the upper teeth), producing an **alveolar.**

5 The midsection of the tongue may be pressed against the hard palate **(palatal),** or against the soft palate or velum **(velar).**

Stops

By entirely closing off the flow of air at some point in the mouth, **stops,** or **plosives,** are formed. Air pressure from the lungs builds up and is suddenly released in a sharp burst of sound. In the production of English stops, the mouth may be sealed off in three major ways. If the lips are pressed together to seal off the air and opened in a sharp burst, the bilabial sounds [p] and [b] are produced, as in the words *pop* and *Bob.* In the alveolar pair of stops, the tip of the tongue is pressed against the alveolar ridge to produce [t] and [d], as in *tot* and *dad.* In the

TABLE 10
PHONETIC REPRESENTATION OF ENGLISH CONSONANTS

		Bilabial	Labiodental	Interdental	Alveolar	Palatal	Velar	Pharyngeal
Stops	Voiceless	p			t		k	
	Voiced	b			d		g	
Fricatives	Voiceless		f	θ	s	š		h
	Voiced		v	ð	z	ž		
Affricates	Voiceless					č		
	Voiced					ǰ		
Nasals	Voiced	m			n		ŋ	
Liquids	Voiced				l	r		
Glides	Voiced	w				y		

ENGLISH CONSONANTS
ILLUSTRATED BY EXAMPLES

[p] *p*at, ma*p*
[t] *t*in, ma*t*
[k] *c*ame, pi*ck*
[ʔ] bo*tt*le
[b] *b*ud, du*b*
[d] *d*in, ma*d*
[g] *g*ame, fla*g*
[f] *f*ine, lea*f*
[θ] *th*in, too*th*
[s] *s*ink, cla*ss*
[š] *s*ure, pu*sh*
[h] *h*and, *wh*o
[v] *v*ine, lea*ve*

[∂] *th*en, fa*th*er
[z] *z*inc, tie*s*
[ž] mea*s*ure, a*z*ure
[č] *ch*ain
[ǰ] *J*ane
[m] *m*an, ca*m*e
[n] *n*o, ti*n*
[ŋ] si*ng*, fi*ng*er
[l] *l*ap, fa*ll*
[r] *r*ap, ta*r*
[w] *w*itch, se*w*
[y] *y*ou, fe*w*

third pair of stops, the velars, the back of the tongue is pressed against the soft palate, or velum, to produce [k] and [g] , as in the words *kick* and *gag.*

The difference between the members of each of these pairs lies in the operation of the **vocal cords,** which are two elastic membranes that can be moved by muscles in the larynx (see Figure 14). The position of the membranes can vary from completely closed to completely open. During the act of swallowing, the vocal cords close to prevent food or drink from going into the lungs; they are open as one breathes. During speech, the vocal cords usually are open in varying degrees. In the production of [p], for example, the vocal cords are completely open and air may pass freely through the larynx. For [b], on the other hand, the vocal cords are almost closed, leaving only a narrow slit. As the lungs force air through this slit, the membranes vibrate in a fashion much like a kazoo. This vibration is called **voicing;** it can be heard by putting your hands over your ears while saying a long, continuous [b] in which the light contact of both lips is maintained. Repeat this experiment, saying a continuous [p]. There will be no vibration; [p] is a **voiceless** consonant, and [b] is its **voiced** counterpart. Voiced sounds are produced when the vocal cords are almost closed and air from the lungs causes them to vibrate; voiceless sounds are produced when the vocal cords are open. Many of the consonants appear in voiceless/voiced pairs like [p] and [b].

The voiceless stops—[p], [t], and [k]—are further characterized by degrees of **aspiration,** or the amount of air that accompanies their production. In initial position—that is, at the beginning of a syllable—the voiceless stops are aspirated, as in *pin, tall,* and *come.* If you hold a lighted match in front of your mouth when saying such words, the flame should go out or at least flicker. When preceded by an *s* or followed by *r* or *l,* as in *spin, tray,* and *clay,* significantly less aspiration accompanies the consonants; these sounds are called **unaspirated.** Finally, when voiceless stops occur in final position, or at the end of a word, they frequently are unreleased or unexploded; *mop, nick,* and *mat* are examples.

FIGURE 14
The vocal cords (from above).

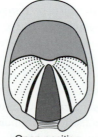

Open position
(voiceless sounds)

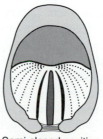

Semi-closed position
(voiced sounds)

These three variations of aspiration can be distinguished in transcription by using the following symbols: [pʰ, tʰ, kʰ] for aspirated stops; [p˙, t˙, k˙] for unaspirated stops; and [p⁻, t⁻, k⁻] for unreleased stops. Because the relative aspiration of these consonants in English is automatic, it often is not designated. For our purposes, only the symbols [p, t, k] will be required.

A different sort of stop is the **glottal stop,** indicated by [ʔ]; (it is not shown in Table 10). This sound is produced by closing off the flow of air at the glottis and suddenly releasing the air. It can be heard between the vowels in the word *kitten, satin,* or *bottle.* All these words are spelled with *t*'s between vowels; but for many speakers, the words do not contain a *t*-sound at all. The glottal sound can be a difficult consonant for the novice to hear, because no part of the mouth functions in its production.

Fricatives

By forcing air through a narrow opening in the oral cavity, a process that creates audible turbulence in the airstream, **fricatives** are made. The constriction may be made in different places of the mouth, as is the case with stops. When the lower lip is pressed lightly against the upper teeth and air is forced out between them, two labiodental fricatives, [f] and [v], may be produced. The voiceless sound [f] occurs in the beginning of the word *fine,* and its voiced counterpart, [v], occurs at the beginning of *vine.*

The next pair of fricatives are the interdentals, [θ] and [ð]. These are spelled *th* in English. Some people pronounce these sounds with their tongues between their teeth; others produce them with their tongues pressed lightly against the upper teeth. The voiceless [θ] appears in words like *thin, thought, pithy, teeth,* and *bath.* The voiced [ð] is present in *then, that, bathe,* and *mother.*

The alveolar fricatives are the voiceless [s] and the voiced [z]. They are formed by placing the tongue in light contact with the alveolar ridge and forcing the air out. The consonant sounds in *sis* and the final sound in *buzz* illustrate alveolars.

The **palatal fricatives,** [š] and [ž], are formed by arching the center of the tongue up toward the hard palate. The [š] is usually spelled *sh* in English, as in *ship,* although the sound occurs also in words like *sure, omission,* and *location.* Its voiced equivalent, [ž], never occurs at the beginning of native English words; it is usually found in the middle of words—as in *measure, seizure,* and *vision —* and at the end of a few borrowed words—as in *rouge* and *garage* —in some dialects of English.

The last fricative, [h], is voiceless and has no voiced counterpart. Strictly speaking, this sound does not meet the definition given for fricatives because [h] does not usually involve turbulence caused by constriction, although there is turbulence when [h] precedes certain vowels, as in a word like *heal.* In any case, many linguists have chosen to include [h] among the fricatives.

Affricates

The **affricates** are a special group of sounds that are formed by combining a stop and a fricative. In English, only one pair of sounds occurs in this category, [č] as in *chain* and *rich* and [ǰ] as in *Jane* and *ridge*. Notice that in pronouncing [č], one seems to pronounce [t] followed by [š]. Similarly, [ǰ] is much like a phonetic compound, consisting of [d] followed by [ž].

Nasals

In English, the three nasals, [m, n, ŋ], are made with the lips and tongue in the same respective positions as they are for [p, t, k]; however, air pressure does not build up as it does in the stops. Instead, the uvula (the flap that controls the opening to the nasal passage) is open, allowing the air to flow through the nose. In English, the nasals are always voiced. Whereas [m] and [n] may occur at the beginning as well as at the end of a syllable in English, as in *mom* and *nun*, [ŋ] occurs only at the end of a syllable, as in *sing*.

Notice that there is no [g] pronunciation inherent in [ŋ] for most speakers of English. On the other hand, in transcribing the word *finger*, both [ŋ] and [g] must be used because the second syllable begins with a [g] sound. Also, the word *rink* would be transcribed as [. . . ŋk].

Liquids

The consonants [l] and [r], as heard in *lilt* and *roar,* are called **liquids.** Both sounds are normally voiced. An [l] sound is formed by touching the tip of the tongue to the alveolar ridge and allowing air to escape to each side. The [r] sound in English is formed by curling the tip of the tongue up behind the alveolar ridge and flipping it forward and upward without actually touching the alveolar ridge.

Glides

The last two consonants are the **glides,** [w] and [y]. A [w] is formed with the back of the tongue arched high and the lips in a rounded position—much as they are in making the sound "oo" (as in *too*). For example, in the word *woo,* a word notoriously difficult for many foreigners to learn to pronounce, the lips begin and end in the same position. The [y] glide, much like the [w], is formed with the tongue and lips in the same position as they are when making the sound "ee" (as in *bee*). Say the word *yeast* and note the position of your lips.

Both [w] and [y] always appear either before or after a vowel in English. In both cases, the sounds "glide" rapidly to or from the articulatory position for that vowel. Since [w] and [y] possess certain vowel-like properties—for example, they lack a definite constriction of the oral cavity—they are not true consonants and are often called **semivowels.**

VOWELS

Vowels are voiced continuous sounds involving no interruption in the flow of air through the oral cavity. Different vowel sounds result from changing the shape of the mouth; each vowel is associated with a different configuration of the tongue and lips. For example, to say "ee" represented phonetically as [i], the lips are somewhat pulled back and the tongue is arched up toward the palate. To say "oo," as in *woo* and *Sue,* represented as [u], the tongue is raised toward the back of the mouth and the lips are rounded and pushed forward. For "ah," as in *father* and *cot,* represented as [a], the tongue is flattened and lowered.

Like the consonants, each vowel is associated with a phonetic symbol. Traditionally, vowels have been described along two dimensions: tongue height and the frontedness or backness of the tongue. Table 11, which is commonly called a **vowel chart,** shows the spatial relationship among vowels in terms of these two dimensions.

The vowels presented in Table 11 generally characterize Standard English or General American speech; that is, a form of speech as free from regional pronunciation variations as possible. English speech sounds, especially vowels, vary considerably from speaker to speaker; in most cases, a finer transcription than the one presented in the vowel chart is necessary to capture these distinctions because vowels lie along a continuum. This means that vowels may be produced slightly higher or lower or more fronted or backed than shown in Table 12.

To represent these variations in vowel sounds, symbols called **diacritics** or **diacritic marks** may be used. Thus, arrows may show how a vowel differs from the Standard English form. For example, [ä] indicates a slightly fronted pronunciation of [a], and [i↓] indicates a slightly lowered pronunciation of [i]. Similarly, dots may be used to show the length of a vowel: one dot following a vowel indicates slight lengthening, [a·]; and two dots indicate greater lengthening, [a:]. A horizontal line above a vowel also may indicate a long vowel, [ī]. In this text we will rarely need diacritics.

TABLE 11
TRADITIONAL REPRESENTATION OF
STANDARD ENGLISH VOWELS

	Front	Central	Back
High	i ɪ		u U
Mid	e ɛ	ʌ	o
Low	æ	a	ɔ

TABLE 12
ENGLISH VOWELS ILLUSTRATED BY EXAMPLES

[i] b*ea*t, k*ey,* f*ee*	[ʊ] b*oo*k, p*u*t
[ɪ] b*i*t, *i*nch	[u] b*oo*t, thr*ou*gh, s*ui*t
[e] b*ai*t, g*ay,* f*a*te	[ʌ] b*u*tter, r*ou*gh, rat*i*fy*
[ɛ] b*e*t, *e*nd, h*ea*d	[ay] b*i*te, f*i*ght
[æ] b*a*t, *a*nd	[aw] h*ow,* s*au*erkr*au*t, ab*ou*t
[a] c*a*lm, f*a*ther	[ɔy] b*oy,* h*oi*st
[ɔ] b*ou*ght, cr*a*wl	
[o] b*oa*t, sn*ow,* h*oe,* th*ou*gh	

*More frequently, the symbol [ə], read as "schwa," is used instead of [ʌ] in unstressed syllables.

The vowels of English are either **monophthongal** or **diphthongal;** that is, they are made up of either a single sound or two sounds in sequence. The major diphthongs of English are [ay], [aw], and [ɔy], as in the words *ride, house,* and *boy* (these are not shown in Table 11). Most linguists treat the English vowels [i], [e], [o], and [u] as diphthongs as well, because most speakers typically pronounce them with following glides. It is not uncommon to find these vowels represented phonetically as [iy], [ey], [ow], and [uw], respectively. Examples of words containing the English vowels are given in Table 12.

DISTINCTIVE FEATURES

So far we have discussed how sounds are produced, but little or no phonetic theory has been involved. Sounds can be classified in a variety of ways to suit a variety of theoretical pursuits. Perhaps the most important of the theoretical approaches is **distinctive-feature theory.** Its purpose is to isolate and identify the relationships between sounds and to provide a universal phonetic system to describe the sounds found in all the world's languages. Again, our application will be restricted to the sounds of English.

A **feature** is ideally a binary attribute; that is, a phonetic aspect that is either present or absent in a specific sound. For example, one of the distinctive features is [voiced]. Thus, such sounds as [b], [m], [a], and [l] can be characterized as [+voiced] whereas such sounds as [p], [f], and [s] are characterized as [−voiced]. In a completely accurate phonetic description, features may be preceded by integers that describe the degree to which a feature is present; for example, [2 nasal]. The vowel [æ] in the word *can't,* for example, is partially nasalized because it is affected by the following nasal [n]; however, it does not possess as great a degree of nasality as [n]. Thus, the [n] in *can't* is [1 nasal], indicating the greatest degree of nasality, and the [æ] is [2 nasal], indicating a secondary degree of nasality. When the features are used for classification, however, they are always either present (+) or absent (−).

The three sounds [p], [t], and [k] all share the feature [−voiced]. Therefore, additional features must be indicated in order to distinguish them from each other. Two additional features are required: [anterior] and [coronal] . The feature [+**anterior**] designates those sounds formed in the front of the mouth; that is, at the alveolar ridge, the teeth, or the lips. The feature [+**coronal**] specifies those sounds made with the front half, or blade, of the tongue. With these features, we can now differentiate the voiceless stops [p], [t], and [k]:

	p	t	k
Voiced	−	−	−
Anterior	+	+	−
Coronal	−	+	−

Thus, the feature [voiced] does not help us distinguish among [p], [t], and [k]; but the three consonants are completely distinguished from each other by the features [anterior] and [coronal]. Tables 13 and 14 list the distinctive features that characterize English sounds. The descriptions are given in articulatory terms because such definitions are simplest, but each feature may be defined in acoustic terms as well (for example, see *strident* in Table 13). This feature system makes possible the complete differentiation of all the sounds of a language.

SUPRASEGMENTALS

Stress and intonation are called **suprasegmentals** because they relate to aspects of pronunciation that go beyond the production of individual (segmental) sounds. Thus, they may be defined better in acoustic terms than in articulatory terms.

Stress

Pitch, length, and loudness are components of **stress.** The basic unit containing stress is the syllable. A **syllable** generally consists of a vowel accompanied by one or more consonants, and the most common syllable form in English is a consonant plus a vowel. In actual pronunciation, one may stress a syllable by giving it a higher pitch, making it louder, or making it longer—or perhaps by a combination of all three. In English, native speakers generally recognize at least three levels of stress: primary, secondary, and unstressed. They are indicated with the following stress marks:

Primary: /
Secondary: \
Unstressed: (no mark)

TABLE 13
THE DISTINCTIVE FEATURES

The following features serve to distinguish between vowels and consonants:

Syllabic—the role a sound plays in the structure of a syllable. [+syllabic] sounds include all vowels, as well as nasals and liquids when they function as the basis of a syllable, as in *rhythm*. The semivowels, [w] and [y], are [−syllabic].

Consonantal—a constriction or occlusion of the oral cavity. [+consonantal] sounds include stops, fricatives, affricates, nasals, and liquids. Note that [h] is [−consonantal], although it has traditionally been classed as a consonant, because [h] does not exhibit the constriction that is typical of consonantal sounds.

Sonorant—the resonance of a sound. Sonorant sounds are produced with a configuration of the vocal tract cavity that allows spontaneous voicing. [+sonorant] sounds include vowels, nasals, liquids, and semivowels.

The following features serve to distinguish among consonants:

Continuant—those sounds that involve a constriction or occlusion of the oral cavity over a period of time. The fricatives, liquids, and glides are [+continuant]; the stops, nasals, and affricates are [−continuant].

Strident—high-frequency noisiness. The sounds [f], [s], [š], and [č]; along with their voiced counterparts, are [+strident].

Nasal—those sounds produced with the nasal cavity open.

Anterior—those sounds formed in the anterior or forward part of the mouth.

Coronal—those sounds formed with the blade of the tongue.

Voiced—the presence of vocal-cord vibration.

The following features principally serve to distinguish among vowels:

High—with the blade of the tongue above a neutral position.

Low—with the blade of the tongue below a neutral position. The midvowels [e], [ε], [ʌ], and [o] are neither high nor low and are marked [−high] and [−low].

Back—with the tongue further back than a neutral position. In utilizing the distinctive features, the central vowels [ʌ] and [a] are considered [+back].

Round—with the lips rounded. The vowels [ʌ] and [a] are unrounded; thus, they are distinguished from the back vowels, which are [+round].

Tense—with the muscles of vocalization tensed. The vowels marked [−tense] are [ɪ], [ε], [ʌ], [a], and [ʊ]; all other vowels are [+tense]. Vowels marked as [−tense] are frequently called **lax vowels;** the articulatory positions for tense vowels are generally maintained longer than for lax vowels. Note that consonants may also be [+tense] or [−tense], although for consonants this feature is best defined acoustically.

Alternatively, stress may be treated as a distinctive feature; thus, the feature [+stress] may be [1 stress] (the syllable with primary stress), [2 stress] (the syllable with secondary stress), and so on.

The distinction between stressed and unstressed syllables in words like *cattle* is easy to hear. In multisyllabic words, three levels of stress often may be perceived. For instance, the word *California* has primary (or greatest) stress on the

TABLE 14
DISTINCTIVE FEATURES

English consonants	p	b	f	v	m	t	d	θ	ð	n	s	z	č	ǰ	š	ž	k	g	ŋ	h	y	w	r	l
Syllabic	–	–	–	–	–	–	–	–	–	–	–	–	–	–	–	–	–	–	–	–	–	–	–	–
Consonantal	+	+	+	+	+	+	+	+	+	+	+	+	+	+	+	+	+	+	+	–	–	–	+	+
Sonorant	–	–	–	–	+	–	–	–	–	+	–	–	–	–	–	–	–	–	+	–	+	+	+	+
Continuant	–	–	+	+	–	–	–	+	+	–	+	+	–	–	+	+	–	–	–	+	+	+	+	+
Nasal	–	–	–	–	+	–	–	–	–	+	–	–	–	–	–	–	–	–	+	–	–	–	–	–
Strident	–	–	+	+	–	–	–	–	–	–	+	+	+	+	+	+	–	–	–	–	–	–	–	–
Anterior	+	+	+	+	+	+	+	+	+	+	+	+	–	–	–	–	–	–	–	–	–	–	–	+
Coronal	–	–	–	–	–	+	+	+	+	+	+	+	+	+	+	+	–	–	–	–	–	–	+	+
Voiced	–	+	–	+	+	–	+	–	+	+	–	+	–	+	–	+	–	+	+	–	+	+	+	+
High	–	–	–	–	–	–	–	–	–	–	–	–	+	+	+	+	+	+	+	–	+	+	+	+
Low	–	–	–	–	–	–	–	–	–	–	–	–	–	–	–	–	–	–	–	+	–	–	–	–
Back	–	–	–	–	–	–	–	–	–	–	–	–	–	–	–	–	+	+	+	–	–	+	–	–
Round	–	–	–	–	–	–	–	–	–	–	–	–	–	–	–	–	–	–	–	–	–	+	–	–
Tense	+	–	+	–	–	+	–	+	–	–	+	–	+	–	+	–	+	–	–	+	–	–	–	–

Note: l, r, and the nasals are [+syllabic] when they serve as the basis for a syllable.

English vowels	i	ɪ	e	ɛ	æ	ʌ	a	ɔ	o	ʊ	u
Syllabic	+	+	+	+	+	+	+	+	+	+	+
Consonantal	–	–	–	–	–	–	–	–	–	–	–
Sonorant	+	+	+	+	+	+	+	+	+	+	+
High	+	+	–	–	–	–	–	–	–	+	+
Low	–	–	–	–	+	–	+	+	–	–	–
Back	–	–	–	–	–	+	+	+	+	+	+
Round	–	–	–	–	–	–	–	+	+	+	+
Tense	+	–	+	–	–	–	+	+	+	–	+

third syllable, secondary stress on the first syllable, and no stress on the remaining two syllables. The word *California* thus may be written phonetically as [kæ̀ləfórnyə] . Notice that in some noun and verb forms of identically spelled words—for example, the noun *cónvict* and the verb *convíct*—stress reflects a parts-of-speech categorization. This fact shows that stress is not independent from higher-level grammatical structure. But stress in fact is a continuum, and its division into discrete levels beyond primary stress is, to an extent, arbitrary. As a result, levels of stress sometimes may be difficult to perceive.

Intonation

The other major suprasegmental is **intonation,** which in English is described as a rising or falling pitch over a group of words. Intonation alone does not normally distinguish between any two words in English; however, it does serve to distinguish among sentences, as in the following examples:

1 Mary had sóup for lunch.
2 Mary had soup for lúnch.
3 Mary had sóup for lunch?
4 Mary had soup for lúnch?

The first sentence indicates that Mary had *soup,* rather than some other food, for lunch. The second sentence indicates that Mary had soup for *lunch,* and not some other meal. The third and fourth sentences are the corresponding questions. It is important to note that intonation, like stress, exists in varying degrees; it is not as simple and uniform as the notation used in these examples suggests.

SUMMARY

Speech sounds are formed by modifying the shape of the mouth to impose characteristic modulations on the flow of air from the lungs. Far more sounds exist in English than the English alphabet suggests; thus, a system of phonetic symbols is required for accurate transcription.

Perhaps the most important division among sounds is that between consonants and vowels. *Consonants* are defined as sounds produced with constrictions or occlusions in the oral cavity. Consonants are further classified according to the degree and location of constriction, whether the nasal cavity is open, and the presence or absence of voicing. *Vowels* are defined as sounds produced through an open oral cavity. They may be classified according to the height and the frontedness or backness of the tongue.

Phonetic transcription makes possible the careful analysis of the sounds of English, as well as any other language, and represents the first step in any linguistic analysis. The next step is the organization of phonetic material into a system of distinctive features. A *feature* is a binary attribute that is used to describe and differentiate the sounds of a language.

The two major suprasegmentals in English are stress and intonation. Stress applies to individual syllables, whereas intonation applies over groups of words.

REFERENCES

Abercrombie, David. 1967. *Elements of General Phonetics.* Edinburgh: Edinburgh University Press.

Catford, John C. 1977. *Fundamental Problems in Phonetics.* Bloomington, Indiana: Indiana University Press.

International Phonetic Association. 1949. *Principles of the International Phonetic Alphabet.* Rev. ed. London: International Phonetic Association.

Jakobson, Roman: Gunnar Fant; and Morris Halle. 1963. *Preliminaries to Speech Analysis.* Cambridge, Mass.: MIT Press.
Ladefoged, Peter. 1975. *A Course in Phonetics.* New York: Harcourt Brace Jovanovich.
———. 1971. *Preliminaries to Linguistic Phonetics.* Chicago: University of Chicago Press.

Theory and Research

Richard E. Hodges

The noted historian James H. Breasted once observed that "the invention of writing and of a convenient system of keeping records on paper has had a greater influence in uplifting the human race than any other intellectual achievement in the career of man" (Breasted 1938, p. 61). This influence, of course, was a direct result of the capacity of writing to record the accumulating cultural heritage so that it could be transmitted across distances and to future generations. In a very real sense, writing was the wellspring that enabled modern civilization to grow and flourish.

Writing often conveys more than its intended message, however; it may also offer subjective information about the writer—his or her social and educational background and quality of thought, among other attributes. Spelling—the mechanism by which language is converted to writing—contributes to these subjective impressions because misspellings are visible, readily identifiable features of written discourse. Whether or not these impressions are warranted, poor spelling can have unfortunate consequences in school, vocational, and personal life.

Yet, the importance attributed to spelling in the larger society is seldom matched by the time and effort given to its study in the school curriculum. Why is this the case? One reason is that spelling has traditionally been relegated to the elementary school curriculum and, in turn, regarded as involving little intellectual effort other than rote memory. A second reason is that the teaching of spelling has generally received scant attention in the professional preparation of teachers. As a result, teachers tend to teach spelling in much the same way that they were taught to spell, and many present-day instructional practices are, in reality, cultural artifacts.

In *Learning to Spell,* my earlier publication in the TRIP series, spelling instruction in the early elementary school was discussed in a very different way. Instead of being regarded as the product of rote memory, spelling ability was described as a complex intellectual accomplishment in which word knowledge is developed over time from many and varied experiences with written language—in short, as a developmental process that continues into adulthood. Indeed, as indicated by emerging research findings which I will describe shortly, some aspects of orthography are probably *best* learned in later school years when instruction can draw upon the greater intellectual maturity of students and their more extensive experiences with written language. From this point of view, then, spelling ability rests to a large degree on a knowledge of the fabric of language itself; rather than being the bland subject it is often thought to be, spelling can be a voyage into a fascinating and beneficial study of our language.

Before exploring how spelling can be presented in this manner, we need to examine briefly two areas where important evidence is accumulating with consequences for spelling instruction. The first of these is how our writing system is structured; the second, how a knowledge of this structure appears to develop, particularly in later school years. We will begin by comparing characteristics of the English writing system to those of other writing systems and then consider recent insights into the development of spelling ability in later school years.

THE STRUCTURE OF ENGLISH ORTHOGRAPHY

Whenever we write, we engage in the process of spelling, the act of transforming our thoughts into a visual record by placing graphic symbols, or graphemes, on a writing surface. Writing, as Breasted observed, is one of our great accomplishments, for it makes possible the preservation of accumulated wisdom and its transmission to future generations. How writing developed is a fascinating story in its own right, but one whose telling is beyond the scope of this booklet. Nevertheless, a brief account of the different kinds of writing systems that have been developed helps us to understand more clearly the advantages and the limitations of our own written code.

Every writing system, or orthography, is made up of a set of graphemes, each representing an element of language such as a complete word, a syllable, or a speech sound. Learning to spell in any orthography involves learning its graphic charcters—their correct production in writing and the unit of language each represents. As we shall see, the ease with which an orthography is learned depends to a large extent on the unit of language that its graphic symbols represent.

The oldest type of orthography is represented by Chinese writing and by the Japanese orthography called kanji, which uses Chinese characters. In these writing systems, graphic characters represent entire words or concepts. In kanji, for example, the graphic symbol 人 ("man") together with the symbol 本 ("root") forms 亻本 or "root of man," which means *human body*. (In scribal practice, 人 is altered to 亻 when written beside another character.) Similarly, the character 人 plus the character 木 ("tree") forms 亻木 or "man resting by tree," which means *rest*. On holidays this is the character a shopkeeper places on the door to indicate the shop is closed (Walsh 1967, p. 56).

A principal advantage of this kind of writing, sometimes referred to as logographic or ideographic writing, is that the graphic symbols can be interpreted without reference to spoken language since they stand for ideas or concepts by themselves. For this reason, a Mandarin-speaking Chinese can communicate in writing with a Cantonese-speaking Chinese even though their spoken languages are different. On the other hand, logographic writing has a major disadvantage: thousands of characters are needed to convey concepts and the words of the language. Learning to read and write in such a system requires much time and effort; indeed, because of the difficulty in mastering the written language, literacy has been a mark of honor and respect throughout the course of Chinese civilization.

A second major type of writing system, the syllabary, is based directly on spoken language and uses graphic symbols to represent the syllables that form spoken words. Thus, combining the graphic characters that represent the spoken syllables of a word enables us to spell that word. Syllabaries are found mainly in languages with simple syllable structures; usually a single vowel, or a consonant and a vowel, forms a syllable. Spoken Japanese is such a language and, in addition to kanji, employs a syllabary called kana in its written language. There are two sets of kana, each containing forty-six graphic symbols. One set, hiragana, is used primarily to form grammatical endings. The second set, katakana, is used to write words adopted from other languages. For example, アメリカ stands for "ah may ri kah" or *America* (Walsh 1967, p. 119).

The advantage of syllabic writing over a writing system that uses symbols to convey whole words is, of course, the significant reduction in the number of written symbols that must be learned in order to read and write. There is a vast difference between learning 9,000 symbols used by Chinese scholars (out of 80,000!) and forty-six kana characters. Nonetheless, few syllabaries exist today because few languages have such simple syllabic structures.

Alphabetic writing, the most highly developed and widespread system of writing in the world today, has proved to be much more convenient and adaptable to spoken language than has syllabic writing. Based on the notion that the separate speech sounds of a language, its phonemes, constitute the units that written symbols represent, alphabetic writing would, ideally, have a distinct symbol for each sound. A spoken language with forty speech sounds, for example, would have an alphabet of forty characters. The simplicity, adaptability, and suitability of alphabetic writing has secured its place as the predominant method of writing in the world today. The alphabet that was derived from the ancient Hebrews, Greeks, and Romans is now used not only in English but in French, Italian, German, Spanish, Turkish, Polish, Dutch, and Hungarian—to name a few of the languages that employ essentially the same alphabetic characters.

But what about the English language and its use of alphabetic writing? The answer to this question is of great importance in our consideration of the teaching of spelling. Let us begin by looking briefly at how English spelling has traditionally been viewed with respect to its allegiance to the alphabetic principle.

To the casual observer, English spelling is a puzzle. One of its problems, its detractors say, stems from the fact that its alphabet contains only twenty-six letters while the spoken language contains more than forty speech sounds. Moreover, many of its speech sounds are spelled in several ways, such as the "f" sound in *far, phone,* and *laugh* or the "u" sound in *cut, tough, done,* and *blood.* That outspoken critic of English orthography George Bernard Shaw once pointed out that *fish* might just as reasonably be spelled *ghoti* because the "f" sound is spelled *gh* in *rough,* the "i" sound is spelled *o* in *women,* and the "sh" sound is spelled *ti* in *nation.* From examples such as these, it is easy to see why there have been many efforts to reform English spelling through the past several centuries, and why the most common practice in teaching spelling has been memorization. As we shall shortly discover, however, Shaw's parody of English spelling itself provides vivid evidence that the writing system is not as erratic as its surface features would indicate.

With the emergence of linguistic science in the twentieth century, a different view of English spelling was proposed, one in which the orthography was described as a flawed but patterned alphabetic writing system, whose errant ways had linguistic and historical explanations. One reason that English spelling does not adhere to the alphabetic principle, some language scholars maintained, is that spoken language changes over time while writing changes very little. As a result, the spelling of many words no longer reflects their pronunciation, for example, *one, two,* and *night.* A second reason, they pointed out, is that the spelling of some words was, for various reasons, changed by sixteenth-and seventeenth-century scribes and other scholars who, with the advent of the printing press, helped to establish English spellings, as in the spelling of *come, love, some,* and *wonder* with *o* instead of the older *u.* A third reason that English spelling appears to stray from its alphabetic base stems from the fact that the language has borrowed many words from other languages, sometimes retaining both the spelling and the pronunciation of the borrowed words, as in *parfait* and *sabotage* from the French, and in other cases changing the spelling and/or the pronunciation to fit English patterns, as in *medicine* from the Latin, *gymnasium* from the Greek, *volcano* from the Italian, and *mosquito* from the Spanish. Thus, as a result of these and other historical forces, present-day English spelling reflects an erosion of its alphabetic base.

The issue remained, however, concerning the extent to which the writing system had strayed from the alphabetic principle and, more important, what this deviation meant for spelling instruction. In response to these questions, linguists and educators interested in English spelling undertook new studies (Robert A. Hall, Jr., 1961; Paul R. Hanna et al., 1966). Let us look for a moment at one of these research efforts, the Stanford University Spelling Project, the basic premise of which was that English spelling is based on the alphabetic principle.

These researchers, headed by Paul Hanna of Stanford University, used computer technology to analyze the spelling of over 17,000 words to determine how individual speech sounds, or phonemes, are spelled in different positions in the syllables of words. The number of different spellings of each phoneme was determined and the number of times each spelling of a given sound occurred in the 17,000 words was counted. The researchers were then able to rank the spellings of each phoneme from most frequent to least frequent and thereby determine which phonemes had "regular" graphic representation and which did not.

Using this information, the researchers developed a computer program that would spell the 17,000 words on the basis of phoneme-grapheme correspondence. The results were revealing. The computer correctly spelled over 8,000 words, or about 50 percent, misspelling another 37 percent of the words with only one incorrect phoneme-grapheme correspondence. Moreover, the misspellings could be explained when certain word-building and historical factors were taken into consideration. Hanna and his associates concluded that English spelling is less capricious than it appears and contains numerous systematic relationships between speech sounds and letters. Shaw's spelling of *fish* as *ghoti* could now be shown to demonstrate the basically rational nature of English orthography: while *gh* represents the "f" sound, it does so only at the ends of words such as *rough;* while *o* represents the "ĭ" sound, the only word in which that spelling occurs is *women;* and while *ti* represents the "sh" sound, that spelling never ends a word and is found only in words that contain the suffix *-tion* as in *nation.*

The Stanford study attracted considerable attention, both favorable and unfavorable. To some observers, the fact that only 50 percent of the words were correctly spelled by the computer, even after applying many complex rules, demonstrated the irrational nature of English spelling. On the other hand, other observers recognized that, although focusing narrowly on phoneme-grapheme correspondence, the study verified the underlying systematic nature of English orthography.

A significant factor of English orthography, however, eluded the Stanford researchers; namely, that the appropriate unit of analysis in looking at English spelling is not phoneme-grapheme correspondences by themselves but how these correspondences are governed by the words in which they occur. Thus, while the researchers had demonstrated how adjacent sounds and letters influence each other (for example, that the final "j" sound of *fudge* is spelled *dge* because it follows a short vowel sound but is spelled *ge* in *huge* and *large* because these words contain other kinds of vowel sounds), their study did not take into account that related words have related spellings despite sound changes (*sane* and *sanity; nation* and *national; derive, derivative,* and *derivation*); nor did it take into account such word-building factors as prefixes and suffixes.

Other scholars did take these factors into account, however. Richard

Venezky, for example, although interested in how the pronunciations of words can be predicted from their written forms, established that English spelling patterns can be effectively described only when both phonological and word-building, or morphological, factors are taken into consideration (Venezky 1967). Noam Chomsky and Morris Hallé (1968) extended this position by asserting that the power of the English writing system lies in its disregard for irrelevant phonetic differences and its focus on the graphic identity of semantically related words *(derive, derivative, derivation)*. The picture that emerges from these studies is one of a writing system that on the surface appears erratic and irregular but is at deeper and more abstract levels quite logical. Our writing system, in short, is not merely a reflection of speech sounds but of other language elements as well—word-building elements, syntax, and meaning.

Although theoretical views of English spelling and research into the nature of its structure are of interest primarily to researchers and scholars, this body of information has genuine significance for spelling instruction. As we are finding out, close parallels exist between what mature, efficient spellers know about the English writing system and what theoreticians and researchers have begun to unearth about that system. Let us turn, then, to a consideration of how spelling is learned.

LEARNING TO SPELL

Just as there have been recent significant advances in our understanding of the nature of English orthography, so have there been major advances in our understanding of how spoken and written language is learned.

The nineteenth-century psychologist William James once commented that we are born into a "kaleidoscopic flux of confusion" and that our basic task as human beings is to make sense of the world about us. Acquiring language is a dramatic example of how we accomplish that task. With the exception of those with severe physical or mental impairment, each individual learns to speak relatively quickly. Within the first year, words are said, and often within the next year rudimentary sentences are produced. By the time children enter school, most show considerable facility with spoken language.

Although major questions remain to be answered about the process of language acquisition, important insights relevant to our examination of spelling have been achieved in recent years. One such insight is that learning to speak is in large measure a developmental process in which language concepts are formed, a process of accumulating generalizations about language through experiencing language. Thus, the acquisition of language is made possible because language is systematic, comprised of "rules" that determine how the sounds, words, and grammar of a language are produced and used to convey meaning. It is worth noting that we do not need linguists to tell us that language is systematic; each of us is well aware of the systematic nature of language, having gained that insight on our own in the first few years of life. A second insight about language learning is that the process is governed by general conditions of intellectual development and that the language displayed by a child at any given time is an expression of that development. A young child's language should not be regarded as inefficient adult language but as a manifestation of that child's model of language at that particular time. Children who say "foots" for "feet" and "hurted" for "hurt" are, in fact, providing eloquent evidence of their active search for the underlying language system. There are, in short, few if any random errors in the speech of children. Related to this observation is a third insight, that learning to speak requires numerous opportunities to be wrong. Errors provide comparisons for children to make with standard speech, enabling them to accommodate their own speech patterns over time to the language standards of the social environment in which they live.

Present research, of course, offers many other insights about the language development of children. For our purposes, however, evidence that language acquisition is an inexorable process in which children naturally and actively engage as they work out the "rules of the game" has important implications for learning to spell. For, as we shall see, there is great similarity between the processes involved in acquiring spoken language and those used to master written language. Children learn to talk by active involvement with the speech environment, and involvement that engages them in identifying, classifying, and applying concepts about the "rules" of spoken language. So, too, does their written language development rely on many of the same intellectual strategies, strategies that develop with maturity and through experiences with the written language.

Only recently has spelling research begun to consider how young learners view the orthography. Instead, earlier studies tended to focus on such factors as the role and kinds of perception involved in learning to spell, the rate of learning, and, most often, comparisons between instructional methods (formal word study versus incidental learning, oral spelling versus silent spelling, test-study versus study-test approaches). Of late, however, researchers have begun to consider both the young learner and the nature of the orthography, and their findings suggest that the ability to spell is not a low-order memory task but is instead a highly complex and active intellectual accomplishment.

Since we are primarily interested in this discussion with the spelling ability of older students, we shall summarize only briefly the recent work concerning the spelling of young children. A more extended discussion of research concerning the beginning stages of spelling ability is found in *Learning to Spell,* the earlier TRIP publication.

One of the first major studies to examine the beginning attempts of children to spell was conducted by Charles Read, a linguist at the University of Wisconsin (Read 1971, 1975a, 1975b). Read looked at the ways in which children four to eight years old used their knowledge of English phonology to spell words. Among his subjects were approximately twenty preschoolers who were able to identify and name the letters of the alphabet and to relate the letter names to the sounds of words. These children then "invented" the spellings of words they wrote or constructed by arranging movable letters. Read found that even at an early age children are able to detect the phonetic characteristics of words that English spelling represents. More important to this discussion of spelling, however, was the observation that these young children, with minor variations, misspelled words in the same ways, for example, *bot* for *boat, fas* for *face, lade* for *lady.* Read's research revealed that even very young children try to make sense of the world around them by using available information, in this instance, applying their intuitive knowledge of the sound structure of English in order to spell words. In addition, Read demonstrated that the judgments of children about relationships between speech and spelling are qualitatively different from those made by adults—that learning to spell, like learning to speak, is a developmental process.

Other researchers have since extended Read's investigations by looking systematically at the spelling of school-aged children. Among the substantive work in this field is that of a number of researchers at the University of Virginia under the direction of Edmund Henderson (Beers and Henderson 1977; Beers, Beers, and Grant 1977; Gentry 1978; Templeton 1979; Zutell 1979). In order to identify and describe the developmental stages of spelling ability, these researchers looked particularly at the kinds of errors children make in free-writing situations. What they found reinforces and extends our growing awareness that ability to spell is a complex intellectual and developmental achievement.

In 1977, James Beers and Edmund Henderson analyzed the spelling errors made by first-grade children over a six-month period and found that these young spellers went through three invariant stages as they developed strategies for spelling. In the first, they used a letter-name strategy in much the same way that Read's preschoolers had. In the second, they showed greater refinement in how they spelled vowel sounds, using letters to represent sounds other than the sounds that resembled letter names. In the third stage, they began to use information about features of the English writing system itself, for example, spelling *made* as *maed* or *hide* as *hied,* thus demonstrating an awareness of the final *e* and how it governs preceding vowels. These young spellers, then, did not lack phonetic knowledge in relation to alphabet letters, but they did lack knowledge about word structure, a knowledge that is gained only through experiences with written language over time.

In a subsequent study (Beers, Beers, and Grant 1977) two hundred children in grades one through four were asked to spell a set of frequently used words and a set of infrequently used words in order to observe the spelling strategies they would employ. Here, as well, children systematically developed strategies based on their experiences with written language, reverting to simpler, more "primitive" strategies, such as assigning letters to words on the basis of letter names, when they were unfamiliar with a word.

These studies give added support to the contention that learning to spell is a developmental process that culminates in an understanding of English spelling rather than a simple knowledge of relationships between speech sounds and their graphic representations. But what about the spelling strategies of older students? Let us turn to several recent examinations of spelling development among youngsters in later school years.

One such examination was undertaken by Shane Templeton (1979). To determine the extent to which knowledge of graphic structure contributes to spelling ability, he studied the abilities of sixth-, eighth-, and tenth-graders to construct and spell derived forms of real and nonsense words. Templeton found considerable evidence that spelling ability does not rely solely on skills for relating sound and spelling, nor upon rote memory. Rather, both phonological knowledge and visual knowledge about words are brought into play when older students spell, the visual knowledge having been acquired, of course, only from extensive prior experiences with written language.

Other evidence indicating that familiarity with the graphic structure of words is employed in spelling was found by Jacqueline Marino (1980), who studied the strategies used by sixth-grade students in a game (Word Mastermind) that requires players to make successive approximations toward identifying and spelling a target word. She found that better players used strategies involving a knowledge of letter frequencies and permissible letter patterns in English spelling and that these players were also the better spellers among the students in the study.

Other studies of the spelling development of older students disclose a developmental shift among better spellers from a reliance upon the phoneme-grapheme strategies used in the early school years toward a strategy of spelling words by analogy to other known words. Thus, while poorer spellers appear to stay with a phoneme-grapheme strategy when confronted with unfamiliar words, better spellers develop more effective strategies that incorporate a knowledge of spelling patterns in related words in order to spell unfamiliar words or words in which sound-letter relationships are insufficient or misleading. (See, for example, Juola, Schadler, Chabot, and McCaughey 1978; Marsh, Friedman, Welch, and Desberg 1980.)

In this same vein, I have observed the strategies of highly proficient ten- to fourteen-year-old spellers who compete yearly in regional "spelling bees." My observations reveal a number of interesting characteristics shared by these extraordinary young spellers. One observation is that these youngsters have a common interest in words generally, not merely in their spelling. A second observation is that word meaning is a crucial element in spelling ability. Time and time again, contestants for whom a target word was not clearly remembered or about which they were unsure was correctly spelled when the word was given in sentence context or when a definition was provided. A third observation is that morphological (word-building) knowledge is a fundamental part of their spelling repertoire. Often, words whose meanings did not elicit a spelling were correctly spelled when information about their roots was provided. In these instances, many contestants were able to reconstruct the correct spelling of the target word on the basis of information about morphological factors reflected in the orthography, even though the word was not completely familiar. A fourth observation is that when the preceding clues failed to elicit a strategy for spelling an unfamiliar word, students resorted to the more primitive strategy of attempting to spell a target word on the basis of sound-letter clues, a practice that only occasionally resulted in a correct spelling.

Although an extensive research literature about the spelling ability of older students is only now emerging, studies such as the foregoing plainly indicate that for most people an ability to spell is a consequence of knowing about words in many guises—their visual or graphic characteristics, their phonological and structural (morphological) properties, and their meanings. These kinds of information enable spellers to develop generalizations about the English writing system that can be used in the spelling task, generalizations that have application to broad groups of words.

IMPLICATIONS FOR INSTRUCTION

What might we conclude about spelling instruction for older students from these linguistic and learning insights? For one, learning to spell involves learning about words and the interrelationships of components of words as these are reflected in the orthography. Because English orthography reflects language sometimes at the level of sound and at more abstract levels at other times, spelling instruction should not be restricted to a study of relationships between letters and sounds but should also entail a comprehensive study of the structural and semantic relationships of words. Consequently, learning to spell is not the exclusive province of spelling lessons. One learns to spell by having opportunities to generate useful "rules" about the written language, an outcome that becomes possible only through a rich interaction with written language in numerous and varied settings. Every instance of writing and reading is a potential moment for learning more about the properties of English spelling.

A second conclusion is that spelling instruction and vocabulary instruction are two faces of the same coin, particularly for older students. Not only does a study of English spelling contribute to spelling ability, but the stability of English orthography makes it possible to explore other aspects of the language—such factors as meaning relationships among words derived from common Latin and Greek roots and how the orthography retains the identity of semantically related words despite pronunciation differences.

A third conclusion is that individuals make few, if any, random spelling errors. Each incorrect spelling has a cause, whether from carelessness or from insufficient or erroneous knowledge about the written language. Spelling mistakes are, therefore, opportunities for teachers to assess the levels of understanding students have about the spelling system and for students to gain new knowledge about the orthography that may have application to other words.

Finally, as we noted in our opening discussion, some aspects of the orthography are probably best learned in later school years when the intellectual maturity of students and their greater range of experiences can be utilized. In this context, it can be argued that a proper goal of spelling study for older students is not only to learn to spell words correctly but to extend interest in and appreciation for the rich, complex fabric of language—its properties, uses, and historical development. In this light, the study of spelling is the study of language itself.

REFERENCES

Beers, James W, Carol S. Beers, and Karen Grant. 1977. "The Logic Behind Children's Spelling." *The Elementary School Journal 77* (January): 238–242.

Beers, James W., and Edmund H. Henderson. 1977. "A Study of Developing Orthographic Concepts Among First Graders." *Research in the Teaching of English* 11 (Fall):133–148.

Gentry, J. Richard. 1978. "Early Spelling Strategies." *The Elementary School Journal* 79 (November):88–92.

Hall, Robert A., Jr. 1961. *Sound and Spelling in English.* Philadelphia, Pa.: Chilton Book Co.

Hanna, Paul R., Jean S. Hanna, Richard E. Hodges, and Erwin H. Rudorf. 1966. *Phoneme-Grapheme Correspondences as Cues to Spelling Improvement.* Washington, D.C.: Government Printing Office, U.S. Office of Education.

Henderson, Edmund H., and James W. Beers, eds. 1980. *Developmental and Cognitive Aspects of Learning to Spell: A Reflection of Word Knowledge.* Newark, Del.: International Reading Association.

Horwitz, Abraham B., and Arthur Goddard. 1969. *Games to Improve Your Child's English.* New York: Simon and Schuster.

Read, Charles. 1971. "Preschool Children's Knowledge of English Phonology." *Harvard Educational Review* 41 (February):1–34.

———. 1975. *Children's Categorization of Speech Sounds in English.* National Council of Teachers of English Research Report No. 17. Urbana, Ill.: National Council of Teachers of English.

———. 1975b. "Lessons to Be Learned from the Preschool Orthographer." In *Foundations of Language Development: A Multidisciplinary Approach,* edited by Eric H. Lenneberg and Elizabeth Lenneberg, vol. 2, pp. 329–346. New York: Academic Press.

Templeton, Shane. 1979. "Spelling First, Sound Later: The Relationship between Orthography and Higher Order Phonological Knowledge in Older Students." *Research in the Teaching of English* 13 (October):255–264.

Venezky, Richard L. 1967. "English Orthography: Its Graphical Structure and Its Relation to Sound." *Reading Research Quarterly* 2 (Spring):75–105.

Walsh, Len. 1967. *Read Japanese Today.* Japan: Asia House Publishers. Also Rutland, Vt.: C.E. Tuttle, 1969.

Zutell, Jerry. 1979. "Spelling Strategies of Primary School Children and Their Relationships to Piaget's Concept of Decentration." *Research in the Teaching of English* 13 (February):69–80.

Helping the Problem Speller Without Suppressing the Writer

Elizabeth Grubgeld

"Sum of my teachers throw out hight school," my student titled his first in-class writing in the noncredit pre-college English course I teach. In the course, I see writers and readers with diverse problems—fluency, difficulty in developing ideas or focusing on one in particular, problems in reading comprehension, syntactic derailment, and a wide variety of errors. Most will soon be called upon to write exams, lab reports, and papers in philosophy, history, or biology, and I have 15 weeks in which to prepare them.

With their problems in focus, organization, and basic fluency, dropped words, articles, and inflections—as well as a fundamental lack of control over the limits of the sentence—there seems little time for spelling. Yet for disabled spellers and their readers, spelling mistakes stand out as the most prominent feature of their writing. The misspellings occasionally obscure meaning even for a basic writing instructor trained to discover significance in the most fractured prose; surely misspellings block the communication of meaning to less searching or tolerant eyes. And because these students have been told for years to "do something about spelling" and are frightened of their capacity for error, most problem spellers are not fluent. When each new word on the page opens another possibility of error, nothing could be more difficult than freewriting or revision. How can we teach composing and spelling simultaneously so that the disabled speller is helped while other writers are equally benefited?

One common response has been to downplay the problem. As Mina Shaughnessy reminds us in her classic work, *Errors and Expectations:*

> Of all the encoding skills, spelling tends to be viewed by most teachers and students alike as the most arbitrary, the most resistant to instruction, and the least related to intelligence. . . .
>
> It is the one area of writing where English teachers themselves will admit ineptness. Outside the academy, however, the response to misspelling is less obliging.

Indeed, the ability to spell is viewed by many as one of the marks of the educated person, and the failure of a college graduate to meet that minimal standard of advanced literacy is cause to question the quality of his education or even his intelligence.[1]

Clearly, it is an abdication of responsibility to allow someone to wander through our high school and college classes who continues to make, perhaps, ten errors in spelling per one hundred words while writing an original composition.

The lists of homonyms and common rules in the back of most handbooks and rhetorics are insufficient, and the common practice of circling errors does little more than provide the instructor with a rationale for assigning a low grade. Instead of searching for the perfect textbook or wasting time circling mistakes, we should begin to teach spelling as part of the students' creation of original texts. Treating spelling as an important—but quite distinct—part of writing allows inexperienced writers to develop fluency and revision skills while providing essential practice. Having students correct spelling as part of publication procedures helps develop motivation. Finally, using student writing as a resource enables us to individualize error analysis and teach students to analyze and recognize their own mistakes.

It's crucial to maintain the distinction between questions of development, shape, or meaning and questions of correctness, just as we maintain a distinction between the reader's demand for worthwhile content and the reader's demand for clean copy. A student, hungry for some empirical evaluation, may focus exclusively upon error. Others, flinching from evaluation, may feel their purposes and meanings are lost upon a reader who jumbles all responses into marginal commentary. How is a student to determine a hierarchy of significance among comments along the page? Spelling errors remain yet another part of the cloud of error, overshadowing or becoming indistinguishable from considerations of meaning. To emphasize the difference between composing well and spelling well, we can use two notebooks, two colors of ink, two rooms, two meeting times, or even two teachers for the two tasks.

Having students correct spelling as the final stage in preparing material for publication acknowledges both its importance for readers and places it, accurately, at the end of the process. Writing can easily be published for a class or school audience, or occasionally for some outside audience, and may include excerpts of reading notes, tests, or journals, as well as entire papers. Students are motivated when they're assured of a genuine, interested audience, and only after some time can we expect a writer to accept the teacher as a reader or the concept of a hypothetical audience. Only after students accept such audiences should we begin to study misspelled words in less overtly public writings, although we can keep a list of those words to make a more accurate analysis of individual error patterns.

---

[1]Mina Shaughnessy, *Errors and Expectations* (New York: Oxford, 1977), pp. 161–62.

As we begin to analyze spelling errors, we see which words students can or cannot spell as they emerge in real writing, and numerous studies suggest that these will differ from the words spelled or misspelled in exercises and quizzes in which they appear unnaturally and out of context. And we are provided with essential guides to the types of errors particular to individual writers; we can find clues to the hodge-podge of rules, visual memories, and systems of logic by which individuals make spelling choices. With some order made of the chaos of their spelling mistakes, students gain confidence in their ability to recognize and correct errors, since they are able to proofread for a limited list of possible mistakes. They may develop a sense of responsibility for *their* words, as they claim ownership and control over them. With guidance, they can begin to see the structures within their words which provide keys to similar words.

Such progress will admittedly be time-consuming and slow. Students will probably not learn to control their errors in one semester, not even one year, but they can learn to use critical eyes. They may not cease making errors, but they can learn to recognize them. Although some students best respond to an approach which emphasizes visual recognition, for most, visual drills must be supported by knowledge of the systems which govern spelling. By isolating words with similar patterns and generalizing from the accumulated examples, students may inductively grasp the nature of such systems.[2] In doing so, they discover not only general principles but strategies for application of those principles to the infinite number of words in their potential vocabularies.

We may select words from students' lists which readily illustrate general principles,[3] recognizing the less classifiable words but perhaps not attempting to find a pertinent pattern or rule to explain them until other, similar, words emerge in the students' writings. Occasionally students may be able to articulate the spelling of words which defy classification, and we may find the residue of some misremembered pattern or misunderstood concept. To succeed at describing such processes, as well as at drawing general principles from more regular words, spellers must have the appropriate vocabulary. They need to be able to use and understand such terms as long and short vowel, consonant and consonant cluster, prefix, suffix, root, diacritic, homophone, missing letter, letter reversal, and word confusion.[4] They also need a workable way to articulate and remember general principles and some understanding of syllabication and pronunciation.

As patterns emerge, we must restrain from recognizing them for our students; students must themselves discover the pattern or rule. Mina Shaughnessy,

---

[2] A helpful source for the instructor is Genevieve Love Smith, *Spelling by Principles* (New York: Appleton Century-Crofts, 1966). Through accumulated examples, it demonstrates how to make educated choices between graphemic options.

[3] Some words may be difficult to classify and are perhaps best ignored, at least for a time; it is crucial to exercise the student's growing ability to classify with confidence.

[4] See Shaughnessy, p. 177.

Thomas Friedman, and Lou Kelly offer different but equally sensible alternatives to the usual way of describing rules. Shaughnessy suggests that rules be written as a series of conditions for which the writer may examine the word in question. Simple rephrasing into question form, she found, gave the writer a set of directions to follow rather than a confusing maxim to memorize. In his argument against the inadvertent visual reinforcement of error, Friedman prohibits the enumeration of exceptions and odd spellings, as well as the common practice of teaching confusing words—like homonyms—"in tandem." He suggests that instead, we teach words within the context of their meaning. Instead of grouping *there* and *their* for example, we should teach *there* in conjunction with *here* and *where.*[5] In *Dialogue to Discourse,* Lou Kelly advises that when students have difficulty with a word, they conversationally write an answer to the question, "What confuses me about this word?" Usually, the answer will expose the rule underlying the correction. Students who discover that they are uncertain when reaching the ending of a word they spell as *potenchul* are ready to discuss suffixes and the *tial* suffix in particular. We need to provide extra drill with other words similar in structure.

Before students can discuss structural patterns, they must understand the concept of a syllable and root words, prefixes, and suffixes, but most basic writers do not think of words as divisible, only as arbitrary groupings of letters. While they may have heard such terms as root, prefix, and suffix, the terms lack clear meaning. Students might practice dividing words as syllabic internals. Their answers need not be dictionary-perfect as long as they demonstrate an increasing awareness of standard divisions. Secondly, spellers who do not hear unstressed syllables may come to hear them more often if trained to read aloud. It is often difficult to make basic writers read their own work sufficiently slowly and even more difficult to help them recognize the discrepancy which so often exists between what is on the page and what they read aloud from the page. The suggestion to "read as slowly and with as much choppiness as someone who can barely read" may help relieve some of the desire to appear fluent which undoubtedly lies at the heart of their overly rapid oral readings.

Oral reading can be combined with practice in recognizing grapheme-phoneme correspondences; it is clear that *tial* commonly represents the sound *chul.* But in many situations, sounding out is insufficient when not supported by drill in visual recognition and application of principles, and it can be disturbingly deceiving. In an observable speech pattern of the Rocky Mountain states, for example, most vowels blur to a short *I*. Thus we see *ixcited, agin,* and *dispair.* Pronunciation cannot be changed, so some alternate method of emphasizing the blurred vowel must be established. In some words, the vowel is more clearly articulated in a variation form of the word: *majer* is less likely to be chosen

---

[5]Thomas Friedman, "Teaching Error, Nurturing Confusion: Grammar Texts, Tests, and Teachers in the Developmental English Class," *College English* 45 (April 1983): 390–399.

when the student thinks of the word *majority*. Admittedly, basic writers often have difficulty thinking of other forms of words, since words—like letters—are viewed as random items. But with practice and considerable drill on syllabication, compounding, and affixation, they may become more adept at the task. If nothing else, they may—as Mina Shaughnessy suggests—become aware what aspects in their speech are likely to be misrepresented by their habitual first choice of graphemes.

We cannot simply make suggestions and tell the students about them; neither does the identification of a structural pattern insure its use. Students must have a way of drilling themselves on visual recognition, application of principles, and contextual usage. In the back of *From Dialogue to Discourse,* Lou Kelly outlines a spelling chart which is the basis for the spelling cards I now use with disabled spellers. I have students buy a set of 5 × 8 cards and punch holes in the top so that the cards may be arranged on rings (cards are more permanent than notebook paper and can be continually looked at). Using large handwriting and skipping lines to reinforce visual impact, the students list *their* words alphabetically. Some other method of indexing—perhaps by type of error—might be more effective, but alphabetical ordering can allow cross-indexing to accommodate recognition of error types. To avoid reinforcing error, I have them write only the correct version of the word and underline the confusing part. If the confusion arose from failing to hear syllables, they may leave spaces between syllables. To the right, students write in their own words why the particular word was difficult. To the right of that column, they record some means of remembering the correct spelling—other words with similar spellings, other forms of the word which highlight the difficult section, some sentence or other mememonic device—whatever the student decides upon. At some point in the semester, the instructor should sort through the cards to list the most frequent types of errors and provide extra drill in those areas.

Writers can practice with these cards to improve their chances of spelling accurately and proofreading efficiently. Besides simply concentrating visually or writing the words repeatedly, they might make up stories or record random thoughts while using the words. They can tape-record the list or their stories and take dictation from the tape. In conference with the instructor, they might try to spell any similar words—including entirely unfamiliar words—which the instructor finds in the dictionary. In its most significant function, the list works as a proofreading guide when writing for public presentation.

With much repeated practice—at least one hour a week with the instructor—severely disabled spellers can begin to make automatic the conceptualizations they have discovered and recognize their own errors when proofreading. Most importantly, spelling error has been lifted out of the morass of undefined error and identified as an act distinct from composition. As readers' needs are recognized and accomodated, spelling is valued yet put into its proper place as a last step before publication of a text.

B

SYNTAX AND THE TEACHING OF GRAMMAR

Revolution in Grammar

W. Nelson Francis

I

A long overdue revolution is at present taking place in the study of English grammar—a revolution as sweeping in its consequences as the Darwinian revolution in biology. It is the result of the application to English of methods of descriptive analysis originally developed for use with languages of primitive people. To anyone at all interested in language, it is challenging; to those concerned with the teaching of English (including parents), it presents the necessity of radically revising both the substance and the methods of their teaching.

A curious paradox exists in regard to grammar. On the one hand it is felt to be the dullest and driest of academic subjects, fit only for those in whose veins the red blood of life has long since turned to ink. On the other, it is a subject upon which people who would scorn to be professional grammarians hold very dogmatic opinions, which they will defend with considerable emotion. Much of this prejudice stems from the usual sources of prejudice—ignorance and confusion. Even highly educated people seldom have a clear idea of what grammarians do, and there is an unfortunate confusion about the meaning of the term "grammar" itself.

Hence it would be well to begin with definitions. What do people mean when they use the word "grammar"? Actually the word is used to refer to three different things, and much of the emotional thinking about matters grammatical arises from confusion among these different meanings.

The first thing we mean by "grammar" is "the set of formal patterns in which the words of a language are arranged in order to convey larger meanings." It is not necessary that we be able to discuss these patterns self-consciously in order to be able to use them. In fact, all speakers of a language above the age of five or six know how to use its complex forms of organization with considerable skill;

426

in this sense of the word—call it "Grammar 1"—they are thoroughly familiar with its grammar.

The second meaning of "grammar"—call it "Grammar 2"—is "the branch of linguistic science which is concerned with the description, analysis, and formulization of formal language patterns." Just as gravity was in full operation before Newton's apple fell, so grammar in the first sense was in full operation before anyone formulated the first rule that began the history of grammar as a study.

The third sense in which people use the word "grammar" is "linguistic etiquette." This we may call "Grammar 3." The word in this sense is often coupled with a derogatory adjective: we say that the expression "he ain't here" is "bad grammar." What we mean is that such an expression is bad linguistic manners in certain circles. From the point of view of "Grammar 1" it is faultless; it conforms just as completely to the structural patterns of English as does "he isn't here." The trouble with it is like the trouble with Prince Hal in Shakespeare's play—it is "bad," not in itself, but in the company it keeps.

As has already been suggested, much confusion arises from mixing these meanings. One hears a good deal of criticism of teachers of English couched in such terms as "they don't teach grammar any more." Criticism of this sort is based on the wholly unproved assumption that teaching Grammar 2 will increase the student's proficiency in Grammar 1 or improve his manners in Grammar 3. Actually, the form of Grammar 2 which is usually taught is a very inaccurate and misleading analysis of the facts of Grammar 1; and it therefore is of highly questionable value in improving a person's ability to handle the structural patterns of his language. It is hardly reasonable to expect that teaching a person some inaccurate grammatical analysis will either improve the effectiveness of his assertions or teach him what expressions are acceptable to use in a given social context.

These, then, are the three meanings of "grammar": Grammar 1, a form of behavior; Grammar 2, a field of study, a science; and Grammar 3, a branch of etiquette.

II

Grammarians have arrived at some basic principles of their science, three of which are fundamental to this discussion. The first is that a language constitutes a set of behavior patterns common to the members of a given community. It is a part of what the anthropologists call the culture of the community. Actually it has complex and intimate relationships with other phases of culture such as myth and ritual. But for purposes of study it may be dealt with as a separate set of phenomena that can be objectively described and analyzed like any other universe of facts. Specifically, its phenomena can be observed, recorded, classified, and compared; and general laws of their behavior can be made by the same inductive process that is used to produce the "laws" of physics, chemistry, and the other sciences.

A second important principle of linguistic science is that each language or dialect has its own unique system of behavior patterns. Parts of this system may show similarities to parts of the systems of other languages, particularly if those languages are genetically related. But different languages solve the problems of expression and communication in different ways, just as the problems of movement through water are solved in different ways by lobsters, fish, seals, and penguins. A couple of corollaries of this principle are important. The first is that there is no such thing as "universal grammar," or at least if there is, it is so general and abstract as to be of little use. The second corollary is that the grammar of each language must be made up on the basis of a study of that particular language—a study that is free from preconceived notions of what a language should contain and how it should operate. The marine biologist does not criticize the octopus for using jet-propulsion to get him through the water instead of the methods of a self-respecting fish. Neither does the linguistic scientist express alarm or distress when he finds a language that seems to get along quite well without any words that correspond to what in English we call verbs.

A third principle on which linguistic science is based is that the analysis and description of a given language must conform to the requirements laid down for any satisfactory scientific theory. These are (1) simplicity, (2) consistency, (3) completeness, and (4) usefulness for predicting the behavior of phenomena not brought under immediate observation when the theory was formed. Linguistic scientists who have recently turned their attention to English have found that, judged by these criteria, the traditional grammar of English is unsatisfactory. It falls down badly on the first two requirements, being unduly complex and glaringly inconsistent within itself. It can be made to work, just as the Ptolemaic earth-centered astronomy can be, but at the cost of great elaboration and complication. The new grammar, like the Copernican sun-centered astronomy, solves the same problems with greater elegance, which is the scientist's word for the simplicity, compactness, and tidiness that characterize a satisfactory theory.

III

A brief look at the history of the traditional grammar of English will make apparent the reasons for its inadequacy. The study of English grammar is actually an outgrowth of the linguistic interest of the Renaissance. It was during the later Middle Ages and early Renaissance that the various vernacular languages of Europe came into their own. They began to be used for many kinds of writing which had previously always been done in Latin. As the vernaculars, in the hands of great writers like Dante and Chaucer, came of age as members of the linguistic family, a concomitant interest in their grammars arose. The earliest important English grammar was written by Shakespeare's contemporary, Ben Jonson.

It is important to observe that not only Ben Jonson himself but also those who followed him in the study of English grammar were men deeply learned in Latin and sometimes in Greek. For all their interest in English, they were conditioned from earliest school days to conceive of the classical languages as superior to the vernaculars. We still sometimes call the elementary school the "grammar school"; historically the term means the school where Latin grammar was taught. By the time the Renaissance or eighteenth-century scholar took his university degree, he was accustomed to using Latin as the normal means of communication with his fellow scholars. Dr. Samuel Johnson, for instance, who had only three years at the university and did not take a degree, wrote poetry in both Latin and Greek. Hence it was natural for these men to take Latin grammar as the norm, and to analyze English in terms of Latin. The grammarians of the seventeenth and eighteenth centuries who formulated the traditional grammar of English looked for the devices and distinctions of Latin grammar in English, and where they did not actually find them they imagined or created them. Of course, since English is a member of the Indo-European family of languages, to which Latin and Greek also belong, it did have many grammatical elements in common with them. But many of these had been obscured or wholly lost as a result of the extensive changes that had taken place in English—changes that the early grammarians inevitably conceived of as degeneration. They felt that it was their function to resist further change, if not to repair the damage already done. So preoccupied were they with the grammar of Latin as the ideal that they overlooked in large part the exceedingly complex and delicate system that English had substituted for the Indo-European grammar it had abandoned. Instead they stretched unhappy English on the Procrustean bed of Latin. It is no wonder that we commonly hear people say, "I didn't really understand grammar until I began to study Latin." This is eloquent testimony to the fact that the grammar "rules" of our present-day textbooks are largely an inheritance from the Latin-based grammar of the eighteenth century.

Meanwhile the extension of linguistic study beyond the Indo-European and Semitic families began to reveal that there are many different ways in which linguistic phenomena are organized—in other words, many different kinds of grammar. The tone-languages of the Orient and of North America, and the complex agglutinative languages of Africa, among others, forced grammarians to abandon the idea of a universal or ideal grammar and to direct their attention more closely to the individual systems employed by the multifarious languages of mankind. With the growth and refinement of the scientific method and its application to the field of anthropology, language came under more rigorous scientific scrutiny. As with anthropology in general, linguistic science at first concerned itself with the primitive. Finally, again following the lead of anthropology, linguistics began to apply its techniques to the old familiar tongues, among them English. Accelerated by the practical need during World War II of teaching languages, including English, to large numbers in a short time, research into the nature of English grammar has moved rapidly in the last fifteen years. The definitive grammar of English is yet to be written, but the results so far achieved are spectacular. It is now as unrealistic to teach "traditional" grammar of English as it is to teach "traditional" (i.e., pre-Darwinian) biology or "traditional" (i.e., four-element) chemistry. Yet nearly all certified teachers of English on all levels are doing so. Here is a cultural lag of major proportions.

IV

Before we can proceed to a sketch of what the new grammar of English looks like, we must take account of a few more of the premises of linguistic science. They must be understood and accepted by anyone who wishes to understand the new grammar.

First, the spoken language is primary, at least for the original study of a language. In many of the primitive languages,[1] of course, where writing is unknown, the spoken language is the *only* form. This is in many ways an advantage to the linguist, because the written language may use conventions that obscure its basic structure. The reason for the primary importance of the spoken language is that language originates as speech, and most of the changes and innovations that occur in the history of a given language begin in the spoken tongue.

Secondly, we must take account of the concept of dialect. I suppose most laymen would define a dialect as "a corrupt form of language spoken in a given region by people who don't know any better." This introduces moral judgments which are repulsive to the linguistic scholar. Let us approach the definition of a dialect from the more objective end, through the notion of a speech community. A speech community is merely a group of people who are in pretty constant intercommunication. There are various types of speech communities: local ones, like "the people who live in Tidewater Virginia"; class ones, like "the white-collar class"; occupational ones, like "doctors, nurses, and other people who work in hospitals"; social ones, like "clubwomen." In a sense, each of these has its own dialect. Each family may be said to have its own dialect; in fact, in so far as each of us has his own vocabulary and particular quirks of speech; each individual has his own dialect. Also, of course, in so far as he is a member of many speech communities, each individual is more or less master of many dialects and shifts easily and almost unconsciously from one to another as he shifts from one social environment to another.

---

[1]"Primitive languages" here is really an abbreviated statement for "languages used by peoples of relatively primitive culture"; it is not to be taken as implying anything simple or rudimentary about the languages themselves. Many languages included under the term, such as native languages of Africa and Mexico, exhibit grammatical complexities unknown to more "civilized" languages.

In the light of this concept of dialects, a language can be defined as a group of dialects which have enough of their sound-system, vocabulary, and grammar (Grammar 1, that is) in common to permit their speakers to be mutually intelligible in the ordinary affairs of life. It usually happens that one of the many dialects that make up a language comes to have more prestige than the others; in modern times it has usually been the dialect of the middle-class residents of the capital, like Parisian French and London English, which is so distinguished. This comes to be thought of as the standard dialect; in fact, its speakers become snobbish and succeed in establishing the belief that it is not a dialect at all, but the only proper form of the language. This causes the speakers of other dialects to become self-conscious and ashamed of their speech, or else aggressive and jingoistic about it—either of which is an acknowledgment of their feelings of inferiority. Thus one of the duties of the educational system comes to be that of teaching the standard dialect to all so as to relieve them of feelings of inferiority, and thus relieve society of linguistic neurotics. This is where Grammar 3, linguistic etiquette, comes into the picture.

A third premise arising from the two just discussed is that the difference between the way educated people talk and the way they write is a dialectal difference. The spread between these two dialects may be very narrow, as in present-day America, or very wide, as in Norway, where people often speak local Norwegian dialects but write in the Dano-Norwegian *Riksmaal.* The extreme is the use by writers of an entirely different language, or at least an ancient and no longer spoken form of the language—like Sanskrit in northern India or Latin in western Europe during the Middle Ages. A corollary of this premise is that anyone setting out to write a grammar must know and make clear whether he is dealing with the spoken or the written dialect. Virtually all current English grammars deal with the written language only; evidence for this is that their rules for the plurals of nouns, for instance, are really spelling rules, which say nothing about pronunciation.

This is not the place to go into any sort of detail about the methods of analysis the linguistic scientist uses. Suffice it to say that he begins by breaking up the flow of speech into minimum sound-units, or phones, which he then groups into families called phonemes, the minimum significant sound-units. Most languages have from twenty to sixty of these. American English has forty-one: nine vowels, twenty-four consonants, four degrees of stress, and four levels of pitch. These phonemes group themselves into minimum meaningful units, called morphemes. These fall into two groups: free morphemes, those that can enter freely into many combinations with other free morphemes to make phrases and sentences; and bound morphemes, which are always found tied in a close and often indissoluble relationship with other bound or free morphemes. An example of a free morpheme is "dog"; an example of a bound morpheme is "un-" or "ex-." The linguist usually avoids talking about "words" because the term is very inexact. Is "instead of," for instance, to be considered one, two, or three words? This is purely a matter of opinion; but it is a matter of fact that it is made up of three morphemes.

In any case, our analysis has now brought the linguist to the point where he has some notion of the word-stock (he would call it the "lexicon") of his language. He must then go into the question of how the morphemes are grouped into meaningful utterances, which is the field of grammar proper. At this point in the analysis of English, as of many other languages, it becomes apparent that there are three bases upon which classification and analysis may be built: form, function, and meaning. For illustration let us take the word "boys" in the utterance "the boys are here." From the point of view of form, "boys" is a noun with the plural ending "s" (pronounced like "z"), preceded by the noun-determiner "the," and tied by concord to the verb "are," which it precedes. From the point of view of function, "boys" is the subject of the verb "are" and of the sentence. From the point of view of meaning, "boys" is the subject of the verb "are" and of the sentence. From the point of view of meaning, "boys" points out or names more than one of the male young of the human species, about whom an assertion is being made.

Of these three bases of classification, the one most amenable to objective description and analysis of a rigorously scientific sort is form. In fact, many conclusions about form can be drawn by a person unable to understand or speak the language. Next comes function. But except as it is revealed by form, function is dependent on knowing the meaning. In a telegraphic sentence like "ship sails today"[2] no one can say whether "ship" is the subject of "sails" or an imperative verb with "sails" as its object until he knows what the sentence means. Most shaky of all bases for grammatical analysis is meaning. Attempts have been made to reduce the phenomena of meaning to objective description, but so far they have not succeeded very well. Meaning is such a subjective quality that it is usually omitted entirely from scientific description. The botanist can describe the forms of plants and the functions of their various parts, but he refuses to concern himself with their meaning. It is left to the poet to find symbolic meanings in roses, violets, and lilies.

At this point it is interesting to note that the traditional grammar of English bases some of its key concepts and definitions on this very subjective and shaky foundation of meaning. A recent English grammar defines a sentence as "a group of words which expresses a complete thought through the use of a verb, called its predicate, and a subject, consisting of a noun or pronoun about which the verb has something to say."[3] But what is a complete thought? Actually we do not identify sentences this way at all. If someone says, "I don't know what to do," dropping his voice at the end, and pauses, the hearer will know that it is quite safe for him to make a comment without running the risk of interrupting an unfinished sentence. But if the speaker says the same words and maintains a

---

[2]This example is taken from C. C. Fries, *The Structure of English* (New York, 1952), p. 62. This important book will be discussed below.

[3]Ralph B. Allen, *English Grammar* (New York, 1950), p. 187.

level pitch at the end, the polite listener will wait for him to finish his sentence. The words are the same, the meaning is the same; the only difference is a slight one in the pitch of the final syllable—a purely formal distinction, which signals that the first utterance is complete, a sentence, while the second is incomplete. In writing we would translate these signals into punctuation: a period or exclamation point at the end of the first, a comma or dash at the end of the second. It is the form of the utterance, not the completeness of the thought, that tells us whether it is a whole sentence or only part of one.

Another favorite definition of the traditional grammar, also based on meaning, is that of "noun" as "the name of a person, place, or thing"; or, as the grammar just quoted has it, "the name of anybody or anything, with or without life, and with or without substance or form."[4] Yet we identify nouns, not by asking if they name something, but by their positions in expressions and by the formal marks they carry. In the sentence, "The slithy toves did gyre and gimble in the wabe," any speaker of English knows that "toves" and "wabe" are nouns, though he cannot tell what they name, if indeed they name anything. How does he know? Actually because they have certain formal marks, like their position in relation to "the" as well as the whole arrangement of the sentence. We know from our practical knowledge of English grammar (Grammar 1), which we have had since before we went to school, that if we were to put meaningful words into this sentence, we would have to put nouns in place of "toves" and "wabe," giving something like "The slithy snakes did gyre and gimble in the wood." The pattern of the sentence simply will not allow us to say "The slithy arounds did gyre and gimble in the wooden."

One trouble with the traditional grammar, then, is that it relies heavily on the most subjective element in language, meaning. Another is that it shifts the ground of its classification and produces the elementary logical error of cross-division. A zoologist who divided animals into invertebrates, mammals, and beasts of burden would not get very far before running into trouble. Yet the traditional grammar is guilty of the same error when it defines three parts of speech on the basis of meaning (noun, verb, and interjection), four more on the basis of function (adjective, adverb, pronoun, conjunction), and one partly on function and partly on form (preposition). The result is that in such an expression as "a dog's life" there can be endless futile argument about whether "dog's" is a noun or an adjective. It is, of course, a noun from the point of view of form and an adjective from the point of view of function, and hence falls into both classes, just as a horse is both a mammal and a beast of burden. No wonder students are bewildered in their attempts to master the traditional grammar. Their natural clearness of mind tells them that it is a crazy patchwork violating the elementary principles of logical thought.

[4]*Ibid.*, p. 1.

V

If the traditional grammar is so bad, what does the new grammar offer in its place?

It offers a description, analysis, and set of definitions and formulas—rules, if you will—based firmly and consistently on the easiest, or at least the most objective, aspect of language, form. Experts can quibble over whether "dog's" in "a dog's life" is a noun or an adjective, but anyone can see that it is spelled with "'s" and hear that it ends with a "z" sound; likewise anyone can tell that it comes in the middle between "a" and "life." Furthermore he can tell that something important has happened if the expression is changed to "the dog's alive," "the live dogs," or "the dogs lived," even if he doesn't know that the words mean and has never heard of such functions as modifier, subject, or attributive genitive. He cannot, of course, get very far into his analysis without either a knowledge of the language or access to someone with such knowledge. He will also need a minimum technical vocabulary describing grammatical functions. Just so the anatomist is better off for knowing physiology. But the grammarian, like the anatomist, must beware of allowing his preconceived notions to lead him into the error of interpreting before he describes—an error which often results in his finding only what he is looking for.

When the grammarian looks at English objectively, he finds that it conveys its meanings by two broad devices: the denotations and connotations of words separately considered, which the linguist calls "lexical meaning," and the significance of word-forms, word-groups, and arrangements apart from the lexical meanings of the words, which the linguist calls "structural meaning." The first of these is the domain of the lexicographer and the semanticist, and hence is not our present concern. The second, the structural meaning, is the business of the structural linguist, or grammarian. The importance of this second kind of meaning must be emphasized because it is often overlooked. The man in the street tends to think of the meaning of a sentence as being the aggregate of the dictionary meanings of the words that make it up; hence the widespread fallacy of literal translation—the feeling that if you take a French sentence and a French-English dictionary and write down the English equivalent of each French word you will come out with an intelligible English sentence. How ludicrous the results can be, anyone knows who is familiar with Mark Twain's retranslation from the French of his jumping frog story. One sentence reads, "Eh bien! I no saw not that that frog has nothing of better than each frog." Upon which Mark's comment is, "if that isn't grammar gone to seed, then I count myself no judge."[5]

The second point brought out by a formal analysis of English is that it uses four principal devices of form to signal structural meanings:

[5]Mark Twain, "The Jumping Frog; the Original Story in English; the Retranslation Clawed Back from the French, into a Civilized Language Once More, by Patient and Unremunerated Toil," *1601 . . . and Sketches Old and New* (n.p., 1933), p. 50.

1 Word order—the sequence in which words and word-groups are arranged.

2 Function-words—words devoid of lexical meaning which indicate relationships among the meaningful words with which they appear.

3 Inflections—alterations in the forms of words themselves to signal changes in meaning and relationship.

4 Formal contrasts—contrasts in the forms of words signaling greater differences in function and meaning. These could also be considered inflections, but it is more convenient for both the lexicographer and the grammarian to consider them separately.

Usually several of these are present in any utterance, but they can be separately illustrated by means of contrasting expressions involving minimum variation—the kind of controlled experiment used in the scientific laboratory.

To illustrate the structural meaning of word order, let us compare the two sentences "man bites dog" and "dog bites man."—The words are identical in lexical meaning and in form; the only difference is in sequence. It is interesting to note that Latin expresses the difference between these two by changes in the form of the words, without necessarily altering the order: "homo canem mordet" or "hominem canis mordet." Latin grammar is worse than useless in understanding this point of English grammar.

Next, compare the sentences "the dog is the friend of man" and "any dog is a friend of that man." Here the words having lexical meaning are "dog," "is," "friend," and "man," which appear in the same form and the same order in both sentences. The formal differences between them are in the substitution of "any" and "a" for "the," and in the insertion of "that." These little words are function-words; they make quite a difference in the meanings of the two sentences, though it is virtually impossible to say what they mean in isolation.

Third, compare the sentences "the dog loves the man" and "the dogs loved the men." Here the words are the same, in the same order, with the same function-words in the same positions. But the forms of the three words having lexical meanings have been changed: "dog" to "dogs," "loves" to "loved," and "man" to "men." These changes are inflections. English has very few of them as compared with Greek, Latin, Russian, or even German. But it still uses them; about one word in four in an ordinary English sentence is inflected.

Fourth, consider the difference between "the dog's friend arrived" and "the dog's friendly arrival." Here the difference lies in the change of "friend" to "friendly," a formal alteration signaling a change of function from subject to modifier, and the change of "arrived" to "arrival," signaling a change of function from predicate to head-word in a noun-modifier group. These changes are of the same formal nature as inflections, but because they produce words of different lexical meaning, classifiable as different parts of speech, it is better to call them formal contrasts than inflections. In other words, it is logically quite defensible to consider "love," "loving," and "loved" as the same word in differing aspects and to consider "friend," "friendly," "friendliness," "friendship," and "befriend" as different words related by formal and semantic similarities. But this is only a matter of convenience of analysis, which permits a more accurate description of English structure. In another language we might find that this kind of distinction is unnecessary but that some other distinction, unnecessary in English, is required. The categories of grammatical description are not sacrosanct; they are as much a part of man's organization of his observations as they are of the nature of things.

If we are considering the spoken variety of English, we must add a fifth device for indicating structural meaning—the various musical and rhythmic patterns which the linguist classifies under juncture, stress, and intonation. Consider the following pairs of sentences:

Alfred, the alligator is sick
Alfred the alligator is sick.

These are identical in the four respects discussed above—word order, function-words, inflections, and word-form. Yet they have markedly different meanings, as would be revealed by the intonation if they were spoken aloud. These differences in intonation are to a certain extent indicated in the written language by punctuation—that is, in fact, the primary function of punctuation.

VI

The examples so far given were chosen to illustrate in isolation the various kinds of structural devices in English grammar. Much more commonly the structural meaning of a given sentence is indicated by a combination of two or more of these devices: a sort of margin of safety which permits some of the devices to be missed or done away with without obscuring the structural meaning of the sentence, as indeed anyone knows who has ever written a telegram or a newspaper headline. On the other hand, sentences which do not have enough of these formal devices are inevitably ambiguous. Take the example already given, Fries's "ship sails today." This is ambiguous because there is nothing to indicate which of the first two words is performing a noun function and which a verb function. If we mark the noun by putting the noun-determining function-word "the" in front of it, the ambiguity disappears; we have either "the ship sails today" or "ship the sails today." The ambiguity could just as well be resolved by using other devices: consider "ship sailed today," "ship to sail today," "Ship sail today," "shipping sails today," "shipment of sails today," and so on. It is simply a question of having enough formal devices in the sentence to indicate its structural meaning clearly.

How powerful the structural meanings of English are is illustrated by so-called "nonsense." In English, nonsense as a literary form often consists of utterances that have a clear structural meaning but use words that either have no lexical meanings, or whose lexical meanings are inconsistent one with another. This will become apparent if we subject a rather famous bit of English nonsense to formal grammatical analysis:

All mimsy were the borogoves
And the mome raths outgrabe.

This passage consists of ten words, five of them words that should have lexical meaning but don't, one standard verb, and four function-words. In so far as it is possible to indicate its abstract structure, it would be this:

All . . . . y were the . . . . s
And the . . . . . s . . . .

Although this is a relatively simple formal organization, it signals some rather complicated meanings. The first thing we observe is that the first line presents a conflict: word order seems to signal one thing, and inflections and function-words something else. Specifically, "mimsy" is in the position normally occupied by the subject, but we know that it is not the subject and that "borogoves" is. We know this because there is an inflectional tie between the form "were" and the "s" ending of "borogoves," because there is the noun-determiner "the" before it, and because the alternative candidate for subject, "mimsy," lacks both of these. It is true that "mimsy" does have the function-word "all" before it, which may indicate a noun; but when it does, the noun is either plural (in which case "mimsy" would most likely end in "s"), or else the noun is what grammarians call a mass-word (like "sugar," "coal," "snow"), in which case the verb would have to be "was," not "were." All these formal considerations are sufficient to counteract the effect of word order and show that the sentence is of the type that may be represented thus:

All gloomy were the Democrats.

Actually there is one other possibility. If "mimsy" belongs to the small group of nouns which don't use "s" to make the plural, and if "borogoves" has been so implied (but not specifically mentioned) in the context as to justify its appearing with the determiner "the," the sentence would then belong to the following type:

(In the campaign for funds) all alumni were the canvassers.
(In the drought last summer) all cattle were the sufferers.

But the odds are so much against this that most of us would be prepared to fight for our belief that "borogoves" are things that can be named, and that at the time referred to they were in a complete state of "mimsyness."

Moving on to the second line, "and the mome raths outgrabe," the first thing we note is that the "And" signals another parallel assertion to follow. We are thus prepared to recognize from the noun-determiner "the," the plural infection "s," and the particular positions of "mome" and "outgrabe," as well as the continuing influence of the "were" of the preceding line, that we are dealing with a sentence of this pattern:

And the lone rats agreed.

The influence of the "were" is particularly important here; it guides us in selecting among several interpretations of the sentence. Specifically, it requires us to identify "outgrabe" as a verb in the past tense, and thus a "strong" or "irregular" verb, since it lacks the characteristic past-tense ending "d" or "ed." We do this in spite of the fact that there is another strong candidate for the position of verb: that is, "raths," which bears a regular verb inflection and could be tied with "mome" as its subject in the normal noun-verb relationship. In such a case we should have to recognize "outgrabe" as either an adverb of the kind not marked by the form-contrast "ly," an adjective, or the past participle of a strong verb. The sentence would then belong to one of the following types:

And the moon shines above.
And the man stays aloof.
And the fool seems outdone.

But we reject all of these—probably they don't even occur to us—because they all have verbs in the present tense, whereas the "were" of the first line combines with the "And" at the beginning of the second to set the whole in the past.

We might recognize one further possibility for the structural meaning of this second line, particularly in the verse context, since we are used to certain patterns in verse that do not often appear in speech or prose. The "were" of the first line could be understood as doing double duty, its ghost or echo appearing between "raths" and "outgrabe." Then we would have something like this:

All gloomy were the Democrats
And the home folks outraged.

But again the odds are pretty heavy against this. I for one am so sure that "outgrabe" is the past tense of a strong verb that I can give its present. In my dialect, at least, it is "outgribe."

The reader may not realize it, but in the last four paragraphs I have been discussing grammar from a purely formal point of view. I have not once called a word a noun because it names something (that is, I have not once resorted to meaning), nor have I called any word an adjective because it modifies a noun (that is, resorted to function). Instead I have been working in the opposite direction, from form toward function and meaning. I have used only criteria which are objectively observable, and I have assumed only a working knowledge of certain structural patterns and devices known to all speakers of English over the age of six. I did use some technical terms like "noun," "verb," and "tense," but only to save time; I could have got along without them.

If one clears his mind of the inconsistencies of the traditional grammar (not so easy a process as it might be), he can proceed with a similarly rigorous formal analysis of a sufficient number of representative utterances in English and come out with a descriptive grammar. This is just what Professor Fries did in gathering and studying the material for the analysis he presents in the remarkable book to which I have already referred, *The Structure of English*. What he actually did was to put a tape recorder into action and record about fifty hours of telephone conversation among the good citizens of Ann Arbor, Michigan. When this material was transcribed, it constituted about a quarter of a million words of perfectly natural speech by educated middle-class Americans. The details of his conclusions cannot be presented here, but they are sufficiently different from the usual grammar to be revolutionary. For instance, he recognizes only four parts of speech among the words with lexical meaning, roughly corresponding to what the traditional grammar calls substantives, verbs, adjectives and adverbs, though to avoid preconceived notions from the traditional grammar Fries calls them Class 1, Class 2, Class 3, and Class 4 words. To these he adds a relatively small group of function-words, 154 in his materials, which he divides into fifteen groups. These must be memorized by anyone learning the language; they are not subject to the same kind of general rules that govern the four parts of speech. Undoubtedly his conclusions will be developed and modified by himself and by other linguistic scholars, but for the present his book remains the most complete treatment extant of English grammar from the point of view of linguistic science.

VII

Two vital questions are raised by this revolution in grammar. The first is, "What is the value of this new system?" In the minds of many who ask it, the implication of this question is, "We have been getting along all these years with traditional grammar, so it can't be so very bad. Why should we go through the painful process of unlearning and relearning grammar just because linguistic scientists have concocted some new theories?

The first answer to this question is the bravest and most honest. It is that the superseding of vague and sloppy thinking by clear and precise thinking is an exciting experience in and for itself. To acquire insight into the workings of a language, and to recognize the infinitely delicate system of relationship, balance, and interplay that constitutes its grammar, is to become closely acquainted with one of man's most miraculous creations, not unworthy to be set beside the equally beautiful organization of the physical universe. And to find that its most complex effects are produced by the multi-layered organization of relatively simple materials is to bring our thinking about language into accord with modern thought in other fields, which is more and more coming to emphasize the importance of organization—the fact that an organized whole is truly greater than the sum of all its parts.

There are other answers, more practical if less philosophically valid. It is too early to tell, but it seems probable that a realistic, scientific grammar should vastly facilitate the teaching of English, especially as a foreign language. Already results are showing here; it has been found that if intonation contours and other structural patterns are taught quite early, the student has a confidence that allows him to attempt to speak the language much sooner than he otherwise would.

The new grammar can also be of use in improving the native speaker's proficiency in handling the structural devices of his own language. In other words, Grammar 2, if it is accurate and consistent, *can* be of use in improving skill in Grammar 1. An illustration is that famous bugaboo, the dangling participle. Consider a specific instance of it, which once appeared on a college freshman's theme, to the mingled delight and despair of the instructor:

Having eaten our lunch, the steamboat departed.

What is the trouble with this sentence? Clearly there must be something wrong with it, because it makes people laugh, although it was not the intent of the writer to make them laugh. In other words, it produces a completely wrong response, resulting in total breakdown of communication. It is, in fact, "bad grammar" in a much more serious way than are mere dialectal divergences like "he ain't here" or "he never seen none," which produce social reactions but communicate effectively. In the light of the new grammar, the trouble with our dangling participle is that the form, instead of leading to the meaning, is in conflict with it. Into the position which, in this pattern, is reserved for the word naming the eater of the lunch, the writer has inserted the word "steamboat." The resulting tug-of-war between form and meaning is only momentary; meaning quickly wins out, simply because our common sense tells us that steamboats don't eat lunches. But if the pull of the lexical meaning is not given a good deal of help from common sense, the form will conquer the meaning, or the two will remain in ambiguous equilibrium—as, for instance, in "Having eaten our lunch, the passengers boarded the steamboat." Writers will find it easier to avoid such troubles if they know about the forms of English and are taught to use the form to convey the meaning, instead of setting up tensions between form and meaning. This, of course, is what English teachers are already trying to do. The new grammar should be a better weapon in their arsenal than the traditional grammar since it is based on a clear understanding of the realities.

The second and more difficult question is, "How can the change from one grammar to the other be effected?" Here we face obstacles of a formidable nature. When we remember the controversies attending on revolutionary changes in biology and astronomy, we realize what a tenacious hold the race can maintain on anything it has once learned, and the resistance it can offer to new ideas. And remember that neither astronomy nor biology was taught in elementary schools. They were, in fact, rather specialized subjects in advanced education. How then change grammar, which is taught to everybody, from the fifth grade up through college? The vested interest represented by thousands upon thousands of English and Speech teachers who have learned the traditional grammar and taught it for many years is a conservative force comparable to those which keep us still using the chaotic system of English spelling and the unwieldy measuring system of inches and feet, pounds and ounces, quarts, bushels, and acres. Moreover, this army is constantly receiving new recruits. It is possible in my state to become certified to teach English in high school if one has had eighteen credit hours of college English—let us say two semesters of freshman composition (almost all of which is taught by people unfamiliar with the new grammar), two semesters of a survey course in English literature, one semester of Shakespeare, and one semester of the contemporary novel. And since hard-pressed school administrators feel that anyone who can speak English can in a pinch teach it, the result is that many people are called upon to teach grammar whose knowledge of the subject is totally inadequate.

There is, in other words, a battle ahead of the new grammar. It will have to fight not only the apathy of the general public but the ignorance and inertia of those who count themselves competent in the field of grammar. The battle is already on, in fact. Those who try to get the concepts of the new grammar introduced into the curriculum are tagged as "liberal" grammarians—the implication being, I suppose, that one has a free choice between "liberal" and "conservative" grammar, and that the liberals are a bit dangerous, perhaps even a touch subversive. They are accused of undermining standards, of holding that "any way of saying something is just as good as any other," of not teaching the fundamentals of good English. I trust that the readers of this article will see how unfounded these charges are. But the smear campaign is on. So far as I know, neither religion nor patriotism has yet been brought into it. When they are, Professor Fries will have to say to Socrates, Galileo, Darwin, Freud, and the other members of the honorable fraternity of the misunderstood, "Move over, gentlemen, and make room for me."

AUTHORS NOTE

This paper was written over thirty-six years ago. During the intervening time, theories of grammar and the views of grammarians, including the author, have changed drastically. But the article reflects faithfully the views of a structural grammarian of its time.

W. Nelson Francis, August 1991

Knowledge of Language

Neil Smith and Deirdre Wilson

[Here] we attempt to clarify the relation between knowledge and language from two quite different directions. First, we want to distinguish between two types of knowledge, linguistic and non-linguistic (and hence between two types of rules, linguistic and non-linguistic); second, we want to distinguish between knowledge of rules and the exercise of that knowledge (and hence, between knowing a language and speaking or understanding it). Our main purpose is to give a general idea of the range and type of facts which fall within the domain of a grammar: of the facts that can be handled by linguistic rule, and those that cannot.

LINGUISTIC AND NON-LINGUISTIC KNOWLEDGE

Granted that a human being can have knowledge at all, it seems obvious that this knowledge can be classified in various ways. One such classification would involve separating linguistic from non-linguistic knowledge. Following Chomsky, we want to argue that such a classification is not only possible but correct: that it is not just imposed by the analyst, but has a basis in human mental organization. In other words, language, though only one among many cognitive systems, has its own principles and rules, which are different in kind from those governing other cognitive systems, and for this reason must be studied separately.

This is one of the claims which most sharply distinguishes Chomsky from others who have thought seriously about the nature of language. While it is a commonplace to say that language is specific to humans, part of the human essence, what crucially distinguishes man from beast, most linguistic theorists have been extremely cautious about concluding from this that humans must have a specific genetic endowment for language-learning. They attempt instead to explain the acquisition of language in terms of whatever general learning theory they espouse. If they believe that knowledge in general is acquired by observation and generalization, then they will claim the same for language. If they believe that knowledge is generally acquired by some form of conditioning, then they will claim the same for language. If they think that knowledge is best analysed as a disposition to behave in certain ways, then they will claim that knowledge of language is best analysed as a disposition to behave linguistically in certain ways. Language will thus be seen as acquired in the course of general intellectual development, and no language-specific endowment, apart from general intelligence and the ability to learn, will be needed for its acquisition. It is clear, though, that there is an alternative to this position. Language may be *sui generis,* different in kind from other cognitive systems, requiring different learning strategies and different genetic programming. The two claims reinforce each other: if linguistic knowledge is different in kind from non-linguistic knowledge, then it is more likely that we need special programming to learn it; and if we have such special programming, then it is more likely that the result of language-learning *will* be different in kind from other systems not so programmed.

There are a number of rather obvious points that support the special-programming view of language acquisition, and disconfirm the general-intellectual-ability approach. If we measure general intellectual development in terms of logical, mathematical and abstract-reasoning powers, these powers are still increasing at puberty, when the ability to acquire native fluency in a language is decreasing rapidly. A child of eight who can beat an eighteen-year-old at chess is something of a prodigy; if an eighteen-year-old acquires native fluency in a language as quickly as an eight-year-old, simply by being exposed to it, and without any formal training, it is the eighteen-year-old, not the eight-year-old, who is the prodigy. If it is thought unfair to compare linguistic skills with powers of abstract reasoning in this way, the point has already been granted; there is a difference between mathematical and linguistic abilities: linguistic knowledge can be distinguished from other types of knowledge, which depend on different intellectual endowments, and are acquired at different rates.

Particularly striking evidence for this mismatch between linguistic and general cognitive abilities comes from the case of the American girl Genie. Genie was discovered in Los Angeles in 1970, at the age of thirteen; she had been kept locked up in conditions of severe sensory deprivation from infancy. In particular, she had heard virtually no speech throughout the period in which children normally learn their first language. Despite this horrifying background, Genie's intelligence turned out to be within normal limits in essential respects, and thus her progress with language learning provides a useful basis for comparison with the language acquisition of more ordinary children. Her early language acquisition was typical of all children in that it passed through stages of one-word, two-word, three-word and then four-word utterances; however, Genie's three- and four-word utterances typically displayed a cognitive complexity not found in the early speech of normal children, and her vocabulary was much larger than that of children at the same stage of syntactic development. In general, her ability to store *lists* of words is very good, but her ability to learn and manipulate rules has been minimal. This is reflected in the fact that whereas the 'two-word' stage lasts for about two to six weeks with normal children, with Genie it lasted over five months:

e.g. Doctor hurt.
     Like mirror.

Moreover, the kind of early negative structures which most two-to-three-year-old children use for a few weeks, where the negative element is initial in the sentence, still persisted with Genie some one and a half *years* after she had first learned to use negatives:

> e.g. No more ear hurt.
>   No stay hospital.
>   Not have orange record.

Indeed, no syntactic rule which is normally taken to involve the *movement* of a word or phrase from one point in a sentence to another . . . has been consistently mastered by Genie as yet. But in contrast with this slow and partial linguistic progress, Genie's intellectual development appears to be progressing extremely rapidly, and to be approaching the normal for her age.

It seems, then, that language-learning abilities are not only different in kind from other intellectual abilities, but that they also become considerably impaired at a time when other intellectual abilities are still increasing. People who retain these language-learning abilities after puberty are as rare as infant mathematical prodigies. One reason for being interested in linguistic knowledge is thus for the light it might shed on human linguistic programming. If it is reasonable to suspect that such programming exists, then one obvious way of investigating it would be to examine the result of language acquisition—linguistic knowledge—and work out what principles would be needed to acquire it. And since the argument works two ways, someone who is not convinced that any linguistic programming exists might become convinced of its necessity simply by examining the contents of linguistic knowledge and asking himself how they could have been arrived at: could they have been acquired by 'general intellectual reasoning' or all-purpose learning strategies?

One common objection to this programme is that it is not always obvious where the line between linguistic and non-linguistic knowledge should be drawn. In fact some people would want to argue that no such line exists: that all knowledge involves both linguistic and non-linguistic aspects. For example, in order to know that children enjoy games—clearly not the sort of knowledge we would want to record in a grammar—one might nevertheless have to know the meanings of the words *children, enjoy* and *games,* and how to combine them into a meaningful sentence. On the other hand, in order to know that *giraffe* is a noun—clearly an item of knowledge that we would want to record in a grammar—one might nevertheless have to have some exposure to the use of English in general; and it is not, practically speaking, possible to acquire such knowledge without having some knowledge of the outside world. Hence, the argument goes, there is no clear-cut division between linguistic and non-linguistic knowledge, or between knowledge of a grammar and knowledge of the world.

This argument is not really sound. It is perfectly possible to distinguish the contents of knowledge from the preconditions for acquiring it. Thus, in order to know the laws of physics, one must be able to breathe: it does not follow that physics cannot be distinguished from human biology. There may be linguistic preconditions for acquiring knowledge of the world, and non-linguistic preconditions for learning a language: this in no way shows that knowledge of language cannot be distinguished from knowledge of the world.

In fact the notion of linguistic knowledge that we shall adopt is a quite narrow and exclusive one, in the sense that not even all knowledge about language is to count as linguistic knowledge. The principle behind this decision is as follows: knowledge about language which is merely a special case of some wider generalization about human beings does not count as linguistic knowledge. Knowledge about language which does *not* emerge as a special case of some wider generalization about human beings is the only knowledge that we are prepared to call linguistic. This of course makes the theoretical distinction between linguistic and non-linguistic knowledge—the claim that language is *sui generis*—true by definition; however, it still leaves open the empirical question of whether anything actually satisfies our definition of linguistic knowledge.

As an example of knowledge about language which does not count as linguistic knowledge in our sense, consider the following. Most linguists have a stock of odd items of knowledge about various languages: that Japanese has the verb in sentence-final position, that Turkish exhibits vowel-harmony, that Latin has no definite article, and so on. This knowledge seems rather clearly to be encyclopedic, of the same type as knowledge that France is a republic, that the capital of Italy is Rome, and that elephants are found in India. Given the capacity to acquire the latter type of knowledge, one should automatically be able to acquire the former; no special abilities would be required.

Similar remarks apply to certain types of knowledge that native speakers have about their own language. For example, most native speakers of English can recognize the social or regional origins of others on the basis of linguistic cues such as accent, intonation, choice of words and syntactic constructions. They can also recognize such things as colloquial, formal, deferential and authoritarian styles of speech, they can tell whether a particular remark is socially or factually appropriate, literally, sarcastically, humorously or otherwise figuratively intended. Although there are certainly rules and principles which make such judgments possible, and which deserve investigation in their own right, we do not want to say that these judgments are evidence of linguistic knowledge, in our sense. The reason for this is that each such principle seems to be a special case of a more general principle which applies to human non-linguistic behaviour too. For example, one can often tell someone's national, regional or social origins by the way he walks, or his gestures, or his clothes, or his facial expressions, as well as by the way he speaks. There are formal, deferential and authoritarian styles of behavior as well as speech—and like language they vary from culture to culture. There are constraints of appropriateness, sincerity, politeness, clownishness and so on, on behaviour, as well as speech. In general, then, we would expect the principles behind all these aspects of language-use to fall together with other human social and behavioural principles, and to be in no way *sui generis.*

Strictly linguistic knowledge, then, will reduce to knowledge of those principles of sentence-construction and interpretation which do not fall together with wider generalizations about human non-linguistic behaviour. Consider, for example, the claim already mentioned, that children pass through regular stages in learning a language. This would be explained on the assumption—which is not specific to language-learning—that there are degrees of complexity in the material to be learned, and that the simplest material is learned first. What *is* specifically linguistic is not the assumption that the learning process passes through successively more complex stages: it is the definition of linguistic complexity itself. Thus there is no generally observable reason why *Not Johnny go* is simpler than *Johnny not go.* The fact that children tend to learn the former before the latter indicates quite strongly that there is a notion of linguistic complexity which does not follow from general cognitive principles—which is specific to language alone and therefore part of linguistic knowledge as we are defining it. The remainder of this chapter . . . is devoted to giving further examples of strictly linguistic knowledge, and to discussing techniques for studying it.

INTUITIONS

A native speaker of English has at his disposal a vast amount of fairly uncontroversially linguistic knowledge. For example, he knows when two words rhyme; he knows when two sentences are paraphrases; when a single sentence has two different meanings; when a change in word order results in a change of meaning, and when it merely results in ungrammaticality. We have argued that the aim of writing grammars is to give a full account of all these facets of linguistic knowledge. How do we go about doing this?

Because, as we have already seen, linguistic knowledge lies well below the level of consciousness, direct questioning of speakers of a language is likely to yield little reliable information about their linguistic knowledge. If we approach a native speaker of English and ask him whether (1) and (2) have the same syntactic structure, there is not the slightest chance of predicting what he will say:

1 I'm leaving, for he makes me nervous.
2 I'm leaving, because he makes me nervous.

He may have his own consciously worked out grammatical theory or he may have no conscious idea of syntactic structure at all. In either case, there is no particular reason for believing the answer that he actually gives us, and his knowledge of language will have to be investigated by rather more indirect means.

Whatever their conscious views on grammatical theory, most native speakers will be able to provide us with evidence of the following kind: they will be able to tell us what each of the following sentence pairs has one grammatical member and one ungrammatical one:

3 a. It was because he was nervous that he left.
  b. *It was for he was nervous that he left.
4 a. Because he makes me nervous, I'm leaving.
  b. *For he makes me nervous, I'm leaving.
5 a. Did you leave because he made you nervous?
  b. *Did you leave for he made you nervous?
6 a. I left, because I was nervous and because I wanted to go.
  b. *I left, for I was nervous and for I wanted to go.
7 a. Maria, who left because I made her nervous, is returning today.
  b. *Maria, who left for I made her nervous, is returning today.

The native speaker of English clearly has some linguistic knowledge which enables him to distinguish *for*-clauses from *because*-clauses, in spite of their similarity in meaning. An adequate grammar must provide some way of replicating this linguistic knowledge. For our present purposes it is not the actual rules which explain the speaker's linguistic judgments that are of interest. What *is* interesting is that such judgments give us good ground for imputing a particular type of linguistic knowledge to the speaker: in this case, knowledge of syntactic structure.[1]

What we have just been suggesting is that one good way of investigating linguistic knowledge is to ask the native speaker for judgments about the sentences of his language: not directly, by asking 'Which of these is a subordinate clause construction?', but indirectly, by eliciting a range of judgments about, say, grammaticality, ungrammaticality, paraphrase and ambiguity, and then constructing a set of rules which will account for these judgments. The relevant judgments are generally called *intuitions*. It is often felt, by both philosophers and linguists, that reliance on native-speaker intuitions is an extremely suspect part of Chomskyan theory: intuitions are 'unscientific,' not amenable to direct observation, variable and untrustworthy. It seems to us that this is not a valid theoretical objection: discovering linguistic rules seems to us exactly analogous to discovering the rules of an invented, uncodified children's game by asking the children concerned whether certain moves are permissible or not, good moves or not, dangerous or not, and so on. How else would one go about discovering unwritten rules?

This is not to say that there are not considerable practical difficulties in deciding how much reliance should be placed on native-speaker intuitions on any

---

[1]In fact, the relevant distinction seems to be that between subordinate and co-ordinate clauses. *For, and* and *but* all link co-ordinate clauses, of roughly equal importance. *Because, although* and *when* introduce subordinate clauses which are in some sense dependent on the main clause which precedes or follows them. It is the fact that co-ordinate clauses have very limited freedom of movement, compared with subordinate clauses, which explains the differential patterns in (3)–(7).

given occasion. Consider, for example, a fairly uncomplicated sentence with more than one meaning:

8 I like Indians without reservations.

A speaker presented with a questionnaire in which he sees (8) divorced from any context, and given a limited amount of time to decide how many meanings it has, might well be unable to produce more than the following two:

9 a. I have no reservations in my liking for Indians.
  b. I like Indians who don't live on reservations.

Given more time, and perhaps some contextual guidance, he might have noticed that there is a further possible interpretation along the following lines:

9 c. I like Indians without reservations (about appearing in cowboy films).

Or he might have noticed another alternative:

9 d. I like Indians without reservations (for seats on the first scheduled flight to the moon).

And there may be still more possibilities. While this indicates that any judgment that (8) has only two interpretations must certainly be set aside, it does not indicate the total unreliability of intuitions. When shown the interpretations in (9a–d), most speakers of English would indeed agree that each was a possible interpretation of (8), and given a suitable context of utterance, most speakers would probably arrive at these interpretations for themselves. In other words, these examples merely indicate that the use of questionnaires is not likely to be a very reliable method of studying linguistic knowledge.

In a similar way, initial judgments about grammaticality, or about the literal interpretation of unambiguous sentences, may well have to be set aside in the light of further investigation. For example, quite often a sentence like (10) will be either judged ungrammatical or wrongly interpreted when heard out of context, even by perfectly competent speakers of English:

10 The train left at midnight crashed.

Where it is wrongly interpreted, it will be taken to mean the same as (11) or (12):

11 The train which left at midnight crashed.
12 The train left at midnight and crashed.

A little thought or prompting, however, should lead to a reevaluation. First, (10) is perfectly grammatical. Second, it means not (11) or (12) but (13):

13 The train which was left at midnight crashed.

An exactly parallel structure which presents no difficulties of interpretation would be (14):

14 The baby abandoned at midnight cried.

We would thus, on consideration, not want to write a grammar which would disallow (10), or interpret it as (11) or (12), even though we can elicit speakers' judgments which would initially support this treatment.

Examples like (10) seem to show that the relation between knowing the grammar of a language and actually producing or understanding utterances may be rather indirect. The grammar of the language, and the speaker of the language on mature consideration, associate (10) with the meaning in (13). However, the speaker's first reaction when presented with (10) out of context, is to associate it with the meaning in (11) or (12). This seems to indicate that the speaker who misunderstands (10) has used something other than the rules of his grammar in arriving at his interpretation. Again, as long as he can be brought to see the correct interpretation, there is no reason why this sort of case should lead to scepticism about the validity of intuitions as a guide to linguistic knowledge: but it does emphasize that intuitions do not give us direct insight into the form of linguistic knowledge, and should be treated with corresponding caution.

The reason why (10) causes difficulties of interpretation, while (14) does not, seems to be that in (10) the sequence *the train left at midnight* could itself stand as a complete (and plausible) sentence, and is initially perceived and interpreted accordingly, with wrong results. The corresponding sequence in (14), *the baby abandoned at midnight,* could not itself be a complete sentence, so that (14) is not misleading in the same way. In other words, speakers of English seem to use the following strategy for analysing complex sentences: 'Take the first sequence of words which sounds like a complete (and plausible) sentence, and interpret it *as* a complete sentence.' This strategy leads, as we have seen, to a misanalysis of (10). Now though this strategy seems to play a genuine part in the interpretation of utterances, we would not want to call it a rule of grammar, since it can so clearly lead to wrong results. What this suggests is that speakers invent shortcuts to the analysis of utterances, by-passing the rules of grammar which they also know, gaining speed but occasionally losing accuracy as a result. Such short cuts are occasionally referred to as *perceptual strategies:* strategies used in the perception (understanding) of utterances; we shall have more to say about them in the next section.

The well-known and deceptively innocent reviewer's comment in (15) is another case where the English speaker's initial interpretation turns out, on closer examination, to be incorrect:

15 This is a book you must not fail to miss.

At first sight, one is tempted to equate it with (16):

16 This is a book you must not fail to read.

It is only on closer inspection that it turns out to mean (17):

17 This is a book you must on no account read.

The problem here seems to be not syntactic, as with (10), but rather semantic or logical: sentences containing a combination of semantically 'negative' items are notoriously difficult to understand, and (15) contains *not, fail* and *miss,* in the space of four words. It is arguable that people who hear sentences like (15) and (16) do not give them a serious linguistic analysis at all: they simply guess what the speaker would be most likely to want to say, and interpret accordingly. In the absence of clues to the speaker's intentions, the process of working out what has actually been said is an exceedingly laborious one, often involving paper and pencil analysis, as the reader of (18) may check for himself:

18 Common courtesy is a virtue that few people would fail to forget unless not specifically forbidden to do otherwise.

Again, this argues for caution in dealing with initial interpretations of certain types of sentence, and for a distinction between the speaker's perceptual or understanding abilities and his actual knowledge of the language. It is to this latter distinction between knowledge of a language and the exercise of that knowledge that we turn in the next section.

COMPETENCE AND PERFORMANCE

Many of the examples we have used have required assessment on two quite different levels. First, do they conform to the principles for correct sentence-formation in standard English: are they *grammatical* ? Second, on an actual occasion of utterance, how appropriate, felicitous or comprehensible would they be: are they *acceptable* ? The first level of assessment is a purely linguistic one: the second involves knowledge and abilities that go well beyond the purely linguistic. Within Chomskyan theory, the first is called the level of *competence,* the speaker's knowledge of language, and the second is called the level of *performance,* the speaker's use of language. The study of competence, then, is the study of grammars which are psychologically real, and which contain all the linguistic knowledge, whether innate or acquired, possessed by a given speaker of the language. Such grammars are often referred to as *competence models.* The study of performance, by contrast, is concerned with the principles which govern language use: here such dimensions as appropriateness to context, ease of comprehension, sincerity, truth and stylistic euphony all play a part. Moreover, a *performance model* would have to include, as a competence model would not, some account of the principles by which sentences are actually produced and understood—and hence occasionally misproduced or misunderstood. Like the notion of intuition, the competence–performance distinction seems to us a theoretically valid one, although like the notion of intuition, it raises certain practical difficulties.

Up till now, we have been able to refer indifferently to the objects of linguistic investigation as either *sentences* or *utterances.* In fact, along with the distinction between competence and performance, grammaticality and acceptability, comes a parallel distinction between sentence and utterance. Sentences fall within the domain of competence models; utterances within the domain of performance models. Sentences are abstract objects which are not tied to a particular context, speaker or time of utterance. Utterances, on the other hand, are datable events, tied to a particular speaker, occasion and context. By contrast, sentences are tied to particular grammars, in the sense that a sentence is not grammatical in the absolute, but only with respect to the rules of a certain grammar; utterances, however, may cross the bounds of particular grammars and incorporate words or constructions from many different languages, or from no language at all. Given a bilingual English-French speaker and hearer, (19) might be a perfectly acceptable utterance, although it could never be a grammatical sentence:

19 [*]John's being a real idiot—I suppose cela va sans dire.

In other words, acceptable utterances need not be the realization of fully grammatical sentences.

There are also grammatical sentences which can never be realized as fully acceptable utterances. This may be because of their semantic, syntactic or phonological content. Thus (20) would be unacceptable in most contexts because it would patently label its speaker as insincere:

20 Your hat's on fire, though I don't believe it.

It is perfectly easy to see what this sentence is claiming: it is not even claiming anything contradictory, since it is perfectly possible for people to make assertions which they do not in fact believe. What is not legitimate, as a matter of human behaviour, is to behave insincerely while explicitly drawing one's audience's attention to the fact. In other words, the oddity in (20) is a performance matter rather than a fact of language. (21) would also be unacceptable in most contexts, this time because of its extreme syntactic complexity:

21 If because when Mary came in John left Harry cried, I'd be surprised.

It is possible, on closer examination, to see that (21) is quite regularly formed according to standard principles of English.[2] However, its syntactic complexity is such that normal speakers would have some difficulty in unravelling its message. Again, this indicates that the oddity in (21) is a performance matter, traceable to whatever principles hearers use in utterance comprehension, rather than a matter of linguistic competence. Finally, (22) would also be unacceptable to many hearers, this time for phonological reasons:

---

[2]The structure of (21) is as follows: If A happened, I'd be surprised. A = Because B happened, Harry cried. B = When Mary came in, John left.

22 We finally sent an Edinburgh man, for for four Forfar men to go would have seemed like favouritism.

There is nothing wrong with the syntax or semantics of (22): it is just that the accidental accumulation of *for* sounds makes it seem like a joke or a play on words, and diverts attention from the intended message.

To say that there is a distinction between competence and performance is not to deny that there is an intimate connection between the two. Perceptual strategies are often based on rules of grammar, and, if they are used often enough, may themselves actually *become* rules of grammar. For example, the perceptual strategy mentioned in the last section: 'Treat the first string of words that *could* be interpreted as a sentence, as being a sentence, and interpret accordingly', is ultimately based on the organization of English grammar. English has a number of ways of showing the start of a subordinate clause: the relative pronouns *who* and *which,* and the complementizer *that,* are the most common. Where these devices are used, the perceptual strategy just mentioned will be inoperative, as in (23):

23 The train which left at midnight crashed.

Thus, when the subordinate devices are omitted, the hearer has a certain right to assume that no subordinate clause is involved: hence the existence of the perceptual strategy. As we have seen, the principles of English grammar are such that this perceptual strategy will occasionally lead to a misinterpretation; nonetheless it is the principles of English grammar which originally gave rise to the perceptual strategy itself.

Conversely, what started out as a perceptual strategy may become so entrenched in the use of language that it gives rise to a rule of grammar. For example, the complementizer *that* which marks the start of a subordinate clause may optionally be omitted in a great many cases, as shown in (24) and (25):

24 a. I believe that John left.
   b. I believe John left.
25 a. I told Mary that Bill was sorry.
   b. I told Mary Bill was sorry.

One of the few places where it may never be omitted is when it introduces a subordinate clause at the very beginning of a sentence: compare (26a) and (26b):

26 a. That John should have left upset me.
   b. *John should have left upset me.

There seems to be no doubt that (26b) is actually ungrammatical, and that English therefore contains a rule of grammar which forbids deletion of a sentence-initial *that.* Returning now to our perceptual strategy, notice that it would invariably lead to a misanalysis of (26b), since the string of words *John should have left* can stand as a sentence on its own, and would thus be taken as the main clause of (26b). Forbidding the deletion of the *that* in (26a) thus guarantees that there will be no wrong application of the perceptual strategy in this case: *That John should have left* cannot stand as a sentence on its own, and hence cannot be treated by the perceptual strategy mentioned. In this case, the rule of grammar is based on the existence of the perceptual strategy, and is designed to prevent its misapplication. Thus there is a clear interaction between rules of grammar and perceptual strategies, either one being capable of giving rise to the other.

Given that there is such a close connection between rules of competence and perceptual strategies, there have been those who are prepared to argue that any clear-cut distinction between the two is impossible to draw. For example, it might be possible to argue that there is not a distinction between competence models and performance models, but merely between more and less abstract rules of performance, each of which has its part to play in the full production and understanding of utterances. And in general, it might be possible to argue that the difference between linguistic and other principles, or linguistic and other rules, is not one of kind, but merely one of degree.

While this is a perfectly reasonable alternative to the view of language that we have been, and shall be, presenting, it is not one we shall pursue ourselves. Our main reason for this is that we have never seen a fully coherent outline of a theory based on a single notion of performance, which could account in an adequate way for the facts which can be accounted for in terms of this competence-performance distinction. . . . [We] have argued that, however easy it is to produce and understand, (27) is actually ungrammatical: it is not formed according to established principles of English grammar:

27 *This is the sort of book that, having once read it, you feel you want to give it to all your friends.

If we incorporated the principles used to form (27) into English grammar, they would immediately give rise to the clear ungrammaticality of (28):

28 *This is a book which I gave it to my friend.

In other words, whatever it is that makes (27) sound natural, it is not, and cannot be, a linguistic rule. It seems to us important that linguistic theory should be able to make this sort of distinction, and we see no way of drawing it without making use of a distinction between competence and performance, language knowledge and language use.

What we have tried to do in this chapter is present a particular view of how knowledge of linguistic rules interacts, on the one hand, with other types of knowledge, and on the other hand with principles of utterance-production and comprehension. The picture that emerges is complex. Firstly, presented with a particular item of knowledge, we must be prepared to argue about how it should be classified, and we have outlined some arguments which might be used.

Where the knowledge can be classified as linguistic, then we claim that it forms part of a grammar—a competence grammar—which incorporates linguistic rules. Secondly, presented with a set of judgments about a sentence—how it should be interpreted, how it relates to other sentences, how it is pronounced—we must be prepared to argue about whether these judgments give direct insight into the competence grammar, or whether the judgments themselves must be set aside, or treated as evidence about performance models rather than grammar. Again, we have outlined some arguments which might be used. Where the judgments do not give direct insight into the competence grammar, we may find that they give us clues to the sort of principles used in utterance-comprehension, which are themselves valid objects of study. However, in general it seems to be both correct and interesting to regard the rules of language as separate from those of other cognitive systems, and to regard knowledge of these rules as only indirectly reflected in linguistic behaviour.

A Study of the Syntactic Skills of Normal Middle-School Males and Females

Joan S. Klecan-Aker

INTRODUCTION

Assessing expressive language has been an important part of speech–language evaluations of children. An effective way of assessing expressive language has been through language sampling (Barrie-Blackley, Musselwhite and Rogister, 1978). Most analyses used in language sampling are syntactic in nature and most appropriate for the child under the age of six (Brown, 1973; Tyack and Gottsleben, 1974). For example, McCarthy (1930) collected 50 responses per child and developed mean length of response (MLR) norms for children at six-month age separations from 18 to 54 months. In addition, Roger Brown (1973) has described the stages of language development in terms of a mean length of utterance (MLU). MLU is counted in morphemes rather than words and is generally used with children between the ages of 12 and 60 months. Both MLR and MLU counts are used widely in the analysis of language samples gathered from pre-school children. Since many speech–language pathologists work in public school systems, where the majority of their caseloads are children older than six, it becomes important to find ways of assessing expressive language in older children.

One means of assessing the language skills of older children that has emerged from the recent literature is that of analyzing their monologues or narratives

(Appleby, 1978; Tannen, 1979; Johnston, 1982; Westby, 1984). There are several reasons why researchers have found the narratives of children fertile data sources. First, nearly every child can respond to the task, "Tell me a story." Additionally, having a child tell a story provides the clinician with an uninterrupted flow of discourse from the child, avoiding certain artificialities of data from conventional elicitation techniques (Bennett-Kastor, 1983, p. 140).

The narratives of school-age children can be examined from several perspectives (Johnston, 1982). Hunt (1970) found that expressive language skills in older children could be measured by an analysis of the syntax found in their monologues. Hunt divided speech into "the shortest units which it is grammatically allowable to punctuate as sentences" (1970, p. 4). He labeled these segments T-units ("minimal terminal units," p. 4). A T-unit is defined as "one main clause plus any subordinate clause or nonclausal structure that is attached or embedded in it" (Hunt, 1970, p. 4), and can be measured in words per T-unit, clauses per T-unit and words per clause. The advantage of words per T-unit is that it is sensitive to language differences characteristic of subjects from age five through adulthood. The T-unit can also be employed to analyze differences in clause length due to adjective and adverb usage and the use of various types of subordinate clauses (O'Donnell, Griffin and Norris, 1967). The analysis of clause length would be particularly useful in assessing the syntactic complexity of the utterances of the middle-school child where the basic rules of adult syntax have been established for quite some time (Entwisle and Frasure, 1974).

O'Donnell *et al.* (1967), using T-units, studied differences in use of syntactic structures at various grade levels. They found differences in use of syntactic structures at various grade levels. They found differential lengthening of T-units in successive grades and believed that this reflected varying degrees of expansion in the exploitation of syntactic resources.

Crystal, Fletcher and Garman (1976) developed a syntactic framework of description that they assert can be applied successfully with children at several age levels. These researchers' grammatical framework is based on the work of Quirk and Greenbaum (1973) and could be used to analyze syntactic structures within a narrative. Three main levels of sentence structure are recognized: patterns of sentence and clause structure, patterns of phrase structure, and patterns of word structure. Crystal *et al.* referred to their procedure as the Language Assessment Remediation and Screening Procedure (LARSP).

In spite of the emerging research on the analyses of children's narratives, there remains a major problem. The majority of the investigations regarding narratives have focused on the language patterns of preschool children (Ames, 1979; Umiker-Sebeok, 1979; Bennett-Kastor, 1983) or studied the expressive language skills of language-disordered school-age children (Johnston, 1982). Very few researchers have examined the expressive language used by normal older school-age children. The assessment tools that are appropriate for the school-age child, however thorough, rarely include an analysis of spontaneous expressive language (Wiig and Semel, 1980; Woodcock and Johnson, 1977). Although all these studies have value in themselves, there remains limited information about the expressive language skills of normal older children. Until a thorough data base is established that documents the expressive language abilities of normal school-age children, the evaluation of language problems in this population is haphazard at best. In an initial attempt to meet this need Klecan-Aker and Hedrick (1983), using T-unit analysis, assessed the syntactic structures used by normal middle-school children during a monologue. We reported significant differences in the length of utterances between the sixth and ninth grade subjects that were tested. In addition to the T-unit analysis we categorized the various types of verb extensions used by the subjects during the same monologue and reported statistically significant differences in the types of verb extensions used within each group. Verb extensions will be defined in detail in a later section of this paper.

Although a syntactic analysis is only one way of examining the narratives or monologues of school-age children, it nonetheless provides valuable information documenting the ways in which normal children use language. In an attempt to enlarge upon the data base established in the prior study the purpose of the present investigation was to extend this previous analysis to include an examination of the syntactic skills of school-age males and females. We controlled for this difference in the earlier study, but did not examine sex as a separate variable. References to the superiority of girls with respect to almost all aspects of language development abound in the literature (Ramar, 1976; Cherry, 1975; Templin, 1957). Winitz (1959), for example, reviewed the literature available to date and found a 2:1 superiority of girls over boys in several areas of language. However, the differences between groups were not statistically significant. A further review of the literature failed to confirm that girls actually acquire words earlier than boys (Darley and Winitz, 1961). In contradiction to these findings, Lynch (1983), in looking at gender differences in language, believed that sex-related differences occur in the language of both children and adults. Evidently, there is ambiguity found in the results of various studies that explore this issue of sex and language. The foregoing considered, it seemed critical to continue to examine the way in which males and females use language.

METHOD

Subjects

Forty-eight children, 24 from both sixth and ninth grades, were selected from a pool of students at the Developmental Research School of a university in the Southeast of the United States. The 24 children at each grade level were evenly divided between males and females. The Developmental Research School is a department of the College of Education and serves as its laboratory for conducting research and developmental activities in education by faculty of the College of Education and other units of the university. In considering students for the school, four specific variables are used: academic ability, social economic factors, sex and race. These variables are used in such a way as to ensure that the children selected for the school represent a cross section of the population living in that area of the country. Therefore the subjects in the present investigation represent that population. In addition to these variables, all students selected for this study passed a speech, hearing and language screening administered by the examiner.

Procedure

All testing was conducted in a 6′ × 8′ room with a one-way mirror. The child and examiner were seated side by side in front of a small table.

A language sample was obtained from each child at the beginning of the experiment. Each child was asked to deliver a five-minute monologue in which he or she explained, in narrative form, the plot of a favorite movie. If the child was unwilling or unable to do this, he was encouraged to discuss a topic of his choice. All narratives were audiotaped and orthographically transcribed.

Transcriptions of Utterances

Transcriptions were made from the middle three minutes of each subject's audiotape. In the event that a subject did not talk for the full five-minute time period, the initial three minutes were transcribed. Each transcription was typed for analysis.

The language sample, once transcribed, was segmented into minimal terminal syntactic units (T-units). An independent judge, a graduate student in speech pathology, checked four randomly selected transcribed samples, two from each grade level. These were checked with the original audiotapes to ensure that the transcriptions accurately represented what the subject had said. Any disagreements between the independent judge and the examiner regarding the transcriptions were resolved by consensus. After T-units had been identified, each one was typed on an analysis sheet for further study.

Measurement and Analysis

The length of utterances of each narrative was measured using Hunt's T-unit analysis (1970). The measurement included words per T-unit, clauses per T-unit, and words per clause. The rules for dividing the narratives can be found in Appendix A.

To examine the reliability of the T-unit analysis, one judge, a graduate student in speech–language pathology, segmented a random selection of transcribed language samples into T-units. A total of four language samples were used, two from each grade level. Interscorer agreement was calculated for number of T-units, words per T-unit, clauses per T-unit and words per clause using a point-by-point percentage of agreement procedure (Prutting, Bagshaw, Goldstein, Juskowitz and Umen, 1978). The interscorer agreement between the judge and the examiner was 96.7% for the number of T-units, 92.6% for words per T-unit, 90.8% for clauses per T-unit and 93.1% for words per clause.

An analysis of the syntactical relationships within the T-units was done using an adaptation of Crystal *et al.'s* Language Assessment Remediation Screening Procedure (LARSP). This adaptation by the first author of the present article consisted of a syntactic description of the verb extensions for each T-unit. The first 10 T-units for each subject were analyzed. Each word, phrase or clause following the main verb was placed in one of the following categories: simple adverbials, complex adverbials, infinitive adverbials, simple objects, complex objects, infinitive objects, simple complements, complex complements, and infinitive complements. For the purposes of this study, the following definitions were utilized: "Simple" was defined as a one-word extension (one word + determiner), and "complex" as any extension longer than one word (two or more words + determiner). "Infinitive" was defined as an extension of the verb phrase consisting of any verb phrase that can be used with *to* to function in a sentence as a noun, adjective or adverb. Examples of each type of verb extension can be found in Appendix B.

To ascertain the reliability of the modified LARSP analysis, one judge, a certified speech–language pathologist experienced in the use of the procedure, analyzed three transcribed narratives (the first 10 T-units in each) from each grade according to the just-cited definitions. Interscorer agreement was calculated by a point-by-point percentage of agreement procedure. The initial interscorer agreement between the judge and the examiner was 84.2%. Differences between the scorers invariably involved disagreement on the classification of one specific category, complements. Following a discussion of these disparities, it became obvious that criteria for coding complements were needed. These guidelines were developed and can be summarized in the following way: any adjective or noun word, phrase or clause that follows a linking verb, thereby referring back to the subject or object of the independent clause, would be categorized as a complement. Reliability was assessed again and this follow-up procedure generated an interscorer agreement value of 97.4%.

Statistical Testing

All inferential statistical tests involved comparisons between males and females within each grade. To analyze for the differences between the sexes, individual *t* tests for independent means were performed on the mean numbers of clauses per T-unit, mean number of words per T-unit, and mean number of words per clause within each grade.

The Chi-Square Test for Independence was used to determine possible differences between males and females in the frequency distribution of the categories of verb extensions within each grade.

RESULTS

Table 15 shows mean performance lengths for words per T-unit, clauses per T-unit and words per clause for sixth-grade males and females. Insofar as inferential statistical analyses are concerned, the difference between group means was not statistically significant for 6th grade males and females for words per T-unit ($t = 0.52$; $df = 22$; $p > 0.05$), words per clause ($t = 1.62$; $df = 22$; $p > 0.05$) and clauses per T-unit ($t = 0.58$; $df = 22$; $p > 0.05$). These same findings held true for the 9th grade males and females as well: words per T-unit ($t = 0.24$; $df = 22$; $p > 0.05$), words per clause ($t = 0.98$; $df = 22$; $p > 0.05$) and clauses per T-unit ($t = 0.44$; $df = 22$; $p > 0.05$).

The second way in which syntax was examined was through an evaluation of verb extensions. The first 10 T-units for each subject were analyzed using the aforementioned adaptation of the Language Assessment Remediation Screening Procedure (LARSP, Crystal *et al.*, 1976). This analysis consisted of an examination and classification of verb extensions. Sixth-grade males had 168 verb extensions compared to 148 verb extensions for the females. Ninth-grade males used 161 verb extensions whereas the females used 145, indicating similar performances of males and females across grades. Even the specific forms of the verb extensions were similar across the groups. This is quite evident upon inspections of Tables 15 and 16. Tables 16 and 17 present the number and type of verb extensions for males and females within each grade. Complex verb extensions were used most often by both males and females across grades. The infinitive verb extensions were used least often.

TABLE 15
COMPARISON OF T-UNIT LENGTH, CLAUSES PER
T-UNIT AND CLAUSE LENGTH OF SIXTH AND NINTH
GRADE MALES AND FEMALES

		Grade	
		6	9
T-unit length	Males	10.06	10.20
(in words)	Females	9.10	10.04
Clauses per	Males	1.26	1.29
T-unit	Females	1.30	1.32
Clause length	Males	7.22	7.33
(in words)	Females	6.41	7.55

TABLE 16
NUMBERS AND TYPES OF VERB EXTENSIONS
USED BY SIXTH AND NINTH GRADE MALES
AND FEMALES

		Grade	
		6	9
Adverb verb	Males	66	68
extensions	Females	56	55
Complement verb	Males	23	47
extensions	Females	37	33
Object verb	Males	59	46
extensions	Females	75	47
Total	Males	148	161
	Females	168	135

TABLE 17
NUMBER AND COMPLEXITY OF VERB EXTENSIONS
USED BY SIXTH AND NINTH GRADE MALES
AND FEMALES

		Grade	
		6	9
Simple verb	Males	35	22
extensions	Females	24	21
Complex verb	Males	99	128
extensions	Females	125	107
Infinitive verb	Males	14	11
extensions	Females	19	17
Total	Males	148	161
	Females	168	145

Inferential statistics were used to further examine within-group differences. A Chi-Square for independent samples was used to determine differences in the use of verb extensions between the sexes within each grade. The results were not significant for the type or complexity of verb extensions used by males and females within each grade level.

DISCUSSION

The results of the present study revealed that, in terms of T-unit analyses and the analyses of verb extensions, there were no significant differences in the way middle-school males and females performed. Each analysis will be discussed separately.

T-unit analysis has been used widely in examining the syntactic skills of children (O'Donnell, Griffin and Norris, 1967; Hunt, 1970; Klecan-Aker and Hedrick, 1983; and Stevens, 1983). Researchers have generally found increases in T-unit length and clause length with increases in age. In addition, it has been found that the number of clauses per T-unit remains approximately the same for subjects from age 5 through adulthood (O'Donnell *et al.,* 1967; Walker, Hardiman, Hedrick and Holbrook, 1982). What becomes apparent as a result of all this research are several points of interest: 1) length of utterances increases with an increase in age; 2) the number of clauses per T-unit remains relatively constant after age 5; and 3) school-age males and females, at least in the grades studied, perform in similar ways. This third factor will be discussed at length since the purpose of the present study was to investigate sex as a possible variable in the use of syntax. Several factors may account for this similarity in syntactic usage between males and females. First, the task itself may have limited the types of responses used by the subjects. In a narrative, if the speaker attempts to be coherent, the length of his utterance must be controlled to some degree. In other types of discourse, a dialogue for instance, different utterance lengths might result for males and females. A second possible explanation for the similar syntactic choices of the subjects might be the fact that by the time children reach middle school their use of the language may be quite similar in structured tasks of any nature.

The second way syntactic complexity was examined in the present study was through an analysis of the types and levels of organization of syntactic structures using an adaptation of the Language Assessment Remediation Screening Procedure (LARSP: Crystal *et al.,* 1976). Recall that syntactic structures following the main verb were classified as simple, complex or infinitive. They were additionally categorized as adverbial, object or complement. This analysis provided information about type or function of syntactic structures that, when added to the data provided by the T-unit analyses, supplies a very thorough view of syntactic development in the middle-school children tested. Essentially it was found that both males and females performed in similar ways within each grade. This similarity included the number, type and complexity of the verb extensions used by the subjects. Again there appear to be two possible explanations. Either the subjects performed in similar ways as a result of the type of task, or males and females, once they reach middle school-age, simply use the syntactic components of the language in similar ways. The majority of the information available at this time regarding children's use of syntax within a narrative is limited in two ways. Either the studies examine the relationship of sex and syntactic usage in discourse (Winitz, 1959; Brown, 1973; Lynch, 1983), or investigations explore syntax within a narrative without consideration of gender (Klecan-Aker and Hedrick, 1983; Westby, 1984). What seems to have been neglected in these explorations of syntax is evidence regarding the relationship between sexes within the narrative style itself.

In view of this gap in our knowledge of school-age children's use of language, it seems feasible to direct future research at an exploration of syntactic skills used by school-age males and females in a variety of narrative situations. There is evidence to support the belief that syntactic structure varies with the function of the language. For example, specifically with narratives, syntax will be different for oral and written texts. In addition, there can be considerable variation depending upon the instructions used in presenting the tasks and the specific materials used to elicit the narratives. Relating a personal narrative generally yields a more orally structured narrative, whereas a request to "make it a story like I would find in a book" will yield a more literal type of narrative (Westby, 1984). Only when it is evident that the findings of the present investigation remain constant under a variety of circumstances can it be assumed that school-age males and females use the language in similar ways. In addition it might be useful to examine different age groups. Males and females may perform differently at different grade levels or ages not previously examined.

A complete investigation of all these factors and how they interrelate is necessary for a thorough understanding of language competency. It is critical for speech–language pathologists to have at their disposal a thorough data base on normal language patterns of school-age children. Only then will it be possible to document systemically and scientifically possible language problems in school-age children.

REFERENCES

Ames, L. (1979). Children as storytellers. *Early Years Magazine,* **10** , 36–37.

Appleby, A. (1978). *The Child's Concept of Story: Ages Two to Seventeen* (Chicago).

Barrie-Blackley, S., C. Musselwhite, and S. Rogister. (1978). *Clinical Language Sampling: A Handbook for Students and Clinicians* (Danville).

Bennett-Kastor, T. (1983). Noun phrases and coherence in child narratives. *Journal of Child Language,* **10,** 135–149.

Brown, R. (1973). *A First Language* (Cambridge, Mass.).

Cherry, L. (1975). Teacher–child verbal interaction: An approach to the study of sex differences. In B. Torns and N. Henley (eds.), *Language and Sex: Differences and Dominance* (Baltimore), pp. 384–402.

Crystal, D., P. Fletcher, and M. Garman. (1976). *The Grammatical Analysis of Language Disorders: A Procedure for Assessment and Remediation* (New York).

Darley, F. and H. Winitz. (1961). Age of first words: Review of research. *Journal of Speech and Hearing Disorders,* **26,** 272–290.

Entwisle, D. R., and N. E. Frasure. (1974). A contradiction resolved: Children's processing of syntactic cues of verbal learning and verbal behavior. *Journal of Verbal Learning and Verbal Behavior,* **18,** 832–837.

Hunt, K. (1970). Syntactic maturity in school children and adults. *Monographs of the Society of Research in Child Development,* **35** (Serial No. 134).

Johnston, J. R. (1982). Narratives: A new look at communication problems in older language-disordered children. *Language, Speech and Hearing Services in Schools,* **13,** 144–155.

Klecan-Aker, J., and D. L. Hedrick. (1983). A Study of the Syntactic Language Skills of Normal Middle School Children. Paper presented at the American Speech, Language and Hearing Convention (Cincinnati).

Lynch, J. (1983). Gender differences in language. *ASHA,* **25,** 37–44.

McCarthy, P. (1930). The language development of the pre-school child. *University of Minnesota Institute of Child Welfare Monograph, Nr. 4,* (Minneapolis).

O'Donnell, R., W. Griffin, and R. Norris. (1967). Syntax of kindergarten and elementary school children: A transformational analysis. *Research Report, National Council of Teachers of English,* **8** 56–133.

Prutting, C., N. Bagshaw, H. Goldstein, S. Juskowitz, and I. Umen. (1978). Clinician-child discourse. *Journal of Speech and Hearing Disorders,* **43,** 123–139.

Quirk, R. and S. Greenbaum. (1973). *A University Grammar of English* (London).

Ramar, A. L. H. (1976). Syntactic styles in emerging language. *Journal of Child Language,* **3,** 49–62.

Stevens, I. (1983). A follow-up study of language impaired children: Narrative analysis. Paper presented at the American Speech, Language and Hearing Convention (Cincinnati).

Tannen, D. (1979). What's in a frame? Surface evidence for underlying expectations. In R. O. Freedle (ed.), *New Directions in Discourse Processing* (Norwood, NJ), pp. 137–181.

Templin, M. C. (1957). Certain language skills in children: Their development and interrelationships. *Child Welfare Monographs,* No. 26 (Minneapolis).

Tyack, D, and R. Gottsleben. (1974). *Language Sampling, Analysis and Training* (Palo Alto).

Umiker-Sebeok, D. J. (1979). Preschool children's intraconversational narratives. *Journal of Child Language,* **6,** 91–110.

Walker, V. G., C. J. Hardiman, D. L. Hedrick, and A. Holbrook. (1982). Speech and language characteristics of an aging population. In N. Lass (ed.), *Speech and Language: Advances in Basic Research and Practice* (Baltimore), pp. 143–202.

Westby, C. E. (1984). Development of narrative language abilities. In F. Wallach and K. Butler (eds.), *Language Learning Disabilities in School-Age Children* (Baltimore), pp. 103–127.

Wiig, E. H., and E. M. Semel. (1980). *Clinical Evaluation of Language Functions* (Columbus).

Winitz, H. (1959). Language skills of male and female kindergarten children. *Journal of Speech and Hearing Research,* **2,** 377–381.

Woodcock, R. W., and M. B. Johnson. (1977). *Woodcock-Johnson Psycho-Educational Battery* (Hingham).

APPENDIX A

The following rules were used for dividing the narratives of subjects into T-units:

1 Exact repetitions of words or phrases were not counted.

2 Syntactic and/or semantic revisions that did not have a complete subject and predicate were not counted.

3 T-units that were not grammatically correct were included.

4 Direct quotations such as, "He said, 'I want to go,'" were considered one T-unit.

5 Subordinate clauses were not counted unless they could logically be placed with a separate independent clause.

6 Unintelligible words were counted as one. If they were an important part of the sentence, such as the subject, then they were not counted.

7 If there was more than one unintelligible word per T-unit, the entire utterance was discounted.

8 Only subject–verb contractions were counted as two words. All other contractions counted as one word.

9 Proper and compound nouns counted as one word.

APPENDIX B:

EXAMPLES OF VERB EXTENSIONS FROM SIXTH- AND NINTH-GRADE SUBJECTS

		Examples	
Category	Type	6th Grade	9th Grade
Adverbial	simple	and he went home	he went there
	complex	this little boy fall over the side	I go to p.e. in the gym
	infinitive	they had to stay in the honeymoon suite	they wanted to play in the streets
Complement	simple	there was midget	it is math
	complex	and he was one of them	it was about an old janitor
	infinitive	they had to act like they were a married couple	they hired him to go find the lost ark
Object	simple	she saved Kirmit	they were threatening
	complex	he dropped the old car	it started out he was looking for his skull
	infinitive	he wanted to go with her	he started to beat up Becky

A Reconsideration of the Definition of Standard English

James C. Stalker

A cursory survey of the literature of linguistics, as well as that of the popular grammarians, gives ample evidence that very few people who write about language reject the existence of some kind of standard English. To my knowledge, no one makes the claim that English is a standard variety of the same sort as German or French in which an official body designates the form of the standard variety. However, most linguists accept a variety of standard Englishes in which standard is determined by appropriateness to such factors as audience, topic, or social setting (Traugott and Pratt, 322), or define standard English as "educated" English, the language of the classroom and public use (Fries, 15; Labov, 220, 241), or as "common" English (Quirk and Greenbaum, 1–9; Wolfram and Fasold, 18–23). Most, if not all, of these definitions carry the assumption, explicitly or implicitly, that standard English carries a higher social status than other varieties. Thus standard English is defined, in one way or another, as a high prestige dialect. The difficulty, as it has been for the past two hundred years, is deciding who uses this dialect and in delineating its features. Both of these tasks have proved to be extremely elusive—so much so that Labov (66) and Wolfram and Fasold (20–21) quite openly and honestly assume, with certain disclaimers, that they use standard English, and in their works, they rely on their "intuitions" about what standard English is.

But, as linguists, we are generally uncomfortable calling a language phenomenon a dialect when we cannot find a core of features, and we have not been able to find that core for the phenomenon labeled standard English because our task is continually confounded by the need to allow for legitimate feature variability caused by regional variation, topic, medium, social demands, and other factors. Given these factors, English that "counts as," is acceptable as, standard English for most people, including linguists, is so diffuse as to defy description.

Because we can find no stable list of features that appears in all occurrences of language use accepted as standard, the best assumption seems to be either that standard English simply does not exist, obviously a position frequently held, particularly by linguists, or that we simply must accept the notion that standard is defined entirely by the context in which it occurs. The latter position seems tantamount to saying that there is no standard English, but rather a number of acceptable variants of English.

However, there is another position available. We can assume that standard English is not a dialect, because it is not definable through a feature list. Rather, it is an attitude toward language use based on the principle of accommodation, of adjustment—a process rather than a product. Language use that evidences accommodation "counts as" standard English, and those whose language use habitually shows accommodation are perceived as users of standard English. This definition shifts our focus from standard English to standard English usage, from an external feature list with which a given text is compared to a consideration of whether the language use has satisfied certain fairly flexible criteria, which, when adhered to, mark the use as indicating a willingness to adapt one's features of discourse to include the audience or provide a common linguistic meeting ground for speaker and audience. Some of these criteria are in fact phonological, morphological, or syntactic features, but some are features of language we are just beginning to understand.

Many definitions of standard English allude to the principle of accommodation. For example, Bolinger attributes language change to a jettisoning of dialect features that interfere with communication, and says in discussing language reformers that they "felt that attaining a standard by unpremediated accommodation would be too slow a process" (575). Traugott and Pratt recognize a number of standard varieties which "serve a combination of unificational, prestige, and frame of reference (or code of correctness) functions" (324). For them, standard varieties obliterate regional and social distinctions "resulting in a group defined not so much by class but by education" (325). In other words, standard varieties are the result of movement from regional and social dialects to some other, but undefined, dialect. Although these definitions, and others like them (cf. e.g., Ferguson, 29–30 and Preston, this volume) do implicitly include the process of accommodation as a feature of standard English, the emphasis in the discussions remains on standard English as a potentially isolable dialect.

Accommodation implies that linguistic movement must occur, but we need not evaluate the movement in terms of a steady state beginning and a steady state ending, in terms of dialect A and dialect B. The clear importance of the need to consider the functions of language within linguistic and nonlinguistic contexts should suggest to us that any definition of standard English must be a functional definition, a definition of language in use, in process, dynamic, not a definition of language in a steady state. Paul Garvin approached this goal in "The Standard Language Problem—Concepts and Methods," where he discusses two "properties" of standard language (flexible stability and intellectualization) and four functions (the ones listed by Traugott and Pratt, plus a separatist function). In discussing the procedure for discovering the details of these properties and functions, Garvin specifies that linguistic movement may be relative when he says that "a given language situation can be described as meeting the criteria for a standard language to a given degree, rather than absolutely" (522), that is we can ask: has movement occurred? how much? and in what directions? But he did not go beyond naming the properties and functions and outlining their gross characteristics and the procedures for exploring them. His article holds the seeds of a definition based on accommodation, but perhaps because he did not elaborate his definition, it seems to have been virtually ignored. Einar Haugen presents a view reminiscent of Garvin's in "Instrumentation in Language Planning," but for the most part, the view that standard language is a dynamic process has lain fallow until the recent interest in such matters as conversational analysis. The focus has been on what standard language is rather than how language use is standard, on which dialect we move to rather than in what kind of movement we engage.

There is at least one exception to this general statement. Over the past few years, Giles has developed explicitly the notion of accommodation that we have seen was implicit in earlier discussion and has conducted a considerable amount of research teasing out some of the facets of the process. His more recent research clearly demonstrates that speakers do adjust features such as speech rate and phonology on the basis of the assumptions and expectations they hold about the listener's language features, and that they are conscious of the adjustment. The adjustment can be either toward or away from the listener's assumed language, depending on whether the speaker wishes to decrease or increase the communicative distance (Thakerer, Giles, and Chesire, 1982). Earlier research (Giles and Smith, 1979) indicates that content adjustment, as well as linguistic features, may be a significant factor in the accommodation process.

However, Giles follows the basic assumption in the field of dialect study that there is a standard dialect which is definable in terms of certain linguistic features, notably phonology (Giles and Smith, 49). Given Giles' research and the plethora of variant definitions of standard English, I would suggest that the process of accommodation is the defining principle of standard English, and I would suggest further that there are three functions that require accommodation in order for a given instance of the use of English to be accepted as standard: social appropriateness, clarity, and register. Before we turn to a discussion of these functions, it is necessary that we briefly reconsider the term "standard English." Bailey's argument that *standard* implies a fixed quantity against which other quantities can be measured is cogent and to the point, particularly for languages which historically have had an academy which specifies the form of the standard dialect. On this basis, we might drop the term *standard* as applied to English and choose another term when we need to discuss this matter. As logical as this suggestion might be, I doubt seriously that it will come to pass. I am adopting as an alternative to "standard English" the phrase "standard English usage" in order to recognize that there is indeed no single variety of English which fulfills the European definition of *standard* as it applies to a particular language. Perhaps linguists themselves need an academy to define the meaning of *standard* as applied to languages.

Of the functions which I have postulated as requiring accommodation in order to qualify language use as standard, social appropriateness is undoubtedly the most commonly discussed, and needs little elaboration, but does need some refocusing. In general, most people, linguists and nonlinguists alike, assume that standard English is some particular, higher social status dialect, and arguments for or against this or that dialect and for or against the basic assumption fill many pages. But, whether we like it or not, we know that we must accept social appropriateness as one of the defining criteria of standard English usage, and most linguists do, however reluctantly. But, we need not accept a single prestigious dialect as the norm to which we must accommodate. For example, many Americans throughout the United States still regard some one of the eastern Massachusetts dialects as the most prestigious of American dialects, but of course make no attempt to alter their native dialect to include features of that dialect. Quite the contrary, they avoid such alterations because the eastern Massachusetts dialect is regarded as snobbish "when used by natives in other regions," so we cannot declare it the standard dialect, although we recognize that it is more prestigious than others. Recently, for obvious economic reasons I think, the dialect of west Texas seemed to be vying with that of eastern Massachusetts, at least for Michiganians, as a prestige dialect, but the typical Michiganian does not mimic that one either.

It is a curious fact that even though the average Michiganian, for example, does not learn and use an eastern Massachusetts or west Texas dialect, or RP for that matter, we are rarely inclined to say that his language is nonstandard. On the contrary, we, and I include all who think in terms of standard English, are reluctant even to say that his language is not prestigious. The most condemnatory comment we are likely to make is that the dialect of a Michiganian probably indicates that he comes from a geographic region which does not bespeak a heritage of power and money.

On the other hand, socially nonprestigious dialects present a different kind of problem. Black English Vernacular, for example, is avoided as a dialect of choice because it belongs to a group of people generally regarded as occupying a social status no one wants to lay claim to. Those of us who desire to be perceived as speakers of a socially acceptable dialect actively avoid adopting features associated with socially nonprestigious groups, while we simply benignly neglect to adopt those of more socially prestigious groups than our own. I feel compelled to specify here that the subject at hand is what *counts* as standard English use. There are contexts in which many of us use features from other dialects, both prestigious and nonprestigious, that are not our own for particular local purposes. We do not avoid that use of features of dialects at all costs; we try to use those features which mark our speech as not nonprestigious, that is as acceptable.

Social appropriateness of language use is not simply a matter of learning and using a prestige dialect or completely avoiding all features of a nonprestige dialect. It is rather learning which features of your own dialect, whatever it may be, are likely to elicit judgments that you are a member of a socially nonprestigious group, or a social outsider. As many studies have shown, only certain features of any nonprestige dialect are judged negatively; those are the ones we must alter. Nor do we need to alter them all, in most cases; we simply need to accommodate our dialect enough so that it is not clearly marked as not the prevailing dialect of the situation. We need not adopt the prevailing one wholesale. In effect, all regional dialects are "standard" dialects because they are highly accommodated, one to another. Regional dialects that have not accommodated are nonstandard—whether they are a regional rural dialect or a long time isolated dialect such as Appalachian. When we can attach negative social beliefs and attitudes to these unaccommodated dialects, they become socially non-prestigious dialects and we add a more stringent accommodation demand—the user must alter a greater proportion of features. As dialects become more or less representative of wealth and power, they need accommodate more or less, and the same is true of individuals who use social dialects. The more socially powerful or positive the individual (or dialect), the less he (or it) need accommodate, regardless of the social judgments made about the dialect. In cases where wealth and power and a particular dialect enjoy a long association, accommodation is toward this stable prestige dialect.

If accommodation according to social setting were the only criterion for standard usage, we could simply rank all variants in terms of social acceptability and choose among them according to current social demands. But it is not the only one. Socially accommodated usage may well be judged as nonstandard, if it is not clear. For example, Edwin Newman's, Richard Mitchell's, and a great many composition teachers' tirades are not so much against socially negative usage as they are against opaqueness and emptiness. In fact, they believe that standard English is language used to enable the clearest communication, and nonstandard language is that usage which obfuscates and hides the meaning. Their point is often lost because they couch their arguments in the correctness tradition, which has its roots firmly planted in the soil of social appropriateness. Were Labov not committed to the view that standard English is primarily a matter of social appropriateness, his discussion of Charles M's disquisition on witchcraft in "The Logic of Nonstandard English" (218–220) could have come to the conclusion that Charles M is not a fully standard speaker. He does conclude that "all too often, standard English is represented by a style that is simultaneously over-particular and vague. The accumulating flow of words buries rather than strikes the target" (222). This statement could as easily have come from Richard Mitchell. More to the point, Labov says that because "it seems likely that standard English has an advantage over BEV in explicit analysis of surface forms" (218), standard English is the better variety of language for the task of presenting linguistic analysis. In other words, standard English is a use of language that attempts to present the message as explicitly as possible, that attempts to accommodate to an audience's potential lack of knowledge, as well as fulfill Garvin's intellectualization category.

Written language is often set as "the standard English" for precisely this reason. It is, when successful, maximally accommodated for clarity. In most cases, spoken language does not have to strive for maximum clarity until the listener demands it. The larger our range of audiences, in spoken or written English, the more likely we are to encounter and converse with strangers, then the greater will be the range of clarity criteria, hence the greater the demand for accommodation. In *American English,* C. C. Fries says that the "most striking difference" between Standard and Vulgar English is that Vulgar English "seems essentially poverty-stricken. It uses less of the resources of the language. . . . The user of Vulgar English seems less sensitive in his impressions, less keen in his realizations, and more incomplete in his representations" (288). In our terms, the user of Vulgar English does not seem to accommodate his language to the richness of his thoughts or to the needs and expectations of his listener. Composition teachers often find the same language use as Fries notes for Vulgar users in their student themes, but hesitate to call it nonstandard because it is socially appropriate even though they regard it as inappropriate from the viewpoint of clarity (Shaughnessy, Chapter 7). As often as not, they ascribe the lack of clarity to poor usage, to an unwillingness or inability to follow correctness rules, and thus provide themselves with a reason for labeling the language nonstandard.

The final of the three categories, situational appropriateness or register, allows for a great deal of variation, perhaps more than the other two categories, but there are limits on the variation. Labov accepts Charles M's disquisition as standard not only because it is socially appropriate language use, but also because it is delivered in a style we accept as appropriate to the interview register, thus Charles M satisfies two of the three criteria. Politicians continue to be regarded as standard English users, by many people, because they select socially appropriate features and use a register we accept for public presentations by politicians. Doctors have long been allowed to use their professional register outside of professional contexts because we accept it as appropriate. This situation seems to be changing because too many people, of many class levels, do not understand doctors—their language use is nonstandard by the clarity criterion—and we are beginning to refuse to allow the medical register as an appropriate register for standard usage.

The following letter from a government agency to a contractor is a prime example of language in the proper register for its immediate, particular audience, but which, when made public, ceases to be standard usage because we do not accept that register as widely appropriate.

Gentlemen:

SUBJECT: Account No. XXXX-XXXXX-XXXXXX
        Repairs to XXXXXXX Building
        Temperature Controls and Steam Valve Repairs

The writer has been advised that our request for $1,430.00 initiated to authorize construction stage professional service disciplines for the subject project has been rejected. Rather than 5 trips for construction supervision, two (2) field trips were offered for authorization to consider.

This is to advise that a contract change order request will be resubmitted considering authorization for two trips against your contract order X-XXXXXXX.

Should you have any strong objections to this action, please advise and support why our resolve will not be appropriately suited to your continued involvement in the project.

Sincerely,
XXXXXXXXXXXXXX

The letter is certainly socially accommodated in that there are no features we would automatically associate with any given socially nonprestigious group (unless we believe that bureaucrats are socially unacceptable). Because we are not familiar with the register we reject it as not falling within the bounds of acceptable English. It elicits the same response that a great deal of academic prose does—why can't those people write in English? Furthermore, because we are unfamiliar with the linguistic features of the register, we have difficulty reading it, and because it is unclear to the average reader what it means, it fails to satisfy the clarity criterion. It is an inappropriate register for our use; it is not accommodated usage for a broader audience, so it is nonstandard usage.

Ideally, standard English usage is that which shows maximum accommodation in all three areas. It is maximally clear, socially appropriate, and falls in some appropriate register. But, of course, there are immediate difficulties. A particular choice of lexicon and syntax may provide maximum clarity for one audience and minimum for another, and the same is true for the other criteria. Furthermore there are tensions among the criteria, as we have implied. A particular situation may demand a particular register choice for the use to be perceived as standard, but the register demand may conflict with the expectation of clarity. Politicians and bureaucrats generally have this problem. They cannot be clear and talk like politicians. If they are clear, they may well lose the election to the opponent who chooses the proper register. Business people must "prioritize their objectives" rather than "rank their goals" or risk being perceived as unprofessional. Academicians must choose the proper register, often at the expense of clarity. Howard Cosell attempts a usage that is supposedly maximally precise and socially prestigious, but which is clearly inappropriate for the sportcasting register.

We cannot always accomodate all categories at once nor can we always do so successfully so the standard English usage we reach for is always illusory, out of reach, but worth striving for. We can teach how to reach for standard English use, how to work at accommodating our language, but we cannot point to a variety of English and say, that is it. Thus, standard English is an attitude about the use of the language which expects accommodation along the three dimensions I have outlined. It is not a particular variety. Those who point at linguists and say, "but you write in standard English; how can you say there isn't one," are right in that when we are addressing them, our language use incorporates an accommodation to their expectations.

This definition raises, of course, the question of who must accommodate and when. Ideally, addressor and addressee accommodate to each other, but in practice, I think power or relative social ranking determines who accommodates most. In any given context, the more powerful accommodates less, but not always. When a great gap in social or economic status exists, often there seems to be the assumption that the inferior member cannot accommodate, so the superior does, and demonstrates in the accommodation his proficiency in standard English usage, or assumes that the inferior can accommodate receptively if not productively, so does not alter his language. Perhaps the focus has been on the social criterion because it is the easiest to correlate with external criteria such as wealth and power. Little organized work has been done on what constitutes clarity, except by philosophers and rhetoricians, because what is clear in one context is not clear in another, and we cannot easily rank contexts for clarity in the same way or with the same ease we rank contexts socially. For instance, a chemistry teacher can explain the same concept clearly in two quite different ways—once for a beginning class, once for an advanced class. Both are regarded as standard usage, because both are accommodated. We are beginning to look more closely at situational accommodation through speech act and discourse studies, but much needs to be done there. We recognize register accommodation, or lack of it, when we hear or see it, but cannot define it very well.

One last factor should be mentioned, the underlying awareness that language is exceedingly complex, that the external defining contexts are equally complex, and that we must exert a continuing effort to achieve a working, useful accommodation, let alone a perfect one. If we tell people that there is no standard English, they will want to listen, to believe, but ultimately they won't because they know there is. They know that they must accommodate somehow, and are asking how. We deny the importance and necessity of accommodation by denying the existence of standard English use and thereby hand the right to define standard English use to those who offer simplistic, and dangerous, definitions, ones that focus only on social factors and correctness rules. We allow it to become rules of etiquette or arcane magic rather than a scientific study.

REFERENCES

Bolinger, Dwight. 1975. *Aspects of Language.* New York: Harcourt Brace Jovanovich, Second Edition.

Ferguson, Charles. 1974. "Language Problems of Variation and Reportoire," in: *Language as a Human Problem.* Ed. Einar Haugen and Morton Bloomfield. New York: W. W. Norton, pp. 23–32.

Fries, C. C. 1940. *American English Grammar.* New York: Appleton-Century-Crofts.

Garvin, Paul L. 1964. "The Standard Language Problem: Concepts and Methods," in: *Language in Culture and Society.* Ed. Dell Hymes. New York: Harper & Row, pp. 521–523.

Giles, Howard, and Philip M. Smith. 1979. "Accommodation Theory: Optimal Levels of

Convergence," in: *Language and Social Psychology.* Ed. Howard Giles and Robert N. St. Clair. Baltimore: University Park Press, pp. 45–65.

Haugen, Einar. 1971. "Instrumentalism in Language Planning," in: *Can Language Be Planned?* Ed. Joan Rubin and Bjorn Jernudd. Honolulu: University of Hawaii Press, pp. 281–289.

Labov, William. 1972. *Language in the Inner City: Studies in the Black English Vernacular.* Philadelphia: University of Pennsylvania Press.

Mitchell, Richard. 1979. *Less Than Words Can Say.* Boston: Little, Brown.

Newman, Edwin. 1975. *Strictly Speaking.* New York: Warner.

Quirk, Randolph, and Sidney Greenbaum. 1973. *A Concise Grammar of Contemporary English.* New York: Harcourt Brace Jovanovich.

Shaughnessy, Mina P. 1977. *Errors and Expectations.* New York: Oxford University Press.

Thakerar, Jitendra N., Howard Giles, and Jenny Cheshire. 1982. "Psychological and Linguistic Parameters of Speech Accommodation Theory," in: *Advances in the Social Psychology of Language.* Ed. Colin Fraser and Klaus R. Scherer. Cambridge, England: Cambridge University Press, pp. 205–255.

Traugott, Elizabeth Closs, and Mary Lousie Pratt. 1980. *Linguistics for Students of Literature.* New York: Harcourt Brace and Jovanovich.

Wolfram, Walt, and Ralph W. Fasold. 1974. *The Study of Social Dialects in American English.* Englewood Cliffs, NJ: Prentice-Hall.

What Makes Good English Good?

John Algeo

Human beings are a peculiar species. We have a rage for order: out of the great booming chaos of the world around us, we obsessively make pattern and regularity. Out of the wilderness, we make cities. Out of experience, we make histories. Out of speech, we make grammars. And in the process of turning chaos into order, we create values.

The human species has been called *homo sapiens,* the earthy one who knows or experiences. But we might as well be called *homo judex,* the judge, because an inescapable human impulse is to distinguish between good and bad. For us, the good is its own warrant. As Mammy Yokum was wont to instruct her physically sound and morally pure, if intellectually disadvantaged, offspring, Li'l Abner: "Good is better than evil because it's so much nicer." Or, as *Webster's New World Dictionary of the American Language,* with which Charlton Laird was associated, defines the word, *good* is "a general term of approval or commendation, meaning 'as it should be.'"

Should is a powerful and distinctly human concept. Wars have been fought over it. Among English speakers, the Grammar Wars began in the seventeenth century, when pedagogues fell out over why and how to teach Latin. One camp wanted to teach grammar as an end in itself, because knowing grammar is good. Another camp wanted to teach grammar only so that young English scholars could read the great works of Latin literature. The two camps were roughly the equivalents three hundred years ago of scientific linguists and literary humanists (if I may use the word *humanist* without calling down the wrath of the Reverend Jerry Falwell). The equivalence is only approximate, however, because the grammar-as-an-end-in-itself advocates of the 1600s had a strong bent toward logic and neatening up the language, whereas the grammar-as-a-tool-for-literature advocates argued that the ancients could hardly have been wrong in the way they used their own language and thus needed no help from grammarians intent on regularizing and improving Latin.

Joseph Webbe, a doughty combatant in the lists of the Grammar Wars, scored against the grammarians in his 1622 book, *An Appeale to Truth,* by writing that

> they haue not onely weakned and broken speech, by reducing it vnto the poore and penurious prescript of Grammar-rules; but haue also corrupted it with many errors, in that they haue spoken otherwise than they ought to doo: well, in respect of rules; but ill, in respect of custome, which is the *Lady and Mistress* of speaking.[1]

Our modern Grammar Wars (chronicled by Edward Finegan in his *Attitudes toward English Usage: The History of a War of Words*) have seen a curious realignment of forces. Today it is those whose principal concern is with studying language as an end in itself who are most in sympathy with Webbe's position "that we can neither in the Latine, nor in any other Tongue, be obedient vnto other rules or reasons, than Custome and our sense of hearing,"[2] whereas it is some contemporary men and women of letters who ignore custom and their sense of hearing in favor of "the poore and penurious prescript of Grammar-rules." And so we have spawned a new subspecies, variously called *pop-grammarians* or *usageasters* (the latter by Thomas L. Clark).[3]

The Grammar Wars go on. And, as they were more than three hundred years ago, they are still concerned with the question of what good English is. What makes good English good? A variety of answers have been given to that question, and since the question has been so long with us, it is useful occasionally to summarize the answers that have been given.

What I propose to do briefly in this essay is to look at ten of the grounds that have been proposed for deciding what good English is. I focus on grounds proposed by Theodore M. Bernstein, mentioning a few other writers on usage to

[1]Joseph Webbe, *An Appeale to Truth, in the Controuersie betweene Art, & Vse; about the Best and Most Expedient Course in Languages* (1622). Reprinted in English Linguistics, 1500–1800, ed. R. C. Alston, no. 42 (Menston, England: Scolar Press, 1967), p. 22.

[2]Ibid., p. 46.

[3]Thomas L. Clark, "The Usageasters," *American Speech* 55 (1980): 131–136.

show that Bernstein is not a linguistic sport. I single out Bernstein, not because he is particularly better or worse than others of the tribe, but because he wrote a good bit on the subject of usage, because he is typical of the modern man of letters, and because he was kind enough to provide a handy list of criteria for determining good usage.

COMMUNICATIVE CRITERION

In *The Careful Writer* (1965), Bernstein equates good English with successful communication: "What good writing can do . . . is to assure that the writer is really in communication with the reader, that he is delivering his message unmistakably."[4] Porter Perrin has a similar criterion for good English: "So far as the writer's language furthers his intended effect, it is good; so far as it fails to further that effect, it is bad, no matter how 'correct' it may be."[5]

These are pious statements, which, like promises never to curtail Social Security benefits, are made to be broken. Bernstein does not even get out of the introduction to his book before he fractures the ideal of communication: "Let us insist that *disinterested* be differentiated from *uninterested*."[6] He urges this difference as essential to the existence of good English, with no concern for communicating with those readers for whom the two words are synonyms. If Bernstein had been really concerned about successful communication, he would not have advised his readers to avoid *disinterested* in the sense 'uninterested' but rather told them not to use it at all, because the word is ambiguous. Bernstein's point about the need for communication is obviously well made, but it is seldom taken seriously by those who make it.

Bernstein goes on to enumerate six other sources for determining good English. It is worth looking at them seriatim.

LITERARY CRITERION

Bernstein adduces "the practices of reputable writers, past and present."[7] This criterion, like that of successful communication, is practically de rigueur in any discussion of usage. It is also a criterion of respectable antiquity. Webbe in 1622 had cited authors like Cicero as models of good Latin, in distinction to the grammarians among his contemporaries who invented rules that imposed more order on Latin than was to be found in classical authors. The authority of the literati was also invoked by Thomas Lounsbury, who used an elegant chiasmus in his

---

[4]Theodore M. Bernstein, *The Careful Writer: A Modern Guide to English Usage* (New York: Atheneum, 1965), p. vii.

[5]Porter G. Perrin, *Writer's Guide and Index to English,* 4th ed. rev. Karl W. Dykema and Wilma R. Ebbitt (Chicago: Scott Foresman, 1965), p. 27.

[6]Bernstein, p. xv.

[7]Ibid., p. viii.

Standard of Usage in English: "The best, and indeed the only proper, usage is the usage of the best."[8]

As appealing as it may be to English teachers, the literary criterion suffers from several weaknesses. One is the difficulty of deciding which authors are reputable or best and which are not; there is a danger of circularity—writers who do not use good English (as the decider conceives it) are clearly not reputable or best, however widely read they may be. Another difficulty is that of deciding how far past or present one will look for models of good English: Joyce Carol Oates? Virginia Woolf? Ralph Waldo Emerson? Fanny Burney? Shakespeare? Chaucer? The Beowulf poet? In fact, popular writers on usage cite reputable writers as exemplifiers of good English rather infrequently. They are rather more apt to quote the words of famous authors as examples of blunders by the mighty, Homer nodding, and all that. Since the days of Bishop Lowth, citing errors from the works of great writers (or of one's opponents) has been a game rivaled only by the current popularity of Trivial Pursuit.

SCHOLARLY CRITERION

Bernstein's next criterion for good English is from "the observations and discoveries of linguistic scholars."[9] He carefully qualifies this criterion in two ways, however. First, "the work of past scholars has, when necessary, been updated," and second, "the work of contemporary scholars has been weighed judiciously." That is, *homo judex* is free to change (update) or to ignore (weigh judiciously) whatever he does not like. Although clearly subordinate to reputable writers, linguistic scholars seem like an authoritative group to invoke, especially if you don't have to pay any attention to them. We like being told that the message we are getting is backed by authorities: 9 out of 10 doctors, 64 percent of economists, any and all linguistic scholars. However, the fact that something is said to be recommended by doctors or economists or linguistic scholars is of no importance. What is important is the evidence on which doctors, economists, and linguistic scholars speak. And therefore this criterion is no criterion at all. It is not evidence, but publicity hype.

PEDAGOGICAL CRITERION

The following criterion is even phonier. It is "the predilections of teachers of English, wherever—right or wrong, like it or not—these predilections have become deeply ingrained in the language itself."[10] It is not at all clear that any predilections of any teachers of English have ever become deeply ingrained in

---

[8]Thomas R. Lounsbury, *The Standard of Usage in English* (New York: Harper, 1908), p. vi.
[9]Bernstein, p. viii.
[10]Ibid., p. viii.

our language. There may be one or two trivial matters for which the sweat of English teachers has dripped so incessantly on the stone of real language that it has finally worn a small indentation—the pronunciation of the *t* in *often* is probably one—but on the whole, not only are English teachers overworked, underpaid, and poorly educated, they are also ineffective.

The archetype of the starched schoolmarm who has devoted her life, at the sacrifice of all personal comfort and happiness, to upholding standards and educating into self-awareness the pliable young minds entrusted to her charge is as mythological as Parson Weems's George Washington. Bernstein seems to be remembering with ambivalent nostalgia some Miss Thistlebottom from the eighth grade, who, in the haze of fifty intervening years, has taken on the epic proportions of Candida, Martin Joos's Muse of Grammar.[11] The reality is likely to have been thinner and more wizened. The predilections of teachers of English that have become deeply ingrained in our language are probably a null set.

LOGICAL CRITERION

Bernstein's next criterion is "what makes for clarity, precision, and logical presentation."[12] This is another mom-and-apple-pie criterion. However important clarity, precision, and logic are, our impression of them in language is likely to be a function of our familiarity with particular words or grammatical structures. Those for whom *disinterested* means 'uninterested' find that use perfectly clear and precise. The difference between *She be here* and *She here* is clear and logical to anyone who understands it. Those who find such expressions muddled, vague, and illogical have got a problem. But the problem is theirs; it is not one for those who use the expressions. Talk about clarity and logic in language is often an unconscious confession of ignorance and ethnocentrism. What we know, we think logical; what we don't, illogical.

This criterion is often expressed by saying that good writing is the expression of good thinking. Ambrose Bierce, for example, held such a position in his delightfully quirky little book *Write It Right,* subtitled *A Little Blacklist of Literary Faults,* in which he says that good writing "is clear thinking made visible."[13] Bierce is probably best known for his advice to prefer *ruined* to *dilapidated* since the latter—coming from Latin *lapis* 'a stone'—"cannot properly be used of any but a stone structure."[14] That is an example of diaphanous, rather than clear, thinking.

A similar standard was adopted by Richard Mitchell, whose *Underground Grammarian* announced in its first issue: "Clear language engenders clear

---

[11]Martin Joos, *The Five Clocks* (New York: Harcourt, 1967).
[12]Bernstein, pp. viii–ix.
[13]Ambrose Bierce, *Write It Right: A Little Blacklist of Literary Faults* (New York: Neale, 1909; New York: Union Library Association, 1934), p. 5.
[14]Ibid., p. 23.

thought, and clear thought is the most important benefit of education."[15] One may subscribe to the idea that clear thought is the best possible result of education, while finding the proposition that clear language produces clear thought to be muddled. However, one can forgive almost any amount of Mitchell's muddling for the sake of his épée, for example, his palpable hit in saying that "so many [college administrators] seem to be born aluminum-siding salesmen who took a wrong turn somewhere along the line."[16]

The link between good language and clear or exact thinking has been made by many writers on usage. One more example, an older one, will have to suffice. John O'London, who dedicated his book *Is It Good English?* to "Men, Women, and Grammarians," thereby expressing his opinion of our tribe, wrote: "Good English follows clear thinking rather than that system of rules called Grammar which youth loathes and maturity forgets."[17]

A problem with the equivalence of good language and clear thinking is that the latter might be defined as thinking that arrives logically at correct conclusions. T. S. Eliot and John Steinbeck, whom one might suppose to use rather good language, have thought themselves into rather different conclusions. It is hard to see how Eliot and Steinbeck can each be said to be clear thinking on social questions. Or, as Jim Quinn points out, "If good thought made good writing, and good writing made good thought, then Immanuel Kant, Hegel, and Ludwig Wittgenstein are not worth reading."[18]

PERSONAL CRITERION

Bernstein's penultimate criterion is the personal preference of the author, of which he asks rhetorically: "And why not? . . . After all, it's my book."[19] Why not, indeed. This is the most honest criterion Bernstein has set forward. By asserting it, he agrees with a cartoon that appeared shortly after the publication of Nancy Mitford's *Noblesse Oblige,* a popular treatment of the difference between U (upper class) and non-U language.[20] In the cartoon, a tweedy, horsy-looking woman says to her companion at the tea table, "I always say, if it's me it's U."

Everyone is certainly entitled to a choice among linguistic options. And if you can get people to buy a book in which you state your choices, why not? First amendment, free enterprise, and all that. Right on, Ted! Let's throw out all that malarkey about communicating unmistakably, reputable writers, linguistic

---

[15]Richard Mitchell, *The Graves of Academe* (Boston: Little, Brown, 1981), p. 27.

[16]Ibid., p. 28.

[17]John O'London, *Is It Good English?* (New York: Putnam's, 1925), p. xi.

[18]Jim Quinn, *American Tongue and Cheek: A Populist Guide to Our Language* (New York: Pantheon, 1980), p. 76.

[19]Bernstein, p. ix.

[20]Nancy Mitford, ed., *Noblesse Oblige* (New York: Harper & Row, 1956).

scholars, English teachers, and logic, and just hunker down with good old ipse dixit. If it's me, it's U. As H. L. Mencken said, "No one ever went broke underestimating the intelligence of the American public."

PROFESSIONAL CRITERION

Bernstein's last criterion is a letdown from the preceding high point. He cites his experience in working with language as the editor of the *New York Times* and congratulates himself on the newspaper's "precision, accuracy, clarity, and—especially in recent years [under Bernstein's editorship, presumably]—good writing."[21] All this criterion does is to establish Bernstein's credentials for ipse-dixiting. It is a sad anticlimax. How much better to finish off with a glorious burst of egotistic self-assertion. Well, we can't all be perfect.

People who earn their living by the word, particularly the written word, know how to use words effectively. If they did not, they would not earn much of a living. But effective journalism and even great literature are obviously not the same thing as good English. If they were, only effective journalists and great writers would be using good English. That Bernstein spent many years as an editor, worrying about the language of others, explains how he came to write five books on usage; it does not warrant his claiming special authority to determine what is good language.

STYLISTIC CRITERION

Other writers have offered still further criteria for good English. Some have identified the stylistic characteristics of bad writing and thus by inference defined what is good. Richard Mitchell, the Underground Grammarian, for example, focuses on the sins of wordiness, weasel words *(attempt to, may)*, passive verbs with no agent, and "needless neologism."[22] Similarly, Edwin Newman castigates cliches, jargon, voguish words, redundancy, and innovations—or what he imagines to be innovations (they frequently are nothing of the kind).

A digression: the subtitle of Newman's first book *(Strictly Speaking: Will America Be the Death of English?)*[23] identifies him as a disciple of the Armageddon school of usageasters. He, like John Simon, whose *Paradigms Lost*[24] is subtitled *Reflections on Literacy and Its Decline,* sees us as living in the time of the end. It is ironic that the demise of English should be predicted at a

---

[21]Bernstein, p. ix.
[22]Mitchell, pp. 27, 49.
[23]Edwin Newman, *Strictly Speaking: Will America Be the Death of English?* (New York: Warner Books, 1974, 1975).
[24]John Simon, *Paradigms Lost: Reflections on Literacy and Its Decline* (New York: Potter, 1980).

time when the language is being used by more people for more purposes in more places around the globe than ever before. Thomas Lounsbury expressed an ironic insight that is as applicable today as it was in 1908, when he wrote it:

> There seems to have been in every period of the past, as there is now, a distinct apprehension in the minds of very many worthy persons that the English tongue is always in the condition of approaching collapse, and that arduous efforts must be put forth, and put forth persistently, in order to save it from destruction.[25]

In a generation between Lounsbury and Newman-Simon, the anonymous "Vigilans" was another of the Dying-Declining-Doomsters. In his book *Chamber of Horrors* he castigated jargon, which he characterized as involving circumlocutions; long, abstract, unfamiliar words using classical roots; phrases where single words will do; padding; cautious wording and euphemism; vagueness and woolliness; and esoteric expressions.[26]

Our thoughts and our language are certainly intimately related, if they are not in fact the same thing. And pompous language is fair game. It is great sport to expose and snicker at egregious examples of linguistic bombast and thick-headedness, as the Armageddon usageasters are wont to do. But such sport is easy to overdo. The cannons of Mitchell-Newman-Simon-"Vigilans" tend to produce, not a bang, but a whimper—kvetching against petty violations of an idiosyncratic standard of style. It is remarkable that so much has been written, so seriously, about such trivia.

DEMOCRATIC CRITERION

A refreshingly different approach to the subject is that of Jim Quinn, whose *American Tongue and Cheek* is a lusty defense of many of the bugbears of contemporary usageasters. Quinn delights in showing that usageasters frequently do not know what they are talking about and that their criteria for defining good language are nonsense. Quinn is straightforward in stating his own criterion: "For me, the only sensible standard of correctness is usage by ordinary people."[27]

And yet Quinn's own usage populism is also nonsense if taken at face value. Ordinary people and extraordinary people alike make mistakes in using language; mistakes are a part of usage. When people notice mistakes—their own or others'—they correct them. Editing language is just as natural as producing it, and so is passing judgment on some forms of language as better than others. The values we attach to our linguistic options are just as much a part of the language as the options themselves. We are value-ridden, judgmental beings. As a piece

---

[25]Lounsbury, p. 2.
[26]"Vigilans," *Chamber of Horrors: A Glossary of Official Jargon Both English and American,* intro. Eric Partridge (New York: British Book Centre, 1952).
[27]Quinn, p. 11.

of rhetoric, a sortie in the Grammar Wars, Quinn's position is great tactics, but it is weak strategy.

ELITIST CRITERION

In America we have no official aristocracy, whose speechways might provide a standard for the commoners of the realm. So we make do with a less well-defined group: educated, respected, important people in the community. Their usage is sometimes held up as a model for the hoi polloi of the citizenry. Bergen and Cornelia Evans in their *Dictionary of Contemporary American Usage* write: "Respectable English . . . means the kind of English that is used by the most respected people, the sort of English that will make readers or listeners regard you as an educated person."[28] William and Mary Morris echo the theoretical sentiment, if not the practical sensibleness, of the Evanses. The Morrises define *standard* (which is not the same as *good,* but is related) as "word usage occurring in the speech and writing of literate, educated users of the language."[29]

Another digression: the *Harper Dictionary of Contemporary Usage,* which the Morrises edited, deserves special acknowledgment as among the most ignorant usage guides to have made the big time. My favorite lapse is their explanation of the use of the objective case for the subject of an infinitive. Under the heading "infinitive, subject of the," they write:

> The confusion about the use of "I" and "me" is reflected in such statements as "The first thing for somebody like you or I to do. . . ." The *subject of the infinitive* "to do" must be in the accusative or objective case. Since the objective case of the first personal pronoun is "me," the statement should be "The first thing for somebody like you or me to do. . . ."[30]

The Morrises tripped over their own grammatical razzle-dazzle. In the example they cite, the subject of the infinitive is *somebody; you or me* is the object of the preposition *like.* So the example is irrelevant to the point for which it is cited. The Morrises are educated users of the language, but grammatically they are booboisie.

CONCLUSION

There are other criteria we might identify. But these ten are enough to show what the tendency has been. In deciding what makes good English good, commentators have tried to correlate variation with some outside factor—success in

[28]Bergen and Cornelia Evans, *A Dictionary of Contemporary American Usage* (New York: Random House, 1957), p. v.

[29]William and Mary Morris, with the assistance of a panel of 136 distinguished consultants on usage, *Harper Dictionary of Contemporary Usage* (New York: Harper & Row, 1975), p. xxii.

[30]Ibid., p. 338.

communication, literary excellence, scholarly authority (at least nominally), pedagogical effort, logic, personal authority, professional expertise, esthetic style, a democratic majority, or an elite model. The unspoken assumption is that good English ought to be good for something.

Efforts to correlate goodness in language with something else are all flawed. Good English is simply what English speakers, in a particular situation, agree to regard as good. There are as many kinds of good English as there are situations in which English is used and sorts of participants who use it. Standard English is one sort of good English—good, that is, in the circumstances that call for it—but it is not the only sort.

Robert Pooley says something similar in *The Teaching of English Usage:*

> The English language is full of possible variations. The term "good usage" implies success in making choices in these variations such that the smallest number of persons (and particularly persons held in esteem) are distracted by the choices."[31]

Good English is the cellophane man—you can see right through it. It does not distract because in any given circumstance it is what the participants expect.

To paraphrase Mammy Yokum, "Good English is so much nicer than bad English because it's better." There is no external criterion by which we can judge what is good in language, either standard English or any other kind. Good language is just what the users of the language have decided is good. Their judgments are exasperatingly inconsistent and unpredictable. Moreover, the bounds they assign to the good are disconcertingly fuzzy; those bounds keep changing, as users of the language push this way and that way against them, continually altering the limits of acceptability. Finally, what is good is wholly relative to the circumstance and the speakers. Despite Wilson Follett's asseveration in *Modern American Usage* that "there is a [i.e., one] right way to use words and construct sentences, and many wrong ways,"[32] good in language is multivalent (that's *mul'ti-va'lent* or *mul-tiv'a-lent,* depending on the circumstances).

Because good English is so diverse, to use it in more than a few circumstances requires an equally diverse knowledge and a fine sense of what is appropriate under varying conditions. Charlton Laird made one of the most sensible comments ever written about usage when he observed, in his introductory essay to *Webster's New World Dictionary,* that "good usage requires wide knowledge and tasteful discrimination; it cannot be learned easily."[33] It is appropriate, especially here, for Laird to have the last word.

---

[31]Robert C. Pooley, *The Teaching of English Usage* (Urbana, Ill.: National Council of Teachers of English, 1974), p. 5.

[32]Wilson Follett, *Modern American Usage: A Guide* (New York: Hill and Wang, 1966), p. 3.

[33]Charlton Laird, "Language and the Dictionary," in *Webster's New World Dictionary of the American Language,* Second College Edition, ed. David B. Guralnik (New York and Cleveland: World, 1970), p. xxv.

Debunking Some Myths About Traditional Grammar

Linda Miller Cleary and Nancy Lund

Learning traditional grammar has been part of coming of age in America. Our parents had to study it, we had to study it, and now, as teachers of English, we struggle with how to teach it . . . or whether to teach it. Well-meaning parents and administrators tell us that grammar is good for our students. However, even though research has told us for over fifty years that traditional grammar does not help with reading or writing or thinking, fifty years' worth of students have spent a good deal of their time in English classes from grades two to twelve studying grammar. This article will examine the myths that have supported the teaching of the rule/exercise approach to grammar.

When strictly used, the term "grammar" refers to the set of rules that deal with the form and function of words and their arrangement of meaningful order, but the word "grammar" has also come to refer to the isolated study of usage, mechanics, punctuation, and even occasionally spelling. In short, it is often seen as anything in that little book of "basics" which accompanies the literature anthology under the arm of the student bound for the English classroom.

Experts in educational research tell us that there is a fifty-year lag between the publication of research and its implementation in the classroom (Lehmann and Mehrens, 1979). Clearly it is time to "re-view" the well-entrenched myths that have sprung up about traditional grammar and to debunk them. The fifty years are up.

MYTH 1: THAT TRADITIONAL GRAMMAR IS AN ACCURATE DESCRIPTION OF STANDARD ENGLISH

Grammars are attempts to describe the structure of language. The problem with our "traditional" grammar is that it has evolved out of the 18th century neoclassicists' attempt to glorify our language by perceiving within it a Latin structure. Crunching the English language into the Latin structure was like crunching a foot into an ill-fitting shoe. It has not been a good fit. Yet to the neoclassicists (who all knew and revered Latin), language was a divine inspiration, originally perfect, but debased by man (Postman and Weingartner, 1969). They implemented the crunch so that English might absorb some of the linguistic purity with which Latin and Greek were imbued. In his book written in 1762, *The Short Introduction to English Grammar* (1762), Robert Lowth outlawed the double negatives that kept popping out of the Latin overlay on the English sentence. At the time, a rising middle class in search of respect and status were only too willing to use language as a mode to get that status. Their children were trained in Lowth's English even though it was not characteristic of even the upper class at the time.

Language has remained a tool for the perpetuation of social class ever since. The irony is that Priestly (the discoverer of oxygen) surveyed the language of the English people to find that from royal to peasants, every social class used double negatives (Priestly, 1768). Writers from Chaucer to Shakespeare used double negatives as well. Now standard English has exorcised the double negative in formal written text, but other structures that Lowth would have fainted over have crept back into acceptable speech and in many cases into acceptable writing. For example, split infinitives and end-of-the-sentence prepositions (both of which were outlawed by Dryden because they didn't occur in the Latin sentence) have reappeared (Postman and Weingartner, 1966).

That traditional grammar is an inaccurate description of the English language should give us some impetus to look at some other myths that claim that the teaching of grammar in the traditional manner has an effect on our use of language or on the use of our minds.

MYTH 2: THAT LEARNING GRAMMAR DISCIPLINES THE MIND

There is no research that has proven that grammar disciplines the mind. Hoyt found no correlation between the study of grammar and the ability to think logically (Sherwin, 1969). In some ways, grammar is confusing instead of clarifying (Hillock, 1986). Once a student has identified the grammatical pattern to be learned, thinking can become rote. Take, for example, the s-v-i.o.-d.o. pattern. If you give a student twenty sentences with this pattern, thinking can become automatic. There may be an original insight, but getting students to internalize the insight seems to fail; hence, the necessity to repeat instruction year after year. Conscious knowledge of what students already know and use unconsciously early in life may not seem relevant or important to the child or adolescent.

Many grammatical concepts are in the abstract, making thinking very difficult for students who are not developmentally ready. In addition, some of the definitions we ask students to understand are not very logical. The definition of a pronoun is "a word that takes the place of a noun." The word "boy" is a noun and not a pronoun. Even the definition of a sentence is confusing: A sentence is a group of words containing a subject and a verb and expressing a complete thought. What is a complete thought? What may be a "complete thought" to one person may not be to another. Children tend to punctuate by complete thoughts rather than by structural completeness until they have read or written to internalize sentence patterns. They have difficulty in seeing the run-ons and fragments that occur in their complete thoughts. They have no difficulty, however, in finding fragments in our best authors who use them to further their craft.

We also have to come to some informed perspectives. What's more important: determining whether a prepositional phrase is adjectival or adverbial or writing about how *Huckleberry Finn* reflects life? If we want students to use higher order thinking skills, then they need to read literature, interpret it, and write about it. Students are often excited about searching for meaning in reading and creating meaning in writing before they are ready to make adjectival and adverbial distinctions.

MYTH 3: THAT GRAMMAR IS BEST LEARNED DEDUCTIVELY, FROM RULE TO EXAMPLES

For some years now linguists have studied the way that children acquire language. Children listen to the language around them and learn to speak by a process of unconsciously building a rule system from the examples of language presented to them. This is an inductive process. "Students need to develop good intuitive sense of grammar, but they can do this best through indirect rather that direct instruction" (Weaver, 1979, p. 5). Correction doesn't affect their language acquisition, though some take it to heart emotionally. Children persist in incorrect forms until they have accumulated enough instances and maturation to figure the rules out for themselves (Moskowitz, 1982). Knowing that the human mind learns concepts more effectively in an inductive manner brings to question our pedagogical strategy in teaching grammar—from rule to example to exercise. Children learn their language from home as well as from their peers. If children learn nonstandard grammar and usage at home (their home dialect), it is difficult to eradicate that grammar by "grammar instruction" of rule and example and exercise at school (Cleary, 1988). Time would be better spent if students read and wrote extensively. They would begin to make inductive distinctions between oral and written language and to develop sentence and story sense.

MYTH 4: THAT LEARNING GRAMMAR HELPS WITH THE STUDY OF A FOREIGN LANGUAGE

For years foreign language teachers have told us that students need to know English grammar before they can learn another language. It is embarrassing and frustrating when we are asked if we teach grammar when we know that our students have studied grammar from grade two to twelve. Not only does it simply not stick, but it doesn't transfer. There are several reasons for lack of transfer. English grammar is unlike other grammars in that it is structured on word order while many languages are based on inflection. Thus, syntactic structure in English may be quite different from those in other languages. Knowing grammatical terminology does not increase a student's proficiency in learning another language. What may be defined as an adjective in one language may be a noun in another. And except for a few pronouns, English does not have grammatical gender; other languages do.

In the last decade or so, grammar has been a sticky issue with foreign language teachers. They're in the same quandary as English teachers: should grammar (not English but that of the language being taught) be taught at all? Their argument is that if the goal of learning a language is proficiency in communication, why spend time on teaching grammar? Time would better be spent on expression and meaning. Their contention is that students can become proficient users of language without memorizing grammatical rules (Garrett, 1986). The same holds true for English, as our first graders come to school with an almost fully developed grammar system.

Actually, foreign language teachers perform an important service for our students of the English language that we as English teachers have difficulty doing in isolation. Instead of English grammar helping with the study of foreign language, quite the opposite is true. Many of us have had the experience of finally making sense of English grammar when we study a foreign language. It is in comparison that the structures of our own language become clear.

MYTH 5: THAT THE STUDY OF GRAMMAR IMPROVES READING AND HELPS WITH THE INTERPRETATION OF LITERATURE

No evidence supports this conclusion. If anything, the reverse is true. As previously stated, the act of reading itself fosters the understanding of the structure of language as grammar exercises never will do. Recent research refers to communicative competence, the unconscious knowledge about the structure and function of language, including meaning, structure, and sound. By the time students enter school when they are five or six, they have a great fund of unconscious knowledge about the spoken language and use it rather well. Whatever is not developed will grow systematically as they learn to read and write. Through reading, these youngsters pick up a lot of information on story grammar or genre schemes (the conventional organization of a particular story or genre, e.g., setting, plot, resolution), the beginning steps in understanding literary elements (Pearson, 1978).

Current practice in reading instruction emphasizes comprehension strategies such as story mapping, clustering, webbing, prereading writing, all of which lead to the understanding of literature and give students experience with sentence structure that models further complexity year by year. Furthermore, research also indicates that preschoolers who write (scribbles, invented spellings, etc.) have a rather sophisticated knowledge of language, especially sound. This might be one of the most important steps in learning how to read. Researchers are also telling us that students who write become better readers, and readers who write, become better writers (Weaver, 1979; Graves, 1983).

This holds true for the first grader as well as for the senior. In short, if we want to improve reading instruction and literary interpretation, we must have our students read and write daily. Not only will comprehension and interpretation be improved, but students will also learn the structure of language.

MYTH 6: THAT THE LEARNING OF TRADITIONAL GRAMMAR IMPROVES SPOKEN AND WRITTEN EXPRESSION

Since the turn of the century, studies consistently and emphatically have shown that there is not a direct correlation between the knowledge of grammar and writing competency. There is a correlation between the amount of exposure to literature and writing, and between oral and written communication. Recent literature in the field cite a number of studies [Harris (1962), Elley (1976)] to support this conclusion. Ingrid Strom (1960), after reviewing over fifty studies, concluded that writing is a far better way of teaching sentence structure, usage, punctuation, and other such elements than are activities such as identifying the parts of speech, diagramming, and memorizing rules (Hartwell, 1985). More research needs to be done to investigate the effects of the functional teaching of grammatical concepts, usage, and mechanics—the folding of language instruction into writing instruction.

Students enter school with syntactic structure nearly intact. Most so-called grammar problems are really usage problems (problems in dialect difference); and writing problems usually deal with usage, mechanics, and organization, or with a student's lack of confidence in having something to say. If students show a lack of growth in writing, it is probably because they have had little opportunity to write (Cleary, 1988). Ironically, it is usually the least successful students who are most often involved in the isolated drills that become roadblocks to good writing.

The hours of remedial exercises that these students do often keep them from becoming fluent in the other language arts and may contribute to a feeling of low self-esteem as students (Cleary, 1988). If, however, instruction in usage is folded into writing instruction, students can formally compare the difference between their home dialect and standard English and can begin to express themselves in both dialects, learning which dialect to use for which audience.

If we want students to become better writers, we need to have them read and write daily, avoiding countless and futile hours of labeling sentences. Students need to create sentences, not tear them apart; it is in these generative activities that they come to an intuitive sense of language. Patrick Hartwell poignantly notes that if knowing grammar makes better writers, then linguists and grammarians would be our best writers, and, he adds, "I can certify that they are, on the whole, not" (Hartwell, 1985, p. 115). Studies reviewed by Hillocks (1986) indicate that exercises in sentence combining and sentence construction are the only exercises that have beneficial effect on syntactic maturity. It is not known, however, how lasting the effects are.

MYTH 7: THAT GRAMMAR INSTRUCTION RAISES SAT SCORES

The verbal section of the SAT is primarily a test of a student's vocabulary and reading comprehension. Parts of speech and parts of the sentence are not tested. The SAT verbal areas include antonyms, analogies, sentence completion (based on vocabulary and sentence sense), and reading comprehension. If we wish to help students perform well on the SAT, then we need to give them many and varied experiences in literature and vocabulary development. It should also be noted that most standardized achievement tests focus on usage, mechanics, spelling, vocabulary, reading comprehension, and knowledge pertaining to composition. It has long been shown that students who read and write often excel on these tests. Time taken away from reading and writing for formal grammar instruction will work to the detriment of students' test scores.

IN CONCLUSION

It's time to take another look at what we really want our students to know. More time is spent in our schools from grades seven to twelve on grammar instruction than on any other English instruction. Many researchers think this is why the time spent on grammar instruction is inversely proportional to progress in writing. While students are spending time on grammar drills and exercises, they are not learning to write by writing or reading. Moreover, students in many schools receive a large dosage of grammar from grade two on. Each fall they come to school with an excitement and eagerness to learn; but each fall we start them out with the same definitions: A noun is the name of a person, place, or thing. This boring repetition year after year shows negligible results; yet, traditional grammar still has a prominent place in the curriculum. By the tenth grade students are still identifying the parts of speech and many still fail tests on them. That in itself should indicate the futility of long term instruction on traditional grammar.

With some of the myths about the teaching of traditional grammar debunked, we can get a clearer picture of how grammar study, or more broadly, language study, should be taught in our schools. Does this mean that attention should no longer be given to the parts and order of the English sentence? No. Knowing the names of the parts of speech (and the parts of a sentence) provides both the student and the teacher with common terminology. Students need these terms for car parts to discuss the adjustment of a carburetor with the owner. More importantly, if the students talk about their writing with other students and the teacher, the students will remember these terms, and they will not have to learn them over every year.

Broader language study, the study of grammar, usage, and mechanics, can be taught with positive results in connection with writing or in mini-lessons right before a writing assignment, for it is in students' own writing that they can see their dialect differences and can consider why it might be economically beneficial to acquire a more standard form. Students should be and can be taught to value their personal language and also be able to vary that language for different audiences. Studying problems that occur frequently in a classroom may alert students to become sensitive to those errors/problems when reading their own or their peers' papers. By eleventh or twelfth grade most students are developmentally ready to rediscover language in all its complexity, and to be challenged by "the tantalizing problems that language has always posed for those who are puzzled and intrigued by the mysteries of human intelligence" (Chomsky, 1982, p. 84). If they haven't been inundated with "grammar" study previously, they are curious and eager. Phrase structure rules, transformational syntax, morphology, phonology, phonetics, and semantics can be fascinating to the student who wants such knowledge. It is also clear that prospective teachers of English must have a thorough understanding of their language to help their students use language effectively (Weaver, 1979).

Debunking some of the myths that surround the teaching of traditional grammar is important so that we, as teachers of English, can consider what to do for our students. The teaching and learning of traditional grammar from grade two through twelve no longer need to be a hurdle for us as teachers or for our students. Our task must be to educate parents and administrators who haven't had the benefit of a close understanding of the research that has been fifty years in the making. It is exciting to see that curriculum guidelines from the State of Minnesota Department of Education are beginning to have some effect on district curriculums, and that inservice teacher training and writing projects in Minnesota are making important steps towards the change that is over fifty years in coming . . . and several years overdue.

REFERENCES

Braddock, R. R. Lloyd-Jones, and L. Schoer. 1963. *Research in Written Composition.* Champaign, IL: NCTE.

Calkins, Lucy. 1986. *The Art of Teaching Writing.* Portsmouth, NH: Heinemann Educational Books.

Chomsky, Noam. 1982. "The Current Scene in Linguistics: Present Directions." In *Readings in Applied Linguistics.* New York: Knopf.

Cleary, Linda Miller. 1988. "A Profile of Carlos: Utilizing the Strengths of a Non-Standard Dialect Writer." *English Journal* (Fall).

D'Eloia, Sarah. 1977. "The Uses—and Limits—of Grammar." *Journal of Basic Writing* 1 (Spring/Summer): 1–2D.

DeStefano, Johanna. 1980. "Research Update: Enhancing Children's Growing Ability to Communicate." *Language Arts,* 57 (October): 807–812.

Dykema, Karl W. 1982. "Where Our Grammar Came From." In *Readings in Applied Linguistics.* New York: Knopf.

Garrett, Nina. 1986. "The Problem with Grammar: What Kind Can the Language Learner Use?" *Modern Language Journal* 70 (Summer): 133–148.

Graves, Donald. 1983. *Writing: Teachers and Children at Work.* Portsmouth, NH: Heinemann Educational Books.

Hartwell, Patrick. 1985. "Grammar, Grammars, and the Teaching of Grammar." *College English* 47 (February):105–127.

Hillocks, George. 1986. *Research on Written Composition: New Directions for Teaching.* Urbana, IL: NCRE, ERIC.

Johnson, Dale D., and David P. Pearson. 1978. *Teaching Reading Comprehension.* New York: Holt, Rinehart, and Winston.

Lamberts, Z. Z. 1972. *A Short Introduction to English Usage.* New York: McGraw-Hill.

Lehmann, Irvin J., and William A. Mehrens. 1979. *Educational Research.* Second Edition. New York: Holt, Rinehart, and Winston.

Moskowitz, Breyne Arlene. 1978. "The Acquisition of Language." *Scientific American* 239.5 L 92–110.

Petrosky, Anthony. 1977. "Grammar Instruction: What We Know." *English Journal.* Vol. 66 (December): 86–88.

Pooley, Robert C. 1974. *The Teaching of English Usage.* Urbana, IL: NCTE.

Postman, Neil, and Charles Weingartner. 1966. *Linguistics: A Revolution in Teaching.* New York: Dell.

Priestly, Joseph. 1768. *Rudiments of English Grammar.* London.

Sanborn, Jean. 1986. "Grammar: Good Wine Before Its Time." *English Journal* 75 (March): 72–79.

Shaunessy, Mina. 1977. *Errors and Expectations: A Guide for the Teacher of Basic Writing.* New York: Oxford University Press.

Sherwin, J. Stephen. 1969. *Four Problems in Teaching English: A Critique of Research.* Urbana, IL: NCTE, 1969.

Weaver, Constance. 1979. *Grammar for Teachers: Perspectives and Definitions.* Urbana, IL: NCTE.

Williams, Joseph M. 1975. *Origins of the English Language: A Social and Linguistic History.* New York: The Free Press: Macmillan.

Grammars and Teaching

Elaine Chaika

Purely theoretical considerations aside, what difference does it make which grammar the English teacher uses? Why isn't traditional, tried and true as it is, as good for pedagogy as the newer transformational grammar? Each provides a framework for discussing language. For composition classes, especially, one would think that's all that's necessary.

Having taught college composition before and after intensive study in linguistics, I have had much experience in teaching via pre- and post-transformational grammars. Unlike the new math which serves only to explain the old, the "new" grammar, henceforth termed "transformational" or T-G, illuminates the workings of language in ways impossible with the old. The explanatory powers of transformational grammar are not only superior to traditional models, but T-G is simpler. Furthermore, the new grammar provides a potent teaching methodology as a natural outcome of its mode of analysis (see below, and Chaika, 1974). These are not trivial concerns in college classrooms, for recent research (Krashen, 1973) suggests that, after puberty, language learning cannot be effected without overt explanation. As noted in Chaika (1974), learning to write may be akin to language learning.

It is disheartening, therefore, to hear English teachers claim that linguistics has nothing to offer rhetoric, or that, if grammar must be taught at all, it makes no difference which. What is ironical is how often those unimpressed by the revolution in syntax are the very ones who have had a course or two in current theory. Apparently the esoteric polemics of many such graduate courses are of little practical value. Indeed, people in English have been known to become downright hostile to linguistics after such exposure.

Yet, polemics about the intricate details of abstract theories aside, the fundamental insights of current syntactic models offer efficacy for teaching rhetoric superior to traditional grammar. Therefore the polemics in this paper are confined to grammars as they pertain to teaching writing. The following offers what has worked for my composition students as well as for teachers-in-service who have enrolled in my writing workshop.

Briefly, by T-G grammar I mean one that recognizes deep as well as surface structure, with transformations from a basic sentence [NP + VP + (Adverb)][1] accounting for the incredible variety of sentence types and constructions found in English. According to such a view, additional sentences may be embedded wherever noun phrases may occur in the deep structure sentence, with subsequent deletions and additions producing surface forms.[2]

Since the same deep structure sentences may be differentially transformed, thereby producing paraphrases or near paraphrases, related sentences in a language must always be considered. Such a grammar has been lately advanced as the basis for sentence combining "grammar-free" writing programs (e.g., O'Hare, 1973). Actually, such methods are grammar free only in their non-use of jargon. Transformations and sentence embeddings can only be effected according to the grammar of a language. In fact, despite all the charges that linguists are "against grammar," T-G methods actually demand a very close atten-

---

[1]Noun phrase + verb phrase + optional adverb.
[2]Since Chaika (1972, 1974) treats the uses of case grammar, a further modification of T-G as it pertains to rhetoric, it is here ignored.

tion to the rules of English. It is precisely here, in its superior evocation of those rules, that T-G grammar is so potent a teaching force, for sentence building, as worth-while as it is, is not enough. Explanation of error so that learners get insights into their own productions is equally important, as is teaching neophyte writers how to analyze language for themselves. No one knows how to write who can only mimic textbook examples or teacher correction. The essence of language use, as Noam Chomsky has so often reiterated, is to say what has never been said before, but, I add, to say it in accordance with the rules of the language. If the literature on first language acquisition has any lesson at all for us, it is that humans use language creatively only after ascertaining its rules.

Basically, traditional grammar is concerned with categorizing and labelling, whereas transformational is concerned with processes. Where traditional grammar defines terms, T-G formulates rules. Where traditional grammar looks for differences, T-G looks for "sames." Thus, where traditional grammar sees subordinate clauses, gerunds, participles, and infinitives, T-G sees only sentence embedding. The difference to pedagogy caused by such variation in approach is tremendous. The natural emphasis of T-G is not on parsing, but on the creative process itself; not what a form is, but why it is selected. The entire presentation of transformational grammar thus becomes easily entwined with the teaching of writing. Perhaps even more important, the new grammar demands the recognition of the linguistic genius of every human being, a powerful morale booster to the non-proficient writer. Often the difference between learning and not is one's belief in one's own power.

Since T-G is always concerned with why language operates as it does and how sentences are related to each other, it often uncovers meaningful explanations for what traditional grammars ignore. Once a student of mine wrote, "He succeeded to do it." My correction noted that he had to change it to "He succeeded in doing it." [(*For*) . . . *to*] can't be used after *succeed*. The student complained, "I'll never remember when to use *to* or *-ing*. It's impossible." My response was to explain that [*for* . . . *to*] typically is used to embed statements which are not necessarily factual, as in:

1a Jack tried to get married.
     (Jack didn't marry.)
2a They reported the storm to have hit the Florida keys.
     (The storm may or may not have hit the Florida keys.)
3a I'd like to live on the Riviera.

Conversely, [(possessive) . . . *-ing*] is used for factual embedding, as in:

1b Jack tried getting married.
     (Jack did marry.)
2b They reported the storm's hitting the Florida keys.
     (The storm did hit.)
3b I like living on the Riviera.

Actually, the student himself was able to ascertain the subtle differences in meaning between the (a) and (b) sentences above. This helped convince him, not only that he has knowledge which he can draw upon to become a competent writer, but that he is capable of thinking about language and making judgments about it. It also reinforced classroom lessons on the necessity of paraphrase to yield the precise meaning. Perhaps, most important, a lively discussion of sentence possibilities and syntactic rules ensued from the correction. It is no accident that T-G grammarians, but not traditionalists, noticed the "fact rule." Since T-G advocates are concerned with why and how all sentences of a language are generated, they constantly search for unifying principles and general processes. A theory with deep structure means searching for underlying unity. It is such a search that led syntacticians to note the deep structure similarity of infinitives and gerunds.

After this experience with my student, I asked six excellent conventionally trained English professors how they would justify such a correction. They all characterized the student error as "awkward" or explained "Because I just know what it has to be." Neither response is likely to stimulate the student to think about language. Indeed, such responses make theme correction seem like placation of an idiosyncratic teacher, not a learning experience.

The vagueness engendered by the lack of coherent theory in traditional grammar can actually be a bar to learning. For instance, *The Holt Guide to English,* published in 1972, cites as an example of "awkwardness" in a chapter on style:

4 When people cease to tolerate themselves is the time hypocrisy comes about.

Irmscher, p. 184

Irmscher (p. 184) asserts that "the awkwardness results from trying to make a 'when clause' the subject of the sentence." Thus, Irmscher implies that (4) results from a violation of syntactic rules. Whereas it does seem most usual for *when* to embed sentences as adverbs, as in Irmscher's suggested revision,

4a Hypocrisy comes about when people cease to tolerate themselves,

there are allowable instances of *when* embedding subject sentences, as

4b When people cease to tolerate themselves is when they become hypocrites.

suggested by Richard Ohmann

In both (4) and (4b) the *when* clause is used as a subject, but the parallelism in the latter makes it more acceptable. Apparently, since "the time" in (4) repeats semantic features of *when,* a stylistic awkwardness results because both clauses in (4) are being used as sentence complements. Neither clause is subordinate to the other, so, stylistically, the repeated elements are best presented by repetition of the same word. Parallelism is stylistically preferable when repeated meanings are grammatically equivalent, but not to employ such parallelism does not create ungrammaticality as Irmscher's second example of awkwardness does:

5 With physical death does not, nor cannot die the existence of the achievements of man.

This sentence violates an important inviolable rule of English grammar: the subject of a sentence cannot be a prepositional phrase. "With physical death" has been placed in subject position. Furthermore, *die* does not allow the object position in a sentence to be filled, but here "the existence" has been placed there. Nor is (5) one of those sentences which allow inversion of subject and predicate because of a proposed negative or locative adverb, as in

5a Never had she run.
5b In the corner sat the frog.

Irmscher's example is not a case of mistaken inversion as the auxiliary and verb aren't interrupted by the subject. These are not matters of stylistic preference or awkwardness, but grammatical necessity.[3] By presenting (5) as well as (4) as an example of awkwardness, *The Holt Guide* makes it appear as if the usage of prepositional phrases in subject position may sometimes also be all right when, in fact, it never is. Unfortunately, students often make that error. Irmscher's easy latching onto a label leads him to lose an opportunity to illustrate an important rule of sentence construction. Similarly, his failure to discuss the proscription of complements after *die* means that *The Holt Guide* fails to make an important point about verbs, namely that lexical rules on verbs determine whether object or indirect object positions may be filled (Fillmore, 1968; Chafe, 1970; Chaika, 1972, 1974). Because traditional grammar, unlike T-G, is content to regard each sentence as idiosyncratic and because it is not concerned with discovery of underlying principles of sentence generation, faulty analysis is inherent in it. Because T-G insists that language is comprised of interrelated rules, it allows an explanation to stand only if it provides usable rules applicable to the student's own writing. As a direct outcome of T-G theory, these rules are related to the language as a whole. They are not presented as chaotic, idiosyncratic instances which are ultimately unlearnable. The traditional catchall "awkward" can only lead to confusion. If a stylistic deficiency is presented as a grammatical error, but a student thinks of an instance in which the supposed error is acceptable, the professor's authority is lessened. It seems to the student that English teachers are privy to mysterious, unlearnable knowledge, or that they are addled.

---

[3]This is not to deny that T-G sometimes finds fuzzy borders between grammar and style. Considering dialectal variation and language change, this is not surprising. However, T-G, because of its emphasis on rule formation and "searching" the whole grammar, is less likely to confuse. Furthermore, it keeps an awareness of grammar vs. style before the student at all times because of the insistence on considering all paraphrases.

Furthermore, the label "awkward" does not tell the student when a given construction may be used, even if the error is accompanied by a sample revision. For the student to be enlightened, several instances of both correct and incorrect usage of a construction must be offered, followed by explication of the principle underlying its use. This explication should follow from the examples. The reader familiar with modern grammars will recognize in this suggestion the typical T-G format for explaining a rule.

Harbrace College Handbook, although traditional, does try to be more precise than "awkward," but it, too, fails to distinguish between grammatical and stylistic criteria. For instance, in a chapter entitled "Unity and Logical Thinking," after cautioning students not to allow "excessive subordination" in a sentence (error 23b), it warns against mixing constructions, (error 23c) with

6 When Howard plays the hypochondriac taxes his wife's patience.
[An adverb clause, part of a complex sentence, is here combined with the predicate of a simple sentence]

Hodges & Whitten, 1972:262

Clearly, this error is grammatical. Its correction is not a matter of personal preference or esthetic judgment, but one of necessity. *Harbrace's* explanation seems to be offering the student a general principle, but as noted above, there is no syntactic rule forbidding adverb clauses as subjects of sentences. For instance,

6a *When Howard finds time to go* remains a mystery.

If the *when* clause in (6a) is permissible, then, clearly, (6) is not in error because of mixing constructions. Whether or not a *when* clause can appear as subject depends upon the verb used as predicate. It has long been known that selectional restrictions on verbs determine their subjects (Fillmore, 1968; Chafe, 1970; Chaika, 1972, 1974). The *Harbrace* warning against "mixed constructions" is not only in error, it denies the student a valid and rhetorically important construction: the embedded sentence as subject.

The *Harbrace* correction of (6) compounds the original misanalysis and does so directly because of the lack of a workable definition of a sentence in traditional grammar. *Harbrace* offers as correction to (6) (letters mine):

A When Howard plays the hypochondriac, he taxes his wife's patience. (*complex sentence*) OR

B Howard's playing the hypochondriac taxes his wife's patience. (*simple sentence*)

Hodges & Whitten, p. 262

Why is the first correction "complex" and the second "simple" when both convey the same meaning and both contain two predications? "Howard's playing" is equivalent to "When Howard plays—", as the text itself admits by offering these as alternates. Furthermore, if "Howard's playing" is not a transformed deep structure sentence, if it is a simple [possessive + NP] subject, one wonders what Hodges and Whitten would propose to do with the fact that "playing" has an object, "the hypochondriac"? There is no way in any theory of grammar that a noun takes a direct object. With T-G, there is no problem. Both of Hodges' and Whitten's corrections are admissible, but the reason is that "Howard plays the hypochondriac" is a deep sentence. In (A) it has been embedded under Adverb, and Howard himself taxes his wife's patience, as shown in the T-G in Figure 15:[4]

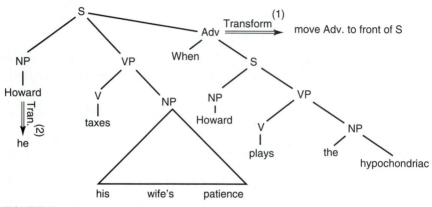

FIGURE 15

Transformation 2, changing *Howard* to *he* takes place after transformation 1. In (B), the sentence "Howard plays the hypochondriac" undergoes [poss - - *ing*] transformation and fills the subject position, creating not only a stylistic difference, but a connotative one, as shown in Figure 16. Note that the T-G explanation not only explains in a manner consistent with the rest of the grammar, but also shows why (A) above actually says that Howard is taxing, whereas (B) says his action is, a distinction Hodges & Whitten don't make. Given the ad hoc, imprecise analyses that their lack of coherent theory leads to, traditionalists often don't seem to have a principled basis to justify such distinctions. Ultimately, traditional terminology like "mixed construction" and "awkwardness" leads to needless complications in the grammar. Because such terms are undefined, if not undefinable, they lack explanatory power. T-G is simpler and more effective not only because of its coherence, but because it always explains in terms of the basic sentence and a few embedding and deletion rules.

Another example of the needless proliferation of terms in traditional grammar is afforded by *Harbrace's* conventional treatment of "misplaced parts, dangling

---

[4]Note that this diagram also suffices for the possible paraphrase of (A):

Al Howard taxes his wife's patience when he plays the hypochondriac.

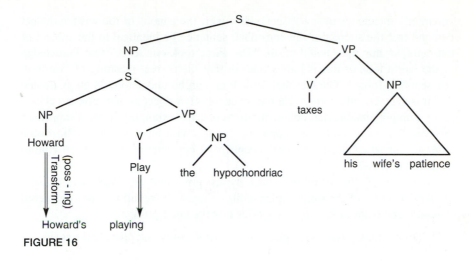

FIGURE 16

modifiers" (Hodges and Whitten, 1972:273–281). Transformational grammar treats these, predictably, as one error. All are caused by improper deletion, as explained below. In contrast, *Harbrace College Handbook* carefully delineates dangling participial, gerund, and infinitive phrases and dangling elliptical clauses. The term *dangling* is defined as

> a construction that hangs loosely within a sentence; the term *dangling* is applied primarily to incoherent verbal phrases and elliptical clauses. A dangling modifier is one that does not refer clearly and logically to some word in the sentence.

p. 277

"Hangs loosely" is, if anything, vaguer than "awkward" to the non-proficient writer. "Incoherent" is precise enough. However, not one example given of dangling anything is incoherent. Each is not only interpretable, but quite usual in ordinary conversation. There's the rub for dangling constructions. Because ordinary speech is so ephemeral, and must be coded so quickly, there seems to be a general rule for understanding: "Interpret on the basis of the nearest thing it could mean given the context." This is why we can understand babies and foreigners. In speech, application of language rules needn't be exact, only exact enough so an interpretation can be made. Furthermore, speech is aided by gesture, tone of voice, and facial expression, all decoding aids denied in writing. Students often carry over speech habits to their writing. They have to be apprised of the difference in convention between the two modes of communicating. An unacceptable construction may be perfectly coherent, yet because it defies literary syntax, mark its writer as uneducated. Thus, the Harbrace example

Taking our seats, the game started.

p. 278

apparently means *we* took our seats. However, the canons of the written dialect demand that the subject of the embedded sentence be identical to the subject of the main, so that this should mean: "The game took our seats." Our knowledge of the world tells us this is impossible, so that the correct meaning of "we took our seats" is forced. The fact that something can be understood is no guarantee that it is syntactically correct. Native speakers often reject as ungrammatical perfectly comprehensible and coherent structures; for example: "John disappeared the cake." Thus, equating ungrammatical items with incoherence, as *Harbrace College Handbook* does, vitiates the concept of correctness in syntax, so vital to the rhetoric class.

Since all of the dangling phrase-types presented in *Harbrace College Handbook* admit of the same explanation, as noted above, all will be considered together, one from each of the categories that the book presents:

7 The evening passed very pleasantly, eating candy and playing the radio.

p.278

8 By mowing the grass high and infrequently, your lawn can be beautiful.

p. 279

9 To write well, good books must be read.

p. 279

Students used to the concept of transformed sentences have no difficulty retrieving the deeper structures. They readily supply:

7a The evening passed pleasantly. We ate candy. We played the radio.
8a Your lawn can be beautiful. (by) You mow the grass high and infrequently.
9a Good books must be ready by anyone (in order to, for) (Anyone, People) write (s) well.

Hodges and Whitten do ask, after (8), "Who is to do the mowing?" (p.279). Actually, no native speaker has any difficulty understanding that the mowing is done by *you,* even in the dangling construction. Furthermore, Hodges and Whitten's correction

> By *mowing the grass* . . . you can have a beautiful lawn

doesn't have a surface subject on *mowing* either.Yet, no explanation is offered for this correction's not being dangling. That is, Hodges & Whitten never say why "By mowing" in one instance doesn't inform us who is doing it, but in the second, does. Using the concept of deep structure and embedded sentences, the students see graphically that the subjects of embedded and main sentences aren't identical in (7–9) above, respectively. Therefore, no subject can be deleted in any of these as they stand. The students learn one simple rule: if a subject of an embedded sentence is deleted, it must be identical to the surface subject of the main sentence. By contrast, teaching students what infinitives, gerunds, and participles are, much less explaining when they "hang loosely," involves needless hours of class time. Then, too, with no notion of deep structure and transformations, no rationale can be offered for when we rightly can or can't supply a particular subject if it hasn't been overtly stated as in (7–9) above.

For instance, *Harbrace* offers as a correction for (7):

7b We passed the evening pleasantly, eating candy and playing the radio.

Hodges and Whitten, 1972:278

Lacking a theory of deep structure and transformations, they offer no rationale for changing the subject of *pass*. The T-G approach demands that reasons be given for all corrections. As just noted, there is a general rule in writing "It can't be deleted unless it's repeated." The subjects of *eating* and *playing* have been deleted, but the only surface subject is *evening*. An *evening* can't eat or play: hence a subject must be provided which can. This subject must be animate and probably human, as humans play radios. *Eat* and *play,* must, of course, share the same deleted subject as they are joined by *and.* Only if the subject is identical may it be deleted and the verbs so joined. Fortunately, *pass* may also have a human subject if the time passed is made an object.[5] Since there is no context provided, any human subject may be selected: hence, the given correction of "The evening passed . . ." to "We passed the evening. . . ." This may seem to be nit-picking. Indeed, for such a simple correction it would be, except that much of what actually occurs in themes is not so obvious. By always insisting upon principled explanations the professor ensures that students become used to analyzing language, paying close attention to sentence structure.

T-G sometimes explains to students why they are prone to certain errors. Thus, one reason for the creation of dangling constructions as in (7) is that the writer is aware of the deep structure noun. Therefore, he embeds sentences with the deep noun in mind, forgetting that, in writing at least, only surface subjects count for deletion.

The correction of (8) also proceeds by supplying a subject for the embedded sentence:

8b If you mow the grass high and infrequently, your lawn can be beautiful.

OR

8c By mowing the grass . . . you can have a beautiful lawn.

Again, this last is offered by *Harbrace* and involves rewriting the main sentence. When this text does such rewriting, it offers no explanation, unlike the T-G corrections which proceed directly from the deep structures of the given sentences.

---

[5]For details of case grammar, see Fillmore, 1968. For its application to rhetoric, see Chaika, 1972, 1974.

Finally, (9) can be corrected to:

9b To write well, anyone must read good books.

Harbrace corrects (9) to:

9c To write well, a student must read good books.

However, there is a general rule of deletion that says that *anyone* or its equivalent can be deleted. This operates throughout the language, as in "To know her is to love her" which means "For anyone to know her is for anyone to love her." The problem in (9) is actually that "good books must be read" is a passive sentence with its agent deleted. It must have an active counterpart. "Anyone must read good books." In the passive, the [*by* + *anyone*] can be omitted by regular rule of agent deletion. *Harbrace's* making *student* the subject of *read* is unmotivated, as there is no rule of "*student* deletion" in the absence of that noun elsewhere in the grammar. Furthermore, patently (9) must refer to all people not just students. Finally, *Harbrace* never explains that (9) dangles only because the main sentence has been passivized, so that the agent no longer appears as subject; thus, their correction simply reinstates that agent subject by conversion back to the active. A paraphrase utilizing the passive transformation might also be discussed for its stylistic effects:

9d For anyone to write well, good books must be read.

T-G encourages paraphrasing as traditional grammars do not. It keeps before the student always that there are many ways to express one idea but that each must conform to the rules of the language.

The dangling elliptical clause as presented by *Harbrace* can be troublesome to students, especially since the given definition is circular: "An elliptical clause—that is, a clause with an implied subject and verb . . ." (p. 280). Structural cues are more helpful. Question words: *who, what, which, when, while, where,* all double as sentence embedders. The NP following them must represent a complete deep structure sentence. Thus, when we see the *Harbrace Handbook* example

10 When only a small boy, Father took me with him to Denver.

(p. 280)

we know this must mean "When I was a small boy," but that the "I was" was erroneously deleted. *Harbrace Handbook* does supply the "I was," but gives no rationale for so doing. This makes correction a matter of mind reading.

T-G grammar automatically considers other possibilities by virtue of its rules. The verb BE and its subject frequently can be deleted in embedded sentences. Here it can't be, only because the surface structure subject of the embedded and main sentences are not identical. If the main sentence is transformed so that "I" becomes its surface subject, the "ellipsis" can remain. That is "I was" can be deleted:

10a When only a small boy, I was taken to Denver by my father.

Harbrace doesn't even consider this quite ordinary alternative, perhaps because it confounds the category of "elliptical clause."

The tree diagrams of T-G grammar are exceptionally useful for two knotty composition problems: comma splices and fragments. It is very easy for students to map their theme sentences on the basic tree. If every position under S is filled and a new S must be started, the student sees where a conjunction or embedder is required. For instance, the following comma splice gets mapped in Figure 17.

11 Oscar's car broke down last week, it's a clunker.

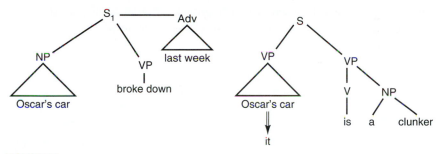

FIGURE 17

There is no place to fit "it's a clunker" under S1. As there is no conjunction or embedder preceding "it's," there is no way to attach it to any part of that sentence. The student readily sees that this must be punctuated as a separate sentence. Alternatively, an embedder like *because* could be employed to heighten the causal relationship between the event and the explanation. Then, too, since "Oscar's car" is mentioned in both sentences, the second could be embedded by *which,* as:

11a Oscar's car, which is a clunker, broke down last week.

For some reason, the act of tree diagraming leads to the cessation of comma splices. There seems to be psychological validity to such an approach to "sentence sense." Peter Blackwell, Headmaster of the Rhode Island School for the Deaf, reports (personal communication) that drawing trees is a potent method of teaching the deaf what a sentence is. He has elementary school children making syntactic trees. Teachers in my workshops found that tree diagraming of their own sentences was an easy task for fourth graders.

Fragments are equally amenable to visual explication. The idea of sentence must be defined in structural terms, for it is structure, not thought, complete or otherwise, that signals an independent sentence. For instance, native speakers have no difficulty distinguishing nonsense sequences as sentences or fragments, despite the fact that no "thought" can be distinguished. Note,

12 The glorbey dale gyred a biffle.

This is a sentence, whereas the following is not:

13 Glinking a darby biffle

The structural cues in (12) show us that a [NP + VP] has been completed, whereas those of (13) show us that the subject NP and *BE* are omitted, as *-ing* on a verb signals an independent predication only if an auxiliary *BE* precedes it, as in *is going, can be going, has been going*. The *-ing* on a verb with no auxiliary always denotes an embedded sentence. Here, there is no sentence into which (13) is inserted; hence, it is a fragment. In order to display such fragments, we must *add* aux (auxiliary) to our VP, as in Figure 18.

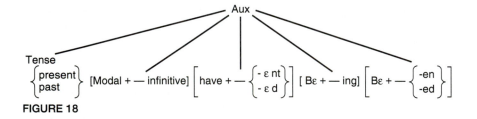

FIGURE 18

(*Note:* Where—indicates, verb or next auxiliary is inserted. *Examples:* will go; will have gone; is going; is gone; shall be going; can have been going; must have been being paid.)

   If an *-ing* has been utilized as a full verb without its requisite auxiliary, this fact leaps up at the student as [one] who is inserting a fragment into the tree. Similarly, if the vital subject NP is missing, its lack is instantly seen, more quickly than from a long-winded verbal explanation. A common fragment type serves as example:

14 Twitching his tail impatiently.

That the subject NP and requisite auxiliary, *BE,* are missing is self-evident.

   Fragments, actually, often are another instance of improper deletion. In conversation, it is usual not to repeat parts of a sentence already uttered. Instead, only the new constructions are supplied with the understanding that they be mentally tacked onto the original. This habit not only speeds communication, but reinforces the unity of discourse. The propensity toward fragments in writing

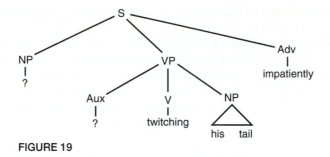

FIGURE 19

is but a carryover of this phenomenon. Indeed, students readily see that deliberate use of fragments is one way to simulate a casual, conversational style.

A complete comparison of traditional and transformational grammars in terms of efficacy for pedagogy would require a fair-sized tome. The foregoing attempts to show that T-G, because of its coherence and simplicity, provides a rational basis for correction for errors and discussion of style. Moreover, because equivalent sentences, paraphrases, are an integral part of T-G syntax, as are the consequences of applying different transformations, students are automatically taught sentence creation in the grammar lessons. Because T-G is so discoverable, whether because it conforms to the speaker's own intuitions, or its simplicity, or both, students can easily supply paraphrases and analyses on their own. This, in turn creates an interest in discussing language which is vital to rhetoric. Using a T-G model, the professor assures students that by virtue of their humanity, they already know a great deal about language. This is reinforced when students see that they can create transformations and judge grammaticality often as accurately as the professor when syntax is discussed. It isn't that the teacher's superior familiarity with written dialect is questioned. It's just that students see they already possess a tremendous body of language knowledge upon which they can build. This is not true of complex, often counterintuitive, traditional models of grammar. Nor does traditional grammar provide a natural basis for exercises in sentence creation. T-G, with its theory of sentence embedding which emphasizes deep structure complete sentences underlying surface fragments, provides a natural model for combining and separating sentences for different effects. Hence, which grammar is chosen for the rhetoric classroom may have a profound effect on what is learned in that class. Transformational grammar, if understood by the teacher, can create a good learning environment.

The question naturally arises whether one must be a full-fledged linguist to use T-G grammar. Teachers in my writing workshop have learned enough in eight weeks to utilize T-G both for devising exciting lessons and for correcting student compositions. They report to me that their students, many very low achievers, not only responded with surprising enthusiasm to grammar discussions, but afterwards produced writing far beyond what anyone had thought possible.[6]

The texts for this workshop were Rosenbaum and Jacobs, *Transformations, Style and Meaning;* Jacobs & Jacobs, *College Writer's Handbook;* and Elgin's *Pouring Down Words.* There are several new and old explications of modern syntax available, but since each has its merits and shortcomings, no titles can be recommended without a review, preferably comparative. For structural definitions of the parts of speech, so much more learnable than the traditional semantic ones, Francis (1958) still stands.

The unwary must be cautioned. Some texts, such as *The Holt Guide,* may actually contain sections describing T-G (pp. 496–500), apparently knowledgeably; yet in no way are they modern grammars. The section is window dressing. Most of the analyses of error are traditional; none, or virtually none, of the insights of T-G are actually applied. Irmscher, for instance, consistently fails to treat the passive as a transformation from an active (pp. 445, 453, 454), just as the bulk of his explanations are wholly pre-T-G. The mere inclusion of trees and terms like "kernel sentence" does not make a transformational grammar. Rather, look to see if the rules are presented only in the context of sentences showing when to and when not to use a construction. Note if several possible paraphrases are offered, with some discussion of when each is most appropriate. Look for discussions of presupposition as a governing factor in choice of transformation. Check whether the text consistently presents sentence types as transformations from kernel(s). Even if the text passes "the T-G test," however, don't be afraid to question any sentence analysis that doesn't accord with your native speaker intuition. Any grammarian occasionally falls into the trap of a glib analysis that doesn't cover enough instances. Besides, improving on some other scholar's rule is delicious.

REFERENCES

Bach, Emmon, and Robert Harms, eds. 1968. *Universals in Linguistic Theory.* New York: Holt, Rinehart and Winston.

Chafe, Wallace. 1970. *Meaning and the Structure of Language.* Chicago: University of Chicago Press.

Chaika, Elaine. 1972. *Models of Grammar and the Pedagogical Problem.* Diss. Brown University.

---

[6]Notions of deep structure and transformations were typically introduced by having students break long sentences into their several kernels; then, where possible, retransforming kernels into paraphrases of the original. It was found that even fourth graders could do this with ease. Furthermore, mapping sentences on trees was not at all difficult, even for the "lowest" high school groups. That they could do it, moreover, spurred these adolescents in subsequent writing assignments. I am especially indebted to Mr. Vincent Ciunci of Pawtucket East High School, RI, and Ms. Bonnie Olchowski of Central High School, Providence, RI, for showing me what such high school students could learn from a T-G methodology. Neither of these teachers had any T-G training beyond my workshop.

———. 1974. "Who Can Be Taught?" *College English,* 35 (Feb.), 575–583.

Elgin, Suzette. 1975. *Pouring Down Words.* Englewood Cliffs, NJ: Prentice-Hall.

Fillmore, Charles. 1968. "The Case for Case." in Bach & Harms, eds. *Universals in Linguistic Theory.* New York: Holt, Rinehart & Winston.

Francis, W. Nelson. 1958. *The Structure of American English.* New York: The Ronald Press.

Hodges, John, and Mary Whitten, eds. 1972. *Harbrace College Handbook, Seventh Edition.* New York: Harcourt, Brace, Jovanovich.

Irmscher, William. 1972. *The Holt Guide to English.* New York: Holt, Rinehart & Winston.

Jacobs, Roderick, and Peter Rosenbaum. 1971. *Transformations, Style, and Meaning.* Waltham, MA: Xerox College Publishing.

Jacobs, Suzanne, and Roderick Jacobs. 1976. *The College Writer's Handbook, Second Edition.* New York: John Wiley & Sons.

Krashen, Stephen. 1973. "Two Studies in Adult Second Language Learning." Paper delivered at Linguistic Society of America, annual meeting, San Diego, CA.

O'Hare, Frank. 1973. *Sentence Combining.* NCTE Research Report #15. Urbana, IL.

The Teaching of English Usage

Robert C. Pooley

THE PROBLEM

The successful use of English in adult life rests on a foundation of habits so thoroughly established as to be automatic. For all ordinary purposes of communication, the proficient adult is generally unconscious of language choices; words, idioms, and constructions appropriate to the nature of the communication flow along unimpeded by conscious effort. Only in unusually formal or difficult situations does a person become conscious of the need for closer discrimination in language choices. Even then, experiences gained in observing the speech and writing of others carry him through.

THE ELEMENTARY SCHOOL

However, sensitivity to the varieties of language usage, particularly to certain forms or constructions frowned upon in many social contexts, is not readily gained in the home. Young children learn speech by ear: the words, idioms, and constructions heard in the home and neighborhood are those that characterize the language which they bring to school. Children acquire both standard and variant habits of speech in the most impressionable years of childhood, reinforcing these habits by countless repetitions prior to the influence of school. But the child who employs nonstandard forms or constructions does not use "bad" language; the choices in language use which he has learned to make were and continue to be quite satisfactory and appropriate in the home and neighborhood environment. Thus usage instruction throughout the school years should not be designed to eliminate such preschool language acquisition but to augment it, so that the child is more steadily guided toward greater proficiency in a wider variety of standard forms.

The child who has heard from the cradle onward the patterns of English which lie within the range of nationally accepted usage may have an advantage in the further mastery of a wider variety of socially approved forms. But his mastery of certain standard forms does not thereby exempt him from usage instruction. For children who employ standard forms as well as for those who do not, the fundamental goals of usage instruction are the same: the development of sensitivity to and proficiency in the use of words, idioms, and constructions according to the nature of the communication. The teaching of certain standard forms to students who know only nonstandard forms is necessarily a part of usage instruction designed to instill a sense of social responsibility for language use, but it is only a part. Unfortunately, because of the prevalence of certain nonstandard forms and because of the high priority schools have placed upon their eradication, drill for "correctness," which is after all only a negative kind of instruction, has tended to overshadow and supplant more positive instruction leading to an appreciation of the ways of the English language. The child whose usage has been made reasonably "correct" or standard, but whose sentences are flat, dull, and inexact, has not been taught good English usage. Language free from dialect variation is not necessarily effective language for being more standard. It becomes effective as the child develops a feeling for the bright, sparkling word or phrase, the exact word for his needs, the sentence which says exactly what he wants to say as clearly as possible and in a manner suiting the tone and purpose of the communication.

This feeling for the fitness of words in their uses is the positive side of usage instruction, and it can be taught well only in situations calling for genuine communication. The goals of language instruction throughout the school years can be achieved only if students become observers of language. Activities which place children in the role of observers are those which establish the attitudes that language is constantly changing and that usage items mastered today may not be the most acceptable ones when they are adults. As observers they will be able to adjust to the culture as it shifts and changes. It is this kind of knowledgeable flexibility which is the ultimate goal of education.

A program of usage instruction will inevitably involve the teaching of speech forms from the standard dialect as substitutions for nonstandard patterns learned in the home and neighborhood environment and reinforced daily out of school. Teachers are thus faced with a very thorny situation. The chief task of language instruction designed to teach certain forms from the standard dialect is to persuade children to substitute new habits for those which they have practiced for many years. But an attack on certain usages of the nonstandard variety may be interpreted as an attack on the child himself and on the culture of his home. From the child's point of view, the language forms he uses are perfectly natural and acceptable. Do not his family and others he holds in esteem use them? The problem is made still more difficult if only a portion of the class regularly employ nonstandard forms. Intensive instruction in standard forms may appear to mean that the teacher favors certain children and not others.

A sound and successful program of teaching usage in the elementary grades can be built upon the understanding and application of four fundamental principles.

1 The teacher must size up the problem of desired usage as it affects the class and plan a campaign to bring about specific results. Every class offers its own challenges which the teacher hopefully will recognize and meet.

2 Children must be aroused to a desire to augment their repertoires to include standard forms in situations requiring them and must be motivated to cooperate actively with the teacher in striving toward the accomplishment of specific results. They must be stimulated to become observers of language, both of their own and of others.

3 Usage instruction must never be divorced from the normal and natural uses of language in the entire school program. This means there should be no language exercise which does not recognize the nature of communication and no use of communication which ignores usage appropriate to the purpose.

4 Students learn standard speech patterns by hearing standard speech patterns. Techniques which provide oral reinforcement are the most effective. Situations which call for the use of oral language, such as storytelling, language games, creative dramatics and role playing, oral reports, etc. are invaluable, but the students must act as observers of the language in order to benefit from the situations.

THE SENIOR HIGH SCHOOL

In the senior high school the teaching of usage is a twofold responsibility. One part is evaluative, the examination of speech patterns that carry over from earlier years, the choices of usage which arise from increased use of language at a higher level, and the increasing need to attain the standard dialect. The other part is constructive, the teaching of effective patterns of speech for wider needs and the refinement of word-choice to increase the interest and effectiveness of expression. Because the first aspect is the more apparent need and is in nature more concrete, it tends to supplant or overshadow the more important constructive responsibility.

In spite of the limiting influence of dialect variations and the evaluative steps necessary to bring about a broadening of usage, the high school program in language development must not be looked upon as purely corrective. Language instruction in the senior high school must be focused upon the constant expansion of powers to use language effectively for the needs of school and adult life. To this end the major portion of time in the English course should be given to two types of constructive activities:

1 Guided practice in oral language by means of reports, discussions, panels, forums, debates, and extemporary dramatics. These exercises should be conducted so as to provide opportunities for every student to take an active part at frequent intervals and to grow in effectiveness of oral presentation through the guidance of the teacher and the suggestions of fellow students.

2 Constant growth in written language by means of composition exercises at regular and frequent intervals. These written exercises should cover a wide range of subjects, with the time allotment fairly equally divided between two types of writings: (a) factual-expository writing, as in reports, summaries, explanations, arguments, reviews, and editorials; and (b) personal-imaginative writing, as in the relation of personal experiences, essays, narratives, class journals, fantasy, humor, and, in some cases, drama and poetry.

In this constructive program of language development, acceptable usage plays an essential but subordinate part. Every language exercise, oral and written, should have an intrinsic purpose of its own, a purpose recognized by the student and ideally one which challenges him to do his best. Good usage, including a conscious effort to employ appropriate standard dialect forms, should be seen as contributory to the accomplishment of the purpose of the exercise, not as an end in itself. Indeed, the best instruction in language use at the high school level is that which arises naturally from the needs of the students as they strive to accomplish effective expression for a definite purpose. Such instruction makes sense and finds immediate application in the task at hand.

USAGE IN CREATIVE COMMUNICATION

Teaching good usage creatively is inseparable from the art of teaching students to communicate. While the illustrations given here are drawn from written composition, the principles of language development apply with equal force to oral communication. The power to communicate effectively and correctly is advanced as the student makes progress in two areas: (1) an ever-increasing knowledge of his total environment through active living, absorbing experiences, developing new interests, and relating each new specific gain to the total body of his knowledge; (2) an increasing command of words, word groups, and sentence patterns together with increasing sensitivity to usage choices which facilitate the expression and interpretation of his experiences. Teaching the student thus to communicate is the art of composition, and composition is here defined as the personal expression of a person who has something to communicate and has also the desire to make his communication influence others.

Unfortunately, it is possible for students to go through high school and receive good grades in English without learning the difference between exercise writing and communicating. They may write neat and often mechanically perfect papers several pages in length, with paragraphs arranged in proper sequence. But the subject and its treatment are entirely secondhand. The student has absorbed from reading or listening certain facts or ideas which he repeats more or less in his own words with a glib facility. The subject has no real significance to him, nor has it raised any internal response. His product contains nothing which he himself has said. In the process of writing he has been not much more than a kind of automatic relay between the source and the product. That there is a great deal of this so-called composition accepted in the high schools is well known. It is accepted because the concept of communication is not clearly recognized.

The requirements of a good composition are, first, that the subject arise from a genuine need or interest of the student which stimulates him to thought and feeling; second, that he find for himself (with help if needed) the form or plan of the writing to develop it in his own way; and, third, that when he finished he has the sense of having made a statement, proclaimed an idea, defended a position, or expressed experiences and feelings in prose or verse which is his own language and in which he can take pride. When these conditions are met in any piece of writing, that writing is truly composition and is genuine communication.

Of equal importance are the evaluations which teachers place on papers. These are not merely grades, or corrections of forms and usages. They should represent appraisal or the measurement of the intrinsic worth of the writing. Such measurement means judgment in three factors: (1) A recognition of what the student set out to do. This will differ for every paper and cannot be taken for granted. Indeed, one of the serious faults in evaluating composition is the confusing of what we think a student ought to do with a subject with what *he* intended to do. So far as in us lies, we must see the project as the author intended. (2) An appreciation of the plan the student adopted to carry out his idea. This means an appraisal of the title and organization of the paper, a recognition of the balance of parts, and a sense of the appropriateness of form and language to the expression of his idea. (3) An evaluation of the success of the communication in terms of what the student set out to do. This judgment comes from a recognition of the clarity of ideas, the sequence of thought, the vividness of illustrations, figures, and conversations, the appropriateness of the usage to these ends, and the sense of completeness of the whole. When the paper has been judged by these three factors, the student is entitled to a statement of appraisal, either orally in a conference or as a written note on the paper.

All these considerations lead to the application of usage standards. There will be questionable usages, of course. The fundamental attitude to take is that the inappropriate forms are not wrong in themselves but are hindrances to the effectiveness of the communication. Every time the reader or listener is confused, irritated, or amused by a detail, the effectiveness of the communication is weakened to some degree. Appropriate usage permits the reader to gain the full impact of the meaning without any interference by the language used.

Since students are often heedless of expected form and imitative of the language they hear, teachers in the past have devoted time and attention to deviations and undesired patterns of sentence structure, idiom and usage, mechanics of writing, and spelling. The best strategy in approaching such deviations and undesired patterns lies in getting students to see that these deviations have interfered with communication. Therefore, in creative teaching the emphasis will be on the communication and not on the form. When the student has something to say, when he wants to say it as well as he can, and when he appreciates the applause and criticisms of his fellows and of his teacher, the correction of details as impediments to the success of his project makes sense and enlists his personal desire for improvement. On the other hand, decades of experience have proved that the correction of errors as errors, and drill on corrective measures in isolation from the need to communicate, result in discouraging returns from the time and effort expended. It cannot be claimed that attention to communication will eliminate errors. It is possible, however, to staunchly defend the position that emphasis on communication will subordinate the correction of errors to an element of the total success and that this emphasis will provide a genuine motivation toward accuracy and sensitivity to good form, a motivation never aroused by red ink, failing grades, or isolated usage drills.

The plea of this section is that the time given to formal drill and grammatical analysis be transferred to the promotion of good communication. Writing should be frequent and as far as possible voluntary. Much time should be devoted to the hearing and evaluating of writing. Compositions should be read aloud and discussed in groups or circulated in the classroom. And the teaching of usage and correctness should feature creative language situations: How should a certain idea be expressed before a certain audience? What effect do certain phrases have on the intent and tone of communication? How would two people of differing age, social status, or degree of education tell the same story or relate the same event? How would one phrase a story or conversation to show the personality of the speaker? and many similar situations. This positive handling of language will stimulate creative expression, will reveal the relative nature of usage choices and prescriptions, and will provide the ground for the consideration of usage and idiom as they affect communication. Finally, of great importance, the student's attitude will shift from the discouragement of being found always in the wrong to the enthusiasm of experimenting with language, all kinds of language, to discover what he can do with it.

DIALECTS AND THE STANDARD DIALECT

It is a fact of English usage that all speakers of English employ a dialect of English which is the product of a number of factors. Each individual's parents and grandparents, the communities in which he spent his formative years, his schools and his teachers, members of the environment whom he admires and perhaps strives to emulate, the media of public communication—all contribute to the formation of each individual's peculiar dialect. Therefore the term *dialect* may not be used in a pejorative sense, for all persons speak dialects. Children in the schoolroom and youth in high school and college reflect the language variations which have arisen from their social environments.

Each city, village, and rural region has its own minor language variations, but has also an overall common content which we call American English. In this American English, language scholars identify three major dialect areas: Northeast, Southern, and General American, the latter spoken in all parts of the United States outside the Northeast and the South. Of course there are minor differences distinguishable within these dialects, but that is a matter for scholars to deal with.

A general, common, widely used dialect known as standard English serves as an agreed-upon standard medium of spoken and written communication in all parts of the United States. This dialect incorporates a wide range of functional variety, having sufficient breadth to permit the shades of difference in language use appropriate to specific occasions. The standard dialect is in no way intrinsically superior to any other dialect. Rather, its value lies in its role as a national standard of commonly accepted form. With minor variations, it has international value as well, for it shares in substance the major part of British standard English, Australian standard English, South African standard English, and the standard English of many other parts of the world. To those students who wish to expand the range of alternatives available to them in their professional lives, the value of attaining proficiency in this dialect must be obvious.

It is part of the strategy of modern usage teaching to lead students to recognize this value; the consequent motivation almost insures acquisition of the skills necessary for fluency in standard English. Some children come to school able to speak and write standard English. Many acquire the distinctive features of standard English in the grades and high school. There should be continuous encouragement and open opportunity for every student to learn and use standard English as an essential part of his general education. In the past many teachers attempted to force this dialect upon unready and unwilling students. In the best of modern teaching students are helped to recognize the values of attaining the standard dialect and are given every opportunity to learn and practice it.

Characteristics of the Standard Dialect

In the senior high school, regardless of the previous education of the student, teachers of English have the duty and privilege of presenting the forms of standard English, of helping students to distinguish the variations from their own dialects and to acquire skill and fluency in their use. To accomplish this end, two factors must operate: (1) the teacher must wisely and skillfully present the usage distinctions of standard English; and (2) the student must actively desire to acquire it.

The informal variety of standard English is a broad dialect embracing a large number of minor deviations. The speakers and writers of this dialect are rarely conscious of these minor variations of usage, or else consider them unimportant. But there are specific usages which are not a part of this dialect and become at once noticeable to the users of informal standard English. The student who has been motivated to acquire and employ informal standard English will find that the major part of his own dialect lies within the scope of informal standard English. What he needs to learn, therefore, are which specific items of usage, though natural to him in his own dialect, must be eliminated if he wants to be fully equipped to speak and write the standard dialect.

As an aid to the teacher and student who are working together to achieve fluency in the standard dialect, the following list will be helpful in identifying those usages which lie outside standard English and are therefore to be avoided in the speaking and writing of the standard dialect.

A Guide to a Standard of English Usage for Today

1 The avoidance of strictly local usages, such as "to home," "I'd admire to go," "The cat wants out," "all the farther."

2 The grammatical uses in speech and writing of *I, me, he, him, she, her, they, them.* (Note: "It's me" is fully acceptable; "It's him" and "It's them" are gaining acceptability in informal speech.)

3 The grammatical uses of *is, are, was, were* with respect to number and tense.

4 Use of the historical past forms of common irregular verbs such as *saw, gave, took, brought, bought, stuck.*

5 Use of past participles of the same and similar verbs as in number 4 above after auxiliaries.

6 Avoidance of the double negative: "We don't have no apples," etc.

7 Avoidance of analogical forms: *ain't, hisn, hern, ourn, theirselves,* etc.

8 Correct use of possessive pronouns: *my, mine, his, hers, theirs, ours.*

9 Mastery in writing of the distinctions between *its* and *it's, of* and *'ve,* etc.

10 Placement of *have* or *has* or of their phonetic reductions to *v* or *s* between subject and past participle, in past participle constructions.

11 Avoidance of *them* as a demonstrative pronoun.

12 Avoidance of *this here* and *that there*.

13 Mastery of the use of *a* and *an* as articles before consonants and vowels. (Note: before a pronounced *h* or long *u*, use of *a* is idiomatic in American English.)

14 Grammatical use of personal pronouns in compound constructions: as subject (Mary and *I*), as object of a verb (Mary and *me*), as object of a preposition (to Mary and *me*).

15 The use of *we* before an appositional noun when subject; *us* when object.

16 Correct number agreement with the phrases *there is, there are, there was, there were. . . .*

17 Avoidance of *he don't, she don't, it don't.*

18 Avoidance of *learn* for *teach, leave* for *let.*

19 Avoidance of pleonastic subjects: "my brother he," "my mother she," "that fellow he."

20 Proper agreement in number with antecedent pronouns *one* and *anyone, each, no one, either, neither.* With *everybody, everyone, somebody, someone,* and *none* some tolerance of number has long been acceptable, particularly in informal contexts. . . .

21 The use of *who* and *whom* as referents to persons. (Note: *who* as an objective case interrogative pronoun in initial position is standard.)

22 Use of *said* rather than *says* in reporting the words of a speaker in the past.

23 The distinction between *good* as adjective and *well* as adverb.

24 Avoidance of *can't hardly, can't scarcely.*

25 Avoidance of *at* after *where:* "Where is she at?"

The study of any usage list should make the student personally aware of his right to choose some forms and to reject others. His understanding of the consequences of his action will be clear to him as he consults current magazine usage or usage handbook authors. In addition, this approach will provide the more talented students with an opportunity to sharpen their language observations as well as "polish" or "refine" the standard English they have already mastered.

It is suggested that teachers and students consider the fact that the following eight items need no longer be "corrected" in the classroom and that these forms are acceptable to many educated speakers and writers today.

A Guide to Usage Items No Longer Considered Nonstandard English

1 Any distinction between *shall* and *will.*

2 Any reference to the split infinitive.

3 Elimination of *like* as a conjunction.

4 Objection to the phrase "different than."

5 Any objection to "He is one of the boys who *is* . . . ."

6 The objection to "The *reason* . . . is *because* . . . ."

7 The objection to *myself* as a polite substitute for *I,* as in "I understand you will meet Mrs. Jones and myself at the station."

8 Any insistence upon the possessive case standing before a gerund.

By no means does the investigation of usage items need to stop with these eight items. If the need and desire to consider other questions grow out of a study of the first group, the teacher will certainly want to continue the work and foster this kind of interest and spirit of investigation. A number of usage reference books are available today to provide additional controversial items which students may wish to study.

C

SEMANTICS AND VOCABULARY

Semantic Properties

Victoria Fromkin and Robert Rodman

"My name is Alice . . ."
"It's a stupid name enough!" Humpty Dumpty interrupted impatiently. "What does it mean?"
"Must a name mean something?" Alice asked doubtfully.
"Of course it must," Humpty Dumpty said with a short laugh: "my name means the shape I am—and a good handsome shape it is, too. With a name like yours, you might be any shape, almost."

Lewis Carroll, *Through the Looking-Glass*

Not only do we know what the morphemes of our language are, we also know what they *mean*. Dictionaries are filled with words and their meanings. So is the head of every human being who speaks a language. You are a walking dictionary. You know the meaning of thousands of words. Your knowledge of their meanings permits you to use them appropriately in sentences and to understand them when heard, even though you probably seldom stop and ask yourself: "What does *boy* mean?" or "What does *walk* mean?"

Most words and morphemes in the language have their own meanings. We shall talk about the meaning of words, even though we already know that words may be composed of several morphemes.

Suppose someone said:

The assassin was stopped before he got to Thwacklehurst.

If the word *assassin* is in your mental dictionary, you know that it was some *person* who was prevented from *murdering* some *important person* named Thwacklehurst. Your knowledge of the meaning of *assassin* tells you that it was not an animal that tried to kill the man and that Thwacklehurst was not likely to

515

be a little old man who owned a tobacco shop. In other words, your knowledge of the meaning of *assassin* includes knowing that the individual to whom that word refers is *human*, is a *murderer*, and is a killer of *very important people*. These, then, are some of the semantic properties of the word that speakers of the language agree to. The meaning of all nouns, verbs, adjectives, adverbs—the "content words"—and even some of the "function words" such as *with* or *over* can at least partially be defined by such properties, or **semantic features.**

The same semantic property may be part of the meaning of many different words. "Female" is a semantic property that helps to define

bitch	hen	actress	maiden
doe	mare	debutante	widow
ewe	vixen	girl	woman

The words in the last two columns are also distinguished by the semantic property "human." The feature "human" is also found in

doctor dean professor bachelor parent baby child

The last two of these words are also specified as "young." That is, parts of the meaning of the words *baby* and *child* are that they are "human" and "young."

The "meaning" of a word can then be specified by indicating a "plus" or "minus" for the presence or absence of all the semantic properties that define the word, as illustrated in the following way:

ACTRESS	BABY	GIRL	BACHELOR	MARE	COURAGE
+human	+human	+human	+human	−human	. . .
+female	. . .	+female	−female	+female	. . .
.	+young	+young	−young	−young	. . .
.	.	.	.	.	+abstract
.	.	.	.	.	.

Of course, words have many more properties which define their meanings than are shown. For example, part of the meaning of *mare* must relate to its "horseness" though whether this is accomplished by including "+horseness" as a feature of *mare* or by some other means is not entirely clear. But note that such semantic properties can be used to classify words into semantic groups—those that are all +human or +abstract and so on. In addition, the presence of certain properties automatically excludes others, so we do not need to indicate that courage is "−human," "−female," and so on, because "+abstract" implies all that. *Baby* is not specified as either "+female" or "+male." A baby can be either sex; this is a fact about the meaning of *baby* that can be indicated by omitting any gender specification. Some properties also mutually exclude each other ("human" and "abstract"), and in some cases one property implies the presence of another ("human" → "animate").

The same semantic property may occur in different parts of speech. "Female" is part of the meaning of the noun *mother*, of the verb *breastfeed*, and of the adjective *pregnant*. Other semantic properties are found usually in words belonging to one particular part of speech. "Cause" is a verbal property, possessed by *darken, kill, uglify,* and so on.

darken	cause to become dark
kill	cause to die
uglify	cause to become ugly

Other semantic properties that help account for the meaning of verbs are shown in this table.

Semantic property	Verbs having it
+motion	bring, fall, plod, walk, run . . .
+contact	hit, kiss, touch . . .
+creation	build, imagine, make . . .
+sense	see, hear, feel . . .

Our linguistic knowledge tells us that for the most part no two words have exactly the same meaning, and this suggests that through semantic properties we can make finer and finer distinctions in meaning. To distinguish *plod* from *walk* we could use the property "slow" and to further distinguish *stalk* from *plod* a property such as "purposeful" is needed.

Evidence for the existence of semantic properties is found in some of the speech errors, or "slips of the tongue," that we all make. In the chapter on phonology some errors were cited that reveal the internalized phonological system of the language. Other errors result in the substitution of a word for an intended word. Consider the following word-substitution errors that some speakers have actually produced:

Intended utterance	Actual utterance (error)
blond hair	blond eyes
bridge of the nose	bridge of the neck
when my gums bled	when my tongues bled
he came too late	he came too early
Mary was young	Mary was early
the lady with the dachshund	the lady with the Volkswagen
that's a horse of another color	that's a horse of another race
he has to pay her alimony	he has to pay her rent

These errors, and thousands of others we and others have collected, reveal that the incorrectly substituted words are not total random substitutions, but share some semantic properties with the intended words. *Hair* and *eyes, nose* and *neck, gums* and *tongues* are all "body parts" or "parts of the head." *Young, early,* and *late* are related to "time." *Dachshund* and *Volkswagen* are both "German" and "small." The semantic relationship between *color* and *race* and even between *alimony* and *rent* are rather obvious.

Other speech errors are word blends such as in the following:

Component words	Blend error
splinters/blisters	splisters
edited/annotated	editated
terrible/horrible	herrible
smart/clever	smever
a tennis player/athlete	a tennis athler
a swinging/hip chick	a swip chick
marijuana/acid	maracid
frown/scowl	frowl
aspect/viewpoint	aspoint

It is almost as if the speakers who produced these errors had the semantic properties or features of the words that would express the meaning they wished to convey and pulled out of their mental dictionaries more than one word that included some of these semantic properties and then couldn't decide between them and so blended them together. Errors in speech thus support what we have been saying about the semantic properties of words.

The meaning of a word, then, is specified in part by a set of semantic properties. Consider, for example, the word *kitten*. Knowing the meaning of this word means knowing that it refers to an animal, a young animal, a young feline animal, and so on. The word does not specify a particular kitten. That is, the meaning of *kitten* does not include the size or color or age of any specific kitten or what its name is or where it lives or who owns it. The meaning signifies what all kittens have in common. It defines "kittenness."

Scientists know that water is composed of hydrogen and oxygen. We know that water is an essential ingredient of lemonade or a bath. But one need not know any of these things to know what the word *water* means, and to be able to use and understand this word in a sentence.

We may know what a word means without knowing anything about the situation in which it is used in an utterance. Some philosophers deny this. Hayakawa believes that "the contexts of an utterance determine its meaning" and that "since no two contexts are ever exactly the same, no two meanings can be exactly the same. . . . To insist dogmatically that we know what a word means in *advance of its utterance* is nonsense."[1]

Nonetheless, we must insist on this "nonsense." It is not important that a word mean *exactly* the same thing each time it is used. What is important is that unless the word has essentially the same meaning from one utterance to another, two people speaking the same language could not understand each other. If we are to understand the nature of language, we must explain the fact that speakers can and do communicate meaningfully with other speakers of their language.

Hayakawa attempts to support his view by the following example. He writes:

> . . . if John says "my typewriter" today, and again "my typewriter" tomorrow, the . . . meaning is different in the two cases, because the typewriter is not exactly the same from one day to the next (nor from one minute to the next): slow processes of wear, change and decay are going on constantly.[2]

But, we would answer, such minute changes can hardly be said to affect the *linguistic* meaning of the *word*.

We have no trouble comprehending the meaning of *typewriter*. We know that what is being talked about is an object readily recognized as a "typewriter," and that the meaning of the *word* does not include the materials of which it is made, how old it is, whether it works well or not, its color, its location, or whether the owner knows how to type. Such information is not included among the semantic properties of the word.

Linguistic knowledge includes knowing the meaning of words and morphemes. Because you know this you can use these words and combine them with other words and understand them when you hear them. This knowledge is part of the grammar of the language.

How Metaphor Gives Meaning to Form

George Lakoff and Mark Johnson

We speak in linear order; in a sentence, we say some words earlier and others later. Since speaking is correlated with time and time is metaphorically conceptualized in terms of space, it is natural for us to conceptualize language metaphorically in terms of space. Our writing system reinforces this conceptualization. Writing a sentence down allows us to conceptualize it even more readily as a spatial object with words in a linear order. Thus our spatial concepts natu-

---

[1]S. I. Hayakawa. 1964. *Language in Thought and Action*, rev. ed. (Harcourt Brace Jovanovich. New York.)
[2]Ibid.

rally apply to linguistic expressions. We know which word occupies the *first position* in the sentence, whether two words are *close* to each other or *far apart*, whether a word is relatively *long* or *short*.

Because we conceptualize linguistic form in spatial terms, it is possible for certain spatial metaphors to apply directly to the *form* of a sentence, as we conceive of it spatially. This can provide automatic direct links between form and content, based on general metaphors in our conceptual system. Such links make the relationship between form and content anything but arbitrary, and some of the meaning of a sentence can be due to the precise form the sentence takes. Thus, as Dwight Bolinger (1977) has claimed, exact paraphrases are usually impossible because the so-called paraphrases are expressed in different forms. We can now offer an explanation for this:

- We spatialize linguistic form.
- Spatial metaphors apply to linguistic form as it is spatialized.
- Linguistic forms are themselves endowed with content by virtue of spatialization metaphors.

MORE OF FORM IS MORE OF CONTENT

For example, the CONDUIT metaphor defines a spatial relationship between form and content: LINGUISTIC EXPRESSIONS ARE CONTAINERS, and their meanings are the *content* of those containers. When we see actual containers that are small, we expect their contents to be small. When we see actual containers that are large, we normally expect their contents to be large. Applying this to the CONDUIT metaphor, we get the expectation:

MORE OF FORM IS MORE OF CONTENT.

As we shall see, this is a very general principle that seems to occur naturally throughout the world's languages. Though the CONDUIT metaphor is widespread, we do not know yet whether it is universal. We would expect, however, that some metaphorical spatialization of language would occur in every language and, whatever the details, it would not be surprising to find such correlations of amount.

An English example of MORE OF FORM IS MORE OF CONTENT is iteration:

He ran and ran and ran and ran.

which indicates more running than just

He ran.

Similarly,

He is very very very tall.

indicates that he is taller than

He is very tall.

does. Extended lengthening of a vowel can have the same effect. Saying

He is bi-i-i-i-ig!

indicates that he is bigger than you indicate when you say just

He is big.

Many languages of the world use the morphological device of *reduplication*, that is, the repetition of one or two syllables of a word, or of the whole word, in this way. To our knowledge, all cases of reduplication in the languages of the world are instances where MORE OF FORM stands for MORE OF CONTENT. The most typical devices are:

Reduplication applied to noun turns singular to plural or collective.
Reduplication applied to verb indicates continuation or completion.
Reduplication applied to adjective indicates intensification or increase.
Reduplication applied to a word for something small indicates diminution.

The generalization is as follows:

A noun stands for an object of a certain kind.
More of the noun stands for more objects of that kind.

A verb stands for an action.
More of the verb stands for more of the action (perhaps until completion).

An adjective stands for a property.
More of the adjective stands for more of the property.

A word stands for something small.
More of the word stands for something smaller.

CLOSENESS IS STRENGTH OF EFFECT

A much subtler example of the way metaphor gives meaning to form occurs in English (and possibly in other languages as well, though detailed studies have not been done). English has the conventional metaphor

CLOSENESS IS STRENGTH OF EFFECT.

Thus, the sentence

Who are the men *closest to* Khomeini?

means

Who are the men *who have the strongest effect on* Khomeini?

Here the metaphor has a purely semantic effect. It has to do with the meaning of the word "close." However, *the metaphor can also apply to the syntactic form of a sentence.* The reason is that one of the things the syntax of the sentence indicates is how CLOSE two expressions are to each other. The CLOSENESS is one of *form.*

This metaphor can apply to the relation between form and meaning in the following way:

If the meaning of form *A* affects the meaning of form *B*, then, the CLOSER form *A* is to form *B*, the STRONGER will be the EFFECT of the meaning of *A* on the meaning of *B*.

For example, a sentential negative like *not* has the effect of negating a predicate, as in

John wo*n't* leave until tomorrow.
The form *n't* has the effect of negation on the predicate with the form *leave.*

There is a rule in English, sometimes called *negative transportation,* which has the effect of placing the negative further away from the predicate it logically negates; for example,

Mary does*n't* think he'll *leave* until tomorrow.

Here *n't* logically negates *leave* rather than *think.* This sentence has roughly the same meaning as

Mary thinks he wo*n't leave* until tomorrow.

except that in the first sentence, where the negative is FURTHER AWAY from *leave*, it has a WEAKER negative force. In the second sentence, where the negative is CLOSER, the force of negation is STRONGER.

Karl Zimmer (personal communication) has observed that the same principle governs differences like

Harry is not happy.

> *versus*

Harry is unhappy.

The negative prefix *un-* is closer to the adjective *happy* than is the separate word *not.* The negative has a stronger effect in *Harry is unhappy* than in *Harry is not happy. Unhappy* means *sad,* while *not happy* is open to the interpretation of being neutral—neither happy nor sad, but in between. This is typical of the difference between negatives and negative affixes, both in English and in other languages.

The same metaphor can be seen at work in the following examples:

I *taught* Greek to *Harry.*
I taught *Harry Greek.*

In the second sentence, where *taught* and *Harry* are closer, there is more of a suggestion that Harry actually learned what was taught him—that is, that the teaching had an affect on him. The following examples are even subtler:

I found that the chair was comfortable.
I found the chair comfortable.

The second sentence indicates that I found out that the chair was comfortable *by direct experience*—by sitting in it. The first sentence leaves open the possibility that I found it out *indirectly*—say, by asking people or taking a survey. In the second sentence, the form *I* is CLOSER to the forms *the chair* and *comfortable*. The syntax of the sentence indicates the directness of the experience with the chair by which I found that the chair was comfortable. The CLOSER the form *I* is to the forms *the chair* and *comfortable*, the more direct is the experience that is indicated. Here the effect of the syntax is to indicate the directness of the experience, and CLOSENESS indicates the STRENGTH OF that EFFECT. This phenomenon in English is verified in detail by Borkin (in press).

The same metaphor can be seen at work in examples like:

Sam killed Harry.
Sam caused Harry to die.

If the cause is a single event, as in the first sentence, the causation is more direct. The second sentence indicates indirect or remote causation—two separate events, Harry's death and what Sam did to cause it. If one wants to indicate causation that is even more indirect, one can say:

Sam brought it about that Harry died.

The *effect that the syntax has* in these sentences is to indicate *how direct the causal link is* between what Sam did and what happened to Harry. The principle at work is this:

The CLOSER the form indicating CAUSATION is to the form indicating the EFFECT, the STRONGER the causal link is.

In *Sam killed Harry*, there is only a single form—the word *kill*—to indicate both the CAUSATION and the EFFECT (death). The forms for this meaning are as close as they can be: one word includes them both. This indicates that the causal link is as strong as it could be: a single event. In *Sam caused Harry to die*, there are two separate words—*cause* and *die*—indicating cause and effect. This indicates that the link between the cause and the effect is not as strong as it could be—the cause and the effect are not part of the same event. In *Sam brought it about that Harry died*, there are two separate clauses: *Sam brought it about* and *that Harry died*, which indicates a still weaker causal link.

In summary, in all of these cases a difference in form indicates a subtle difference in meaning. Just what the subtle differences are is given by the metaphor

CLOSENESS IS STRENGTH OF EFFECT, where CLOSENESS applies to elements of the syntax of the sentence, while STRENGTH OF EFFECT applies to the meaning of the sentence. The CLOSENESS has to do with form, while the STRENGTH OF EFFECT has to do with meaning. Thus the metaphor CLOSENESS IS STRENGTH OF EFFECT, which is part of our normal conceptual system, can work either in purely semantic terms, as in the sentence "Who are the men closest to Khomeini?," or it can link *form* to *meaning*, since CLOSENESS can indicate a relation holding between two *forms* in a sentence. The subtle shades of meaning that we can see in the examples given above are thus the consequences not of special rules of English but of a metaphor that is in our conceptual system applying naturally to the *form* of the language.

THE ME-FIRST ORIENTATION

Cooper and Ross (1975) observe that our culture's view of what a prototypical member of our culture is like determines an orientation of concepts within our conceptual system. The canonical person forms a conceptual reference point, and an enormous number of concepts in our conceptual system are oriented with respect to whether or not they are similar to the properties of the prototypical person. Since people typically function in an *upright* position, see and move *frontward*, spend most of their time performing *actions*, and view themselves as being basically *good*, we have a basis in our experience for viewing ourselves as more UP than DOWN, more FRONT than BACK, more ACTIVE than PASSIVE, more GOOD than BAD. Since we are where we are and exist in the present, we conceive of ourselves as being HERE rather than THERE, and NOW rather than THEN. This determines what Cooper and Ross call the ME-FIRST orientation: UP, FRONT, ACTIVE, GOOD, HERE, and NOW are all oriented toward the canonical person; DOWN, BACKWARD, PASSIVE, BAD, THERE, and THEN are all oriented away from the canonical person.

This cultural orientation correlates with the fact that in English certain orders of words are more normal than others:

More normal	Less normal
up and down	down and up
front and back	back and front
active and passive	passive and active
good and bad	bad and good
here and there	there and here
now and then	then and now

The general principle is: Relative to the properties of the prototypical person, the word whose meaning is NEAREST comes FIRST.

This principle states a correlation between form and content. Like the other principles that we have seen so far, it is a consequence of a metaphor in our normal conceptual system: NEAREST IS FIRST. For example, suppose you are pointing out someone in a picture. If you say

The *first* person on Bill's left is Sam.

you mean

The person who is on Bill's left and *nearest* to him is Sam.

To summarize: Since we speak in linear order, we constantly have to choose which words to put first. Given an otherwise random choice between *up and down* and *down and up,* we automatically choose *up and down.* Of the two concepts UP and DOWN, UP is oriented nearest to the prototypical speaker. Since NEAREST IS FIRST is part of our conceptual system, we place the word whose meaning is NEAREST (namely, UP) in FIRST position. The word order *up and down* is thus more coherent with our conceptual system than the order DOWN AND UP.

For a detailed account of this phenomenon and a discussion of apparent counterexamples, see Cooper and Ross (1975).

METAPHORICAL COHERENCE IN GRAMMAR

An Instrument Is a Companion

It is common for a child playing with a toy to act toward it as if it were a companion, talking to it, putting it on his pillow next to him at night, etc. Dolls are toys designed especially for this purpose. Behavior like this occurs in adults, who treat certain significant instruments like cars and guns as companions, giving them names, talking to them, etc. Likewise, in our conceptual system, there is the conventional metaphor AN INSTRUMENT IS A COMPANION, which is reflected in the following examples:

AN INSTRUMENT IS A COMPANION

Me and my old Chevy have seen a lot of the country together.

Q: Who's gonna stop me?
A: Me and old Betsy here [said by the cowboy reaching for his gun].

Domenico is going on tour with his priceless Stradivarius.

Sleezo the Magician and his Magic Harmonica will be performing tonight at the Rialto.

WHY *WITH* INDICATES BOTH INSTRUMENTALITY AND ACCOMPANIMENT

The word *with* indicates ACCOMPANIMENT in English, as in:

I went to the movies *with* Sally. (COMPANION)

The fact that it is *with* and not some other word that indicates ACCOMPANIMENT is an arbitrary convention of English. In other languages, other words (or grammatical devices like case endings) indicate ACCOMPANIMENT (e.g., *avec* in French). But given the fact that *with* indicates ACCOMPANIMENT in English, it is no accident that *with* also indicates INSTRUMENTALITY, as in:

I sliced the salami *with* a knife. (INSTRUMENT)

The reason that this is not arbitrary is that our conceptual system is structured by the metaphor AN INSTRUMENT IS A COMPANION. It is a *systematic*, not an *accidental*, fact about English that the same word that indicates ACCOMPANIMENT also indicates INSTRUMENTALITY. This grammatical fact about English is *coherent* with the conceptual system of English.

As it happens, this is not merely a fact about English. With few exceptions, the following principle holds in all the languages of the world:

The word or grammatical device that indicates ACCOMPANIMENT also indicates INSTRUMENTALITY.

Since the experiences on which the metaphor AN INSTRUMENT IS A COMPANION are based are likely to be universal, it is natural that this grammatical principle holds in most languages. Those languages where the principle holds are coherent with the metaphor; those languages where the principle does not hold are not coherent with this metaphor. Where the INSTRUMENT IS A COMPANION coherence does not appear in a language, it is common for some other conceptual coherence to appear in its place. Thus, there are languages where INSTRUMENT is indicated by a form of the verb *use* or where ACCOMPANIMENT is indicated by the word for *and*. These are other, nonmetaphorical, ways in which form may be coherent with content.

The "Logic" of a Language

The use of the same word to indicate INSTRUMENTALITY as well as ACCOMPANIMENT makes sense. It makes such form-content links coherent with the conceptual system of the language. Similarly, the use of spatial words like *in* and *at* for time expressions (e.g., *in* an hour, *at* ten o'clock) makes sense given that TIME is metaphorically conceptualized in terms of SPACE. Metaphors in the conceptual system indicate coherent and systematic relationships between concepts. The use of the same words and grammatical devices for concepts with systematic metaphorical correspondences (like TIME and SPACE) is one of the ways in which the correspondences between form and meaning in a language are "logical" rather than arbitrary.

CONCLUSION

Subtle Variations in Meaning

Is paraphrase possible? Can two different sentences ever mean exactly the same thing? Dwight Bolinger has spent most of his career showing that this is virtually impossible and that almost any change in a sentence—whether a change in word order, vocabulary, intonation, or grammatical construction—will alter the sentence's meaning, though often in a subtle way. We are now in a position to see *why* this should be so.

We conceptualize sentences metaphorically in spatial terms, with elements of linguistic form bearing spatial properties (like length) and relations (like closeness). Therefore, the spatial metaphors inherent in our conceptual system (like CLOSENESS IS STRENGTH OF EFFECT) will automatically structure relationships between form and content. While some aspects of the meaning of a sentence are consequences of certain relatively arbitrary conventions of the language, other aspects of meaning arise by virtue of our natural attempt to make what we say coherent with our conceptual system. This includes the *form* that we say things in, since that form is conceptualized in spatial terms.

Regularities of Linguistic Form

We have seen that metaphors play an important role in characterizing regularities of linguistic form. One such regularity is the use of the same word to indicate both accompaniment and instrumentality. This regularity is coherent with the conceptual metaphor INSTRUMENTS ARE COMPANIONS. Many of what we perceive as "natural" regularities of linguistic form are regularities that are coherent with metaphors in our conceptual system. Take, for example, the fact that questions typically end in what we perceive as a "rising" intonation, while statements typically end in what we perceive as a "falling" intonation.

This is coherent with the orientational metaphor UNKNOWN IS UP; KNOWN IS DOWN. This conceptual metaphor can be seen in examples like:

That's still *up in the air.*
I'd like to *raise* some questions about that.
That *settles* the question.
It's still *up* for grabs.
Let's *bring it up* for discussion.

And the reason that the verb *come* is used in *come up with an answer* is that the answer is conceptualized as starting out DOWN and ending where we are, namely, UP.

Questions typically indicate what is unknown. The use of rising intonation in questions is therefore coherent with UNKNOWN IS UP. The use of falling intonations with statements is therefore coherent with KNOWN IS DOWN. In fact, questions with falling intonation are understood not as real questions but as rhetorical questions indicating statements. For example, "Will you ever learn?" said with falling intonation is a way of saying, indirectly, "You'll never learn." Similarly, statements with rising intonation indicate uncertainty or inability to make sense of something. For example, "Your name's Fred" said with rising intonation indicates that you're not sure and want confirmation. "The Giants traded Madlock" said with rising intonation indicates an inability to make sense of something— that it doesn't fit with what you know. These are all examples of the use of rising and falling intonation coherently with the UNKNOWN IS UP, KNOWN IS DOWN metaphor.

Incidentally, WH-questions in English have falling intonation, for example, "Who did John see yesterday?" Our guess as to the reason for this is that most of the content of WH-questions is known, and only a single piece of information is taken to be unknown. For instance, "Who did John see yesterday?" presupposes that John saw someone yesterday. As might be expected, tone languages generally do not use intonation to mark questions at all, usually making use of question particles. On the whole, where intonation signals the difference between questions and statements, rising intonation goes with the unknown (yes-no) questions and falling intonation with the known (statements).

Examples like this indicate that regularities of linguistic form cannot be explained in formal terms alone. Many such regularities make sense only when they are seen in terms of the application of conceptual metaphors to our spatial conceptualization of linguistic form. In other words, syntax is not independent of meaning, especially metaphorical aspects of meaning. The "logic" of a language is based on the coherences between the spatialized form of the language and the conceptual system, especially the metaphorical aspects of the conceptual system.

The King of France *Is* Bald: An Introduction to Cognitive Linguistics[1]

Seth R. Katz

THE PROBLEM WITH LOGICAL SEMANTICS

Semantics is the study of how words mean. For most of Western history, semantics has been a part of the study of philosophy and logic. Only since about 1900 has it been commonly considered a part of the larger field of language studies. Modern semantic study has, for the most part, remained rooted in logic. Most theories of how words mean have treated sentences as logical propositions with truth values. According to these studies, the most important thing to determine about the meaning of a sentence is whether it is true or false in relation to the "real-world." For example, in a classic work of the logical-semantic tradition, Bertrand Russell (1956 [1905]) analyzes the sentence,

The king of France is bald.

Russell treats "The king of France is bald" as a logical proposition and describes its meaning in the following way. The sentence is a "definite description" of a person, "The king of France." The use of "the" in "The king of France is bald" implies that there exists a king of France, and only *one* king of France (*the* king of France), and he is bald. Therefore, there are three situations in which "The king of France is bald" would, logically, be false:

1 It would be false if there were no king of France;
2 It would be false if there were more than one king of France; and
3 It would be false if there were only one king of France and he is not bald.

Since there is, in fact, no king of France, "The king of France is bald" is false. And, according to Russell, this is how this sentence means; this is what it is important to know about how this sentence means; and this is all this sentence means.

Logically, Russell's analysis is indisputable; intuitively, it is not very useful. For the most part, we don't look for the truth value of the sentences we hear and read. We are usually more concerned with whether we understand them, and whether they are relevant, informative, and interesting. Russell's analysis tells us very little about how we get meaning from "The king of France is bald."

Russell also assumes that his sample sentence has only one possible reading—that is, he only imagines one context or world in which it might be used, which he might think of as the "real world." In that world, there is a country

[1]I wish to thank Linda Miller Cleary, Mike Linn, and Mark Turner for all their comments and suggestions.

called France which once had a king but no longer does. We can easily imagine contexts in which the *sentence* "The king of France is bald" means something different and is therefore true. It might be uttered truthfully by a character in a historical novel: someone who is close to the king and speaking from personal knowledge in the "here" and "now" of the novel could tell a friend, or even think, "The king of France is bald." Or, say we are at a costume party and observe a man dressed as Louis XIV. As he leans over to get a potato chip, his elaborate wig falls off, into the punchbowl, revealing that he is bald. At that moment, I say to you, "The king of France is bald." The sentence is true—even if we are both consciously aware as I utter it that the "real" France hasn't had a monarch for many years. But Russell's analysis, and all such logical analyses, assume that individual words point directly to individual objects and concepts in the "real world," and that, therefore, the sentences people utter can be called true or false on the basis of whether they name objects and relationships that "really" exist.

We conventionally use words as though they point directly to or are labels on objects. But, as Ferdinand de Saussure (1966 [1915]) shows, the relationship between words (signifiers) and the things they name (signifieds) is arbitrary. It is simply chance that we use the sound [dog] to name the object we call "dog." Other languages use other sounds to signify "dog" (e.g., in French [*chien*] means "dog") (65–9). Ludwig Wittgenstein (1953) shows further that, even conventionally, many words cannot be thought of as pointing to individual objects in the world. Wittgenstein uses the example of the word "game." He shows that there are many different kinds of games and that all games possess no single quality in common. Some games are played alone, some in pairs, some with teams; some games involve physical skill, some mental skill, some luck, and some any combination of the three; some games are played on fields, some on boards; some are played with cards, or balls, or special equipment. Therefore, we cannot point to one thing and say, "That is 'game.'" We can only point to objects and say something like, "That is an *example* of a game." Even if we take the name of a specific game, like "checkers," there are a potentially infinite number of checker sets and games of checkers which that word might refer to or "be used to mean." We can also invent a new thing and legitimately call it a "game" if it has enough features in common with an already-established member of the category of "games."

In the logical tradition, Keith Donnellan (1966) proposed a way different from Russell's for thinking about language use. Say, at another party, I see someone I don't know and ask you, "Who is the woman drinking the martini?" I may be asserting to you that the woman is, in fact, drinking a martini (just as "The king of France is bald" may assert that there is "really" a king of France); or I may simply be identifying her for you even though she may have chicken soup in her martini glass. But say we are at a party being thrown by the local "Teetotalers Union" and I, as the chairperson, am informed that one of the female members has been spotted drinking a martini at the party. I might ask my informant, "Who is the woman drinking the martini?" In this situation, the question has a different meaning: I am asserting that the woman is drinking a martini and am asking my informant to identify her (285–287). Donnellan's point is that language use is *situational* : the meaning of any utterance, expression, or word is not fixed in relation to the "real world" but is based on the situation of its use [just as "game" will mean different things in different situations (e.g., ball game, board game, dice game) and "checkers" will mean whatever checker set or game of checkers the situation dictates].

Logical semantics has, like most theories of grammar, syntax, and semantics, tried to separate language from how it is actually used. But the relationship between words and the things they name is not fixed; rather, it is arbitrary and conventional. An individual word may refer to a potentially infinite number of different objects, events, or concepts. And the meaning of words varies from one situation to another. Yet, for the most part, we understand what people mean when they use words, often very clearly and specifically. How do words mean, and how do we know what they mean when they're used?

THE COGNITIVE LINGUISTIC SOLUTION

Logical-semantic theories have assumed that the meaning of a word is the thing it names or, at least, the inherent properties of the thing (e.g., Russell 1956 [1905]; see also Fromkin and Rodman 1983). But this clearly leads to some problems in explaining how we actually use and understand language. Cognitive linguistic theory proposes that the mind and experience of the language user mediate between language and the world. Language does not refer directly to things but evokes "mental images," or concepts, in the mind of the hearer or reader. These concepts are not only sensory or visual but also include emotive and kinesthetic sensations, as well as a person's awareness and knowledge "of the physical, social, and linguistic content," context and implications of the act of language use (Langacker 1988, 4–7). When we hear or read language, we don't find the meaning by just "looking up the words" in a mental "dictionary of the real world" and stringing word meanings together to find the meaning (and truth value) of the whole. Rather, to understand or find the meaning of what we hear and read, we draw on our relevant knowledge about how individual words and expressions may mean, the context or situation they are being used in, and other contexts in which we have experienced their use or which have been similar in terms of sensory, emotive, or other experience.[2]

We often find distinct examples of the personal aspect of meaning, as when a

---

[2]C.f. Frank Smith (1988, 164–179) on the connection between the whole context of the act of reading (type of text, reader's experience, reader's purpose for reading, etc.) and the reader's comprehension of the text.

particular word or tone will annoy or anger someone. If I say to you, "Hey, that's life," and you think or feel, "I hate when you say that—that's what my boyfriend said before he dumped me," then that thought or feeling is part of your understanding of the meaning of the expression "Hey, that's life." Similarly, if there is a particular tone of voice that your father used when telling you to "do your homework," and I use that tone of voice when saying something to you, your experience of that vocal tone is going to be part of the meaning of what I say to you. Regardless of the supposedly objective reality of a situation, particular words, expressions, sensory experiences, events, places, contexts, etc., will "set a person off" or "get a person down" or "pick a person up" because of his or her experience of those words, expressions, etc. Meaning is not, as in the logical-semantic view, inherent in objects and events. Things are only meaningful to *someone* within a *context* (Lakoff 1987, 292; see also Lakoff and Johnson 1980, 159–84). And all of the interpreter's potentially relevant experience becomes part of a word or expression's meaning.

If we bring all of this experience to bear in understanding individual words and expressions, how do we use language at all? Why don't we collapse under the weight of all this mental processing effort? And if meaning is subjective, how do people understand each other? Recent psychological research has shown that knowledge is acquired, organized, and stored in human memory in systematic ways which make it easily accessible.[3] The ways in which we can and do use and understand language directly reflect that organization. We basically organize knowledge in memory by means of *schemas, categorization, metonymy,* and *metaphor*.

Though we retain many memories of specific events, our memories of events that bear any similarity to each other become, for the most part, cross-referenced, conflated, and generalized into schemas, scripts, or frames.[4] These schemas (or scripts or frames) are made up of the most common or typical objects, actions, and ideas which make up the event. If I say to you, "I'm getting married!" your immediate question might be, "Who's the lucky woman?" Your "natural" assumption is that, since I am a man, if I am getting married, there must be a bride who is an adult human female. You do not actually know that there is a woman involved; I have not mentioned one and could be marrying anyone or anything for all you know. But given your overwhelming and repeated experience of "getting married" in America—not only weddings you yourself have witnessed but weddings on TV, in movies, books, that you've heard about

---

[3]See Rosch 1975, 1978; Rosch, et al., 1976; Nelson 1977; Berlin 1978; Rosch and Lloyd 1978; Reddy 1984 [1979]; Lakoff and Johnson 1980, 1984; Mervis 1980; Black 1984; Hirst 1984; Fauconnier 1985; Neisser 1986; Reiser, Black, and Kalamarides 1986; Johnson 1987; Lakoff 1987; Turner 1987; Langacker 1987, 1988, 1989; Lakoff and Turner 1989; and Sweetser 1989.

[4]For further information on schemas, see Rumelhart (1975); on scripts, see Schank and Abelson (1977); and on frames, see Goffman (1974), Minsky (1975), and Fillmore (1982). See also Kintsch (1974, 4) and Seamon (1984).

from other people, or seen pictures of, and so on—you have developed, in your "store" of knowledge about the world, a generalized "wedding-schema" that contains and assumes all the people, objects, emotions, concepts, and events that a "typical" American wedding would have. The simple mention of "marriage" (or any of the major parts of the wedding schema, its most important or salient features—e.g., "bride," "groom," "toss the bouquet") is enough to evoke a concept of the whole schema, as well as particular instances and versions of that schema (e.g., "The band was so good at our wedding." "Remember your friend Lenny fainted when he was standing up for his brother?").

If Todd and Nancy have been dating for five years and Todd tells his mother, "We went to talk to Reverend Harkovy today," and she interrupts him with, "Oh! I've waited so long for this!" it is probably because she has taken Todd's statement to mean, "We're getting married." Her assumption would be based on a "courtship schema" (in which, typically, dating someone for a long time leads, ultimately, to marriage and in which one would visit a clergyperson with one's significant other only when seriously contemplating marriage), as well as on her hopes for and anxieties about her son. We generalize experiences into schemas from very early in our lives and have a tremendous number of them by the time we are mature language users. Events, activities, and objects become schematized very quickly, and repeated experiences extend and develop our schemas.[5] Though every individual's experiences are different, the sum of those experiences—their generalization into schemas—is similar enough from person to person that in most commonly occurring situations, people have essentially the same expectations about what will "normally" happen. Schemas make up our expectations about the world to such a degree that we do not notice those expectations until they are violated. Todd's mother would be surprised if he continued by replying, "Huh? Well, the Reverend wants us to join the choir." My friend would be surprised if I told him that I wasn't marrying a woman.[6]

Our expectations about what people will say (and how they will say it) and our understanding of the meaning of words are based largely on our schematic understanding of the world. Even our expectations about word choice depend on our schema-based knowledge. "Julius came into the shop. He wanted to buy a watch" makes sense in part because of "what we know about going into shops and buying watches" (Bosch 1985, 307). By contrast, "Julius came into the shop. He wanted to buy Julius" is strange because, even if we imagine a world

---

[5]See Schank and Abelson (1977, 225–227); Anderson and Shifrin (1980); Brown (1980); c.f. Vygotsky (1962 [1934]).

[6]We also do not remember everything that happens to us and frequently use schemas to reconstruct how events "must have" occurred (Collins, et al., 1980; Spiro 1980; Brewer 1986; Barclay 1986; Neisser 1986). For example, I do not remember the actual act of typing the beginning of this article, but given that I have a great deal of experience of typing which has become generalized in my memory into a "typing schema," I can reconstruct what I probably did. In court testimony, people will use their schematic knowledge to reconstruct their memories of events (Neisser 1981; Loftus and Yuille 1984).

in which "people" were among the things that fit into the schema of "what one can buy in stores," it is still strange to imagine buying oneself. The use of "Julius" at the end of the second sentence violates our schema-based expectations. Likewise, "Julius came into the shop. She wanted to buy a watch" also strikes us as strange, since we assume, from the concept evoked by the name "Julius," that Julius is a "he," not a "she." While telling someone they are "in error," "wrong," "mistaken," or that they "screwed up" can all "mean the same thing," each evokes a different concept and so has a different effect. That effect is an essential part of the meaning.

Most of our concepts are organized into categories: we store and recall concepts of objects and events of the same type together. These categories are themselves organized in a number of ways. Many categories are *graded* : that is, they contain a variety of instances of the same object or event, but some instances are more typical (or "higher-grade") examples of the category than others. For instance, given the category "bird," for most Americans or Europeans, a "robin" is a more typical example of the category (is "more birdish") than an "ostrich"; and a bird with wings that flies is a better example than a wingless and/or flightless bird (Rosch 1975; Rosch, et al., 1976). Likewise, a wedding at which the bride wore black and didn't throw a bouquet would not be the most typical example of a wedding. When we hear the word "bird," the concept it evokes is something more like a robin than an ostrich, and when we hear "wedding," we have a concept of (and so expect) a bride dressed in white who will throw a bouquet. If everything else were typical but the bride wore black, it would still be a wedding; it just would not be the most typical example of a wedding. In the same way, an ostrich is a bird, just not our most typical concept of a bird.

Some categories are organized in terms of *family resemblances*. As noted above, a category like "game" is made up of members that all have no single property in common. Football and baseball are both played with balls and involve physical skill and competition. Baseball and poker both involve competition. Poker and clock solitaire are both card games. Clock and craps both involve luck. All of these are, nonetheless, games, and the word "game" might be used to refer to any of them (Lakoff 1987, 16). In different situations, "game" will refer to different subsets within the category; e.g., mother says to father, "Why don't you teach the children a game?" as opposed to one stereotypical adult male saying to another, "I haven't seen a game in weeks." "Game" probably means very different things in these sentences.

Knowledge in general is organized and can be accessed *metonymically*. Metonymy is when some part of a schema is used to stand for another part, or for the whole schema. Metonymy is common in our language use.[7] Generally, the word or phrase used metonymically must name an important or focal part of the schema. In "Check out my new *wheels*," "wheels" refers metonymically to

---

[7]See Lakoff and Johnson (1980, 35–40); Lakoff (1987); Turner (1987, 21); Lakoff and Turner (1989, 100–106).

the whole car, the wheels being an important part of the whole (note that in British English, one would say, "Come see my new *motor*") (Thrall and Hibbard 1960, 481). In "*The White House* today announced new tax increases," the PLACE WHERE SOMETHING HAPPENED (the White House) is used metonymically to refer to the PERSON OR INSTITUTION WHICH RESIDES THERE (the President or another representative of the executive branch of government). Other common types of metonymy include

PRODUCER FOR PRODUCT: You should have bought a *Sony* (for *a Sony tape deck*); I hate reading *Plato* (for *the works of Plato*).

OBJECT USED FOR USER: The *sax* has the flu today (for *the saxophone player*); The *ham sandwich* left without paying! (for *the customer who ordered the ham sandwich*).

CONTROLLER FOR CONTROLLED: *Bush* bombed Baghdad (for *the military which Bush controlled*); A Mercedes rear-ended *me* (for *my car*).

INSTITUTION FOR PEOPLE RESPONSIBLE: *Exxon* destroyed Prince William Sound (for *the people who actually spilled the oil that destroyed the Sound*); The *university* will never agree to that (for *the university's administration*).

Lakoff and Johnson 1980, 38–9

We organize our thoughts and actions in terms of these metonymic relationships. That is, though Bush didn't actually drop the bombs on Baghdad, "via the CONTROLLER FOR CONTROLLED metonymy we not only say 'Bush bombed Baghdad' but also think of him as doing the bombing and hold him responsible for it." "The ham sandwich left without paying" shows that the waitress is thinking of the person who ate the sandwich not as a human being, but only as a customer— in her thinking, the customer is depersonalized and dehumanized (Lakoff and Johnson 1980, 35–40). We use language to refer to people, objects, and events metonymically because we conceive of them metonymically: we know that a whole has parts which relate to each other and to the whole in certain ways. This knowledge comes from our schematic understanding of the world and from the fact that the mention of a part of a schema can evoke the whole schema, the mention of the whole can evoke a part, and the mention of one part can evoke others. We know that a "bride" is part of a "wedding," so that mentioning a bride (the part) can and will evoke a wedding schema (the whole), just as mentioning a wedding will evoke a concept of its parts. The mention of a bride also evokes such related concepts as "groom," "bridesmaids," and "tossing the bouquet."

Our knowledge is also organized *metaphorically*. A metaphor consists of describing one thing in terms of another, as in "Money is the *key* to our success" or "The wind has a real *bite* to it." Money is not literally a key, nor success something with a lock on it that needs to be opened; likewise, the wind does not have teeth. But, in our thinking, money is somehow like a key and the wind somehow like something that has teeth and bites. Lakoff and Johnson (1980, 1984) have described how much of our use of language and our corresponding thinking about the world is organized metaphorically—that we think and talk about many things as if they were actually other things. They cite the example of the metaphor LOVE IS WAR:

> He is known for his many *conquests*.
> She *fought for* him, but his mistress *won out*.
> He *fled from* her *advances*.
> She *pursued* him *relentlessly*.
> He is slowly *gaining ground* with her.
> He *won* her hand in marriage.
>
> 1980, 49

Love is not actually war, there is no battlefield across which armies advance and retreat, with an ultimate winner (and an implied loser); but we talk and think about it as though it were. A metaphor can be thought of as a mapping in which the names for concepts in one schema or "domain" are used to name concepts in another domain, and the relationships between concepts in the former domain are "mapped onto" (used to characterize relationships in) the latter domain (Turner 1987; Lakoff and Turner 1989). In LOVE IS WAR, the lovers are called combatants, and the act of wooing and the response to that wooing are the movements of an army in battle. This metaphor is so entrenched in our thinking about love that it influences our actions: if we *fail to win* in love, we think we need to be more *forceful* or *aggressive* in our *pursuit*. It's very rare that the object of our affections actually runs away. There are several other metaphoric ways in which we talk about love, including:

LOVE IS A PHYSICAL FORCE: I could feel the *electricity* between us. They *gravitated* to each other.

LOVE IS A PATIENT: This is a *sick* relationship. They have a *strong, healthy* marriage.

LOVE IS MADNESS: I'm *crazy/mad* about her. She *drives me out of my mind*.

LOVE IS MAGIC: She *cast her spell* over me. The *magic* is gone. I'm *charmed* by her.

(Lakoff and Johnson 1980, 49)

Each of these metaphors, like LOVE IS WAR, partially shapes and reflects—and limits—our understanding and experience of love, as well as the ways in which we talk about love. We use them because they adequately express some part of the experience of love. At the same time, they limit the ways in which we will understand, talk about, experience, and be able to act in the context of love. Love, by these metaphors, is something beyond our control (magic, disease, madness, disembodied physical force) or which we are striving to control by force or conniving (war); and because of these metaphors, we think and behave as though love is something we cannot control, or can control only by the methods of war. Think how different our understanding and experience of love would be if our dominant metaphor for it were LOVE IS A COLLABORATIVE WORK OF ART. Such a metaphor would entail that love is work, requires cooperation, creativity, and self-expression—in short, that a love schema consists of all those things that a "collaborative work of art schema" consists of (Lakoff and Johnson 1980, 139–55). Rather than thinking, acting, and talking as though love is "beyond our control" or "must be won (by force)," by LOVE IS A COLLABORATIVE WORK OF ART, love would be something which we could control, through cooperation, in order to *create a work of beauty* or *genius*, something that was *aesthetically pleasing* and that would be *an object of enduring interest and study.* Though it is possible to create new metaphors such as this, most of our metaphoric (and metonymic) understanding of the world is so deeply entrenched that it would be very difficult to change. Note how, often, it is very hard to conceive of and talk about things in new ways.

SOME APPLICATIONS TO TEACHING WRITING

Cognitive linguistics claims that certain principles underlie our use and comprehension of language. Learning these principles can help writing students at any level. A frequent teacher comment on student essays is "Explain more" or "Tell more." And the standard student reply is, "But you *know* what I *mean*." To an extent, the student is right: given a few cues, a reader can sketch out the schema of the typical version of a situation suggested by a student's words. But students don't realize that every reader's construal of a schema will be different—in their own minds, readers will emphasize different parts of or ideas in a typical version of an event. Students have to learn that in writing, and in essay prose particularly, they must explicitly mention those parts of the schema which they wish their reader to focus on. Since there will be common variations on the typical version of any schema, they must say which one they intend. Students have to be sure to explicitly mention enough of the details of a schema so that a reader can readily understand why they mention it at all and what its connection is to the essay's subject. Writers must provide enough explicit information so as to be sure that readers will choose the writers' intended meaning over their own. Questioning whether a writer creates enough context or mentions enough explicit details of schemas is one way in which students can read and critique each other's writing.

Words may have different meanings (evoke different concepts) in different contexts. This provides clear motivation for the old editing saw, "Question every word." If it becomes apparent to students that every word choice can affect meaning, it becomes more reasonable to ask, "Does *this* word evoke the concept I want it to in the context of this sentence/passage/essay? Is this word expected here, given the wording I've used so far? If it is unexpected, what concepts does/might it evoke? Are those concepts consistent with the tone and effect of the whole, and with my goals in writing this essay?" These questions become significantly more concrete.

A cognitive linguistic approach can also help students improve their vocabulary and general language usage. Studies have shown that students do not learn how to use words merely by memorizing vocabulary lists (see Coomber and Peet 1981). Cognitive linguistics emphasizes that the concepts evoked by words are stored, recalled, used, and comprehended only in the context (schematic, categoric, metonymic, metaphoric) of other concepts. Therefore, students cannot learn new words without learning them in context. They must rehearse new words and their evoked concepts together with related words and concepts with which they are already familiar. To be effective, vocabulary drills must involve some kind of context. But the best method for learning new words is practice through actual usage: reading, writing, and speaking.

The systematicity underlying metaphor as described by Lakoff and Johnson (1980, 1984) provides a way to create new metaphors and so new ways of thinking. Many common schemas have particularly rich vocabularies for expressing concepts and relationships, and so can be excellent sources for new ways of talking and thinking about other schemas. Some examples of domains of knowledge with interesting concepts and complex relationships are GARDENING or PLANTS (1980, 47; Lakoff and Turner 1989), DANCE (Lakoff and Johnson 1980, 5), COLLABORATIVE WORK OF ART (1980, 139–53), WORK OF LITERATURE, CHEMICAL (1980, 143–9), THE HUMAN BODY (see Johnson 1987; Sweetser 1987), and even the WRITING PROCESS itself. All of these domains of knowledge can form a basis for new ways of understanding other domains. If we think of love in terms of the metaphor LOVE IS THE WRITING PROCESS, the lovers can be named and described as the writers (coauthors), and the relationship can be described as the text. This produces some interesting images:

> We've been *revising* our relationship.
> They should have *done more research* before they got together.
> Our love isn't *written in stone* : we can *revise* the *text*.

The lovers could also be writer and text:

> I've decided to *edit* her out of my life.
> The way he's trying to *revise* my life, I wonder if he'll ever produce a *draft* he likes!

CONCLUSION

Meaning is not inherent in objects or in words; meaning only exists in a person's understanding of objects, ideas, and events within contexts. According to cognitive linguistics, we construct meaning on the basis of generalizations of experience or "schemas," which are organized in our minds in terms of categories, metonymy, and metaphor. The systematicity of our storage and retrieval of knowledge permits us to access both general and specific knowledge quickly and efficiently. Our generalized, schematic knowledge permits us to understand the world and share expectations about it with each other.

Our schematic knowledge of the world and the organization of that knowledge are deeply entrenched in our thinking and closely interwoven with each other. We, therefore, often cannot talk or think about something other than in the way in which we habitually do. In our experience and in our thinking and in our language use, love *is* war and madness and magic; and our experience reinforces how we think and talk about it, our thinking reinforces how we experience and talk about it, and the way we use language to discuss and describe love reinforces how we experience and think about it. The meaning of "love" is not *necessarily* "war" or "madness" or "magic." But our experience, thinking, and language use, within the context of our culture, create and reinforce "war," "madness," and "magic" as part of the meaning of "love." Language works to communicate meaning because we share so many experiences in common and generalize, organize, and talk about them in the same, systematic ways.

Cognitive linguistics shows how language use draws on, taps into, and operates inseparably from our experience of language and the world. Underlying language use is a vast systematicity—an organization of memory, experience, knowledge, and language that directs and predisposes us in the ways in which we can and will use and understand language. Schemas, categorization, metonymy, and metaphor appear to be universal among human cultures as ways in which concepts are stored, recalled, and expressed in language. Different cultures will focus on different parts of schemas (as sources of metonymy) and different features of similarity (in defining categories), but the basic principles of organization remain the same.[8] The basis for this organization seems to be human beings' tremendous facility for making connections (finding relationships between concepts) and finding and matching patterns. Language is not an independent entity. It is part of an intricate system made up of our knowledge and experience, our cultures and environments, and the structure of our minds and our bodies.[9] Cognitive linguistics recognizes the integrity of this system and develops its theory of language use and comprehension from there.

REFERENCES

Anderson, Richard C., and Zohara Shifrin. 1980. "The Meaning of Words in Context." Spiro, Bruce, and Brewer 331–348.

Barclay, Craig R. 1986. "Schematization of Autobiographical Memory." Rubin 82–99.

Berlin, Brent. "Ethnobiological Classification." *Cognition and Categorization*. Rosch and Lloyd 9–27.

[8]See Johnson (1987); Lakoff (1987); Sweetser (1989).
[9]See Lakoff and Johnson (1980, 14–24; 1984, 127–30); Langacker (1987, 1988, 1989).

Black, John B. 1984. "Understanding and Remembering Stories." *Tutorials in Learning and Memory: Essays in Honor of Gordon Bower*. Eds. John R. Anderson and Stephen M. Kosslyn. San Francisco: Freeman. 235–255.

Brewer, William F. 1986. "What Is Autobiographical Memory?" Rubin 25–49.

Brown, Ann L. 1980. "Metacognitive Development and Reading." Spiro, Bruce, and Brewer 453–481.

Collins, Allan M., John Seely Brown, and Kathy M. Larkin. 1980. "Inference in Text Understanding." Spiro, Bruce, and Brewer 385–407.

Coomber, James E., and Howard D. Peet. 1981. "Vocabulary Teaching: Toward System and Reinforcement." *SRA Position Paper*. Chicago: Science Research Associates.

Donnellan, Keith. 1966. "Reference and Definite Descriptions." *Philosophical Review* **75** : 281–321.

Fauconnier, Gilles. 1985. *Mental Spaces: Aspects of Meaning Construction in Natural Language*. Cambridge, MA: MIT Press.

Fillmore, Charles. 1982. "Frame Semantics." *Linguistics in the Morning Calm*. Ed. Linguistic Society of Korea. Seoul: Hanshin. 111–138.

Fromkin, Victoria, and Robert Rodman. 1983. "Semantic Properties." *An Introduction to Language*. New York: Holt. 164–168.

Goffman, Erving. 1974. *Frame Analysis: An Essay on the Organization of Experience*. Cambridge, MA: Harvard University Press.

Hirst, William. 1984. "Factual Memory?" *The Behavioral and Brain Sciences* **7**: 241–242.

Johnson, Mark. 1987. *The Body in the Mind: The Bodily Basis of Reason and Imagination*. Chicago: University of Chicago Press.

Kintsch, Walter. 1974. *The Representation of Meaning in Memory*. Hillsdale, NJ: Lawrence Erlbaum.

Lakoff, George. 1987. *Women, Fire, and Dangerous Things: What Categories Reveal about the Mind*. Chicago: University of Chicago Press.

Lakoff, George, and Mark Johnson. 1980. *Metaphors We Live By*. Chicago: University of Chicago Press.

———. 1984. "From *Metaphors We Live By*." *The Harper and Row Reader*. Eds. Wayne C. Booth and Marshall W. Gregory. New York: Harper. 121–130.

Lakoff, George, and Mark Turner. 1988. *More Than Cool Reason: A Field Guide to Poetic Metaphor*. Chicago: University of Chicago Press.

Langacker, Ronald. 1987. *Foundations of Cognitive Grammar*. Volume I. *Theoretical Prerequisites*. Stanford University Press.

———. 1988. "An Overview of Cognitive Grammar." *Topics in Cognitive Linguistics*. Ed. Brygida Rudzka-Ostyn. *Current Issues in Linguistic Theory 50*. Philadelphia: John Benjamins. 3–48.

Langacker, Ronald. 1989. *Foundations of Cognitive Grammar*. Volume II. *Descriptive Application*. Chapters 1–4. ms.

Loftus, Elizabeth F., and John C. Yuille. 1984. "Departures from Reality in Human Perception and Memory." *Memory Consolidation: Psychology of Cognition*. Eds. Herbert Weingartner and Elizabeth S. Parker. Hillsdale, NJ: Lawrence Erlbaum. 163–183.

Mervis, Carolyn B. 1980. "Category Structure and the Development of Categorization." Spiro, Bruce, and Brewer 279–307.

Minsky, Marvin. 1975. "A Framework for Representing Knowledge." *The Psychology of Computer Vision*. Ed. P. H. Winston. New York: Cambridge University Press.

Neisser, Ulric. 1981. "John Dean's Memory: A Case Study." *Cognition* **9** : 1–22.

———. 1986. "Nested Structure in Autobiographical Memory." Rubin 71–81.

Nelson, Katherine. 1977. "Cognitive Development and the Acquisition of Concepts." *Schooling and the Acquisition of Knowledge*. Eds. Richard C. Anderson, Rand J. Spiro, and William E. Montague. Hillsdale, NJ: Lawrence Erlbaum. 215–239.

Reiser, Brian J., and John B. Black. 1982. "Processing and Structural Models of Comprehension." *Text* **2** (1–3):225–252.

Reiser, Brian J., John B. Black, and Peter Kalamarides. 1986. "Strategic Memory Search Processes." Rubin 100–121.

Rosch, Eleanor. 1975. "Universals and Cultural Specifics in Human Categorization." *Cross Cultural Perspectives on Learning*. Eds. Richard W. Brislin, Stephen Bochner, and Walter J. Lonner. New York: Wiley. 177–206.

———. 1978. "Principles of Categorization." Rosch and Lloyd 27–49.

Rosch, Eleanor, and Barbara L. Lloyd. 1978. *Cognition and Categorization*. Hillsdale, NJ: Lawrence Erlbaum.

Rosch, E[leanor], C. B. Mervis, W. D. Gray, D. M. Johnson, and P. Boyes-Braem. 1976. "Basic Objects in Natural Categories." *Cognitive Psychology* **8**: 382–439.

Rubin, David C., ed. 1986. *Autobiographical Memory*. New York: Cambridge University Press.

Rumelhart, David E. 1975. "Notes on a Schema for Stories." *Representation and Understanding*. Eds. Daniel G. Bobrow and Allan Collins. New York: Academic. 211–236.

Russell, Bertrand. 1956[1905]. "On Denoting." *Logic and Knowledge: Essays 1901–1950*. Ed. Robert Charles Marsh. New York: Macmillan. 41–56.

Saussure, Ferdinand de. 1966[1915]. *Course in General Linguistics*. Eds. Charles Bally, Albert Sechehaye, and Albert Riedlinger. Trans. Wade Baskin. New York: McGraw-Hill.

Seamon, John G. 1984. "The Ontogeny of Episodic and Semantic Memory." *The Behavior and Brain Sciences* **7** (2):254.

Smith, Frank. 1988. *Understanding Reading: A Psycholinguistic Analysis of Reading and Learning to Read.* 4th ed. Hillsdale, NJ: Lawrence Erlbaum.

Spiro, Rand J. 1980. "Constructive Processes in Prose Comprehension and Recall." Spiro, Bruce, and Brewer. 245–278.

Spiro, Rand J., Bertram C. Bruce, and William F. Brewer, eds. *Theoretical Issues in Reading Comprehension: Perspectives from Cognitive Psychology, Linguistics, Artificial Intelligence, and Education*. Hillsdale, NJ: Lawrence Erlbaum.

Sweetser, Eve. 1989. *From Etymology to Pragmatics: The Mind-as-Body Metaphor in Semantic Structure and Semantic Change*. Cambridge: Cambridge University Press.

Thrall, William Flint, and Addison Hibbard. 1960. "Synechdoche." *A Handbook of Literature*. New York: Odyssey. 481.

Turner, Mark. 1987. *Death Is the Mother of Beauty: Mind, Metaphor, Criticism*. Chicago: University of Chicago Press.

Vygotsky, Lev. 1962 [1934]. *Thought and Language*. Cambridge, MA: MIT Press.

Wittgenstein, Ludwig. 1953. *Philosophical Investigations*. Trans. G. E. M. Anscombe. New York: Macmillan.

Truth Is a Linguistic Question

Dwight Bolinger

The drift of this paper can be summed up in an expression that first saw the light of day in 1942. For almost three years, from 1937 to 1939, American volunteers had been part of the army that fought against Hitler and Mussolini in Spain. After the vortex of Hitlerism had finally sucked us in, one would have expected those trained and seasoned young soldiers to be admired for their foresight and sought out for their experience. But nothing of the sort happened. In one of those perverse labelings that propagandists are so good at, they were passed over as 'premature antifascists'. To have admitted their foresight would have been to admit our own lack of it.

Every generation has to rediscover love. So, I suppose, every generation must rediscover jargon. Here is a 1972 definition by L. E. Sissman: 'all of these debased and isolable forms of the mother tongue that attempt to paper over an unpalatable truth and/or to advance the career of the speaker (or the issue, cause or product he is agent for) by a kind of verbal sleight of hand, a one-upmanship of which the reader or listener is victim.' Stepping back to 1955 we hear James Thurber calling for a psychosemanticist, or for anybody, who could treat us for what he called 'the havoc wrought by verbal artillery on the fortress of reason', by a language 'full of sound and fury, dignifying nothing'. Going back another quarter century to my own college days, there was Sir Arthur Quiller-Couch with his essay 'On jargon' (1916). Running the film in reverse a good 200 years more, Sir Ernest Gowers (1948) quotes an admonition 'delivered to the Supervisor of Pontefract by the Secretary to the Commissioners of Excise'. It reads: 'The Commissioners on perusal of your diary observe that you make use of many affected phrases and incongruous words, such as "illegal procedure," "harmony," etc., all of which you use in a sense that the words do not bear. I am ordered to acquaint you that if you hereafter continue that affected and school-boy way of writing, and to murder the language in such a manner, you will be discharged as a fool.' It would be a simple matter to round out the history with quotations from Erasmus and Thucydides.

All very interesting, you may admit, but what does it have to do with us? There was a time when it would have been hard to believe that any linguist could admit that it had anything to do at all. Those of us who trekked across the semantic desert of the forties and fifties could hardly have been blamed for feeling that life had lost all meaning, except perhaps differential meaning. Not that there were no respectable scholars interested in how meaning can be abused in language. In 1941 there was a group calling itself the Institute for Propaganda Analysis, numbering among its officers Clyde Beals, W. H. Kilpatrick, and Charles Beard, along with other notables. (I insert at this point, as a sign of the times, the fact that after thirty years of suspended animation the Propaganda Analysis group began to show signs of life again this fall, and was calling on linguists for cooperation. But the original group had no linguists in it.) Of course there existed at about the same time a flourishing school of General Semanticists, very much involved in such questions. Yet I don't need to remind any of the veterans in LSA how these lower-class people were looked down upon. Leonard Bloomfield regarded their leader, Alfred Korzybski, as a kind of soothsayer, and Korzybski's own jargonesque prose did little to dispel that impression. In any case, linguistic engineering (to use a bit of jargon from our own side) was totally absorbed in establishment activities such as army specialized training, literacy programs, and language policy in emerging nations. This was where the money went and where the action was. The linguist up to very recently has been a more or less useful social sideliner, but not a social critic.

Happily, I think we can say that this aloofness has begun to thaw somewhat. In a sense we are repeating the two phases of the protest movement. First came civil rights. In our terms, this has meant studies of Black English and Harlem Spanish and so-called deficit language in general. Now we are approaching something akin to peace and welfare demonstrations in the form of demands on the 'white standard' for accountability. The National Council of Teachers of English is one step ahead of us. In November they set up a Committee on Public Doublespeak; one of its members, Wayne O'Neil, is also a member of LSA, so we may expect the gospel to be spread any day now. What makes me more certain of this is the fact that the Boston *Globe*, when it carried the account of the Committee on Public Doublespeak, identified Wayne as Rabbi Wayne O'Neil. Robert Hogan, Executive Secretary of NCTE, described the charge of the committee in these terms: "The question is not just whether subjects and verbs agree, but whether statements and facts agree."[1]

Though I suspect that a majority of linguists would still want to reject it, there is also the plea made recently (1972) by Congressman Robert F. Drinan. He was addressing himself to teachers of English, and he had this to say (279): 'In the matter of officially proclaimed marshmallow prose, it does seem to me that you have some professional responsibility.' Whether we deny this or not, we are being pushed toward it by events both in our field and from outside. Take the grammar of the sentence. There aren't many big nuggets left in that gold mine. Right now the prospectors are swarming over presuppositions, higher sentences, and other things whose purpose or effect is exactly to make explicit what writers and speakers get away with in their self-serving prose. Context is in, both linguistic and social. And we have rediscovered the lexicon, including the morass of connotations, euphemisms, and general chicanery. The last refuge left for the weakhearted seems to be phonology. The rest of us are finding it more and more difficult to keep ourselves undefiled.

[1]Boston *Globe*, 22 November 1972, p. 5.

As for events outside the field, our government—the very government that is the greatest abuser of language—finds itself caught in the embarrasing necessity of enforcing honesty in order to collect its taxes. Only so much money can be squeezed out of a family budget; so, in true gangster fashion, the small-time operators are being liquidated. There are the dealers who for years levied usurious rates of interest and were allowed to get away with it by the neat semantic trick of labeling them 'carrying charges'; also the local rent gougers, and the minor medicine men with their pill-promoting prodigies and their end-product, the drug culture. Government hits back by giving us truth in lending, truth in labeling, and truth in advertising. These are narrow gains. If we want the truth that government requires of its own business partners—e.g., which insurers give value for their premiums or which automotive manufacturers build safe transmissions—we still have to go to court to get it. All the same, there is a danger for those bent on concealment. A taste of truth is like a taste of blood. The subject should never have been brought up at all. Now that it has, truth is in the headlines, pushed there by the two-way struggle between governors and governed, each bent on finding out about the other—the governors to sniff out our private feelings, which could pose a threat to our control; the governed to know the decisions that affect them, but of which they may not be the beneficiaries. The medium of all this knowing is language, and linguists are in the line of fire.

If this widespread clamor for truth only embraced the way language is used, it might affect us less intimately. But it is also directed at the way language is. Here the target is not so much government as the whole of society. Julia Stanley (1972a) shows us a lexicon replete with terms of barter referring to women, and few or no counterparts referring to men. Robin Lakoff in a similar study (1973) exposes the undertow of condescension and depreciation even in two such innocent-looking terms as *woman* and *lady*. Women are taught their place, along with other lesser breeds, by the implicit lies that language tells about them. Now you can argue that a term is not a proposition; therefore merely having the words does not constitute a lie about anybody. The words may be there, but it takes people to put them together, and so people may be liars but words are not. This argument has a familiar ring. We hear it every time Congress tries to pass legislation restricting the possession of guns. A loaded word is like a loaded gun, sometimes fired deliberately, but almost as often by accident. And even when you feel like firing one on purpose, it has to be in your possession first. Lots of casualties, some crippling ones, result from merely having weapons around.

I'm sure that many linguists will sympathize with these social concerns and agree that they should do something about them—but as citizens, not as linguists. How is truth to be defined so as to involve us professionally? Before I try to answer that, let me at least see if I can show that linguists who already accept some responsibility for language use can't consistently say that truth is irrelevant to linguistics. Here, adopting a suggestion made to me by Julia Stanley, I raise the question of appropriateness in language. Appropriateness is just as pertinent to content as it is to form. If linguists allow themselves a professional interest in how well a dialect or a code fits a place or situation, they cannot logically turn their backs on the fitness of language to facts. Let's hope that this comparison will satisfy at least some of the sociolinguists among us. It will not be quite so easy to convince those who feel that linguists who tangle themselves in anything having to do with messages and contexts thereby cease to be scientific. Still, we can snatch a reminder from what has been happening to us in the last decade or so. We are now fully involved with meaning, and from the meanings of the parts to the meaning of the whole is only one more step in the same direction.

The definition I propose for truth will not make it more precise, but it will establish the right connections. Consider how we use the verbs *inform* and *misinform*. They require either human subjects or message subjects. We say *He misinformed me with his letter* or *His letter misinformed me*, but not *The clouds misinformed me about the coming rainstorm*. Truth is that quality of language by which we inform ourselves. This rules out the logician's analytic truth, which is no more than consistency within language. Literal truth it includes only partially, because literal truth—the kind one swears to tell on the witness stand—permits any amount of evasion. I think it also has to be distinguished from historical truth, because in language that informs there has to be an element of timeliness. We can say of truth what is said of justice: truth delayed is truth denied. But the most insidious of all concepts of truth is that of literalness. Advertising capitalizes on the legal protection that it affords. The California prune-growers tell us that prunes, pound for pound, offer several times more vitamins and minerals than fresh fruit; literally true. The oil industry advertises that no heat costs less than oil heat, which has to be true because no heat costs nothing at all. These cases of verbal thimblerigging depend on an old ethic that winks at the clever and laughs at the gullible. In simpler times they were part of our education; but in today's complex world everyone is an ignoramus about something—about diet, about the workings of our electronic whigmaleeries and arcane bureaucracies, about the flammability of fabrics, the potability of water, or the meaning of Form 1040A. The possibilities of deception have passed the bounds of tolerance. It is no longer innocent fun when the Barnums and Baileys hang up their sign reading 'This Way to the Egress'. The egress has lost her imaginary feathers and shivers out there in the cold with the rest and the best of us.

I have tailored my definition of truth to fit what speakers mean to have understood. Within a social setting, any other definition is a game. Appropriateness is not to be taken between facts and abstract sentences, but between facts and sentences plus their contexts—and contexts include intentions. Not because I can justify it if anyone wants to debate the point, but just to get this kind of truth as pure as I can distill it, I'll go a step farther and say that when two parties are in communication, anything that may be used which clogs the channel, and is not the result of accident, is a lie. I am trying to paint the lie as black as I can by not requiring that it be intentional. There are consciously intentional lies, of course; but there are also lies by habit, and people who believe their own propaganda, and chiefs of state who surely harbor such a concept as that of a little lie being part of a larger truth, on the analogy of War is Peace or what you don't know won't hurt you. So I'd rather make falsehood embrace the hidden and unconscious, as well as the barefaced and deliberate. By contrast, truth would always be prompted by the active willingness to share what we know. There are some people for whom this willingness may be almost habitual. We still try to make it that way with our children, in the small society of the home.

Now I hope I am ready for the linguist who wants to maintain his scientific integrity. I quote from Robin Lakoff again (1972: 907). She writes: 'In order to predict correctly the application of many rules, one must be able to refer to assumptions about the social context of an utterance, as well as to other implicit assumptions made by the participants in a discourse.' The ingredient of the social context that is relevant to truth is the disposition to share what we think or know, and it is reflected in our choice of words and often in our choice of grammar. The very existence of a large part of the lexicon depends on it, and it explains at least part of the survival value of some constructions.

Let me start with some examples from grammar. The easiest to document from current discussions are the ones that involve deletion, so my first example is the case of the missing performative. Parenthetically, if you prefer to believe that a performative is inserted when it is present rather than deleted when it is absent, it makes no difference, since nobody doubts that WHEN they are present, performative verbs are explanatory. Take the case where somebody in authority makes a pronouncement like *America is lagging behind Russia in arms production*. With no indication of the evidence, we have to take the claim on faith. But if the speaker says *I think that America is lagging*, or *My chief of staff informs me* or *I'll just bet America is lagging*, then there is a measure of honesty about how reliable the information is.

Compared with other omitted elements, the missing performative is the least of the deceptions. It is a mere peashooter in the liar's arsenal, because as long as a proposition is straightforward, whether it has an explicit performative or not, most people can muster enough skepticism to ask for proof. It is when other less conspicuous things are deleted that dubious propositions are able to slip past our guard. A number of these have been getting attention of late, especially by Stanley, in studies of what she terms 'syntactic exploitation' (e.g. 1972b).

My first example of these is the old story of the deleted agent of the passive. This is the prime syntactic means for sophisticated gossip. In place of *they say*, where a listener who is on his toes will ask 'Who's *they*?', the speaker removes this temptation by putting the performative verb in the passive and keeping quiet about *they*. In our culture this is a commonplace of newspaper headlines. Shanks and Shaughnessey are having a dispute over a medical bill. Shanks says that Shaughnessey sewed him up with a couple of sponges and a scalpel still inside. Shaughnessey says that's a dirty lie. Depending on how friendly the editor is with one or the other, the headline comes out *Shaughnessey charged with malpractice* or *Shanks charged with slander*. Either way, the reader is invited to fill in the empty slot with more than one agent. The effect is to magnify the guilt of one or the other party.

There are other instances of deleted agents that are more insidious. Stanley (1972c: 17) quotes a paragraph from Dostoevsky in which eight passive constructions without agents succeed one another, creating the impression 'of a faceless society in which the individual has no power, and all activities affecting citizens are carried out by a nameless, impersonal "they"' (1972c: 19). To the extent that such a view is accepted, the passive becomes a means of lying on a large scale.

Another of Stanley's examples is the passive adjective. When we use sentences like *In the 5th century the known world was limited to Europe and small parts of Asia and Africa*, what do we mean by *known world*? Known to whom? Since the phrase is a 'syntactic island', it is not open to question, and we are able to get away with ignoring three-fourths of the world's population. As Stanley puts it, 'our attention is focused on the major predication' (1972b: 11), so that we can wonder about the accuracy of the geographical claim, but not about who did the knowing. When Mutual of Omaha proudly announces on its ecology-minded program 'Wild kingdom' (31 December 1972) that *Man protects threatened animals*, it is able to give credit to the well-known human race without at the same time explicitly taking credit away.

Donald Smith 1972 adds a further case of an omitted element and its exploitation, which he terms 'Experiencer deletion'. The most typical sentences are those with the verb *seem*—which, as Smith says (20), 'are favored in certain types of prose and speech such as by bureaucrats, educationalists or anybody who may wish, among other things, to disguise the sources of impressionistic assertions about the world'. One of Smith's examples is this (21), from *Beyond freedom and dignity* by B.F. Skinner: *The need for punishment seems to have the support of history*. Seems to whom? The lack of frankness of this score makes the claim irresponsible.

Not to overstate the case, we should recognize that some inept deletions are not due to attempts at concealment, but to having overlearned a rule of high-school rhetoric: if you're a writer, make your references to yourself as few as possible. The passive with deleted agent is fine for this; it works out well in scientific writing where the emphasis is on processes, not on the people who carry them out. But some writers carry the prescription for self-effacement to the point of passivizing even a performative. So you get successions of more or less normal passives, capped by a sentence like *It is believed that these instructions will prove easy to follow*. This is a fair exchange of modesty for muddleheadedness.

We could go on with more examples from syntax, but it would be tedious because there are probably no two things that can be put together in a sentence that can't be used for some kind of fakery. Linguists make a great thing of the duality that developed between meaningless sub-units and meaningful higher units as defining human language; but long before that, there must have grown up a deadlier kind of duality whereby meanings were divorced from reality. As soon as signs were fully detached from things, it became possible for them to point at something non-existent or at the opposite of what they are supposed to point at. The practical joker who today turns the arrows from right to left on a one-way street surely had his caveman counterpart. This is not to say that bluffing and other forms of disingenuousness are unknown in the animal kingdom; but what distinguishes human mendacity is its capacity for elaboration. By the simple act of negation, any truth we utter can be turned into falsehood. By merely changing the intonation, any doubt can be rendered a certainty.

But the power of the lie carries beyond the realm of elaboration into the realm of invention. We elaborate with syntax. We invent in the lexicon. I suspect that some syntactic lies are beyond our control. When a child is caught redhanded and says *I didn't do it,* it may be an instinctive reaction of self-defense. But the act of coining a new expression is conscious, and any lying there is deliberate. The very act of naming has consequences for our attitudes. Take a sentence like *He responded to her cry of distress*: this uses a syntactic means that is at least neutral as regards sympathy. But in a sentence like *He responded to her distress cry*, you sense an incongruity. *Distress cry* adds something to the lexicon; it sets up a classification, and does it in a clinical way—for observation, not for pity or for hate. Karl Zimmer, in a recent study of nominal compounds (1971: 14), finds that one necessary condition is that they be 'appropriately classificatory' for the speaker—i.e., represent a slice of reality and not a passing event. So by using them we can represent a happening as a thing. Now happenings can be prevented by attacking their causes or their causers, but things have a life of their own. They are independent of us; and if we fail to change them, it is because THEY are capable of resistance. The person who refers to migratory workers as wetbacks or weed-pullers excuses himself from responsibility for illegal entry and bad working conditions. That class of people simply exists.

The act of naming, plus some favorable or unfavorable overtone in the terms selected for it, is the favorite device of the propagandist and the ultimate refinement in the art of lying. Syntax you can penetrate. In a phrase such as *intelligible remark* or *acceptable excuse,* there's a submerged predication, all right; but it's at least represented by a detachable adjective, and if you think of it you can ask 'Intelligible to whom?' But the nominal compound is impervious: the predication is not only buried out of reach but out of sight.

This helplessness, I think, is what has focused the attention of political commentators on the lie of naming. Henry Steele Commager (1972:10) accuses the Nixon administration of replacing the Big Lie with great quantities of lies; but the interesting thing is that all the examples he identifies, as far as language is concerned, are nominal compounds. Here is the paragraph containing them (11): 'Corruption of language is a special form of deception which this Administration, through its Madison Avenue mercenaries, has brought to a high level of perfection. Bombing is "protective reaction," precision bombing is "surgical strikes," concentration camps are "pacification centers" or "refugee camps" . . . Bombs dropped outside the target area are "incontinent ordnance," and those dropped on one of your own villages are excused as "friendly fire"; a bombed house becomes automatically a "military structure" and a lowly sampan sunk on the waterfront a "waterborne logistic craft".' 'How sobering,' he adds, 'that fifteen years before 1984 our own government should invent a doublethink as dishonest as that imagined by Orwell.' Congressman Drinan, after saying that 'Language is not merely the way we express our foreign policy; language is our foreign policy' (279), goes on to add that 'The systematic use of such opaque terms as "protective reaction", and the hollow sentences of war planners, do far more to hide the decision-making process from the people—and from Congress—than any secrecy classification rules' (281). Charles Osgood (1971:4) is equally impressed with the effectiveness of naming; he mentions the title *Camelot* which 'conferred a romantic, even chivalrous, tang to an ill-fated U.S. Army project designed to study the causes of revolutions,' and he says that 'to name an ABM system *Safe-guard* certainly must make its possessors feel more secure. A touch of nobility is added to raw power when intercontinental ballistic missiles are named *Thor, Jupiter, Atlas, Zeus,* and *Polaris* although I miss the ultimate in semantic deception which would be a missile named *Venus.*'

Again I should pull back an inch or two, so as not to make it appear that I think all the abuses of naming have an ulterior motive. If the habit had not already been there, officialdom could never have made capital of it. Out of its passion for supplying needs and dealing with problems frontally, this society has bred a mania for making everything tangible. It arrests every motion, solidifies every event. The lowly clerk exhibits it when he lets you know that he is *in receipt of* your message—nothing so ordinary as that he has simply received it. The advertiser exhibits it when he offers you, not a product that will make your battery last longer, but one that will give you longer *battery life.* The bureaucrat merely follows suit when, instead of talking about the side that has the most and most powerful planes, he talks about the side that has *air superiority.*

The nominal compound at the service of bureaucracy is only the wholesaling of those embodiments of prejudice that every speech community allows to flourish in its vocabulary, terms in which neutral semantic features are mingled with valuative ones. Most likely everyone here has his own pet collection, from business, government, or daily life. My favorite is this quotation from *The Sonoma County Realtor* of Santa Rosa, California: 'An alert real estate salesman should learn how to express himself well and to use psychology . . . Don't say "down payment"; say "initial investment." Don't ask for a "listing"; ask for an "authorization to sell." Don't say "second mortgage"; say "perhaps we can find additional financing." Don't use the word "contract"; have them sign a "proposal" or "offer" . . . Don't use the word "lot"; call it a "homesite." Don't say "sign here"; say "write your name as you want it to appear on your deed." '[2] Here we see the unremitting struggle to keep concepts free of their associations. A term such as *military conscription* picks up unpleasant connotations along the way, and is replaced with *draft*. *Draft* starts to pick them up in turn and is replaced with *selective service*. Since a nation such as ours no longer wages war but only defends itself, it became necessary many years ago to change the name of the old War Department to the Department of Defense. In all these examples the exploiters of words are fighting to keep them free of certain semantic features. The other side of the coin is when they cling to features even though the actual conditions are absent, to use the word as a weapon. Calling a person a traitor is like throwing him in prison; both are symbolic acts. *Traitor* is a disgraceful name, prison is a disgraceful place. This works as long as people can be kept from their habit of re-interpreting in the light of the facts, and discovering perhaps that the whole prison concept is a fake. Either way you take it—whether fighting off semantic features from words, or trying, in the teeth of the evidence, to keep them—there is an accelerated rate of semantic change and greater confusion when we try to communicate, and to that extent we can speak of the corruption of language, for it is caused by deliberate and well-financed interference.[3]

I mentioned valuative features. The study of them is one that has gone on sporadically, but has never been central to our discipline. It would be timely to revive it now, especially in the context of paralinguistics, because there is an unmistakable tie with gesture. The more we learn about the concepts of attraction and repulsion, the better we see how pervasive they are in our ways of thinking and in most of our words. Within language, valuative features are transmitted from one part of the lexicon to another by hidden link-ups that doubtless reflect some basic fact about where and how the lexicon is stored in our brains. A few linguists were interested in this a decade or so ago and studied it under the rubric of phonesthemes, a certain type of sound symbolism. Let me give just one example. I was recently struck by the peculiar contrast in a pair of synonyms that, in any literal sense, ought to be about as close in meaning as any two words can get. The Merriam-Webster Third regards them as identical: *baseless* and *groundless*. I was puzzled as to why *baseless* struck me as the stronger of the two; so I put the question to a seminar of three Harvard freshmen I was

---

[2] Quoted in *Consumer Reports*, October 1972, p. 626.

[3] As far as advertising is concerned, no further examples are needed, for the mercenary bias is clear. As for government, to quote Drinan again (281), 'the use of empty words by the Defense Department is not the accidental by-product of a metastasized bureaucracy; rather, it is an essential part of a pervasive scheme to keep Defense Department decision-making a secret—unknown and unknowable by any potential critics.'

teaching, and one of them came up with the same explanation that had occurred to me: *baseless* echoes *base*. A baseless accusation, for instance, is one that is not only groundless, but also mean and unworthy. Language is a jungle of associations like this one, where a malevolent guide can lose any simple-minded wayfarer. For us to lead one another without leading one another astray requires a conscious act of will. Truth is not a highway. It is a trail hacked through snake-infested undergrowth.

One form of lying uses all the tricks so far described, but is distinguished from them by sheer quantity. I refer to what we might term obfuscation, more the province of the stylist than the linguist. A piece of obfuscatory prose may contain a message somewhere, but it is lost in the murk of rhetorical self-importance. Stanislav Andreski 1972 cites an example from Talcott Parsons:

> Instead of saying simply that a developed brain, acquired skills, and knowledge are needed for attaining human goals, Parsons writes: 'Skills constitute the manipulative techniques of human goal attainment and control in relation to the physical world, so far as artifacts or machines especially designed as tools do not yet supplement them. Truly human skills are guided by organized and codified KNOWLEDGE of both the things to be manipulated and the human capacities that are used to manipulate them. Such knowledge is an aspect of cultural-level symbolic processes, and, like other aspects to be discussed presently, requires the capacities of the human central nervous system, particularly the brain. This organic system is clearly essential to all of the symbolic processes. . . .'

Getting back to things of more direct concern to linguists, what if enough of them were to turn their attention to truth and falsehood for it really to make a difference? It is a risky business when scientists start developing tools that are capable of misuse. To bring to light the mechanisms of Machiavellianism may be to provide future Machiavellis with easy access. But I doubt we can teach today's Machiavellis much that they do not already know. This is one game where the con men have less to learn than their victims. Knowing how to lie—brazenly, delicately, urbanely, esoterically—is a question of survival for officials dedicated to fundamentally unpopular causes. For this we can partly blame our own eager acceptance of a cosmetic society. 'America', I once wrote (Bolinger 1962), 'is the first society to achieve a virtual taboo on the unpleasant.' Our advertising has convinced us of it, and our officials are afraid to say otherwise. Language is called upon to do the same thing as psychiatry—in Sissman's words, 'to paper over unpalatable truths'. The most pathetically pertinent example of psychiatric paper-over was aired recently on a Boston radio station. It seems that a psychiatric service has been set up to treat those abnormal people who are afraid of flying. It will not do for a traveling public to harbor any pathological fears about being trapped at thirty thousand feet with no place to go but down. Compare this attitude with that of the maritime regulations, according to which common carriers not only stock up with life preservers and lifeboats, but also conduct regular lifeboat drills among their passengers. Imagine the effect on travel if airline passengers were required to take part in parachute drills; and contrast that with the sweetly offhand voice of the stewardess giving perfunctory safety directions, trusting that her tone and her legs will distract you from her ominous words. This may not be dedication to the utmost in safety, but it is at least dedication to the utmost in playing down the need for it. Forget the parachutes and give us piano bars. When you have government, business, and camp-following psychiatrists teamed up in this fashion to make the normal in OVERT behavior seem abnormal, what can you expect with as pliant a medium as language?

Let's suppose that an aroused public were to begin paying as much attention to linguistic ecology as to environmental ecology. What might some of the reactions to this be—on the part of those who oppose truth—against which we should be forearmed? In business they are already visible as a reaction to the comparatively feeble jabs of the truth-in-this and truth-in-that campaigns (observe, please, that there is as yet no campaign for truth, period). Another possible effect is the heightened reliance on war, especially the selling of war materials. War is popular, among other reasons, because it enables business to get along without customers. There are no finical housewives to complain that the plastic pellets in smart bombs are not penetrating deep enough. Another effect, of more direct concern to us, is the retreat from language. What I outlined in the first part of this talk was the retreat from PROPOSITIONAL language. Things are said, but said in such a way that even professional skeptics have trouble pinning them down. But after all that comes to light; then what? First there's the recourse of not making any claims yourself, but putting them as testimonials. Terence Langendoen (1970), in his critique of the Federal Trade Commission, points out (7–8) that 'all an advertiser needs to do to convert a misleading statement of fact into a misleading statement of opinion (which is hence exempt from sanctions) is to put it in the mouth of a celebrity or "average consumer."' Of late there has been a further refinement in testimonials, which consists in not making any outright claim, but staging a little dramatization. A pre-Columbian pedant announces that the world is flat, and this proceeds through a series of non-sequiturs to the conclusion that not all aspirins are the same. As a last resort, after the testimonial in its various forms direct and indirect, there remains the recourse of not using language at all, but merely making agreeable noises. We now leave the left hemisphere of the brain and move over to the right. In my personal count of radio and TV ads, I came up with about one in three that uses just language. The rest feature a mixture of language and music or other sound effects. With TV of course there are the dimensions of color and image. It tells us something about the importance of truth to language that the more you insist on truth, the farther those who care little for the truth retreat from language.

Truth is a linguistic question because communication is impossible without it. Unless social interaction is to break down, the lie must always be the exception.

Robin Lakoff (1972:916) sets up five rules which she says 'define an appropriate conversational situation.' Here are the first three:

Rule I. What is being communicated is true.
Rule II. It is necessary to state what is being said: it is not known to other participants, or utterly obvious. Further, everything necessary for the hearer to understand the communication is present.
Rule III. Therefore, in the case of statements, the speaker assumes that the hearer will believe what he says (due to Rule I).

Government and business are making two arrogant assumptions. The first is that it is possible to have one-way monopolistic communication, with the public consuming official verbiage as it consumes the handouts from industry and welfare. The second is that Lakoff's rules are not important, only the illusion of them. Public officials hide behind the images that Madison Avenue creates for them, and lies hide behind the face of truth.

Linguists cannot excuse themselves from these uses of language, though they may find various ways of approaching them. Lloyd Anderson (1970:1) sees our field 'reopening itself to the study of rhetoric and literature, to communications and psychology, to continuous and fuzzy phenomena of the real world'—including, among its possible contributions, 'new rigorous principles of "false advertising" and "false communicating" for legal guidelines, for journalistic ethics, to support a new interpretive reporting distinct from propaganda'. It can't come too soon.

REFERENCES

Anderson, Lloyd B. 1970. Journalism and linguistics: some mutual interests. Talk at student-faculty seminar. School of Journalism, University of North Carolina, Chapel Hill, October.

Andreski, Stanislav. 1972. *Social sciences as sorcery*. London: Andre Deutsch. (Cited in *Time* , 25 September 1972, p. 67.)

Bolinger, Dwight. 1962. The tragedy must go on. *American Liberal*, November, p. 26.

Commager, Henry Steele. 1972. The defeat of America. *New York Review of Books*, 5 October, pp. 7–13.

Drinan, Robert F. 1972. The rhetoric of peace. *College Composition and Communication* 23:279–282.

Gowers, Sir Ernest. 1948. *Plain words*. London: His Majesty's Stationery Office. (Cited by Joseph Jones, *American Speech* 24:121, 1949.)

Lakoff, Robin. 1972. Language in context. *Lg.* 48:907–927.

———. 1973. Language and woman's place. *Language in Society* 2:45–80.

Langendoen, D. T. 1970. A study of the linguistic practices of the Federal Trade Commission. Paper read at LSA, 29 December.

Osgood, Charles E. 1971. Conservative words and radical sentences in the semantics of international politics. *Social psychology and political behavior: Problems and prospects,* ed. by Gilbert Abcarian and J. W. Soule, 101–129. Columbus, Ohio: Charles E. Merrill.

Quiller-Couch, Sir Arthur. 1916. *On the art of writing.* Lectures delivered in the University of Cambridge, 1913–1914, pp. 83–103. Cambridge: University Press.

Sissman, L. E. 1972. Plastic English. *Atlantic Monthly,* October, p. 32.

Smith, Donald. 1972. Experiencer deletion. MS.

Stanley, Julia. 1972a. The semantic features of the machismo ethic in English. Paper read at South Atlantic Modern Language Association.

———. 1972b. Syntactic exploitation: passive adjectives in English. Paper read at Southeastern Conference on Linguistics VII, 21 April.

———. 1972c. Passive motivation. MS.

Thurber, James. 1955. The psychosemanticist will see you now, Mr. Thurber. *New Yorker,* 28 May, pp. 28–31.

Zimmer, Karl E. 1971. Some general observations about nominal compounds. Working papers in language universals, Stanford University, 5.

Placing Meaning at the Center of Language Study

Nancy Mellin McCracken

Generals, clergymen, advertisers, and the rulers of totalitarian states—all have good reasons for disliking the idea of universal education in the rational use of language. To the . . . authoritarian mind such training seems (and rightly seems) profoundly subversive.

Aldous Huxley

While national test scores indicate that more students than ever before are achieving skill in decoding written language, there has been no such growth in students' ability to interpret written language. Calls for attention to "critical thinking" abound. In elementary schools brave voices proclaim the benefits of a "whole language" approach versus the segmented skills approaches loosely classified as "phonics." The high school curriculum, however, has most often remained impervious to sporadic professional calls for "integrated language arts instruction." The trivium remains: literature, grammar, and writing with its own separate strands—often illustrated by separate books—for vocabulary and spelling. Sometimes separate units on "critical thinking" are taught. Occasionally one finds a unit on mass media or persuasion analysis. Almost always there is a brief review of "logical fallacies." But these separate units are insufficient to help students to move beyond decoding and Hirshian "cultural literacy" to interpretation of the language they will hear and read in their lives.

I. A. Richards believed that the proper purpose of language studies or rhetoric should be "a study of misunderstanding and its remedies." In most schools, however, far more time is spent on the study of linguistic etiquette than on the study of communication and "misunderstanding and its remedies." For example, in Warriner's *English Grammar and Composition*, 3rd course, Franklin Edition, the grammar text required in the school in which I am now a visiting teacher, students will read all the way to pages 705–707, the final pages of this popular text, before they are advised to "distinguish facts from opinions" and "Watch out for propaganda devices" notably, "Name-calling," "Slogans," "The Testimonial," and "The Bandwagon." In the first seven hundred pages, Warriner manages to include quite a bit of advice about proper usage in language, even including "Choose appropriate stationery."

Even with just the minimal six-week unit on language study taught each year in grades 1–12, students graduate from American high schools with 72 weeks of instruction on polite, prestigious, "standard" usage, yet there is no guarantee that they will have had any instruction in semantics and rhetoric as it is reflected in the language usage of nonliterary texts.

Too often, even when we do make time to teach semantics in English classes, we do so in a vacuum—as though it were something separate from the regular English curriculum—a kind of gimmick thrown in between grammar review and short stories. A common approach is to arm the kids with a list of propaganda techniques with catchy names, prove to them that those techniques are bad things done by bad people out to get their money or their votes, and then move on to what is seen as more central to the English curriculum—literature, parts of speech, and five-paragraph essays. The students' interest in analyzing the ordinary uses of language seldom lasts beyond the unit, and rarely extends beyond the classroom. There are serious problems with this approach. Not only is it insufficient to prepare students to deal with language and meaning in our culture; much worse, it is a disservice because it perpetuates the falsehood that only bad people manipulate language for their own ends while good people speak a pure and simple language that reveals the truth directly. Furthermore, by segmenting the study of meaning in language from the rest of the curriculum, the brief unit approach prevents students from applying the critical reading skills they practice all year through literary studies to the areas where they most need them.

For those teachers who do want to try to place the study of semantics at the heart of the English curriculum, it is not easy to find textbooks which integrate literary studies and critical analysis of ordinary language. English teachers are usually well "trained" to teach writing, literary analysis, grammatical analysis, and polite English usage, but without textbooks that focus on analysis of meaning in public language, new teachers may feel they lack the backgrounds to teach semantics. In this essay I want to describe an approach to teaching about language that I have used successfully with advanced students in grades nine and twelve as well as in college. (My first efforts with this approach are described in an earlier essay entitled "A Student-Centered, Process-Oriented, Interdisciplinary Non-Unit on Doublespeak.") The approach builds on the literature skills we know and teach and moves the classroom focus back and forth between the language of literature and the language of public persuasion. This approach is not difficult, but it does require planning and at least one major change in the curriculum—live public language must find entry to the classroom. My approach is built on the principle that the heightened attention to language provided in literature study is the best preparation for making students close readers of the language that permeates the vast nonliterary zones of their lives.

The approach has two vital components: (1) The study of semantics is integrally related to the literature-centered, high school English curriculum, and thus it offers a way in for teachers to the newer and compelling integrated approaches to language arts; and (2) students are afforded opportunities over an extended period of time, both in class and out, to read about and examine language environments which directly affect their lives. The first component of the approach is essential because it allows us to teach about meaning in language through the medium we know best. I like to begin with poetry. It has always interested me that novice students of poetry find it so difficult to accept ambiguity—it takes so long for them to stop asking what a poem *finally* means; yet when confronted with ordinary language, they readily accept not only ambiguity but gobbledygook, blatant propaganda, and general vacuous nonsense.

There are a few reasons for this. First, we teach students that their interpretations of poetry are important—they will be graded. We don't do this with political, commercial, or other powerful nonliterary language even though ability to interpret it may be the most important skill we can teach. Secondly, adolescent students often feel so inundated with the language of authority that they acquire a defensive "deafness" to all but the immediate language of their peers. In a memorable Charlie Brown cartoon, the words that Marcie's teacher speaks in class come through to Marcie only as garbled droning. It is likely that the words coming over the airwaves in news reports are similarly garbled for many of our students. Without real efforts of attention, our students can miss the meanings of most of the public rhetoric they hear outside school. Thirdly, it is possible that much of what we do with language in the classroom—as when we insist on single meanings of literary texts or when we try to teach traditional grammar as a rational system—results in the students' loss of faith in their own interpretive abilities, so much so that they are eager to accept someone else's interpretation. If we can get students to respond to the art of poetry and to trust their own responses, we will have gone a long way toward teaching them how to deal with language manipulation in the hands of those nonliterary masters they must interpret in everyday life.

Poetry works in several ways toward developing semantic discrimination in interpreting nonliterary language. In the first place, poetry uses many of the same devices that propagandists use. In teaching poetry, we teach analogy, imagery, symbolism, ambiguity—in short, the techniques of propaganda. Although the critical terms differ, the difference between language manipulation by poets and propagandists is often only one of purpose. In the hands of a poet, literary devices are used to communicate the most intense personal response to the reader. In the hands of a propagandist, they may be used to thwart that communication. We might begin with MacLeish's dictum: "A poem should not mean, but be," and reverse it for public rhetoric: "A statement must mean, not just be." There are some very instructive pairs to be made of poem and public statement. The Marine Corps' "Rifleman's Creed" and Randall Jarrell's "The Death of the Ball Turret Gunner" make one such pair. To some students' initial frustration, Jarrell's poem subverts attempts at purely intellectual analysis of meaning.

> From my mother's sleep I fell into the State,
> And I hunched in its belly till my wet fur froze.
> Six miles from earth, loosed from its dream of life,
> I woke to black flak and the nightmare fighters.
> When I died they washed me out of the turret with a hose.

The language here bypasses logic to create in the reader a more immediate sense of the subject (war). In contrast, while the Rifleman's Creed also subverts attempts at logical analysis, it does so to create a greater distance between the reader and the subject (also war).

> My rifle is human, even as I, because it is my life.
> Thus, I will learn it as a brother. . . . We will become
> part of each other. . . . Before God I swear this creed.
> My rifle and myself are the defenders of my country. . . .
> We are the saviors of my life.

Here poetic devices are used to create a personal response, but surely *not* to the real business of war.

In another example, e.e. cummings's poem "Next to of course god America i" and almost any political press statement aimed at making the speaker appear patriotic while withholding the truth make an instructive pair. There is an abundance of examples to choose from. Testimony given during congressional investigations work well: Haldeman in the Watergate hearings, Ollie North in the Iran-Contra hearings. On the international scene Iraqi leader, Saddam Hussein, recently raised the possibilities for analysis of deceptive patriotic rhetoric to new heights. (A review, printed in Lutz's *Doublespeak* of the recipients of the NCTE Committee on Public Doublespeak's "Doublespeak Award" given annually since 1974 will provide a nice overview of the possibilities.) In both cummings's poem and in political press statements that aim to obscure meaning, the language is gibberish punctuated with patriotic slogans, but while a poem can be termed "inoperative" (we frequently ask of a poem, "does it work?"), a press statement termed "inoperative" is a lie.

Members of the Watergate administration were heard in taped transcripts speculating, whether their fabricated cover-ups would "*play* in Peoria." In the Reagan and Bush administrations, the press coined the term "Spin Doctor" for the public relations specialist who finds ways to put a good "spin" on bad news. Analyses of political language supports the notion that the language of literature is often usurped by public speakers, not to enhance communication as in poetry but to subvert communication. Students who can analyze the language manipulation devices of literature (imagery, tone, metaphor, characterization) are certainly well trained to analyze language manipulation in the hands of political leaders when they hear it.

Another way literature study works to develop attention to meaning in language is to counteract the numbing effect of the sheer verbosity of our culture. The language of literature is concentrated while that of public speech is often inflated to the point where meaning is entirely obscured. My ninth-graders read *The Miracle Worker* to experience Helen's silence and subsequent joy in acquiring simple language. The twelfth-graders read Flannery O'Connor and portions of James Joyce's *Portrait of the Artist as a Young Man* to experience language which reveals character at its most essential level. Coming to know Hazel Motes or Stephen Dedalus from the inside out, and reading the language of interior monologue, language stripped of conventional filler, is good preparation for analysis of much public language. The contrast is so startling that it reawakens the students' sense of impatience with and dislike for political jargon and commercial hyperbole, even before they read Orwell's "Politics and the English Language."

Poetry works as an antidote to the antiseptic abstractions of much public language. While public speech dulls our senses with phrases like "revenue enhancement," "terminal living," "friendly fire," and "global economic downturn," poetry continues to keep us sensible of the loss of human life and dignity, bigotry, pain, and hunger. In the ninth-grade English class I am currently teaching, we began with two poems from the anthology *Patterns in Literature* that express a reverence for life and are especially vivid in their imagery of old people: Joseph Bruchac III's "Birdfoot's Grampa" and Ramona C. Wilson's "Keeping Hair." After reading and discussing these poems, the students were asked to look in their own language environments for examples of counterlanguage, words used to treat similar subjects with quite opposite effects. The poets we read use language to make us connect most personally with the subjects. "Keeping Hair" is a childhood reminiscence of a grandmother who knew how to brew a hair rinse from willows steeped in water. The old woman kept her hair long after she had lost her teeth, and the poet writes,

> The thought that once
> when I was so very young
> her work-bent hands
> very gently and smoothly
> washed my hair in willows
> may also keep my heart.

The students brought in an amazing array of advertisements for hair-care products, high-tech shampoos and color rinses claiming to "revitalize" hair. They wrote about the differences and similarities between poem and advertisement: both used strong visual and tactile images, for example, but the poem left them feeling a bond with the older woman, while in the advertisements the models were isolated. The poem suggested a continuity between youth and old age; the advertisements suggested that old age is a fate to be denied as long as possible.

Similar pairings were brought in to class in response to the poem "Birdfoot's Grampa" in which an old man stops the car each time a toad jumps into the road. The speaker complains about this constant stopping, for they have places to go,

> "But, leathery hands full
> of wet brown life,
> knee deep in the summer
> roadside grass,
> he just smiled and said
> they have places to go to
> too."

The students sympathized with Birdfoot's Grampa and understood the poem to be a celebration of the value of all living things. The "leathery hands" of the man and the "wet brown life" of the toads made it easy for the students to experience the life in the poem. The samples of counterlanguage students brought in worked in the opposite way, using language to put distance between reader and subject: an article on women's fashion noting that mink, beaver, and fox are very popular this season in new shades of green, red, and plum; an editorial complaining about the overabundance of deer in a local county; a news article on the new practice of "Grandma Dumping"—adults abandoning healthy, but troublesome, elderly parents in hospital emergency rooms around the country.

The English teacher who begins her year this way can expect some noticeable changes in her classroom. Suddenly, right in there with literature and grammar comes language from sources that have traditionally been excluded and topics usually submerged in the class discussions of character, plot, and setting. After reading Langston Hughes's "Daybreak in Alabama," for example, students brought in articles about racism on college campuses, violence erupting between Jews and blacks in Crown Heights in New York, racially motivated violence in Howard Beach and Bensonhurst, and the rise of white supremacist groups and increasing racial intolerance among groups of young adults. Such topics aren't found in most courses of study for English/language arts, but they are the result of adolescent students beginning to listen and read closely the texts that surround their lives.

Building on the heightened language awareness and skills the study of poetry brings to the analysis of nonliterary language, I assign a research project on language and meaning that will involve students in a long-term collaborative study of language beyond the literature anthology. To start off the research project, I assign chapter 10 from Lakoff and Johnson's *Metaphors We Live By*, which provides a good variety of examples of metaphors used in ordinary expressions such as that love is madness (for example, "I'm crazy about her . . .") or that ideas are for cutting (". . . an incisive idea . . . a cutting remark . . . a razor wit"). Current examples are discussed in class (President Bush's war-as-football-game metaphor during the Iraqi war and the peculiar Russian Communist Party metaphor of coup d'etat-as-illness are recent examples.) Most important in the Lakoff and Johnson work is that it opens discussion of the effects of the powerful "hidden meanings" that occur not only in literature and in propaganda, but everywhere in the language we all use.

I also like to assign excerpts from Postman's essay, "Demeaning of Meaning" in *Language in America*, and discuss his helpful metaphor of language as a "semantic environment" capable of being polluted: "The semantic environment is polluted . . . when language obscures from people what they are doing and why they are doing it." Postman explains that because there are many different purposes governing language use, there are many different semantic environments to be studied: "Science is a semantic environment. So is politics; commerce; war; love-making; praying; reporting; law-making: etc." (15–16).

In keeping with the scientific metaphor introduced in the Postman essay, I assign students to field work in a semantic environment of their choosing. They are asked to determine what they believe to be the proper function of language in the environment they choose to study, and then to analyze the language used in order to determine whether it performs that function. At the end of a semester of observation, note-taking, and recording, they report to the class on the pollution index of their specific language environment. The only restriction I make is that the students have to choose language environments which have high interest for them and to which they have frequent access.

I make additional resources available on reserve in the library. Deborah Tannen's *You Just Don't Understand* intrigues students with its evidence that boys and girls talk differently (e.g., men report and women "rapport.") Goshgarian's *Exploring Language* provides a good collection of essays on semantic topics ranging from advertising and political language to the language of racism and sexism. Lutz's *Doublespeak* is a popular resource for the study of doublespeak in advertising, business, and politics. Out of a sense of fairness, I even provide an essay on the pollution of teacher-language, "The Language of Education: the Great Trivia Contest" by Terence P. Moran. This essay is a popular choice because it focuses semantic analysis on the field of greatest concern to the students—the language of tests. Moran reminds us of a line by John Dewey: "Education is what remains after the facts are forgotten," and offers a series of paired test questions—questions from school tests matched with trivia game questions. For example:

I A silver bullet is used as an identifying symbol by (a) Tom Mix, (b) the Durango Kid, (c) the Lone Ranger, (d) Hopalong Cassidy.

II A silver bullet ends the life of the principal character in (a) *Orpheus Descending*, (b) *The Emperor Jones*, (c) *The Silver Cord*, (d) *The Great God Brown*.

The similarity between the two sets of questions is obvious to the students and they recognize the metaphor of education-as-game of trivial pursuit. Other sources on reserve include Postman's *Amusing Ourselves to Death*, essays from Charles Osgood's *The Osgood File* and William Safire's *Language Mavin Strikes Again* that discuss contemporary euphemism and other forms of obfuscation in public discourse.

In addition to the resources placed on reserve, students bring in materials to share, both language usage samples and essays about meaning in language. Gradually, we fill a wall-length bulletin board with examples of interesting uses of language. Students are encouraged to examine the language used in their own environment, and they do so with an intensity which is surprising. The language environments the students have chosen to investigate and their conclusions are worth sharing here. Several students have chosen to focus on the language of the school environment.

While adolescence is generally a time for rebellion against authority, in students who have spent a semester in close reading of texts both literary and nonliterary, the rebellion often takes a different form—one not easily dismissed with short answers. One year, for example, the political science teacher was interrupted so frequently with questions that he had to break into his tightly structured schedule of lectures to allow for discussion of terms previously memorized and bandied about by students as though they had clear single meanings ("communism," "free enterprise system," etc.). We later invited him to spend two hours in our class discussing the merits of ambiguity in the phrasing of major public documents (e.g., "the pursuit of happiness").

The students asked the science teacher the purpose of studying physics and then pointed out that the kinds of questions she asked on their objective tests belied her answer. They convinced her to give an alternative problem-solving test to those who preferred to practice "thinking as physicists." In my own class, we had begun reading *Anna Karenina* from several different translations. The students pointed out that in several cases it was not possible to come to agreement about even the literal meaning of certain passages, let alone the nonliteral meanings because the choice of *language* differed from one translator to another. The student council, led by one of the students in our class, launched the yearly campaign against several school regulations and at least temporarily baffled the administration by taking up the argument that the regulations were at variance with the *language* of the official school philosophy. These students were reexamining the language environment that controls their lives and demanding attempts at semantic honesty in school.

Other students looked well beyond the school in their study of meaning in language. One student brought a tape recorder to three of the homes where she regularly babysat. With the parents' permission, she taped the conversations of three- and four-year old children under several different conditions (anger, solitary play, and anxiety). She found that much of the children's language was used to express an inner reality quite distinct from observable reality—and that the children were aware of the distinction while often the listening adults were not. She concluded that communication is thwarted when the adult language does not take into account the function of child language.

A student who had recently attended the funeral of a grandparent reported on the language of funeral directors. She interviewed several funeral directors in the neighborhood and examined copies of their professional journals (one was happily entitled *Sunnyside and Casket*). Going on the premise that the function of funeral director language should be to provide assistance to a mourning family and a clear explanation of technical services offered and their costs, she concluded that semantic environment was grossly polluted. She reproduced pages from the journals which openly stated ways for funeral directors to obscure language for the purpose of playing on a family's grief while making a greater profit.

Another student "forced" herself to begin watching the local television news station regularly. She perceived a blatant editorializing in the drawings which were flashed behind the anchorman to illustrate each news item. The student called the television station to make a complaint, but noted that she was thwarted by the language of bureaucracy.

Other students have looked into the language of political speeches, international diplomacy, sermons, college applications, book reviews, local newspaper editorials, advertisements, sports, adolescent males and females, physicians and dentists, popular music, and M-TV. The interest in semantics remains high throughout the year, continuing to influence other classes and language environments outside the school. The students become adept at recognizing doublespeak when they hear or read it and even begin to recognize it when they speak it themselves. In these classes, analyzing the language of literature and that of everyday language continues to have a reciprocal benefit for interpreting both.

Given a chance to apply what they have learned through literature study to other semantic areas, and the freedom to explore the languages that they see as vital to them, students can become more discriminating semantically. But I remain convinced that separate units on semantics will not have their desired effect unless they can be incorporated into an entire curriculum aimed at semantic study. Given the information and entertainment explosion in our culture and the concurrent increase of public language pollution, we must place meaning at the center of our English language curriculum. And we must make room for the analysis of public discourse along with literary discourse in the classroom. It is clear that knowing the difference between *lay* and *lie* has no relationship to knowing the difference between news reports and government-sponsored "disinformation." And a cursory look at voting patterns over the past decade indicates with equal clarity that even those students who learn to recognize the trickery of Iago and the bombast of Polonius cannot be expected to automatically recognize these uses of language in their contemporary public counterparts.

REFERENCES

Clark, Virginia P., Paul A. Escholz, and Alfred F. Rosa, eds. 1985. *Language: Introductory Readings*, 4th ed. New York: St. Martin's.

Farrell, Edmund J., Ouida H. Clapp, and Karen J. Kuehner. 1987. *Patterns in Literature: America Reads*, 7th ed. Glenview, IL: Scott, Foresman.

Goshgarian, Gary. 1989. *Exploring Language*, 5th ed. Glenview IL: Scott, Foresman.

Huxley, Aldous. 1962. "Education on the Nonverbal Level." *Daedalus,* Spring. Quoted in Postman, Weingartner, and Moran, vii.

Lakoff, George, and Mark Johnson. 1980. *Metaphors We Live By*. Chicago: University of Chicago Press.

Lutz, William, ed. 1989. *Beyond Nineteen Eighty-Four: Doublespeak in a Post-Orwellian Age*. Urbana, IL: NCTE.

———. 1990. *Doublespeak*. New York: HarperCollins.

McCracken, Nancy. 1976. "A Student-Centered, Process-Oriented, Interdisciplinary Non-Unit on Doublespeak." *Teaching About Doublespeak*. Ed. Daniel Dieterich. Urbana, IL: NCTE. 135–142.

———. 1975. "Public Doublespeak: A Modest Proposal on Teaching Sisyphus the Use of the Pulley." *College English* **37**: 324–327.

Moran, Terence P. 1969. "The Language of Education: The Great Trivia Contest." *Language in America*. Ed. Postman, Neil, Charles Weingartner, and Terence P. Moran. New York: Bobbs-Merrill-Pegasus. 103–113.

Orwell, George. 1989. "Politics and the English Language." *Exploring Language*. Ed. Gary Goshgarian, 5th ed. Glenview, IL: Scott, Foresman.

Osgood, Charles. 1991. *The Osgood Files*. New York: Putnam's.

Postman, Neil. 1985. *Amusing Ourselves to Death: Public Discourse in the Age of Show Business*. New York: Elizabeth Sifton/Viking.

———. 1969. "Demeaning of Meaning: Or What's the Language-Pollution Index Today?" In Postman, Weingartner, and Moran. 13–20.

Postman, Neil, Charles Weingartner, and Terence P. Moran, eds. 1969. *Language in America*. New York: Bobbs-Merrill-Pegasus.

Richards, I. A. 1965. *The Philosophy of Rhetoric*. New York: Oxford University Press.

Safire, William. 1990. *Language Maven Strikes Again*. New York: Doubleday.

Tannen, Deborah. 1990. *You Just Don't Understand*. New York: Morrow.

Warriner, John E. 1982. *English Grammar and Composition: Third Course*, Franklin Edition. New York: Harcourt.

How the System Is Used to Make Meaning

John Mayher

The language system so acquired has many uses. Some of them are private, including whatever role language plays in the processes of thought, but most of them are public, or rather communal, in the sense that they enable us to interact with others. Even the private uses of language are influenced by the cultural nature of the particular language system we have acquired, and there is a long tradition in language study of exploring the influence of language on thought stretching, from Humboldt (1836/1988) to Sapir (1921) to Whorf (1956) to Lakoff and Johnson (1980). Anthropologists have long recognized that studying the language of a culture is essential to understanding it, and in some ways the two cannot be meaningfully separated since so many of a culture's assumptions and practices are embedded in and revealed by the particulars of its language system. In the familiar Whorfian examples this can involve vocabulary—the contrast between Eskimo and English terminology for types of snow—syntax— the contrast between Hopi and English ways of talking about explosions (a noun in English, a verb in Hopi)—or semantic properties—how time is expressed relatively in Hopi, absolutely in English.

Although it has proved difficult to substantiate empirically the strong version of the Sapir-Whorf hypothesis that our language categories and forms literally limit or restrict our perceptions, it does seem plausible that our language shapes our typical approach to problems. Our commonsense ways of thinking about language and communication are powerfully influenced by our characteristic language of how they function. So without committing ourselves to a position of absolute limitations, we should nonetheless be alert to the likelihood that our particular culture and the language which characterizes it do provide us with sets of categories and ways of talking which influence our thinking and even, in Berger and Luckmann's (1966) sense, our very conception of reality.

The overwhelmingly common and normal way in which we use language, aside from thinking itself, is to communicate with others. While we can and do communicate by other means, including the way we dress, the way we move and posture ourselves, our facial expressions, and so on, verbal communication through language is such a natural part of our daily lives that only on those occasions when we cannot use it, for example, in a place where we don't speak the language, are we aware of how pervasive and essential it is. The centrality of communication as the major use of language has led some students of language and language acquisition to argue that it is the communicative function of language that provides its essential defining characteristics.

Unlike Chomsky and the generative linguists, for whom internal processes provide the best approach to understanding the nature of language, scholars like Bates (1976), Givon (1979), Bruner (1975), and Halliday (1978) have built theories of language and language acquisition on the basis of the functions of language which center on communication. They have argued, in effect, for the priority of social and cultural constraints on the process of language learning, since children are driven to acquire language out of their need to become part of the language and culture in which they are growing up and to become fully communicative members of the group.

These two approaches are not necessarily incompatible, since it seems clear that both *internal* (hypothesis testing, mental grammar building based on innate constraints) and *external* (learning how to communicate in socially and culturally appropriate ways) processes are operating throughout the course of language acquisition and development. As individuals, we develop our capacity to participate in the culture by learning to communicate both within and against its grain. That is, the culture's ideas, beliefs, and even its language system can provoke dissent as well as assent. One source of language change and the development of dialects is individual and small group efforts to rebel against its ideational constraints. To understand language and its uses fully, we will need to look at both the inside-out role of the individual language acquirer and the constraints, models, and influences which come to the learner from the outside in.

COMMONSENSE COMMUNICATION: THE CODE THEORY

Like the nature of the language system itself, communication and other aspects of language use are generally regarded as straightforward and essentially one-way processes from the commonsense perspective. As Michael Reddy (1979) and others have pointed out, the basic commonsense metaphor for communication is transmission, or as he calls it, "the conduit metaphor." The assumption is essentially what Sperber and Wilson (1986) call the code theory: The speaker or writer encodes her thoughts in language, which is then transmitted by a variety of channels or conduits—voice to air, pen to paper, key to electronic display, and so on—to a receiver, who then decodes the language and receives the thought. As Reddy points out, this conduit metaphor is deeply embedded in our language of language use in such phrases as "putting one's thoughts into words," "getting one's ideas across," "putting one's thoughts down on paper," and so on.

All of these expressions articulate the commonsense theory that communication is a matter of putting one's message or content into words which can then be sent off through a conduit or channel to be received and unpacked by the recipient. As Sperber and Wilson comment, however, "the power of these figures of speech is such that one tends to forget that . . . they cannot be true. In writing [*Relevance*], we have not literally put our thoughts down on paper. What we have put down on paper are little dark marks, a copy of which you are now looking at. As for our thoughts, they remain where they always were, inside our brains." (1986, p. 1). That is, although the conduit metaphor suggests that it is, literally, *ideas* which are sent from one person to another, Reddy and Sperber and Wilson are pointing out that what gets sent is a *representation of our ideas,* not the ideas themselves. Similarly when we receive a message, we must interpret it, not merely directly decode it for the ideas it contains. The conduit metaphor or the code theory in effect omits a crucial step in both the sending and the receiving of linguistic messages. It therefore makes the process seem simpler and more straightforward than it really is.

But it is not only common sense which holds firmly to the code theory; it has been advocated in various forms by most of the Western intellectual tradition from Aristotle through Shannon and Weaver to modern semantics, which generalizes the code model from verbal communication to all forms of communication. The basic hypothesis of the code theory, that thoughts are directly and literally encoded in sounds (or written symbols), seems so natural that it has been taken for granted by most commentators.

*   *   *   *

COOPERATING IN COMMUNICATING

Just as Aristotle, Shannon and Weaver, and many others have developed the code model of communication, the importance of inferential processes in communication has been discussed by many writers. It has played a key role in theories of reading, particularly the reading of literature as explored by such critics as Iser (1978) and Rosenblatt (1978). It has also been a crucial problem for theorists of discourse, both written and oral. Foremost among them in recent years has been the philosopher H. Paul Grice (1967/forthcoming), who has developed the view that communication, and particularly conversation, is governed by a "cooperative principle" and "maxims of communication."

Grice argues:

> Our talk exchanges . . . are characteristically, to some degree at least, cooperative efforts; and each participant recognizes in them, to some extent, a common purpose or set of purposes, or at least a mutually accepted direction . . . at each stage, *some* possible conversational moves would be excluded as conversationally unsuitable. We might then formulate a general principle which participants will be expected to

observe, namely: Make your conversational contribution such as is required, at the stage at which it occurs, by the accepted purpose or direction of the talk exchange in which you are engaged.

Grice, 1975, p. 45

Grice went on to elaborate his cooperative principle through a series of maxims of communication which govern how participants in conversation can enact the cooperative drama of a conversation. The particulars of Grice's proposals need not concern us here, but it is important to recognize, as Sperber and Wilson (1986) point out in their critique of Grice, that "this account of the general standards governing verbal communication makes it possible to explain how the utterance of a sentence, which provides only an incomplete and ambiguous representation of a thought, can nevertheless express a complete and unambiguous thought . . . to communicate efficiently, all a speaker has to do is to utter a sentence only one interpretation of which is compatible with the assumption that she is obeying the cooperative principle and maxims" (p. 34).

What Grice has accomplished, therefore, is to begin to give a theoretical framework to account for the aspect of appropriateness in the normally creative use of language identified by Chomsky. Even if someone we are talking to makes what we at first consider to be an inappropriate contribution to the conversation, our assumption that he is abiding by the cooperative principle helps us try to find a way to make it comprehensible. Consider, for example, the following dialogue:

Bernie: Would you like to go to the movies?
Barbara: I have a lot of work to do.

Clearly Bernie needs to do some inferring in order to understand that Barbara is intending to mean something like: no, I don't have time to go, but not that she doesn't want to. Depending on how fully they understand each other's mental models and conversational rule systems, this might be the end of the topic, or it might be the beginning of an attempt by Bernie to persuade Barbara to take the night off because the break would do her good. But at the minimum, Bernie would have to assume that the reason Barbara mentioned her workload was cooperatively responsive to his question; and he would then have to use his own inference system to make the appropriate connection and then come up with an appropriate interpretation.

It was not, of course, the only response Barbara could have made. She could have said, with the same, or quite similar, intended meaning:

a We don't have a babysitter.
b My mother is very ill.
c I hate films with subtitles.
d It's going to rain.
e That won't solve the problem.

And, of course, she could have said a potentially infinite number of other things. Bernie's capacity to interpret these responses would depend on how fully he and Barbara share the same reference systems: that he knows how difficult or easy it will be to get a babysitter (a); whether or not Barbara is likely to want to be near a telephone waiting for news of her mother (b); that she knows that the film he wants to see has subtitles (c); that the only nearby theater is a drive-in (d); or that they have been having a fight and his suggestion of a movie was an attempt at peacemaking (e). Insofar as he can't make such inferences, or makes different ones, his interpretation may likewise be different, but the point here, from a Gricean perspective, is that conversers have both a vested interest in cooperation in order to communicate, and that they possess models of appropriateness which enable them to make relevant interpretations of potentially or seemingly inappropriate utterances. The meaning being made is essentially dialogic, not monologic as the code theory suggests.

While we can, for example, make some guesses as to what there is about their shared context which enables Bernie to make the inferences he does about Barbara's reply, it is hard to see how to make those contextual principles sufficiently systematic to be a guide to interpretation. What is lacking is a principled way of determining how people make the interpretations they do, and why these are, in effect, the only ones which would be consistent with the conversational rule system.

RELEVANCE THEORY

To remedy this weakness and those we have noted with the code system, Dan Sperber and Deirdre Wilson (1986) have developed a combined code and inferential theory which they call relevance theory. It seems to be a more adequate and explanatory theory than any proposed so far, and whatever its final virtues turn out to be, it does contain a number of powerful implications for language education. The essence of their theory is that coded, in particular, linguistic, communication is not autonomous but depends on, and is subservient to, a variety of inferential processes. The principle of relevance enables us to determine which of the possible implications of an utterance should be inferred in order to do the most efficient information processing possible.

For Sperber and Wilson, the relevance theory contains a way of determining how we can make inferences based on the combination of what we already know and what we are receiving. The essentials of their approach are given briefly here.

> Some information is old: it is already present in the individual's representation of the world. Unless it is needed for the performance of a particular cognitive task, such information is not worth processing at all. Other information is not only new but entirely unconnected with anything in the individual's representation of the world. It can only be added to the individual's representation as bits and pieces, and this usual-

ly means too much processing cost for too little benefit. Still other information is new but connected with old information. When these interconnected new and old items of information are used together as premises in an inference process, further new information can be derived: information which could not have been inferred without this combination of the new and old premises. When the processing of new information gives rise to such a multiplication effect, we call it *relevant*. The greater the multiplication effect, the greater the relevance. . . .

Our claim is that all human beings automatically aim at the most efficient information processing possible. This is so whether they are conscious of it or not; in fact, the very diverse and shifting conscious interests of individuals result from the pursuit of this permanent aim in changing conditions. In other words, an individual's particular cognitive goal at a given moment is always an instance of a more general goal: maximizing the relevance of the information processed. . . . This is a crucial factor in human interaction. . . .

Information processing involves effort; it will only be undertaken in expectation of some reward. There is thus no point in drawing someone's attention to a phenomenon [through human intentional communication] unless it seems relevant enough to be worth his attention.

1986, pp. 47–49

Part of the point, Sperber and Wilson argue, is that the principle of relevance is an inevitable part of deliberate, intentional communication. We don't choose to "'follow' the principle of relevance . . . [we] could not violate it if we wanted to. The principle of relevance applies without exception" (p. 162). What we do choose, as speakers and writers, is what we believe will be relevant on the basis of our understanding of the social and cognitive context of our listeners or readers. And reciprocally, as listeners and readers we use the principle of relevance to make the most significant (multiplicative) meanings we can by using the new information we've received together with the old we've appropriately foregrounded in a variety of inferential processes, all of which go far beyond simply receiving, through decoding, the thought of the speaker or writer.

This contrast with the transmission code-conduit theory is crucial to education, since commonsense theory, ironically, often seems to ignore both sides of the relevance equation. Far too often the oral and written texts of teachers and schools are not chosen with any attention at all to the social and cognitive context of listeners and/or readers, but rather in terms of some organizing principle dictated by the subject or discipline. (And, as noted earlier, decisions about what texts to choose are usually made by people far from the actual site of the transaction.) The reciprocal use of the learners' own experiences and prior knowledge is frequently denied to them in school, on the mistaken assumption that they are not relevant. So rather than being asked to use the knowledge they have already acquired (the "old information") to make the kind of multiplicative meanings made possible by the relevance process, such connections are actively discouraged as children are urged, in effect, to act as tape recorders, merely memorizing and repeating the information given.

In relevance theory, in contrast, "Communication [is] a matter of enlarging mutual cognitive environments, not of duplicating thoughts." In fact, strictly speaking, such duplication is impossible, since no two people have exactly the same world representations. They have neither had exactly the same experiences to build on, nor can they have exactly the same set of intentions in a communicative situation. The success of a communicative event, therefore, does not depend on exact duplication but on using the principle of relevance to make our own meaning from the transaction between the received utterance and our own existing cognitive environment. This is, among other things, one of the differences between our minds and those of contemporary computers: We can identify category similarities on the basis of less than identical representations. It is this flexible ability to make category connections which enables us to build relevance connections even though we have not had identical experiences.

*   *   *   *

METAPHORS AND SCHEMAS: STRUCTURING OUR WORLDS

In addition to relevance theory, there are a number of other aspects of language which determine how it is used and which have implications for language educators. One of the most interesting and provocative to be developed in recent years has already been touched on briefly, the work of George Lakoff and Mark Johnson, who have together and separately been developing a theory of metaphoric schemas which attempts to explain some aspects of the ways our perceptual and conceptual systems interact with our language system. For Lakoff and Johnson, the key basis for our language and conceptual systems stems from the properties of our bodies. In the words of Johnson's (1987) title we carry *The Body in the Mind* and we use our bodily experiences as the basis for our meaning making, imagination, and reason. This extends from such relatively simple body-based schemas as *up is good, down is bad* to considerably more complex metaphors like *the body as a container.* The former derives from our upright posture and is associated with ideas ranging from growing *up* to a *raise* in pay, and even the traditional location of heaven (*up*) and hell (*down*). The latter, which derives from our sense of ourselves as having an inside and an outside, turns out to structure a lot of our thinking, in ways ranging from the relations of "in-groups" and "out-groups" to the structure of arguments expressed as *journeys from one contained position to another.*

In several instances we've already seen the body as container metaphor in action. The conduit metaphor of communication draws on and extends the container metaphor since thoughts are put into the container of the words that express them and sent out from a speaker to be taken in by a listener. In another sense, the conversation between Elizabeth and her mother about the uses of ashes on the garden showed Elizabeth's mother using her bodily imagination to enable Elizabeth to understand that just as she needs to take a variety of foods from outside into the container of her body to keep her healthy, so plants, too, need to do the same thing. In neither case, of course, is the metaphor deliberately or consciously chosen—like most of the language system, such schemas function completely out of awareness—but our shared experience with our bodies and their relation to the world enables us to use our imaginations to make such connections for ourselves and with each other.

Lakoff (1987) also stresses the uses of such metaphors in our category systems, and through them to the ways we make meaning and develop our knowledge of the world. We develop our initial category systems from the ways we experience the world, but experience does not come to us in neatly prepackaged form; we impose meaning upon it in terms of our earliest bodily experience. For Lakoff, "Meaning is not a thing; it involves what is meaningful to us. Nothing is meaningful in itself. Meaningfulness derives from the experience of functioning as a being of a certain sort in an environment of a certain sort" (p. 292). For Lakoff, the important thing about our category systems is that they are the result of our imaginative minds operating within real bodies by means of metaphors enabling us to see connections and build our understanding of the world. . . .

Since a child knows that living things "move," "grow," and "die," it seems eminently reasonable (and, in this sense at least, imaginable) at least to raise the question that clouds may be living, since they certainly move and they do seem to grow and to disappear if not actually die. While clouds may be a decidable case once the criteria are clearer, the discussion itself illustrates that Lakoff and Johnson's approach is speaking to real human problems of the relations between ourselves and our world. For Lakoff and Johnson, there is a real world, but its categories derive not from properties which are exclusive to the things being categorized, but from the relations between the things being categorized and the categorizers; that is, they derive from human beings with human perceptual and cognitive systems speaking a human language.

Of course, much of schooling is to a certain extent a matter of learning categories and the labels for these categories that are assigned by the culture into which the children are being initiated. This is, in a sense, a more adequate view of cultural literacy than Hirsch's (1987) list. Whether the categories are "living, not living, and never lived" or "progressive versus regressive taxes" or "poems, stories, plays, and essays," children learning to participate in a culture must learn the concepts and their associated labels. Further, Lakoff insists, in strong contrast to Hirsch, that these categories and labels are dynamic and interrelated systems which derive from our active attempts to understand the world, not static lists of cultural artifacts and ideas. Since they derive from our imaginative projection of likenesses and contrasts based on our bodily experiences, they are continually subject to modification and refinement as our understanding grows and develops.

They are, in effect, world theories, which develop as we discover their limits and find new explanations more successfully encompassing. The word *atom,* for example, was initially coined to coincide with the view that atoms were the indivisible building blocks of matter. We still use the term metaphorically to mean indivisibility, but as our understanding of the nature of matter has developed, we also understand that atoms are actually composed of a multitude of smaller particles, and even now the precise nature and role of the more fundamental particles is still the subject of active inquiry and considerable scientific debate. As we know more our schemas change, whether we are scientists at the frontiers of human knowledge or more pedestrian human beings trying to understand the world we live in. In fact it is probably the case that trying to understand the world we live in is the real knowledge frontier, and this pursuit is certainly far more relevant than what most scientists do. These ideas are consistent with the notions of Piaget, Vygotsky, and particularly George Kelly (1955), whose characterization of human beings as scientists making predictions on the basis of their interpretation of their experience is consistent with Lakoff and Johnson's view. For Kelly, as for Lakoff and Johnson, our experience of the world does not come interpreted or labeled; we actively interpret and label on the basis of our current understanding. And when our categories or constructs don't help us make accurate predictions, we have the capacity to modify them because we have the imaginative power to build new ones.

For language educators, one essential element of the contribution that Lakoff and Johnson are making to an uncommonsense view of language development is their insistence upon both the experiential (and therefore bodily) basis of knowledge and learning, and their view that such development depends upon our imaginative capacities. Imagination, like creativity, has often been considered a kind of superfluity "hard" to be a subject worthy of attention in school. For Lakoff and Johnson, in contrast, the capacity to form mental images, to image the world and to imagine alternatives and connections, is so basic to our mental processes as to be said to constitute them. For Johnson (1987), "Imagination is central to human meaning and rationality for the simple reason that what we can experience and cognize as meaningful, and how we reason about it, are both dependent upon structures of imagination that make our experience what it is. In this view, meaning is not situated solely in propositions; instead, it permeates our embodied, spatial, temporal, culturally-formed, and value-laden understanding. The structures of imagination are part of what is shared when we understand one another and are able to communicate within a community" (p. 172).

Since language education is preeminently concerned with developing our pupils' powers of thinking and communication, developing their structures of imagination is clearly one of the most natural and effective ways to do so. These imaginative powers derive from our initial bodily experiences of the world but they are then extended as we acquire language and use it to think and communicate. Since the imagination is most naturally developed by the experience of reading and writing narratives, it is also consistent with the best of the traditions of language education, which derive from both the common and uncommonsense approaches. These structures of imagination are part of what we use to make the inferences which relevance theory has shown to pervade the processes of comprehension, of how we relate one thing to another. Similarly the notion that such things are shared within a community enables us to understand how we can use the language which embodies them for meaning making with others as well as for ourselves.

Although I've already argued that narratives function as an important way of structuring our experience as well as communicating it to others, it should be stressed here that narratives, too, are something we impose on our experience. They are constructs, not mere tape recordings of our lives. Even participants in the "same" experience will tell its story differently depending on the interpretation they impose on the events. My own autobiographical accounts of my high school teaching of English, for example, are *my story told from my perspective twenty plus years after the events occurred.* It isn't the story I told about it when the events were occurring, it isn't the story that the other participants in the events would have told then or would tell now, and it is a story I can tell only from the perspective of many years of intervening teaching experience and many years of thinking, reading, writing, and talking about teaching. There would, of course, be some similarities among all those stories, and they all could be mutually shared with profit and understanding, but each story would be a product of the individual's own imaginative interpretation of the meaning of the events.

Uncommonsense language education recognizes that learners are the ones who must do the learning, but that does not mean that teachers, texts, and curricula have no role to play. Our new task is not to present or transmit the world of knowledge to our students, but to find, instead, new ways to help them learn how to do it for themselves. In this role we are not all-knowing experts with all the facts, but guides, coaches, listeners, and questioners who encourage children to stretch their imaginations to understand and solve problems and who build our curriculum to exploit their relevance systems and their intentions.

FUNCTIONS AND FORMS OF LANGUAGE USE

We have concentrated a log on the *hows* of meaning making through language and not so much on the *whats* of either the *functions* which language can serve, or the *forms* which enable us to use language most effectively and efficiently. Since the time of the Greek rhetoricians these aspects have been the subject of intense study and debate, and various category systems have been proposed to account for them. In recent years such concerns have been studied in various ways by anthropologists, by literary theorists, by contemporary students of rhetoric, and by discourse linguists, as well as by language educators.

Sorting out which comes first is in some respects a chicken-and-egg problem, but aside from the intellectual difficulties involved, such decisions have had pedagogical consequences. Those who advocate the importance of forms have tended to try to teach them to writers and speakers. Those who believe in the priority of function have emphasized the prior importance of getting one's purposes clear before deciding on a form to embody it. Either approach has meant that categories tend to become reified and static by the time they are taught in schools. That is, whatever was tentative and fuzzy in the original attempt to distinguish between form or function hardens and takes on an independent existence once it is used as part of teaching. This hardening of the categories is, in a way, another aspect of the common sense of language education, and in educational terms from the formal side it has led to teaching such things as narrative, descriptive, expository, and argumentative or persuasive prose, or the five-paragraph theme, or, from the functional side, transforming descriptive distinctions like James Britton's among transactional, expressive, and poetic writing (1970) into things which should be taught.

While I am sure that we have much more to learn and to explore about these connections and interactions, for the most part the effort seems to be doomed to failure if it is intended to provide a definitive categorization of either forms or functions. Worse, it is pedagogically counterproductive to teach children that there is a finite number of forms which must be employed or functions which can be fulfilled by language. The creative nature of the language system and its possibilities for infinite varieties of utterances, metaphors, and schemas make it hard to pin down the characteristics of particular types or genres of language use. The situation is made even more complicated by the fact that any particular instance of language use is likely to be multifunctional and to mix forms as well. In this book, for example, I have told stories and presented examples of talk, reported on research and theory and explored beliefs and attitudes, been serious and funny, straight-forward and ironic, and so on. And this seems to be typical of most language use.

Form, whether it is grammatical—at the sentence level—or rhetorical—at the discourse level—happens almost completely unconsciously during the process of producing language itself. There may be times when we attend to it more closely, as when we deliberately set out to compose a haiku or a sonnet, but even there the consciousness of form is more likely to play a role after some text has been produced than while we are producing it. It is the case, of course, that our experience in producing and receiving language does help us internalize a wide range of possible forms so that they are available when needed. But as Jasper Neel (1988) noted, when we assign a cause-effect essay we get a cause-effect essay, regardless of what its "content" is supposed to be.

Function does seem to play a more active role in consciousness since we are aware of our communicative purposes and intentions, but even there what we attend to is not some category of possible functions, but the particular intention we have to say something to somebody. We don't abstractly and independently choose a function and then embody it (except, of course, in school exercises).

And since functions can be achieved by a multiplicity of possible forms, depending on the culture, attending to our purpose and intention does not in itself dictate the form we will use.

At the highest level of categorization into function versus form, that of distinguishing between narratives and arguments, there seems to be widespread belief that the distinction is both psychologically and culturally real. In addition to a long history of such genre distinctions which have been embodied in such commonsense categories as fiction versus nonfiction and creative versus expository writing, it has also been embodied in some of the most thoughtful recent work of language and language education. This distinction is essentially the one Britton (1970) draws between transactional and poetic uses of language, that Rosenblatt (1978) makes between efferent and aesthetic reading, and that Bruner (1986) develops between what he calls "a good story and a well-formed argument" (p. 11).

I find, however, in my own writing and reading that while there are differences between reading, say, Jerome Bruner and Iris Murdoch, there are also some similarities, and even when reading Bruner I find myself unconvinced of the "irreducibility" of the distinction. He is, after all, a great storyteller even in his "logico-scientific" books, (see in particular his *Child's Talk* [1983]), and Murdoch's characters often engage in highly logico-scientific talk. Because stories value and evaluate experience, and even in some ways help to create experience, they too are a form of argument, and certainly the stories I have told within this text have been intended to further and support its general argument.

This muddying of the distinction exists, in part, because stories always have a point and that point can be expressed in logico-scientific language even though doing so loses much of the storyness of the narrative. I am perfectly willing to grant that there are real differences in standards of truth, or proof, or verification between the two modes. We should observe and understand the different kinds of logic at work in each case. But for me the fact that stories can serve as examples which prove the rule, and that they are so used in normal everyday language use, as well as in more "logico-scientific" discourse, suggests some overlap between the two rather than a rigid distinction. Even science and mathematics can be and are learned through stories, whether of the cause-and-effect sort of physics and chemistry, the word problems of mathematics, or the life-cycle stories of biology. It is important not to think of narrative as an exclusively literary device; its structures pervade all knowing and learning.

My overall conclusion about forms and functions, therefore, is that while they are certainly worthy of exploration and study, they play little direct role in our processes of using language. Language use is multilayered as the centrality of inference in relevance theory has shown. Trying to fit it into compartments denies the possibility that more than one thing is happening at once and focuses our attention on the wrong sorts of characteristics. Just as the traditional distinction between cognitive and affective domains of thought is vitiated by the recognition that every thought embeds a feeling and every feeling is entwined with a thought, so, too, making categorical distinctions can lead to exclusivity and distortion. If we use them at all we must be continually aware of their partial and tentative nature and, above all, of the fact that they are constructed by human beings for human purposes.

This is not to say that children should not be exposed to and given opportunities to employ a wide range of genres to fulfill a wide variety of functions. The inevitable leakage of our category systems, as layers conflict with categories, doesn't mean that there aren't differences of form, style, tone, and means of argument and proof which children should experience as producers and receivers. What it means, instead, is that *we can count on children to internalize unconsciously the useful distinction of forms and functions as long as they have the opportunity to transact with them for real purposes.* If their attention can keep focused on the meanings they are making as speakers and listeners, readers and writers, the experiences they have will provide adequate exemplars for building their own discourse competence systems in much the same way that they build their language competence systems.

It may be helpful, from time to time, to reflect on those meaning-making efforts, to explore with learners the ways in which their efforts do and don't work effectively. This reflection should not have the goal of bringing them into closer conformity to a preexisting model, but to see how, within the limits of their current purpose, their strategies are enabling them to fulfill it. However, as Vygotsky (1962) has pointed out in respect to other scientific concepts, we can't reflect on that which we haven't experienced, and so the crucial first step always has to be the experience.

REFERENCES

Bates, Elizabeth. 1976. *Language and Context: The Acquisition of Pragmatics.* New York: Academic Press.

Berger, Peter, and Thomas Luckmann. 1966. *The Social Construction of Reality.* New York: Doubleday.

Britton, James. 1970. *Language and Learning.* Harmondsworth: Penguin.

Bruner, Jerome. 1983. *Child's Talk.* New York: Norton.

Givon, Talmy. 1979. *On Understanding Grammar.* New York: Academic Press.

Halliday, Michael A. K. 1978. *Language as Social Semiotic: The Social Interpretation of Language and Meaning.* London: Edward Arnold.

Hirsch, E. D. 1987. *Cultural Literacy: What Every American Needs to Know.* Boston: Houghton Mifflin.

Humboldt, Wilhelm von. 1836/1988. *On Language: The Diversity of Human Language—Structure and Its Influence on the Mental Development of Mankind.* (Translated by Peter Heath.) Cambridge, England: Cambridge University Press.

Johnson, Mark. 1987. *The Body in the Mind: The Bodily Basis of Meaning, Imagination and Reason.* Chicago: University of Chicago Press.

Kelly, George. 1955. *The Psychology of Personal Constructs.* New York: Norton.

Lakoff, George. 1987. *Women, Fire, and Dangerous Things: What Categories Reveal about the Mind.* Chicago: University of Chicago Press.

Lakoff, George, and Mark Johnson. 1980. *Metaphors We Live By.* Chicago: University of Chicago Press.

Neel, Jasper. 1988. *Plato, Derrida, and Writing.* Carbondale, IL: Southern Illinois University Press.

Reddy, Michael. 1979. "The Conduit Metaphor." In Ortony, A., ed. *Metaphor and Thought.* Cambridge, England: Cambridge University Press.

Rosenblatt, Louise M. 1978. *The Reader, the Text, the Poem: The Transactional Theory of the Literary Work.* Carbondale, IL: Southern Illinois University Press.

Sapir, Edward. 1921. *Language.* New York: Harcourt Brace.

Sperber, Dan, and Wilson Deirdre. 1986. *Relevance: Communication and Cognition.* Oxford: Basil Blackwell.

Vygotsky, Lev S. 1962. *Thought and Language.* Cambridge, MA: MIT Press.

Whorf, Benjamin Lee. 1956. *Language, Thought and Reality: Selected Papers of Benjamin Lee Whorf.* Carroll, J. B., ed. Cambridge, MA: MIT Press.

Vocabulary Teaching: Active Involvement in Contexts

James E. Coomber and Howard D. Peet

"When our words change, we change," Edgar Dale and Joseph O'Rourke stated in *Techniques of Teaching Vocabulary* (1971), their classic work on vocabulary teaching. Using as an illustration the word *serendipity,* "making happy and unexpected discoveries by accident," they suggest that in learning that word, the learner has done much more than add a word to her lexicon; she is more aware of the concept of serendipity in the world in general, more "serendipity-sensitive" (1971:9). As we learn new words, we change, and our world changes.

Words are labels for what we know; as our store of words grows, it is no wonder that our knowledge of the world grows as well. Sapir and Whorf's "linguistic relativity hypothesis" (1964) suggests that the structure of a language predisposes speakers of that language to view the world around them in distinctive ways. An Eskimo, they claim, has many different names for our word for *snow;* Aztecs, on the other hand, have only one word for the meanings of the English words *cold, ice,* and *snow* (216). Think of Eskimos and Aztecs—and children from Pennsylvania—and how each of their vocabularies for snow might affect how they view the same winter scene. In schools we see another manifestation of the vocabulary-knowledge relationship in high correlations between students' lexicons and measures of intelligence and reading comprehension.

What research has told us about learning in general seems to apply also to learning words: the more involved the learner, the more effective the learning. A recent review of research on vocabulary learning by Karen Mezynski (1983) highlights three teaching factors associated with effective vocabulary study:

Amount of practice given to the words
Breadth of training in the use of the words
The degree to which active processing is encouraged (273)

In addition to being effective, these factors also lead to more enjoyable vocabulary learning. As our students—and we—become involved in meaningful words and contexts, there will likely be engaging discussions, even laughter. Yes, vocabulary study can mean lively interest and good times! And why not? As we have suggested elsewhere, "The history of words is the history of people, with all of the inherent pathos, poetry, and pleasure imaginable. To study words is to study ourselves and our world" (Coomber and Peet 1981). It is interesting to read in an early review of vocabulary research by Manzo and Sherk (1971–72) that word games are effective in word study and that teacher enthusiasm is a significant factor in effective vocabulary teaching (81).

In this paper we will focus on these three factors Mezynski (1983) identified in effective vocabulary teaching and discuss practical ways of implementing Mezynski's findings in the classroom. We will also cite other studies that have useful implications for teaching.

AMOUNT OF PRACTICE

How many times must a learner be exposed to a word before it becomes part of her lexicon? This, of course, is a challenging question to deal with, fraught with difficult-to-control variables, as some behavioral psychologists have noted (e.g., Underwood and Schulz 44–62). Some reading educators have given rough estimates ranging from ten to twenty exposures needed for making a word one's own, depending of course on factors within the learner, the word, and the text. More recently, cognitive psychologists would ask not how many times a student must be exposed to a word but how rich those exposures might be. Several truly meaningful experiences with a word will probably accomplish more than drilling on the word ten times. Exact number of exposures are, of course, impossible to state; the important point is that meaningful review is needed if students are to remember the words they learn. Presenting a word one day, having the students use it in a sentence or give a synonym, and then quizzing them over it several days later is not likely to add significantly to their lexicons. Research also seems to tell us that drilling on definitions and synonyms is not the most effective way to teach vocabulary—if the purpose of vocabulary study is to enhance reading comprehension or develop enthusiasm for language. We have discussed system and reinforcement elsewhere (Coomber and Peet 4–5).

The Role of Wide Reading

Rather than teaching specific words at all, some educators have assumed that wide reading is adequate as a vocabulary program, without direct or systematic instruction in specific words, structures, or meaning-seeking strategies. Children reading widely, they reason, encounter numerous new words. They see these words in their reading materials and figure them out via context. Thus the best vocabulary program is one that does little more than stimulate students' interest in reading; vocabulary development, on the whole, comes naturally, without direct instruction.

Reading widely is vital for helping students develop vocabulary and comprehension skills. But reading a wide variety of material without direct vocabulary instruction is not likely to lead to optimal vocabulary development. Exposures to words or reflections on word meanings is necessary for those word meanings to be retained, and most students, reading on their own, do not give much thought to the words they meet. Whether or not ten to twenty exposures to a word are needed for retention, we know that reflection of some kind is vital for remembering lexical items. Most of us are well aware of the typical student who skips a difficult word rather than use context or dictionary or any other means of dealing with it. While he may understand the passage without knowing that word, we suspect that if he dealt seriously with at least some of these words, he would strengthen his ability to deal with texts generally. He would also be more likely to move these words into his active vocabulary, using them in his own writing and speaking.

Students apparently benefit from both direct and indirect vocabulary instruction, as research seems to indicate. H. Alan Robinson (1963) and Rankin and Oberholser (1969) found that many students had considerable difficulty learning words from context. As Manzo and Sherk (1971–72) conclude in their research, wide reading by itself, with no teaching of specific words and word structures, "is usually not very effective for influencing rapid and marked achievement" (81). In their more recent review of research on vocabulary teaching, Stahl and Fairbanks (1986), while pointing out that students learn many words from context, recommend vocabulary instruction in conjunction with learning lexical items from context. They conclude that specific words taught add significantly to students' lexicons, especially for those students, often poor readers, who have difficulty determining word meanings from context (100). And if those specific words are taught in context, working with individual words can also strengthen the student's sense of context as a word recognition skill.

Syntactic and Semantic Context

As important as word study is, a vocabulary program that focused only on individual words would surely be inadequate. To function in this world, students must learn far more words than the schools would ever have time to teach.

Systematic word study can encourage vocabulary growth with a cluster of words, preferably words that students will encounter and use, to be learned well.

But along with that cluster of words an effective program also develops strategies in coping with strange words. How does a proficient reader obtain meaning from unfamiliar words? If we monitor our own reaction to problem words in our reading, we will almost surely find that context is the first strategy we try. It has been said that a word "is known by the company it keeps." Unless the reading material is very difficult, context should be the first choice even for most fourth-graders. However, even many teen-agers have weak context skills and can benefit from figuring out new words in context.

Sometimes the reader cannot successfully determine a word's meaning from context. Word structure is generally the next strategy to try—or, more accurately—structure combined with context. Imagine that the student stumbles on *supersede* in the following sentence:

Rulings by the United State Supreme Court *supersede* rulings on the same case by any other court.

In dealing with *supersede,* she might use *super* as a key. If she knows that *super* means "over" or "above" and realizes that the Supreme Court is higher than any other Court, she should be able to determine the meaning of *supersede.*

The effective reader draws on two types of context: syntactic and semantic. Syntactic context focuses on relationships of words in phrases and sentences, the grammar of the sentence. In the following sentence the location of *plitzed* and its *-ed* ending are clues that *plitzed* is probably a verb:

One dancer *plitzed* the bandleader to play "Mockingbird Hill."

However, we would have difficulties with a phrase like *the alligator green* because a modifier immediately following a noun doesn't typically fit the syntactic structure of English.

Semantic context focuses on meaning and the way various word meanings interrelate in context (see Fromkin and Rodman, "Semantic Properties," in this volume). In the above sentence, *dancer, bandleader, play,* and the title of a song suggest the meaning "requested" or "asked." The verb slot in this sentence requires a transitive verb that takes a concrete object, a human subject, and a prepositional phrase. For this reason, the verb could not be an intransitive verb, such as *lie* or *sat.*

Similarly, words that do not "fit" illustrate semantic context (as well as alert a reader to problems of meaning), as in the following sentences:

The 1991 high school homecoming queen was an all-conference linebacker.
Out behind the barn, hogs dined on garden refuse and field corn.

In the first sentence, homecoming queens are pictured as petite, attractive females, and all-conference linebackers are large, tough males. So there is a semantic contradiction between these two words, making the sentence contradictory. In the second sentence, the verb *dined* normally occurs with human subjects and adverb phrases that describe elegant eating locations so that when the subject is *hogs* (nonhuman) and the adverb phrase is *behind the barn* (normally a nonelegant location), and the food is *garden refuse* and *field corn* (nonelegant matter), there is again a semantic jar. Thus studying words in isolation does not help students learn meaning vocabulary because it is necessary for them to understand the semantic context with which the word is associated.

Rather than automatically defining words for students, we should, with some coaching, encourage risk taking so that students learn to determine word meanings on their own. We might prompt them with questions that focus on the parts of a sentence relevant to the difficult words. We encourage responses appropriate to the context. If, for example, a student defined *supersede* in the above sentence as "depend upon," we would ask him whether his response makes sense. We might model for our students how we use context and structure when we encounter difficult words, talking through the processes we have used. In short, we want to convince students that context really works, that there is logic in the English language, that risk taking often pays off.

Thus effective vocabulary teaching strives for balance between emphasis on specific words on the one hand and on vocabulary independence strategies like context and word structure on the other. The two can grow simultaneously.

Concepts, Words, and Meanings

In considering effective vocabulary learning, we might reflect on relationships between words and concepts. Carroll described concepts as "abstracted and often cognitively structured classes of 'mental' experience learned by organisms in the course of their life histories" (180). Many concepts acquire labels so that members of a speech community can communicate their common experiences to others; these mutually agreed upon labels are words. The meaning of a word, according to Carroll, is "a societally standardized concept" (187) shared by people of the same speech community. According to Deighton, words, like concepts, are not acquired in a single exposure but with many exposures (86); our knowledge of a word or concept should continue to grow. What does this mean for word *study?* Each time a student encounters a "new" word, he should be doing more than reviewing definitions; he should be deepening his knowledge of that word and the concept that word represents—deepening, we could say, his knowledge of the world. Encounters with a word should result in expanded word meanings, new associations with that word, and knowledge of how that word is used in various contexts, a knowledge that should become ever more complex.

If, then, we view vocabulary acquisition as similar to concept learning, we will probably not regard lexicon building as simply mastering the definitions in a list of words in an either-he-knows-it-or-he-doesn't fashion; the learner might know the word in some contexts and not in others. We also need to remember that most language-users have four vocabularies: listening, reading, writing, and speaking. We should not be surprised when a student recognizes a word when he reads it or hears it but cannot use that word in his writing or speaking. A model of word knowledge in terms of several concentric circles, developed by Henry Bamman (1971), effectively depicts these levels of word knowledge: In the center are words that are known very well, words that one can use actively as well as respond to passively; in the middle circle are words that are known when one encounters them in most contexts but are rarely used in writing and speaking; in the outermost circle lie words that might be recognized in some contexts but not in others (190).

Moving the lesser-known words from the outer circles to the inner core is as important a vocabulary-teaching objective as learning new words. All of us as teachers have been frustrated by the student who we believe has strong reading and listening vocabularies but refuses to use many of the words he knows in his writing, probably because his knowledge of those words is superficial or because he avoids taking risks. Furthermore, one of the best reviews of a word is using that word in writing or speaking.

If we believe that learning a new word comes with successive exposures to, and experiences with that word, vocabulary teaching will include opportunities to become increasingly familiar with the word, beginning with perhaps a definition or an experience in a single context and progressing toward gradually widening and refining knowledge of its meanings and how it is used in different contexts. Contrast this with the "one-shot" treatment of unfamiliar words that is all too typical in classrooms. This view of word learning and Bamman's model of word knowledge also have implications for evaluation. If we test knowledge of a word shortly after that word has been introduced, we may measure only superficial knowledge. Also, we might best replace definition and synonym test items with items calling for students to use words meaningfully in varied contexts, an ability that comes after numerous encounters with those words.

A Nucleus of Frequently Used Words

Learning a word well, then, means encountering it a number of times in varying contexts. This may require more class time per word, time that we believe is well spent. Realizing how limited class time is, we find one of Manzo and Sherk's conclusions pertinent: Words that are selected for intensive teaching should be words that belong to a learner's "verbal community" (81). "Verbal communities" can refer to the many contexts in which we live, including home, job, and school. What we use we are more likely to remember—one reason that students are more likely to remember words that they naturally encounter and use.

If we take word frequency seriously and consider the likelihood that students will later encounter the words we teach, we will avoid one questionable but common vocabulary-teaching habit: holding students responsible for difficult words in a reading assignment without regard for the frequency of those words. We may chuckle at the awesome non sequitor of the professor who exhorted his class, "You'd better learn this word now because you might never see it again!" But sometimes we, too, have not considered word frequency in words we have taught nor remembered the adage "If you don't use it, you'll lose it." We can remember teaching Shakespearean drama and quizzing high school students over words like *nonce*. What were our students' chances of ever encountering that word again? And how likely were they to need to use that word? These are two questions we should ask ourselves when we select certain vocabulary for careful teaching. Words that may cause problems for a certain reading assignment but are not likely to be used beyond the present assignment can simply be defined for the class before they begin their reading, with no more attention given to them after that. But words that denote key concepts and are important beyond our classrooms are the words we should consider emphasizing in vocabulary study.

As we choose words for intensive study, then, word frequency becomes a significant factor. Most indexes of word frequency list the number of times a certain word occurs in a given body of published material; the higher the frequency of occurrence, the more likely the reader will encounter that word. The pioneers in word frequency were Edward Thorndike and Irving Lorge, with their classic *Teacher's Word Book of 30,000 Words* (1944). Several more recent word frequency lists are also available (e.g., Carroll, Davies, and Richman, *The American Heritage Word Frequency Book,* 1971; Dale and O'Rourke, *The Living Word Vocabulary,* 1976; and Kucera and Francis, *Computational Analysis of Present-Day American English,* 1967). Guides like these can supplement, but not replace, our judgment of which words our students are likely to use and which words will help them better understand the concepts they are being taught, in our class and in other classes.

Verbal communities can also be taken to mean that each academic discipline has its own vocabulary, the key to understanding texts in that area. That is why vocabulary teaching is as important in the sciences, social sciences, and mathematics as it is in English. In fact, several science educators have stated that the biggest reason students have trouble with science is the vocabulary.

Word Games as Word and Concept-Builders

Think of the many books of word games on the newstands and the fascination of newspaper readers with crossword puzzles. These can even be traced back to Sophocles. According to one wordsmith, humankind's first words were the palindrome used by Adam when he greeted Eve, "Madam, I'm Adam."

Again, research tells us that a learner must encounter a word a number of times before he can call it his own. Word games properly used may become a delightful system for providing those multiple exposures. Hundreds of word games and activities are available for the various stages of word learning, with different games to meet different objectives. (For information on the rich possibilities for word games and activities, see, for example, Dale and O'Rourke 1971; Johnson and Pearson 1978; McCarthy 1990; Nagy 1988; Nation 1990; and Wallace 1984.) Word activities, in addition to enhancing vocabulary growth, can also contribute to other areas of language development.

BREADTH OF TRAINING

Reading researchers and educators have generally agreed that context is the choice means of dealing with words, and for several reasons: First, when a student determines a word's meaning from context (as opposed to being told its definition), she learns that word's semantic and syntactic features inductively, an approach that shares in the advantages of inductive teaching generally. Trying to figure out a word's meaning means becoming involved with that word, which enhances retention. The learner might even feel some ownership of his definition and his associations with the word—more so, surely, than if the teacher supplied a definition. Second, students see the target word "in action"; in fact, one might argue that apart from a sentence a word has no stable meaning, for a word's meaning depends considerably on the words around it. Finally, when students encounter a new word in sentence context and try to determine its meaning, they are practicing context as a word recognition skill and hence developing greater vocabulary independence.

As we teach context, we often think of context at the sentence or paragraph level, or perhaps the context of a story or chapter of a textbook. We would suggest also teaching context as a larger situation. Someone tapping you on the shoulder and asking "How do you spell *stick-up*?" will elicit one type of reaction if you are helping a class of second-graders write stories but a much different reaction if you are standing in the teller's line at the bank. Different reactions to the same statement are due to different contexts. Think of the many jokes and humorous stories that depend on differences in contexts.

Considering contexts beyond the sentence leads to pertinent implications for teaching. Kathleen Nitsch (1977) found in her research that providing examples with word definitions yielded superior results to providing definitions only; the examples helped students place new words in some kind of context. But more than that, she also found that students who reviewed words in several different contexts could recall those words better and use them more effectively than students who reviewed those words in a single context. We learn words best by relating them to situations—and the more situations we relate them to, the better. In fact, have you ever noticed that you are able to produce the definition of a word best after thinking of it in several contexts? Notice how children often define words by specific context rather than by definition, as, for example, "A *davenport* is what we sit on after dinner and watch the news."

Other studies support the use of several contexts in learning a word well. Karen Mezynski (1983) concluded from her review of research that effective vocabulary learning, learning which enhanced a student's reading comprehension, was characterized by "multiple-context" word review (266). Stahl and Fairbanks (1986) state that word knowledge depends on both definitional knowledge and contextual knowledge. The latter they define as "knowledge of a core concept and how that knowledge is realized in different contexts" (74). We tend to learn a word in a particular context, but words are most usable when they become "decontextualized," i.e., not limited to a single context.

Word activities that encourage thinking in contexts are not difficult to construct. Even the familiar true-false format can be used to present a lexical item in context:

A *belligerent* person is easy to get along with.

The fact that we have fireworks at homecoming for the first time this year makes it a *tradition*.

One thing that is *reliable* is the sunrise.

Notice that whether the statement is true or false depends on how the student defines the target word and understands the context in which that word appears, a context larger than the sentence. In order to answer the item correctly, it is necessary to think about the meaning of the word and imagine the situation or context.

Applying words to situations may also be accomplished by various kinds of checklist or matching exercises. Students may indicate which situation or situations illustrate a target word by responding yes or no to each of the items, with the possibility that more than one item might be applicable:

Unison

_____ three dogs in a dogfight
_____ a whole choir singing
_____ two moose locking horns
_____ all fans cheering on
the count of three

Distinctive

_____ the car that won the
Indianapolis 500
_____ four people playing bridge
_____ a bag of barley
_____ an elm tree

Pondering the target word in relation to contexts not only makes vocabulary more interesting than reviewing definitions and synonyms; words also become easier to remember. Context-based items may generate more disagreement about the right answer than the more clear-cut definition or synonym questions.

For example, in the *distinctive* example cited above, a student might argue that "a bag of barley" might be distinctive if it was unusual to grow barley in a particular region or if the producer won an award—unlikely situations but possible. If we are willing to tolerate some ambiguity, this kind of discussion nurtures in-depth thinking about the word and the context and strengthens knowledge of the vocabulary item. Having studied possible contexts of a word, the student is more likely to apply the word in writing and speaking, as Mezynski suggested.

Furthermore, exercises emphasizing contexts or situations can be ways of studying multiple meanings of words, as different situations can illustrate different definitions of the same word. How, for example, is *range* used in each of the following sentences?

_____ 1 Fran's truck has a *range* of three hundred miles.

_____ 2 Uncle Jack remembers cooking many meals on the old kitchen *range* at the Coffee Cup Cafe.

_____ 3 *Range* wars were often sparked by land disputes.

In determining which meaning applies in each sentence, students are working with the same word in several contexts.

Multiple meanings are very important to content-area vocabulary. Words that students have known well in everyday life may be completely unfamiliar when they appear in the context of mathematics, science, or the social sciences with a more specialized meaning. For example, in the social sciences, *office, term,* and *recall* denote different concepts than they do in everyday usage. When a social studies teacher speaks of a public office, for example, she is probably not referring to a room with desk, chair, computer terminal, and file cabinets.

When students get involved in situational activities, they become involved in contexts. Again, for them to deal with a word in several contexts makes that word more likely to become part of Bamman's inner circle of well-known words. Relating words to larger contexts could also be regarded as application. It has often been said that until a learner has applied a concept, he does not truly understand it.

ACTIVE PROCESSING

After students have become accustomed to responding to teacher-made situations, the students might create, for words they have recently learned, situations of their own. Psychologists specializing in memory have demonstrated the power of generational effects: Review tends to be even more effective when learners are creating something rather than responding to materials created for them (e.g., Slamecka and Graf 1978). Shouldn't this also work in teaching vocabulary? One study has indicated that learners creating their own contexts for words tend to retain word meanings better than do subjects reviewing contexts provided for them (Coomber, Ramstad, and Sheets 1986). Students can experiment with sentences and change various words in those sentences to see the effect of word change on context as well as the effect of context on words. In vocabulary notebooks students might write new words, but with examples, situations, stories, or personal associations they have with those words, instead of definitions.

Writing is another means to active processing in vocabulary teaching. Janet Emig (1977) and others have pointed out the many learning behaviors inherent in writing that make writing such an effective mode of learning. Writing, according to Emig, encourages learning by doing, provides a visible record of what one learns, and helps the learner make connections between what he is learning and what he already knows. (123–124). This has obvious possibilities for vocabulary study.

If we ask students for the most common ways their teachers review vocabulary, many would probably mention using targeted words in sentences, for example, being asked to compose a sentence with the word *inquiry* properly used. Using a new word in a sentence, after a student has had meaningful encounters with that word in context, has real possibilities for vocabulary review; we are asking the student to create a context as well as use the word appropriately. But sometimes the responses we get from students may not prove that they in fact know the meaning of the word. (Imagine, for example, that a student tries to demonstrate that he knows *ponder* by giving the sentence "Uncle Fred likes to *ponder*.") To encourage students to produce sample sentences with better sense of context, some teachers have shared with us a strategy of asking students to use two or even three targeted words in the same sentence. This seems to force more specific, more easily evaluated responses, probably because specifying several words for the same sentence narrows the context significantly.

We can also ask students to answer questions containing target words with sentences that also contain those words, perhaps applying those words to their own experiences:

What is an important *issue* for people in your town?
Name what you believe is the greatest *obstacle* to happiness.

Using the word in contextual writing is one way of achieving the active process Mezynski (1983) identifies as effective vocabulary-teaching strategy. Applying the words to themselves is likely to evoke personal images and associations that will help anchor that word in their minds. This kind of writing should also help move that word from passive to active vocabulary.

Active involvement with significant words in various contexts is what research suggests learners need for building strong vocabularies. As teachers we can provide that kind of active involvement through class discussions, word games, and other language activities.

John Dewey once described becoming educated as a matter of seeing things from different perspectives. Isn't vocabulary study an example of looking at things from multiple perspectives? Wouldn't the habit of looking at words from different perspectives, in different contexts, be an education in itself? That is what the research seems to be telling us.

REFERENCES

Bamman, Henry A. (1971). Promoting Vocabulary Growth. *Claremont College Reading Conference Yearbook* **35**: 190–193.

Carroll, John B. (1964). "Words, Meanings, and Concepts." *Harvard Education Review* **34**: 178–202.

Carroll, John B., Peter Davies, and Barry Richman. (1971). *The American Heritage Word Frequency Book.* Boston: Houghton Mifflin.

Coomber, James E., and Howard D. Peet. (1981). *Teaching Vocabulary: Toward System and Reinforcement.* Position Paper on the Teaching of English. Ed. Jayne Moliterno. Chicago: Science Research Associates.

Coomber, James E., David A. Ramstad, and DeeAnn R. Sheets. (1986). "Elaboration in Vocabulary Learning: A Comparison of Three Rehearsal Methods." *Research in the Teaching of English* **20**: 281–293.

Dale, Edgar, and Joseph O'Rourke. (1976). *The Living Word Vocabulary.* Palo Alto, CA: Field.

———. (1960). *Techniques of Teaching Vocabulary.* Palo Alto, CA: Field, 1971.

Deighton, Lee C. "Developing Vocabulary: A Look at the Problem." *English Journal* **49**: 82–88.

Emig, Janet. (1977). "Writing as a Mode of Learning." *College Composition and Communication* **28** (1977): 122–127.

Johnson, Dale D., and P. David Pearson. (1978). *Teaching Reading Vocabulary.* New York: Holt, Rinehart and Winston.

Kucera, Henry, and W. Nelson Francis. (1967). *A Computational Analysis of Present-Day American English.* Providence, RI: Brown University Press.

Manzo, A. V., and J. K. Sherk. (1971–1972). "Some Generalizations and Strategies for Guiding Vocabulary Learning." *Journal of Reading Behavior* **4** (Winter): 78–89.

McCarthy, M. (1990). *Vocabulary.* New York: Oxford University Press.

Mezynski, Karen. (1983). "Issues Concerning the Acquisition of Knowledge: Effects of Vocabulary Training on Reading Comprehension." *Review of Education Research* **53** (Summer): 253–279.

Nagy, William E. (1988). *Teaching Vocabulary to Improve Reading Comprehension.* Urbana, IL: National Council of Teachers of English.

Nation, I. S. P. (1990). *Teaching and Learning Vocabulary.* New York: Newbury House.

Nitsch, Kathleen E. (1977). "Structuring Decontextualized Forms of Knowledge." Diss. Vanderbilt University.

Rankin, Earl F., and Betsy M. Overholser. (1969). "Reaction of Intermediate Grade Children to Contextual Clues." *Journal of Reading Behavior* **1**: 50–73.

Robinson, H. Alan. (1963). "A Study of the Techniques of Word Identification." *The Reading Teacher* **16**: 238–241.

Slamecka, N. J., and P. Graf. (1978). "The Generation Effect: Delineation of a Phenomenon." *Journal of Experimental Psychology: Human Learning and Memory* **4**: 592–604.

Stahl, Steven A., and Marilyn M. Fairbanks. (1986). "The Effect of Vocabulary Instruction: A Model-Based Meta-Analysis." *Review of Educational Research* **56** (Spring): 72–110.

Thorndike, Edward L., and Irving Lorge. (1944). *The Teacher's Word Book of 30,000 Words.* New York: Teachers College Columbia University.

Underwood, B. J., and R. W. Schulz. (1960). *Meaningfulness and Verbal Learning.* Chicago: Lippincott.

Wallace, Michael J. (1989). *Teaching Vocabulary.* London: Heineman, 1984.

Whorf, Benjamin Lee. (1964). *Language, Thought, and Reality: Selected Writings of B. L. Whorf.* Ed. John B. Carroll. New York: Wiley.

Spoken Words: Quality Exposure to Vocabulary Concepts

Steven Grubaugh

The teacher asked the class to prepare for the Spoken Words Vocabulary Activity. Mr. Urban turned to the vocabulary section of his grade book and took a seat among his students. Slightly restless, the students behaved like a troupe of actors on the opening night of a performance.

Mr. Urban randomly called the name of Linda J. from his grade book. Linda strode to the front of the class, selected a piece of chalk, and wrote the word *deluge* on the board. She turned to face her waiting classmates and began: "My word today is *deluge*. It means 'a flood'." Then Linda related her word-story. She told of babysitting a spirited three-year-old boy who was usually into everything. One evening, the child had disappeared from the living room and had been too quiet too long. Linda's search led her to the bathroom door from behind which came the sounds of gurgling water. As she opened the door, a deluge of cold water washed over her feet and ran out into the hallway. The child was at the toilet attempting to flush his E.T. doll down the pipes and water was spilling over the bowl in a flash flood.

Linda threw some towels on the floor to sop up the water and rescued the E.T. doll. She told the class that she had to explain the mess to the child's parents, but they were used to such mischievousness and gave her an extra three dollars for "combat pay."

"Fine, Linda, and a useful word," commented Urban, noting the interest she had sparked. He reminded students to take notes. "Any questions or comments about the word *deluge*?"

Everyone wanted to react to her *deluge* story. Two students added their own examples. One told about helping neighbors fortify their homes with sandbags during the New Orleans May 3rd flood. Another reported that one of his favorite tunes was "Before the Deluge" by Jackson Browne.

Urban encouraged brief anecdotes which served as examples of the concept under study, but the class knew that he would move quickly to cut short any story which did not relate to the concept of the presented word.

The teacher had worked hard to develop a positive attitude toward the study of vocabulary. His objective was not only to expose students to new words but to enable them to extract meanings from unfamiliar words. Initially, explaining and demonstrating Spoken Word methodology had required part of one class period. The students had been taught how to select words from their language environment, to "lift" the words in context, to define the words through personal contact with adults, and to get across the meaning of words through a story.

The Spoken Word performances were short and smoothly executed and might have looked easy to the casual observer. But the students worked hard to prepare their presentations. Because he required students to select their own vocabulary words, Linda listened more closely to new words, dutifully collecting and recording them in their spoken or written contexts. Linda also followed Urban's suggestions for defining her words by bringing them to the dinner table, relying on her parents to explain the meaning and offer examples. Then she looked at the dictionary to check for accuracy. Linda's parents were flattered to be included in their daughter's academic concerns. Linda's final step was to generate a story and share it with her class. It was challenging, yet satisfying.

SELF-SELECTING WORDS

Using the Spoken Words vocabulary technique, students can be taught to select usable, high-frequency words. The rationale for self-selection is that everyone operates in a world of language where words reflect school subjects, employment, family life, reading, viewing, and other interests. These words are clearly more important and surely easier to learn than esoteric terms from a graded word list (Rapp-Haggard, 1982).

Students should be asked to acquire words they have heard or seen before and about which they have only a speculative idea of the meaning. Dale, O'Rourke, and Bamman (1971) suggest that the learning potential of such words is greater than learning totally unknown words. During the first weeks of Spoken Word presentations, the teacher should ask students where and how they chose their words. Discussions should guide students to become more observant of language and to increase their sensitivity to words.

As they present their words in class, students should feel they have something worthwhile to offer, no matter what their academic standing. As a suitable classroom climate is developed, speakers before the class and members of the audience should come to appreciate their differences as rich veins of information to be explored.

TO DEFINE NEW WORDS

Once a word has been selected, it must be defined. Students should be taught to guess at the meaning from the context, and students must present the word within its context. Students can then proceed to a more refined definition through word interviews, i.e., asking parents, teachers, or peers to define the word. That will offer students a chance to probe for the word's meaning as well as hear the word in different examples. The opportunity for an exciting story about the word may materialize during these interviews.

A good dictionary should be consulted to clear up any confusion. Dictionary skills and reading context clues should be pretaught or taught concurrently with the Spoken Word method.

MEDIATING WORD CONCEPTS THROUGH EXPERIENCE STORIES

Once the concept of the word is understood, students must probe their memories to locate experiences which match the concept. These can be real or vicarious, personal or second-hand, but not made up or invented on the spot. Experiences must be put into anecdote or story form and must illustrate the concept of the word, a task within the capabilities of students from fourth grade to adult levels of language development (Labov, 1967; Menig-Peterson & McCabe, 1977).

Students often begin with a general idea or a broad categorization of a concept and rework and adjust that idea to a more precise or specialized meaning (Ortony, 1975). For instance, the concept of *bug* can represent to a child any small, crawling thing. Later, the same youngster learns to distinguish bugs or insects from reptiles and mammals. And if students study entomology, they will learn how to attribute features and nonfeatures of insects to develop entomological categories and label these groups.

The teacher who uses Spoken Words should trust students to have experiences stored and accessible from memory and available through language. When youngsters learn new words, they must realize their experience is a resource to probe and question, to build upon, and to be used to form new meaning. Essentially, Spoken Words is show-and-tell with new vocabulary and within the framework of a story.

The story has served humanity as a teaching tool for centuries in such diverse forms as the psalms and poetry of the Old Testament lessons, the parables of Christ, the moralizing of *Aesop's Fables,* and the rich oral folklore from countries all over the world. In the modern schoolroom, the story is used to entertain, to develop critical thinking, and to study literary devices. Spoken Words methodology uses the story as a useful organizer for associative learning and as a means for capturing student interest and developing a positive attitude about the study of vocabulary.

IMPLEMENTATION AND TESTING

Spoken Words can be used for one class period a week, but the method can also serve as a change-of-pace activity or as a reward to the class for good work. This means that students need to be prepared at all times for Spoken Words.

As students present their Spoken Word stories, the teacher should require that others take notes to record the words and story ideas, along with the definitions. Devine (1981) states that making a written record of oral presentation enhances listening comprehension because the speaker's ideas are transformed and then recorded into the listener's own words. Notes on words can be written in a special vocabulary notebook. Students should be required to write a sentence with each new word at some time during or directly after each speaker's presentation.

Since Spoken Words is an individualized vocabulary method, it must be tested individually in a way that does not overburden the teacher. After students have accumulated 20–30 words, a vocabulary test may be given. To examine students on their own vocabulary words, the teacher goes to each student and checks-off five words on a sheet of paper on which the student has written only the word. To examine students on words presented to the entire class, the teacher notes the best of these words and allows students to study or review them from their own notes.

To demonstrate mastery of each word on either of these tests, students must, in order of preference: (1) write a definition, (2) write a synonym, (3) provide an associative word, or (4) write "no response." Then, they must compose a sentence using each word in a suitable context. That not only gives the teacher a good idea how well the concept of the target word is understood but also provides insight into each student's ability to manipulate these words as they would be used in real life.

OPPORTUNITIES TO TEACH TRADITIONAL
VOCABULARY STRATEGIES

Using Spoken Words also creates opportunities to teach students traditional strategies to determine word meanings. Students can be depended upon to present a variety of types of words requiring different word attack strategies. The teacher will have a chance to demonstrate strategies for words in context, combining forms, terms with multiple meanings, words with interesting etymologies or histories, abstract and concrete lexical items, symbols, dictionary usage, etc.

Because students are required to select and use words in context, the most common *context clues* (Quealy, 1969) should be taught and reinforced during

Spoken Words. The teacher may experiment with the context of particular Spoken Words giving students a chance to inflect new words as practice for actual use (Dale, O'Rourke and Bamman, 1971). Oral *modified cloze* activities are versatile and can be used to help students understand the semantic and syntactic elements of context clues. And words such as *arch* will occur with multiple meanings, in various context areas, giving the teacher a chance to explore different meanings of the word in various contexts.

Compound words like *clearinghouse* and derived words like *metamorphosis* and *amoral* will give the teacher a chance to teach structural analysis and offer a list of common prefixes and root words with their meanings (Roe, Stoodt, and Burns, 1978). For help with pronouncing words in the student's reading vocabulary, the teacher may wish to review common prefix pronunciation and teach the *sound-structure-context-dictionary* (SSCD) word attack strategy (Devine, 1981).

Word association exercises can generate categorization exercises-identifying features and non-features of a word, naming groups of items, or listing items which fall into a certain category—contributing to vocabulary growth (Pearson & Johnson, 1978). Students see words in their relationship to other words and word groups which helps them refine concepts. Students can be taught to consider the relative power of a word when compared with synonyms. A student might ask the class if they would rather eat a *tenderloin steak* or *carrion,* thus contrasting the *connotation* and *denotation* of words (Hayakawa, 1972).

Dictionary skills can be explored, questioned, and debated by class members. Roget's *Thesaurus,* in indexed or dictionary format, can help locate a concept word to develop an interesting story the student might wish to tell. But words chosen this way may be so esoteric as to make their use questionable. Professional journals and other research tools can be cited and investigated by students who find a difficult word, like *relativity,* where investigation could extend understanding of the concept as the story and examples unfold in the Spoken Word presentation.

Finally, *etymological* searches and word history development could be encouraged for students interested in words, their origins, and their evolution. Origins and etymologies could enrich the learning for the students and provide the teacher with an unobtrusive chance to introduce the *Oxford English Dictionary* and other lexical resources to the class.

For the most part, a person's ability to express thoughts and to receive the thoughts of others is dependent upon an ability with language. Much of this ability can be attributed to the knowledge of words (Terman, 1916; Carroll, 194; Davis, 1968). The Spoken Words approach places subtle pressures on students to notice the language in their environment and to methodically select useful words to learn. Through word interviews students define words and generate specific examples. They tell amusing word-stories and learn from and enjoy other students' word-stories. When students use the words they begin to master them in both speaking and writing.

For teachers, the Spoken Word approach provides opportunities for instruction and sharing student attitudes. Seated among the learners, the teacher guides students to select useful and challenging words, coaches their speaking delivery, and develops the use of vocabulary strategies. The Spoken Words format offers a chance for teachers and students to become better acquainted as their words and stories reveal their lives, interests, hobbies, readings, etc. Spoken Words generates its own momentum as teachers and students together contribute to a learning climate where exposure to vocabulary concepts is enjoyable and valuable.

REFERENCES

Allen, Roach V. 1976. *Language Experiences in Communication.* Boston: Houghton Mifflin.

Ashton-Warner, Sylvia. 1963. *Teacher.* New York: Simon & Schuster.

Bartlett, Frederic. 1932. *Remembering: A Study in Experimental and Social Psychology.* Cambridge, England: Cambridge University Press.

Carroll, John B. 1964. "Words, Meanings and Concepts." *Harvard Education Review* 34 (Spring): 178–202.

Dale, Edgar, Joseph O'Rourke, and Henry A. Bamman. 1971. *Techniques of Teaching Vocabulary.* Menlo Park, NJ: Benjamin/Cummings Publishing Company.

Davis, Frederic B. 1968. "Research in Comprehension in Reading." *Reading Research Quarterly* 3 (Summer): 499–545.

Devine, Thomas. 1981. *Teaching Study Skills.* Boston: Allyn & Bacon.

Duffelmeyer, Frederic A. 1980. "The Influence of Experience-based Vocabulary Instruction on Learning Word Meanings." *Journal of Reading* 24 (October): 35–41.

Hayakawa, Samuel. 1972. *Language in Thought and Action.* New York: Harcourt, Brace, Jovanovich.

Hunter, Madeline. 1967. *Motivation Theory for Teachers.* El Segundo, CA: TIP Publications.

Labov, William, and J. Waltezky. 1967. "Narrative Analysis: Oral Versions of Personal Experience" in *Essays on the Verbal Visual Arts,* June Helm, ed. Seattle: University of Washington Press.

Lockhart, Robert S., Fergus M. Craik, and Larry Jacoby. 1976. "Depth of Processing, Recognition and Recall" in *Recall and Recognition,* J. Brown, ed. London: Wiley.

Menig-Peterson, C. L., and A. McCabe. 1977. *Structure of Children's Narratives.* ED 138376, New Orleans: ERIC Documents.

Ortony, Andrew. 1975. "Why Metaphors Are Necessary and Not Just Nice." *Educational Theory* 25 (Winter): 45–53.

Pearson, David P., and Dale D. Johnson. 1978. *Teaching Reading Vocabulary.* New York: Holt, Rinehart & Winston.

Piaget, Jean, and B. Inhelder. 1973. *Memory and Intelligence.* New York: Basic Books.

Quealy, Roger J. 1969. "Senior High School Students Use of Contextual Aids in Reading." *Reading Research Quarterly* 4 (Summer): 512–533.

Rapp-Haggard, Martha. 1982. "The Vocabulary Self-Selection Strategy: An Active Approach Toward Learning." *Journal of Reading* 26 (December): 203–207.

Roe, Betty, Barbara Stoodt, and Paul Burns. 1978. *Reading Instruction in the Secondary School.* Chicago: Rand McNally.
Smith, Frank. 1978. *Reading without Nonsense.* New York: Teachers College Press.
Stein, Nancy L. 1978. *How Children Understand Stories: A Developmental Analysis.* ED 153205. Urbana, IL: Center for the Study of Reading, 1978.
Terman, Louis M. 1916. *The Measurement of Intelligence.* Cambridge: Riverside Press.
Vacca, Richard T. 1981. *Content Area Reading.* Boston: Little, Brown, 1981.

TEACHING ENGLISH AS
A SECOND LANGUAGE

As more English classrooms include students who are not native speakers of English, it becomes more important for teachers to know some of the fundamentals of teaching English as a second language (ESL). The two articles in this section provide useful methods for students whose first language is not English.

In the first article, James Nattinger discusses the "communicative language teaching method" of teaching English as a second language in which the goals are developing communicative competence and developing exercises that emphasize the interaction between language users and their environment. This permits the learners to communicate their meaning in different situations beyond the classroom. This article discusses methods for teaching speaking, reading, and writing. The second article by David Freeman and Yvonne Freeman discusses the six principles of the student-centered, whole-language approach to writing for these students. In doing this, they provide practical applications, examples, and exercises to help teachers with their own classrooms.

Those of you who would like more information about teaching English as a second language should browse through the *TESOL Quarterly*. It has both theoretical articles and practical classroom applications. You will also find the following reading helpful:

Broselow, Ellen. "Second Language Acquisition," in *Linguistics: The Cambridge Survey, Vol. III. Language: Psychological and Biological Aspects,* edited by Frederick J. Newmeyer (New York: Cambridge University Press, 1988), pp. 194–208. This is a comprehensive article with an excellent bibliography; it will be difficult reading for beginners.

Johnson, Donna M., and Duane H. Roen (eds.). *Richness in Writing: Empowering ESL Students* (White Plains, N.Y.: Longman, 1989). This collection of essays will provide assistance to teachers working with ESL students in the writing classroom.

Cleary, Linda Miller. "Chapter Six Jenny: Second Language Blues," in *From the Other Side of the Desk: Students Who Speak Out About Writing* (Portsmouth, N.H.: Boynton/Cook, 1991), pp. 118–144. Cleary provides a helpful discussion of the problems faced by students whose native language is not English and who are tracked in the mainstream classrooms. Included are practical classroom suggestions.

Rigg, Pat, and Virginia G. Allen (eds.), *When They Don't All Speak English: Integrating the ESL Student into the Regular Classroom* (Urbana, Ill.: NCTE, 1989). This is another source for teachers who have ESL students mainstreamed in their classes.

Rodrigues, Raymond J., and Robert White, *Mainstreaming the Non-English-Speaking Student* (Urbana, Ill.: NCTE, 1981).

Spolsky, Bernard. "Contrastive Analysis, Error Analysis, Interlanguage, and Other Useful Fads," *The Modern Language Journal* 13 (1979): 250–257. This is an older article, but it is still useful and easy reading.

Communicative Language Teaching: A New Metaphor

James R. Nattinger

Currently, a method for second language teaching that calls itself "communicative" is developing; specifically, this method is known as Communicative Language Teaching (CLT). Although work on it is still preliminary, CLT has the possibility of being less vague than former "communicative competence" methods, less limited than notional-functional ones, less ethnocentric than many humanistic methods, and less psycholinguistically objectionable than audiolingual ones. CLT practice is quite diverse, yet underlying all of its variations are these similarities: 1) communicative competence is the goal at each level of instruction, 2) interaction between language users and their environment is a primary objective of all exercises, and 3) the processes involved in using language, that is, the strategies for making sense of something and for negotiating meaning, are the center of attention.

This article will first describe some of the ways that CLT is being used in classrooms to teach conversation, writing, and reading and will then suggest how this method is related to current theory building in second language acquisition research, in linguistics, and in artificial intelligence. Before that, however, it is necessary to consider how method is linked to metaphor in general, for one of the problems in talking about CLT is that this method seems to have moved away from the metaphors commonly used to describe language teaching and has yet to fasten firmly onto one of its own.

METAPHOR AND METHOD

A metaphor helps us understand by suggesting likenesses between something whose outlines are vague and imperfectly understood and something whose shape is distinct and familiar. In suggesting such a relationship, a metaphor provides us with a framework for organizing our knowledge and gives shape to the unknown. The more likenesses between the two entities it suggests, the better the metaphor seems to be, so that often the border between the two blurs, creating a confusion of the metaphor with psychological reality (Seliger 1983). When this happens, we understand one thing to be exactly like another and, whether consciously or not, we tend to act as if they were the same in all of their details and implications. If metaphor were only rhetorical flourish, this problem would be essentially trivial and would have little to do with language teaching, but it is clear that it is much more.[1] Any model, any theory, any description is a

---

[1] Lakoff and Johnson (1980) make dramatic claims for metaphor and, in fact, put it at the very center of our lives. Our conceptual system itself operates almost wholly metaphorically, they feel.

metaphor of a sort, so most of the explaining and learning we do takes place metaphorically. Language learning and teaching are also closely tied to metaphor, as Herron claims: "what we teach (or think we are teaching) and how we teach, along with the complementary perceptions of value, are intimately linked to metaphor" (1982:241). Yet, in spite of this link, there has been little written about the relationship between metaphor and language learning, or between metaphor and education in general, for that matter. Herron's article, one of the best in tracing the history of the metaphors that have characterized language teaching, summarizes the situation well.

According to Herron, the grammar-translation method was accompanied by a *gymnastic* metaphor, one which equates training and exercise of the body with that of the mind. The main thrust of the equation is that as muscles become stronger and more flexible through rigorous exercise, the mind becomes more dexterous through classroom training. And just as the body becomes generally stronger as a result of this training, learning results in generally increased intellectual powers. Some of the implications of this metaphor are that students are full of latent abilities which, because of lack of training, have never been developed; that teachers are trainers who will discipline them into practicing these unused powers; and that language, the focus of this exercise, is a formal object which consists of meanings to be extracted and mastered.

A more recent method, audiolingualism, carries with it quite another metaphor, one that Herron calls the *production* metaphor, which links language teaching to the development of marketable and usable skills. The implications here are that schools are factories in which teachers, who are supervisors, oversee the products being molded (i.e., the students), who are essentially passive receptacles for the learning that is poured into them by the teachers. Learning itself is broken down into uncomplicated sub-tasks in order to avoid snags on the production line. Language is seen as a formal, grammatical object, much as in the gymnastic metaphor, and is to be poured into the students bit by bit.

Post-audiolingual methods, those that have called themselves "humanistic" and "learner-centered," are based on yet another metaphor, one which shifts from defining teaching to defining learning. In this metaphor, second language learners are equated with children learning their first language: just as children learn first languages actively and automatically in natural, informal environments, second language learners go about acquiring language best in similar naturalistic situations in which the meaning and function of language become much more important than the memorization of the forms of the language. Further implications of this metaphor are that teachers, who are something like guardians of the child language acquirers, must concentrate on the emotional as well as the cognitive needs of their students and that the students themselves, unlike students in the gymnastic and industrial metaphors, actively go about learning in an environment to which they are intimately attached. The language they learn is a communicative rather than a grammatical construct, one whose meanings are not inviolable and self-contained but rather are created in the very act of students' relating to their environment and to each other. Meaning itself is something that emerges as it is negotiated.

Considering all language learning to be comparable to first language learning, as this metaphor does, is in many ways quite stimulating, for it has made us reconsider many of our assumptions about teaching. But there are, as Herron admits, many things about it that are unsatisfactory. The basic equation of the metaphor itself is intuitively jarring: second language learners are *not* children who are tied completely to the immediate environment and who are approaching a language for the first time; rather, they are experienced language users (no matter how young) with a great deal of common sense about the world, and they have knowledge of the linguistic patterns of their first language as well as of the strategies necessary for using those patterns. A more intuitively accurate metaphor will have to change this basic analogy, while retaining the parts that are satisfying.

Whether the new metaphor will be simply an adaptation of the humanistic one to accommodate new criteria, or whether it will be a completely different one, is not certain at this point, although it seems likely that if the basic analogy changes, the resulting metaphor will also be quite different. But even though this metaphor has yet to take a definite shape, some of its general characteristics are clear: it would again describe language as a communicative rather than a grammatical construct, and would define meaning as that which emerges in students' communicative interactions with each other. Teachers would still look to the emotional as well as the cognitive needs of the students and would provide as natural a language learning environment for them as possible. This new metaphor, however, would describe students not as beginning language learners but rather as sophisticated processors of language who use what they already know about language and the world to make sense of a new linguistic system. This new metaphor, when it is finally articulated, will be the one to characterize CLT.

CLT IN THE CLASSROOM

Strategy, interaction, process—the keys to CLT; how are they guiding classroom practice? Let me describe some work in three different areas of language teaching in order to give an idea of the variety they have generated and, in this way, suggest more specifically what it is that the new metaphor will need to account for.

Conversation

In "The Open-Ended Scenario: A New Approach to Conversation," DiPietro (1982) expands upon the typical roleplaying activity by proposing that new information be introduced into rather set situations in order to force students to make quick choices about the direction of their conversations. The intention, he says, "is to emulate those occasions which often occur in real life wherein people are called upon to redirect their communication in response to newly introduced facts and events" (1982:16). This sort of oral interaction requires not only sudden changes of expression and content but also draws on both receptive and productive skills.

In open-ended scenarios, new information is handed out in phases rather than given all at once:

Phase One: The teacher selects one male and one female student. The male must invite the female to dinner at a restaurant. The female may either accept the invitation or reject it. The interactants are to develop a conversation in either case.

Phase Two: If the female accepts, the two go to the restaurant where they encounter another male who appears to be the boyfriend of the female. Develop a conversation among the three individuals. If the female rejects the offer to dinner, the male asks another female, who accepts. Then they go to a restaurant where they encounter the first female seated at a table having dinner with another male. Develop a conversation with the four persons (DiPietro 1982:17).

The teacher divides the class into small groups, assigning each group a role to play in the scenario, and allows time for preparation and rehearsal. The groups discuss the desired goal of their interaction in each situation and the verbal strategies they might use to achieve it, which leads to considerations of possible speech functions for each strategy and the grammatical ways of expressing them. DiPietro feels that "matters of grammatical form are best explained in strategic contexts" (1982:19) like these, which provide a natural connection of function and form. The problem for the students, of course, is that they must allow for a number of possibilities in the future interaction by preparing for the verbal countermoves of the interlocutors, since what is said *by* speakers depends crucially on what is said *to* them. Students thus experience firsthand the ways in which extended discourse affects conventional language and, at the same time, they develop verbal strategies.

Writing

The teaching of writing can be described in a similar way. It may, at first, appear odd to think of writing in the same terms as conversation for it seems, on the surface at least, to be an isolated and solitary activity. But the two are in fact very similar. Writing, like speaking, is almost always directed toward an audience whose expectations shape the form and content of the message, making interaction an integral element of the process. Furthermore, writers discover solutions as they go along. They modify their discourse as they attempt to get closer to their intended meaning; they try out different strategies, much as speakers do in ever-shifting conversations, and as they write and rewrite, and approximate more closely their intended meaning, the form with which to express the meaning suggests itself. Many ESL writing texts, based on structural approaches, prescribe the form first and then ask that the meaning be tailored to fit, a procedure which reflects just the opposite approach. Zamel (1982, 1983) has done a good deal of work to develop a writing program that follows the new directions.

For Zamel, revision becomes the main component of instruction as students are taught to view their writing as someone else's reading. As students assume the roles of both writer and reader, they try to predict what problems the reader will have and what possible reactions there will be to what they are writing. The first part of such a course gets the students to articulate ideas they want to write about. Then the teacher helps them to order these ideas by getting them to consider their intention, or the goal they have in mind for what it is they will write. This comes about in conversations with the teacher and with members of a small group to which the students have been assigned and, throughout the process, questions are raised not only about the goal but also about the written strategies and forms most likely to be useful in achieving that goal. In this way it is extremely similar to the kinds of "rehearsals" that DiPietro proposes for his open-ended scenarios. Once the writing begins, it usually takes the form of sketchy notes, quickly jotted ideas, perhaps more fully developed sentences, but never formal, cohesive outlines. Students have to be constantly reassured that they are not supposed to know exactly what they are going to say before they begin. The teacher then allows ample time for revision. Students write down ideas, rethink them, rewrite them, rewrite them again, not exactly sure of what is going to appear next on the page. New insights can occur anytime in the process, and, as they do, they are jotted down and incorporated into future revisions. Fluency—letting ideas flow—is an immediate result and happens in the context of goal and reader expectations. As the revisions get closer to the intended meaning, accuracy of form begins to be attended to. Zamel finds that first revisions usually address very general issues such as content, organization, or purpose of the entire piece, while each subsequent revision turns to more formal considerations and, finally, to sentence polishing.

Reading

Reading, a third area of language teaching, can also be described in similar terms. Readers are seen as not passively absorbing but rather as actively creating meanings on the basis of the discourse clues they find, just as in speaking and writing. Readers assess these clues against their experience and expectations—against their *schemas* (see Carrell 1982, Carrell and Eisterhold 1983), and they make tentative guesses about meanings, which will then be rejected or confirmed as the reading progresses (Smith 1978, Van Dijk 1981, Purves 1983). The tie to writing is extremely close, as suggested above. Widdowson, for example, regards reading "not as a reaction to a text but as *interaction* between writer and reader mediated through the text" (1979:174). This is certainly contrary to any idea of a text being complete in itself and independent of any context, which has been the assumption of many traditional and audiolingual theorists (Fries 1963, Lefevre 1964). The idea that a text can be so self-contained was no doubt reinforced by the gymnastic and industrial metaphors, which suggest that words are containers that hold exact amounts of meaning waiting to be released. In the new metaphor, however, meaning is seen as being attached to words when they are used in particular contexts.[2] Thus, reading, as described by this metaphor, is not seen as a process of imperfectly extracting meaning from a text, since the process of writing the text was equally imperfect in encoding meaning. This is why Widdowson says there is "no possibility of recovering complete meaning from a text [because] it is never there in the first place" (1979:174). It is best to think of encoding, he says, "not as the formulation of messages, in principle complete and self-contained, but as the devising of a set of directions" (1979:174) which will indicate to readers where they are to look in their own experience for the writer's meaning. Readers understand and carry out these directions as well as they can by means of the strategies they have already learned.

How does this work in practice? Widdowson (1978) has the students progress from simple to complex prose by "gradual approximation," the building up of dialogue sequences into more and more complex units. He interposes each passage with numerous points called "interpretive checks" (which are essentially questions that direct the students to consider the meaning and organization of what they have been reading) and in this way adroitly links problems of grammatical choice with those of rhetorical constraints, such as operate in the real world (Eskey 1983). In other words, he provides a natural connection between function and form, which is very similar to the sort of thing DiPietro works for in his conversational exercises. Weaver (1980) offers something quite different. Whenever students find stop signs drawn at various points in her narratives, they must stop and consider—often aloud—what is going to happen next. In this way they learn about other students' strategies for predicting, as well as recognize the ones they themselves use. Stories with an element of suspense or mystery are especially good for predicting, Weaver suggests, and so are folktales, because they often contain interculturally predictable patterns and because they can be used with students of various ages and language backgrounds.[3]

---

[2]This is *not* to say that we have finally reached the "perfect" metaphor, which will never be supplanted by another; it is only to suggest that metaphors guide us and influence our thinking. The matter is entirely relative. It would be possible to come up with many different metaphors for the same situation, for example, each influencing us differently. Furthermore, as one anonymous reviewer of this article suggested, "using metaphors for certain situations is an ad hoc way of looking at that situation; it is, in fact, another metaphor!"

[3]For these reasons, a modified cloze procedure and a Grimm's fairy tale may be a very good combination for an ESL reading class. To fill in the blanks, students select words that make sense with what went before as well as what they think will come later; they then refine or reject these choices as the reading progresses. This is the very sort of thing that Lebauer (1984) proposes for helping students better comprehend academic lectures. Her students practice with cloze exercises drawn from transcripts of lectures in order to enhance their ability to extract relevant information, to predict future information, and to relate their background knowledge to new information.

RELATED RESEARCH

The emerging metaphor that underlies these specific ESL practices also directs current research in other areas. In work on second language acquisition, for example, interest is turning from viewing input and language product independently to viewing the interaction between the input and the product. As Larsen-Freeman points out, "structure in a child's competence may at first develop out of a construction that the child builds jointly with other speakers," and from interactions like these, she continues, it may be that "a child learns how to produce topic-comment constructions" (1908:vi–vii). Hatch feels the same can be said for second language learners. Rather than first learning correct structures, then learning how to apply them in discourse, it is much more likely that the learner "learns how to do conversation . . . how to interact verbally, and out of this interaction syntactic structures are developed" (1978:404). Most agree that the learner's developing ability to empathize with an audience affects language learning. Differing strategies are also being investigated to account for differences in the ability to acquire language (Rubin 1975, Naiman, Frohlich, Stern and Todesco 1978, Cohen and Aphek 1981, Tarone 1981). Scarcella and Higa, for example, note that

> older second language acquirers utilize conversational strategies to a greater extent. They are better at keeping conversations going ("sustaining the talk") and can use several strategies to improve the comprehensibility of the input they receive, [which means] they are therefore better at getting the comprehensible input they need for acquisition (1982:173) . . . Adult native English speakers do much more negotiation work in conversation with younger L2 learners than they do with older learners. They provide larger quantities of simple input, a more supportive atmosphere, and a constant check to see that the input a child receives is both attended to and understood (1982:193).

Work in linguistics has, traditionally, been concerned with describing the formal properties of linguistic knowledge, not with how that knowledge is used, so this work has only been of indirect value in guiding language teaching practice, as Chomsky (1966) suggested long ago. Two principles that underlie most current linguistic theory, in fact, immediately contradict the basis upon which CLT methods and research are carried out: that monologue rather than dialogue is the linguistic basis of language; and that basic meanings are independent of an individual's particular experience (Habermas 1970, Sampson 1982). Recently, however, some linguists have begun to explore the relationship between these formal properties of linguistic knowledge and how they are used by working on cognitive models of language structure and on models of discourse processing, and many are finding a tight link between language comprehension and production, and language context and existing knowledge (Ortony 1975). Chief among these linguists is Chafe, who has been exploring the relationship between language and consciousness, and language and memory (1970, 1973, 1974, 1980). He has examined the problem of how we make meaning from language and how we remember it and has suggested that language users primarily focus on semantic information when they perceive a message. They "translate" surface structures as quickly as possible into meaningful sequences of propositions, then store that information in memory. These stored semantic facts, he says, are "schematic" structures consisting of an "event," "action," "process," or "state," and a number of "participants" having expected case roles. These schematic structures are themselves further integrated into the user's world knowledge, which is itself organized in terms of prototypical situations called *frames* and *scripts*. These are complex cognitive units that represent series of cause and effect relationships about particular subjects and frequently occurring episodes in our lives (Van Dijk 1981). Such knowledge-based structures are seen to provide a framework for comprehension patterns in discourse as well as to account for inference strategies, which are an extremely important part of discourse processing.

Much of Chafe's work, as well as that of other linguists who have turned to more performance-based research, echoes work in artificial intelligence (AI). Researchers here also study underlying processes of discourse production, comprehension, and storage and, as they attempt to model computers after the way the mind works, have had to turn away, just as these linguists have had to, from static models of information storage and retrieval. The old metaphor in this field, which many still accept as common sense, equates human intelligence with "the result of applying rules of inference to a large data base of static facts, a process idealized in mathematical theorem proving" (Waltz 1982:14). But many AI researchers, not believing this analogy to be a good one, are looking for new ways of thinking about thinking.

A nice example of this occurs in AI's attempts to develop a chess program. AI researchers have had to shift from a power strategy (a brute-force, trial-and-error search of all possible moves and countermoves) to more efficient "knowledge strategies that more clearly approximate human mental processes and employ heuristics" (Welles 1983:53) for two reasons: first, they have found that chess masters do not consider all possible moves but instead use their vast experience to limit, drastically, the number of choices they have; and second, they have realized that it is the way that chess masters store knowledge in their memory that gives them such an advantage.[4] Novices see positions on the chessboard simply as individual pieces on individual squares, but masters, who have organized their knowledge more hierarchically, see the same positions as clusters or

---

[4]Recently, however, many AI researchers have abandoned heuristic chess programs because "the intelligent programs kept making mistakes, although slower brute force programs that simply tried all possible moves did not. As the technology of computer hardware advanced, brute force increasingly became the method of choice; in the past five years chess programs have become dumber, faster, and much harder to beat" (Hunt 1982:327). As a result of this and other such work, the major direction of AI research currently is to discover what the human mind can do better than the computer and to describe these skills with programs that minimize brute force and that deduce general principles instead.

chunks of several pieces which are themselves grouped into more general chunks, and these grouped into still more general ones (Hunt 1982). The masters can recall these chunks just as easily as novices can recall individual pieces. This is similar to research in natural language processing, which finds that we recall many more words if they are chunked into coherent groups rather than if they are learned individually (Miller 1956, Simon 1974), and similar to work in cognitive psychology, which finds that new information is retained by aggregating it into more comprehensive chunks, which are then made accessible by linking them in as many ways as possible to information that is already stored (Miller, Galanter, and Pribram 1960, Simon 1969, Hofstadter 1980, Hunt 1982).

There is, then, a great deal of interaction between AI and cognitive psychology: mechanical processes for chunking and linking information imitate human processes of perception and memory; methods of information retrieval reflect human strategies for inference and production. The two fields also share an elusive goal—to be able to model "common sense." To do this will require linking perception, reasoning, and action simultaneously, in as yet unknown ways, because ultimately the intelligent use of concepts depends on all three. Research that results from this will have much to say to CLT teachers, who make such "common sense" performance the goal of their classroom activities.

FUTURE RESEARCH

CLT not only guides classroom practice and aligns ESL teaching with current theory in other fields, but also offers clear directions for future research. Foremost among the issues that are unresolved is the question of what ought to be the starting point in the design and implementation of a second language program. Should it be the development of a communicative methodology or the specification of the content of CLT courses? Should it, to use Richards' (1984) terms, be basically a "learning-centered" method, whose methodology is developed through a theory of learning processes and instructional procedures, or should it be basically a "language-centered" method, which is developed through the syllabus and concerned with the way language content is defined and organized? As Yalden (1983) suggests in her summary, CLT has been defined variously as both kinds of method. This variety can, perhaps, be seen as both the result and the cause of there being no clear metaphor guiding CLT at the present. As learning-centered variants, she cites the work of Krashen (1981), Terrell (1982), and the immersion model of bilingual education (Stern 1980), which she feels are all "naturalistic" versions of CLT and "in which methodology is of far more interest than syllabus design, if indeed the latter figures at all" (Yalden 1983:236). Another learning-centered variant of CLT, most clearly articulated by Candlin and Breen (1979), she says, "not merely ignore[s] the classic procedures of functional syllabus design but is opposed to it" (1983:236). Language-centered interpretations of CLT also abound, and several models of syllabus types have been proposed, from structural ones (Brumfit 1980), to the completely functional models used in English for Science and Technology (EST) and English for Academic Purposes (EAP), to the more communicative syllabus types (Yalden 1982). Interestingly, many of these combine their descriptions of syllabus content with methodological concerns. Brumfit's (1980) model, for example, "grafts functional teaching on to a structural core" (Yalden 1983). Yalden's own "proportional model" uses topics "as a framework for a gradual change of proportion in the time devoted to language forms on the one hand and language function and discourse structure on the other" (Yalden 1982).

Just what sorts of syllabus components will eventually be determined to be the most efficient, whether these be structural, semantic, functional, or more process-oriented strategic units, is certainly unclear at this point. Whatever decisions are made, either in syllabus specification or in communicative methodology, will come from research in the three areas upon which CLT is based, and they will provide answers to questions such as these:

Strategies: What sorts of strategies do we have for perceiving, producing, learning, and acquiring language? How do these differ from each other? How can they best be made use of in the classroom?

Interaction: How does the learner's developing ability to empathize with an audience affect language learning? What sorts of interactions are possible, and what are their effects?

Processes: What are the psychological units of perception and production? How are these integrated into larger structures of knowledge? How can they be incorporated into a class syllabus?

A COMPUTATIONAL METAPHOR

Such questions of strategy, interaction, and process have more to do with the processes of comprehension and production than with the forms of language, and they are very similar to the questions now being asked by researchers in cognitive science, a new discipline that combines the sorts of investigations in linguistics, AI, and cognitive psychology mentioned previously. Let me return to that research briefly to consider whether one possible metaphor from that discipline might offer a compatible one for CLT.

The metaphor involves the computer. In cognitive science, many researchers are guided by a computational metaphor to help them build precise models of mental processes. This metaphor provides a special way of looking at language, a view which is somewhat different from the ones offered by other language theories, and has been very useful in helping these researchers to conceptualize and develop their work. As Winograd (1983) describes it, this metaphor is built on four assumptions: 1) The proper domain of study is the structure of the knowledge possessed by a language user, not the form of the text itself or the social context in which the text occurs. 2) This knowledge can be understood, completely, as formal rules concerning the structure of symbols. 3) Instead of concentrating on "competence," an abstract characterization of a user's knowledge of language which is independent of any rules for manifesting this knowledge, the computational metaphor directs attention to the organization of "performance," to the processes of comprehension and production that put the underlying competence to work. Thus, these processes assume a central rather than a peripheral role. Finally, 4) the computational metaphor assumes that knowledge structures and processes are shared with other aspects of intelligence; the metaphor directs researchers to ask in what ways language fits into larger contexts of action and knowledge, not to view language, as most generative grammarians do, as the product of some special, autonomous, language faculty. If we understand how language works, cognitive researchers feel, we will be far along the path to understanding how the mind works—in reasoning, learning, and remembering.

As compatible as the computational metaphor seems to be with many of the issues raised previously, it has two immediately apparent limitations which may make it inappropriate for CLT. The first is its basic assumption that knowledge can be completely modeled as a set of formal structures. This may simply be too narrow a view of language use to be intuitively satisfactory for language teachers. As Winograd notes,

> Many critics of artificial intelligence argue that much of our skill in using language is not in the nature of formal rules, but is more akin to physical skills like walking or playing tennis. They do not believe that the individual's ability to use language can be explained by any formal characterization analogous to the data structures of computers or the rules of formal logic. They see the success of computer programs that deal with natural language in specialized domains as due to the constrained nature of those domains.

1983:29

In light of some of the ways in which CLT is currently being described, perhaps an even more immediate limitation of the metaphor is its relegation of the social aspects of language use to a decidedly secondary role. It is not clear, in fact, whether there would even be a place for descriptions of social interaction in this metaphor. If it turns out that CLT is defined largely in terms of affective variables, then this computational metaphor will not offer a useful way of conceptualizing it or of describing it further.

A FINAL MATTER

In spite of the uncertain metaphor, the unanswered questions, and the diverging methods, there is already enough agreement about basic matters in CLT to permit empirical research to discover what sorts of classrooms provide better environments for second language learning and what sorts of syllabus designs work best. The need for such rigorous evaluation procedures is great, as Richards (1984) suggests, especially since new methods often go unmeasured and their claims remain unevaluated. Gathering empirical data of this kind should be a main thrust of future research in CLT. Such data will determine the most effective types of classroom interactions and will help validate the selection of items for the syllabus. When this happens, many of the variations in methodology and content mentioned above will disappear. As the specific details of CLT practice become clearer, so will the general outlines of a compatible metaphor to guide it.

REFERENCES

Brumfit, Christopher. 1980. From defining to designing: communicative specifications versus communicative methodology in foreign language teaching. In *The foreign language syllabus and communicative approaches to teaching: proceedings of a European-American seminar,* Kurt Muller (Ed.), 1–9. Special Issue of *Studies in Second Language Acquisition* 3(1).

Candlin, Christopher, and Michael Breen. 1979. Evaluating and designing language teaching materials. *Practical Papers in English Language Education* 2:172–216. Lancaster, England: University of Lancaster.

Carrell, Patricia. 1982. Cohesion is not coherence. *TESOL Quarterly* 16(4):479–488.

Carrell, Patricia, and Joan Eisterhold. 1983. Schema theory and ESL reading pedagogy. *TESOL Quarterly* 17(4):553–573.

Chafe, Wallace. 1970. *Meaning and the structure of language.* Chicago: University of Chicago Press.

———. 1973. Language and memory. *Language* 49:261–281.

———. 1974. Language and consciousness. *Language* 50:111–133.

———. (Ed.). 1980. *The pear stories: cognitive, cultural and linguistic aspects of narrative production. Advances in Discourse Processes* 3. Norwood, New Jersey: Ablex.

Chomsky, Noam. 1966. Linguistic theory. In *Northeast Conference on the Teaching of Foreign Languages: reports of the working committee,* Robert Mead, Jr. (Ed.), 43–49. New York: Northeast Conference on the Teaching of Foreign Language.

Cohen, A., and E. Aphek. 1981. Easifying second language learning. *Studies in Second Language Acquisition* 3(2):221–236.

DiPietro, Robert. 1982. The open-ended scenario: a new approach to conversation. *TESOL Quarterly* 16(1):15–20.

Eskey, David. 1983. Meanwhile, back in the real world . . . : accuracy and fluency in second language teaching. *TESOL Quarterly* 17(2):315–323.

Fries, Charles. 1963. *Linguistics and reading.* New York: Holt, Rinehart and Winston.

Habermas, J. 1970. Towards a theory of communicative competence. *Inquiry* 13(4):360–375.

Hatch, Evelyn. 1978. Discourse analysis and second language acquisition. In *Second language acquisition: a book of readings,* Evelyn Hatch (Ed.), 401–435. Rowley, Massachusetts: Newbury House.

Herron, Carol. 1982. Foreign language learning approaches as metaphor. *The Modern Language Journal* 66(3):235–242.

Hofstadter, Douglas. 1980. *Gäodel, Escher, Bach: an eternal golden braid.* New York: Vintage Books.

Hunt, Morton. 1982. *The universe within: a new science explores the human mind.* New York: Simon and Schuster.

Krashen, Stephen. 1981. *Second language acquisition and second language learning.* New York: Pergamon Press.

Lakoff, G., and M. Johnson. 1980. *Metaphors we live by.* Chicago: University of Chicago Press.

Larsen-Freeman, Diane. 1980. Introduction. In *Discourse analysis in second language research,* Diane Larsen-Freeman (Ed.), v-xi. Rowley, Massachusetts: Newbury House.

Lebauer, Roni. 1984. Using lecture transcripts in EAP lecture comprehension courses. *TESOL Quarterly* 18(1):41–54.

Lefevre, Carl. 1964. *Linguistics and the teaching of reading.* New York: McGraw-Hill.

Miller, G. 1956. The magical number seven, plus or minus two: some limits on our capacity for processing information. *Psychological Review* 63:81–97.

Miller, G., E. Galanter, and K. Pribram. 1960. *Plans and the structure of behavior.* New York: Holt, Rinehart and Winston.

Naiman, N., M. Frohlich, H. Stern, and A. Todesco. 1978. *The good language learner.* Toronto: Modern Language Center, Ontario Institute for Studies in Education.

Ortony, A. 1975. Language isn't for people: on applying theoretical linguistics to practical problems. *Review of Educational Research* 45(3):485–504.

Purves, Alan. 1983. Language processing: reading and writing. *College English,* 45(2):129–140.

Richards, Jack. 1984. The secret life of methods. *TESOL Quarterly* 18(1):7–23.

Rubin, Joan. 1975. What the "good language learner" can teach us. *TESOL Quarterly* 9:41–51.

Sampson, Gloria. 1982. Converging evidence for a dialectical model of function and form in second language learning. *Applied Linguistics* 3(1):1–28.

Scarcella, Robin, and Corrine Higa. 1982. Input and age differences in second language acquisition. In *Child-adult differences in second language acquisition,* Stephen Krashen, Robin Scarcella, and Michael Long (Eds.), 175–201. Rowley, Massachusetts: Newbury House.

Seliger, Herbert. 1983. The language learner as linguist: of metaphor and realities. *Applied Linguistics* 4(3):179–191.

Simon, Herbert A. 1969. The architecture of complexity. In *The sciences of the artificial,* Herbert A. Simon (Ed.), 192–229. Cambridge, Massachusetts: MIT Press.

———. 1974. How big is a chunk? *Science* 183:482–488.

Smith, Frank. 1978. *Understanding reading.* New York: Holt, Rinehart and Winston.

Stern, H. 1980. Some approaches to communicative language teaching in Canada. In *The foreign language syllabus and communicative approaches to teaching: proceedings of a European-American seminar,* Kurt Muller (Ed.), 57–63. Special Issue of *Studies in Second Language Acquisition* 3(1).

Tarone, Elaine. 1981. Some thoughts on the notion of communication strategy. *TESOL Quarterly* 15(3):285–295.

Terrell, Tracy. 1982. A natural approach. In *Innovative approaches to language teaching,* Robert Blair (Ed.), 160–173. Rowley, Massachusetts: Newbury House.

Van Dijk, Teun. 1981. Discourse studies and education. *Applied Linguistics* 2(1):1–26.

Waltz, David L. 1982. Artificial intelligence. In *Perspectives in cognitive science,* David Farwell, Stephen Helmreich, and William Wallace (Eds.), 11–28. Urbana, Illinois: Linguistics Student Organization, University of Illinois.

Weaver, Constance. 1980. *Psycholinguistics and reading: from process to practice.* Cambridge, Massachusetts: Winthrop Publishers.

Welles, Chris. 1983. Teaching the brain new things. *Esquire* 99:49–54.

Widdowson, H. G. 1978. *Teaching language as communication.* Oxford, England: Oxford University Press.

———. 1979. *Explorations in applied linguistics.* Oxford, England: Oxford University Press.

Winograd, Terry. 1983. *Language as a cognitive process: syntax.* Reading, Massachusetts: Addison-Wesley Publishing Company.

Yalden, Janice. 1982. *The communicative syllabus: evolution, design and implementation.* New York: Pergamon Press.

———. 1983. Chicken or egg? Communicative methodology or communicative syllabus design. In *On TESOL '82,* Mark Clarke and Jean Handscombe (Eds.), 235–242. Washington, D.C.: TESOL.

Zamel, Vivian. 1982. Writing: the process of discovering meaning. *TESOL Quarterly* 16(2):195–209.

———. 1983. The composing processes of advanced ESL students: six case studies. *TESOL Quarterly* 17(2):165–187.

A Road to Success for Language-Minority High School Students

David Freeman and Yvonne S. Freeman

Emilia, Miguel, Feliciana, and David graduated from high school in June. The year before their parents, teachers, counselors, and even the students themselves had little hope that they would receive their diplomas with their classmates. A special summer program made the difference for them and many of their peers (Freeman, Freeman, and Gonzales 1987). This program was developed by teachers, consultants, and administrators working together to approach the teaching of content to secondary students in a way that would help language-minority students succeed in school. By examining how the program was set up, how the teachers were prepared, how the lessons were approached, and how the students came to view learning, we are able to draw some conclusions about how secondary teachers with no knowledge of their students' first language can help second-language students succeed in content-area classrooms.

The key elements of the program are indicated in Figure 20: the *who, what, when,* and *where* set the scene, and the *how* describes the principles that the

Who:	Students whose first language was not English.
	Students with low standardized test scores.
	Students who had failed at least three classes.
	Two content-area teachers hired by the district.
	Two ESL student teachers.
What:	Intensive summer classes in required United States history and biology courses.
When and Where:	Two three-week sessions of summer classes meeting from 7:00 a.m. to noon, in an urban school in Arizona.
How:	Teachers applied four learning principles.

FIGURE 20
Key elements of the special summer program.

teachers applied to help these language-minority students reach their potential and discover that learning can be worthwhile. We will discuss each of these key elements in some detail, because we think that what helped these teachers and students can also help other similar students in secondary content-area classrooms.

WHO: THE PEOPLE

The Students

The forty-six students involved in the summer program had just finished their freshman or junior years of high school. The home language survey administered by the district indicated that their first language was either Spanish or Yaqui. However, the students had not had the benefit of instruction in their native language, and had been in mainstreamed classes during all of their schooling in the United States.

The minority status of the students was not the only criterion used to determine placement in the program. In addition, the participants had experienced little previous academic success. All had scored below the forty-first percentile on the California Achievement Test, and all had failed at least three courses during the previous school year. They were high-risk students. Such students often drop out of school when they reach the legal age to do so (Wong Fillmore 1986; Duran 1983). The classes, then, were made up of students who were identified by the district to be potential dropouts.

Emilia, Miguel, Feliciana, and David are representative of the group as a whole. They demonstrated oral proficiency in their second language, English. Although they spoke Spanish or Spanish and Yaqui, they had never received any schooling in either of these languages and had never developed academic skills in their first language. Therefore, instruction in their first languages—with the extensive vocabulary that would be necessary for the study of the science and social studies courses—did not seem appropriate, nor was it available through the school district. None of the four students appeared to have developed the literacy skills necessary for academic success in either their first language or in English. What they needed was a special kind of classroom instruction in English that differed from the traditional instruction they had experienced in school thus far.

The Teachers

The two content-area teachers for the classes were regular classroom teachers with no previous experience in this type of program. Rob, the history teacher, teaches gifted classes during the regular school year and originally took the summer job because he wanted the extra salary. Ruben, the biology teacher, has taught science in regular and bilingual classrooms for several years. Ruben did not usually teach summer school, but took the job at the last minute when the teacher originally scheduled could not teach.

The two student teachers, Carrie and Sue, were completing their master of arts degrees at the local university and wanted their student teaching experience in a high school classroom. Though these ESL teachers were not experts in biology or history, they understood language acquisition theory and methods of teaching English as a second language.

WHAT: THE COURSES

Two required courses were offered during the summer: biology and United States history. The courses were specifically designed to help academically troubled language-minority students succeed. The district administration, which fully supported these courses, insisted that the content be the same as during the regular year. The difference in these summer courses was the instructional approach of the teachers, which was supported by the student teachers and local university consultants. Staff from the university not only conferred with administrators, resource personnel, and teachers, but also with the school board itself so that approval for the program came from the district's main governing board.

Initially, Stephen Krashen made a presentation to the school board. He reviewed his theory of language acquisition (1981, 1985), emphasizing the need for comprehensible input. Once the board approved the plan, the university consultants came to the school for pre- and inservice meetings with the teachers, student teachers, district administrators, and resource people.

An important condition set by the board was that the materials and tests not be "simplified" and that the students be required to do the same work that students did during the regular school year. As a result, the challenge for all involved was to find ways to make the academic coursework "comprehensible input" to these students.

WHEN AND WHERE: TIME AND PLACE

The program was held in two three-week sessions. Classes met daily from 7:00 a.m. to noon during June and July. This, of course, meant that the coursework was intense, because it condensed a full year's course into six weeks of instruction. Daily attendance was mandatory since each day represented a week's work.

The classes were held in Arizona at an urban school site. The biology class and the United States history class were only two of the many classes held there that summer. Although these two classes were considered pilot classes by the district, other students at the school were not aware that these courses were anything more than regular summer "makeup" classes.

HOW: APPLYING PRINCIPLES

In the preservice training and during the time the classes were being taught, the consultants asked the teachers to apply four principles of learning that have been suggested at different times for first-language learners and second-language elementary school students (Goodman 1986b; Goodman and Goodman 1981; Harste, Woodward, and Burke 1984; Goodman, Goodman, and Flores 1984; Cazden 1986; Hudelson 1984, 1986; Rigg 1986; Urzúa 1986; Enright 1986; Enright and McCloskey 1985). During the preservice sessions the principles were discussed and sample lessons were demonstrated. As teachers and consultants worked together with students in the classroom, they used the principles as a base to help them reflect upon what was happening in the classroom.

The principles are:

1 Learning occurs most easily when language is kept whole.

2 Classes should be learner-centered and include activities that are meaningful and functional.

3 Learning takes place in social interaction that employs all four modes of language.

4 Learning requires that teachers have faith in learners.

We next describe each of these principles, and we give examples of how they were applied in the two content classes.

Language Is Learned Best When Kept Whole

Researchers and theorists in first-language acquisition have argued that language learning is a gradual differentiation of wholes into parts, not a building up of parts into the whole (Vygotsky 1962; Smith 1973; Cochrane et al. 1984; Rich 1985; Goodman 1986b). Often second-language students are given more drill and practice on isolated bits and pieces of language than native speakers of English are because it is assumed that whole, meaningful language is too difficult for them. But many second-language educators disagree. Allen (1986) points out, "The kinds of language arts experiences which support English-speaking children to develop and shape their skills in communicating in their native language are also the kinds of experiences that can support the LEP child as he or she takes on a new language" (61). Enright and McCloskey (1985) note, "Children learn language as a medium of communication rather than as a curriculum subject with sets of isolated topics, facts, or skills" (434).

In the summer program, the teachers were encouraged to apply the principle that learning takes place from whole to part in their content classrooms. Rather than having their students memorize bits and pieces of information about biology or history, the teachers began with whole concepts and let the details fall into place as students developed an understanding of the concepts.

For example, in the United States history class, Rob and Carrie began the unit on the American Revolution by asking students to talk about what *revolution* meant, why countries had revolutions, where there were revolutions right now, and finally, what they knew about the American Revolution. Students and teachers brought in current periodicals with articles about present-day revolutions. Carrie read the students a short story about the American Revolution to help make the characters and setting of the period come alive (Brozo and Tomlinson 1986). Students then read the social studies text, compared what they read with the information about revolutions they had already gathered, and worked in groups to decide what the major causes of the American Revolution were, what events and people were important to the outcome, and how the American Revolution could be compared to other revolutions discussed in class.

Classes Should Be Learner-centered, with Meaningful, Functional Activities

The teachers in the summer program began by focusing on what the students already knew in order to build upon their strengths and interests. Often, content-area classes begin by finding out what the students don't know. These classes operate on the assumption that there is a great deal of information that students lack and that the teacher and textbooks will impart that information to the students. Teachers who hold this assumption view students as plants waiting passively to be fed and watered (Lindfors 1982). The teachers in this summer program were asked to view their students as explorers (Lindfors 1982), active learners who bring a great deal to the learning process and at the same time, draw from their environment as they develop new understandings.

The American Revolution unit which Rob and Carrie taught was designed to begin with what the students already knew and understood. The students shared their knowledge of revolutions in general and brought in information from newspapers and magazines about current revolutions. Then they compared these revolutions with what they read about the American Revolution. In this way, their understanding of the American Revolution was framed by their previous knowledge and experiences.

The unit on plants which Ruben and Sue taught also was designed to involve the students from the start. To begin the unit, students and teachers brought in fruits and vegetables from home for class. Then, the students worked in groups. They were given knives and told to study the fruits and vegetables at their tables and to record their discoveries. After a few minutes, students were making hypotheses about fruit parts, seeds, seed coverings, and plant growth. Feliciana, for example, noticed that onions are different from apples because onions have so many layers.

The following day students read the plant chapter in their textbooks. In the same groups, they compared what they read with what they had already discovered. Later in the unit they again used real fruits, vegetables, and plants as they drew and labeled plants, fruits, and seeds. As they worked with fruits and vegetables, conversations about what the students ate came up naturally. These conversations led to a lively discussion on nutrition. This evolved into a comparison of the kinds of fruits and vegetables that are traditionally present in typical American food and in the food the students eat at traditional family festivities. For example, in the American South, many people eat black-eyed peas on New Year's Day; on that day, tamales are usually served in the homes of these students.

By involving students actively and by making sure that the content of the units related personally to them, the teachers made the lessons meaningful and functional for their students. Student involvement extended from initial activities to final evaluation. Students wrote questions and answers about the content material that was covered. These questions were used by the students in cooperative groups to quiz each other on facts (Kagan 1986) and formed the basis of classroom quiz games. The teachers also made a point of including some of the student-generated questions on unit tests. In these ways, classes were learner-centered. All class activities involved students in the learning process from the beginning of the units to the end when they were evaluated.

Language Is Learned in Social Interaction

Most of the activities in the classrooms involved pairs, small groups, or large groups. In fact, when students were left to work on their own, some did not enjoy it. David complained in his journal, "The thing I don't like is when we have to go off on our own and do our own notes."

First-language researchers (Halliday 1975; Wells 1985) have shown that language develops in social interaction. Second-language researchers and theorists also support group work for language-minority students (Long and Porter 1985; Enright and McCloskey 1985; Kagan 1986). When students work in groups they actually use more language, take greater risks, and help each other learn more.

In both the American Revolution unit and the plant unit, students worked together constantly. Students came up with ideas together, discussed concepts together, turned in joint projects at the end of the units, read and responded to textbooks together, wrote and answered questions about the content together, and even shared their journal writing with one another.

As the students worked together, they used all four modes of language—writing, listening, reading, and speaking. In many secondary classrooms, the role of the teacher is to talk while the students' role is to listen, read the textbook, and answer questions. The summer school teachers changed these traditional roles which both teachers and students usually take on. Students did much more of the talking as they shared what they knew, and read and discussed the class content materials together. As a result, students also listened to each other more as they worked together to understand the concepts they were studying.

Both the students and the teachers noticed the difference. Miguel pointed out that when he walked down the hall, other classrooms were quiet, with the students writing and reading alone at their desks, and the teachers sitting at their desks. "The only two classrooms where there is anything interesting going on are our United States history class and that biology class down the hall." Rob made a similar observation from the teacher's point of view:

> The first day I came in and, despite the inservice suggestions, I started lecturing as usual. I soon realized the students were not listening and that my usual use of sarcasm to discipline and get their attention was not as effective as I had always assumed it was. Now that I have involved students and used group work, I will never again depend solely on lecture, textbooks, and tests to teach. Involvement in this summer program has changed my teaching with all students.

Social interaction extended beyond oral language activities to writing. Students wrote daily. They did not simply answer questions on tests or from their textbooks; instead, they kept daily journals that either their teachers or their peers responded to. In these journals, the students reacted to events that had happened in class or to the class content. They used the journals to ask questions, to express their opinions, and to work out ideas they were beginning to understand. Emilia, when studying the Civil War, asked, "Why didn't the first Constitution get rid of slavery?" Feliciana wrote about a brainstorming session, "I enjoyed when we got into a group today and how we thought of what to write on the board from what we could remember. It was long but fun. . . ." David wrote about the seeds in fruits and vegetables, "The seeds were different sizes, but the size of the seeds doesn't match what grows. . . ."

The history and biology classrooms became communities of learners using all four modes of language in social interaction to explore the content areas.

Language Is Learned Best When Teachers Have Faith in Learners

The responses that Emilia, Feliciana, and David gave in their journals reflect an atmosphere in which they were willing to take risks. They felt free to ask questions, express opinions, and make hypotheses because they knew that their teachers and peers would accept what they said or wrote as something that was potentially valuable and worth considering. For many of the students in this summer program, this was the first time that they had been in a classroom where they were encouraged to take risks and supported when they ventured opinions.

At the preservice sessions, the consultants and the teachers talked about how classes usually start out. In many high school classes, the first day is spent going over course requirements and rules. The course begins with the teacher setting out her or his expectations: "In order to pass this course, you must . . ." or "Unless you do this and this and this, you will fail," or "In my course, I expect you to . . ." or "If you do this, the penalty will be. . . ."

The teachers of these summer courses agreed to try another approach. They took the attitude that their students could succeed and that they *would* succeed. They started the first day by explaining that their course would be different. They stressed that everyone in the course was going to succeed, and that the teachers and students were going to succeed, and that the teachers and students were going to work together to help each other succeed. From the first day, the teachers made it clear to students that they could do the work successfully and that there would be a support group to help them.

As teachers drew on students' background knowledge, encouraged them to express their opinions and ask questions, and allowed them to work together to discover answers, students gained confidence in themselves as thinkers and learners. In an atmosphere where the teachers made it clear that they had faith in their students, the students were able to revalue themselves as learners (Goodman 1986a). At the same time, they began to revalue the coursework and to see it as something worth doing. Because their teachers had faith in them as learners, the students developed faith in themselves that they could learn. This change in self-perception for these particular students was the most important result of the program, because the attitude that they could succeed in school carried over into the regular school year.

RESULTS

The results of the program were exciting. Students experienced success in school, some of them for the first time. They became actively involved in their own learning and succeeded. Even though he had seldom written to express himself before, Miguel wrote, without hesitation, his appreciation for the class and how it helped him:

> I think class helps me out a lot because in my other classes they never really explain and you people always explain everything that is about the subject that we are studying and i think that this class is pretty fun to be in because we have nice teachers for the class and if the teachers wasn't here to help us where would we be we all would be dumb. teachers help alot its seemed that this class i'm in i'm learning more then i learned last year and on the first test i took in here was the best test i have ever had and i thank you teachers for the help

Besides responding in their journals, students had an opportunity to evaluate the class by completing a questionnaire on their perceptions and attitudes (Figure 21).

It is significant that ninety-five percent of the students responding to the survey either strongly agreed (#5) or agreed a little (#4) that "working in groups helped me." Ninety percent agreed by marking #4 or #5 that they would like more classes conducted like this one, and seventy-three percent agreed they were ready for tests because of the way the material was reviewed. Perhaps the most significant percentage for these students, who were considered potential dropouts, was question eleven: seventy-four percent agreed with the statement "I feel better about school because of the help I got in class."

Student grades also reflected the students' feelings about school. All but two students in the two classes passed the course and those students failed because they did not fulfill strict attendance requirements. Some students received an *A* or *B* for the first time since elementary school. One girl wrote: "This is the first class I've had since seventh grade that I passed a test without cheating." Students felt the classes helped them and that their time was well spent. Emilia sums up the attitude of many of the students in realistic terms:

> I think this class is not to bad, this is my first time in summer school, and I have began to like it. eventhough its kind of boring sitting in your seat for 5 hrs. but with the work we do it makes it alot easier to go threw the day. Working in groups is not to bad either because you get to meet oouther classmates and it gives you an oppurtunity to see how much their interested in this class too, and it make work alot easier cause you can all work and help each other I feel that the time I will be here it will be worthwhile and I will be getting something out of it.

By working on whole concepts, drawing on student strengths and understandings, encouraging group interaction, and having faith in the learners themselves, teachers were able to help these students change their view of themselves as learners. The success of this program suggests that other schools with similar student populations might benefit from trying out and refining the techniques outlined here.

On a scale of 1-5, show how you feel about the items listed. Agree or disagree by checking (√) your responses as follows:

Check: #5 if you *strongly agree*

#4 if you *agree a little*

#3 if you *are undecided*

#2 if you *disagree a little*

#1 if you *strongly disagree*

	5	4	3	2	1
1. I was able to participate more in this class because of the way it was conducted.	58%	30%	10%		2%
2. Working in groups helped me.	70%	25%	5%		
3. I liked working in groups.	62%	25%	10%	3%	
4. The teacher(s) made an extra effort to help us understand the material and learn more.	68%	15%	11%	6%	
5. The class was presented in an interesting way.	49%	35%	8%	8%	
6. There were many different types of activities that benefited us.	27%	50%	13%	10%	
7. I was ready for the tests because we studied, discussed, and reviewed the material in class several different ways.	48%	25%	5%	12%	10%
8. I liked this class because I learned.	55%	35%	8%	2%	
9. I would like more classes conducted like this one.	70%	20%	5%		5%
10. I got to know many of the students in class.	60%	26%	7%	7%	
11. I feel better about school because of the help I got in class.	53%	21%	18%	8%	
12. I learned some skills in this class that I can use in my other classes next year.	43%	47%	10%		

FIGURE 21
Students' perceptions and attitudes.

REFERENCES

Allen, V. G. 1986. Developing Contexts to Support Second Language Acquisition. *Language Arts* 63:61–66.

Brozo, W. G., and C. M. Tomlinson. 1986. Literature: The Key to Lively Content Courses. *The Reading Teacher* 40:288–293.

Cazden, C. 1986. ESL Teachers as Language Advocates for Children. In *Children and ESL: Integrating Perspectives,* edited by P. Rigg and D. S. Enright, 7–22. Washington, D.C.: TESOL.

Cochrane, O., D. Cochrane, S. Scalena, and E. Buchanan. 1984. *Reading, Writing, and Caring.* Winnipeg: Whole Language Consultants.

Duran, R. P. 1983. *Hispanics' Education and Background.* New York: College Entrance Examination Board.

Enright, D. S. 1986. Use Everything You Have to Teach English: Providing Useful Input to Young Language Learners. In *Children and ESL: Integrating Perspectives,* edited by P. Rigg and D. S. Enright, 113–162. Washington, D.C.: TESOL.

Enright, D. S., and M. L. McCloskey. 1985. Yes, Talking! Organizing the Classroom to Promote Second Language Acquisition. *TESOL Quarterly* 19:431–454.

Freeman, D., Y. S. Freeman, and R. D. Gonzalez. 1987. Success for LEP Students: The Sunnyside Sheltered English Program. *TESOL Quarterly* 21:361–367.

Goodman, K. S. 1986a. Revaluing Readers and Reading. Occasional Paper no. 15, Program in Language and Literacy, College of Education. University of Arizona.

———. 1986b. *What's Whole in Whole Language?* Portsmouth, N.H.: Heinemann.

Goodman, K. S., and Y. Goodman. 1981. Twenty Questions about Teaching Language. *Educational Leadership* 38:437–442.

Goodman, K. S., Y. Goodman, and B. Flores. 1984. *Reading in the Bilingual Classroom.* Rosslyn, Va.: National Clearinghouse for Bilingual Education.

Halliday, M. A. K. 1975. *Learning How to Mean: Explorations in the Development of Language.* London: Edward Arnold.

Harste, J. C., V. A. Woodward, and C. L. Burke. 1984. *Language Stories and Literacy Lessons.* Portsmouth, N.H.: Heinemann.

Hudelson, S. 1984. Kan Yu Ret an Rayt en Ingles: Children Become Literate in English. *TESOL Quarterly* 18:221–238.

———. 1986. ESL Children's Writing: What We've Learned, What We're Learning. In *Children and ESL: Integrating Perspectives,* edited by P. Rigg and D. S. Enright, 23–54. Washington, D.C.: TESOL.

Kagan, S. 1986. Cooperative Learning and Sociocultural Factors in Schooling. In *Beyond Language: Social and Cultural Factors in Schooling Language Minority Students,* 231–298. Los Angeles: University of California, Evaluation, Dissemination, and Assessment Center.

Krashen, S. 1981. Bilingual Education and Second Language Acquisition Theory. In *Schooling and Language Minority Students: A Theoretical Framework,* 51–79. Los Angeles: University of California, Evaluation, Dissemination, and Assessment Center.

———. 1985. *Inquiries and Insights.* Hayward, Calif.: Alemany Press.

Lindfors, J. 1982. Exploring in and through Language. In *On TESOL '82,* edited by M. Clarke and J. Handscombe, 143–156. Washington, D.C.: TESOL.

Long, M. H., and P. A. Porter. 1985. Group Work, Interlanguage Talk, and Second Language Acquisition. *TESOL Quarterly* 19:207–228.

Rich, S. 1985. Whole Language—A Quick Checklist. *Whole Language Newsletter* 3:5–6.

Rigg, P. 1986. Reading and ESL: Learning from Kids. In *Children and ESL: Integrating Perspectives,* edited by P. Rigg and D. S. Enright, 55–92. Washington, D.C.: TESOL.

Smith, F. 1973. *Psycholinguistics and Reading.* New York: Holt, Rinehart and Winston.

Urzúa, C. 1986. A Children's Story. In *Children and ESL: Integrating Perspectives,* edited by P. Rigg and D. S. Enright, 93–112. Washington, D.C.: TESOL.

Vygotsky, L. S. 1962. *Thought and Language.* Edited and translated by W. Hanfmann and G. Vakar. Cambridge, Mass.: MIT Press.

Wong Fillmore, L. 1986. Teaching Bilingual Learners. In *Handbook of Research on Teaching,* edited by M. C. Wittrock, 648–670. New York: Macmillan.

Wells, C. G. 1986. *The Meaning Makers.* Portsmouth, N.H.: Heinemann.

ACKNOWLEDGMENTS

For specific permission to reprint the articles in this anthology we are grateful to the living authors and to these publishers.

Ablex Publishing Corporation. For James Collins, "The Development of Writing during the School Years," in *The Development of Oral and Written Language in Social Contexts,* edited by Anthony Pellegrini. Norwood: Ablex, 1984, pp. 201–211. Reprinted with the permission of the publisher.

Academic Press. For Jenny Cheshire, "The Relationship Between Language and Sex in English." *Applied Sociolinguistics,* edited by Peter Trudgill. New York: Academic Press, 1984, pp. 33–49. Copyright © 1984 by Harcourt, Brace and Jovanovich, Inc., reprinted with permission by the publisher.

Cambridge University Press. For Roger D. Abrahams, "Black Talking in the Street," in *Explorations in the Ethnography of Speaking,* edited by Richard Bauman and Joel Sherzer. New York: Cambridge University Press, 1974, pp. 240–262. Reprinted with permission of Cambridge University Press.

Cambridge University Press. For Walt Wolfram, "Varieties of American English," in *Language in the USA,* edited by Charles A. Ferguson and Shirley Brice Heath. New York: Cambridge University Press, 1981, pp. 44–69. Reprinted with the permission of Cambridge University Press.

James E. Coomber and Howard D. Peet. For "Vocabulary Teaching: Active Involvement in Contexts." Printed with permission of James E. Coomber and Howard D. Peet.

Ben L. Crane, Edward Yeager, and Randal L. Whitman. For "Phonetics," in *Introduction to Linguistics.* Boston: Little, Brown, and Co., 1981, pp. 57–70. Permission granted by authors.

Georgetown University Press. For William Leap, "American Indian English and Its Implications for the Bilingual Education." *Georgetown Roundtable on Language and Linguistics.* Georgetown, Va.: Georgetown University Press, 1978, pp. 657–69.

Harcourt, Brace and Jovanovich, Inc. For Jerome Bruner, "Learning the Mother Tongue." *Human Nature* (September 1978). pp. 42–49. Copyright © 1989 by Harcourt, Brace and Jovanovich, Inc., reprinted with permission by the publisher.

Harcourt, Brace and Jovanovich, Inc. For Edward Finegan and Niko Besnier, "The Relationship Between Language and Thought," in *Language: Its Structure and Use,* by Edward Finegan and Niko Besnier. Orlando, Fla.: Harcourt, Brace and Jovanovich, 1989, pp. 20–22. Copyright © 1989 by Harcourt, Brace and Jovanovich, Inc., reprinted by permission of the publisher.

Linguistic Society of America. For Dwight Bolinger, "Truth Is a Linguistic Question." *Language* **49** (1973), pp. 539–550. Reprinted with permission by the publisher and author.

Nancy McCracken. For "Placing Meaning at the Center of Language Study."

Minnesota English Journal. For Linda Miller Cleary and Nancy Lund, "Debunking Some Myths About Traditional Grammar." *Minnesota English Journal* **19,** 2 (1989), pp. 1–8. Reprinted with permission of the publisher and authors.

MIT Press. For Lev Semenovich Vygotsky, "The Genetic Roots of Thought and Speech, Section III and IV," in *Thought and Language,* translated, revised, and edited by Alex Kosulin. Cambridge: MIT Press, 1986, pp. 84–95. Copyright © 1986 by MIT Press.

William Morrow & Company, Inc. For Deborah Tannen, "Assymetries: Men and Women Talking at Cross-Purposes." *You Just Don't Understand: Women and Men in Conversation.* New York: Ballantine Books, 1990, pp. 49–73. Copyright © 1990 Deborah Tannen. Copyright © by permission of William Morrow & Company, Inc.

National Council of Teachers of English. For Elaine Chaika, "Grammars and Teaching." *College English* **39** (1978), pp. 770–783. Copyright 1978 by the National Council of Teachers of English. Reprinted by permission of the publisher and Elaine Chaika.

National Council of Teachers of English. For Linda Miller Cleary, "A Profile of Carlos: Strengths of a Nonstandard Dialect Writer." *English Journal* (September 1988), pp. 59–64. Copyright 1988 by the National Council of Teachers of English. Reprinted by permission of the publisher and Linda Miller Cleary.

National Council of Teachers of English. For Karl W. Dykema, "Where Our Grammars Came From." *College English* **27** (1966), pp. 455–465. Copyright 1966 by the National Council of Teachers of English. Reprinted by permission of the publisher and Karl W. Dykema.

National Council of Teachers of English. For Margaret Early, "The Act of Reading." *Literature in the Classroom: Readers, Texts, and Contexts,* edited by Ben F. Nelms. Urbana, Ill.: NCTE, 1988, pp. 31–44. Copyright 1988 by the National Council of Teachers of English. Reprinted by permission of the publisher and Margaret Early.

National Council of Teachers of English. For David Freeman and Yvonne S. Freeman, "A Road to Success for Language-Minority High School Students." *When They Don't All Speak English: Integrating the ESL Student Into the Regular Classroom.* Urbana, Ill.: NCTE, 1989, pp. 126–138. Copyright 1989 by the National Council of Teachers of English. Reprinted by permission of the publisher, Davis Freeman, and Yvonne Freeman.

National Council of Teachers of English. For Yetta Goodman, "I Never Heard Such a Long Story Before." *English Journal* **63** (1974), pp. 65–71. Copyright 1974 by the National Council of Teachers of English. Reprinted by permission of the publisher and Yetta Goodman.

National Council of Teachers of English. For Steven Grubaugh, "Spoken Words: Quality Exposure to Vocabulary Concepts." *English Journal* (January 1985), pp. 64–67. Copyright 1985 by the National Council of Teachers of English. Reprinted by permission of the publisher and Steven Grubaugh.

National Council of Teachers of English. For Elizabeth Grubgeld, "Helping the Problem Speller." *English Journal* (February 1986), pp. 58–61. Copyright 1986 by the National Council of Teachers of English. Reprinted by permission of the publisher and Elizabeth Grubgeld.

INDEX